AMERICAN SONG AND STRUGGLE FROM COLUMBUS TO WORLD WAR II

Long before anyone ever heard of "protest music," people in America were singing about their struggles. They sang for justice and fairness, food and shelter, and equality and freedom; they sang to be acknowledged. Sometimes they also sang to oppress. This book uncovers the history of these people and their songs, from the moment Columbus made fateful landfall to the start of World War II, when "protest music" emerged as an identifiable brand. Cutting across musical genres, Will Kaufman recovers the passionate voices of America itself. We encounter songs of the mainland and the conquered territories of Hawai'i, Cuba, Puerto Rico, and the Philippines; we hear Indigenous songs, immigrant songs and Klan songs, minstrel songs and symphonies, songs of the heard and the unheard, songs of the celebrated and the anonymous, of the righteous and the despicable. This magisterial book shows that all these songs are woven into the very fabric of American history.

WILL KAUFMAN is Professor of American Literature and Culture at the University of Central Lancashire in Preston, England. He is the author of *Woody Guthrie, American Radical* (2011), *Woody Guthrie's Modern World Blues* (2017), and *Mapping Woody Guthrie* (2019). His other books include *The Comedian as Confidence Man* (1997), *The Civil War in American Culture* (2006), *American Culture in the 1970s* (2009), and, co-authored with Ronald D. Cohen, *Singing for Peace: Antiwar Songs in American History* (2015).

AMERICAN SONG AND STRUGGLE FROM COLUMBUS TO WORLD WAR II

A Cultural History

WILL KAUFMAN

University of Central Lancashire

CAMBRIDGE
UNIVERSITY PRESS

University Printing House, Cambridge CB2 8BS, United Kingdom

One Liberty Plaza, 20th Floor, New York, NY 10006, USA

477 Williamstown Road, Port Melbourne, VIC 3207, Australia

314–321, 3rd Floor, Plot 3, Splendor Forum, Jasola District Centre, New Delhi – 110025, India

103 Penang Road, #05-06/07, Visioncrest Commercial, Singapore 238467

Cambridge University Press is part of the University of Cambridge.

It furthers the University's mission by disseminating knowledge in the pursuit of education, learning, and research at the highest international levels of excellence.

www.cambridge.org
Information on this title: www.cambridge.org/9781316514337
DOI: 10.1017/9781009086769

First published 2022

Printed in the United Kingdom by TJ Books Ltd, Padstow Cornwall

A catalogue record for this publication is available from the British Library.

ISBN 978-1-316-51433-7 Hardback

Praise for American Song and Struggle

Will Kaufman has uncovered a massive hidden history, one that none of us can ignore. Get the book, be in the know.

—Chuck D

Will Kaufman's extraordinary book is a sprawling, multicentury cavalcade of how the peoples of America sought freedom through song. Its range is extensive: the centrality of singing in Native cultures, the continuing resistance of African American music, stirring labor songs, satiric antiwar songs, lyric expressions of sexual freedom, and cries of pain during hard times. In a time of endless wars over who owns American culture, Kaufman brilliantly demonstrates that song is not just integral to the struggle for freedoms in the United States but its most stirring, truest expression.

—Michael Bronski, author of *A Queer History of the United States*

Will Kaufman has gifted us with a deep and panoramic story of songs of struggle throughout US prehistory and history.

—Roxanne Dunbar-Ortiz, author of *An Indigenous Peoples' History of the United States*

Since song is such a crucial part of who we are as humans, it should not be surprising to find out that it is central to all our struggles for justice; yet we needed to wait for Will Kaufman's groundbreaking book to truly show us that protest music was going on long before Woody and Pete. Such important work – a first in American music history; it is amazing that no one has ever covered it before.

—Matt Glaser, Artistic Director, American Roots Program, Berklee College of Music

Will Kaufman is already known for his unsurpassed scholarship on the great American songwriter Woody Guthrie. In this wonderful book we are given the soul and spirit of the countless people who came before him. Their songs remind us of our common humanity and the need to get to the heart of the truth.

—Ralph McTell

So much of what I learned about postwar America began with a song – by Woody Guthrie, Bob Dylan, Phil Ochs, or Buffy Sainte-Marie, who sang so eloquently about the plight of Native Americans. And from Joan Baez I learned that protest – struggle, resistance – is a way of meaningful life, not merely a song. From *American Song and Struggle*, I've learned how much *more* there is to learn about this often misunderstood and debased genre. And Will Kaufman is the best of teachers.

—Elizabeth Thomson, author of *Joan Baez: The Last Leaf*

Will Kaufman has written a deft, wide-ranging exploration of six centuries of politics and songs in the United States up to the eve of World War II, with much emphasis on the pre-Independence centuries. This is a significant, heavily researched, highly detailed, and very welcome addition to musical as well as political and historical scholarship.

—Ronald D. Cohen, author of *Rainbow Quest* and *Depression Folk*

We sing to affirm that the lives we lead are real, that what happened really happened, and that there is a future worth living. Will Kaufman has turned over all the rocks on the long road of American song and struggle. These songs carry the truth of the American experience, and they chart the course of our evolution.

—Ani DiFranco

Will Kaufman has been one of our most valuable and trusted Woody Guthrie authorities. Now with *American Song and Struggle* he's broadened his reach and in the process artfully corrected the notion that Woody was solely responsible for the creation of the protest song. This is a powerful work that is a must read for anyone interested in songs of conscience and how they helped shape our nation.

—Robert Santelli, Founding Executive Director, Grammy Museum

For two men named Ralph –
one, my father,
the other,
a good friend who walked me through a lonesome valley

Contents

Figures

Preface

First of all, this is not a book about protest music – at least, I don't think it is. I've always had great trouble wrestling with the concept of "protest music" or "protest songs." For many people, I suspect, "protest music" conjures up a somewhat cranky field of musical complaint, one that didn't really make its mark until the 1960s, with the Vietnam War and the Civil Rights Movement. A "protest singer" is someone – most likely white – who hectors at you from behind an acoustic guitar or maybe a long-necked banjo in honor of their father figure, Pete Seeger. It's someone who's pointing fingers all the time. Protest singers get on your nerves – they're so . . . earnest. So self-righteous! This is a caricature, of course, but apparently one so common that, in 1965, Tom Lehrer could skewer it in a live recording of his song "Folk Song Army." As he introduced it:

> One type of song that has come into increasing prominence in recent months is the folk song of protest. You have to admire people who sing these songs. It takes a certain amount of courage to get up in a coffee house or a college auditorium and come out in favor of the things that everybody else in the audience is against, like peace and justice and brotherhood and so on.

His verses didn't let up, either:

> We are the folk song army,
> Every one of us cares.
> We all hate poverty, war, and injustice
> Unlike the rest of you squares.

At some point, "protest music" became a serious problem for Bob Dylan, not least because the culture and the media were so intent on shoving him into the "protest singer" box and slamming the drawer shut. He wasn't having it. "I'm not part of no Movement," he said. "If I was, I wouldn't be able to do anything else but in 'The Movement.' I just can't have people sit around and make rules for me." He was done with "finger-pointing songs." That was in 1964. The following year, when he set aside his acoustic guitar and plugged in a Fender Stratocaster at the Newport Folk Festival, he set up a chain reaction that would end with his being absurdly branded a "Judas." His acolytes felt that he had betrayed them by giving up on both "folk music" and critical engagement with the world – in other words, "protest music." In fact, he'd done no such thing.

By then, "protest music" had long been virtually synonymous with "folk music." For that reason, no other genre was so relentlessly targeted by the FBI and various incarnations of the House Un-American Activities Committee as folk music. The FBI files on Woody Guthrie, Pete Seeger, Burl Ives, the Almanac Singers, Alan Lomax, Josh White, Aunt Molly Jackson, and Paul Robeson are bursting at the seams. Even after the fall of Senator Joe McCarthy – that is, in the early 1960s and well into the 1970s – right-wing ideologues were still calling folk music "a tool of Communist psychological or cybernetic warfare to ensnare and capture youthful minds." The country singer Tex Ritter said, "At one time I called myself a folk singer. [But] it got to the point there for a few years where it was very difficult to tell where folk music ended and Communism began. So that's when I quit calling myself a folk singer."

It was as early as 1940 that "folk music" and "protest music" had so dovetailed as to become practically indistinguishable from one another. This was aided by the expansion of the recording industry and a celebrated folk revival dominated by the pantheon of Guthrie, Seeger, Lead Belly, Josh White, and others under the patronage of Alan Lomax. In the 1950s, academics and sociologists began agonizing over how to categorize the protest song. Was it a song of "criticism," "persuasion," or "complaint"? Was it "rhetorical" or "magnetic"? Was it "deliberative" or "epideictic"?

Heck, was it even a "protest song"? "If you want to call it that," Martin Carthy said. Even one of England's greatest practitioners couldn't quite tell. Neither, apparently, could Woody Guthrie when he proposed to his producer, Moe Asch, the organizing principle of an album that was posthumously released under the title *Struggle* (1976). As Asch explained in the liner notes, it was "Woody's insistence that there should be a series of records depicting the struggle of working people in bringing to light their fight for a place in the America that they envisioned." This went so far beyond mere "protest."

* * *

In this book, I take my cues from Woody. For me, "struggle" most accurately captures what the songs in this book reflect: the struggle for access – access to fairness, justice, food and shelter, equality and freedom; the struggle to be recognized and acknowledged for one's own worth; sometimes a struggle over the act of singing itself – how to sing, what to sing, where to sing, even whether one might sing at all. "Struggle" cuts across time periods and musical genres in a way that "protest music" does not.

In terms of the songs themselves, I have looked far beyond the folk and singer-songwriter genres that have been most readily associated with "protest music." My sources come from a wealth of repositories: Aztec codices and the writings of the conquistadors; Indigenous songs of struggle and cultural assertion (well into the twentieth century); colonial journals and reports; Puritan hymns and psalms; broadsides and newspaper ballads; printed sheet music; opera, operetta, and art songs; political pamphlets and songsters; work songs; spirituals; suffrage songs; abolitionist songs; strike songs; parlor songs; minstrel songs; ragtime songs; vaudeville, cabaret, and musical theater songs; songs from the Yiddish theater, the German American theater, the Italian American theater, and Chinese opera; Tin Pan Alley songs; war songs; peace songs; songs of immigration and assimilation, translated from many languages; songs of despair scrawled on the walls of the Angel Island and Ellis Island detention centers; songs of queer struggle; blues songs; jazz songs; folk songs; symphonies. Indeed, my source material comes from wherever song has been used to express and reflect the currents of American struggle between 1492 and 1940 – that is, the period before the emergence of "protest music" as an industry or a brand.

* * *

The songs in this book do reflect – to repeat Asch – people's "fight for a place in America," an America "that they envisioned." But – given the realities of conquest, settler colonialism, slavery, imperialism, racism, nativism, religious bigotry, sexism, and rampant capitalism – perhaps it is an "America" that had been thrust upon them. Arguing in these terms – and foregrounding these realities – undoubtedly puts this book in the company denounced by Donald Trump when he launched his "1776 Commission" in September of 2020 to combat what he called "decades of left-wing indoctrination in our schools." As he proclaimed on that miserable day:

> Our children are instructed from propaganda tracts, like those of Howard Zinn, that try to make students ashamed of their own history. The left has

> warped, distorted, and defiled the American story with deceptions, falsehoods, and lies. There is no better example than the *New York Times'* totally discredited 1619 Project. This project rewrites American history to teach our children that we were founded on the principle of oppression, not freedom. . . . Critical race theory, the 1619 Project, and the crusade against American history is toxic propaganda, ideological poison that, if not removed, will dissolve the civic bonds that tie us together. It will destroy our country.

Howard Zinn has been an angel on my shoulder throughout the writing of this book, as have the architects of the 1619 Project, the aim of which has been to situate African American slavery and its aftermath as controlling forces in the development of the USA and its democracy as we know it. These historians have inevitably – and bravely – uncovered difficult historical truths that don't sit well with any uncritical, "patriotic" mission to present US history in only the most celebratory and effusive terms. Thankfully, one of President Joe Biden's first acts was to dismantle Trump's 1776 Commission. Trump himself may be gone (for the time being, at least); but the same can't be said for either Trumpism or the retrograde spirit behind his 1776 Commission. Many, if not most, of the songs and events discussed in this book are unlikely to be included in any curriculum sanctioned by such a reactionary project. That doesn't mean that these songs weren't sung, or that the events never happened. Let the reader decide the value of an encounter with them; and let no reader imagine that it is either "un-American," "anti-American," or "unpatriotic" to face up to a discussion that for good, historical reasons refuses to disappear. As Wynton Marsalis has said of this discussion: "The more we run from it, the more we run into it." Denial certainly won't make it go away.

I began my research in the late spring of 2016, three years into Barack Obama's second term. The writing proper began in June of 2020, toward the end of Trump's burning trash heap of a presidency and in the early months of a deadly COVID pandemic with, at that time, no end in sight. I completed the book in May of 2021, with some signs of hope on the horizon but still feeling that we were all standing amidst piles and piles of smoking wreckage and toxic lies, with no guarantee that a clean-up was to come or what it might look like. In spite of this, the songs and stories I have encountered in the course of writing this book have given me a long view and enabled me to maintain a sense of historical perspective. They have reaffirmed my belief that struggle is, was, and always will be at the heart of any step forward, even in the darkest of times.

The chapters in this history unfold chronologically, beginning with the Spanish invasion of America in 1492 and concluding at the dawn of the Second World War, with Marian Anderson singing "America" from the steps of the Lincoln Memorial, Paul Robeson broadcasting "Ballad for Americans" coast to coast, and Woody Guthrie holed up in a cheap rooming house in New York City, wrestling with the question, "Whose land is this, anyway?" The unifying subject, and the filter through which this entire history is presented, is song. The tradition of song and struggle in what is now known as the USA – the tradition inherited by Anderson, Robeson, Guthrie, and all their successors – began at the moment of the first encounter between the invading Europeans and the Indigenous Americans. For the Taínos who first greeted Christopher Columbus off the coast of Guanahani, entranced and enticed by the musical tinkling of the Admiral's hawks' bells, songs and singing were fundamental in the making and understanding of their world. It remains so to this day, for all of us.

Acknowledgments

So many people have helped and encouraged me, beginning with my dear wife Judy Blazer, ever the professional's professional on the Broadway stage, in the concert hall, and in the recording studio. Judy drew me out of my habitual comfort zone of folk music and Guthrie studies and into *her* territory: musical theater (including Yiddish theater), opera, and art song. Moreover, she critiqued my work at the end of each writing day in a twilight-and-wine ritual that I already miss, now that the writing is over. She was determined, as she said, to "keep the rhythm of the writing on track," and this book – like its author – would be nowhere without her.

Ray Ryan and Edgar Mendez at Cambridge University Press have taken the words "patience," "understanding," and "professionalism" to new levels of meaning for me.

For commenting on draft chapters, pointing me to source material, sacrificing their time on my behalf, boosting my morale, or otherwise helping me bring this project to fruition, I am grateful to David Amram, Chris Barton, Lorrie Boula, Richard Brandt, Michael Bronski, Jonathan Butterell, Martin Carthy, Cara Chamberlain, Ron Cohen, Kim Criswell, Chuck D, Kevin Lane Dearinger, Roxanne Dunbar-Ortiz, Anne Nathans Eddy, Will Eddy, Clyde Ellis, Glen Fretwell, Matt Glaser, Jason Graae, Nora Guthrie, Bucky Halker, Stephen Hunt, T. R. Johnson, Christopher Kennedy, Sean Latham, Deana McCloud, Rose McMahon, Ralph McTell, Reg Meuross, Kathy Morath, Max Morath, Carla Rios-Neumeier, Michelle Rios-Neumeier, Bob Santelli, Paula Sides, Gus Stadler, Mary Testa, Elizabeth Thomson, Pete Townshend, Nigel Wells, Benjamin Williamson, Neil Wynn, Douglas Yeager, and Natalie Zacek.

For familial encouragement all along the way I am grateful to Mike and Suzanne Kaufman, Steve and Donna Kaufman, David and Regina Blazer, all my beloved Rosenbergs, and all of their children.

And to my sons, Reuben and Theo Kaufman: I love you with my all. Always will.

Introduction
The Work of Recovery

> *When we entered the cabin of this Savage, we found a Fire lighted, near which a Man beat (singing at the same time) upon a Kind of Drum: Another shook, without ceasing his Chichkioue, and sang also. This lasted two Hours, till we were quite tired of it; for they always said the same thing, or rather they formed Sounds that were but half articulate, without any Variation. We begged the Master of the Cabin to put an End to this.*

The Jesuit traveler and historian Fr. Pierre de Charlevoix included this account of an Iroquois "Fire-Dance" in his narrative, *Voyage to Canada, and Travels through that vast Country* (1763). His impression tells us much about the cultural incomprehension and presumed superiority that marked European encounters with Indigenous American song in the colonial era. For Charlevoix, the musical experience was simply an ordeal: "Their songs, whether of war or devotion, harvest or hunting, consisted of but few words and scanty intonations, repeated in the most monotonous way."

How this French traveler could have distinguished between songs of "war or devotion, harvest or hunting" is perplexing, given that – as far as he could tell – Iroquois songs conveyed no meaning, only "Sounds that were but half articulate." In the subsequent centuries, music historians and ethnomusicologists have worked hard to rectify such early Eurocentric and logocentric ignorance (not to say arrogance), and to make sense of what one historian has called "songwork," that is, the "place and efficacy of song" in society. But this task has often been difficult, not only because of the impossibility of accurately recreating the music of Indigenous societies prior to the advent of sound recording but also because, in the colonial era, Indigenous musical expression was typically shoehorned into established European frameworks of notation and rhythm: "When it came to nondiatonic pitches, the polyrhythmic interaction of singing and drumming, and the vocal timbre of Indigenous song, colonial transcriptions floundered."

The retrieval of song lyrics has been equally beset with difficulty. Through the violence of conquest and colonialism, Indigenous cultures throughout the Americas were uprooted, scattered, and destroyed – wholly or partially – so that previously discrete languages and practices melded and intermixed, becoming blurred. Hence the fate of many cultures reliant for millennia upon oral transmission suddenly facing the preservative of the European written record: "Indian words passed down in official and unofficial records have no doubt been garbled or twisted – inadvertently or for political reasons – by the people who translated and recorded them. Some even have been fabricated." Indeed, there are Indigenous people today who have no access to the meaning of lyrics that they themselves have inherited through oral transmission. Even societies that have managed, through their relative isolation, to escape the more immediate or violent whirlwinds of cultural disruption have suffered through a traumatic loss of access to meaning. In 1902, a collector of Inuit songs noted that "the singers in many cases did not understand the words of the songs," although they had been singing in "the language of their ancestors." As late as 1991, a Paalirmiut Inuit from Nunavut lamented the diminished communicative power of her people's tradition of "throat singing" (*qiaqpaarniq*): "The words ... are words that were used by our remote ancestors. People have forgotten the meaning behind the words and that, I assume, adds to why people don't have any knowledge of their meaning. ... They came from the mouths of the ancients."

The centrality of singing in Indigenous American life has long been recognized, even by those colonial commentators who could otherwise make neither head nor tail of it. Songs on either side of the Columbian invasion were "acts of world- and even self-making," filtering a people's existence through music "in non- (or anti-) European ways, even in the bleakest moments of conquest and early colonization." Singing throughout Indigenous America – North, Central, and South – was (and remains) associated with rituals: rituals of hunting, of healing, of warfare; rituals of mourning, of play, of communication and communion with the gods. The instruments accompanying Indigenous vocal music are themselves "power objects," developed from weapons of the hunt and the struggle against starvation: the earliest stringed instrument was derived from the hunter's bow; the earliest percussion instruments being the "sticks and stones that dealt death in the chase."

Given the importance of music and song, it can be disheartening to confront the relative inaccessibility of Indigenous songs of struggle before the twentieth century, when – in North America, at least – the interest of ethnographers and collectors culminated in the field work of Alice Cunningham Fletcher, Natalie Curtis, and Frances Densmore. Even today, the sole Smithsonian Folkways recording marketed as Indian protest music contains only contemporary songs sparked by the waves of resurgent Indian protest movements in the 1970s. And yet, we know that the Hunkpapa Lakota chief Tȟatȟáŋka Íyotake (Sitting Bull) was himself known as a protest song writer: "Once a famous warrior I was. It is all over and now a hard time I have."

The accumulated caveats about the slipperiness of translation mean, of course, that these lyrics of Sitting Bull must be considered, to some extent, suspect – as must the Diné (Navajo) ode, "*Hlin Biyin*" (Song of the Horse), collected by Natalie Curtis in the early twentieth century and described by her as a song of "blessing and protection" for a family's herd of horses:

> How joyous his neigh!
> Lo, the Turquoise Horse of Johano-ai,
> How joyous his neigh,
> There on precious hides outspread standeth he.

The caveats must apply equally to all translations of Indigenous songs discussed in this book. Yet, such translations still help us understand the central place of struggle in the songs of the Americas before the Spanish invasion of 1492 and in the centuries that followed; for songs of struggle are everywhere in Indigenous America. Struggle is imbued in the "Song of the Horse" as an expression of the rituals, taboos, and customs surrounding the solemn (and economically necessary) quest for horses – not only by the Navajos but by the Apaches as well. For these and other North American tribes, horse raids were "sacred missions to bring home 'the things by which men lived,'" and as such they were the subjects of holy song.

Looking southward, a leading historian of pre-Columbian music, Gary Tomlinson, has made a study of one of the earliest remaining repositories of Aztec song, the ninety-one Mexica Songs (*Cantares mexicanos*) initially preserved in pictographic imagery – "songs to be sung, drummed, and danced" but represented visually in fragile codices and on painted murals, monuments, sculpture, and carvings throughout Mesoamerica, with "elaborate volutes extending from the mouths of singing figures." Various song categories, including war songs (*yaocuicatl*) and songs of "misery or grief" (*icnocuicatl*), as well as songs of implicit "ethnic pride," are indicative of struggle against forces of both human and natural origin. But, again, the precision of meanings contained within them remains beyond our grasp. Eventually translated into an "alphabetalized Nahuatl" form sometime in the late 1500s, the *Cantaras mexicanos* remain, in Tomlinson's words, "inescapably colonized," rooted in "any number of specifics we are not in a position to recover." However, one specific that we *are* in a position to recover is the importance of instrumental and vocal music in the struggles of conquest and resistance between the Indigenous Americans and the invading Europeans. This is where we will begin, with the arrival of three strange ships from beyond the horizon.

CHAPTER 1

Broken Spears and Songs of Sorrow

It all began with Columbus and his little tinkling bells. It was October 12, 1492, the day the invading Europeans first met Indigenous people of America, on the shore of the island called Guanahani by its inhabitants. A remarkably unwarlike society, with "no war music or signals or artifacts" yet recovered by historians, the welcoming Taínos of Guanahani were apparently ripe for musical seduction from the moment of the first encounter. Other than "the songs of the birds and the chirping of crickets," the only remotely musical reference in Columbus's *Journal of the First Voyage* is to the "small bells" that were quickly recognized as useful, if relatively worthless, items of exchange in the conquistadors' quest for items they considered more valuable – in particular, gold. Coming ashore, Columbus distributed a handful of "small bells" to his delighted Taíno hosts. The next day, he was seen giving "a hawk's bell and glass beads" to a Taíno in exchange for a pair of solid gold nose rings – a practice that he repeated as a sure bargain on subsequent dates at various locations during the first voyage. On December 26, Columbus recounted the arrival of a Taíno cacique and his emissaries in a canoe, as his journal describes in the third person employed by his transcriber:

> [They had with them] some pieces of gold, which the people in the canoe wanted to exchange for a hawk's bell; for there was nothing they desired more than these bells. They had scarcely come alongside when they called and held up the gold, saying *Chuq chuq* for the bells, for they are quite mad about them. After the king had seen this, and when the canoes which came from other places had departed, he called the Admiral and asked him to give orders that one of the bells was to be kept for another day, when he would bring four pieces of gold the size of a man's hand. The Admiral rejoiced to hear this, and afterwards a sailor, who came from the shore, told him that it was wonderful what pieces of gold the men on shore were getting in exchange for next to nothing.

Clearly, the Taínos' delight in the musical sounds of the *chuq chuq* was matched only by the cynicism of the invading Spaniards; but this was only the beginning of the part that music was to play in the conquest of America – and the Indigenous resistance *to* that conquest.

Columbus returned on his second voyage in late 1493, landing on what he immediately claimed as *La Isla Española*, thereby erasing the Indigenous names of *Haiti* and *Quisqueya*. He and the first contingent of Spanish settlers promptly sang a mass upon coming ashore, thus weaponizing church music as the initial instrument of conquest. This marked "the first recorded instance of European music in the Western Hemisphere." By the time of the third voyage (1498–1500), the terms of musical engagement had heightened and darkened even further. Much of what we know of this voyage comes through Bartolomé de Las Casas's *Historia de las Indias* (completed 1561), which relied on Columbus's own papers, including fragments of his journal. Through Las Casas, we learn that, upon the admiral's encounter with, and naming of, the island of Trinidad (from time immemorial called *Iere* by the native Arawak), "with great rejoicings and merriment the *Salve Regina* was sung with other devout songs which contain praises of God and our Lady," punctuating the rite (and presumed right) of taking possession. But Columbus was not done with music as a weapon of enticement. Anchoring off the Point of Arenal, Trinidad, on August 2, 1498, he was approached by "a large canoe . . . in which came twenty-five men." Seeing their hesitancy, Columbus ordered what resulted in apparently the first of many musical misunderstandings between the Europeans and their Indigenous hosts:

> They approached somewhat, and afterwards became terrified of the ship; and as they would not approach, the Admiral ordered a tambourine player to come up to the poop deck of the ship and that the young boys of the ship should dance, thinking to please them. But they did not understand it thus, but rather, as they saw dancing and playing, taking it for a signal of war, they distrusted them. They left all their oars and laid hold of their bows and arrows; and each one embracing his wooden shield, they commenced to shoot a great cloud of arrows. Having seen this, the Admiral ordered the playing and dancing to cease, and that some cross-bows should be drawn on deck and two of them shot off at them, nothing more than to frighten them.

"This escalating exchange," a historian writes, "would not only exemplify the lack of understanding between European explorers and America's First People, but also emphasize the seriousness of music among the Indigenous."

Not that the "European explorers" were particularly interested in examining "the seriousness of music among the Indigenous." Certainly

Columbus, on his second voyage in 1495 ("after his search for gold faltered"), was more concerned with abducting roughly 1500 Arawak men, women, and children, to be shipped to Europe as slaves. "Of the five hundred slaves shipped to Spain, only three hundred arrived alive and were put up for sale by an archbishop." Indeed, the early conquistadors' contempt for Indigenous culture was such that they "rarely took the trouble to record descriptions of it. As a result, little is known of their music." There were, fortunately, noteworthy exceptions – not only Las Casas but two Spanish missionaries deserving of mention and the gratitude of posterity: Bernardino de Sahagún and Diego Durán, who did what they could to thwart the conquistadors' mission of systematically destroying all Indigenous centers of culture and education. As their late champion, the Mexican historian and anthropologist Miguel Leon-Portilla, argued,

> Their major accomplishment was to save a great many of the old songs and narratives that were still faithfully remembered after the Conquest. They worked out means of writing the native languages with the Latin alphabet, and this enabled them – and their Indian pupils – to record the texts in the original words.

Among these recovered texts is the collection of Aztec song relating to one of the grimmest episodes in the history of the Spanish invasion, beginning with the arrival of Hernán Cortés on the Mexican mainland in 1519. Music, in this episode, was again central to the drama, starting with the "small bells" that seem to have played such a surprising role in the conquest of the Americas. As Howard Zinn succinctly relates the initial encounter,

> When a Spanish armada appeared at Vera Cruz, and a bearded white man came ashore, with strange beasts (horses), clad in iron, it was thought that he was the legendary Aztec man-god who had died three hundred years before, with the promise to return – the mysterious Quetzalcoatl. And so they welcomed him, with munificent hospitality.

The "bearded white man" was Cortés; and, as an anonymous Aztec historian recounted in one of the codices rescued by Sahagún, the emissaries of the Aztec king Moctezuma attempted to bestow upon him their highest honor, the "divine adornments" of Quetzalcoatl:

> Then they arrayed the Captain in the finery they had brought him as presents ... Next they fastened the mirror to his hips, dressed him in the cloak known as "the ringing bell" and adorned his feet with the greaves used by the *Huastecas*, which were set with *chalchihuites* and hung with little gold bells.

Figure 1.1 Moctezuma receiving Cortés. Lithographer unknown, 1907.
Library of Congress Prints and Photographs Division

The contemptuous ingratitude of Cortés still rings down through the centuries:

> The Captain asked them: "And is this all? Is this your gift of welcome? Is this how you greet people?" They replied: "This is all, our lord. This is what we have brought you." ... Then the Captain gave orders, and the messengers were chained by the feet and by the neck. When this had been done, the great cannon was fired off. The messengers lost their senses and fainted away.

Thus began the Aztecs' ultimately fatal encounter with the conquistadors.

Within a year of his arrival, Cortés marched on the Aztec capital, Tenochtitlan, and had Moctezuma put under house arrest for the growing Indigenous resistance to Spanish encroachment. On the fateful night of May 22, 1520, Cortés's deputy, Pedro de Alvarado (called "The Sun" by the Aztecs), ordered the massacre of celebrants in the city's main temple during a fiesta for the god Toxcatl. As it unfolds in one of the narratives rescued by Sahagún, the musicians and singers were the first to fall:

> The celebrants began to sing their songs. That is how they celebrated the first day of the fiesta. On the second day they began to sing again, but without warning they were all put to death. The dancers and the singers were completely unarmed. They brought only their embroidered cloaks, their turquoises, their lip plugs, their necklaces, their clusters of heron feathers, their trinkets made of deer hooves. Those who played the drums, the old men, had brought their gourds of snuff and their timbrels.

> The Spaniards attacked the musicians first, slashing at their hands and faces until they had killed all of them. The singers – and even the spectators – were also killed. This slaughter in the Sacred Patio went on for three hours. Then the Spaniards burst into the rooms of the temple to kill the others: those who were carrying water, or bringing fodder for the horses, or grinding meal, or sweeping, or standing watch over this work.

Why were the celebrants caught so off guard? Sahagún recalled: "The Indians thought that [the Spanish] were just admiring the style of their dancing and playing and singing, and so continued with their celebration and songs." By the time they realized their peril, it was too late:

> The first Spaniards to start fighting suddenly attacked those who were playing the music for the singers and dancers. They chopped off their hands and their heads so that they fell down dead. Then all the other Spaniards began to cut off heads, arms, and legs and to disembowel the Indians.

In a separate recollection of the same moment, another of Sahagún's anonymous historians proposed, "When the dance was loveliest and when song was linked to song, the Spaniards were seized with an urge to kill the celebrants."

The next time the Spanish encountered Aztec music, song had become an Indigenous battle weapon, not only for the Aztecs but also for Cortés's temporary allies, the Tlaxcaltecas, enemies of the Aztecs. One of the recovered codices recounts the Spanish and their Indigenous allies marching on the Aztec formations:

> They advanced cautiously, with their standard-bearer in the lead, and they beat their drums and played their *chirimias* as they came. The Tlaxcaltecas and the other allies followed close behind. The Tlaxcaltecas held their heads high and pounded their breasts with their hands, hoping to frighten us with their arrogance and courage. They sang songs as they marched, but the Aztecs were also singing. It was as if both sides were challenging each other with their songs. They sang whatever they happened to remember and the music strengthened their hearts.

Although we will never know precisely what they were singing, we do know that the Aztecs briefly gained the ground in this instance, driving the Spaniards away and taking prisoners. But the Spanish regrouped and returned to Moctezuma's capital, Tenochtitlan, blockading and besieging the city until the inhabitants were half-starved and smallpox began to decimate the population. Moctezuma was killed, along with most of the Aztec priesthood.

Indigenous enslavement, massacres, and other "genocidal enterprises" became the order of the day under Cortés and his rivals in brutality, notably Nuño de Guzmán, the conqueror of western Mexico. In one instance, Las Casas recalled, in the Aztec religious center of Cholula, it was the Spaniards' turn to sing in the midst of carnage:

> It is said, that while those five, or six thousand men were being put to the sword in the courtyard, the captain of the Spaniards stood singing.
>
> Miro Nero de Tarpeya
> A Roma como se ardia.
> Gritos dan ninos ye viejos,
> Y del de nada se dola.

This ode, chanted in sarcasm over the dismembered bodies of the Aztecs, was an ancient Spanish ballad depicting the emperor Nero standing on the Tarpeian Rock, rejoicing as Rome burned below him, unmoved by the screaming of the young and the old.

Figure 1.2 The conquest of Michoacán, c. 1530. Nuño de Guzmán depicted upper left. Detail from a facsimile of the Lienzo de Tlaxcala (c. 1550), reproduced in William Sievers, *Allgemeine Landeskunde: Amerika* (1914).
Public domain via Wikimedia Commons

For Las Casas, looking back from the vantage point of the 1550s to the swift period of what he called "the destruction of the Indies," the Spanish recompense for the gift of Indigenous music had been perceptible from day one of the invasion:

> In many provinces, indeed in all those that they entered . . . the people would come out to greet and receive them with songs and dances and with many presents of gold in great quantity. The payment that the Spaniards gave them, though, in order to sow fear throughout the entire land, was to put them to the sword and hack them utterly to pieces.

As for the Aztecs themselves, one retrieved codex reveals what remained in the wake of the conquistadors' wrath:

> Nothing but flowers and songs of sorrow are left in Mexico and Tlatelolco, where once we saw warriors and wise men. . . . We are crushed to the ground; we lie in ruins. There is nothing but grief and suffering in Mexico and Tlatelolco, where once we saw beauty and valor.

Las Casas knew these "songs of sorrow" and agreed:

> From this day until the end of the world, or the Spaniards do away with them all, they shall never cease lamenting and singing in their *areitos* and dances . . . that calamity and loss of the succession of all their nobility, which for so many years past they had treasured and venerated.

In fact, the extant threnodies – the laments, or "songs of sorrow" – tell of Aztec grief over more than just the "loss of succession of all their nobility." Within seven years of the Spanish conquest – that is, in 1528 – the anonymous authors of Tlatelolco were singing of a broader, more desolate landscape:

> Broken spears lie in the roads;
> we have torn our hair in our grief.
> The houses are roofless now, and their walls
> are red with blood.
>
> Worms are swarming in the streets and plazas,
> and the walls are splattered with gore.
> The water has turned red, as if it were dyed,
> and when we drink it,
> it has the taste of brine.
>
> We have pounded our hands in despair
> against the adobe walls,
> for our inheritance, our city, is lost and dead.
> The shields of our warriors were its defense,
> but they could not save it.

> We have chewed dry twigs and salt grasses;
> we have filled our mouths with dust and bits of adobe;
> we have eaten lizards, rats and worms.

As the histories of the conquest make clear, it was not simply the lust for gold, land, slaves, and natural resources that drove the brutality of the European invaders. It was also a conviction that the Indigenous peoples were less than human, in a fallen state made apparent not only by their dark skin and their sacrificial rituals but also by the apparently meaningless songs they howled to the moon as if from out of Satan's own bowels – a conviction uttered with tedious regularity before the officers of the Spanish Inquisition. The unfolding logic was merciless and deadly: "When a religion was bad, its people were necessarily also bad. It did not matter that they had never done wrong to the Christian contemplating them; they were enemies to God. They were therefore also enemies to God's people." For Las Casas, the surest way of saving both the bodies and the souls of the Indigenous Americans would be to turn them into Christians – and he aimed to enlist music in his mission of mercy. In 1540, he sailed to Spain to argue his case before the Council of Charles V, urging the king to send music teachers and musical instruments into the wilds of America to help convert the people to the true belief. He knew it would work, because he had tried it himself, composing couplets in native tongues about "the creation of the world and the story of Eden; man's fallen state and need of redemption; the birth and miracles of Our Lord and finally His death upon the Cross."

So began a new chapter in the history of music in America. By the close of the 1500s, Spanish musical instruments and songs, both sacred and secular, were fanning out toward the far corners of New Spain. Indigenous musical instruments were noted along the way – the whistles, flutes, and "simple cane flageolets" observed in Florida by Cabeza de Vaca in 1528 and Hernando de Soto in 1539; the "fife" heard by Pedro de Casteñada during Coronado's 1540–1542 expedition to New Mexico, played by a Zuni herdsman and accompanied by the singing of women rattling "stones to the music." But these instruments were tainted by their diabolical associations; as one Spanish missionary was later to claim in California, "[The Indians] are fond of music and song, but their instruments also remember the pagan tunes."

Spain sent out more and more music teachers and choirmasters; thousands of choirs and church bands sprouted up among Indigenous converts, entranced by the liturgical chants and the vernacular songs composed by priests to naturalize the new religious doctrine:

> The folk-tinged Catholicism of Spain turned out to be surprisingly congenial to the Indians, not only because they responded to its colourful liturgy, music, and ceremony, but also because it enabled the natives to retain many of their old gods by renaming and reimaging them among the numerous saints venerated by the Spanish.

But the musical way to salvation was a narrow one, even for such a relatively sympathetic commentator as Sahagún, who observed in 1576: "If, after their conversion here, they sing some songs they have composed, which deal with the things of God and His saints, they are surrounded by many errors and heresies."

Still, the musical conquistadors persevered, stamping out when they could the holdouts of Indigenous song and instrumentation encountered along the royal roads leading from Mexico City outwards to the far reaches of the Spanish empire – along "the trail of the Camino Real de Tierra Adentro northward into the region of the Río Grande del Norte." In 1598, where the Río Grande met the Río Chama, the disciples of both Cortés and Las Casas – with sword in one hand and Bible in the other – established their settlements "to the beat of their own music." That same year, Fray Cristóbal de Quiñones saw to it that the first organ in what is now the United States was installed in the monastery chapel at San Felipe Pueblo (New Mexico) and began teaching its inhabitants to sing hymns. Elsewhere throughout the empire – whether along the Río Grande or the California coast – Indigenous laborers sweated under the lash and the Bible to build missions and military posts; "and the Spanish settlers enjoyed a gracious and easy lifestyle. Music for their recreation and entertainment was provided by natives playing popular Spanish and Mexican songs on guitars and violins."

The imperial scramble for the Americas was well under way. Over the next two centuries more than a dozen European powers, large and small, staked their claims to Indigenous lands in the so-called New World. The Portuguese had already seized Brazil and Barbados; they soon had parts of Uruguay and took various stabs at Labrador and Nova Scotia. The French set up the massive empire of New France, a swath of territory that stretched from Canada to the Gulf of Mexico, to add to their presumptive possessions in the Caribbean and – until it was violently seized by the Portuguese – Brazil. Parts of the West Indies, as well as the entirety of Greenland, somehow ended up belonging to the Kingdom of Denmark. (Greenland was used goods, though, having been previously claimed by the Kingdom of Norway, which also snatched – or tried to snatch – lands in the north of Canada and in the West Indies.) The Dutch took possession of what they named New Netherland, stretching from today's Chesapeake Bay to Cape Cod, adding to the territories they claimed as theirs in the Caribbean, the Guianas, and Brazil. For two decades, Sweden had imperial footholds in Delaware and, by the 1780s, the Caribbean islands – one of which, St. Barts, had somehow wound up previously in the loving care of the Knights of Malta. Even Scotland took a stab at the imperial project with the short-lived colony of Darién in Panama. Russian sailors had spotted Alaska in the 1640s; it became "Russian America" by 1733. A handful of German and Italian colonizing ventures also made their brief marks in places like Venezuela, the Caribbean, and the Guianas. In all of these instances, it was presumed that America was there for the taking, the legacy of a "crusader ideology" inherited and honed by Europeans who were "mostly Christian by profession and mostly Caucasian by heredity."

In 1578 Queen Elizabeth I of England joined the scramble, instructing one of her most loyal and brutal henchmen, the soldier-adventurer Sir Humphrey Gilbert, to explore and seize the "remote heathen and barbarous lands" of North America. Gilbert had already proved his mettle, to Elizabeth's satisfaction, in the subjugation of Ireland, which was marked by his ingenious ritual of lining the path to his tent with the decapitated heads of resistant Irish, no matter their age or gender: "[It brought] greate terrour to the people when thei saw the heddes of their dedde fathers, brothers, children, kinsfolke, and friends." A commemorative plaque unveiled in 1998 in St. John's, Newfoundland, reads:

CLOSE TO THIS COMMANDING AND
HISTORIC SPOT SIR HUMPHREY GILBERT
LANDED ON THE 5TH DAY OF AUGUST 1583
AND IN TAKING POSSESSION OF THIS
NEW FOUND LAND IN THE NAME OF HIS
SOVEREIGN QUEEN ELIZABETH THEREBY
FOUNDED BRITAIN's OVERSEAS EMPIRE.

No expression of Europe's supreme imperial arrogance was ever put more succinctly. But Gilbert was not the first Englishman to make the acquaintance of North America's Indigenous people. In July 1576, the Inuit of Hall's Island, off Baffin Island in today's Nunavut, met their first Europeans, the crew of the barque *Gabriel* captained by Martin Frobisher, on the lookout for the fabled Northwest Passage to Asia. Frobisher had taken a leaf from Columbus's book when it came to identifying the sharpest practices in what must have appeared, to the European gaze, an easy and unequal bargain. As his second in command, Lieutenant George Best, recalled, Frobisher presented his welcoming hosts with "bells, looking-glasses and other toys" in exchange for "coats of seal skins and bear skins." The Inuits' next encounter with Frobisher, exactly a year later, did not go well. Relations between the Hall's Islanders and their European guests had deteriorated with the disappearance of five English sailors and Frobisher's retaliatory seizure of a local emissary named Kalicho. Lieutenant Best later wrote of the subsequent warfare between the Inuit of Jackson Sound and Frobisher's crew: "That point has since been named Bloody Point because of the slaughter that occurred there that day." The musical accompaniment to that "slaughter" was hardly the tinkling of bells. The Inuit numbers swelled as they surrounded the English camp, lining up "in plain sight on the top of a hill, holding their hands over their heads and dancing and singing with great gusto."

This is not to say that the early musical encounters between the English and the Inuit were uniformly belligerent. Seven years after the christening of Bloody Point, two ships under the command of John Davis dropped their anchors in the Cumberland Sound, on the east coast of Baffin Island. Indigenous villagers ran out to greet them, at which point Davis ordered his shipboard musicians to play: "They [the Inuit] tooke great delight, and fals a dauncing." This time, the "amicable relations" between the English and the Inuit lasted as long as a week. At another location during the same voyage, Davis's crewman John Janes recalled their shoreline camp being approached by Indigenous villagers in a canoe:

> When they came unto us, we caused our Musicians to play, our selves dauncing, and making many signes of friendship. At length there came 10 Canoas from the other Ilands, and two of them came so neere the shoare where we were, that they talked with us . . . and one of them came on shoare, to whom we threwe our caps, stocking and gloves, and such other things as then was had about us, playing with our musicke, and making signs of joy, and dancing. So the night coming we bade them farewell, and went aboord our barks.

There is no record of these earliest English explorers making any serious attempt to understand or accurately describe Indigenous music. That was left to French travelers in the first years of the seventeenth century. In 1606, the first transcription of North American Indigenous music in European notation was made by the explorer (and composer) Marc Lescarbot, who "transcribed three Micmac melodies using solfege syllables without rhythmic indications." The earliest French transcriptions were clearly aimed at reinforcing the broader European narrative of Indigenous peoples as "primitive, heathen, and inferior to Europeans," with the transcribers presenting their songs as

> short and unsophisticated in melody and rhythm, and lacking any longer formal structure, instrumental accompaniment, variation in vocal texture, or other complication for refinements of musical style. [They] reinforced the idea that American Indian music was crude and inferior to European music by linking native music to the sounds of nature, animals, and children.

Samuel de Champlain amplified these reductive assumptions in his description of an "Algoumenquin" (presumably Algonquin) victory celebration in his narrative *Des Sauvages* (1603). To him, Indigenous song was simply evidence of heathenish "false opinions" and communion with "devils":

> Now, after having brought their Tabagie to an end, they began to dance by taking up the heads of their enemies, which were hanging behind them. As a sign of rejoicing, one or two of them sing, synchronizing their voices by the beat of their hands, which they strike upon their knees; then they pause sometimes, crying out "*ho, ho, ho,*" and begin again to dance, panting like a man out of breath. They were making this celebration for the victory that they had won over the *Irocois,* of whom they had killed about a hundred, from whom they had cut the heads that they had with them for their ceremony.

Champlain, like his Spanish counterparts to the south, was correct in identifying Indigenous music as inextricably linked to religious ceremony. But through their benighted imperial arrogance, the European colonizers embarked – as we have seen – on a systematic program of eradication and conversion, to wipe out all vestiges of Indigenous music and ritual, to bring the original inhabitants of America into the saving embrace of Christianity. Psalms and hymns increasingly infiltrated the soundscapes of the American wilderness, reassuring many white colonizers that the natives could indeed become "civilized." It was an assumption and a program that continued into the early years of the twentieth century, in what had by then become the USA. The determination of Indigenous peoples to resist such eradication and to keep singing their world into being is part of the larger story of song and struggle in America.

CHAPTER 2

Good Newes from Virginia

Queen Elizabeth's first substantial colonization project in what became the USA began with predictable brutality and ended in mystery. The year 1585 saw the arrival of seven ships under the command of Sir Richard Grenville on Roanoke Island off the coast of North Carolina. Grenville and his men were met and welcomed by the Algonquian inhabitants of a village called Aquascogoc. After a few days, one of the Englishmen's silver drinking cups vanished. In retaliation, Grenville had the entire village burned to the ground. The establishment of the Roanoke military colony continued apace. Grenville went back to England. Five years later, a supply detachment headed by Captain George White returned to Roanoke, to find that all the colonists had disappeared. The settlement was intact and fortified, but completely abandoned, the only possible clues to their whereabouts being the letters "CRO" carved into a tree and "CROATOAN" carved into the palisade of the fort. Possibly this meant that the colonists had relocated to the nearby island of that name (now called Hatteras), but they were never seen again.

The story of the "Lost Colony" of Roanoke is a well-known chapter in American history. Less known is the invocation of song in the desperate search for the colonists. As White recalled, approaching the emptiness of the settlement, his men "sounded with a trumpet a call, and afterwards many familiar English tunes of songs, and called to them friendly, but we had no answere." What particular English songs were sounded out into the vastness of the American wilderness, we shall never know. Nor can we know how they might have been received by any Indigenous ears within hearing distance. Such is the injustice of historical silencing, an unequal contest in which the victors hold the pen, as well as the sword; for we know enough about what the English colonizers felt about the Indigenous music *they* heard along the coast of Virginia and the Carolinas. With the settlement of the Jamestown colony in 1607, Captain John Smith had the opportunity to play the disinterested musicologist in his description of the Indigenous instruments he'd heard – the "thicke cane, on which they pipe on as a Recordor"; the "drumme" fashioned from skin stretched over "a great deepe platter of wood"; the "Rattels made of small gourds or Pumpion shels," a huge variety spanning the "Base, Tenor, Countertenor, Meane and Trible" ranges. His conclusion, however, betrayed his sense of Europe's cultural superiority: "These mingled with their voices sometimes 20 or 30 togither, make such a terrible noise as would rather affright then delight any man." The instruments were played by "Priests" with their faces "painted as ugly as they can devise."

The Jamestown colony was set up in the midst of an Algonquian confederacy headed by a chief, Wahunsenacawh, commonly known as the Powhatan. Wahunsenacawh was initially patient as he watched the English settlers encroaching on his people's territory. There is no record of his response, if he had one, to Smith's description of his people's singing as "the most dolefullest noyse." What we *do* have, if by way of a possibly embellished translation, is Wahunsenacawh's plea to Smith as the English grew more and more aggressive and acquisitive: "What will it availe you to take that by force you may quickly have by love, or to destroy them that provide you food." By the winter of 1610, the year after Wahunsenacawh made his plea, the Jamestown settlers were going through what they called the "starving time," a period so desolate that many of them abandoned the colony to live among Wahunsenacawh's people. When Smith and the colonial governor, Thomas Gates, demanded that the Powhatan return the runaways, they were firmly rebuffed:

> Some soldiers were therefore sent out "to take Revendge." They fell upon an Indian settlement, killed fifteen or sixteen Indians, burned the houses, cut down the corn growing around the village, took the queen of the tribe and her children into boats, then ended up throwing the children overboard "and shoteinge owtt their Braynes in the water." The queen was later taken off and stabbed to death.

Twelve years of brazen English encroachment and sporadic violence followed, until the Powhatan struck back, killing 347 settlers – men, women, and children. This was all the colonists needed to unleash their vengeance and to give their territorial greed full reign and justification. As one settler gloated:

> We, who hitherto have had possession of no more ground then their waste ... may now by right of Warre, and law of Nations, invade the Country, and destroy them who sought to destroy us: whereby wee shall enjoy their cultivated places ... Now their cleared grounds in all their villages (which are situate in the fruitfullest places of the land) shall be inhabited by us.

No Powhatan war songs have come down to us commemorating what became known as the "Powhatan Uprising" of 1622. Thus, it was left to the anonymous English ballad makers to tell their side, and only their side, of the story. Within a year of the "uprising," a broadside ballad entitled "Good Newes from Virginia," published in London, was harping on the paganism and bloodlust of the "salvages," with the blatant aim of justifying the presumed right of colonial conquest. The ballad also showed that, when it came to savagery and bloody retribution, the English settlers could give like for like:

> No English heart but heard with griefe,
> the massacre here done:
> And how by savage treacheries,
> fell many a mother's sonne:
> But God that gave them power and leave,
> their cruelties to use,
> Hath given them up into our hands,
> who English did abuse.

The ballad's author, known only as "a Gentleman in that Country," dwelled with relish upon the details of the "abuse" consequently suffered upon the Powhatan by the English, lauding the "bould," "worthy," and "stout" Englishmen who "set fire of a Towne of theirs, / and bravely came away," who "landing slew those enemies, / that massacred our men: / Tooke prisoners, corne, & burnt their townes / and came abord again." To cap it all off, and with no hint of irony, the "Gentleman in that Country" pointed out that this grim account was best sung "to the Tune of *All those that be good fellowes.*"

Naturally, "Good Newes from Virginia" makes no mention of the conflicts leading up to the Powhatan "uprising" – nothing about the violence of the colonists during the "starving time" of 1610; nothing about John Smith descending with fire and pillage upon the Powhatan villages; nothing about the murder of Wahunsenacawh's wife or the abduction of his children; nothing about the colonists' "guile and merciless treatment of captives," nor, incidentally, about the treacherous use of music by Governor Gates, who at the opening stage of the conflict had "lured some Indians into the open with a music-and-dance act by his drummer, then slaughtered them." No, the primary aim of the ballad was to establish the English right – and determination – to seize from the "salvages" what the cleric Samuel Purchas described as "that unmanned wild Countrey, which they range rather than inhabit." Thus, the classic fiction of settler colonialism – later expressed by Israel Zangwill as "a land without people for a people without a land" – was inscribed into countless ballads of the

Elizabethan age. "Salvages" were, by definition, less than people. And the "aural landscape" or "soundscape" of their dispossession was one in which the music of "civilization" was pitted against the "whoops, shouts, and drum beats" of Indigenous "savagery." Who were the civilized, and who were the savage, remained – and remains – open to discussion.

That question is also germane to the European construction of the other group uniformly slandered as "savage" by settler colonists for the justification of theft and exploitation: the sons and daughters of Africa. The introduction of kidnapped Africans as slaves on the North American mainland did not occur in 1619 in Jamestown – as is conventionally

Figure 2.1 Landing the first kidnapped Africans at Jamestown, 1619. Illustration in *Harper's Monthly*, January 1901.
Library of Congress Prints and Photographs Division

taught – but rather in 1526 in the short-lived Spanish colony of San Miguel de Gualdape, founded by the explorer Lucas Vázquez de Ayllón on Sapelo Sound, south of today's Savannah, Georgia. The colony existed only for some four months, and it holds the distinction of hosting the first North American slave rebellion; but the historical records are sketchy, and we know little about the African people there, including their number. So we must look to the twenty kidnapped souls brought to Jamestown in 1619 to join the roughly million other Africans already thrown into slavery in South America and the Caribbean.

That they sang, there can be no doubt; but what they sang, we shall never know. One scholar of African American music explains the "anomalous situation" in which the music of these involuntary immigrants has been lodged: "The blacks arrived in the colonies in 1619, but almost nothing about their music has been found before the end of the seventeenth century, when they were already playing the fiddle." The silences in the historical record resonate well into the next century, ironically for a body of song that, when it was sung, must have been "so discernible, so palpable, so loud." But it now comes down to us only as

> passing comments in diaries and legal documents that recorded acts in the control and discipline of slaves. Among the first was that of the British traveller, John Josselyn, who, during a visit to Noddles Island, off the coast of Massachusetts, witnessed in 1639 an African woman, a former "Queen," who, "in her own Countrey language and tune sang very loud and shrill . . . [to] express her grief" over her forced mating with another slave.

This Josselyn was not unique in his willingness to declare with certainty the meaning of an African's song, although white observers were just as likely to reflect little beyond their own perplexity at the otherness of the music. Some ventured to surmise, at best, about the meaning of the songs they attempted to describe. A brief and telling digest comes from a British surgeon, Alexander Falconbridge, asked by members of the House of Commons in 1791 if he had ever heard Africans singing on board his slave ship during three voyages in the 1760s. Falconbridge replied that "the poor wretches" would indeed sing, "but when they do, their songs are generally, as may naturally be expected, melancholy lamentations of their exile from their native country." Another shipboard surgeon, Ecroyde Claxton, likewise testified:

> They were ordered to sing by the captain, but they were songs of sad lamentations. The words of the songs used by them were, Madda! Madda! Yiera! Bemini! Madda! Aufera! that is to say, they were all sick, and by and

> by they should be no more; they also sang songs expressive of their fears of being beat, of their want of victuals, particularly the want of their native food, and of their never returning to their own country.

A third witness, ship's carpenter James Towne, reflected on the African singing he had heard at sea: "I never found it any thing joyous, but lamentations. What I did not understand I made it my business to learn what the subject was . . . and from their information it was complaints for having been taken away from their friends and relations."

No surprise there, then: human beings were distressed and distraught at having been kidnapped and separated from all they knew and all they loved. But on the other side of the musical coin, one of the most abominable aspects of the Middle Passage – one with far-reaching cultural consequences – was the masquerade of merriment enforced by the coercion of the white man's whip. As Katrina Dyonne Thompson has shown in her harrowing study of slave performance, kidnapped Africans were dragged up, out of the filth and suffocation of the mid-decks, on to the upper decks of the ships and forced to sing and dance – not only for exercise but also to create the impression of their own happiness in bondage. "One slaver testified before Parliament that during his voyage they taught the captives lyrics that 'they are compelled to sing while they are dancing.' On one ship the captives were forced to sing 'Meffe, meffe, Mackarida,' which translated to 'Good Living or Messing well among White Men.'" This coercion was to continue in the slave-labor camps of America ("politely called plantations") for as long as the practice of slavery persisted. African bondsmen and women were forced, upon pain of injury or death, to keep dancing and singing happily at the white man's behest, laying the groundwork for the degrading minstrel stereotypes of the "happy darkey" that dominated American popular culture throughout the nineteenth and early twentieth centuries.

Supercilious musicology often marked the observations of Europeans first encountering the sounds and songs of Africans. Hence one Captain Richard Jobson, sent on a mission in 1621 to explore the commercial possibilities along the Gambia River:

> They have little varieties of instruments; that which is most common in use, is made of a great gourd, and a necke thereunto fastened, resembling in some sort, our Bandora. . . . In consortship with this they have many times another who playes upon a little drumme which he holds under his left arme, and with a crooked stick in his right hand, and his naked fingers on the left he strikes the drumme, and with his mouth gaping open, makes a rude noyse, resembling much the manner and countenance of those kinde of distressed people which amongst us are called changelings.

However much they were dismissed offhand as "rude noyse" by European commentators, the African songs brought to America in fact spanned from "the relatively simple to the complex, and served a range of purposes, not all of them readily appreciated by outsiders." Often these took the forms of musical "calls":

> Particularly when African influences were strong – in the early years of slavery, for example, or wherever groups of newly arrived slaves were kept together – calls functioned as an alternative communication system, conveying information through the medium of sounds that whites could neither confidently understand nor easily jam. Calls constructed from the language of the slaves' homeland were, of course, unintelligible to whites, and to many slaves. But, just as West African drums could "talk" by imitating the rhythmic and tonal characteristics of speech, so too, in all probability, could some of the wordless calls of the North American slaves.

There were the "calls" and there were the "cries" – not the same thing, according to the late Ethiopian composer, Ashenafi Kebede. "Calls" were meant to convey factual information. "Cries," however, were meant to express

> a deeply felt emotional experience, such as hunger, loneliness, or lovesickness. They are half-sung and half-yelled. Vocables are often intermixed in the text. The melodies are performed in a free and spontaneous style; they are often ornamented and employ many African vocal devices, such as yodels, echolike falsetto, tonal glides, embellished melismas, and microtonal inflections that are often impossible to indicate in European staff notation.

Out of these calls and cries came the African foundations of American music. They morphed into work songs and spirituals, blues and jazz; and they became vehicles of cultural preservation and resistance to oppression.

Slave owners and overseers, as well as legislators in slaveholding societies, often didn't know what to do with African music. They might outlaw the use of drums, out of fear of clandestine communication for an uprising; but at the same time they were frightened by silence, which just as well may have signalled malign plotting underway. "A silent slave was not liked by master or overseers. 'Make a noise, make a noise' was the injunction to slaves when they were silent." So, "shouts," "hollers," "calls," and "cries" from the field were accepted and, when slow and mournful, explicable enough as lamentations, even to plantation masters. But the presumed lamentations often heard and commented upon by white observers may well have been devised for strategic purposes other than lament or complaint. As one historian of slavery has observed, "the masters encouraged quick-time singing among their field slaves, but the slaves proved themselves masters of slowing down the songs and the work."

As chattel slavery expanded and became more firmly entrenched in the colonial economy, slaveholders would often clamp down on overtly African forms of musical expression, with or without the use of drums. The poet Amiri Baraka (writing as LeRoi Jones) saw this as constituting

> the basic difference between the first slaves and their offspring. The African slave continued to chant his native chants, singing his native songs, at work, even though the singing of them might be forbidden or completely out of context. But being forbidden, the songs were after a time changed into other forms that weren't forbidden in contexts that were contemporary.

Among those "permitted" forms was the spiritual, most likely "the first black music performed in English," eventually leaving its mark on the entire spectrum of American music – on "martial, entertainment, and art music, while providing a precedent for both black and white songs of protest."

It would be impossible to date the composition of the first African American spiritual. Emanating from the gradual and complex adoption of Christian theology melded with inherited African traditions, spirituals served a number of communicative purposes facilitated by the "coded meanings" they contained – a process and phenomenon named by Henry Louis Gates, Jr., as "signifying." Spirituals, accompanying ring shouts and dances in the praise houses that were the forerunners of the African American churches, were instruments of cultural cohesion through which "the new African Americans were able to survive the loss of their shared languages and customs." They transmitted not only "religious truth but information that was vital for survival in the face of ferocious opposition." A man, woman, or child designated a slave might be tortured or put to death for speaking of freedom, or for learning to read and write; but they might sing of crossing the River Jordan and get away with it. As one historian of musical subversion observes: "Protest songs do not always advertise their protestations, and often reveal extraordinary adaptability to the dictates and values of the authorities." But as far as spirituals go, we will have to wait until the mid-nineteenth century before the historical record offers up any clues as to what actual words may have been sung, even for generations prior. Not until 1861 will the first complete text of an African American spiritual be published.

Settler-colonial exploitation – and songs arising from it – did not end with Indigenous Americans and kidnapped Africans. From the early 1620s onward, countless numbers of the destitute from England's workhouses, Ireland's fields and prisons, Scotland's rebellious Highlands, and Roma (or "Gypsy") encampments everywhere were "spirited," "nabbed," "kidnapped" (literally "to seize a child"), and "trepanned" ("to entrap or ensnare a person for labor"), to be shipped to American plantations as indentured servants. A vast number of these were children. Indentured servitude shared many degrading qualities with the institution of chattel slavery, with one important difference (besides the overriding determinant of skin color): indentured servants could hold out the hope of their servitude expiring after a finite number of years.

A thriving trade developed, with British city merchants combining with ships' captains and nefarious press gangs to ensure a steady supply of cheap, mostly white, labor to augment the ongoing kidnapping and transportation of Africans. The indentured servant's ordeal was typically hellish: "These people . . . had to turn over their pay for five or seven years to cover the cost of passage. They were packed into ships almost as densely as were the black slaves from Africa, in journeys that lasted months. On board they were plagued by sickness and many died, especially the children." Once in America, the survivors "were bought and sold much like slaves. From that point on, their lives were completely controlled by their masters, the women subject to sexual abuse, the men beaten and whipped for disobeying orders."

Unsurprisingly, a history of resistance and uprising among indentured servants marked the colonial landscape as long as the practice persisted. In Maine in 1636, Virginia in 1661, Maryland in 1663, and on into the eighteenth century, rebellions broke out up and down the colonial seaboard. Some of these uprisings were characterized by alliances between indentured servants and escapees from chattel slavery, both African and Indigenous. But there is also evidence that, once their period of indenture had ended, many former servants became landowners in their own right and active agents in the dispossession of Indigenous people's lands.

Indentured servitude also left its mark on colonial protest balladry – unsurprisingly, as among the "rogues and vagabonds" habitually swept up for transportation to the colonies were "common Players of Interludes and Minstrells wandring abroade." We cannot say who it was that wrote the broadside ballad variously printed in London, Edinburgh, and elsewhere as "The Virginia Maid's Lament," "The Distressed Damsel," or "The Trappan'd Maiden." But we can surely appreciate, through three short stanzas, the depths of abuse that would naturally spark concerted resistance to the practice of indentured servitude:

> Seven long years I serv'd
> To Captain Welsh, a laird,
> In the lands of Virginia, O;
> And he so cruelly
> Sold me to Madam Guy,
> And O but I'm weary, weary O.

We are yoked in a plough,
And wearied sair enough,
In the lands of Virginia O;
With the yoke upon our neck,
Till our hearts are like to break,
And O but I'm weary, weary, O.

When we're called home to meat,
There's little there to eat;
In the lands of Virginia, O;
We're whipt at every meal,
And our backs are never heal,
And O but I'm weary, weary O.

In the new Puritan colony six hundred miles to the north of Jamestown, a different, more carnivalesque style of resistance – one with both song and indentured servitude at its heart – was unfolding. In 1624, a mere four years after the "Pilgrim" separatists on the *Mayflower* (hoping to reach the northernmost area of the Virginia colony) had found themselves on the shore of Cape Cod Bay, where they established the Plymouth colony, a liberal English barrister "founded a decidedly non-Puritan colony in Wollaston, now the township of Quincy outside of Boston." Thomas Morton and a band of associates – among them "thirty male indentured servants" – named their proto-hippy commune "Merrymount, punning on Mare-Mount and Mary-Mount, direct references to bestial sodomy and Roman Catholicism." Morton freed the indentured servants, naming them his "consociates" in equality. He had long been a critic of the Plymouth Puritans' social and legal austerity as well as their hostility towards the Indigenous people, particularly the Algonquians, with whom he had become friendly – to the point of providing them with arms for their self-defense against raids from hostile neighbors, a major affront to the Plymouth authorities.

In 1628, Morton hosted a May Day celebration at Merrymount. Knowing full well the red rag he was waving before the "precise Separatists" of Plymouth (as he called them), he and his "consociates" erected a maypole decked in the most provocative pagan imagery, and invited scores of their Indigenous friends to mingle with the colonists and drink their fill. In what may well be the first significant American example of a secular song coming up against the wrath of the governing establishment, Morton composed a not-so-implicit musical challenge to the reigning Puritan prohibitions, nailing it to the maypole and inviting all the revellers to sing its verses aloud. They began with an ode to Hymen, the pagan deity of "the wedding feast and of the virgin's marriage bed," as accompaniment to a series of ritualistic marriages "concluded between whites and Indians, all of whom [were] reeling with drink and dressed in the heads and hides of forest beasts or in the traditional garb of the Indians":

> Drink and be merry, merry, merry boys,
> Let all your delight be in Hymen's joys,
> Io to Hymen now the day is come:
> About the merry Maypole take room.
> Make green garlands, bring bottles out
> And fill sweet Nectar freely about,
> Uncover thy head, and fear no harm,
> For her[es] good liquor to keep it warm.
> Then drink and be merry, & c.
> Io to Hymen, & c.

In a further provocation to Puritan sensibilities, as he poured out the drinks for his guests, Morton explicitly invoked "the archetypical male lovers in Greek mythology," Zeus (Jupiter) and Ganymede (whom Morton called "Gammedes"). And with its emphasis on drinking and sexual abandon (both gay and straight), Morton's song contained one further affront, the explicit invitation to Indigenous women to join in the revels: "Lasses in beaver coats come away, / Ye shall be welcome to us night and day."

Years later, William Bradford, the erstwhile Governor of the Plymouth Colony, looked back on the events at Merrymount with high-handed disdain:

> They then fell to utter licentiousness, and led a dissolute and profane life. Morton became a Lord of Misrule, and maintained (as it were) a School of Atheism. And after they had got some goods into their hands, and got much by trading with the Indians, they spent it as vainly in quaffing and drinking, both wine and strong waters in great excess (and, as some reported), £10 worth in a morning. They also set up a maypole, drinking and dancing about it many days together, inviting the Indian women for their consorts, dancing and frisking together like so many fairies, or furies, rather; and worse practices. As if they had anew revived and celebrated the feasts of the Roman goddess Flora, or the beastly practices of the mad Bacchanalians.

Bradford placed special emphasis on the part played by Morton's song in securing his infamy: "Morton likewise, to show his poetry, composed sundry rhymes and verses, some tending to lasciviousness, and others to the detraction and scandal of some persons, which he affixed to this idle or idol maypole."

The Merrymount celebrations were brought to an abrupt end by a militia under the command of Captain Myles Standish (whom Morton later derided as "Captain Shrimp"). Morton was arrested, tried, and subsequently exiled back to England, where he acquitted himself before the Inns of Court and published "political tracts that accused the Puritans of many crimes, including a fear of the native peoples that manifested itself in near-genocidal behavior." In a supreme gesture of retribution, the Plymouth elders sent their angel of vengeance, in the form of the notoriously zealous future governor of Massachusetts Bay, John Endecott, out to Merrymount to make a grand show of chopping down Morton's maypole.

Endecott's ritualistic act inspired Nathaniel Hawthorne to compose one of the most celebrated of his *Twice-Told Tales*, "The May-Pole of Merry Mount" (1832). In this story, "Jollity and gloom were contending for an empire," as Hawthorne says of Puritan Massachusetts, where the innocent revelers around a maypole – to the accompaniment of "pipe, cittern, and

Figure 2.2 A nineteenth-century engraving of Captain Myles Standish and his men observing the May Day festivities at Merrymount. Engraver unknown.

viol, touched with practised minstrelsy" – are set upon and vanquished by the pious, bloodthirsty militiamen under Endecott's command. "Their weapons were always at hand to shoot down the straggling savage," Hawthorne's narrator observes.

> When they met in conclave, it was never to keep up the old English mirth, but to hear sermons three hours long, or to proclaim bounties on the heads of wolves and the scalps of Indians. Their festivals were fast days, and their chief pastime the singing of psalms. Woe to the youth or maiden who did but dream of a dance!

When Endecott's sword finally slices through the maypole, ending the revels, his mercilessness sets the tone for the unfolding history of Puritan America:

> And with his keen sword Endicott [*sic*] assaulted the hallowed Maypole. Nor long did it resist his arm. It groaned with a dismal sound; it showered leaves and rosebuds upon the remorseless enthusiast; and finally, with all its green boughs and ribbons and flowers, symbolic of departed pleasures, down fell the banner staff of Merry Mount. As it sank, tradition says, the evening sky grew darker, and the woods threw forth a more sombre shadow.

We now know that Hawthorne's description of Puritan cultural severity, not least with regard to secular music, was somewhat overstated – a charge he was to repeat in his novel *The Scarlet Letter* (1850), in his depiction of the grim society that persecutes the protagonist, Hester Prynne, for adultery. Hester's Boston offers "no rude shows of a theatrical kind; no minstrel, with his harp and legendary ballad, nor gleeman, with an ape dancing to his music." Historians have subsequently pointed out that surviving diaries from the Puritan period, such as that of Judge Samuel Sewall, and the poetry of Anne Bradstreet (North America's first published poet), express both the knowledge and enjoyment of music outside religious settings. As we will shortly see, however, music and song *do* become a battleground as New England society develops; but for now it is important to acknowledge one area in which Hawthorne was correct in his depiction of the Puritan brutality that led to the destruction of Thomas Morton's utopian colony. It is encapsulated in one phrase, to repeat: "the straggling savage."

To put it plainly, and with all humane exceptions admitted, the Puritan colonists came to see the elimination of the Indigenous presence as a "wonderful preparation" for the establishment of their "New Jerusalem," their "City upon a hill" (as Massachusetts Bay Governor John Winthrop called it). The Indigenous people lived their lives out of doors, in the midst of the satanic "howling wilderness" that the Puritans had come to redeem for the glory of God. The "saints" (as the Puritan elders modestly called themselves) saw their Indigenous neighbors as filthy, and

> "filthiness" was sin. . . . [Indigenous people] showed small concern about covering their nakedness. They were happily loose about premarital sex. Women were mistresses of their own bodies. They had no real marriage at all in the eyes of some Europeans. Divorce was easy, and – utterest abomination – male homosexuality was tolerated openly, even institutionalized.

Indeed, one historian has concluded that "alternative genders" were "among the most widely shared features of North American societies" in the period of initial European contact.

More to the point, the Indigenous people were impediments to colonial expansion. For Winthrop, among others, their associations with the "untamed" wilderness meant that, as in Virginia, their land was England's for the taking. This assumption, of course, was a falsehood, as the tribes of Massachusetts had their own demonstrable systems of land cultivation. Nevertheless:

> Responding to scrupulous objections against seizing Indian property, Winthrop declared in 1629 that most land in America fell under the legal rubric of *vacuum domicilium* because the Indians had not "subdued" it and therefore had only a "natural" and not a "civil" right to it. Such natural right need not be respected in the same way as civil right; only the latter imposed the obligations of true legal property.

Some historians have argued that this dubious rationalization was at the bottom of "New England's first Anglo-Indian War," the so-called Pequot War of 1636–1637 in what is now Rhode Island and southeastern Connecticut. The war began with the killing of an Englishman, John Stone, "a white trader, Indian-kidnapper, and troublemaker." Under Endecott's command, Stone's murder was repaid by a punitive raid and pillage on Block Island in the Long Island Sound. The war ended not only with the physical obliteration of the Pequot tribe, but also its "executive termination": "In 1638, at the conclusion of the Pequot War, the Treaty of Hartford stipulated that the surviving Indians 'shall no more be called Pequots but Narragansetts and Mohegans.'" The treaty also stipulated that the Pequot River would now be called the Thames, and that the village formerly known as Pequot would be called New London "in remembrance . . . of the chief city in our dear native country." And how cruel and gloating was the recollection of one of Endecott's comrades in conquest, Captain John Mason, who described the silencing of the singing and dancing he had heard among the roughly four hundred Pequot men,

Figure 2.3 A figure depicting the Puritan settlers' attack on the Pequot village at Mistick. From John Underhill, *Newes from America* (London, 1638).
Library of Congress Rare Book and Special Collections Division

women, and children of Mistick, before his army of ninety men slaughtered them: "We were like Men in a Dream; and then was our Mouth filled with Laughter, and our Tongues with Singing; thus we may say the Lord hath done great Things for us among the Heathen, whereof we are glad. Praise ye the Lord!"

When Oliver Cromwell's Puritans colonized Ulster in Ireland (1649–1653) and subdued the clans of Scotland (1650), they made a point of forbidding, upon pain of death, the singing of "native bardic myth-historians." In New England, the subjugation of Indigenous song was often, though not always, pursued by subtler means. Just as the Spanish missionaries in Mexico and the Southwest had worked to infiltrate the Indigenous consciousness and soundscape with hymns, Gregorian chants, organs, guitars, and bassoons, in Massachusetts the task of converting "heathens" into "praying Indians" fell to the Puritan minister John

Eliot, known as the "Indian Apostle." Eliot taught the villagers of Nontaum (now Newton) to sing approved song texts in their native Algonquian and translated the catechism for them in 1646; this became "the first book published in a Native tongue." His Algonquian translations of the New Testament (1661) and Old Testament (1663) followed. By the time his work was done, Eliot had succeeded in converting over 1100 heathenish souls and established fourteen communities of "Praying Indians" in Massachusetts. To be sure, Puritan auditors, including Endecott and Eliot himself, were unsettled by hearing "our ordinary English tunes" set to Massachusett Algonquian, these tunes being unavoidably filtered through the unfamiliar, non-Western musical nuances of the Indigenous voice, which Eliot crudely reduced to "Ululation, Howling, Yelling, or Mourning."

But in Puritan Massachusetts, who was permitted to sing what? And how should they be permitted to sing it, whatever "it" was? In the realm of sacred music, there were battles over musical doctrine that extended well into the eighteenth century. Indeed, not until then would the singing of hymns be officially sanctioned. Hymns, so the argument went, were created by lesser mortals and had "no Biblical sanction." But psalms were something else, for they came directly from the Old Testament and had been composed by King David himself; and in the New Testament, St. Peter had declared: "If any be merry, let him sing psalms." So, with such an imprimatur, there appeared the first book to be printed in the British colonies of North America, *The Whole Booke of Psalmes Faithfully Translated into English Meter*, or – as it is more commonly known – the *Bay Psalm Book*, published by Stephen Daye of Cambridge, Massachusetts, in 1640.

The Bay Psalm Book was the product of a rejection by the Massachusetts Bay colonists of the psalters brought to America from Holland two decades earlier and which were still in use by the "separatists" of the neighboring, somewhat rival, Plymouth Colony. The Massachusetts Bay elders were particularly unhappy with the translations from Hebrew in the imported psalters – not only for their perceived ecclesiastical mistakes but also for their stylistic embellishments. In the preface to the first edition of the *Bay Psalm Book*, the Reverend John Cotton made this point plain:

> If therefore the verses are not always so smooth and elegant as some may desire or expect; let them consider that God's Altar needs not our polishings ... for we have respected rather a plain translation, than to smooth our verses with the sweetness of any paraphrase, and have attended Conscience rather than Elegance, fidelity rather than poetry, in translating the Hebrew words into English language, and David's poetry into English metre.

One doesn't immediately think of the Puritans in connection with "protest music," but in fact protest was central to the body of church music in the New England colonies – protest against competing forms and expressions of religious doctrine, protest against the temptations of secular thought, and protest against the practice of music itself, both in terms of lyrical content and in terms of musical form and instrumentation. To repeat: music itself was a battleground in Puritan society. As one historian has noted (and with such exceptions as Sewall and Bradstreet admitted):

> The Protestant ethic, reinforced by the wilderness experience, led the Puritans and other religious zealots to consider music a waste of time unless specifically contributing to the task at hand. The power of music to affect human emotions caused the Calvinist denominations especially to view it with more suspicion than fondness and therefore to restrict its role even in worship.

But there was something else. Musical practice could be a symbol of holy – or unholy – allegiance. Organs, choirs, even reading and writing musical notation (as opposed to rote singing) sailed perilously close to Catholicism if not to "outright witchcraft." Such prejudices held sway in New England until the early eighteenth century, when musical literacy and "note-singing" were increasingly encouraged by liberal church reformers. "The Old Way," or "Usual Singing," gave way to the practice of "Regular Singing," that is, the note-reading introduced by the wave of "singing schools" championed by the Reverend Thomas Symmes of Bradford, Massachusetts. In his manifesto, *The Reasonableness of Regular Singing* (1720), Symmes pleaded: "Would it not greatly tend to the promoting [of] Singing Psalms, if Singing Schools were promoted; Would not this be a Conforming to Scripture Pattern? Have we not as much need of them as GOD's People of *Singing*, and more than that of *Reading*?" An unhappy correspondent to the *New England Chronicle* reflected what Symmes was up against, writing in 1723: "If we once begin to sing by note, the next thing will be to pray by *rule*, and preach by rule; and then comes Popery." Such objections notwithstanding, even the Puritan divine Cotton Mather eventually came on board with a tract championing the singing-school movement. Mather's *The Accomplished Singer* (1721) justifies the adoption of formal music education in New England: "Intended for the assistance of all that sing psalms with grace in their hearts, but more particularly to accompany the laudable endeavours of those who are learning to sing by Rule, and seeking to preserve a REGULAR SINGING in the Assemblies of the Faithful."

Gradually the ironclad domination of the psalm gave way to an acceptance of hymns, notably with the importation and reprinting of the

English clergyman Isaac Watts's *Hymns* (1707) along with his *Psalms of David Imitated in the Language of the New Testament* (1719). Watts had proved himself very congenial to the imperial designs of settler colonialism, as his brazen reworking of Psalm 100 indicated. The King James Bible had originally proclaimed, "Make a joyful noise unto the LORD, all ye lands. / Serve the LORD with gladness: come before his presence with singing." But for Watts, this *really* meant: "Sing to the Lord with joyful voice, / Let ev'ry land his name adore; / The British isles shall send the noise / Across the ocean to the shore."

Such British "noise" could prove useful in a variety of ways. It certainly helped, for instance, in the pacification and indoctrination of the Mohegan tribes of Connecticut, as the converted Mohegan missionary and teacher Samson Occom recalled in his *Short Narrative of My Life* (1768): "My Method in our Religious Meetings was this; Sabbath Morning we Assemble together about 10 o'C and begin with Singing; we generally Sung Dr. Watt's Psalms or Hymns. I distinctly read the Psalm or Hymn first, and then gave the meaning of it to them, and after that Sing, then pray, and Sing again after Prayer."

But there was also some "noise" that needed to be filtered out. This was one of the objectives of the singing-school movement. As Symmes argued, a rigorous musical education was needed "to divert young people . . . from learning idle, foolish, yea pernicious songs and ballads, and banish all such trash from their minds." Ah, the poor, maligned ballad, with its associations with the alehouse, the street, the high seas, the largely secular folk tradition, the oral tradition, the working-class tradition, the traditions of resistance and rebellion. Ballads were, in short, popular; and they were relatively cheap to obtain, printed not in expensive bound volumes but rather on halfpenny or penny broadsides – "single sheets of paper printed on one side only . . . [and] sold on the street by hawkers and pedlars – street performers in their own right." While the Puritan authorities in New England were, overall, "not friendly to ballad making," broadside ballads were remarkably resilient in spite of their ephemeral nature. Moreover, they might be used as easily for conservative or reactionary purposes as for progressive or revolutionary ones. Indeed, they sometimes proved directly useful to the Puritan mission itself. Since "an austere religious interpretation of life reduced any subject matter to an illustration of either God's wrath or favour," a ballad might effectively become "a sermon." Thus the eminent John Winthrop was elegized through a ballad composed by Percival Lowell (d. 1665), "the ancestor of the Lowell family in America," who also used the opportunity to take a swipe at the Puritans' avowed enemy, "Popery": "Death like a murth'ring Jesuite / Hath rob'd us of our hearts delight."

By the last quarter of the seventeenth century, Indigenous people across the continent had had more than enough of European encroachment on their lands, pacification (whether through psalms and hymns or by harsher means), and the attempted eradication of their cultures. Wars of resistance erupted from sea to shining sea. From Florida in the east to California in the west, the Spanish colonists fought rear-guard actions and faced a particularly stunning defeat with the so-called Pueblo Revolt of 1680 in New Mexico, which cleared the territory of Iberian settlers for a dozen years. In New England, the second full-scale war between Puritan colonists and Indigenous people broke out in 1675. During this conflict, subsequently known as King Philip's War, sound and song became part of the military arsenal – "psychological weapons" on both sides.

The Puritan war against the Wampanoags began with a convenient charge of murder leveled against their chief, Metacom, known to the settlers as "Philip" – ironically, "the name he [had] asked for as a compliment to the English." As Howard Zinn encapsulates it, the murder charge proved a useful pretext for the Puritans to begin

> a war of conquest against the Wampanoags, a war to take their land ... The Indians certainly did not want war, but they matched atrocity with atrocity. When it was over, in 1676, the English had won, but their resources were drained; they had lost six hundred men. Three thousand Indians were dead, including Metacom himself.

During the early days of the war, on August 3, 1675, the English inhabitants of Brookfield, Massachusetts, took refuge in a garrison house as a band of Nipmuc warriors – former "Praying Indians" who were no longer "pacified" by Christian counsels of meekness – stormed the adjacent town church and began loudly mocking the settlers and firing their weapons at them. One witness, Captain Thomas Wheeler, recalled:

> They continued *shooting & shouting*, & proceeded in their *former wickedness blaspheming the Name of the Lord*, and *reproaching* us *his Afflicted Servants*, scoffing at our *prayers* as they were sending in their *shot* upon all quarters of the house. And many of them went to the Towns *meeting house* (which was, within *twenty Rods* of the house in which we were) who mocked saying, *Come and pray, & sing Psalms*, & in Contempt made an hideous noise *somewhat resembling singing*.

And just as their Virginian counterparts had done in response to the "Powhatan Uprising" of 1622, the Puritan colonists drafted in the broadside ballad to demonize the Indigenous people, to exculpate the English, and to justify their vengeance. Such is the example of Captain Wait Winthrop's ballad composed in December 1675 under the torturous title, "Some Meditations Concerning our HONOURABLE Gentlemen and Fellow-Souldiers, In Pursuit of those Barbarous NATIVES in the NARRAGANSIT-Country; and Their Service there." Of Winthrop's thirty-two stanzas, two stand out for their intimations of cruelty and menace to come, lathered with pious assertions that any Indigenous attacks, and subsequent English losses, could only have been the result of some inscrutable divine chastisement, rather than for any meaner, greedier, more earthly reasons:

O New-England, I understand,
with thee God is offended:
And therefore He doth humble thee,
till thou thy ways hast mended.

Repent, therefore, and do no more,
advance thy self so High.
But humbled be, and thou shalt see
these Indians soon will dy.

King Philip's War produced other ballads protesting Indigenous "treacheries" against a curiously mixed backdrop of presumed English innocence and divine displeasure. Unsurprisingly, we have no record of what any Indigenous participants may have themselves been singing (barring the mocking singing of psalms noted by Wheeler). However, their music was remarked upon by one colonial woman, Mary Rowlandson, who was held hostage for eleven weeks by a coalition of Narragansett, Wampanoag, and Nipmuc fighters who had attacked the settlement of Lancaster, Massachusetts, in February 1675. In her best-selling captivity narrative (published in 1682), Rowlandson noted the "roaring, and singing and dancing, and yelling of those black creatures in the night, which made the place a lively resemblance of hell." Continually removed to different locations during her captivity, she recalled the sounds of her twentieth and final "remove," where Indigenous people danced to the accompaniment of "two others singing and knocking on a kettle for their music." We will never know whether the singers overheard by Rowlandson were singing in celebration; in worship; in protest against continued English incursion into their territories; in lament over their own relatives lost to smallpox, typhoid, and other diseases introduced by the Europeans; in outrage over the humiliation of their chief, Metacom, who had been forced by the Massachusetts Bay authorities in 1671 to surrender his tribal arms; or in contempt for the kangaroo courts and death sentences of Wampanoag tribesmen in the Plymouth Colony. All these affronts had contributed to the "cold war mentality" between the Wampanoag and the English that finally drove the opposing parties to full-scale war.

Compounding the fractures of racial and religious schism in the settler-colonial enterprise was the enduring reality of class struggle, a thread running through some of the earliest expressions of musical protest in British America just as it ran through the wider society. As we have seen, a ballad such as "The Virginia Maid's Lament" could powerfully express the discontent of a white involuntary immigrant in the earliest years of English settlement, against the backdrop of plots and rebellions among indentured servants from Maine to Virginia. Another ballad, "An Invitation to North America," which appeared as a London broadside sometime in the early eighteenth century, extols the lures of *voluntary* emigration specifically as an antidote to class exploitation from a host of oppressive interests. There are the "farmers in England" who "sell their corn so dear / They do what they can to starve the poor here. / They send it to France, which sure is not right, / To feed other nations that against us do fight." These wealthy, unscrupulous farmers are allied to the "landlords in England" who "raise the lands high" and to the "priests in England" who "come into the field" to "tithe as they please." All this carries on, regardless of a depressed economy in which "for weavers and combers no work's to be had." The answer: "Poor men had better go to North America." Such ballads, when read against the catalog of late seventeenth- and early eighteenth-century uprisings and strikes in the British American colonies – among fishermen in Maine; coopers, shoemakers, and ships' carpenters in Boston; carters in New York City; and indentured servants everywhere – indicate how class antagonisms were transported to America along with the hopes of working-class emigrants, both voluntary and involuntary.

One of the most monumental and complex uprisings of the early colonial period was Bacon's Rebellion of 1675–1676 in Virginia, actually a conflation of two separate waves of resistance. First, there were the middling farmer-settlers challenging the colonial authorities who, they believed, had been negligent in protecting them from Indigenous attacks in spite of the high taxes imposed upon them. Secondly, there were a host of escapees from slavery and indentured servitude who had combined to fight against the governor's forces. Although the leader of the uprising, Nathaniel Bacon, was himself a wealthy, landed planter, he was denounced in broadsides and parliamentary speeches as "a Leveller" and eulogized in balladry by an anonymous indentured servant as "Our hopes of safety, liberty, our all." But even such a revolutionary moment – and movement – was compromised in the messy landscape of conquest and colonization, as the Indigenous people of Virginia were well aware. Any progressive associations with Bacon's Rebellion must be tempered by the understanding that "the Anglo settler-farmers" of Bacon's army "took into their own hands the slaughter of Indigenous farmers with the aim of taking their land." Consequently, "Bacon's Rebellion affected the development of genocidal policies aimed at the Indigenous peoples – namely, the creation of wealth in the colonies based on landholding and the use of landless or land-poor settler-farmers as foot soldiers for moving the settlement frontier deeper into Indigenous territories."

In the immediate wake of Bacon's Rebellion in the south came a series of disruptive labor strikes in New York City between 1677 and 1684, the Boston Revolt of 1689 (which pitted disaffected militia and provincial citizens against the New England authorities), Leisler's Rebellion of 1689–1691 in New York State (small farmers, artisans, shopkeepers, and sailors versus the ruling "patroon" class of landholders), and the Knowles Riot of Boston in 1747, one of many eighteenth-century riots against the practice of impressing poor colonial freemen against their will into the Royal Navy. The immediate decades before the French and Indian War of 1754–1763 saw class divisions so deepen that municipal tax records could show 40 percent of Boston's wealth in the hands of "the richest one percent of the property owners." In April of 1734, near Exeter, New Hampshire, destitute tenant farmers invaded wealthy estates to chop down trees for firewood. When a British officer arrived with a militia, his men were attacked and driven back by "local residents."

It was in the context of such prevailing class antagonisms that a popular balladry emerged to celebrate the outlaw or the escaped prisoner. "The Escape of Old John Webber," otherwise known as "Billy Broke Locks," was based on a Salem, Massachusetts, prison break sometime around 1735: "Billy broke locks and Billy broke bolts, / And Billy broke all that he came nigh, / Until he came to the dungeon door, / And that he broke right manfully." The ballad ends with the rescued prisoner celebrating on the riverbank with the friend who had sprung him: "And then they called for a room to dance / (And who but they danced merrily), / And the best dancer among them all / Was old John Webber who was just set free."

Ballads of outlaws and rebellion might be sung to the rafters in taverns by free white men, if only within the hearing of friendly ears. Printing them was another matter, as John Peter Zenger, editor of the *New York Weekly Journal*, found to his discomfiture in 1734, having been indicted for printing "scandalous and Seditious Songs or Ballads" lampooning the colony's royal governor. The grand jury ruled that, in the event of the authors never being identified, the ballads themselves should be "burnt before the City Hall ... by the hands of the Common hangman or Whipper."

Such a surreal judgment was nothing compared to the judicial rulings faced by Black musicians and singers held in bondage – not least in South Carolina, which saw the Stono rebellion of 1739 begin with African drumming and song, as one official account reported:

> On the 9th day of September last being Sunday which is the day the Planters allow them to work for themselves, Some Angola Negroes assembled, to the number of Twenty; at a place called Stonehow. ... Several negroes joined them, they calling out Liberty, marched on with Colours displayed, and two Drums beating, pursuing all the white people they met with, and killing Man Woman and Child. ... They increased every minute by new Negroes coming to them, so that they were above Sixty, some say a hundred, on which they halted in a field, and set to dancing, Singing and beating Drums, to draw more Negroes to them, thinking they were now victorious over the whole Province, having marched ten miles & burnt all before them without opposition.

A wave of repressive legislation immediately followed. South Carolina banned the enslaved from "using or keeping of drums, horns, or other loud instruments, which may call together, or give sign or notice to one another of their wicked designs or purposes." In North Carolina, even "free Negroes" – let alone the enslaved – were forbidden from gathering to sing and dance. African drums were banned as dangerous communicative instruments. But as Baraka has explained, musical adaptation proved a key survival strategy:

> Where the use of the African drum was strictly forbidden, other percussive devices had to be found, like the empty oil drums that led to the development of the West Indian steel bands. Or the metal wash basin turned upside down and floated in another basin that sounds, when beaten, like an African hollow-log drum. The Negro's way in this part of the Western world was adaptation and reinterpretation.

As we have seen and shall again see, the spiritual was a product of similar "adaptation and reinterpretation" in the realm of song.

As class divisions – racialized or otherwise – deepened in the colonial economy, songs preserved their potency as an outlet for the expression of profound discontent. In times of war, the developing store of labor songs dovetailed with those against military exploitation and involuntary servitude. In particular, the lamentations of Irish boys and men dragooned into the British army became almost a ballad subgenre in itself. One well-remembered example is "Felix the Soldier." No one knows who wrote it; it has come down to us as a folk memory of the French and Indian War:

They took away my brogues
And they robbed me of my spade,
They put me in the army
And a soldier of me made.

But I couldn't beat the drum,
And I couldn't play the flute,
So they handed me a musket
And taught me how to shoot . . .

But the Injuns they were sly,
And the Frenchies they were coy,
So they shot off the left leg
Of this poor Irish boy . . .

I will bid my spade adieu,
For I cannot dig the bog,
But I still can play a fiddle
And I still can drink my grog.

The ten years following the end of the French and Indian War saw an exponential growth of American ballads appearing as broadsides. Many of these marked a middle-class reaction against the revenue policies of the British government in the colonies, where – in order to recoup the expenditures of war – such hated impositions as the American Revenue Act (or Sugar Act) of 1764 and the Stamp Act of 1765 sowed the seeds of the colonial backlash that would end in the establishment of the USA. As we shall see, that colonial backlash – and the British backlash *against* that backlash – are well represented in song.

CHAPTER 3

A Capital Chop

In the immediate aftermath of the French and Indian War, the popular musical landscape of the American colonies reflected the increasingly heated atmosphere of protest against the British parliament's habit of legislating for the colonies without colonial input. Broadside ballads spilled from printing presses all up and down the seaboard, and, while many dealt with a variety of subjects, "the majority mention Britain's oppression of America." These musical developments were, in fact, less a departure from than a continuance of the British tradition of "itinerant ballad-singers who stood on London street corners, singing the latest news and gossip to well-known tunes and selling printed copies of the verses." Indeed, many colonial protest songs were meant to reinforce the connection to a British musical, as well as political, tradition. Lyrics of resistance were, more often than not, set to traditional or popular British tunes, from "God Save the King" on the high end to the lowest gutter ballad: "To the English colonists this music was a part of their cultural heritage, just as singing it for political protest was a part of their natural birthright." Even the physical form in which most colonial protest songs were disseminated was of British origin: broadside sheets "printed from woodcuts and distributed in the streets of colonial cities and villages for a penny apiece, a custom practiced in England since the early sixteenth century."

There was, of course, one further tradition inherited from Britain: that of working-class resistance. The fire that had driven the first of England's major peasant rebellions – Wat Tyler's Rebellion of 1381 – had not been extinguished with that revolt's suppression. It carried on across the centuries through a succession of rebellions against the seizures and enclosure of common lands in England, against clerical and monarchical impositions, against so-called poor laws, and against landowners. Wat Tyler's fire was reignited in Britain's North American colonies:

> For a hundred years before the Revolution, the colonies were torn by class conflict: tenants against landlords, riots of the poor. That internal conflict would now be temporarily obscured by the struggle against England. But it was still there, bursting out now and then even during the war, and emerging again after victory over the British Empire.

Thus, acts of colonial resistance at the conclusion of the French and Indian War – acts that included the composition and dissemination of protest songs – should be recognized in the broader context of an ongoing, if often eclipsed, class struggle:

> By the year 1760 there had been eighteen uprisings aimed at overthrowing colonial governments. There had also been six black rebellions, from South Carolina to New York, and forty riots of various origins. That rebellious energy soon began to be turned against England by the important people in the colonies who saw great advantages in freedom from British rule ... With the French out of the way, the colonial leadership was less in need of English protection. At the same time, the English were now more in need of the colonies' wealth. So the elements were there for conflict, especially because the war had brought glory for the generals, death to the privates, wealth for the merchants, and unemployment for the poor. The resulting anger could now be turned against England rather than against the rich men of the colonies.

One particular class of working people – enslaved Black men and women in both the northern and southern colonies – had their own peculiar battles to fight. Historians have increasingly placed their struggles in the context of the developing schism between the colonies and the so-called "Mother Country":

> On the North American continent, the reverberations of rebellion intensified after 1765, as slaves seized the new opportunities offered by splits between the imperial and colonial ruling classes. Runaways increased at a rate that alarmed slaveholders everywhere, and by the mid-1770s a rash of slave plots and revolts had sent white fears soaring. Slaves organized uprisings in Alexandria, Virginia, in 1767, Perth Amboy, New Jersey, in 1772, Saint Andrew's Parish, South Carolina, and in a joint African-Irish effort, Boston in 1774; and Ulster County, New York, Dorchester County, Maryland, Norfolk, Virginia, Charleston, South Carolina, and the Tar River region of North Carolina in 1775.

If one reads the few contemporary accounts of Black music in the waning years of the colonial period, one might think that there was very little beyond the "very droll" songs sung by the enslaved in "a very satirical stile and manner" against "the usage they have received from their Masters or Mistresses" (as noted by the English traveler Nicholas Cresswell in the mid-1770s). Yet, emerging from the general shadowland of Black protest music in the eighteenth century is one precious example to the contrary: the choral work *Promise Anthem*, composed by a musically educated man in Rhode Island called "Newport Gardner" by his enslavers – his African name was Occramer Marycoo – and based on passages from the Book of Jeremiah and the Gospel of St. Mark. There was certainly nothing "droll" about these words as they were sung on two occasions in Newport and Boston, heralding the dawn of a "Back to Africa" movement that would persist well into the twentieth century:

> For lo! the days come, saith the Lord, that I will bring again the captivity of my people
> Israel and Judah, saith the Lord;
> and I will cause them to return to the land that I gave to their fathers, and they shall possess it.
> Therefore, fear thou not, O my servant Jacob, saith the Lord; neither be dismayed, O Israel;
> For lo! I will save thee from afar, and thy seed from their captivity,
> And Jacob shall return and be in rest and quiet, and none shall make him afraid.
>
> Hear the words of the Lord, O ye African race, hear the words of promise.
> But it is not meet to take the children's bread and cast it to the dogs.
> Truth, Lord, yet the dogs eat of the crumbs that fall from their master's table.

The timing of this anthem's appearance (1764) tenuously validates by one year the claim that "few songs radical in sentiments were published between 1765 and 1768." Yet this is not to say that *no* songs "radical in sentiments" were published during those three years – much less to say that no such songs may have been composed, sung, and *not* published. The year 1765 is especially important because it saw the imposition of one of the most contentious of British levies following the French and Indian War: the Stamp Act, which taxed the use of every single page of printed paper in the colonies, provoking violent backlashes and riots. These outbreaks in turn provoked a wave of imperial repression – arbitrary arrests, deportations for trial, seizures of property, and military occupation. Hence the Quartering Act, imposed that same year, obliging the colonial subjects to provide, at their own expense, room and board for British soldiers.

The most violent of the Stamp Act riots occurred in Boston, where residents attacked the homes of both Andrew Oliver, the local agent with the unenviable task of collecting the stamp duties, and Thomas Hutchinson, the Lieutenant Governor of Massachusetts. Effigies of these and other British officials (along with Satan for good company) were soon to be seen hanging from the trees of Boston, increasingly called "Liberty Trees" by the populace. Hence the anonymous broadside ballad "Liberty, Property and No Excise," which became a rallying cry reproduced on badges and cockades worn during subsequent anti-tax protests and rebellions on both sides of the Atlantic. This particular broadside was subtitled, "A Poem, compos'd on occasion of the sight seen on the Great Trees (so called) in Boston, New England, on the 14th of August, 1765" – the "sight seen" being not only the abundance of effigies hanging like the fruits of the most fertile season but also the growing crowd numbers turning out to gaze upon them, the warning of a gathering popular storm: "But while I stood to gaze upon the tree, / Another and another came to see; / Each moment I beheld a diff'rent face, / For on they prest 'till thousands fill'd the place."

In the early days of the colonial backlash, American ire was for the most part directed at the British parliament and the colonial agents of the crown. The king himself was largely off limits for criticism. Thus, even in the midst of the Stamp Act riot in Boston, as well as a subsequent riot in Newport the following month, colonial wrath was generally restricted to the political strata below the monarchy, as the Liberty Trees proliferated along with their hangings in effigy. The *Boston Evening-Post* reported on September 2, 1765, that the Liberty Tree of Newport was being protected through a stark warning nailed to the trunk: "Whoever attempts, in any Way whatsoever, to render ineffectual this Mark of public Contempt, will be deem'd an Enemy to Liberty, and incur the Resentment of the Town." But a ballad affixed to the tree pointedly kept the monarch above the fray. "To our King we'll be loyal," the balladeer proclaimed, but "All infernal Taxes let us then nobly spurn, / These Effigies first – next the Stamp Paper burn."

It is now clear that the propertied, elite leaders of the anti-British movement sought to direct "mob energy against England," at least in part to deflect poor and working-class resentment away from themselves and colonial monied interests. Hence the calculated employment of the first-person collective – "our" – that peppers so many ballads of the period: "This was to become a critically important rhetorical device for the rule of the few, who would speak to the many of 'our' liberty, 'our' property, 'our' country."

By the close of 1765, all the gloves were off, even against the king. Hence the ballad that has been called "the opening anthem of the revolution." This was "Taxation of America," a belligerent thirty-six-stanza diatribe composed by a schoolteacher, Samuel (or possibly Peter) St. John, in Norwalk, Connecticut, reflecting in rhetoric the same outrage that had turned the streets of Boston and Newport into battle zones. The modest schoolmaster St. John threw down the gauntlet to George III himself: "To what you have commanded, we never will consent, / Although your troops are landed upon our continent; / We'll take our swords and muskets, and march in dread array, / And drive the British red-coats from North America."

In spite of such attacks against the monarch and Parliament, colonial balladeers continued to assert both their political and cultural identities *as Britons*. Such assertions were inscribed into the borrowed imagery as well as the borrowed sources. In 1766, one year after the imposition of the Stamp Act, both the *Boston Post-Boy and Advertiser* and the *Virginia Gazette* published a new ballad adapting David Garrick and William Boyce's 1759 ode to the British Navy, "Hearts of Oak." The anonymously composed colonial adaptation derisively implied that the Americans had taken up the mantle of British righteousness, now that the British themselves had seemingly abandoned it. "Hearts of Oak Are We Still," the balladeer proclaimed: "On our brow while we laurel-crowned Liberty wear, / What Englishmen ought, we Americans dare."

The Stamp Act was repealed in March of 1766 after months of colonial protest and an appeal before the House of Commons by Benjamin Franklin. However, the same day as the hated act's repeal, Parliament passed the Declaratory Act asserting firmly the British right and intention to legislate howsoever for the American colonies. Parliament made good its threat the following year by imposing the Townshend Acts (named after the Chancellor of the Exchequer, Charles Townshend), which levied duties on paper, lead, glass, paint, and tea, almost all of which had to be imported from Britain. The aims of these acts were twofold: to provide salaries for loyal colonial governors and judges, and to punish the colony of New York in particular for its steadfast resistance to the Quartering Act.

The Townshend Acts brought to the fore one of the most influential propagandists and protest songwriters of the Revolutionary era, John Dickinson, claimed as a native son by both Pennsylvania and Delaware. Somewhat misleadingly cast as the antagonist of John Adams and independence in the Broadway musical *1776* as well as the film that followed, Dickinson – in spite of his acknowledged conservatism – issued the first major alarm over the erosion of British rights in America (for white male property holders, at any rate): *Letters from a Farmer in Pennsylvania, to the Inhabitants of the British Colonies* (1767–1768). First serialized in the *Pennsylvania Chronicle and Universal Advertiser*, Dickinson's twelve letters were reprinted and circulated throughout the colonies, as well as Britain and the Continent, damning the Stamp Act, the Quartering Act, the Townshend Acts, the punitive suspension of the New York colonial legislature, the parliamentary prohibition against colonial importations from anywhere other than Britain, and Parliament's assumption that it had any right to impose taxes on the American colonies – especially without colonial representation in that Parliament. "HERE then, my dear countrymen," Dickinson's Farmer pleads, "ROUSE yourselves, and behold the ruin hanging over your heads" – the ruin of "*American* liberty."

But Dickinson didn't stop there. On the July 4, 1768 – unwittingly eight years to the day before the adoption of the Declaration of Independence – he sent a letter to his friend James Otis of Massachusetts: "I inclose you a song for American Freedom. I have long since renounced poetry, but as indifferent songs are very powerful on certain occasions, I venture to invoke the deserted muses." He also invoked the memory of a French predecessor known for *his* revolutionary agitation through music: "Cardinal de Retz always enforced his political operations by songs. I wish our attempt may be

Figure 3.1 John Dickinson. Reproduction after 1772 illustration.
Library of Congress Prints and Photographs Division

useful." Dickinson's song, first published in the *Boston Gazette* of July 18, 1768, had for its musical setting Garrick and Boyce's "Hearts of Oak," but its title did not derive from the earlier ballad. Initially called, simply, "A New Song," it soon became known in the popular imagination as "The Liberty Song," sung with verve at meetings of the Sons of Liberty throughout Massachusetts. Dickinson, deliberately or otherwise,

> created as forcible an impact with his "Liberty Song" as he had with his *Farmer's Letters*. By popular insistence it was printed and reprinted throughout the colonies. The "Liberty Song" became an obsession, being sung everywhere: at political demonstrations, protest meetings, patriotic celebrations, dedication ceremonies for liberty trees, for pure enjoyment, and also for nuisance value to enrage the British and their American sympathizers.

In "A New Song," Dickinson begins with a clarion call – not for revolution, but rather for the withholding of money from the British exciseman, presumably until a tax system of, by, and for Americans can be established. He makes clear that his argument is not about taxation in principle, but about the ultimate destination of the revenue: "HOW sweet are the labors that Freemen endure, / That *they* shall enjoy all the Profit, secure – / NO more such sweet Labors AMERICANS know / If Britons shall *reap* what Americans sow." There are, then, some grounds for questioning the song's revolutionary potential:

> Given Dickinson's moderate – if not conservative – political views, his "Liberty Song" becomes even more remarkable a reflection of the growing chasm between England and the colonies. And yet, the song is cautious. It calls on Americans to give their money, not their lives, for "Liberty," not independence and separation.

The song calls for one further significant action: a *united* front against imperial usurpation of British rights in America – the first major intimation of a fledgling national consciousness: "Then join Hand in Hand brave AMERICANS all, / By *uniting* We stand, by *dividing* We fall." It was a mark of Dickinson's influence as a major – if not *the* major – protest balladeer at the dawn of the Revolution that his "Liberty Song" should have immediately inspired a rash of parodies and counter-parodies appearing in the colonial press, dominated by increasingly martial rhetoric.

The expanding body of colonial protest song exhibited significant attempts to include women in the ranks of resistance, even from within the restricted confines of the domestic sphere. The year 1769 saw the appearance of an anonymous appeal "To the Ladies" (alternately "Young Ladies in Town") to thwart the Townshend Acts by refusing to purchase tea, paper, glass, paint, lead, cloth, or any other items imported from Britain and to rely wholly on domestic or home-made products. In "Young Ladies in Town," a woman's patriotic duty becomes an overtly sexualized issue: "And as one, all agree that you'll not married be / To such as will wear London factory; / But at first sight refuse, tell 'em you will choose / As encourage our own manufactory." As a result, the "Ladies" are assured: "Though the times remain darkish, young men will be sparkish, / And love you much stronger than ever."

If the times were already "darkish" in 1769, they grew decidedly more so on the fifth of March the following year, when what John Adams called a "motley rabble of saucy boys, negroes and molattoes, Irish teagues, and outlandish Jack Tarrs" violently provoked a thin line of outnumbered, unprepared British soldiers into firing their flintlocks, sparking what has come down in history as the "Boston Massacre." Adams defended and ultimately secured the acquittal of the soldiers on the grounds of an appeal to *British* justice; but the "motley crew" had "provided an image of revolution from below that proved terrifying to Tories and moderate patriots" (such as, at that time, Adams himself). Recent history problematizes the received narrative of the "Boston Massacre" as a straightforward story of reckless British militarism against unoffending, law-abiding colonial subjects, with no element of class conflict muddying the lines of opposition. In the realm of topical song, however, there is no such problematizing. On the contrary, the broadside ballad "On the Death of Five Young Men Who Was Murthered, March 5th 1770, By the 29th Regiment" draws the lines ever so neatly, if not crudely, inflating the small British regiment into a virtual army: "By cruel Soldiers, five Men were slain, / Their everlasting happiness to gain; / And when fierce Troops urg'd thick on ev'ry Side, / They spurned their fate, and spread Destruction wide."

Indeed, the confused judicial mess that was the "Boston Massacre" proved enormously useful in the propagandist mission to transform the British colonial realm into an American one, as a second ballad – "A Song for the 5th of March," published that month in the *Newport Mercury* – demonstrated to the tune of the British patriotic ode, "Once the Gods of the Greeks": "When the *Foes* of the Land, our Destruction had plan'd, / They sent *ragged* TROOPS for our *Masters*: / But from former Defeat they must now understand, / Their *Wolves* shall not prowl in our PASTURES."

A three-year period of relative calm followed the "Boston Massacre," with the British parliament repealing the hated Townshend duties – a period so calm, in fact, that agitators for American independence began to worry over the soothing of public anger. Parliament gave them a gift, however, in the Tea Act of 1773, which gave the British East India

Company a monopoly on the importation of tea into the colonies. American merchants were outraged, none more so than in Boston, where, on the night of December 16, 1773, a contingent of the Sons of Liberty disguised themselves (some, though not all, in Mohawk headdress), stole aboard three cargo ships on the quay, and dumped a total of 342 chests of tea – nine thousand pounds' worth – into the harbor. (At today's value, the loss would amount to approximately $1.5 million.) Parliament responded with the imposition of the so-called Coercive Acts (or, as the colonials called them, "Intolerable Acts"), closing the port of Boston, suspending self-government in Massachusetts, transporting suspects to Britain for trial, and, once again, enforcing the quartering of British troops among the populace. What came to be known as the "Boston Tea Party" thus became a rallying point for expressions of middle-class colonial resistance, not least in song.

One of the earliest musical responses, titled "The Destruction of the Tea" (alternately "A new Song, to the plaintive tune of 'Hozier's Ghost'"), appeared in the *Pennsylvania Packet* in late December 1773. It argued what was increasingly becoming a minority position, that is, that the rights being protected through the drowning of the "Cursed weed of China's coast" were "British rights" – rights that should "ne'er be lost." Otherwise, the ballads evoking the tea protest aimed to reinforce a distinctly *American* identity at odds with foreign – including British – impositions. Hence the broadside ballad "Tea Destroyed by Indians," which appeared shortly after the protest, proclaiming that "KING and PRINCE shall know that we are FREE," such familial estrangement being the price of Britain's betrayal of her own children: "Could our Fore-fathers rise from their cold Graves, / And view their Land, with all the Children SLAVES; / What would they say! how would their Spirits rend, / And, Thunder-strucken, to their Graves descend."

And, in spite of the overwhelmingly masculine ownership of the "Boston Tea Party" and other dramatic events as they have been reflected in history, women in their own right were at the forefront of the protest. Abigail Adams, known for admonishing her husband John to "remember the ladies" or face "rebellion" from them, wrote to him about the Boston "coffee party" staged by women at the expense of a profiteering coffee merchant:

> A number of females, some say a hundred, some say more, assembled with a cart and trunks, marched down to the warehouse, and demanded the keys, which he refused to deliver. Upon which one of them seized him by his neck and tossed him into the cart. Upon his finding no quarter, he delivered the keys when they tipped up the cart and discharged him; then opened the warehouse, hoisted out the coffee themselves, put it into the trunks and drove off.

Balladeers duly invoked the image of rising womanhood to challenge the imperial decrees. Hence "The Rich Lady over the Sea," the "island queen" whose "pockets were filled with gold," commanding her "daughter [who] lived off in the new country" to "pay her a tax / Of thruppence a pound on the tea." The consequent rebellion is owned by women, implicitly the Daughters of Liberty, the organization formed in 1765 alongside the Sons of Liberty to protest the Stamp Act and subsequently active in challenging the Townshend Acts and the Tea Act. The rebellious daughter taunts "the island queen" as the spilled tea is carried by the tide back towards England: "'O mother, dear mother,' called she, / 'Your tea you may have when 'tis steeped enough, / But never a tax from me.'"

Figure 3.2 "Society of Patriotic Ladies." Satirical print on American women pledging to boycott English tea. London, 1775.
Library of Congress Prints and Photographs Division

It is possible that even Benjamin Franklin joined the fellowship of protest songwriters utilizing the mother/child opposition, although – if a surviving text in his handwriting is indeed his own composition – his song "The Mother Country" still retains a shred of familial loyalty, however grudging: "Her Orders so odd are, we often suspect / That Age has impaired her sound Intellect; / But still an old Mother should have due Respect, / *Which nobody can deny, &c.*" (We do know that Franklin had a great interest in the art of popular ballad composition, having critiqued his brother Peter's attempt sometime before 1765, pointing out the importance of simple phrasing; short syllables; "the beauties of common speech"; and setting lyrics to old, familiar tunes rather than even "the best new tune we can get composed for it.")

The Coercive/Intolerable Acts succeeded in little else but unifying the colonies in opposition to Parliament; igniting campaigns of resistance spreading far beyond the cauldron of Massachusetts; and culminating, in September 1774, in the establishment of the First Continental Congress in Philadelphia. One of the earliest and least known congressional acts was a resolution adopted in October 1774 to "encourage frugality . . . and discourage every species of extravagance and dissipation," including "shews, plays, and other expensive diversions and entertainments." Inadvertently this spurred on the composition and printing of broadside ballads, as singing at public meetings and at home filled the vacuum left by the "suspension of civic amusements."

Among the many broadside ballads circulating were those encouraging and celebrating campaigns throughout the colonies to defend the people of Boston and to provide them with money, provisions, and moral support while their port remained punitively blockaded by the British. Anonymous balladeers took up the baton from Dickinson, himself having taken up "Hearts of Oak" as a template for his "Liberty Song," to proclaim solidarity in songs like "The Glorious Seventy-Four," first printed in the *Virginia Gazette* of October 6, 1774, and subsequently reprinted throughout the colonies: "Hearts of oak were our sires, / Hearts of oak are their sons, / Like them we are ready, as firm and as steady, / To fight for our freedom with swords and with guns." This belligerent chorus is attached to verses outlining the resolve of the colonies to come as one to the aid of besieged Boston: "Now, unasked we unite, we agree to a man, / See our stores flow to Boston from rear and from van: / Hark, the shout how it flies! freedom's voice how it sounds! / From each country, each clime, hark the echo rebounds!"

The growing colonial resistance movement inevitably sparked an outpouring of Loyalist balladry, igniting a singing war similar to that inspired by Dickinson's "Liberty Song" the previous decade. Thus, in mockery of the solidarity for Boston evinced in "The Glorious Seventy-Four," *Rivington's New York Gazetteer* – perhaps the leading publisher of Loyalist ballads – offered its anonymous "Epigram," which both denied the dire straits of Boston's poor and argued that they should be "Employed in Paving the Streets" rather than being the unworthy recipients of charity from outside the colony: "Instead of *Bread*, give only *Stones*." As the resistant spirit spread from Massachusetts to Virginia, Loyalist balladeers cheered the arrival of General Thomas Gage as the new Governor of Massachusetts, with his proclamation demanding colonial obedience. "Bostonia first shall feel my power," declares the narrator of "Gage's Proclamation," published in the *Virginia Gazette* as a "friendly warning": "Then shall my thundering cannons rattle, / My hardy veterans march to battle, / Against Virginia's hostile land, / To humble that rebellious band."

On April 19, 1775, open military hostilities began with the battles of Lexington and Concord, which first pitted local Massachusetts militia groups – soon called "Minutemen" for their ability to mobilize quickly at the first alarm – against regular British regiments. Two days later, Ezekiel Russell's *Salem Gazette, or Newbury and Marblehead Advertiser* published the broadside "Bloody Butchery, by the British Troops: Or, the Runaway Flight of the Regulars," which included an elegiac song for the American militiamen killed in securing the first British defeat of the war: "At *Lexington* they met their foe / Completely all equipp'd, / Their guns & swords made glit'ring show, / But their base schemes were nipp'd. / *Americans*, go drop a tear / Where your slain brethren lay! / O! Mourn and sympathize for them! / O! Weep this very day!" Less stately were the verse taunts sung against the retreating British, such as that published by one "Paddy" in the *Pennsylvania Magazine* of May 1775: "How brave you went out with muskets all bright, / And thought to befrighten the folks with the sight; / But when you got there how they powder'd your pums, / And all the way home how they pepper'd your bums, / And is it not, honics, a comical farce, / To be proud in the face, and be shot in the a-se."

Lexington and Concord also marked the first occasion when a tune previously used by British martial bands to mock American protesters was thrown back into the faces of the British themselves. Since the earliest days of the colonial protests, British bandsmen had been playing their old marching tune from the French and Indian War, "Yankee Doodle," as a mark of derision (and, in one horrific instance, to accompany their tarring and feathering of a protester in Boston). As one Patriot newspaper reported on the British retreat from Concord back to Boston:

> When the Second Brigade marched out of *Boston* to reinforce the First, nothing was played by the Fifes and Drums but *Yankee Doodle* (which had become their favourite tune ever since that notable exploit, which did such *honour* to the Troops of *Britain's* King, of tarring and feathering a poor countryman in *Boston*, and parading with him through the principal streets, under arms, with their bayonets fixed). Upon their return to *Boston*, one asked his brother officer how he liked the tune now? "Damn them (returned he), they made us dance it till we were tired." Since which *Yankee Doodle* sounds less sweet to their ears.

The origins of "Yankee Doodle" are a matter of historical debate. By one account it "probably originated as a Dutch harvest song." Another claims it arrived "from England, Ireland, or Scotland" and that "'doodle' stems from 'tootle,' which in turn comes from the 'tooting' of the German flutes so characteristic among eighteenth-century gentlemen." Other possible origins include "Hungarian, Hessian, Basque, and Indian, to name but a few." Most disturbingly, "Yankee Doodle" has some of the earliest associations with the ethnically degrading musical form later known as the "coon song," having first been seen in print in the script of an unproduced ballad opera by Andrew Barton, *The Disappointment, or, The Force of Credulity* (1767). As the stage directions indicate, the song would already have been familiar to audiences; what was new was putting minstrel-dialect lyrics into the mouth of a possibly blackface character named "Raccoon":

> *Raccoon*
> (Air – "Yankee Doodle")
> O! how joyful shall I be,
> When I get de money,
> I will bring it all to dee
> O! my diddling honey!
> (*Exit, singing the chorus, Yankee Doodle, etc.*)

Whatever its origins, "Yankee Doodle" would become one of the defining songs of the War of Independence and the country that sprang from it.

In May 1775, after the American capture of Fort Ticonderoga in New York, three British generals – Burgoyne, Clinton, and Howe, the so-called Junto – arrived to reinforce imperial authority and martial law in Massachusetts. In the process, they subjected themselves so extensively to defiance and mockery in colonial song that scholars have referred to the "Junto song" as a subgenre. One such "Junto song" damns both the Boston Harbor blockade and the Tea Act while declaring outright that there is now "no cure but a capital chop" (in other words, American independence): "Three generals these mandates have borne 'cross the sea, / To deprive 'em of fish and make 'em drink tea; / In turn, sure, these freemen will boldly agree, / To give 'em a dance upon Liberty Tree."

The military escalation led the Continental Congress to appoint George Washington as commanding general of a unified Continental Army in June 1775. Unsurprisingly, his appointment was met with musical burlesque from the pens of Loyalist balladeers, as in the mocking "Adam's Fall" ("The Trip to Cambridge"):

When Congress sent great Washington
All clothed in powder and breeches,
To meet old Britain's warlike sons
And make some rebel speeches;

'Twas then he took his gloomy way
Astride his dapple donkeys,
And traveled well, both night and day
Until he reach'd the Yankees.

More surprising, perhaps, is the treatment of Washington at the hands of American Patriots such as Edward Bangs, himself a Minuteman at Lexington, to whom the authorship of the most well-known version of "Yankee Doodle" is attributed. His song, alternately titled "The Yankee's Return from Camp" or "The Farmer and his Son's return from a visit to the Camp," is riddled with implicit class resentment at Washington's expense (even though Bangs himself was a relatively privileged sophomore at Harvard):

And there was captain Washington,
And gentlefolks about him,
They say he's grown so tarnal proud,
He will not ride without them.
Yankee doodle, &c.

What is to come, it is implied, is the proverbial rich man's war and poor man's fight:

I see another snarl of men,
A digging graves they told me,
So tarnal long, so tarnal deep,
They 'tended they should hold me.
Yankee doodle, &c.

Such class resentment was hardly uncommon, although it has been little remarked upon in the more celebratory histories of the "American

Revolution." In fact, not only was the summary seizure and impressment of poor seamen brutally carried out by the Continental Navy, but the Continental Army was deliberately structured along stark class lines, with resultant antagonisms arising from the "petty privileges of the officers, the frequently gross disparity in provisions and accommodations, and the general authoritarian tone inherited from the limited military experience some of the American officers had had with the British Army." As one of Washington's chaplains wrote, "New lords, new laws. The strictest government is taking place and great distinction is made between officers & men. Everyone is made to know his place & keep it, or be immediately tied up, and receive not one but 30 or 40 lashes." The wealthy could avoid conscription "by paying for substitutes; the poor had to serve. This led to rioting and shouting: 'Tyranny is Tyranny let it come from whom it may.'" Until the end of the war, Washington would be plagued by high levels of desertion and organized mutinies among Massachusetts, Pennsylvania, Connecticut, and New Jersey troops. Unsurprisingly, class discontent found its way into anonymous ballads such as "A New Song, Written by a Soldier": "And to you my lovely officers, a word I have to say, / Before you go to battle, consider well I pray, / See you kept our wages back, and robbed us of our clothes, / That we so dearly paid for in hard fatiguing blows."

Military events took a decidedly dark turn with the Battle of Breed's Hill (conventionally known as the Battle of Bunker Hill) and the British destruction of the Charlestown area of Boston in June 1775. Colonial militia had occupied the hills around Boston to forestall a British seizure of the territory, and after two deadly frontal assaults by the imperial forces, they retreated, leaving the British in control of the heights but sobered by the casualties they had suffered, far greater than those of the Americans. The burning of Charlestown brought to the fore the lyrics of Joel Barlow, the Connecticut poet known as one of the "Hartford Wits" and the author of two celebrated works, "Columbiad" and "The Hasty-Pudding." During the war years he was a chaplain for a Massachusetts regiment, but as he wrote to a friend: "I do not know, whether I shall do more for the cause in the capacity of chaplain, than I could in that of poet; I have great faith in the influence of songs; and shall continue, while fulfilling the duties of my appointment, to write one now and then ... One good song is worth a dozen addresses or proclamations." From his pen came one of the earliest responses to the Battle of Bunker Hill, "Breed's Hill" ("The Burning of Charlestown"): "To see a town so elegantly form'd, / Such buildings graced with every curious art, / Spoil'd in a moment, on a sudden storm'd, / Must fill with indignation every heart." Barlow also satisfied the requirement of many protest songwriters, that of naming names – in this case, respectively, the British prime minister, Lord North, and the military governor of Massachusetts: "Thy crimes, oh North, shall then like spectres stand, / Nor Charlestown hindmost in the ghastly roll, / And faithless Gage, who gave the dread command, / Shall find dire torments gnaw upon his soul."

The carnage of war inspired other known pioneers of American protest and topical music. Francis Hopkinson – signer of the Declaration of Independence, first Secretary of the US Navy, member of the Constitutional Convention, and, by some accounts, designer of the American flag stitched by Betsy Ross – is remembered for "a series of incendiary ballads aimed at destroying the legend of British invincibility." Hopkinson was also a prolific composer of chamber music, opera, and oratorio, audaciously claiming "the Credit of being the first Native of the United States who has produced a Musical Composition" (a claim subsequently debunked by historians of American music).

Even more significant, in terms of American music history, was the tanner and amateur composer from Boston, William Billings, whose "Lamentation Over Boston" (composed 1774; published 1778) updated the 137th Psalm to excoriate the British siege and partial destruction of the city: "By the Rivers of Watertown we sat down & wept, / We wept, we wept, we wept / When we remembered thee, O Boston." The stirring music of Billings's "Chester" (1770), when "played on fifes and drums and used as a march," was the Continental Army's call to arms, becoming "one of the most popular of all Revolutionary War tunes." Even more renowned were his words, which Billings withheld from publication until he could ensure they would be printed on American paper, and which were as central to the propaganda of resistance as were the writings of Thomas Paine: "Let tyrants shake their iron rod, / And slavery clank her galling chains; / We fear them not; we trust in God – / New England's God forever reigns."

But it is from the pens of countless anonymous balladeers that we have received the widest body of song to reflect the crosscurrents of the colonial – and indeed, anticolonial – struggles of the period. As folksong editor Irwin Silber argued:

> The essential contradiction of all colonial wars is that soldiers of the imperialist army have little to die for, other than their mercenary's pay. In every colonial war the foot soldier of the imperial force is plagued by doubts as to the justice of his cause and the worth of the struggle. And so it is not surprising, in the wake of Bunker Hill, to encounter a song literature by dispirited British soldiers reflecting a bitterness towards their own command and a respect for the rebel cause.

Out of this literature comes "The Soldier's Lamentation," expressing regret that former comrades during the French and Indian War were now mortal enemies atop Breed's Hill:

> I am a jolly soldier,
> Enlisted years ago,
> To serve my king and country
> Against the common foe.
> But when across th' Atlantic
> My orders were to go,
> I grieved to think that English hearts
> Should draw their swords on those
> Who fought and conquered by their side
> When Frenchmen were their foes.

There were also the songs of anonymous prisoners of war on both sides. One rebel soldier wrote, in the third person, of "the CRUELTY exercised by the [British] Regulars and Hessians Upon our poor Prisoners in New-York." He sings of them "in a stinking dungeon laid, / All sustenance denied them"; "stript . . . of their cash & clothes, / Deny'd . . . any fuel"; "With poison . . . infected"; succumbing to "the want of food" and "the small-pox." A British soldier in "PHILADELPHIA PRISON" reflects, "In vaults, with bars and iron doors, confin'd / They hold our persons, but can't rule the mind." These voices are tenuous and few, but at least they have been preserved.

The same cannot be said for those doomed to be sung *about,* to be described, defined, and utilized by others. The Quakers, persecuted by the Massachusetts Bay Puritans from the moment of their arrival in the 1650s, were now damned for their pacifism in the midst of the rebellion. John Adams, for instance, called them "dull as beetles," capable of demonstrating "neither good . . . nor evil." This was useful to the Loyalist balladeer Joseph Stansbury, who added mistreatment of the Quakers to the list of Patriot hypocrisies and their cant of freedom: "When Quakers and Churchmen have suffer'd your pleasure – / Their Worship and Consciences shap'd to your measure – / The Catholics then may expect penal laws, / Whereby we shall have one Religion and Cause. / This, this is the Freedom for which we are fighting: / And let all who think so, call it inviting."

We are also missing – and are condemned to miss until the archives yield up some as yet undiscovered holdings – the musical responses from one of the most important constituencies in the struggle for and against

American independence, the enslaved Black men and women. After all, they were central to the worried slaveholder Thomas Jefferson's charges against the British king in the first draft of the Declaration of Independence – the king he damned for "prompting our negroes to rise in arms among us." Indeed, thousands of escapees from slavery joined the British forces from the outset of hostilities, having been promised freedom in exchange for their military service. They were thus instrumental in sealing "the Patriots' decision to escalate the revolt to a full-blown war of independence." Yet, for all the Black Americans' struggle to gain *their* "independence," *their* "liberty," *their* "freedom from tyranny" (all the watchwords of the Patriots' cause), their songs are out of reach: "No one bothered to record the music of the black servicemen, and so it is lost, as are most of the names of those who sang and played it."

Equally resounding is the silence – at least in terms of song – of the Indigenous people caught in the middle of what appeared to them a civil war – a "family quarrel" – between factions of Europeans. On the one side were the Anglo-Americans, French, and Spanish, along with the Dutch merchant class; on the other, the British and their Hessian mercenaries. Indigenous tribes found themselves coerced into alliances they had not themselves invited. Like the kidnapped Africans, they had to endure their demeaning use as pawns by Jefferson in his list of outrages against George III in the Declaration of Independence: "He . . . has endeavored to bring on the inhabitants of our frontiers, the merciless Indian Savages, whose known rule of warfare, is an undistinguished destruction of all ages, sexes, and conditions" – a crude, undifferentiated, one-sided slander that survives in the final, published draft of the Declaration. The Iroquois watched helplessly as George Washington's armies invaded their territory, burned down their villages and crops, and cut down their orchards; Washington would be forever after known by them as "Town Destroyer." Meanwhile, Jefferson, as the rebel governor in Virginia, "urged a war of extermination against the Shawnees in Ohio, and the Shawnees saw their villages burned time and again by Kentucky militia who crossed the Ohio River." The Delawares, upon concluding an alliance with Washington at Fort Pitt in 1799, found that their words, as represented in the treaty, were not their own. As one chief wrote to Washington's agent: "I have now looked over the Articles of Treaty again & find that they are wrote down false, & as I did not understand the Interpreter what he spoke I could not contradict his Interpretation."

The British, for their part, used the lure of trade and promises of sanctuary to win over Indigenous tribes as allies. Overall, they were successful, as "most tribes eventually supported the British," not least because the British "had demonstrated in the past that they would try to restrain trespass onto Indian lands" – notably through the Proclamation of 1763 that forbade settler incursion into Indigenous territory west of the Appalachians. But, at the mercy of a Loyalist balladeer's pen, woe to those tribes who joined forces with the Americans, the French, the Spanish, and the meddling Dutch merchants:

Choctaws, Chickasaws, and Catawbas,
Are all engaged to fight us:
Keep off you Mynheers with your yaws,
And England's gun shall right us.

We don't mind Monsieur's copper lace,
Nor solemn Don in cloak;
Once let us meet them face to face,
And fighting is no joke.

Such bravado notwithstanding, in 1776, an English ballad that was recirculated as a broadside in the colonies warned of the price to be paid in British resources and blood, should the colonial war persist: "America, the song hints, is not a second Ireland – a tiny country that may be overridden with impunity by British military might: it is a vast continent, whose permanent occupation in the face of American resistance will be impossible." The anonymous balladeer counsels:

What though your cannon raze their towns,
And tumble down their houses;
They'll fight like devils, blood and bones,
For children and for spouses ...

For further than your bullets fly
A common man may run, sirs;
And wheat will grow beneath a sky
Where cannot reach a gun, sirs.

Effectively, this unknown English balladeer accurately predicted, in broad strokes, the outcome of the American war. The British exchequer could not indefinitely sustain the cost of an expensive imperial conflict three thousand miles across the ocean, and, facing defeat by American and French forces at the Battle of Yorktown in 1781, the British surrendered and left the Americans to their own devices. Newspapers up and down the eastern seaboard posted classified ads for the sale of "genteel furniture" and other items flogged by Loyalists taking up the British offer of transportation out of the new United States. A ballad appeared in the *Brooklyne-Hall Super Extra Gazette* on June 8, 1782, under the title, "Unhappy Times":

Unhappy times of late we've seen,
Unhappy days indeed,
For such the rueful hours have been,
Did make our hearts to bleed.

Rebellion did with all its force,
Pour down upon our heads,
The stream took such a rapid course,
It drove us from our beds.

This anonymous – presumably Loyalist – balladeer succeeds in capturing the disorienting whirlwind of history as it sometimes unfolds. Legend has it that the defeated British forces at Yorktown ceremoniously withdrew to the tune of "The World Turned Upside Down" played by their fife and drum band (a legend subsequently debunked by military historians). The armed struggle that gave birth to the USA may have been over; but the new country's struggle in life and in song had only just begun.

CHAPTER 4

If I Had but a Small Loaf of Bread

The ink was barely dry on the Treaty of Paris, formally establishing US independence (1783), when cultural arbiters such as Noah Webster began agitating for a USA that was "as independent in *literature* as she is in *politics* – as famous for arts as for arms." This was easier said than done, as cultural practitioners from across the spectrum – from literature to opera, from painting to popular song – struggled to slough off the received forms and baggage of British culture; and there *were* some resounding declarations of cultural independence. Indeed, even before the end of the war – in 1770 – William Billings, often considered the first national composer, had declared himself free and independent of "any Rules for Composition laid down by any that went before me." After the war, in his *Continental Harmony* of 1794, he was no less strident in his declaration: "I am not confined to rules prescribed by others, yet I come as near as I possibly can to a set of rules which I have carved out for myself." These were stirring words; but in practice, Billings remained, until the end of his life as a composer, "influenced by the British models he knew."

Devotees of opera flocked to the urban concert halls that had reopened after the congressional ban on wartime performances was finally lifted in 1793; but the repertoire remained dominated by "vernacular British opera." Popular song remained "English music to the core: written by English composers for performance in England by English musicians; performed in America in pleasure gardens and opera houses modeled on those in England; sung by singers brought over from England. This was music in America, not American music." As we shall see, the struggle to articulate an "American music" would continue beyond the next century, dovetailing with broader questions concerning American identity and the rights of Americans *as* Americans.

It is perhaps ironic that "the most popular song in America before 1800" – based on printings and sales of sheet music – should have been about a slave: "The Galley Slave," taken from James Cross and William

Reeve's one-act opera, *The Purse; or, the Benevolent Tar* (1794). White audiences could wipe away their tears to the pathos of Will Steady, an English seaman captured on the high seas by an "Algerine force" – a reference to the North African corsairs attacking and raiding European and US ships in the Mediterranean for both plunder and slaves. Will Steady's "melancholy ditty," as related by his noble friend, Edmund, is designed to tug at the genteel heartstrings, whether in the opera house or around the pianoforte in the parlor:

> Oh! think on my fate, once I freedom enjoy'd,
> Was as happy as happy could be! –
> But pleasure is fled; every hope is destroy'd;
> A captive, alas! on the sea!
> I was ta'en by the foe – t'was the fiat of fate
> To tear me from her I adore!
> When thought brings to mind my once happy state,
> I sigh! – while I tug at the oar.

This song's popularity suggests that, although it is distanced through the safe filter of a *white* slave's ordeal, the original sin of American slavery – sidestepped completely in the final draft of the Declaration of Independence and soon to be enshrined and protected by the US Constitution – remained a potent force in the national consciousness. Nor did some white songwriters shy away from compositions in service of the dawning abolitionist movement, including Reeve, whose "The Desponding Negro" was published in *The American Musical Miscellany* of 1798 – notably without the demeaning minstrel dialect that was to characterize so many antislavery songs of the nineteenth century, however well-intentioned:

> On Afric's wide plains where the lion now roaring,
> With freedom stalks forth the vast desert exploring,
> I was dragg'd from my hut and enchain'd as a slave,
> In a dark floating dungeon upon the salt wave,
> Spare a halfpenny, Spare a halfpenny,
> Spare a halfpenny to a poor Negro.

Even in the South – as in Charleston's *City Gazette* of November 18, 1789 – an anonymous white balladeer could offer an abolitionist plea entitled simply "Favorite Song":

> May the head be corrected, subdu'd the proud soul,
> Who would fetter free limbs and free spirits control!

Be th' gem or in ebon or in ivory enshrined,
The same form of heart warms the whole human kind.
And nature's great charter the right never gave
That one mortal another should dare to enslave.

But what were the enslaved African Americans themselves singing in the immediate wake of US independence? We have precious few hints, but they indicate that a powerful body of African song had been retained in the collective Black consciousness. In 1786, eighty West Africans were dragged in as slave labor to drain the swamp at Phelps Lake, North Carolina, for a canal to be built. An overseer recalled:

> At night they would begin to sing their native songs, and in a short while would become so wrought up that, utter oblivious to the danger involved, they would grasp their bundles of personal effects, swing them on their shoulders, and setting their faces towards Africa would march down into the water singing as they marched till recalled to their senses only by the drowning of some of the party.

This eyewitness account prefigures – and perhaps validates – the later legend of the mass suicide at Igbo Landing in 1803 off Saint Simons Island, Georgia, where the newly arrived Igbos jumped from the decks of their kidnappers' ship to drown in their chains rather than face continued slavery. All the while they sang an appeal to "the great water spirit, *Mami Wata*, to take the tribe back across the ocean to their loved ones: 'Mami Wata carry us here, Mami Wata carry us back!'"

There is evidence, too, that as early as 1795 enslaved Africans and their American offspring were equipped to adapt European resistance songs to their own ends. In Spanish-controlled New Orleans, a cabildo administrator reported hearing the "singing of Jacobin songs which threatened the lives of the officials of the province. In one of the more popular songs, the slaves sang of the time when they would become republicans and freedmen, promised to guillotine the 'swine governor' and hang the treasurer and auditor." From the same time and territory comes a translated ballad – so valuable because of its rarity amidst the generally deafening historical silence – that continued to be sung by Black Americans into the nineteenth century. It honors Jean St. Malo (Juan San Malo), who led a community of escapees from slavery – maroons or, in Spanish, *cimarrones* – in the bayous around New Orleans. The precise date of the community's establishment is unknown, but they succeeded in carrying out plantation raids until St. Malo was captured and executed by the Spanish colonial authorities in 1784. "The Dirge of St. Malo" commemorates the bravery of his final moments:

> They hauled him from the cypress swamp –
> His arms they tied behind his back,
> They tied his hands in front of him;
> They tied him to a horse's tail,
> They dragged him up into the town
> Before those grand Cabildo men.
> They charged that he had made a plot
> To cut the throats of all the whites.
> They asked him who his comrades were;
> Poor St. Malo said not a word!
> The judge his sentence read to him.
> And then they raised the gallows-tree.
> They drew the horse – the cart moved off –
> And left St. Malo hanging there.
> The sun was up an hour high
> When on the Levee he was hung;
> They left his body swinging there,
> For carrion crows to feed upon.

The Spanish colonial authorities had further musical headaches to contend with. In 2014, the scholar Carla Gerona unearthed records of the 1795 court proceedings from Nacogdoches, near the Texas–Louisiana border. There, the colonial authorities had "conducted two trials against citizens who sang songs that offended them and challenged their authority" – first, a group of French Creoles and, subsequently, Spanish Creoles, who had composed traditional *décimas* ("poems of ten octosyllabic verses") and dared to sing them in the town square. Their songs lambasted a local landowner ("Vicente is a rich man / and he has beaver oil / he has a woman in his house / and for him there is no prison") as well as the Spanish commander and some local bankers:

> With quarrels every day
> and the injustice is constant
> our commander lives
> with a great fantasy
> everything is melancholy
> which makes us bothered
> so to avoid this
> and take away this difficulty
> we will throw out [illegible]
> the bank that is in this town.

There is no record of the trials' proceeding beyond the information-gathering stage; but whether or not these prototypical singer-songwriters were convicted or sentenced, it was yet another early example of the place of song in America's anticolonial struggles.

Back east, in what was now the USA, there was, as could be expected, an avalanche of triumphalist songs and musical compositions appearing in the wake of independence. One (out of many possible examples) came from the pen of Alexander Reinagle, Philadelphia's leading composer. The jingoism of "America, Commerce and Freedom" from Reinagle's "ballet pantomime" *The Sailor's Landlady* (1794) is brimming with the cockiness and cant of "freedom" that characterized so much US song in the early national period: "Then under full sail we laugh at the gale / And the landsmen look pale, never heed 'em, / But toss off the glass to a favorite lass: / To America, Commerce and Freedom."

Off the pantomime stage, women were still struggling for the same "freedom" after the supposed Revolution as before it. Hence the truly pioneering US anthem "Rights of Woman," composed "By a Lady" and printed in the *Philadelphia Minerva* of October 17, 1795. Its stanzas, meant to be sung to the tune of "God Save the King," but with echoes of Mary Wollstonecraft and Thomas Paine, make it clear that the usurpation of natural "rights" was still ongoing in the new nation:

Oh let the sacred fire
Of Freedom's voice inspire
A Female too; –
Man makes the cause his own,
And fame his acts renown, –
Woman thy fears disown,
Assert thy due.

Free laborers were also questioning how truly free, equal, and independent they were. Philadelphia was fast becoming a hotbed of labor agitation. In 1791, the city's carpenters carried out the first US strike in the building trade. That same year, the country's first labor union was constituted by Philadelphia's shoemakers: the Federal Society of Journeyman Cordwainers, whose recruiting song, written by John McIlvaine, was "the first trade union song in American labor history": "Cordwainers! Arouse! The time now has come! / When our rights should be fully protected; / And every attempt to reduce any one / By all should be nobly rejected." Their struggle had only begun. The Cordwainers union would be dogged by the repressive legal apparatus until 1806, when it was finally broken with the judicial ruling: "guilty of a combination to raise wages."

The judicial fear of labor power should be seen in the context of the class struggle that had been carried on since before the War of Independence, and which had broken out during the war in the form of the desertions and mutinies that plagued George Washington. In 1786, the struggle exploded into an open revolt by small farmers in western Massachusetts who, in spite of their own service in the war, found themselves impoverished by punitive state taxes, their land and livestock impounded. To the fore came the army veteran Daniel Shays with his lieutenant, Luke Day, who led thousands of angry farmers to surround the courthouses in Worcester and Boston. Another of the compatriots in the so-called Shays Rebellion, known only as "Plough Jogger," articulated their grievances:

> I have been greatly abused, have been obliged to do more than my part in the war; been loaded with class rates, town rates, province rates, Continental rates and all rates ... been pulled and hauled by sheriffs, constables and collectors, and had my cattle sold for less than they were worth ... The great men are going to get all we have and I think it is time for us to rise and put a stop to it, and have no more courts, nor sheriffs, nor collectors nor lawyers.

The Riot Act read to them from the Boston courthouse steps was composed by none other than the celebrated Patriot of the Revolution, Sam Adams. After the rebellion was suppressed, with some of its leaders hanged and Shays escaped to Vermont, the founders of the nation met in Philadelphia to draw up a new constitution securing – with the Shays Rebellion in mind – "a central government strong enough to put down such uprisings." At least one anonymous balladeer expressed profound gratitude to the framers of "The Grand Constitution" upon its ratification in 1787: "Here Plenty, and Order, and Freedom shall dwell, / And your Shayses and Dayses won't dare to rebel."

As for the Indigenous people who woke up to find themselves in some new place called the United States of America, the nightmare hadn't ended. If anything, it was just beginning. A year after the Treaty of Paris was ratified, a desperate group of Iroquois, Shawnee, Chickasaw, Choctaw, Cherokee, and Loup representatives appealed for an alliance with Spain, telling the Spanish governor in St. Louis: "The Master of Life willed that our lands should be inhabited by the English, and that these should dominate us tyrannically, until they and the Americans, separating their interests, formed two distinct nations." US independence, they said, was "the greatest blow that could have been dealt," short of their "total destruction." Through the Treaty of Paris, Britain had ceded to the USA

> a vast empire, starting at the Appalachian Mountains and extending to the Mississippi River. This meant profit for the likes of many Founding Fathers, including Washington, Jefferson, Franklin, Hamilton, and Henry. The "deed game" of early colonial times reemerged in the West after American independence; the only obstacle to wealth was the American Indian.

This is when the motif of the "disappearing Indian," the doomed "noble savage," entered the catalog of US popular music, as white songwriters and librettists scrambled to exploit shamelessly the cash cow of white American sentimentality. Beginning with such songs as Sarah Wentworth Morton and Hans Gram's "The Death Song of an Indian Chief" (1791) and Anne Hunter and James Hewitt's "Alknomook, the Death Song of the Cherokee Indian" (1794), a sturdy and long-lasting musical theme was forming. "Operatic melodrama" based on this theme proliferated, culminating with the likes of *The Indian Princess; or, La Belle Sauvage* (1808) by James Nelson Barker and John Bray, "the first surviving play on the story of Captain John Smith and Pocahontas." Meanwhile, what the Indigenous people *themselves* might have been singing in this early national period, we may never know. As the late Haitian scholar Michel-Rolph Trouillot put it, historical sources "are not created equal." Thus, the songs of Hunter and Hewitt's Alknomook and Barker and Bray's Pocahontas (not to say Walt Disney's) have drowned out those of the people who inspired them.

Of the victorious "Great White Fathers" in the nation's capital, of course, the songs were (and are) legion. One collector, basing his findings on printed sheet music alone, numbers songs for Washington at 632 (followed by Jefferson at 76, and, running a poor third, John Adams at 29). These numbers would surely be dwarfed by the more ephemeral musical commentaries printed on broadsides and in newspapers, and it is in such sources that we would find evidence of the most trenchant, and nastiest, singing wars. Washington, revered as he was, remained largely untouchable. Adams, however, brought a ton of negative musical commentary down on his head, not only for his "monarchical" tendencies and his suspected Anglophilia (vis-à-vis revolutionary France), but also – and in particular – for his administration's passage of the Alien and Sedition Acts of 1798, which criminalized writing, saying, or publishing anything deemed "false, scandalous and malicious" against the president or the Federal government. The First Amendment be damned, apparently; and it was this act that sealed the ideological and political rivalry between Adams and Jefferson. "Adams and Liberty," sang one Federalist balladeer, Robert Treat Paine, who had signed the Declaration of Independence on behalf of Massachusetts: "Let our patriots destroy Anarch's pestilent worm, / Lest our Liberty's growth should be checked by corrosion." A Jeffersonian shot back: "Men in power too oft betray / Full of wild ambition, / Their commands we must obey, / Or they'll cry – 'sedition.'" In closing, this anonymous balladeer advised: "If you peace and freedom love, / Act with circumspection, / Every foe to these remove, / At your next election; / Choose for chief, Columbia's son, / The immortal Jefferson."

Voters heeded the advice, and Jefferson was swept into office in 1801. Neither peace nor freedom followed – no peace either on the Indigenous frontiers or on the high seas, where British warships preyed on US commerce and impressed US sailors into the Royal Navy; and no freedom for the enslaved men and women at Jefferson's Monticello or, for that matter, anywhere else under the protection of a "Grand Constitution" that officially equated the value of one Black person to three-fifths of a white person.

A particularly dangerous flashpoint came with the British naval attack on the US frigate *Chesapeake* in June of 1807. Jefferson, into his second term, sought to cripple Britain (and keep France at bay) with an embargo on US exports to both countries – a strategy that backfired, throwing the economy into depression and launching a thriving black market. Merchants and exporters damned Jefferson in balladry: "Our ships all in motion / once whitened the ocean; / They sail'd and return'd with a Cargo; / Now doom'd to decay, / They are fallen a prey, / To Jefferson, worms, and EMBARGO." In particularly dire straits were the "jobless jack tars," the suddenly unemployed and destitute sailors haunting the empty wharves of US seaports. In New York, some dropped their old, revered sea chanteys for new plaintive songs: "Here's milk, ho!" from those now hawking the landlubber's hated beverage out of desperation; "Tumble Up! Tumble Up! Old Rope!" from former ship's mates who were now rag-and-bone men; and, from those proud seamen who had traded climbing the masts for sweeping a chimney, "Sweep, O—O—O—O / From the bottom to the top, / Without a ladder or a rope, / Sweep, O—O—O—O."

With the expiration of Jefferson's second term, his Secretary of State, James Madison, was elected president in 1808. Madison had steered Jefferson's Louisiana Purchase from France in 1803, not only doubling the territory of the USA with a signature but in the process ensuring that Britain's Proclamation of 1763 outlawing further Anglo incursion into Indigenous lands west of the Appalachians would be but a distant memory. Indeed, the US acquisition of territory had by 1803 already brought the country's western border to the banks of the Mississippi, whether through piecemeal, localized force of arms or (often conveniently) misunderstood treaties and land deeds. As the Oneida chief Good Peter had said in the wake of a treaty concluded with the State of New York in 1788, "The Governor of New York said to us; – 'You have now leased to me all your territory, exclusive of the reservation, as long as the grass shall grow and the rivers run.' He did not say, 'I buy your country.' Nor did we say, 'We sell it to you.'" Now, with the Louisiana Purchase, the USA had assumed the old French claims from eastern Montana to Minnesota in the north, and from eastern New Mexico to Louisiana in the south, prompting one fawning, historically misinformed balladeer to proclaim: "Without arms, without dread, / Or a drop of blood shed / Great Jefferson adds to the wealth of a Nation."

On the bewildering merry-go-round of colonial buying and selling, one of the most bizarre episodes concerned the so-called War of the Quadrilles that erupted only two weeks after the transfer of Louisiana from France to the USA. Residents of New Orleans could remember the days of Spanish control, before France's reacquisition of the territory in 1800. (France had lost it to Spain in a treaty of 1763.) These new wards of the USA drew their battle lines in a public ballroom on January 8, 1804. The issue was what kind of music the band should be playing – a French or an Anglo-American quadrille: "When an American raised his walking stick at a fiddler, 'bedlam ensued.'" One of the French Creole attendees was heard to say: "We have been Spaniards thirty years and the Spaniards never have forced us to dance the Fandango. We do not wish to dance either the reel or the jig." Later that year, the New Orleans City Council was forced to issue a stark warning: "If good order is to be maintained, the orchestra of the hall can-not be subject to fanciful demands to play this or that tune . . . No person by bringing up any request in this regard shall disturb either the orchestra or the audience without running the risk of being brought before the magistrate." For decades afterwards, nationalist disruptions continued to mar the performances of French opera in New Orleans and elsewhere, with strident Americans calling out for "Yankee Doodle" – a growing habit that earned the notice of the English writer Frances Trollope: "When a patriotic fit seize[d] them, and 'Yankee Doodle' was called for, every man seemed to think his reputation as a citizen depended on the noise he made."

The expansionist mission of the early national period also spawned the "Injun fighter" as a figure of mythic heroism. In 1811, that mantle fell upon the shoulders of William Henry Harrison, governor of the Indiana Territory and future US president, at the so-called Battle of Tippecanoe. Harrison had already built an effectively acquisitive reputation under both Jefferson and Madison through "'negotiating' the cession of millions of acres of land from the Indians in the Northwest Territory." But the "battle" that earned him the popular nickname "Old Tippecanoe" was in fact a sneaky preemptive attack by Harrison's forces on a Shawnee settlement on Tippecanoe Creek while its beleaguered chief, Tecumseh, was away. (Tecumseh had long been fighting against US incursion into Shawnee lands, having sought a pan-Indigenous alliance with his celebrated oratory: "Where today are the Pequot? Where are the Narraganset, the Mohican, the Pocanet, and other powerful tribes of our people? They have vanished before the avarice and oppression of the white man, as snow before the summer sun.") In between lauding Harrison and racially abusing the Shawnees, an anonymous songwriter seized the opportunity to also take a swipe at the British in Canada, popularly suspected of backing Tecumseh's resistance campaign:

Hark hark, ye sons of liberty,
Of what is this we hear?
It is the voice of agony,
It comes from our frontier.
The savage massacre's begun,
Hark, hear the infants cry,
The father, mother and the son,
And daughter slaughtered lie.

Great Britain's tawny brethren,
That cruel savage crew,
Set on by British agents,
This bloody work to do.
The tomahawk and scalping knife
They arm them in with speed.
The bloody weapons to take life,
And do the cruel deed.

Tecumseh had traveled to Alabama in 1811 to make an appeal to the Creeks for an intertribal resistance campaign. In the subsequent "Creek War" of 1813–1814, other "Injun fighters" such as Davy Crockett and – with resounding historical significance – future president Andrew Jackson emerged. Whatever else he may have been, Jackson was also

> a land speculator, merchant, slave trader, and the most aggressive enemy of the Indians in early American history. He became a hero of the War of 1812, which was not (as usually depicted in American textbooks) just a war against England for survival, but a war for the expansion of the new nation, into Florida, into Canada, into Indian territory.

It is in this context that one of the most musically documented wars in US history should be viewed: "Mr. Madison's War," the "Second War of Independence" – the "War of 1812" that gave us "The Star-Spangled

Banner" from the pen of Francis Scott Key, who set it to the tune of an English drinking song, "To Anacreon in Heaven." A politically broader view of the war is not to detract from the very real menaces of Britain's impressment of US sailors on the high seas or the danger brought to the streets of US cities facing attack. The British destruction of Washington, DC, and the burning of both the White House and the Library of Congress are the more well-known and, perhaps, emotionally charged examples; but it was the working people defending New York who inspired "one of the most popular songs of the war." This was "The Patriotic Diggers," which eulogized the citizens – "Labor in succession" – who came out to confront the invading British on Brooklyn Heights: "Plumbers, founders, dyers, / Tin men, turners, shavers, / Sweepers, clerks and criers, / Jewellers, engravers, / Clothiers, drapers, players, / Cartmen, hatters, tailors, / Gaugers, sealers, weighers, / Carpenters and sailors!"

Like all wars, the War of 1812 offered jingoistic songwriters the convenient opportunity, from the safety of their armchairs, to sneer – on broadsides and in newspapers – at those who might later be called "conscientious objectors": "Is there one – a milky heart, / Curdling at the thought of death; / Shrinking from a valiant part, / To prolong a puny breath?" And amidst the avalanche of literally countless nationalistic and patriotic odes predicting the bloody nose to be given by the Yankees to John Bull, one compassionate balladeer, at least, could spare a thought for a young US Marine named James Bird, a wounded veteran of the Battle of Lake Erie, subsequently court martialled and convicted for deserting his guard post. Sentenced to die, Bird was refused clemency by President Madison. A Pennsylvania newspaper editor, Charles Miner, published a heartfelt plea: "Lo! he fought so brave at Erie, / Freely bled and nobly dared. / Let his courage plead for mercy, / Let his precious life be spared." Twenty-nine-year-old Bird was executed on the deck of the warship *Niagara* in October of 1814.

The broad canvas of war will always obscure what goes on behind it. Andrew Jackson was catapulted to national renown through his stunning victory against the British in the Battle of New Orleans in January 1815; but relatively few know that the Treaty of Ghent, which ended the war, had already been signed – three weeks earlier. Few have learned, at least through the history textbooks, how, at the war's conclusion, "Jackson and friends of his began buying up the seized Creek lands. He got himself appointed treaty commissioner and dictated a treaty which took away half the land of the Creek nation." Fewer still, perhaps, know of other struggles, other groups, pushed to the margins of national attention in the midst of a full-blown war. Had, for instance, the ongoing struggle for women's rights dropped below the nation's radar, a struggle for the right of personal autonomy within the institution of marriage? At least one obscure songwriter from Baltimore thought so in 1813, half-way through the war, and offered a polite reminder:

When a maiden's about to be wedded,
Her heart beats with joy and with fear,
As the hour so wish'd for and dreaded,
Of meeting her husband, draws near; draws near,
Of meeting her husband draws near.

The ring when you take from your lover,
To him when you're giv'n away.
Remember one word to slip over,
Remember one word to slip over;
And that you will guess is OBEY.

The war's conclusion in 1814 ushered in a brief, deceptive period of calm and economic prosperity, helped along by the Napoleonic Wars hobbling European commerce. But when the benefits of wartime production began to wear off in 1819 and a three-year depression set in, the USA saw the first of its "unending cycles of industrial-age joblessness." Twenty thousand were soon out of work in Philadelphia, with the same number in New York, where a song began to circulate through the taverns: "If I had but a small loaf of bread, Bobby Buff, / If I had but a small loaf of bread, / How happy I'd be, and we'd go and hab tea, / If I had but a small loaf of bread, Bobby Buff!" The 1820s saw a burst of union organization among the women tailors of New York (whose strike in 1825 marked the first instance of US women striking on their own), among the mechanics of Philadelphia, and among combined trades with the first efforts at national "workingmen's" associations. This was the pioneering period of "organized labor's song tradition," which "developed in earnest when journeymen's organizations became full-fledged trade unions in the 1820s."

It is no coincidence that the dawning of the nation's trade union movement should coincide with the dawning of its industrial age, marked in 1832 by an anonymous songwriter in a curious parlor number, "The Washerwoman versus the Steam Washing Company":

Adieu, my weekly wash, adieu,
  A weeping heart thy loss bewails;
Perhaps I never more may view
  Thy stiffen'd collars, draggled tails;
No thou art fled – my only hope,
  Thy smoke and dirt are lost to me;
Adieu to pearlash, farewell soap,
  Oh, base Steam Washing Company!

Equally forlorn was the song of the "Hackney Coachman" thrown onto the scrap heap with the arrival of "the railroads [that] has ruin'd us" and "them curs'd omnibuses": "Then pity poor Jarvey, kind gentlefolks, pray, / For he's sadly in debt, without money to pay." Indeed, at the very time such sentimental songs were being sung in middle-class parlors, "five out of every six prisoners in New England and the Middle States jails were debtors, most of whom owed less than $20."

Already nostalgia for the disappearing American pastoral was setting in, triggered by the rapidly industrializing processes memorably framed by historian Leo Marx as "the machine in the garden." This nostalgia is seen (and heard) in the enormously popular parlor ballad of 1837, George Pope Morris and Henry Russell's "Woodman, Spare That Tree!": "Woodman, spare that tree! / Touch not a single bough; / In youth it shelter'd me, / And I'll protect it now." One online publisher claims that this might be "the first environmental American protest song." (In fact, that honor probably belongs to the Massachusetts Puritan Samuel Sewall's obscure ballad of 1719, "Upon the Drying Up that Ancient River, the River Merrymak": "Thus *Merrymak* kept House secure, / And hop'd for Ages to endure / . . . And unawares, at one Huge Sup, / Hydropick *Hampshire* Drunk it Up!")

In terms of the depletion of resources, one of the greatest stress points triggered by rapid industrialization was the labor of women and children, none more so than the mill workers of the burgeoning textile industry. The first industrial spinning machines in the USA had been introduced in 1789, followed by power looms in 1814. With spinning and weaving combined under one factory roof, the textile powerhouse of Lowell, Massachusetts, grew into an epicenter of labor agitation, particularly on the part of the young women who made up between 80 and 90 percent of the industry's workforce – women initially and deliberately chosen by the mill owners because they were thought "docile and easily managed." After a steady diet of wage cuts, twelve-to-sixteen-hour work days, deteriorating conditions, summary firings, and the tyrannical paternalism of the mill owners and managers, the Lowell operatives organized and struck, first in 1834 and again in 1836. A body of song grew to fortify the movement, and the women and girls marched out, singing: "Oh! Isn't it a pity that such a pretty girl as I / Should be sent to the factory to pine away and die? / O, I cannot be a slave; I will not be a slave. / For I'm so fond of liberty / That I cannot be a slave."

In Paterson, New Jersey, fifteen hundred children between the ages of eight and sixteen, with their parents behind them, marched into the streets for a six-week-long strike in the summer of 1835. They faced down hostile strikebreakers and the threat of the militia before being joined by adult workers from other industries – masons, machinists, and carpenters. New York newspapers reprinted ephemeral ballads from the Lancashire cotton mill towns to comment on the conditions of children in the US mills: "Oh! who would wish to have a child; / A mother who would be!!" In a ballad from this period, one Thomas Mann – himself the son of a mill-owning family in Pawtucket, Rhode Island, where the first industrial spinning machine had been introduced – expressed regret for what his own family's industry had wrought: "Hark! Don't you hear the fact'ry bell? / Of wit and learning 'tis the knell. / It rings them out, it rings them in, / Where girls they weave, and men they spin." By the end of 1836, there were 140 strikes crippling the textile mills throughout the eastern states and as far west as Ohio.

The US economy was careening toward what came to be known as "the Panic of 1837," a crushing depression that saw rioting for flour in the streets of New York City, the hobbling of the trade union movement (to ballad cries of "the mill has shut down! Good God, shut down!"), and roundly sung hatred for the banking system:

Oh – curse upon the banks!
No credit's there.
They issue naught but blanks –
No cash is there.
Hard times! the men do cry,
Hard times! the women sigh,
Ruin and misery –
No cash is here.

Meanwhile, on the fringes of the rising industrial powerhouse, US expansionists had been working to extend the country's borders even further southward. In the decade since the end of the War of 1812, "three-fourths of Alabama and Florida, one-third of Tennessee, one-fifth of Georgia and Mississippi, and parts of Kentucky and North Carolina" had fallen into US hands, largely through a series of slippery treaties – or "land grabs" – engineered by Andrew Jackson and his cronies; and with every treaty signed and every parcel of land ceded, white settlers flooded the region, leaving the Indigenous tribes "to sign another treaty, giving up more land in return for security elsewhere." Nervous eyes in Washington were particularly directed toward Spanish Florida. Jackson spoke of the "Seminole Indians inhabiting the territories of Spain [who have] visited our Frontier settlements with all the horrors of savage massacre – helpless women have been butchered and the cradle stained with the blood of innocence." Secretary of State John Quincy Adams added that the Seminoles had for years offered sanctuary to escapees from slavery and had been actively facilitating slave rebellions – compounding his horror over the wars of liberation throughout Latin America, which he compared to the "slave revolts in the late Roman Republic, which according to the historian Plutarch contributed to its fall."

It was with such pretexts that the US launched the first of two "Seminole Wars" in 1816 under Jackson's orders, with the firebombing of the so-called Negro Fort on the Apalachicola River in Florida, which had been protecting a community of fugitives from slavery and Choctaw people who had fled US attacks. Jackson justified the carnage – in which scores of men, women, and children were killed – as self-defense in the midst of a "savage and Negro war." The ultimate aim was not simply the securing of more territory or quashing slave uprisings, but also the "ethnic transfer" of the Indigenous people ultimately realized through the Indian Removal Act of 1830 under Jackson's presidency – the classic settler-colonial policy of "turning Indigenous peoples into refugees . . . by definition Indigenous to somewhere else – the very opposite of 'Aboriginal.'" Thus began the Choctaw removal of 1831; the Creek removal of 1836; the Chickasaw and Cherokee removals of 1837; and the Seminole removal of 1838 – each tribe destined to follow its own "trail of tears" to the unfamiliar lands west of the Mississippi.

Of the translated Indigenous "removal songs" that have come down to us – the handful that must be, in any case, "inescapably colonized" by their presentation in English language and form – one from the Creeks succeeds in conveying the desolation of those along, and at the end of, "The Trail Where They Cried":

I have no more land,
I am driven away from home,
driven up the red waters,
let us all go,
let us all die together.

And from the Seminoles: "They are taking us to the end of our tribe."

Utterly swamping these faint Indigenous voices are those of the white songwriters of the mid-nineteenth century who, perhaps taking their leaf from James Fenimore Cooper's tremendously popular *Last of the Mohicans* (1826), set out to "elicit our pity, but also our resignation to inexorable progress." Their parlor ballads are peopled with "noble but primitive savages [who] cannot adapt to civilization," products of "a fabled, vanished land," "examples of civilization's injustice, the objects of nostalgia, and the symbols of idealized love." Hence J. M. Smith and Charles Edward Horn's "The American Indian Girl" (1835): "O give me back my forest shade, / Where once I roam'd so blithe and gay"; Eliza Cook and William R. Dempster's "O Why Does the White Man Follow My Path?" (1846): "Does the flush of my dark cheek waken his wrath! / Does he covet the bow on my back!"; "The Indian's Lament" (1846) from the Hutchinson Family Singers: "I once had a sister, the pride of the vale, and a brother whose features were ruddy and hale, / Who often would join me in innocent play, / But the steel of the white man has driv'n them away"; or S. S. Steele and Benjamin Franklin Baker's "The Death of Osceola" (1847): "Oh, bring me the arrow'd raven, / That I may send his plume, / To tell my hunted nation / Their fallen chieftain's doom." All of these songs are couched in a stately, even "exalted musical style" matched only by "the strangely elevated rhetoric of their texts."

The same can surely not be said of the mass of songs composed by white lyricists attempting to replicate the voices of enslaved Black Americans, in the process providing fodder for the leading popular culture craze of the nineteenth century, the minstrel show – the world-renowned "theatrical practice, principally of the urban North, in which white men caricatured blacks for sport and profit." As we have seen, prototypes of the minstrel figure can be found at least as far back as 1767 with the first printing of "Yankee Doodle." But it was in the 1820s that the minstrel show came into its own, beginning with the caricatures of the Albany, New York-based George Washington Dixon, "probably the first [white] American to specialize in stage portrayals of blacks." Dixon's most popular figure was "Ole Zip Coon . . . a larned skoler . . . / Sings possum up a gum tree an coony in a holler." "Zip Coon" was surpassed in popularity only by Thomas Dartmouth ("Daddy") Rice's "Jim Crow": "Weel about and turn about and do jis so, / Eb'ry time I weel about I jump Jim Crow." Other individuals and minstrel troupes followed with the dehumanizing mission of racial caricature, from Edwin P. Christy and his "Christy Minstrels" to Daniel Decatur Emmett's "Virginia Minstrels," otherwise known as the "Ethiopian Delineators." Regardless of the name, the stage practice of white men "blacking up" was roughly the same, as laid out in a theatrical stage manual instructing in the application of burned cork or shoe polish to the face, followed by "a broad streak of carmine to the lips, carrying it well beyond the corners of the mouth. . . . Put on the wig, wipe the palms of the hands clean, and the makeup is completed." Cue the "fiddle, banjo, bones, tambourines, and . . . other instruments of music used on the Southern Plantations," and there you had the complete picture of the

Figure 4.1 Thomas D. Rice in the costume of his character "Jim Crow." Lithograph by George E. Madeley, c. 1833.
Library of Congress Prints and Photographs Division

happy or melancholy "darkey" pining for the old slave cabin and the country that kept him in chains, as represented by none other than the most popular American songwriter of the nineteenth century, Stephen Foster: "We'll put for de souf – Ah! dat's the place, / For the steeple chase and de bully hoss race – / Poker, brag, euchre, seven up and loo, / Den chime in Niggas, won't you come along too."

Christy, for one, claimed to have observed and studied African American musical performance in New Orleans, picking up what he called the "queer words and simple but expressive melodies" of the city's street performers. Most likely, Christy would have encountered his models in the regular festivals staged in the city's Congo Square, by then "one of the few places in the United States where it was possible to hear pure African music." Pianist and historian Terry Waldo notes: "Slaves representing six African tribes could be seen there on Sunday afternoons engaged in so-called wild dancing, singing, and playing to the accompaniment of such instruments as drums, crude banjos, rattles, and the like." When the city fathers, increasingly fearful of such gatherings, shut down the Congo Square festivals in 1843, "the music survived in underground form in taverns and other nightspots ... This is the beginning of what we have come to call jazz."

But for Christy and his fellow minstrel performers, musical and cultural authenticity was hardly the aim; and this is what incensed many Black commentators. Frederick Douglass saw the minstrel troupes as "the filthy scum of white society, who have stolen from us a complexion denied to them by nature, in which to make money, and to pander to the corrupt taste of their white fellow citizens." Later, W. E. B. Du Bois condemned the "caricature" and the "debased melodies which vulgar ears scarce know from the real." Perhaps the most eloquent condemnation came from a former slave, John Little, who wrote:

> They say slaves are happy, because they laugh, and are merry. I myself and three or four others, have received two hundred lashes in the day, and had our feet in fetters; yet at night, we would sing and dance, and make others laugh at the rattling of our chains. Happy men we must have been! We did it to keep down trouble, and to keep our hearts from being completely broken ... I have cut capers in chains.

As Katrina Dyonne Thompson has shown in her groundbreaking study of coercion in slave music, singing "to keep down trouble" was a survival strategy of the greatest import; and it surely reinforced the minstrel-stage caricatures of the ever-happy "darkey" slave. While white audiences, Northern and Southern, laughed along to the "capers" cut in front of them onstage, slaves were being driven along the Southern byways, double-chained together in coffles, and forced to sing aloud – "walking advertisements announcing to potential customers that they could buy not only labor but docile, happy, submissive bodies." And what might they have been singing? – "The fiddle sing, the banjo ding, Virginia never tire: / To laugh and sing is just the thing we darkies admire. / Oh happy is the darkey's life, when, hunting for the coon, / He has the fun with the dog and gun to catch him very soon."

Perhaps one of the greatest historical ironies lies in the fact that the minstrel show was approaching its zenith in antebellum popularity just as white terror of slave rebellions was nearing *its* height – as though there were some cultural need to reduce the outrage of an entire enslaved people,

A Slave-Coffle passing the Capitol.

Figure 4.2 Slave coffle passing the US Capitol, around 1815. Unknown engraver. Library of Congress Prints and Photographs Division

demonstrably militant, to the figure of a grinning minstrel who could indeed "cut capers in chains." The public memory of Denmark Vesey's uprising of 1822 in South Carolina was still fresh; Vesey and his comrades were said to have sung an anthem put to the tune of "Hail Columbia" by an enslaved African American who had been fully capable of avoiding minstrel dialect: "Blow the clarion's warlike blast; / Call every Negro from his task; / Wrest the scourge from Buckra's hand, / And drive each tyrant from the land!" Nat Turner's rebellion of 1831 in Virginia was still being recalled in African American song: "You mought be rich as cream, / And drive you a coach and four horse team; / But you can't keep the world from moving around, / And Nat Turner from the gaining ground." To be sure, singing such anthems – or indeed, singing anything – could be risky business, as one Charity Bowery, formerly enslaved in North Carolina, recalled of the immediate aftermath of the Nat Turner uprising: "After that, the low whites would fall upon any slaves they heard praying, or singing a hymn, and often killed them before their masters or mistresses could get to them . . . They thought we was going to *rise*, because we sung 'better days are coming.'" The suspicion of doubled meanings in African American song had finally begun to seep into the slaveholding consciousness; Turner and his co-conspirators were known to have sung "Steal Away, steal away home; / I ain't got long to stay here" as "a summoning code for the secret meetings to plot the rebellion."

Slave ship mutinies were also firmly in the public mind, such as the attempted takeover of the *Decatur* by African Americans in 1826 on the seas between Baltimore and Georgia, and the *Amistad* takeover of 1839 which – in 1841, in the midst of minstrel-show craziness – was declared a just and justified act by the US Supreme Court. That same year witnessed the successful takeover of the slave ship *Creole*, bound for New Orleans from Richmond, Virginia, and sailed to the British West Indies, where the ship's 134 African American "mutineers" secured their freedom. In the following year, 1842, a band of escapees successfully overpowered their Cherokee and Creek enslavers in Oklahoma's "Indian Territory." (The so-called "Five Civilized Tribes" – the Cherokee, the Chickasaw, the Choctaw, the Creek, and, to a lesser extent, the Seminole – did practice variations of African American slavery.) Suffice it to say, the militant participants of these and other slave rebellions could hardly be accommodated through the "capers" and "Ethiopian Delineations" of the minstrel show.

There was also a host of earnest songwriters – white and Black – composing and singing in the service of the abolition movement. Many have remained anonymous, their words coming down to us only through the ephemera of newspaper columns. Others, such as the celebrated Hutchinson Family Singers, are enshrined in the history books. The Hutchinsons are there for good reason. In spite of their occasional forays into the dubious championship of westward expansion (through such songs as "Westward Ho!" and "Uncle Sam's Farm") as well as the "vanishing Indian" motif (even then, it must be said, with a steady finger pointed at the white man's crimes), it was through their abolitionist singing that the Hutchinsons became effectively the country's first supergroup. Hailing from "the Old Granite State" of New Hampshire, as they boasted in their signature theme song of the same title, the Hutchinsons toured the northern states from 1842 to 1849, avoiding the south, "as one visit to Baltimore convinced them that abolitionists, even musical ones, were unwelcome." Their most famous anthem, "Get Off the Track" (1844) stood minstrelsy on its head in appropriating the familiar tune of the Virginia Minstrels' "Old Dan Tucker" and infusing it with the irresistible imagery – and energy – of the new-fangled railroad engine, towing behind it "Freedom's Car, Emancipation":

> Hear the mighty car wheels humming!
> Now look out! *The Engine's coming*!
> Church and Statesmen! hear the thunder!
> Clear the track! or you'll fall under.
> Get off the track! all are singing,
> While the *Liberty Bell* is ringing.

Slavery was driving the country inexorably toward what William Seward would call the "irrepressible conflict" between the north and the south, between the slave power and free-labor power. But there were other "irrepressible conflicts" shuddering through the foundations of US society in the decades before the Civil War. The Hutchinsons sang at temperance meetings and women's rights conventions, where their songs dovetailed with the currents of industrialization and labor agitation, as in their adaptation of Thomas Hood's "The Song of the Shirt" (1847):

> With fingers weary and worn,
> With eye-lids heavy and red,
> A woman sat in unwomanly rags,
> Plying her needle and thread.
> Stitch, stitch, stitch,
> In poverty, hunger and dirt,
> And still with a voice of dolorous pitch,
> She sang the song of the shirt.

Meanwhile, less celebrated, largely unremembered singers and songwriters sang their way through New York's "Anti-Rent War" of 1839–1841, when tenant farmers turned out en masse – to the blare of their signature tin horns – to fight against the Dutch landholding class of the Hudson Valley's near-feudal "patroonship system." "Old Dan Tucker" was drafted in again, this time in the form of "the most popular of the Anti-Rent songs" celebrating the thrashing of "a universally despised deputy sheriff who was imported by the landholders in 1841 to serve writs": "Keep out of the way – big Bill Snyder, / We'll tar your coat and feather your hide, Sir!" In nearby Rhode Island, and allied with the

Figure 4.3 Hutchinson Family Singers. Theatrical poster. Boston, c. 1881.
Library of Congress Prints and Photographs Division

Anti-Rent struggles in New York, was the "radical insurgency" prompted by the state's charter – a holdover from the days of Charles II – restricting voting rights to landowners. In 1842, the new "People's Party" of Rhode Island elected Thomas Wilson Dorr as the people's governor, in opposition to the landholders' governor-elect, Samuel King. There were thus two rival governments claiming authority. King – with Federal backing – imposed martial law, declared Dorr a "traitor," and jailed scores of his supporters. After two years in exile, Dorr returned to face a foregone conviction of treason, and was slapped with a life sentence. (He was released in 1845 after a year in solitary confinement.) The so-called Dorr Rebellion gave rise to a catalog of ballads condemning the landholders ("These are the men who love to rule the State / And have their laws decide the poor man's fate") and championing the state's own Bonnie Prince Charlie: "Although our chosen guide / Is exiled from his home, / The day approaches near, / When he'll no longer roam. . . . / Farewell to 'Martial law'; / The conquering hero comes! / Hail! Thomas Wilson Dorr."

This momentous decade of the 1840s was also approaching the peak of Irish Catholic immigration to the USA, with 260,000 having arrived directly from Ireland by 1840, "while tens of thousands more re-migrated from Great Britain or Canada." Genteel American parlors had long been shimmering to the sweet sounds of Thomas Moore's multivolume collection, *Irish Melodies* (1808–1834), which, along with the songs of Stephen Foster, were by far "the most popular, widely sung, best-loved, and most durable songs in the English language of the entire nineteenth century." Moore's ballads walked a tightrope between safe sentimentalism and nationalist agitation, invoking Ireland's "glorious past" while lamenting its "dismal present" ("The harp that once, thro' Tara's halls, / The soul of Music shed, / Now hangs as mute on Tara's walls / As if that soul were fled"). Lining up behind Moore were scores of songwriters tapping into the tropes and motifs of emigration and parting – such as F. N. Crouch in "Kathleen Mavourneen" and William Dempster in "Lament of the Irish Emigrant." There was even a sentimental buck to be made from Irish starvation, as in A. M. Edmond's "Give Me Three Grains of Corn":

> Give me three grains of corn, mother,
> Only three grains of corn;
> It will keep the little life I have
> Till the coming of the morn.
> I am dying of hunger and cold, mother,
> I am dying of hunger and cold,
> And half the agony of such a death
> My lips have never told.

More muscular and militant were the ballads of the Irish laborers, the "navvies" who for the previous two decades had been the backbone of the expanding road, railway, and canal systems, suffering "the cold in winter, the heat in summer, the swamps, the poor food and housing, the lack of sanitation in the Paddy Camps, the bad whiskey that contractors offered as part of the pay." Such conditions would inevitably give rise to calls for a workers' revolution, as in the "The Tarriers' Song," written from the depths of a prison cell in 1845 by the now-forgotten Mike Walsh: "Arise! Degraded sons of toil! / Too long you've foully bent the knee." After all, as one ballad-mongering veteran of the New Orleans New Canal gang had written in the 1830s: "Ten thousand Micks, they swung their picks / To dig the New Canal. / But the cholera was stronger'n they, / An' twice it killed them all."

In spite of their contributions to the building of the nation, Irish Catholic immigrants were subject to horrific attacks at the hands of largely Protestant nativists in the eastern cities. For their part, the Irish could give as good as they got, as recorded in "De Philadelphia Riots" of 1844, a minstrel song which, in spite of its corrupt comedic voice, accurately informs "Mr. Mayor" and everyone else that it is all too easy to blame the Black man for urban unrest:

> Oh, de "Natives" dey went up to meet,
> At de corner ob Second an' Massa Street,
> De Irish cotch dar Starry Flag,
> An' tare him clean up to a rag.
>
> Oh, de peaceful Natives go away,
> An' meet up dar an odder day,
> Den de Irish get half shot all round,
> An' den dey shoot de Natives down.

Some commentators obviously thought that the USA was already getting too crowded. Germans and Irish were flooding into the northern cities. In the south, the slaveholding powers were flexing their muscles for the acquisition of new territory, not only to prevent their "peculiar institution" of slavery from exhausting itself along with the harshly overworked lands of "King Cotton" but also to increase their representative power against the increasingly hostile northern free-labor bloc in Congress. In the *Democratic Review* of July–August 1845, influential New York editor John L. O'Sullivan called for the US annexation of western territories, notably Oregon and Texas, the latter of which had been prised away from Mexico by proslavery US insurgents. Mexico had abolished slavery in 1829 – everywhere except Texas, where the dominant constituency of American settlers, fronted by Stephen F. Austin, had fiercely protected the institution. Mexico's renunciation of slavery as a "palpable violation of the first principles of a free republic" was at the basis of the Texan separatist movement. Mexico was unable to prevent Austin's faction from declaring Texas the independent "Lone Star Republic" in 1836, with a constitution confirming citizenship upon all those then residing in Texas except "Africans, the descendants of Africans, and Indians" and outlawing the emancipation of slaves without congressional consent.

The Texan Revolution's holy trinity of martyrs were Jim Bowie, William Travis, and – at the cultural apotheosis – Davy Crockett, killed at the Battle of the Alamo in March of 1836. Three years later, the popular stage play *Crockett in Texas* played to packed houses, while Crockett was worshiped in a song set to the tune of "The Star-Spangled Banner," R. T. Conrad's "The Alamo, or the Death of Crockett," which appeared in *Crockett's Free and Easy Song Book, a New Collection of the Most Popular Stage Songs* (1839). Crockett had been a national hero since the Seminole wars, already famous for his cocksure motto, "Be sure you're right – then

Figure 4.4 *American Progress*, by George A. Crofutt, c. 1873.
Library of Congress Prints and Photographs Division

go ahead!" Hence the publication, a year before his death, of "Go Ahead . . . A March Dedicated to Colonel Crockett."

Crockett's motto may as well have been that of the US president John Tyler, who signed off on the annexation of Texas in March of 1845 – "a certain provocation to war with Mexico." It may as well have been the motto of Zachary Taylor, general of the US forces moving toward the Río Grande in June of that year, as recalled in the diary of his subordinate, Colonel Ethan Allen Hitchcock: "He is to expel any armed force of Mexicans who may cross that river. . . . Violence leads to violence, and if this movement of ours does not lead to others and to bloodshed, I am much mistaken." And it may as well have been the motto of John L. O'Sullivan, proclaiming the "Manifest Destiny" of US expansion westward across the continent: "We are the nation of human progress, and who will, what can, set limits to our onward march? Providence is with us, and no earthly power can."

CHAPTER 5

Where Today Are the Pequot?

Following the annexation of Texas, the marching of US troops to the banks of the Río Grande was yet another provocation to Mexico. The border between the "Lone Star Republic" and Mexico had been in dispute for ten years. In March of 1846, Zachary Taylor's troops arrived in what had long been cultivated Mexican territory; *campesinos* and villagers fled in advance of the invading Americans. What Washington needed was a pretext to start a war – the war that future president Ulysses S. Grant, who served in it, would later deem "one of the most unjust ever waged by a stronger against a weaker nation." The USA, he said, had aimed "to provoke a fight, but it was essential that Mexico should commence it." With the disappearance of Taylor's quartermaster and a subsequent Mexican ambush of a US patrol, the pretext was granted, and the Mexican–US War began. It took eighteen months for Taylor's forces to fight their way to the heights of Chapultepec outside Mexico City. Meanwhile, the US Army and irregular forces conquered swaths of what is now New Mexico and fanned out into California, which was prised away from Mexico and declared the independent "Bear Flag Republic." Mexico's surrender came with the fall of Mexico City. In signing the Treaty of Guadalupe Hidalgo in February of 1848, the Mexicans lost over half of their territory to the United States. The international boundary was now, firmly, the Río Grande; California and New Mexico became US territory, as well as parts of today's Arizona, Colorado, Nevada, and Utah. The USA and its territories now extended in an unbroken empire from the Atlantic to the Pacific Ocean. In the wake of the $15 million pittance paid to Mexico, one self-satisfied US journalist declared, "We take nothing by conquest, thank God." One hundred fifteen thousand Mexicans now found themselves living in US territory and subject to the laws – and the "racialization" – of the white-dominated USA. As they and their descendants would ever after say: "*Nosotros no cruzamos la frontera, la frontera nos cruzó* (We didn't cross the border; the border crossed us)."

This massive expansion of the USA was heavily marked by song, not least in the so-called songsters that flew off the presses all across the country. They were cheap, pocket-sized booklets, usually containing only lyrics, hawked by booksellers and street vendors who advertised their contents as "sentimental, patriotic, and moral" (although they were just as likely to be racist and jingoistic to an appalling degree). One particularly noxious example was *The Rough and Ready Songster* (1848), so titled in honor of Zachary Taylor, long nicknamed "Old Rough and Ready." It boasted such jingles as "We're the Boys for Mexico" ("The Mexicans are doomed to fall, / God in his wrath forsook 'em, / And all their goods and chattels call / On us to go and hook 'em") and "Remember the Alamo!" ("O heed not the Spanish battle yell, / Let every stroke we give them *tell*, / And let them fall as Crockett fell, / Remember the Alamo!"). Even worse was the blatant racism of what became a cowboy favorite, "Way Down in Mexico": "O Boys, we're goin' far to-night, / Yeo-ho, yeo-ho! / We'll take the greasers now in hand / And drive 'em in the Rio Grande, / Way down in Mexico." Jingoistic celebrations of the Texas Rangers proliferated, as did "Grand Triumphal Marches," "Victory Quick Steps," and "Grand Entrée Quick Steps" dedicated to the generals and the "Volunteers for Glory" who had avenged Davy Crockett and done their "All for Texas!"

However, there were notable song examples that resisted the triumphalist tide. Sea chanteys of Black American origin, often adopted by British seamen, were a case in point. (One historian of chanteys notes that "quite a number of British seamen deserted their ships to join [Mexican general] Santa Anna's wild and ragged army.") By far, the most curious of these chanteys is "Santy Anno," which goes so far as to brazenly reverse the historical outcome and project the Mexicans as the victors:

Oh, Santy Anna gained the day,
Heave away, Santy Anna,
He gained the day at Monterey,
All on the plains of Mexico.

Zachary Taylor ran away,
Heave away, Santy Anna,
He ran away at Monterey,
All on the plains of Mexico.

It might be a bit of an overstatement to claim that "American anti-war songs originated with this war," but it certainly generated the first large body of song against American war-making, providing the soundtrack to an anti-war movement dovetailing with the anti-slavery movement. The leading abolitionist William Lloyd Garrison's newspaper, *The*

Liberator, printed a raft of songs against the war, while the Hutchinson Family Singers reminded the nation that the expansion of slave territory was at the basis of Washington's annexation policies. As the Hutchinsons sang in a revised version of their signature song, "The Old Granite State": "War and slavery perplex us / And ere long will sorely vex us, / Oh, we're paying dear for Texas, / In the war with Mexico." Henry David Thoreau – himself jailed for refusing to pay the taxes funding the war – conceived of his revolutionary thesis "Civil Disobedience" with "the present Mexican war" in mind. It was, to him, "the work of comparatively a few individuals using the standing government as their tool."

"Disobedience" was also on the minds of entire regiments – volunteers from North Carolina, Mississippi, and Virginia – who mutinied in Northern Mexico in August 1847. It was on the minds, in particular, of many deserters from the US ranks, including John Riley and his Irish, German, British, and US comrades who formed the St. Patrick's Battalion (*San Patricios*) to fight for Mexico, a weak Catholic nation being mauled by a strong, overwhelmingly Protestant one. One period ballad, set to the old English tune of "Derry Down," was composed by defecting US troops near Chapultepec, where most of the *San Patricios* were wiped out. It survives to give us at least a partial account of many a deserter's motivation, beyond politics or ideology. This was the brutality faced by troops at the mercy of sadistic officers whose pleasure was to "buck and gag" them, tying them spread-eagled to stakes driven into the ground, with a gag shoved into their mouths: "'Sergeant, buck him and gag him,' our officers cry, / For each trifling offense which they happen to spy, / Till with bucking and gagging of Dick, Tom, Pat, and Bill, / Faith, the Mexicans' ranks they have helped to fill."

Of all the bodies of song to have emerged from the Mexican–US War and its subsequent border conflicts, the most striking is the corrido or "border ballad" eulogizing outlaws and champions of social justice, "graphic testimony to the resistive bent of the Texas-Mexicans . . . when they and their whole way of life were still reeling from the catastrophic defeat at the hands of the Anglos and their powerfully ascendant economic order." Hence, for example, the corrido "*El General Cortina*," celebrating the border raider Juan Nepomuceno Cortina, who with a force of 1200 men attacked and briefly captured Brownsville, Texas, in protest against the cession of his family's lands to the USA: "That General Cortina / is very sovereign and free; / the honor due him is greater / for he saved a Mexican's life." Other ballads celebrated the "mustangers, buffalo hunters, trail drivers, and vaqueros" who were now "wandering pioneers" in the lands that once were Mexican. The borderlands of California and Mexico gave rise to corridos honoring such "social bandits" as Tiburcio Vásquez,

Juan Flores, and – above all – Joaquín Murieta, whose figure "looms large against the climate of racial prejudice and violence in California society of the 1850s." In Murieta's story, "historical fact, legend, and myth are intermingled." So murky – yet general – was the popular knowledge of Murieta that "five or perhaps more Mexican bandits of the early 1850s used the name of Joaquín Murieta/Murietta."

One constant running through the musical versions of Murieta's life is his stature as an agent of nearly Olympian justice, if not vengeance:

Murieta does not like
To be falsely accused.
I come to avenge my wife,
And again I repeat it –
Carmelita, so lovely,
How they made her suffer.

Through bars I went,
Punishing Americans.
"You must be the captain
Who killed my brother;
You grabbed him, defenceless."

Figure 5.1a Joaquín Murieta shortly before his death in 1853, painted by a priest at Mission San Carlos del Carmelo.
Courtesy of the University of Southern California Libraries and the California Historical Society

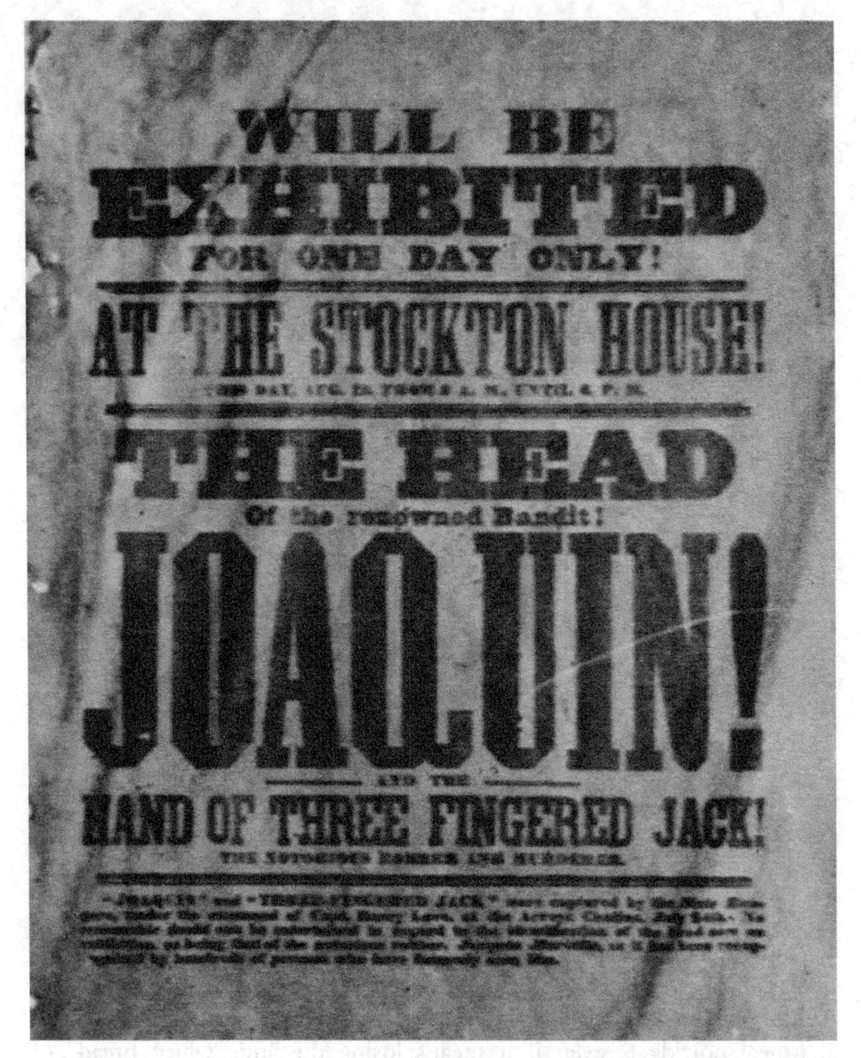

Figure 5.1b Poster advertising the exhibition of Murieta's pickled head, c. 1855. Courtesy of the University of Southern California Libraries and the California Historical Society

Today's state of California was carved out of the territory that the Mexicans – and before them, the Spanish colonials – had known as *Alta California* (Upper California). Only two years before Californian statehood in 1850, a vein of gold was discovered at Sutter's Mill on the South Fork of the American River, sparking the "Gold Rush" that would bring three hundred thousand gold-hungry and land-hungry immigrants to California over the next seven years, many of them making the voyage by steamship either around South America's Cape Horn or via the Panama Isthmus. Few songs emerged to depict one's striking it rich. By far, the vast number of songs appearing in the likes of *The Golden Songster* and *Put's Original California Songster* presented "The Lousy Miner" and "The Fools of Forty-Nine" taken for a ride by the "Steam Navigation Thieves" and "Humbug Steamship Companies" (all verbatim song titles) as well as a host of other unscrupulous exploiters in the transportation, hotel, and service industries. Some hopeful emigrants never even made it as far as their California claim, as depicted in a magazine ballad based on a letter from a "Dying Californian" to his brother:

> Listen, brother, catch each whisper
> 'Tis my wife I speak of now,
> Tell, oh, tell her how I missed her
> When the fever burned my brow.
> Tell her she must kiss my children
> Like the kiss I last impressed,
> Hold them as when last I held them
> Held them closely to my breast.
>
> It was for them I crossed the ocean,
> What my hopes were I'll not tell;
> But they gained an orphan's portion,
> Yet He doeth all things well;
> Tell them I have reached the haven
> Where I sought the precious dust,
> But I gained a port called Heaven
> Where the gold will never rust.

And, from further afield, among the massive store of Norwegian emigrant songs is that of the "Adventurer Who Has Seen the States and California" but has decided that it would be better to return to his "oatmeal porridge," even if it means losing the "fine wheat bread" of America:

> You journeyed away to the distant
> West, to Columbia, where there is no
> Oppression, and liberty and equality
> for all . . .
>
> And you went still further, far beyond
> the states, to where men dig for gold on
> the steep slopes of the hill . . .

> Then let him go who will to the distant
> West. He will long to return
> home, I know, for it is good to be
> there.

Such songs reflect the skepticism of many over the lure of California's fabled riches. Sweden and Denmark, too, boasted their share of returned, disappointed gold-seekers, sarcastically presenting the USA in impossibly utopian terms. A Swedish returner's "America Ballad: Song in Praise of Far-Off America" boasted that

> Ducks and chickens rain right down,
> A roasted goose flies in,
> And on the table lands one more
> With fork and knife stuck in

while a Danish version proclaims

> This is where bird Phoenix lives,
> Gold and silver sprout on the ground,
> And in woods and meadows
> There grows only money.

Indeed, it was partially skepticism over the Gold Rush that prompted the celebrated Norwegian violinist, Ole Bull, to establish his ill-fated colony, Oleana (New Norway), in Pennsylvania, earning him the musical sobriquet, "*Bedre End Guld* (Better than Gold)":

> Good men of Norway, strong of arm
> and brave of soul, behold a friend who
> does not scorn you! He is worth more
> to you than gold. You know him well:
> his name is Ole Bull.

Norwegian posterity was unkind to Bull with the collapse of his project at the hands of unscrupulous land speculators amidst a host of other difficulties. Henrik Ibsen's utopian phantasmagoria, Gyntiana, in *Peer Gynt*, was said to be based on Bull's Oleana, while Ditmar Meidell wrote "the most famous of all the [Norwegian] 'America Songs,'" "Oleana," with its mocking chorus: "Ole—Ole—Ole—oh! Oleana!"

For abolitionists such as the Hutchinsons, far from prompting skepticism, the Gold Rush appeared to open the golden gate to freedom and victory over slavery, as California entered the Union officially as a "free state." And so they sang triumphantly: "Then, ho! Boys ho! / To California go. / No slave shall toil on God's free Soil / On the banks of the

Sacramento." Yet, as one historian grimly catalogs it, behind the promises of freedom in the newly acquired territories, a darker history was unfolding:

> Though California was admitted to the United States as a "free state" in 1850, slavery was tacitly tolerated throughout the state, and California passed a fugitive slave law in 1852. Whites impatient with the pace of legal disenfranchisement launched assaults against Mexicans and Indians. In California, hundreds were lynched in the decades after California statehood, while in Texas, Afro-Mestizo landowners were driven off of their lands by white usurpers.

The western lands between California and the Mississippi were also fast becoming mid-century magnets for Anglo-European settlers. A store of ballads, parlor numbers, and minstrel songs invoking the westward migration have come down to us, some of them first sung for collectors in the 1930s by elderly settlers themselves or by their children. "The Wisconsin Emigrant" is one, recreating a would-be settler's attempt to persuade his resistant wife to leave their New England farm for the new lands of the west. Unsurprisingly, the fear of Indigenous savagery becomes part of the rhetorical arsenal:

> Oh, husband, remember, that land of delight
> Is surrounded by Indians who murder by night.
> Your house they will plunder and burn to the ground,
> While your wife and your children lie murdered around.
> Oh, stay on the farm, and you'll suffer no loss,
> For the stone that keeps rolling will gather no moss.

And yet, the historical record makes it clear that, far from offering a steady diet of scalping and arrows in the back, the Indigenous people encountered on the westward trek were likely to be hospitable to those who meant them no harm and treated them with human decency. Indeed, a number of accounts place musical exchange at the center of benign encounters: "Plains Indians seemed especially to delight in providing music and dances for emigrants whom they had found to be friendly and receptive to Indian ways . . . Overlanders also entertained appreciative audiences with music of their own." Details of such exchanges are heartwarming:

> While camped near Fort Laramie in 1854, Mary Burrell played her melodeon for a small group of Sioux men and women, while her brother playfully resisted the women's efforts to dance with him. At about the same time, William Woodhams shared his food with a few Paiutes, who soon

became an appreciative audience for his accordion playing. In return for Sioux performances of song and dance, the Mormons of George Benjamin Wallace's Emigrating Company reciprocated with a dance that was accompanied by violin, fife, and drums.

Indeed, the Anglo "emigrants" and "overlanders" heading westward shared a bitterly ironic fellowship with the displaced eastern tribes forced into exchanging their status from *aboriginal* ("Indigenous to here") to *refugees* ("Indigenous to somewhere else"). Among the many odes in the songsters enticing white easterners to turn their backs on the crowded cities and seek fulfilment and fortune in the West, at least one directed specifically at the Choctaws and Cherokees – from the *Virginia Warbler* of 1845 – deserves reprinting in full for its chilling change of voice from Mephistophelean seduction to Jacksonian menace. Either knowingly or otherwise, it reveals the true colors of settler colonialism and Manifest Destiny:

March, march, Choctaw and Cherokee,
Pull up your stakes, and march forward in order,
March, march, where white men no more you'll see,
All the red chieftains are over the border.
Many a blanket spread lies there to be your bed,
Many a wigwam that is famous in story;
Mount and make ready then, chieftains and fighting men,
Arkansas's prairies are quite captivating.

Come from the woods where your rifles are ringing,
Come from the land where the golden ore grows,
Come from the fount where the sweet waters are springing,
Come from the wigwam, your arrows and bows,
Will money content you – here's dollars in plenty,
Gird on your leggings and march forward in order,
Or else you may rue the day you have resolved to stay,
Hunting the deer in the pale faces' border.

A major impetus for westward expansion was a long-held anxiety over the impact of eastern urban dominance, with the cities swelling through a steady influx of immigrants. Witness Thomas Jefferson's letter to James Madison as early as 1787, urging the acquisition of "vacant lands in any part of America. When they get piled upon one another in large cities, as in Europe, they will become corrupt as in Europe." By the 1850s, anti-German and anti-Irish nativism was firmly entrenched in the culture as well as the body politic, as demonstrated in the rise of the "Know Nothing" movement and its political wing, the American Party (or, as it was sometimes called, with no hint of irony, the Native American Party).

A leading historian writes: "Immigration during the first five years of the 1850s reached a level five times greater than a decade earlier. Most of the new arrivals were poor Catholic peasants or laborers from Ireland and Germany who crowded into the tenements of large cities."

Germans, in particular, were associated with the European revolutions of 1848, the suppressions of which spawned a raft of emigrant songs proclaiming America as the haven of liberty: "Since freedom has been lost / in all of Europe / So, brother, let us travel, / To America, la la la." The 1848 revolutions, though largely bourgeois and more concerned with the overthrow of monarchy than capitalism, were construed as dangerous radical movements by reactionary US nativists – a misapprehension helped along by the fact that the writers of the *Communist Manifesto* (1848), Karl Marx and Friedrich Engels, were both German. German-language newspapers in the USA, such as Philadelphia's *Die Republik der Arbeiter*, published song-poems like "The Little Communist" (January 1853), whose words seem innocuous enough, and fully in keeping with the gospel preached every Sunday in US churches:

I am a little Communist
And never need anything more
Than what I need to live
All else I give away to others . . .

I am a little Communist
And don't ask for money
Since our master Jesus Christ
Neither valued it.

Lyrics and sentiments such as these only added fuel to the nativist fires.

As for the Irish, already a substantial immigrant population before midcentury, the onset of the Great Famine in 1850 swelled the ranks of the diaspora to over two million, sparking the composition of sentimental minstrel songs such as L. V. H. Crosby's "The Emigrant's Farewell" (1852) as sung by the Boston Harmoneons:

Then the famine came stalking with gaunt bony finger;
And our landlord was ruthless and pitiless sure;
And sweet Kathleen, our blue-eyed – but why should we linger,
Recounting our sorrows – who cares for the poor?

Yes, God careth for us. Then no more repining,
Though we fly from this desolate country away
To the free happy West; as each day is declining
For the land of our fathers we'll fervently pray.

A mere two years after this song appeared, the *New York Times* published a small classified advertisement utilizing for the first time the phrase that was to resound in the annals of anti-Irish bigotry in the US: "GIRL WANTED – In a small private family. . . . She must have good references. . . . No Irish need apply." As we shall see, this phrase was to take on enormous significance in songs of the Civil War.

Although most public attention on midcentury immigration was focused on the crowded cities of the east, conflict was brewing on the West Coast between the Anglo nativists – already hard at work demonizing the Mexican and Indigenous people whom they were determined to displace – and the Chinese, who, like many other immigrant groups, had been attracted by the California gold strikes. Their arrival in large numbers – over forty thousand between 1851 and 1860 – triggered not only a "vicious campaign to force them out of the mines by violence and restrictive legislation" but also a tradition of anti-Chinese songs that "were already popular in California as early as 1855." One of these was the truly appalling "John Chinaman" from San Francisco's *California Songster* of that year:

I thought you'd cut your queue off, John,
And don a Yankee coat,
And a collar high you'd raise, John,
Around your dusky throat.

I thought of rats and puppies, John,
You'd eaten your last fill,
But on such slimy "pot-pies,"
I'm told you dinner still.

Oh, John, I've been deceived in you,
In all your thieving clan,
For our gold is all you're after, John,
To get it as you can.

Indeed, the "John Chinaman" figure, ubiquitous in anti-Chinese songs of the 1850s and 1860s, had a similar function to that of Jim Crow or Zip Coon on the minstrel stage, reinforcing an exclusionary racial difference that, in the case of the Chinese, would be codified in national law before the century's end. Of course, few minstrel performers would have thought of the humanity behind those they were caricaturing in "yellowface." Rare was the exception, such as Mart Taylor's "John Chinaman's Appeal," which – in spite of its recourse to insulting "Oriental"-sounding nonsense syllables for comic effect – manages to convey credible sympathy for the mistreated Chinese immigrant:

Oh, now my friends, I'm going away
From this infernal place, sir;
The balance of my days I'll stay
With the Celestial race, sir;
I'll go to raising rice and tea;
I'll be a heathen ever,
For Christians all have treated me
As men should be used never.

The first Chinese to come to California had settled in what was then called Yerba Buena – subsequently "San Francisco" – in 1838; but it was the Gold Rush ten years later that sparked the first major migration, mostly from Canton. For these people, the USA was *Gamsaan* (*Jinshan*): "Gold Mountain." Many composed their own songs reflecting the struggles of arrival, settlement, separation, labor, and racist victimization. One body of vernacular song, by immigrants from the Taishan region of Guangdong, includes this ode of departure:

With a pillow on my shoulder, I begin the perilous journey:

Sailing a boat with bamboo poles across the sea,
Leaving wives and sisters behind in search of wealth,
No longer lingering to the woman in the bedroom,
No longer paying respects to parents at home.

Others reflected the hardship and hopes of the gold mines (often abandoned claims left by Anglo-European miners, for which the Chinese were obliged to pay "a hefty foreign miners' tax"):

O, sojourner from Gold Mountain:
If you have not one thousand in gold,
  You must have at least eight hundred.

O, uncle from the South Seas:
Just look at your money bag,
  It's empty, it's empty.

And still others reflected the longing of those left behind in Canton:

My husband, because of poverty, has gone to Gold Mountain.
With only a petty sum of capital, he cannot make the journey home.
The road to Gold Mountain is extremely perilous and difficult;
At home, in grief and pain, my longing eyes piercing through the horizon,
  Waiting.

These were the voices never heard on the minstrel stage, where "John Chinaman" took his place alongside all the other racially dehumanized figures whose labor had built, and was to continue building, the USA.

The social and political struggles of the mid-nineteenth century often expressed themselves in seemingly disconnected or even bizarre ways – for example, "the futile violence over nationality [and] religion" that manifested itself in the "Astor Place Riot" of May 10, 1849, in New York City. In that instance, it was an opera house that proved the locus of working-class antagonism, sparked by rival supporters of two actors playing Macbeth at the same time in different productions: the English actor William Charles Macready in one, and the American Edwin Forrest in another. Forrest's supporters, mostly Irish Catholic workers fronted by the "Bowery B'hoy" gangs with whom they were linked, stormed what they called "the English ARISTOCRATIC opera house" on Astor Place, where Macready was appearing. Their battle cry was: "WORKING MEN shall AMERICANS or ENGLISH RULE in this city?" The consequent fight between the attackers and the militia left twenty-two dead. As an opera historian has noted: "The Astor Place Opera House was built to demonstrate the wealth and power of New York's social elite. The Bowery B'hoys didn't have to attend opera there to know what it meant in cultural terms for them and for their antagonists. Opera was foreign and upper-class."

The US economy was careening toward what has been called "the Panic of 1857," caused by "the boom in railroads and manufacturing, the surge of immigration, the increased speculation in stocks and bonds, the stealing, corruption, manipulation [that] led to wild expansion and then crash." The "Panic" had been foretold by the recession of 1853–1854, which saw a run on the banks in New York and, through the inevitable ripple effect, elsewhere. Hence a topical song published in Louisville, Kentucky, in 1854: "Money Is a Hard Thing to Borrow." It was composed by one George Morris, with "Song and Chorus to Suit the Hard Times, as Sung by the Well Known Campbell Minstrels":

> The times are so "tight" for the cash is hard to get,
> Though all hope they'll have some tomorrow.
> And ev'ry one looks "blue" and are in such a pet,
> Finding: money is a hard thing to borrow . . .
>
> So take down your "shingle" and shut up your shop,
> For money is a hard thing to borrow.
> "Yes indeed."

Money would have been a particularly "hard thing to borrow" for women in the mid-nineteenth century, as most states had yet to legally enshrine women's right to manage a separate economy or to control property in their own name (except in instances of a spouse's incapacitation). By 1848, a state such as New York might attempt to address this injustice through passing its Married Women's Property Act; but that very year Elizabeth Cady Stanton "cited the lack of married woman's property rights as one of her main points at the Seneca Falls convention, perhaps realizing that most other states did not yet have such legislation." This historic convention – the first dedicated to the securing of women's rights in the USA – rocked the political dimension as it rocked the popular music dimension. The most comprehensive catalog of suffragist sheet music numbers, in that medium alone, thirty songs published in the USA between 1850 and 1860. This would not include the countless lyrics published in national, state, and local newspapers, society journals, and other ephemeral organs, let alone the unknown number of unpublished songs composed spontaneously for women's rights rallies. However, two events appear to have particularly marked the midcentury musical landscape. One was the Seneca Falls Convention itself, which attracted its share of reaction, as witnessed in Kate Horn's mocking "Women's Rights" (1853), which the composer declared was "Rightly written for the 'Woman's Rights Conventions'":

> 'Tis "woman's Right" a home to have
> As perfect as can be,
> But "Not her right" to make that home
> To every lover free;
> 'Tis "woman's Right" to rule the house,
> And petty troubles brave,
> But "not her right" to rule the head
> And treat him as her slave.

Just as this song reduced the political complexities of the women's rights struggle to a wild campaign for free love and men's emasculation, other reactionary numbers reduced it to a mere fashion statement, such as one published in 1852 with "Words written for this Work by a Lady":

> Come prepared, each free-born daughter!
> Cut the skirt still shorter, shorter,
> Don the waistcoat and cravat!
> Let each leader, each retainer,
> Booted, spurred, in full slatana,
> Come and join the grand debate.

Indeed, the songwriters' fixation on fashion was crudely connected to the serious issue introduced into "the grand debate" by Stanton's friend from Seneca Falls, Amelia Jenks Bloomer, editor of the women's magazine *The Lily*. In 1851, Bloomer "hurled her first spear in defense of women's rights when she made the following comment on a news story concerning two fashionably dressed New York women who had been seen openly smoking cigars on the street: 'Surely we have an equal right to do it.'"

That same year, Bloomer "embodied her advanced editorial policy by appearing on the streets of Seneca Falls in a pair of Turkish-looking trousers topped by a knee-length overdress or tunic." Thus was born what became known as "the Bloomer," aimed at liberating women from the uncomfortable and debilitating whalebone corsets that crushed their internal organs and the caged hoop skirts that weighed down and exhausted their muscles.

Composers of parlor music had a field day, briefly flooding the market with piano pieces such as "The Bloomer Polka," "Bloomer Waltz," "The Bloomer Quick Step," and more than one "Bloomer Schottische." Amidst the flurry of these instrumental responses, one anonymous lyricist – whose gender remains unknown – published "The Bloomer's Complaint: A Very Pathetic SONG" (1851), which appears to support Bloomer's position while ridiculing the public hysteria – and male hypocrisy – over the issue:

> Dear me, what a terrible clatter they raise,
> Because that old gossip Dame Rumor
> Declares, with her hands lifted up in amaze
> That I'm coming out as a Bloomer,
> That I'm coming out as a Bloomer.
> I wonder how often these men must be told
> When a woman a notion once seizes,
> However they ridicule, lecture or scold
> She'll do, after all, as she pleases,
> She'll do, after all, as she pleases.
>
> They know very well that their own fashions change
> With each little change of the season,
> But Oh! it is "monstrous" and "dreadful" and "strange"
> And "out of all manner of reason,"
> And "out of all manner of reason."

Of all the voices that have come down to us from the women's rights movement of the mid-nineteenth-century, one that has resonated well into the twenty-first century is that of Sojourner Truth, born into slavery in New York roughly thirty years before that state abolished the practice in 1827. Speaking at a women's rights convention in Akron, Ohio, in 1851, Truth is said to have uttered these famous words:

> And ain't I a woman? Look at me! Look at my arm! I have ploughed and planted, and gathered into barns, and no man could head me! And ain't I a woman? I could work as much and eat as much as a man – when I could get it – and bear the lash as well! And ain't I a woman? I have borne thirteen

Figure 5.2 Sheet music cover of "Bloomer Waltz," composed by William Dessier, c. 1851.
Library of Congress Prints and Photographs Division

> children, and seen most all sold off to slavery, and when I cried out with my mother's grief, none but Jesus heard me! And ain't I a woman?

There has been considerable scholarly debate as to whether these are Truth's actual words or a dramatic recasting of them by the white feminist Frances Gage. But there is no doubt that Truth, like Stanton, Susan B. Anthony, Frederick Douglass, and many others, saw an inextricable connection between the women's rights movement and the anti-slavery movement. Truth is known to have written songs that she herself would sing at abolitionist meetings, such as "I Am Pleading for My People," which she set to the tune of "Auld Lang Syne":

> I am pleading for my people,
> A poor downtrodden race,
> Who dwell in freedom's boasted land,
> With no abiding place.

I am pleading that my people
May have their rights restored;
For they have long been toiling,
And yet have no reward.

They are forced the crops to culture,
But not for them they yield,
Although both late and early
They labor in the field.

Whilst I bear upon my body
The scars of many a gash,
I am pleading for my people
Who groan beneath the lash.

Figure 5.3 Sojourner Truth, undated image.
Library of Congress Prints and Photographs Division

Slavery, along with Indigenous genocide the nation's greatest original sin, had been eating away at the cultural and political foundations since before independence. By the mid-nineteenth century – as the Hutchinsons sang – slavery was still "a hard foe to battle":

> The South have their school where the masters learn to rule,
> And lord it o'er the free states accordin';
> But sure they'd better quit e'er they raise the Yankee grit,
> And we tumble 'em over t'other side of Jordan.
> Then wake up the North, the sword unsheath,
> Slavery is a hard foe to battle!

The ramped-up anti-slavery rhetoric was directly connected to the US seizure of lands west of the Mississippi. Would these territories eventually be converted into free states or slave states, with their attendant power in Congress and the judiciary? The Fugitive Slave Act of 1850, obliging the return of escapees back to bondage in the South, even if they had been apprehended in the northern free states, had already eliminated the North as a safe haven. The Kansas–Nebraska Act of 1854 succeeded in overturning the decades-old prohibition against slavery in territories north of the 36°30′parallel. So now, theoretically, any new state – North or South – could be admitted to the Union as a slave state.

It was in the midst of this turmoil that Harriet Beecher Stowe emerged to publish what was arguably the most influential American novel of the nineteenth century, *Uncle Tom's Cabin* (1852), based heavily on the slave narrative *The Life of Josiah Henson, Formerly a Slave* (1849). The novel's impact reached far beyond mere political debate, at home and abroad; it transformed popular culture, inaugurating the proliferation of "Tom Shows" on the stage and commercial spin-offs from children's toys to candies, crockery, jigsaw puzzles, and household decorations all based on characters from the novel. The minstrel show was particularly influenced, just as, arguably, it had influenced Stowe in the creation of her characters. Without the protection of today's copyright laws, there was nothing to prevent the avalanche of parody shows – as often as not debunking the antislavery narrative – such as *Happy Uncle Tom*, *Uncle Dad's Cabin*, *Aunt Dinah's Cabin*, and *Life Among the Happy*, all offering the spectacle of the novel's main characters mugging and dancing to such edifying lyrics as "Oh, white folks, we'll have you to know / Dis am not de version of Mrs. Stowe; / Wid her de Darks am all unlucky / But we am de boys from Old Kentucky."

The treatment of Stowe and her characters on the minstrel stage is not surprising, given the medium's long hosting of sentimental plantation narratives purportedly from the mouths of slaves themselves ("Hurrah, hurrah, for massa's old plantation. / Hurrah, hurrah, I'm going back again, / Dere's not a spot on all the earth, / Not yet in all creation, / Dat's half so near dis darkie's heart / As massa's old plantation"). Stowe had her champions, too, in popular music. Midcentury progenitors of Tin Pan Alley flooded the sheet music market with the likes of "Poor Uncle Tom," "Eliza's Flight," "Little Eva; Uncle Tom's Guardian Angel," "Uncle Tom's Glimpse of Glory," and "The Georgian Slave (Ballad). To Mrs. Harriet Beecher Stowe."

Escapees from slavery were also honored in song, either through fictional characterization or real-life eulogizing. We may never know the names of some of the most influential composers, such as the anonymous "cotton hoosiers of Mobile" who introduced ocean-going sailors to the chantey "Alabama," otherwise known as "John Cherokee," which celebrates the near-supernatural abilities of a mixed-race trickster and fugitive:

Oh, this is the tale of John Cherokee,
Alabama – John Cher'kee!
The Injun man from Miramashee,
Alabama – John Cher'kee!
With a hauley high, an' a hauley low!
Alabama – John Cher'kee!

They made him a slave down in Alabam,
Alabama – John Cher'kee!
He run away every time he can,
Alabama – John Cher'kee!
They shipped him aboard of a whaling ship,
Alabama – John Cher'kee!
Agen an' agen he gave 'em the slip,
Alabama – John Cher'kee!

The mythical John Cherokee had a real-life counterpart, at least in terms of bravery and ingenuity, in Henry "Box" Brown, who had escaped from slavery in 1849 by concealing himself in a wooden crate shipped from Virginia to Philadelphia. At least one anonymous balladeer took note:

Here you see a man by the name of Henry Brown,
Ran away from the South to the North,
Which he would not have done but they stole all his rights,
But they'll never do the like again.
Brown laid down the shovel and the hoe,
Down in the box he did go,

No more Slave work for Henry Box Brown,
In the box by *Express* he did go.

Beyond such daring individuals, whether mythical or historical, the Underground Railroad – the intricate system of secret routes and safe-houses designed to aid fugitives escaping to Canada or other free havens – was a particularly fertile source of songwriting inspiration, not least for the amateur composer and geologist George Nelson Allen, whose "Underground Rail Car! Or, Song of the Fugitive" (1854) was dedicated to "Fred. Douglass, Esq." Known primarily for providing the music to other people's religious texts (such as the hymn "Take My Hand, Precious Lord"), Allen cast the Underground Railroad as an instrument of divine execution:

I'm on my way to Canada, a freeman's rights to share.
The cruel wrongs of slavery I can no longer bear;
My heart is crush'd within me so while I remain a slave.
That I'm resolved to strike the blow for Freedom or the Grave!

O Great Father! do Thou pity me.
And help me on to Canada where the panting slave is free!

The greatest ownership of odes to the Underground Railroad must belong, in the end, to Black Americans themselves, who were certainly not silent in spite of concerted repression sparked by white terror. After all, even the spectacle of free Black men whistling on a street corner in Lynchburg, Virginia, prompted editorial complaints that "unless something was done the whites would . . . hand over control of the streets to a motley crew of free blacks and slaves." So, from the depths of the southern swamps, bayous, canebrakes, and cottonfields emerged songs of instruction. They might be cast as spirituals – "Steal Away to Jesus," "Run to Jesus," "Seeking for a City," "Brother Moses, Go to de Promised Land," "Oh Sinner, You'd Better Get Ready." Or, they might be even more inscrutable, such as the ode to one Peg Leg Joe, who – according to a report in the journal of the American Anti-Slavery Society – was a "peg-legged sailor" charged with the task of guiding escapees to the way stations of the Underground Railroad. "Follow the Drinking Gourd" was, in part, a reference to the Big Dipper or the Plough constellation pointing ever northward. It was also an instruction to secrecy and to follow the markings left by Peg Leg Joe:

Foller the drinkin' gou'd
Foller the drinkin' gou'd

No one know, the wise man say,
Foller the drinkin' gou'd

The riva's bank am a very good road
The dead trees show the way
Lef' foot, peg foot goin' on
Foller the drinkin' gou'd.

Since the passage of the Fugitive Slave Act, a number of high-profile escapes had caught the attention of the northern public, often showing the free people's readiness to challenge both the act and the authorities attempting to enforce it. In February of 1851, a fugitive from Virginia, Shadrach Minkins, was apprehended and put on trial in Boston. A determined crowd stormed the courtroom, freed Minkins, and spirited him away to Montreal, where he became one of the founders of that city's Black community. A similar event in Syracuse, New York, that same year, saw a fugitive known only as "Jerry" rescued from a courthouse by a crowd with crowbars and battering rams facing down a posse of armed marshals. But with the Southern-dominated Supreme Court's ruling in the *Dred Scott* v. *Sandford* case (1857), in which the enslaved Scott family had attempted to sue for their freedom on the grounds of having been brought into free territory, the screws were further tightened against Black Americans, even in the North. Chief Justice Roger B. Taney had ruled not only that Black people should not be construed as US citizens under the Constitution but that they were "so far inferior that they had no rights which the white man was bound to respect." This was a position, as one legal scholar notes, that "probably represented the views of the vast majority of whites in American society" in 1857 (if not, sadly, long afterwards).

One white American, we know, did not share these views. John Brown was an antislavery crusader who, with his sons, led bloody battles against slaveholding settlers in Kansas in 1856, in one instance cutting down five of them with broadswords on the banks of Pottawatomie Creek and helping to secure the disputed territory's reputation as "Bleeding Kansas." In 1859, Brown attempted to seize the Federal arsenal at Harper's Ferry, Virginia (now West Virginia), in hopes of sparking an armed slave uprising. Overwhelmed by local militia and US marines under the command of Robert E. Lee, Brown was captured, tried for treason, and hanged on the morning of December 2, 1859. His final words on that day ring down through history: "I, John Brown, am quite certain that the crimes of this guilty land will never be purged away but with blood. I had, as I now think vainly, flattered myself that without very much bloodshed it might be done." As W. E. B. Du Bois wrote in his biography of Brown (1909): "These were the last written words of John Brown, set down the day he died – the culminating of that wonderful message of his forty days in prison, which all in all made the mightiest Abolition document that America has known." To Herman Melville, "Weird John Brown" was, more than anyone else, "the Meteor of the war." Possibly the tune to the song by which Brown is best remembered was written by a South Carolinian named William Steffe. The lyrics are attributed to at least three authors; but when the Hutchinson Family Singers began to storm the country, singing "John Brown's body lies a-mouldering in the grave / His soul is marching on," they may well have "converted more people to the antislavery cause than all the speeches and sermons of the time."

John Brown had argued on his last day in court: "The New Testament teaches me to 'remember them that are in bonds, as bound with them' . . . [the] millions in this slave country whose rights are disregarded by wicked, cruel, and unjust enactments." The Fugitive Slave Law; the Dred Scott decision; the "peculiar institution" of slavery itself, bolstered by a host of complicit forces, both Northern and Southern – all of these had contributed to the "disregard" of which Brown spoke. So did the popular culture that reinforced the impression that Black Americans were indeed "so far inferior that they had no rights which the white man was bound to respect." For Frederick Douglass, the main cultural culprit in the dehumanizing mission was minstrelsy. He called on performers to "cease to exaggerate the exaggerations of our enemies; and represent the colored man rather as he is, than as Ethiopian Minstrels usually represent him to be."

Black challenges to the culture of antebellum minstrelsy were legion. In literature, there was Douglass's own novel, *The Heroic Slave* (1853), published the year after *Uncle Tom's Cabin* and deliberately responding to Stowe's roster of passive, feeble-minded, meek slaves with a narrative based on the story of Madison Washington, the leader of the *Creole* slave-ship rebellion of 1841. There were the short stories of Frances Ellen Watkins Harper – the first published by an African American woman – as well as her poetry; there were the novels, plays, and autobiographical narratives of the former fugitive from slavery William Wells Brown – all published before the Civil War. The great Shakespearean actor Ira Aldridge and the Creole dramatist and poet Victor Sejour had long abandoned the USA for the freer cultures of Europe; but in the 1850s they were still remembered and revered in Black cultural circles.

On the concert and operatic stage, the prodigious soprano Elizabeth Taylor Greenfield, born into slavery in Mississippi, paved the way for her successors with a premiere at New York's Metropolitan Hall in March of 1853. On that occasion, as the *New-York Tribune* reported, "the bills of the Concert stated that no colored persons would be admitted, and a strong police was there in anticipation of riot." White critics had advised Greenfield to begin her concert while hidden behind a curtain, so that her (again, white) audience would give her debut a "blind listening." The *Tribune* reviewer's sombre conclusion, defeatist as it was, validated all that John Brown and Frederick Douglass had highlighted about their "guilty land": "Under these circumstances we advise Elizabeth Greenfield to go to Europe and there remain. . . . She has had everything to contend against – an education neglected – a spurned thing in social life." Greenfield did tour Europe; but she returned to the country that was rightfully hers, to establish an opera company in Philadelphia along with her former student Thomas Bowers, who himself recalled: "What induced me more than any thing else to appear in public was to give the lie to 'negro serenaders' (minstrels), and to show to the world that colored men and women could sing classical music as well as the members of the other race by whom they had been so terribly vilified."

Those "members of the other race" included, at the peak of his popularity, Stephen Foster, who in 1852 had apparently concluded that an association with minstrelsy – for white people, at least – was not such a bad thing after all. He wrote to the leading minstrel show performer, Edwin P. Christy, asking for his name to be restored to such songs as "Old Folks at Home," for which he had happily seen Christy receive composer's credit: "I had the intention of omitting my name on my Ethiopian songs, owing to the prejudice against them by some which might injure my reputation as a writer of another style of music, but I find that by my efforts I have done a great deal to build up a taste for the Ethiopian songs among refined people."

Let us remind ourselves of some of the lyrics of "Old Folks at Home," as they appeared in the first printed sheet music edition:

> Way down upon de Swanee ribber,
> Far, far away,
> Dere's wha my heart is turning ebber,
> Dere's wha de old folks stay.
> All up and down de whole creation,
> Sadly I roam,
> Still longing for de old plantation,
> And for de old folks at home.
>
> CHORUS.
> All de world am sad and dreary,
> Ebry where I roam,

Oh! darkeys how my heart grows weary,
Far from de old folks at home.

This is the popular culture sensation that African American performers were up against in the antebellum years. As one song historian observes, Foster's "fluency in black culture was a studied pose that makes white rapper Vanilla Ice look like a paragon of authenticity by comparison."

Towards the end of the decade, on the eve of the Civil War, the white abolitionist and feminist, Frances Gage – herself possibly guilty of assigning a dubious minstrel tinge to the voice of Sojourner Truth – looked into the future and proposed, to a tune by John Hutchinson, what the USA might look like "A Hundred Years Hence":

One hundred years hence what a change will be made,
In politics, morals, religion and trade;
In statesmen who wrangle or ride on the fence,
These things will be altered a hundred years hence . . .

The woman, man's partner, man's equal shall stand,
While beauty and harmony govern the land,
And to think for one's self will be no offence,
The world will be thinking a hundred years hence.

Oppression and war will be heard of no more,
Nor the blood of a slave have its print on our shore;
Conventions will then be a needless expense,
The world will be thinking a hundred years hence.

Looking back from the vantage point of well over "a hundred years hence" – indeed, closer to two hundred – one can only smile ruefully. There was, as now, still so much work to do, and so much struggle, as the country and its people dragged, fought, and sang themselves toward an ever-elusive grail. For some, that grail would be the grand abstraction of "a more perfect union." For others, it would simply be a place that they could truly call "home."

CHAPTER 6

There Is a Fountain Filled with Blood

The Civil War years of 1861–1865 are among the most studied and written about in all the nation's history. The war itself, the biography and administration of Lincoln, and of course the central issues of slavery and abolition have so dominated the historical discourse that one can almost be forgiven for thinking that nothing else of importance was going on.

Who will have heard, for instance, of Pablita Angel, who had the unhappy (if disputed) fate of being "the first woman to be legally executed in New Mexico" for murdering her married, womanizing lover, Juan Miguel Martín? She was hanged on Friday, April 26, 1861 – exactly two weeks after the first shots of the Civil War were fired at Fort Sumter, South Carolina. The gruesome manner of her death still casts a shade over the topic of capital punishment:

> On the appointed day, Sheriff Herrera took his condemned prisoner to a cottonwood tree, stood her in the back of a wagon, and slipped the noose over her head. He whipped away the team of horses, having forgotten to bind Pablita's wrists. The dangling woman desperately sought to avoid strangulation by holding onto the rope with her hands. The sheriff caught her by the waist and tried to use his own weight to finish the job. This proved too much for the assembled crowd, who stopped the proceeding and demanded her release. After a brief delay, Pablita was bound, placed back in the wagon, renoosed and hanged again, this time until dead.

For a brief moment – when the crowd "demanded her release" – a change of direction might have been possible. But in the end, it was left to an unknown balladeer to remind posterity of the cruelty of her death: "In the countryside I went to die / hanged like a dog, / in the countryside I went to die, / hanged like a dog."

Who is aware that in 1862 – one year into the Civil War and three years into statehood – "Oregon passed a 'race tax' that required African Americans, Hawaiians, Chinese, and 'Mulattos' (individuals of mixed race) to pay an annual five-dollar penalty for residing in the state"? How many people know that in 1863 – midway through the war – the first railroad labor union, the Brotherhood of the Footboard (subsequently called the Brotherhood of Locomotive Engineers) was founded? – or that the following year saw the founding of the National Cigar Makers Union? Is it common knowledge that more Indigenous people were killed by US forces during the Civil War years than in any other period in the country's history? Or that President Lincoln signed off on the execution of thirty-eight Minnesota Dakota men following the so-called Dakota War (or "Sioux Uprising") of 1862 – that he wrote down each of their names "in his own hand on executive mansion stationary"? (Or that he commuted the death sentences of 294 others?) None of these examples are meant to diminish the overwhelming importance of the war for what Lincoln called "a new birth of freedom" in his Gettysburg Address of 1863. They are meant to serve as reminders that, for so many, the Civil War years saw the continuation of ongoing struggles pushed beyond the margins of the central conflict.

As for the conflict itself, so much of it was sung into history. Lincoln was ushered into the White House to the tune of campaign songs such as "Honest Old Abe," "Rail Splitter's Polka," "Lincoln's Log Cabin March," "Old Abe Lincoln Came Out of the Wilderness," the Hutchinsons' "Lincoln and Liberty" ("They'll find what by felling and mauling / Our rail-maker statesman can do"), and "The Old Chieftain" ("Old Abe Lincoln is the man for me, /However long and lean he may be, / He's honest and bold and never fails, / He knows how to fight and split old rails"). Such songs were part of the arsenal developed by Lincoln and his image-makers to reinforce in the public mind the candidate's humble wilderness origins, his self-education, his emergence through adversity, and – most importantly – his association with hard manual labor: "Sprung from the race of yeomen, their country's boast and pride, / His stalwart form has braved the storms that lash the mountain's side; / His manly forehead dripping with the sweat of honest toil, / And side by side he labor'd with the tillers of the soil."

Even Karl Marx mined that vein, presenting Lincoln as "the single-minded son of the working class" (his words) and eliding one significant dimension: Lincoln's "quintessential bourgeois occupation," that of the corporate lawyer who became quite wealthy working on behalf of, among other entities, the Illinois Central Railroad. Naturally, few campaign songwriters would choose to emphasize this aspect of Lincoln's background in reinforcing the "log cabin to White House" narrative. Still, it was a mark of

Lincoln's political acumen, if not genius, that he could "skilfully blend the interests of the very rich"; the "white, up-and-coming, economically ambitious, politically active middle class"; and, bringing up the rear, the Black Americans in bondage – "not at the top of his list of priorities, but close enough to the top so [they] could be pushed there temporarily by abolitionist pressures and by practical political advantage."

In his first inaugural address, on March 4, 1861, Lincoln reaffirmed his fealty to the Constitution, to the Fugitive Slave Act, and to his campaign promise to the South that he would not interfere with slavery where it already existed. All of this led Frederick Douglass to conclude that Lincoln had proved himself "preëminently the white man's President, entirely devoted to the welfare of white men. He was ready and willing at any time during the first years of his administration to deny, postpone, and sacrifice the rights of humanity in the colored people in order to promote the welfare of the white people of this country." This opinion was obviously not shared by the partisans of slavery, who painted Lincoln as the "Black Republican," caricaturing him "for his perceived support of abolition in various ways, including symbolic 'blackening.' Opponents suggested that he had 'African' origins, while a related strand of satire caricatured the president as Othello, 'Blacked . . . all over to play the part.'" In 1861, a group of Northern anti-Lincoln Democrats (otherwise known as "Copperheads") drafted a satirical play, *Abraham Africanus I*, which presented Lincoln as revealing, under hypnosis, not only his secret African bloodline but also an undisclosed biographical detail: as a young man on a flatboat voyage to New Orleans, he had "picked up a good deal of money by dancing jigs and singing n——r songs." (This was a particularly vicious inversion of the apocryphal story that Lincoln had first acquired his hatred of slavery when witnessing a slave auction in New Orleans.)

As we know, one of the most committed anti-Lincoln partisans, the actor John Wilkes Booth, assassinated the president on April 14, 1865, not for any perceived likeness to Shakespeare's Othello, but rather to his Julius Caesar. As Booth wrote in his diary while on the run: "After being hunted like a dog through swamps, woods, and last night being chased by gun boats . . . with every man's hand against me, I am here in despair. And why; For doing what Brutus was honoured for." Before the year was out, a New Orleans music publisher, A. E. Blackmar, writing as "E. B. Armand," composed the ode "Our Brutus" in honor of Booth, calling for "a sepulcher broad as the sweep of the tidal wave's measureless mountain." As Blackmar explained in a note inside the sheet music, he wrote the song "at the time when it was proposed to bury its illustrious subject in the ocean, so that no trace of his resting place could be found by those who might wish to honor his remains."

For his part, Lincoln, on his way to his inauguration in 1861, had had his own classic premonition, stopping in New York to attend a performance of Verdi's opera, *A Masked Ball* (*Un ballo in maschera*). It was, an opera historian writes, "an ironic glimpse of the future, this opera about the assassination of a ruler." Lincoln had developed a passion for opera in his mature years, so during that same visit to New York he also attended a performance of Rossini's *Barber of Seville* (*Il barbiere di Siviglia*) with one of the country's first native-born opera stars, the soprano Isabella Hinckley, in the role of Rosina, interjecting "The Star-Spangled Banner" into the celebrated "singing lesson" scene – one of many occasions immediately preceding and during the Civil War in which opera texts were appropriated and crudely adapted to reflect the tense political currents and stances of the time.

Music historians have long pointed to the power and importance of music during the Civil War, so much so that one could almost be forgiven for concluding that "the Civil War was the first American war fought to music" (a conclusion that the preceding pages of this book should call into question). Still, it would be true to say that, as the last US war fought on home soil, the Civil War was inevitably "a people's war, drawing into its political and military events a vast majority of the people of the country. Its music likewise was a people's music, written and sung by probably the widest range of Americans ever to be involved with popular song." It would be equally true to point out that, North and South, "common soldiers and citizens wrested control of the musical landscape, ensuring that lively minstrel ditties, maudlin sentimental ballads, and chest-thumping patriotic numbers dominated the day" – these, of course, being mostly the product of white songwriters' efforts. For the African Americans in the fields, in the praise houses, in the urban workshops, on the river and seacoast wharves, and along the pathways of the Underground Railroad, there were not only spirituals expressing the yearning for deliverance but also songs often adapted from a variety of sources. (Hence a curious aural snapshot described by an unnamed son of the composer Lowell Mason, who had witnessed Black stevedores unloading cargo to the whistled tune of the "Anvil Chorus" from Verdi's *Il Trovatore* medleyed with George Frederick Root's prisoner song, "Tramp! Tramp! Tramp!")

The Civil War was in fact a boom time for US popular music. How ironic, then, that of all people, Stephen Foster should have expressed – *in song* – the difficulties of being a popular songwriter in this period: "We live in hard and stirring times, / Too sad for mirth, too rough for rhymes, / For songs of peace have lost their chimes, / And that's what's the matter." It is doubly ironic because, in another song – titled "The Song of All Songs" – Foster himself remarked upon the musical boom time – "Old songs! New songs! Every kind of song" that he saw in the form of "the penny ballads sticking up, in a row," tacked to "fences and railings, where ever you go":

> "When this Cruel war is over," "No Irish need apply;"
> "For, every little thing is lovely, and the Goose hangs high;"
> "The Young Gal from New-Jersey," "Oh! wilt thou be my bride?"
> And "Oft in the Still Night" "We'll all take a ride."
> "Let me kiss him for his Mother," "He's a Gay Young Gambolier;"
> "I'm going to fight mit Sigel" and "De bully Lager-bier."
> "Hunky Boy is Yankee Doodle" "When cannons loudly roar;"
> "We are coming, Father Abraham, six hundred thousand more!"

The war brought to the forefront a host of Foster's professional competitors. In the North, there were, besides the prodigiously prolific Root ("The Battle Cry of Freedom," "Just Before the Battle, Mother," "The Vacant Chair," and "Tramp! Tramp! Tramp!" among others), Walter Kittridge ("Tenting on the Old Camp Ground"), Henry Clay Work ("Kingdom Coming," "Come Home, Father," "Grafted into the Army," "Wake Nicodemus," and "Marching Through Georgia"), and the ever-present Hutchinson Family Singers. A smaller cohort came from the South, the likes of John Hill Hewitt ("All Quiet Along the Potomac"), Harry Macarthy ("The Bonnie Blue Flag"), George Henry Miles (using the pen name of Earnest Halphin), and Charles Ellerbrock ("God Save the South"). Their songs lay in piles of sheet music and bound volumes atop the pianos of middle-class households, while soldiers on both sides carried cheap pocket songsters into camps and onto the battlefields – for the Federals, *The Camp Fire Songster*, *War Songs for Freedom*, and *Beadle's Dime Songs for the War*; for the Confederates, *The Soldier Boy's Songster*, *The Stonewall Jackson Song Book*, and *Hopkins' New Orleans 5 Cent Song-Book*. In between bouts of slaughter, Union and Confederate soldiers would swap shared songs and contrasting versions with each other. A lieutenant in a Virginia regiment wrote to his father: "We are on one side of the Rappahannock, the enemy on the other. . . . Our boys will sing a Southern song, the Yankees will reply by singing the same tune to Yankee words." Another soldier reported both sides joining together in a moment to sing a Christian hymn with unavoidable wartime overtones, "There Is a Fountain Filled with Blood." Again, another described two encamped riverside bands challenging each other with their own patriotic tunes before joining together to play "Home, Sweet Home."

Unremarked by music critics and publishers' catalogs, and largely unknown until revealed by former slaves in interviews recorded by the Works Progress Administration (WPA) in the 1930s, were obscure plantation laments of family separation: "Mammy, is Ol' Massa gwin'er sell us tomorrow? / Yes my chile. / Whar he gwin'er sell us? / Way down South in Georgia." There were songs of outrage over dreams deferred: "My old Mistis promised me / Dat when she died, she gwine set me free. / But she lived so long en got so po / Dat she lef me digging wid er garden ho." And there were songs of premonition and reckoning, clothed as spirituals: "My army cross ober, / My army cross ober, / O Pharoah's army drownded, / My army cross ober ... We'll cross de riber Jordan / We'll cross the danger water."

A persistent and perverse failure to appreciate slavery as the central factor in the Civil War is what enabled the publication of such songs as "My God! What Is All This For?", noted on the sheet music by its anonymous composer as "the dying words of a Federal soldier on the Battle field of Manassas, 1861." Indeed, slavery *was*, officially at least, the North's elephant in the room, as Lincoln himself indicated in his famous reply to Horace Greeley's open letter of August 20, 1862, in the *New-York Tribune*, the "Prayer of Twenty Millions" challenging the president to state plainly his objective in prosecuting the war. Lincoln replied: "My paramount object in this struggle *is* to save the Union, and is *not* either to save or to destroy slavery. If I could save the Union without freeing *any* slave I would do it, and if I could save it by freeing *all* the slaves I would do it; and if I could save it by freeing some and leaving others alone I would also do that."

Lincoln had in fact already drafted the Emancipation Proclamation by then, but was delaying its release until it could be backed up by a credible military victory for the North, which only came with the battle of Antietam in September of 1862. Still, as long as slavery remained the official blind spot – as it was for all those batting back and forth the mantras of "Union" versus "States' Rights" – it was perhaps no surprise for abolitionist stalwarts like the Hutchinsons to see their performances disrupted even by Union soldiers and to have their passes revoked by Union Army officials on the grounds that their camp concerts were simply pretexts for "political pow-wowing."

In terms of a career move, then, it was far better for a successful singer to pack the concert bill with tearjerkers such as Charles Carroll Sawyer and Henry Tucker's "Weeping, Sad and Lonely; or, When This Cruel War Is Over," a sheet music bestseller in both the North and the South and beloved on the home front as well as in the army camps, where generals on both sides forbade its singing "because it was so destructive of morale."

One might follow with an encore of Henry Clay Work's "Come Home, Father" or William Shakespeare Hays's "The Drummer Boy of Shiloh," one of many songs to exploit the combination of "death on the battlefield with the tragic death of children." This was a winning strategy also enjoyed by Stephen Foster and George Cooper in "For the Dear Old Flag I Die!", these being the final words of "a brave little drummer boy who was fatally wounded in the battle of Gettysburg." Failing these, one might fall back on Work's "Little Major," Albert Fleming's "Drummer Boy of Antietam," S. Wesley Martin's "Little Harry, the Drummer Boy," J. C. Koch and L. Grube's "The Dying Drummer Boy," or – for those with their hearts in the Southland – "The Drummer Boy of Vicksburg," all calculated "to tug at the heartstrings."

These were all eminently safe songs; but this is not to say that it was universally assumed that all popular singing was safe. For instance, in New York, the state legislature passed the "Anti-Concert Saloon Bill" in 1862, "a watershed in the history of variety entertainment." It barred any proprietor from holding simultaneously an entertainment license and a liquor license – the argument being that New York City, a gathering place for young, rural and "naïve" recruits for the Union Army, would see them lured by "innocent" singing into the dens of depravity and vice. Better, then, to seek your musical solace in the parlor or, if a public venue, one without a liquor license.

It is in the ephemera of newspapers, magazines, song sheets, and political songsters where one finds the most evidence of songs written against the commercial tide of the popular music industry. In the North, it would be in Garrison's *The Liberator* or in the journal of the Anti-Slavery Society or in *The Continental Monthly*, where one would encounter emancipation songs like George Boker's "Hymn of the Freedman" (with music by "A. Contraband"). Occasionally, the most obscure publication might be downright historic, such as the *National Anti-Slavery Standard*'s printing of Harriet Tubman's favorite spiritual, "Go Down, Moses," in 1861. This was "the first publication of the complete text of a Negro spiritual," the song by which Tubman conducted her "passengers" along the Underground Railroad and that earned for her the honorable sobriquet "Moses."

In the South, local newspapers printed songs and poems aimed at reminding readers of *their* honorable sobriquet, *rebel*: "Washington a rebel was, / Jefferson a traitor, / But their treason won success, / And made their glory greater." As the war dragged on and privation set in, Southern papers printed – and music publishers duly reprinted – the likes of "The Southern Girl, Or the Homespun Dress": "My homespun dress is plain, I know, / My hat's palmetto too, / But then it shows what Southern girls / For Southern rights will do." In the border state of Maryland, a trip-wire state ever on the verge of pitching itself into the arms of the Confederacy, a privately printed and circulated song sheet condemned Lincoln's suspension of the writ of habeas corpus, by which he took the liberty of jailing without trial Baltimore newspaper editors expressing Confederate sympathies:

> They called them by a traitorous name,
> And with a fiendish hate
> Heaped on their heads a load of shame,
> Such as on felon's wait.
> They dragged them from their peaceful hearths
> Upon a despot's word,
> Although the vilest man on earth
> Should by law be heard.

As we know, the Emancipation Proclamation of 1862 actually freed no slaves upon its issuance. It was effectively a *promise* to free the slaves in the Southern territories yet to be conquered by the Union forces; and it refrained from freeing the slaves precisely in the areas where it might have done so, the border states such as Maryland, which had – so far – remained loyal to the Union. In part, it was aimed at forestalling Great Britain and other European powers from intervening on the side of the Confederacy, for these nations would have to think twice about choosing the wrong side in what was now, officially and finally, a war against slavery. That the Proclamation carried enormous symbolic weight there is no doubt – a fact represented as much in song as anywhere else. William Wells Brown recalled hearing "a sister," joined by "a vast assembly," improvising a new verse to "Go Down, Moses" upon hearing the Proclamation read aloud: "Go down, Abraham, / Away down in Dixie's land; / Tell Jeff Davis / To let my people go."

Lincoln and his commanding general, George McClellan, had already designated any Black fugitives to reach the Union lines as "contraband of war" – not quite human beings, but rather confiscated enemy property. It was not until 1863, in the wake of the Emancipation Proclamation, that Black men were finally uniformed and armed to fight for the Union. One broadside ballad implied that it was better late than never:

> McClellan went to Richmond,
> With two hundred thousand braves,
> Says he, "Keep back the Negroes,
> And I'll the Union save."
> But little Mac, he was defeated,
> Now the Union is in tears,
> Now they are all calling on the Colored Volunteers.

In June of 1863, Harriet Tubman led a contingent of 150 Black soldiers of the Massachusetts Fifty-fourth regiment on a raid along the Combahee River in South Carolina to free 750 slaves to swell the ranks of the Union army. This was "the only wartime effort designed specifically to liberate slaves," which incidentally made Tubman the "first woman in US history to plan and lead a military raid." Regiments such as the Massachusetts Fifty-fourth and the First Arkansas (Negro) Regiment undoubtedly were instrumental in turning the tide against the South, which was no assured thing in the first half of the war. As the (white) commander of the First Arkansas wrote to the tune of "John Brown's Body": "Oh, we're the bully soldiers of the 'First of Arkansas,' / We are fighting for the Union, we are fighting for the law, / We can hit a Rebel further than a white man ever saw, / As we go marching on."

In the South, the screws of the Northern blockade were turned tighter. Bread riots, mostly carried out by women, broke out in cities across the Confederacy throughout 1863 – in Richmond, Columbus, Macon, Atlanta, Augusta, and Mobile. In Richmond, Jefferson Davis reportedly emptied his pockets before the women, throwing them a wad of Confederate notes and telling them it was all he had (to which they replied it was "worthless"). Songsters reminded civilians – and the troops in the field – of the holy significance of the "Homespun Dress":

Now Northern goods are out of date;
And since old Abe's blockade,
We Southern girls can be content
With goods that's Southern made.
We send our sweethearts to the war;
But, dear girls, never mind,
Your soldier-love will ne'er forget
The girl he left behind.

In the North, too, the costs of a seemingly endless war began to show cracks in the economy. The printing of so-called "greenbacks" – wartime currency backed up by neither gold nor silver but simply the Federal government's promise to pay – prompted minstrel parodies such as Dan Emmett's "How Are You, Greenbacks," which began with a swipe at Lincoln's call for one hundred thousand more recruits: "We're coming, Father Abra'am, one hundred thousand more, / Five hundred presses printing us from morn till night is o'er; / Like magic, you will see us start and scatter thro' the land / To pay the soldiers or release the border contraband."

The Northern home front was further rocked by Lincoln's Conscription Act of 1863, which established a lottery selection for all male citizens between the ages of twenty and forty-five, unless they had the magical sum of three hundred dollars to buy themselves out and provide a substitute. In July of 1863, the New York Draft Riots broke out. Largely poor Irish workers, most of whom could not afford a substitute payment – and most of whom were Catholic – vented their rage at the Conscription Act and its recruiters alongside the apparent agents of other grievances: Jewish and German shopkeepers, Chinese street peddlers, wealthy Protestant property owners, and – most of all – Black people, whether the free who were competitors in the labor market or, in absentia, the enslaved whom they blamed as the cause of the war (as well as, for some reason, the children in the Colored Orphans' Asylum, which they sacked and torched). After a week, "somewhere between the documented figure [of 105] and the sober contemporary estimate of 500" people lay dead. Among them were at least eighteen lynched and five drowned Black Americans. Beyond these fatalities, "thousands of blacks – many with untreated injuries – went into hiding or fled the city altogether." Smaller antidraft riots broke out in Toledo, Evansville, Troy, Newark, and – fatally – Boston, where soldiers fired on Irish workers storming a Federal armory.

Songwriters broke out their pens, which were generally savage and satirical, occasionally masquerading as sentimental, such as in "He's Gone to the Arms of Abraham" by Septimus Winner, the composer of less controversial favorites such as "Listen to the Mockingbird" and "Where, Oh Where, Has My Little Dog Gone." Although a Northerner, Winner also gave a sympathetic nod to the Southern boys swept up by the Confederate Conscription Acts of 1862:

My true love is a soldier
In the army now today.
It was the cruel war that made him
Have to go away;
The "draft" it was that took him,
And it was a "heavy blow,"
It took him for a Conscript,
But he didn't want to go.

Chorus:
He's gone – He's gone – As meek as any lamb,
They took him, yes, they took him, to the Arms of Abraham.

Oh should he meet a rebel,
A pointin' with his gun,
I hope he may have courage
To "take care of number one."

If I were him, I'd offer
The fellow but a dram;
For what's the use of dying
Just for Jeff or Abraham?

Lyricists were particularly unforgiving of the three-hundred-dollar substitute provision. For Henry Clay Work, it meant being "Grafted into the Army," the words of a widowed, working-class Mrs. Malaprop in a comic song with dark, double-meant undertones: "Oh, Jimmy farewell! Your brothers fell / Way down in Alabarmy: / I thought they would spare a lone widder's hair, / But they grafted him into the army." For John L. Zieber of Philadelphia, it meant flush times for "The Substitute Broker":

I am a broker, Sirs, and living in this city;
In substitutes I deal, and do it without pity,
I'm always on the hunt for some poor verdant fellow,
I ply him with "soft-soap" and liquor till he's mellow;
That's the way we do, ain't we Jolly Jokers!
Making money too, all by being brokers.

And, for an unknown Copperhead, it meant a final round for the poor Irish boys who could never buy a substitute, singing to the tune of the newly composed patriotic hit by the Irish-born Patrick Sarsfield Gilmore, "When Johnny Comes Marching Home":

The Conscription Act it now is passed,
Hurrah! hurrah!
And we'll be drafted all at last;
Hurrah! hurrah!
The Conscription Act it now is passed,
And we'll be drafted all at last;
Then we'll all drink stone blind –
Johnny, fill up the bowl.

Across the water, Irish leaders like Daniel O'Connell had called upon their compatriots in the USA to join the fight against slavery. Frederick Douglass himself had seen during his journey through Ireland that there were indeed friends of abolition all over the Emerald Isle. But, as he wrote in 1853: "The Irish, who, at home, readily sympathise with the oppressed everywhere, are instantly taught when they step upon our soil to hate and despise the Negro." While it is the case that the Civil War era witnessed a collision between "the Irish effort to gain the rights of white men" and "the black struggle to maintain the right to work" as free laborers, it is important not to cast the Irish in the USA as uniformly opposed either to abolition or to the Union cause.

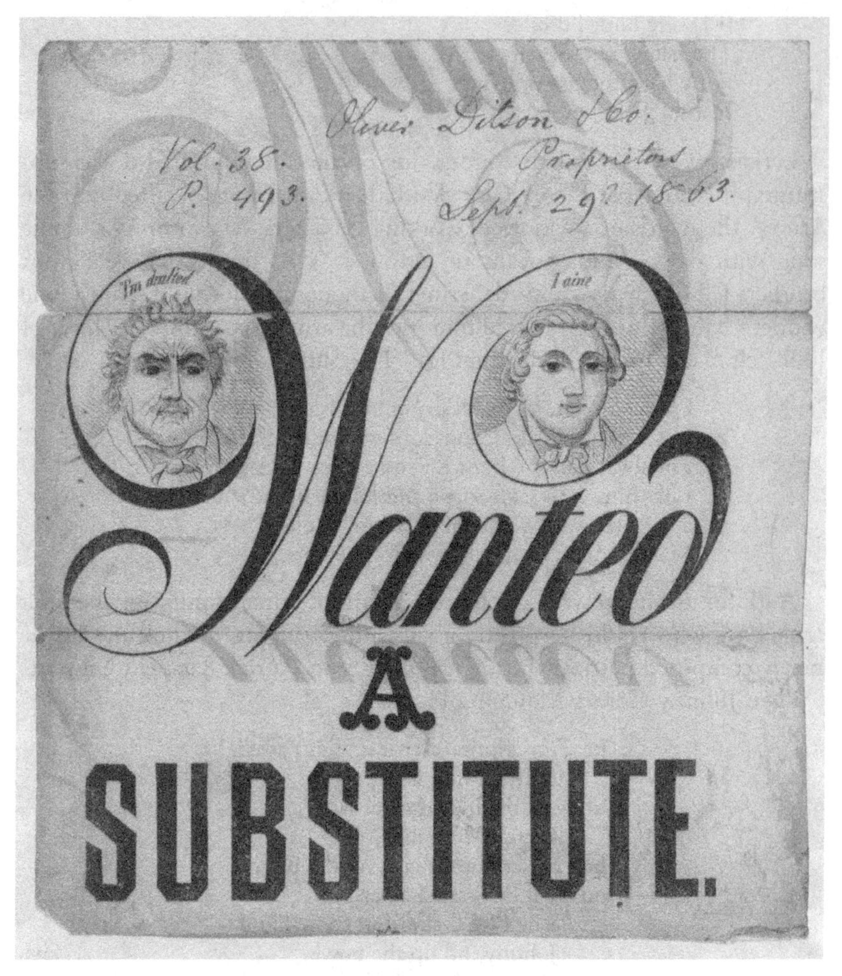

Figure 6.1 Sheet music cover of "Wanted: A Substitute," composed by Frank Wilder, 1863.
Library of Congress Prints and Photographs Division

"No Irish Need Apply" had become a slogan common enough to prompt more than one protest song with that title. In one, perhaps the best known on the music hall circuit, John F. Poole covered the home front in his depiction of the insult received by an Irish job-seeker on the streets of New York: "'No!' he says, 'You are a Paddy, / And no Irish need apply.'" But Poole also reminded listeners of the proven prowess of the "Irish brigades" in the Union Army: "Ould Ireland on the battle-field a lasting fame has made; / We all have heard of Meagher's men, and Corcoran's brigade. / Though fools many flout and bigots rave, and fanatics may cry, / Yet when they want good fighting-men, the Irish may apply." The leading star of the music hall, Tony Pastor, roused his audiences with this song as well as "The Irish Volunteer," which praised the Irish-born Union brigade leader Michael Corcoran and accurately predicted the rank he was to receive upon his release from Confederate captivity during a prisoner exchange following the First Battle of Bull Run:

> But now a bright sunshine has followed the rain
> And back in New York we'll soon have him again
> At the head of his regiment then he'll be seen.
> And as such a valor and worth he displayed,
> A Brigadier-general he's sure to be made
> Then the insults he met from the vile rebel crew
> He'll pay them all back; aye, and interest too
> Or he'll die for the Stars and the banner of green.

Other songwriters turned the slogan "No Irish Need Apply" on its head to affirm the value of the Irish in uniform. The "Irish Vocalist" Kathleen O'Neil cast the slogan as positively "un-American," not only because of the Irish soldier's proven military prowess on battlefields from Sebastopol to India but also because of what he could now offer to "the 'Home of Liberty!'" Another anonymous songwriter borrowed the setting of Poole's music hall hit in order to turn the negative into a positive: "But now on every side a different cry is heard, / And the public feeling is – an Irishman preferred." The phrase "on every side" is indeed apt, for there were roughly 30,000 Irish troops fighting for the Confederacy against 150,000 in the Union ranks.

Amidst all the patriotic tub-thumping, a lone voice sang of the human costs suffered by the Irish on the battlefield. John Ross Dix, a British immigrant and former alcoholic turned temperance activist who wrote a number of ballads in support of the Union, published a comic-pathetic music hall number called "Paddy's Lament," which appears to have been the basis of the better-known Irish American folk standard, "Paddy's Lamentation." Both versions focus on the crippling of an Irish recruit suddenly thrown onto the scrap heap – a morose déjà vu of "Felix the Soldier" from the days of the French and Indian War: "Och! de Rebels dey are savages to sarve poor Paddy so, / For I'm afraid on crutches I must hereafter go, / And when I come back Molly to you and to de pig, / I don't think I'll be able to dance an Irish jig!"

Another tragic dimension to the Civil War was the fate of its prisoners. Although the Union and the Confederacy had initially agreed to a policy of prisoner exchanges, the practice became complicated not only by the increasingly unwieldy numbers of prisoners swept up in the larger battles but also by the arming of Black men after the Emancipation Proclamation. A prison historian writes: "The Confederacy, outraged by the Union's affront to white supremacy and the encouragement of slave resistance, increasingly adopted a 'black flag' policy toward these African American troops. Perhaps no other aspect of the war reveals the reprehensible nature of Confederate racism more than these repeated slaughters." This "black flag" policy meant that Confederate soldiers would take no Black prisoners: they would either kill them on the battlefield or – as at Fort Pillow, Tennessee, in 1864 – massacre them en masse. If a Black soldier managed to avoid either fate, he would be denied prisoner-of-war status by the Confederates and either executed summarily or sent into slavery. It was in this context that the system of prison camps, North and South, developed. By the end of the war, 30,000 Federal prisoners had died in the Southern camps, while 26,000 Confederates died in the North, amidst unspeakable conditions.

As the revelation of these conditions began to filter back into the public consciousness through newspaper reports and official testimonies, songwriters on both sides took up the subject with a mission that cannot simply be dismissed as the cynical exploitation of tragedy. The subject of the prisoner's fate was too sensitive, the pathos too raw, the public outrage too real. No one negotiated the subject more fervently than Root. His "Tramp! Tramp! Tramp!" of 1864 (subtitled "The Prisoner's Hope") has remained firmly lodged in the cultural memory, returning as the musical setting for hymns (C. Herbert Woolston's "Jesus Loves the Little Children"), labor songs (Joe Hill's "The Tramp"), and Irish freedom songs ("God Save Ireland"). Root's narrator sings from the depths of a Southern dungeon: "Tramp, tramp, tramp, the boys are marching, / Cheer up comrades, they will come, / And beneath the starry flag / We shall breathe the air again / Of the free land in our own beloved home." As was the case with so many other songs of the war, an anonymous lyricist on the opposing side took up Root's original and refashioned it, replacing "the starry flag" with "the stars and bars" and exchanging the Union prisoners, staring with "hollow eye" at "the iron door," for the Confederates dreaming of "the warm delights of home" as they "freeze and starve in Northern prison walls."

Root flung back the charge of starvation the following year with the revelation of the conditions in the notorious Andersonville prison camp in Georgia, for which its commandant, Henry Wirtz, was hastily and sensationally tried and convicted of war crimes. Wirtz was hanged with the cry of "Remember Andersonville" screamed at him from the spectators' gallery. Root's "Starved in Prison," to be played (as the sheet music instructs) "*With deep feeling*," could hardly contain more outrage:

Had they fallen in the battle,
With the old flag waving high,
We should mourn, but not in anguish,
For the soldier thus would die;
But the dear boys starv'd in prison,
Helpless, friendless and alone,
While the haughty rebel leaders
Heard unmov'd each dying groan.

Had they died in ward or sickroom,
Nursed with but a soldier's care,
We should grieve, but still be thankful
That a human heart was there –
But the dear boys starv'd in prison,
Helpless, friendless and alone,
While the heartless rebel leaders
Heard unmov'd each dying groan.

In the final months of 1864, US General William Tecumseh Sherman ended the Southern dream with his "scorched earth" march from Atlanta to Savannah, cutting the Confederacy in two and breaking the back of the rebellion. Upon capturing Atlanta, Sherman issued an order expelling all civilians from the city, with his justification: "War is cruelty and you cannot refine it" (popularly rephrased as "War is Hell"). He backed up this belief in what became known as "Sherman's March," the Savannah Campaign that left a swath of destruction across Georgia two hundred miles long and fifty miles wide, the mark of his vow to "make old and young, rich and poor, feel the hard hand of war." Out of this devastation came the war's final popular song hit, Work's "Marching Through Georgia," which gleefully recounted the liberated slaves' shouting "when they heard the joyful sound" and the flight of "treason" itself before the marauding armies. In Work's lyrics, the devastated earth is not the scar of Sherman's vaunted "cruelty," but rather "a thoroughfare for Freedom and her train." In the North, the tune became one of the most frequently played of triumphalist marches. In the South, schoolchildren covered their ears whenever they heard it sung, one later recalling that she could not bear "to listen to a song that declares such a tyrant and coward as Sherman and his disgraceful and horrible march through Georgia . . . to be glorious." Sherman himself was underwhelmed by the song, saying, "I wish I had a dollar for every time I have had to listen to that blasted tune."

Work's was the most famous, but not the only, song to come from the scorched earth of Sherman's March. A former slave, James Calhart James, recalled in one of the WPA narratives the singing of Black men and women on a plantation as they heard of Sherman's approach:

> Oh where shall we go when de great day comes
> And de blowing of de trumpets and de banging of de drums.
> When General Sherman comes.
> No more rice and cotton fields
> We will hear no more crying
> Old master will be sighing.

James explained, "I can't remember the tune. People sang it according to their own tune."

From the Black perspective, there was great reason for rejoicing, beyond the fact of emancipation itself. When he reached Savannah, Sherman met with "twenty Negro ministers and church officials, mostly former slaves," who told him: "The way we can best take care of ourselves is to have land, and till it by our labor." In good faith, Sherman issued "Special Field Order No. 15," which designated "the entire southern coastline 30 miles inland for exclusive Negro settlement" – the famed promise of "forty acres and a mule" for each family. By June of 1865, there were "forty thousand freedmen" working farms in the area. But two months later, they were forced off their land, "some at bayonet point," under the orders of President Andrew Johnson, who promptly "restored this land to the Confederate owners." How bitter must have been the recollection of one Susie Melton, who recalled for the WPA her fellow Black Americans singing upon the news of the Confederate surrender at Appomattox:

> Sun, you be here and I'll be gone
> Sun, you be here and I'll be gone
> Sun, you be here and I'll be gone
> Bye, bye, don't grieve after me
> Won't give you my place, not for yours
> Bye, bye, don't grieve after me
> Cause you be here and I'll be gone.

Four days after the Confederate surrender, on April 14, 1865, Booth murdered Lincoln at Ford's Theatre – an ironic historical twist, as "Lincoln, himself, made a point of seeing Booth's *Richard III* at a Washington theatre in April of 1863." An equally ironic folk song, which dubiously purports itself to have been written three weeks after the assassination, quotes Lincoln's imaginary last words: "Of all the actors in this town, / I loved Wilkes Booth the best." Lincoln was laid to rest to literally scores of odes, funeral marches, and musical elegies: "President Lincoln's Funeral March," "The Nation in Tears," "Toll the Bell Mournfully," "Rest, Spirit, Rest," "Our Flag Is Half Mast High," "Lincoln Lies Sleeping," and on and on.

Amidst this avalanche, some spared a thought for the lowlier, broken veterans. Among them were Thomas MacKellar and J. Henry Wolseiffer, two northerners who published a song "for the benefit of the Soldiers and Sailor's Home":

> Shall we let our soldiers perish,
> Now the victory is won?
> Coming from the Southern prison,
> Spectres from the tomb arisen,
> Woeful men to look upon!
> Ghastly, gaunt, and shadowy creatures,
> Scarcely human in their features,
> Brother freemen, see them come!
> They who fought for Freedom's sake!
> Will you bid their brave hearts break,
> Shall the homeless have no home?

Others thought of the cruel fate of the disabled who belied Louisa May Alcott's claim in *Hospital Sketches* (1863) that "all women thought a wound the best decoration a brave soldier could wear." This was an experience not shared in song by a young amputee returned from the war, only to be spurned by his fiancée:

> To accept my hand she had agreed,
> "Her love would ne'er grow cold."
> But when I lost my hand, she said,
> The bargain didn't hold.
>
> I offered her my other hand
> Uninjured by the fight;
> 'Twas all that I had left, I said,
> She said, 'twould not be right.

"The Union Restored!" proclaimed newspaper headlines across the North, a celebratory cry picked up by giddy songwriters confident of their prediction that, though "Care was lost, secession sought / . . . we'll e'er united be, / As brothers to brothers band, / In the land of Liberty." Some composers were so transported by the phrase as to feel no need to amplify it with lyrics, as in William Willing's piano march, "The Union Restored," composed "To the Memory of Abraham Lincoln." For the labor movement, the word "Union" naturally took on added significance. Early in 1865, one Northern paper, the *Boston Daily Evening Voice*, issued its declaration of labor's renewed war – a war that had been sidelined only temporarily by the battles between the Blue and the Gray: "Arouse ye! arouse ye! the foe draweth nigh! / Arouse, to the battle, sound the rallying cry! / Be just and fear not – in Union there's power; / Soon Labor will triumph – God speed the hour!"

And who, or what, was the adversary in this renewed war? One answer lies in popular songwriters' responses to the Appalachian oil boom of 1861–1865. While the Northern and Southern armies were busy slaughtering one another, the oil-producing basin had been quietly spreading from western Pennsylvania through western New York State and down through Ohio, Kentucky, and West Virginia. It soon became the country's major oil-producing region, destined to remain so for another fifty years. In a mirror image of the "Nobody Knows You When You're Down and Out" motif, songwriters such as one C. Archer marveled at the quick change of status once it was discovered that "Pa Has Struck Ile":

> Tis strange what attention a fortune does bring,
> At home or abroad how friends to one cling;
> And now even strangers are courteous and bland,
> To pay their addresses or take by the hand.
> When before, on a walk if a neighbour I'd meet,
> Cold was his look and quick his retreat.
> But now in my carriage he greets with a smile,
> And it's simply because my "Pa has struck ile."

It was the season of "Oil on the Brain," as Joseph Eastburn Winner sang (four years before writing his hit, "Little Brown Jug"): "The lawyers, doctors, hatters, clerks, / Industrious and lazy, / Have put their money all in stocks, / In fact, have gone 'oil crazy.'" That same year (1865), the pseudonymous O. I. L. Wells composed "Petroleum, Petroleum," echoing what had become a songwriter's catchphrase: "'Tis very strange, but I declare, / The world seems half insane. / The new disease, as all will swear, / Is 'oil upon the brain.'" But at least one anonymous songwriter noted that, beyond any individual's greed, the problem was systemic and massive. The song "Famous Oil Firms" advertises itself playfully on the sheet music cover:

To Messrs. Swindle'em & Co.,
Brokers and Dealers in Oil Stocks.
Famous Oil Firms.
A SERIO-COMIC BALLAD,
During the singing of which, people are requested not to laugh.
WORDS BORED FOR NEAR OIL CREEK, BY
E. PLURIBUS OILUM
MUSIC COMPOSED AND WELL GREASED SO AS TO RUN
SMOOTHLY, BY
PETROLEANA.

Fully four stanzas of lyrics follow in a catalog of corporate corruption: "There's 'Ketchum & Cheatum,' / And 'Lure 'em & Beatum,' / And 'swindle 'um all in a row; / Then 'Coax 'em & Lead 'em,' / And 'Leech 'em & Bleed 'em,' / And 'Guzzle 'em, Sink 'em & Co.'"

Indeed, there had been no surrender of corporate greed at Appomattox, no surrender of systemic oppression. A host of struggles were to continue. Black Americans would see June 19, 1865 – "Juneteenth" – as the true date of liberation in the USA, the day when emancipation was proclaimed in the Confederacy's most remote outpost, Texas. They were now, at least nominally, in the ranks of "free labor," a status confirmed by the Thirteenth Amendment to the Constitution ratified on December 6, 1865. That amendment outlawed slavery and "involuntary servitude" anywhere in the country – "except as a punishment for crime." Historians and legal scholars have referred to a consequent criminalization of Blackness – effectively slavery by other means – that set in with the overthrow of Reconstruction in the following decade, along with a racially marked caste system, "a system of control that would ensure a low-paid, submissive labor force." The resultant struggles, as we shall see, are well represented in song.

Neither did Appomattox cancel out (a partial list): systemic patriarchy and women's struggles against it; the fights of organized labor against capitalism; the continued cultural and physical genocide of Indigenous peoples; resistance to US militarism, expansionism, and imperialism; the insult of minstrelsy; cyclical economic panic and collapse; hunger and homelessness; the oppression of nonwhite or non-Protestant immigrant groups. These were old struggles in new contexts, perhaps, but old struggles all the same – and all of them are captured in the songs we have yet to explore.

CHAPTER 7

A Tragedy That Beggared the Greek

The Civil War was over. Henry Clay Work began the year 1866 by asking one of many questions on people's minds:

> Who shall rule this American Nation?
> Say, boys, say!
> Who shall rule this American Nation?
> Say, boys, say!
> Shall the men who trampled on the banner?
> They who would now their country betray?
> They who murder the innocent freedmen?
> Say, boys, say!

The "innocent freedmen" themselves were asking the same thing. In Louisiana, former plantation slaves sang of a time when there would be – as there once had been – "*Pas Nègres, pas rubans, / Pas diamants / Pour dochans*": "No Negroes, no ribbons, / No diamonds" for the *dochans* or *des gens* – "common white Americans." Yet it was clear that the "common white Americans," both Northern and Southern, would combine to ensure that, emancipation and Reconstruction notwithstanding, there would be neither equality nor real freedom for the freedpeople. Lincoln's then-vice president – now president – Andrew Johnson, had grandly proclaimed in his 1864 "Speech to the Freedmen": "I will be your Moses, and will lead you through the Red Sea of struggle and servitude to a future of Liberty & Peace," a quote reprinted on the sheet music cover of J. H. McNaughton's "Where Is Our Moses? (Song of the Freedman)" in 1866. As though Andrew Johnson could ever have adopted the mantle of Harriet Tubman – Johnson, who personally, and to Frederick Douglass's face, spurned the appeal for Black suffrage that year. It was the same Johnson who ordered the return of confiscated Confederate lands earmarked for freedpeople back to their prewar owners. (When the head of the Freedmen's Bureau, O. O. Howard, delivered – as he wept – the news of Johnson's dictum to a group of freedpeople, they sang in mournful response, "Nobody Knows the Trouble I've Seen.") In spite of the "Reconstruction Amendments" to the Constitution – the Thirteenth abolishing slavery (1865), the Fourteenth confirming citizenship and equal protection under the law for all those born in the United States (1868), and the Fifteenth prohibiting denial of voting rights based on a citizen's "race, color, or previous condition of servitude" (1870) – white Americans, Northern and Southern, were swept up in what a leading Civil War scholar calls the "romance of reunion." It was a "conciliatory culture" in which North–South (white) solidarity was ultimately effected at the expense of Black Americans' rights and progress.

Politically, the brief twelve years of Reconstruction (1865–1877) promised the brightest, most hopeful period for Black Americans in the South. It was the period that saw the first surge of Black voting and officeholding at all levels of government; the period that saw the introduction of state-funded public schools, "more equitable" taxation, and the outlawing of racially discriminatory practice in public services and transportation. But it was also a period of great white fear and resentment, enshrined in social practice and culture, and reflected in a host of songs such as "I'm a Good Old Rebel" by the Virginia lawyer Innes Randolph:

> O I'm a good old rebel,
> Now that's just what I am,
> For this "Fair Land of Freedom"
> I do not care a dam;
> I'm glad I fit against it –
> I only wish we'd won;
> And I don't want no pardon
> For anything I done.

Musicologist Alan Lomax believed that, rather than being an affirmation of unreconstructed rebeldom, Randolph's song was in fact a "satire on the unreconstructable rebel." But whether or not Randolph was playing the satirist, his song managed to capture the very real hatred felt by a cross-section of the white South for "the Freedmen's Buro, / In uniforms of blue" and the "lyin', thievin' Yankees":

> Three hundred thousand Yankees
> Is stiff in Southern dust;
> We GOT three hundred thousand
> Before they conquered us;
> They died of Southern fever
> And Southern steel and shot,
> I wish they was three million
> Instead of what we got.

I can't take up my musket
And fight 'em now no more,
But I ain't a going to love 'em,
Now that is sarten sure;
And I don't want no pardon
For what I was and am,
I won't be reconstructed
And I don't care a dam.

If indeed this song "was received with shouts of joyous, healing laughter at Confederate Army conventions," as Lomax believed, it is unlikely that it would have given rise to the same among those Black Americans attending the Freedmen's Conventions that were also held after the war. The brotherly handshakes between the Blue and the Gray at Civil War reunions would continue for decades over the heads of Black veterans, who found themselves barred (for instance) from the segregated fiftieth anniversary commemoration of the Battle of Gettysburg in 1913, where "the only role for blacks was as laborers distributing blankets."

These same excluded Black veterans might well have remembered singing a new song when it first appeared in 1866:

I fought beneath the dear old flag
For freedom, peace and right,
And saw the dark clouds roll away
Before our country's might;
And now that I am truly free
Upon Columbia's shore,
A slave I never more will be
As in dark days of yore.

Some might even have recalled a series of events in Charleston, New Orleans, and Richmond, in 1867 – events that were not to feature in D. W. Griffith's *Birth of a Nation* (1915), Margaret Mitchell's *Gone With the Wind* (1936), the Victor Fleming/David O. Selznick film based on it (1939), or any other Confederate-friendly cultural productions that presented Reconstruction as an unmitigated period of tragedy and Northern vengeance, peopled by avaricious carpetbaggers, eye-rolling mammies, predatory Black "bucks," endangered white maidens, and tyrannical Radical Republicans. Throughout 1867, Black Americans in these cities set out to test the new laws against racial discrimination in public transport – boarding streetcars and refusing to move when ordered by conductors and policemen. Such was the promise of the Reconstruction freedoms, eighty-eight years before Rosa Parks was obliged to confront the Montgomery Bus Company with the very same challenge.

It was precisely this promise that sparked the vicious white backlash that ended the dream of Reconstruction, which W. E. B. Du Bois called "the finest effort to achieve democracy for the working millions which this world had ever seen," and its end "a tragedy that beggared the Greek." Songwriters were certainly resolute in the defense of Reconstruction, but some were also complicit in its downfall. Thus John Hutchinson, of the singing family, could offer his paean to Reconstruction, "The Fatherhood of God and the Brotherhood of Man" (notably including in the verses, in spite of the excluding title, his everlasting promise to the "stricken sisters" of the nation to "sing for woman's cause"):

Now, peace on earth, the hosts above
 Proclaim the nation's free,
And all both black and white enjoy
 The boon of liberty,
We claim no creed for class or clan,
 But cherish all the good,
While round the world
 There soon will be our common brotherhood.

But for the more cynical, there was always a songwriter ready to exploit the baseless conspiracy theory about the huge swarm of Northern opportunists – "carpetbaggers" – descending in droves upon the prostrate (white) South, ready to milk the losers out of every last penny and ounce of self-respect. This task fell upon the able shoulders of T. E. Garrett, Esq., and Alfred von Rochow in "The Carpet-Bagger," whose sheet music boasts the song as "sung with immense èclat by the inimitable BILLY EMERSON," the Irish-born minstrel performer:

I'm a gay old Carpet-Bagger!
 O! don't you understand?
'Mong the color'd folks I swagger
 Down in the cotton land.
Now I got no eddication;
 Of brains I does not brag,
But I owns a big plantation
 All in my carpet bag . . .

In the North I was Nobody,
 O! don't you understand?
Now I drinks my wine, and toddy,
 King of the cotton land!
For I drives the old slave master;
 He calls me scallawag
While he cusses fast, and faster,
 I fills my carpet bag.

The immediate postbellum years brought out some particularly nasty impulses in the realm of song, as counterpoint to even nastier impulses in the political sphere, mostly having to do with the preservation and perpetuation of white supremacy. There was, for instance, the state of Oregon's brazen abrogation of the Fourteenth Amendment, "just in case African Americans had not received the message that they were persona non grata in the Pacific Northwest." And, further to the north, tens of thousands of Indigenous people – Sugpiat, Alutiiq, Yupiget, and others, conveniently lumped together as "Eskimos" – had seen their land sold out from under them the previous year in an exchange between one old colonial power (Russia) and a new, rising one (the USA). William Seward, Lincoln's Secretary of State – and now Johnson's – "considered it the destiny of the United States to dominate the Pacific Ocean," and his "purchase" of Alaska was a manifest part of that destiny. The Alaskan people, of course, had their own store of songs – hunting songs, dance songs, game songs, ceremonial songs – that would remain misunderstood and discounted for many decades, just like those of their Indigenous neighbors to the south. The Bureau of Indian Affairs (BIA) set out to "Christianize and 'civilize' Alaska Natives" and teach them "what a white man wants of them," just as they intended for the Indigenous people in the lower states. Indeed, within the decade, the BIA agent to the Dakota would report: "The 'medicine dances' and 'singing doctors' keep their superstition alive through fear of sickness and death if disobedient. . . . [These] are deplorable obstacles in the way of Christianizing this generation."

The opening of the Chisholm Trail in 1867 further cemented the foundations of Anglo expansion in the West. Also known as the Kansas Trail, the Chisholm Trail became the locus and subject of well-known cowboy balladry. It also gave birth to one of the earliest corridos to eulogize the Mexican vaqueros, or cattle drivers, whose seasonal migration northwards was a source of both legend and "intercultural conflict." "*El corrido de Kiansis*" depicts, among other episodes, the mocking contempt of an American cattleman for the vaqueros crossing the Salado River, as well as the Mexicans' assertion of their own skills and heroism:

We got to the Salado River,
And we swam our horses across;
An American was saying,
"Those men are as good as drowned."

I wonder what the man thought,
That we came to learn, perhaps;
Why, we're from the Rio Grande,
Where the good swimmers are from.

Meanwhile, roughly ten thousand Chinese workers had been toiling on the western half of the transcontinental railroad, begun during the Civil War. Swinging picks alongside them were roughly three thousand Irish workers. George F. Root was one of the first songwriters to cast his celebratory eye on the grand object of their labor, sidestepping the blood-loss and struggle that had undergirded the laying of the gleaming steel rails:

> We reach out towards the Golden Gate,
> And eastward to the oceans;
> The tea will come at lightning rate,
> And likewise Yankee notions.
> From spicy islands of the West,
> The breezes now are blowing,
> And all the world will do its best
> To keep the cars a-going.

The transcontinental railroad was completed in 1869 with the hammering of a golden spike at Promontory Summit in Utah. The Chinese and Irish workers dispersed to find other means of survival. One cowboy ballad, "Westward Ho," predicted a dismal outlook for the Chinese in the rush for western settlement (throwing into the mix some derogatory Indigenous stereotypes):

> Shall Arizona woo me
> Where the meek Apache bides?
> Or New Mexico where natives grow
> With arrow-proof insides?
>
> Nay, 'tis where the grizzlies wander
> And the lonely diggers foam,
> And the grim Chinese from the squatter flees
> That I'll make my humble home.

And to where would these "grim Chinese" have "fled"? They would have returned to such cities as San Francisco to face the indignities of minstrel singers capitalizing, for comic effect, upon the universally acknowledged competition for low-waged, low-skilled labor – particularly between Chinese and Irish workers. The popular variety entertainer Tony Pastor was only one of many to make light of what was in reality a bitter, racialized scramble for scraps thrown under the table:

> Now Coolie labor is the cry,
> "Pat" must give way to Pagan "John,"
> Whom Christian bosses, rich and sly,
> Have anxiously the heart set on.

For he's a nice, cheap Chinaman,
Who ne'er turns Turk or "strikes" his work
For more pay, like the Irishman.
And won't he a fine Christian make?
The gentle, lamb-like Chinaman,
And for much toil small wages take,
The sweet, soft, yielding Chinaman?
The weak, tea-drinking Chinaman,
The unassuming, unpresuming,
Rice-consuming Chinaman.

California songsters contained anonymously composed verses supposedly sung from the point of view of a jaded Irish washerwoman (itself a hackneyed stereotype) fuming over her lot "Since the Chinese Ruint the Thrade":

For I kin wash an' iron a shirt,
An' I kin scrub a flure;
An' I kin starch a collar as stiff
As any Chineseman, I'm sure;

Figure 7.1 "What Shall We Do with John Chinaman?" Racist cartoon in *Frank Leslie's Illustrated Newspaper*, September 25, 1869.
Library of Congress Prints and Photographs Division

But there dhirty, pigtailed haythens,
An' ther prices they are paid
Have brought me to the state you see –
They've entirely ruint the thrade.

Across the country, people were recovering from the 1868 electoral battle between the Democratic candidates for president and vice-president, Horatio Seymour and Francis P. Blair, and the Republican champion of the Union and Reconstruction, Ulysses S. Grant. Seymour and Blair had some telling campaign songs written on their behalf, such as Thomas von La Hache and W. M. F. Bigney's "The White Man's Banner" – one of many Seymour/Blair songs published not only in the South but also in New York, Chicago, St. Louis, Philadelphia, and Cleveland. Even worse, under the leadership of the "Grand Wizard," former Confederate general Nathan Bedford Forrest, the "Invisible Empire of the Ku Klux Klan" had emerged to fight against Reconstruction with all the terrorizing means at their disposal, to the tune of published dance numbers like "The Ku Klux Polka," "Ku Klux Klan Schottische and Mazurka," and "Bloody Moon (Polka Brillante)." For his part, Grant, though a moderate as opposed to a Radical Republican, was an inveterate hater of the Klan and campaigned against them, not least through song – as in "K. K. K.," one of the numbers bulking out *The Grant Songster* of 1868 and sung to the tune of "When Johnny Comes Marching Home":

Upon the breeze our banner blue, hurrah! hurrah!
We'll spread for Grant and Colfax too, hurrah! Hurrah!
For him who leads to vict'ry on,
And Indiana's favorite son,
And the Ku-Klux-Klan is
A-shiverin' in its shoes.
A-shiverin' in its shoes.

Once in office, Grant and the Forty-second US Congress set about to hobble the Klan through the Civil Rights Act of 1871, also known as the Ku Klux Klan Act or the Enforcement Act, empowering the president to suspend the writ of habeas corpus in combatting the Klan. This was one of the major achievements of Reconstruction legislation alongside the constitutional amendments, providing the backdrop to individual milestones such as Thomas Mundy Peterson's casting of the first Black American vote – in Perth Amboy, New Jersey, the day after the ratification of the Fifteenth Amendment – and the election of Hiram Rhodes Revels as the first Black American in the US Senate, representing Mississippi.

But the writing was on the wall for Reconstruction, and none saw that more clearly than Frederick Douglass, who looked ahead to a predictable

Figure 7.2 Sheet music cover of "K.K.K., or Bloody Moon Waltz," composed by Gusavus Dolfuss, 1878.
Library of Congress Civil War Sheet Music Collection

weakening of the reforming spirit as Northern and Southern whites sank themselves deeper into the "romance of reunion." Speaking at the Republican National Convention in 1876, Douglass threw down the gauntlet:

> You say you have emancipated us. You have; and I thank you for it. You say you have enfranchised us. You have; and I thank you for it. But what is your emancipation? – what is your enfranchisement? What does it all amount to, if the black man, after having been made free by the letter of your law, is unable to exercise that freedom, and, after having been freed from the slaveholder's lash, he is to be subject to the slaveholder's shot-gun?

That year's presidential election ended in dispute, with the Democratic candidate, Samuel Tilden, winning the popular vote by a margin of

250,000, but with one vote shy of the needed 185 Electoral College votes. As Howard Zinn summarizes it:

> Three states not yet counted had a total of 19 electoral votes; if [Republican candidate Rutherford B.] Hayes could get all of those, he would have 185 and be President. This is what his managers proceeded to arrange. They made concessions to the Democratic party and the white South, including an agreement to remove Union troops from the South, the last military obstacle to the reestablishment of white supremacy there. . . . It was a time for reconciliation between southern and northern elites.

How bitterly ironic now were the words of Tilden's campaign song, given that in the end it was *Hayes* who delivered what Tilden had promised: "The South will from her shackles spring, / For Tilden brings relief."

Reconstruction was dead and buried. For Black Americans in the South, it meant a certain future of further disfranchisement, peonage and penury, the erosion of educational provision, Klan terror, lynchings, and the entrenchment of the "Black Codes" that marked the landscape of what became known as the Jim Crow era. Thus was born the genre known as the "Exodus song," reflecting the mass uprooting and departure from the South of, initially, over fifty thousand Black Americans for parts northward: "For Tennessee is a hard slavery state, and we find no friends in that country, / Marching along, yes, we are marching along. / We want peaceful homes and quiet firesides; no one to disturb us or turn us out. / Marching along, yes, we are marching along." They had "fled" and would continue to flee, in Isabel Wilkerson's words, "as if under a spell or a high fever." In their wake, the popular music arena continued to resonate with songs of nostalgia for the old plantation, from David Braham's "Where the Sweet Magnolia Grows" (1877) to Henry Newman's "Dem Good Ole Times" (1877) to Stephen S. Bonbright's "Dar Sleeps Massa and My Missus Side by Side" (1884). Such songs were, in a sense, the accompanying soundtrack to the white southerner Joel Chandler Harris's *Uncle Remus: His Songs and Sayings* (1880) and its numerous sequels appearing between 1883 and 1910, in which the aged retainer and former slave, Uncle Remus, enchants a young white boy with tales out of African American folklore – the stories of Brer Rabbit, Brer Fox, and Brer Bear. Harris created a utopian antebellum dreamworld of loyal slaves worshipping their benign white masters, "one of the most hackneyed clichés in American history."

Fortunately, we have a strong record of contemporary Black music challenging the minstrel motifs of both the ante- and postbellum decades, not least through the publication of *Slave Songs of the United States* (1867) by three white abolitionists, Lucy McKim Garrison, William F. Allen, and Charles P. Ware. The appearance of this volume was later deemed by one musicologist as "something like our first orbital lunar flight." That same year, the Unitarian minister Thomas Wentworth Higginson published his influential essay "Negro Spirituals" in *The Atlantic Monthly*. Both these publications, it is true, emphasized religious singing at the expense of secular song, but at least they showed that Black music had finally begun "to find platforms for expression that presented it with a modicum of dignity." And in the last half of the nineteenth century, no vocalists were more influential in bringing spirituals to the world's attention than the Fisk Jubilee Singers, "an unlikely band of former slaves and the children of slaves," whose story is "one of the few bright spots in the otherwise grim history of post-Reconstruction African American history."

The Fisk Jubilee Singers began as a student fund-raising group in 1871 for the historically Black institution Fisk University in Nashville, Tennessee. The next decade saw their fame spread across the USA and Europe through their singing of "the slave songs," in Du Bois's words, "so deeply into the world's heart that it can never wholly forget them again," and sparking a rash of imitative choral groups. By then, there was no more

Figure 7.3 The Fisk Jubilee Singers, c. 1875. Photographer unknown. Library of Congress, Prints and Photographs Division

expectation that they, like Elizabeth Taylor Greenfield two decades earlier, should begin their concerts while hidden behind a curtain – as they, too, had been initially advised, lest the white audiences "see their black faces before they heard their heavenly voices." The Fisk Jubilee Singers' classically arranged "glee club" style of singing prompted some later critics, such as Zora Neale Hurston, to dismiss it as a "trick style of delivery." (Hurston: "I say again, that not one concert singer in the world is singing the songs as the Negro songmakers sing them. If anyone wishes to prove the truth of this, let him step into some unfashionable Negro church and hear for himself.")

If it is indeed true that the Fisk Jubilee Singers' versions of "Go Down, Moses," "O Brother, Don't Stay Away," and other spirituals "reflect white musical practice," it is also the case that other contemporary practices carried their own mixed blessings, none more so than the minstrel shows increasingly featuring Black performers themselves. Composers and singers such as James Bland, Sam Lucas, Billy Kersands, Ernest Hogan, and the Bohee Brothers – all Black Americans – seized the double-edged sword of blackface minstrelsy in order to carve out financially rewarding careers that would otherwise have been unattainable. As the writer and civil rights activist James Weldon Johnson later reflected, minstrel troupes – demeaning and racially defamatory as they were – "did provide stage training and theatrical experience for a large number of colored men. They provided an essential training and theatrical experience which, at the time, could not have been acquired from any other source." There is no telling how uncomfortable it must have been for a Black performer like Charles B. Hicks to have a minstrel song personally dedicated to him by its composer, "a Republican Yankee from Boston," and to be obliged professionally to sing its lyrics at the head of an all-Black troupe: "Oh, the old home ain't what it used to be, / The banjo and fiddle has gone, / And no more you hear the darkies singing, / Among the sugar cane and corn." Suffice it to say that the tenacity of the minstrel show and its racially disparaging motifs would continue to challenge Black actors, singers, composers, and lyricists well into the next century.

And just as the central (military) struggle had threatened to marginalize other important struggles of the Civil War years, the same is true of the sectional and racial struggles of the Reconstruction period. In November of 1872, just shy of three years after Peterson had cast the first Black vote, Susan B. Anthony and thirteen of her female associates registered to vote in the presidential election and cast their ballots. Anthony alone was arrested, tried, convicted, and fined one hundred dollars for "knowingly voting without having a lawful right to vote." She refused to pay the fine. In her address before the court, she argued that – especially after the adoption of the Fifteenth Amendment – all citizens of the United States had the right to vote and that, until that right was enjoyed by women, the USA would remain "an odious aristocracy; a hateful oligarchy of sex ... which makes father, brothers, husband, sons, the oligarchs over the mother and sisters, the wife and daughters, of every household." If the hard-won gains of Reconstruction had proved anything, it was that "every discrimination against women" was "null and void, precisely as is every one against Negroes."

The fellowship between former abolitionists and suffragists had remained strong during Reconstruction. In 1871, William Lloyd Garrison composed the verses to "Human Equality," specifically set to the tune of the 1750 Jacobite song, "For A' That" and arguing in the same uncompromising, anti-oligarchical terms used by Anthony: "A vassal state her heritage, / Dependent, poor, and a' that. / For a' that, and a' that, / Most deeply wronged, and a' that; / Though subjugated from her birth, / She still aspires, for a' that!" Predictably, male supremacist songwriters stuck their oars in, too, such as the deservedly obscure R. A. Cohen, whose "Female Suffrage" (1867) must mark one of the lowest points in the musical debate:

But when from her position
A careless woman's hurled,
She's the loathing of our manhood,
The scorn of all the world;
She loses her identity,
With all that's noble then,
And seeks the common level,
Of the commonest of men ...

Then mothers, wives, and sisters,
I beg you keep your place;
And remain what nature made you –
The help-meets of our race.
Let no temptation lead you,
Nor any wily fox,
To descend unto the level
Of the nation's ballot-box.

Between the two opposing poles of anti-suffrage and full suffrage was the curious position of "partial suffrage," a halfway house allowing women to vote in minor elections, usually at the local or schoolboard level. The confusion of this grudging position is reflected in a contradictory stanza in

Elizabeth B. Dewing and Joseph Philbrick Webster's "All Rights for All!" (1868), which appears to argue for something less than what the title suggests:

> O, men whom the people have trusted,
> The status of Freedmen to fix.
> Remember the great Declaration,
> By the Fathers in seventy-six;
> In God given rights, we are equal,
> Man, woman, white, black, great and small,
> Then legalize in partial suffrage,
> And guaranty "All rights for all!"

Women would not achieve the guarantee of unrestricted suffrage until August of 1920 with the ratification of the Nineteenth Amendment to the Constitution. Until then, the struggle for women's equal rights would continue.

So, too, would the class struggle continue, as it had all through the Civil War. It went far beyond the sentimental evocation of starving children in popular parlor song, such as Charles A. Van Anden's "Poverty's Child" of 1870:

> Shiv'ring and cold, a young girl stood,
> With clothing scant, and feet all bare;
> Seeking a shelter from the chill wind,
> And sleet that fill'd the wintry air,
> Leaning against a cold stone wall.
> With thread-bare shawl round her shivering form,
> Stood poverty's child, asking alms from all,
> To pay for shelter from the storm.

What was needed, beyond tear jerking, was a movement, and for struggling farmers in the South and the Midwest this was realized in 1867 with the establishment of the National Grange of the Patrons of Husbandry. The so-called "Grange Movement" was meant to unite small farmers across the country to combat a host of adversaries, from exploitative railroad interests to punitive credit institutions, as well as their political enablers. As the economy careened toward the disastrous Panic of 1873, the nexus of capitalist and political corruption brought Mark Twain and Charles Dudley Warner to the fore with their collaborative novel, *The Gilded Age* (1873), satirizing, among other ills, the postwar mania for land speculation. As the narrator describes the eternally optimistic and infectious schemer Colonel Sellers: "The Colonel's tongue was a magician's wand that turned dried apples into figs and water into wine as easily as it could change a hovel into a palace and present poverty into imminent future riches." Looking at the western lands and the farmers ripe for exploitation, Sellers practically salivates, "there's whole Atlantic oceans of cash in it, gulfs and bays thrown in."

But outside the world of the text, less endearing financiers, oil men, and "robber barons" were making their fortunes, hand over fist – the likes of John D. Rockefeller, Cornelius Vanderbilt, Andrew Carnegie, and Jay Gould (who famously boasted: "I can hire one half of the working class to kill the other half.") As a Grange historian writes, there was "a further irritant to farmers and other citizens": postwar corruption and sleaze in the Federal government, as revealed by such debacles as the Crédit Mobilier scandal, "which consisted of financial hijinks by the directors of the Union Pacific Railroad abetted by certain members of Congress." As if predatory land speculation on behalf of the railroads weren't enough, the agricultural sector was traumatized by the return to the gold standard after the wartime "experiment" with greenbacks, resulting in "precipitous" price crashes and financial insecurity for the majority of the country's farmers.

Across the hardscrabble southland and on the western plains, farmers saw themselves growing poorer while eastern industrialists and speculators gathered in the riches. Out of this turmoil came one of the most enduring songs to be associated with radical agrarianism and the Grange Movement. Knowles Shaw's "The Farmer Feeds Us All" (1874) sparked numerous subsequent versions recorded by artists well into the twentieth century, from Fiddlin' John Carson to Pete Seeger to Ry Cooder: "There are speculators / All about, you know, / Who are sure to help each other roll the ball. / As the people they can fleece, and then take so much apiece, / While the farmer is the man that feeds them all."

The industrial sector was also hammered by crisis. In January of 1874, unemployed workers lobbying for public works projects clashed with police in New York's Tompkins Square. As one newspaper reported: "Police clubs rose and fell. Women and children ran screaming in all directions. Many of them were trampled underfoot in the stampede for the gates. In the street bystanders were ridden down and mercilessly clubbed by mounted officers." If the police and the civic authorities were unable to account for the desperation behind such demonstrations, at least one anonymous broadside balladeer, known only as "J. C. J.," could:

> It's true what you say, Uncle Samuel,
> We've plenty of gold laid away,
> Mouldy with mildew and rust, sir,
> Guarded by night and by day . . .

I'm sure you will own, Uncle Sam, sir,
Temptation is hard to resist.
Just look at our poor working girl, sir,
Striving her best to exist!
Can you wonder at weak constitutions,
When your blood-sucking firms barely give
Enough to keep off destitution,
A girl though she's poor, she must live.

In fact, both the Civil War and Reconstruction had succeeded in obscuring one of the longest labor struggles the country had seen:

> Agitation against the traditional sunup-to-sundown working day began in 1791, when Philadelphia carpenters struck for shorter hours. During the decade of 1825–35 the movement for a ten-hour day spread like fire through labor's ranks and resulted in numerous strikes. The mechanics and artisans, who were well organized in trade unions, first succeeded in gaining the ten-hour day, but for textile operatives and other industrial workers, the working day remained twelve hours or more.

At the end of the Civil War, the Boston machinist Ira Steward spearheaded the organization of the Grand Eight Hour League of Massachusetts, a movement that was repeated in cities and states across the country. The movement's leading balladeer was Steward's fellow New Englander, E. R. Place, hailed by Steward as "the poet of the Boston Eight Hour League." Place knew that the struggles of the Civil War would resonate in the hearts of the people who had gone through it, so he adapted the war's most rousing tunes for the cause in such numbers as "A Song of Eight Hours" (to the tune of "Marching Through Georgia") and "James Brown" (to the tune of "John Brown's Body"):

James Brown's body toils along the rocky road,
James Brown's body bends beneath a crushing load,
James Brown's body feels the point of hunger's goad,
His soul cries out for help.

Come, O bearer of Glad Tidings,
Bringing joy from out her hidings,
Come, O bearer of Glad Tidings,
O come, O come, Eight Hours!

Indeed, a great surge of labor unification marked the years immediately following the Civil War. Beginning with the establishment of the country's first national labor federation, the National Labor Union in 1866, and, in 1869, the Colored National Labor Union (led initially by Isaac Myers and subsequently by Frederick Douglass), the movement culminated with the founding of the "Noble and Holy Order of the Knights of Labor" by Uriah Stephens, also in 1869. Reaching the peak of its influence in the mid-1880s, the Knights of Labor marked the checkered landscape of US labor activism, so progressive in some ways and so reactionary in others. This was particularly so when it came to race. Hence the Knights' culpability in the appalling anti-Chinese riots of 1885 and 1886 in Rock Springs, Wyoming, in which twenty-eight Chinese railroad workers were killed in "a mass action by the Knights' members." It is true, however, that other chapters of the Knights actively pursued a policy of "racial egalitarianism" and by 1887 the union could nationally boast a Black membership of 90,000. At their best, the Knights of Labor were worthy of the words they sang at the close of each session of their general assembly:

> Base oppressors, cease your slumbers,
> Listen to a people's cry . . .
>
> Iron hands are giving way –
> Kingcraft, statecraft, base oppression,
> Cannot bear our scrutiny –
> We have learned the startling lesson,
> If we will, we can be free,
> If we will, we can be free.

Nowhere was the labor struggle more intense in the postbellum years than in the anthracite coal fields of northeastern Pennsylvania. Since the late 1820s, when the first coal fields were opened up for speculation, the region had become the major producer of the prime energy source that would propel industrial production, home heating, and – eventually – the railroads. Periods of boom and bust destabilized the coal mining industry, sometimes resulting in labor conflicts such as the Schuylkill County coal strike in 1842, "the first major uprising of coal miners in the history of the United States – the first battle in a century-long war between coal miners, the so-called 'shock troops' of labor, and the coal companies." A second strike, in 1868, led to the establishment of the Workingmen's Benevolent Association (WBA), an important but divided union whose major accomplishment was securing the nation's first written contract between coal miners and operators in 1870. However, the contract was not strong enough to prevent the coal operators – some of whom were also directors of the railroad companies that had bought up the fields in the rush of speculation – from imposing wage cuts whenever prices dropped. This naturally led to strikes and lockouts, the basis of which was explained in a store of mining ballads, such as the anonymously penned "What Makes Us Strike?" from the Schuylkill mine patch:

> What's that you say? What makes us strike?
> Well, now you've hit a subject which I like
> To talk upon to strangers, for you'll understand,
> A very wrong impression fills the land –
> That we are lazy, bloody, reckless men,
> Who live beneath the ground, in cave and den;
> And come out once a while to get the light
> To burn a breaker, kill a boss, or fight . . .
>
> We oft get hurt, and sometimes lost, pard'
> And consequently we good wages like,
> And when we can't get that, why, sir, we strike.
> That's how it comes – I don't see we're to blame,
> For any other men would do the same.

As for the coal bosses themselves, the pioneering ballad collector George Korson noted: "Having more potent weapons, the operators rarely employed balladry in their battles with workers." Hence the rarity and consequent importance of a broadside ballad circulating in Schuylkill in 1871, lampooning the WBA and directed at its predominantly Irish members, cruelly mocking their dialect and stirring the pot of ethnic conflict and competition:

> Go back to yer work, me broth of a boy,
> An' shtop all yer strikes an' yer fuss.
> Or divil a wun will get any employ,
> An' ye'll soon be shtarvin' or wuss.
>
> It's d—d little minin' yer doin' at all;
> There's others work betther nor you.
> Yer fit but for ditchin' out in the canawl,
> Or workin' wid some railroad crew.
>
> So shtart or be off – (we're wanting no such)
> An' lit those min who want to work, be:
> We've miners enough, both English and Dutch,
> An' in your place we'll get the Chinee.

This balladeer's fixation on the Irish belies the fact that the Pennsylvania mine patch was a salad bowl of other ethnicities: Welsh, English, Scottish, German (which the balladeer calls "Dutch"), and – often drafted in as strikebreakers – Italians. But the Irish dominated the coal fields, not only in terms of their numbers but also because of their association with the folklore of the region, not least that arising out of the case of the "Molly Maguires," a band of labor activists and alleged coal-mine saboteurs dubiously convicted of murder in 1875 and subsequently executed. The band had taken their name from a legendary resistance group against landlords' evictions in Ireland. Because of their connections with both the WBA and the Ancient Order of Hibernians, a benevolent Irish fraternity, they were used by the coal-mine and railroad bosses (one of whom was also, conveniently, district attorney during the trial) to demonize the Irish as "a drunken underclass" and to tar "organized labor with the label of terrorism."

The trial and execution of twenty suspected "Molly Maguires" brought to the fore one Martin Mulhall, perhaps the most intriguing and least known of Woody Guthrie's predecessors. Musician-historian Bucky Halker introduces him:

> The intensity of class conflict in Pennsylvania's collieries encouraged one miner to desert the mines for a career as itinerant singer, writer, minstrel, and hawker of ballads. Upon witnessing the hanging of the Molly Maguire defendants, sixteen-year-old collier Martin Mulhall felt moved to compose a song-poem for each victim. A local printer offered them in broadside form and Mulhall sang and hawked them as he wandered the state's coal camps. Mulhall rapidly established his reputation as singer-composer and his talents earned him the title Poet Mulhall.

George Korson adds further precious details:

> He was self-taught not only in poesy, but in music and painting. He was also a superb story teller, a folk artist if there ever was one! To one of his artistic temperament, mine work was irksome. He deserted the trade in his early teens, eking out a precarious living by his minstrelsy and performing odd jobs. The early habit of riding the rods, his principal mode of traveling as he grew older, ultimately proved his undoing. It was while hopping a freight that he was killed in the Altoona yards about a quarter of a century ago.

At the time of Korson's writing, "about a quarter of a century ago" would place Mulhall's death at 1912, the year of Guthrie's birth. (Believers in metempsychosis or the "transmigration of souls" may draw their own conclusions.)

Only a handful of Poet Mulhall's ballads have survived. Of these, his elegy on the executed Thomas Duffy is particularly strong in its indictment of centuries of legal chicanery weighted against the Irish on both sides of the Atlantic:

> Thomas Duffy and James Carroll as you can plainly see,
> They were murdered by false perjurers all on the gallows tree.
> Thomas Duffy on the brink of death did neither shake or fear,
> But he smiled upon his murderers although his end was near.

He took his brother by the hand and kissed him o'er and o'er
Saying, "Farewell, my faithful brother, I shall never see you more,
Till your spirit from this world has fled to that celestial shore
Where perjurers can't enter to shake loving hearts any more.

"Take my advice, dear Patrick, and follow in my wake.
Let perjurers do all they can, my heart they will never shake."
He scorned his prosecutors although he stood alone,
As did many a gallant Irishman before England's king and throne.

The Molly Maguires affair was only one of many episodes arising from the fierce conflict between labor and capital in the postbellum decades. This conflict was encapsulated in one of the century's most popular workers' ballads, "Labor's Ninety and Nine," written by Elizabeth Rose Smith for the Knights of Labor. In 1868 Smith condemned the mismatch in wealth between the laboring poor (the 99 percent) and the idle rich (the 1 percent). This was almost 150 years before David Graeber and his fellow activists in the Occupy Wall Street Movement shook the world with their battle cry, "We Are the 99 Percent":

They toil in the fields, – the ninety-and-nine –
  For the fruits of the mother earth;
They dig and delve in the dusky mine,
  And bring its treasures forth;
But the wealth released by their sturdy blows
To the hands of the one forever flows . . .

But the one owns cities and homes and lands,
While the ninety-and-nine have empty hands.

What were the "ninety-and-nine" to do about it? Their battle against "the one" would go on and – of course – they would continue to sing their songs of struggle as the gilding on the age wore thinner and thinner still.

CHAPTER 8

Muscle, Blood, and Steel

Labor's gloves were off. Much of the fight was directed against the rapidly expanding railroad networks and their hubristic owners, the robber barons, who could cynically boast of hiring (to repeat Jay Gould) "one half of the working class to kill the other half." Fed up with an increasing spiral of wage cuts in the face of fattening profits, US railroad workers embarked on the "Great Railroad Strike" of July 1877, "the first nationwide work stoppage," which ended only with the drafting in of US Army troops fresh from their butcheries of the Lakota on the western plains. The "Battle of the Viaduct" in Chicago left thirty protesters dead and over one hundred wounded. The following year saw the founding of the Socialist Labor Party of America, the Greenback Labor Party, and the International Labor Union. As the balladeer B. M. Lawrence asked rhetorically in his *National Greenback Labor Songster* of 1878, "Shall banks and railroad kings unite / For base and selfish ends, /And those who labor for the right, / Prove false and not true friends?" The answer (implicitly in the negative) lay in the title of his song, "When Workingmen Combine."

If anyone needed proof, they could look at the pitiful fate of the unorganized freight handlers working on two New York railroads, the Central & Hudson River and the Lake Erie & Western, who had gone on strike for a pay increase of three cents per hour in the summer of 1882. The railroad barons – Gould, Cyrus Field, and William Henry Vanderbilt – broke the strike by drafting in replacement laborers, many but not all of them immigrants, and stirring the pot of nativist bigotry in the process. An anonymously penned satirical ballad, "The Freight Handlers' Strike" – meant to be sung to the tune of "Rambling Rake of Poverty" – relied on some fairly coarse national scapegoating as well as (given the strike's outcome) some misplaced muscular bravado:

> There's Field, Jay Gould, and Vanderbilt, their millions they did save
> By paying starvation wages and working men like slaves;

They hum round honest labor as the bee does round the flower,
And suck the sweetness of your toil for 17 cents an hour.

They advertised in English, French, Irish, and Dutch,
They got a sample of all nations to work in place of us;
They marched them to the depot and told them not to fear,
And to shake their courage up in them, they gave them lager beer.

The lager beer and sandwiches with them did not agree;
In place of handling merchandise they all got on the spree.
The Russian Jews soon spread the news about their jolly times,
And all the bums from Baxter Street rushed for the railroad lines.

The Italians made themselves at home and soon began to call
For William H., the railroad king, to pass the beer along;
Jay Gould was making sandwiches and Field began to cry
Because he couldn't snatch the man that blew up his English spy.

"Combination" – the archaic phrase for organization – was on everyone's lips, whether labor or capitalist. The next four years saw the launch of the Federation of Organized Trades and Labor Unions, the Brotherhood of Carpenters and Joiners, and the Revolutionary Socialist Labor Party. The first Labor Day parade, in September 1882, had thirty thousand workers marching in New York – a city that by then could boast an estimated one hundred thousand homeless children on its streets. Antimonopoly activists declared fierce war on the rising railroad barons, one front of that war being musical, as in the anonymously composed "Anti-Monopoly War Song":

As it moves o'er hill and dale
Riding on its iron rail,
Will you let the idol grim
Tear ye, brothers, limb from limb?
And your breath of Freedom choke
With its clouds of poisoned smoke?

No! then onward to the fray,
Hurl the monster from your way,
Let your cry of battle be,
Death to all Monopoly!

Another call to arms, "Our Battle Song," leapt out of James and Emily Tallmadge's collection of twenty-nine *Labor Songs Dedicated to the Knights of Labor* (1886). It traveled across the country, then to Britain, Australia, and beyond, returning to the USA as "Hold the Fort." The song's music

Figure 8.1 "The Tournament of Today – A Set-To between Labor and Monopoly," by F. Graetz in *Puck*, August 1, 1883.
Library of Congress Prints and Photographs Division

carried even more militarily offensive overtones, for the lyrics were set to an existing tune called "Storm the Fort":

Strong intrenched behind their millions,
  Sit the money kings;
Salary grabbers, thieves and traitors
  Join them in their rings.

Vile injustice fills their coffers
  With their blood bought gold;
And the might of their oppression
  Ruins young and old.

Who will dare to shun the conflict!
  Who would be a slave?
Better die within the trenches,
  Forward, then, be brave!

The wave of strikes continued all across the country – by the cotton mill workers of Cohoes, New York (1882); cowboys in Texas, tobacco workers in Lynchburg, Virginia, and iron puddlers everywhere (1883); workers in the Fall River, Massachusetts, textile mills and on the Union Pacific

Railroad (1884); cloak makers in multiple states; carpet weavers in Yonkers, New York; workers at the McCormick Harvesting Machine Company in Council Bluffs, Iowa; and – against Jay Gould's Union Pacific and Missouri Pacific railroads – two hundred thousand workers in the "Great Southwest Railroad Strike." The latter conflict inspired Ella Lodge to compose her battle song, "Come Join the Knights of Labor," which perhaps overstated the case in declaring that, against "famine, floods, and earthquakes, / Fires, wars and drouths," even "worse than all the rest" was "the railway strike."

On May 1, 1886 – "the first time May Day had been celebrated by organized workers" – strikes and demonstrations undercut national production, primarily in agitation for the eight-hour work day. Striking marchers sang as much against the strikebreakers – or "blacklegs" – as against the miserable working conditions: "If Satan took the blacklegs, I'm sure 'twould be no sin; / What peace and happiness 'twould be for us poor workingmen. / Eight hours we'd have for working, eight hours we'd have for play; / Eight hours we'd have for sleeping in free Amerikay."

In Wisconsin, the next four days saw two thousand building and steel workers swell to sixteen thousand facing the state militia outside the rolling mills at Bay View. Many of them were Polish workers, belying the all-too-common equation of "strikebreaker" with "immigrant." At the end of the conflict, known afterwards as the Bay View Massacre, fifteen lay dead on the streets, including one child. The Knights of Labor's balladeers churned out their screeds at full tilt:

> Ev'ry day that passes by, they increase and multiply,
> The great knights, the noble knights of labor.
> Let the millionaire reflect that their force cannot be check'd,
> The great knights, the noble knights of labor.
> In the Senate when they sit, all the frauds will have to git.
> Or they'll drive them from the country in a hurry;
> Ev'ry dog has got his day; our mechanics want fair pay,
> And in Union they will get it, don't you worry.

On the same May Day, in Chicago, a protest meeting against police brutality in the city's Haymarket Square ended with someone – it was never determined who – throwing a bomb into the midst of the police ranks, "killing one policeman at once and wounding five others, who died soon after; some 50 others were injured." Eight demonstrators were arrested: "None was accused of having thrown the bomb, but merely with having encouraged that act by virtue of their other political activities." In fact, some of them had not even been at the protest; their crime lay in the fact that they were prominent in Chicago's anarchist movement. All eight were convicted in a highly compromised trial; seven were sentenced to hang. Of these doomed men, two had their sentences commuted and one committed suicide in prison. The remaining four were executed in November of 1887, the same month that up to sixty unarmed Black sugar workers were killed by local white militia and racist gangs in Thibodaux, Louisiana, while striking for a wage increase to a dollar a day. The eventual pardons for all eight of the Haymarket defendants (including the four executed and the one suicide) came after a storm of international protest, which included songs such as Arthur Cheesewright's "A Shout of Protest": "Let us save our noble brothers! / Raise your voices loud and high! / Noble men who lived for others, / Cannot, will not, must not die!" But no songs honoring or mourning the victims of the Thibodaux Massacre would be written until the twenty-first century.

The strikes continued into 1889 – by the longshoremen in New York City; workers on the Chicago, Burlington and Quincy Railroad; textile operatives in Fall City; and shoemakers in Cincinnati. The "Baseball Players' Revolt" of 1889–1890 saw the first great "struggle between players and owners for control of the sport." A chantey from the Georgia Sea Islands, first printed in 1888 by the English song collector Laura Smith – and later adapted by the Kingston Trio, Pete Seeger, and the Weavers in the twentieth century as well as Bruce Springsteen in the twenty-first – seemed to sing well for the times: "Pay me my money down / Pay me or go to jail / Pay me my money down."

However, as the Molly Maguires and the Haymarket tragedy had shown, it was more likely that the striking workers, rather than their bosses, would be the ones to end up in jail. It is no surprise, then, that many would abandon their faith in the law, if they ever had any in the first place. In New Mexico, Mexican farmers and ranchers had been consistently "defrauded in land grabs" for the half century since the territory was seized from Mexico. With the laying of the Santa Fe, Atchison & Topeka railway line from Kansas to northern New Mexico Territory in the 1890s,

> land speculators organized into the "Santa Fe Ring" and engineered schemes in which hundreds of Hispanic landowners lost their farms and ranches. In response, the Mexicans organized into bands of hooded night riders known as *Las Gorras Blancas* (the White Caps) and set out in forays to tear down fences and derail trains, hoping to frighten Anglo land developers and railroad companies into abandoning New Mexico.

When forty-seven suspected fence cutters were arrested in 1889 and tried on "flimsy evidence" in Las Vegas, their families and supporters marched through the streets, singing in Spanish "the abolitionist and labor song 'John Brown's Body.'"

Aware of the hypocritical contempt for organized labor on the part of capitalist interests that flourished happily through their own "combinations," US farmers combined in 1888–1889 into Farmers' Alliances. Their aim was to target "banks, for refusal to reduce interest rates"; "railroads, for discriminatory freight rates"; and "local law officials, for laxity in prosecuting cattle thieves." One of their most popular songs famously held the mirror up to the capitalist "combinations":

I once was a tool of oppression
As green as a sucker could be
And monopolies banded together
To beat a poor hayseed like me

The railroads and old party bosses
Together did sweetly agree
And they thought there would be little trouble
In working a hayseed like me.

Sadly, the Alliance movement failed to capitalize on the potential of biracial cooperation, with the Colored Farmers National Alliance boasting over one million members across the South before its ultimate demise in the face of white fears of a return to the egalitarianism of Reconstruction. This was a sad and self-defeating betrayal of the spirit in which Black and white members had briefly sung together, once again to the tune of "John Brown's Body": "Let us work and vote together, with a due respect to law; / Let us choose our ablest workmen, to represent our cause; / Let us say to all monopolies, just loosen up your claws! / So we go marching on. Glory, Glory, hallelujah . . ."

In 1892, New Orleans faced a general strike. Railroad switchmen in Buffalo, New York, walked out; and copper miners in Coeur d'Alene, Idaho, fought and died in pitched gun battles with strikebreakers and militia. In Tennessee, the Knights of Labor were into the second year of a strike against the Tennessee Coal, Iron, and Railroad Company. The strike at the Coal Creek mines had escalated in rancor with the company's drafting in of mostly Black convicts as replacement labor through the state's "convict-lease" system. The conflict continued for another two years, provoking interventions by the state legislature, the National Guard, and balladeers like the blind fiddler James W. Day ("Coal Creek Troubles"), Pete Steele ("Coal Creek March" and "Pay Day at Coal Creek"), and the contested author of what would become an Uncle Dave Macon classic on the Grand Ole Opry in the 1920s, "Buddy, Won't You Roll Down the Line":

Way back yonder in Tennessee,
They leased the convicts out.
They worked them in the coal mines
Against free labor stout.
Free labor rebelled against it;
To win it took some time.
But while the lease was in effect,
They made 'em rise and shine.
Oh, Buddy, won't you roll down the line?
Buddy, won't you roll down the line?
Yonder come my darling, coming down the line . . .

That same year – 1892 – Henry Clay Frick, manager of the Carnegie Steel plant at Homestead, Pennsylvania, took it upon himself, with his boss Andrew Carnegie's blessing, to cut the steelworkers' wages, lock them out, break their union, draft in replacements, and fortify the plant with barbed-wire fences and three hundred Pinkerton agents as company guards. On July 6, 1892, strikers and Pinkertons battled one another with firearms and projectiles, leaving at least fourteen dead between them. The state militia was called in and by August the strike as well as the union were broken. A steelworker named Michael McGovern, known as "the Puddler Poet," captured the workers' ire in his song, "The Homestead Strike": "When a bunch of bum detectives came without authority / Like thieves at night, while decent men were sleeping peacefully, / Can you wonder why all honest hearts with indignation burn, / Or why the worm that treads the ground, when trod upon, will turn?" By far, the most widely known song to emerge from the Homestead Strike was William W. Delaney's "Father Was Killed by the Pinkerton Men," which captures the outrage prompted not only by the strike and the bloodletting but also by Carnegie's lavish reception of the Freedom of the City of Aberdeen on the very day of the Pinkertons' arrival at the steel works:

Ye prating politicians, who boast protection creed,
Go to Homestead and stop the orphans' cry.
Protection for the rich man, ye pander to his greed,
His workmen they are cattle and may die.
The freedom of the city in Scotland far away
'Tis presented to the millionaire suave,
But here in Free America with protection in full sway
His workmen get the freedom of the grave.

As if capitalist greed were not enough, by the end of 1893 the country was in the midst of the worst depression it had ever seen. Out of a workforce of fifteen million, three million were jobless. "A third of the railroads with 225,000 miles of track fell into receivership, and 32 iron and steel companies and 642 banks closed. In sparsely settled Colorado 30,000 were jobless. Chicago's 200,000 unemployed had to sleep on stairways, floors, or in police stations." The crisis brought to the fore Eugene V. Debs, who with his colleagues established the American Railway Union (ARU). In 1894 the ARU took up the battle against wage cuts in the Pullman Car Company in Illinois, briefly forcing a nationwide rail stoppage before the Federal government crushed the strike with army troops. Debs was imprisoned, along with other ARU leaders. Debs maintained that the union had been undermined by its official color bar, which, over his protests, had kept Black workers out of the ranks, understandably leaving them "in no mood to cooperate with the strikers."

A store of mournful ballads emerged from the failed Pullman strike, reflecting the misery of thousands of blacklisted ARU members who "drifted to other railroads, got jobs under new names, were detected, dropped from the pay rolls, and . . . put 'on the hog,' riding hog and cattle cars." As one anonymous railroad drifter sang:

> Been on the hummer since ninety-four,
> Last job I had was on the Lake Shore,
> Lost my office in the ARU.
> And I won't get it back till nineteen-two.
> And I'm still on the hog train flagging my meals,
> Ridin' the brake beams close to the wheels.

By no means did the defeat of the ARU mean the defeat of the organized labor movement. On Easter Sunday, 1894, a mass of demonstrators – many of them Civil War veterans – led by Jacob S. Coxey marched out of Massillon, Ohio, headed for Washington, DC. Their numbers were swelled by marchers from Montana as well as San Francisco, Oakland, and Los Angeles, California, arriving at the capital on the first of May. The march on Washington by "Coxey's Army" was an historic first, laying down the template for the suffragist marches of 1913, the "Green Corn Rebellion" of 1917, the Bonus Army March of 1932, the Civil Rights March on Washington in 1963, the Vietnam moratoria of the 1970s, the Million Man March of 1995, and the Black Lives Matter (or Commitment) march against police brutality in 2020. Contemporary activists called the Coxey tactic "petition with boots."

Coxey's Army – or, as they formally called themselves, the United States Industrial Army – carried with them "A Petition of the Unemployed" calling for the nationalization of the major industries, "immediate employment on public works at fair wages," and, in the nativist spirit of much

American labor activism, an end to "the immigration of foreign laborers . . . until there is a demand for their labor or until the serfdom of the wage earner is abolished." The marchers were barred from presenting their petition to the US Congress; Coxey and his comrades were arrested "for the trivial offense of stepping on the grass," and the demonstration was broken up. But the marchers were memorialized in song, most glowingly by William Delaney (under the pen name of "Willie Wildwave"), who aimed to resurrect the righteousness of the Civil War to the tune of "Marching Through Georgia": "Yes, we have Union men – men who fought in sixty-one, / Who faced ev'ry danger 'neath the broiling Southern sun, / Out of work, they're marching on to Washington – / Marching in the Coxey Army!" Their ignominious defeat, however, was also musically noted, anonymously, to the tune of "The Star-Spangled Banner":

O say, can you see, by the dawn's early light,
That grass plot so dear to the hearts of us all?
Is it green yet and fair, in well-nurtured plight,
Unpolluted by the Coxeyites' hated foot-fall?
Midst the yells of police, and swish of clubs through the air,
We could hardly tell if our grass was still there.
But the green growing grass doth in triumph yet wave,
And the gallant police with their buttons of brass
Will make sure the Coxeyites keep off the grass.

Three years later, in the Appalachian coal fields, "the spontaneous uprising of an enslaved people" (as the miners described their strike) led to "the first agreement organizing a major industry in the United States," spearheaded by the United Mine Workers (UMW), now in its fourth year. Among the major aims of the UMW was the elimination of "company scrip" as the mode of wage payment, a practice that had kept miners and their families in a continuous state of debt peonage at the mercy of the "company store." Isaac Hanna's 1895 song of that title is a forerunner of Merle Travis's twentieth-century classic, "Sixteen Tons," in which a poor miner owes his very "soul to the company store":

We sign then a contract
   As agreed between men;
Though it holds us like slaves,
   It never holds them;
And when they've exhausted
   The old contract score,
They capped the climax
   With the company store.

In the context of such industrial turmoil, it is unsurprising that one socialist activist, Katherine Lee Bates, should have put her thoughts on paper in verse, composing a song that, like Woody Guthrie's "This Land Is Your Land" half a century later, could easily be considered a second national anthem – even a conservative one, were it not for a provocative verse rarely, if ever, sung at political conventions and sports events: "America! America! / God shed his grace on thee, / Till selfish gain no longer stain / The banner of the free!" And, as the social historians William Loren Katz and Laurie Lehman write:

> Into this boiling cauldron walked the world's greatest migration. By the mid-1890s a million men, women, and children a year, largely society's uprooted from eastern and southern Europe, arrived in packed ships and settled in crowded urban slums. Millions of Americans in rural areas were also drawn to cities for work where they jostled the newcomers for jobs and breathing space.

German immigrants established socialist and anarchist singing societies, with their folk songs and traditional drinking songs buttressed by odes to revolution and the proletarian struggle: "*Das Leid von der Kommune*" (Song of the Commune), "*Arbeitmanner*" (Workingmen), "*Die rote Fahne*" (The Red Flag), and "*Hoch die Anarchie!*" (Long Live Anarchy!). Polish singing societies and a Polish Singers Alliance flourished, preserving not only hymns and folk songs but also patriotic songs to boost national and cultural pride in the face of nativist hostility and alarm. (Not to say ignorance: "Immigrants from southern and eastern Europe were frequently lumped together as an indistinguishable mass of foreigners from a distant land, under such pejorative terms as 'hunky.'") The fact that the Polish population in the USA had doubled from half a million to a million between 1880 and 1890, and again to two million by 1900, insured that nativist hostility would rear its head repeatedly, particularly in periods of economic depression and industrial conflict.

Italian immigrants were a minor group before 1880, numbering a little over 81,000 at their peak; but between 1881 and 1890 that number had nearly quadrupled to over 300,000. They paid for it by being the subject of vaudeville and minstrel show stereotypes along the lines of "the Organ Grinder" and "the Dagoe Banana Peddler." Even sympathetic portrayals such as the anonymously composed "Song of an Italian Workman," which appeared in New York's social reform newspaper *The Survey*, sometimes perpetuated the stereotype of inarticulacy in an almost minstrel fashion:

Nothing work, nothing work,
  Bad time is this;
Nothing work, nothing work,
  How lean is my face.

Nothing job, nothing job,
  I come back to Italy;
Nothing job, nothing job.

In Russia, the assassination of Czar Alexander III in 1881 led to the vicious targeting of Jews throughout the Russian empire, in the form not only of discriminatory, repressive legislation but also of terror attacks – pogroms – in which Jewish towns and villages were burned and the inhabitants killed or driven into exile. Thus began the first large-scale emigration of Jews from eastern Europe to the USA, swelling to 2.5 million over the succeeding four decades. Russia's Jews had been restricted to living in an imposed "Pale of Settlement" since 1791, eking out meager livings as artisans and small-scale service workers, belying the anti-Semitic stereotypes and conspiracy theories of "the Jews" as the wizards and manipulators of global finance – a slander already firmly entrenched in the late nineteenth century. As one Jewish immigrant song has it:

Ponder on these bitter times
In every occupation.
At every step you see paupers,
And even more from the Jewish nation.

We are fleeing on foot to America
To earn a crust of bread there.
We will sell ourselves for slaves,
So long as we can live in peace.

This was the time of "sweatshops" in New York's Lower East Side, where lone Jewish tailors – male and female – worked day and night in their cramped apartments to save enough money to bring their families over from Russia, as memorialized in song by one celebrated immigrant, the Yiddish writer Sholem Aleichem (Solomon Naumovich Rabinovich), whose stories would later form the basis of the musical *Fiddler on the Roof*:

Your daddy's in America,
Your daddy, little son,
But you are still a child,
Sleep then, hushaby.

There they eat even on the weekdays
White bread, little son;
I will cook chicken broth there for you,
Sleep then, hushaby.

He will send us twenty dollars
And his picture, too,
And will take us – long life to him! –
To America.

Amidst the burgeoning garment industry in New York, one anonymous balladeer sang not only of the unremitting toil in the sweatshop, but also of the organizational energies that led to "the first victories" of unionization in the industry:

Weary days are a tailor's,
Weary days are his.

From dawn till dusk he sews away,
A cent and a song are all his pay.

From dawn till dusk he sits and sews,
Hunger and pain are all he knows.

From dawn till dusk we work away
Time was, we worked a twelve-hour day.

The union broke the twelve-hour day,
Brought us shorter hours and better pay.

Indeed, far from validating the conspiracy theories that would lead to the Holocaust and the persecution of Jews as capitalist "bloodsuckers" within the next half-century, the early wave of Jewish immigration brought to America a fabled fellowship of "Sweatshop Poets," a group of influential Yiddish versifiers and songwriters that included Morris Rosenfeld, David Edelshtadt, Joseph Bovshover, and Morris Winchevsky, the latter "regarded as founder of the Socialist press and literature and referred to as the 'first Yiddish proletarian poet.'" Upon settling in New York in 1894, Winchevsky threw down the gauntlet to "capital" and "foretold the workingman's realization of his power":

Everywhere, on both sides
Of the Atlantic, he is stirring!
He refuses to let
His bloodsuckers ride him anymore.
He refuses, like a blind horse,

To trudge under the yoke anymore,
He wants to be free, dear children,
The workingman wants to be fed!

Although Jewish immigrant songwriters would soon come to dominate Tin Pan Alley and lay the foundations of American musical theater with the Yiddish theater of Abraham Goldfaden, Boris and Bessie Thomashefsky, Jacob Adler, and others, late nineteenth-century vaudeville worked hard to perpetuate the stereotypes of Jewish avarice and financial wiliness. Among the more appalling examples is Frank Dumont's "Jacob and Solomon Rosenstein" (1890):

The merchants are jealous of our bargain store,
But we'll stay in business until they are poor,
We move thro' the crowd and the both of us cry,
Sleeve buttons, shoe laces, who wants to buy.
As we go peddling in our second-hand suits,
We don't watch the customers, we watch the goods,
For two smarter sheenies you never will find,
Like Jacob and Solomon Rosenstein.

With much more nuance, the popular vaudeville team of Edward "Ned" Harrigan and David Braham (the latter of whom was himself Jewish) problematically turned the spotlight on the stereotype of the Jewish schemer obsessed with moneymaking and appearing to have forgotten his own origins in the sweatshops, tenements, and pushcarts of the Lower East Side. The question remains as to whether Harrigan and Braham did more to perpetuate the stereotype than to challenge it:

They say some of our people are hungry today,
To me that is awfully funny,
Find Hebrews a tramp, oh you can't with a lamp,
They're bankers with plenty of money,
There's many a case, when some of our race,
Let dollars like water to flow,
We're out [of] the dust and riches or bust,
But I never tell all what I know.

The explosion of arrivals from eastern and southern Europe threatens to dominate the picture of US immigration in the last two decades of the nineteenth century. But, at the same time, other groups – with their own songs of struggle – were enriching the canvas. Mexicans still crossed the Río Grande, as they had done for centuries, but now they were officially "immigrants" and subject to the same exploitation as other seekers of contract labor. One late-century corrido reflects upon the fate of laborers working on the southwestern railroads. It is known by two titles – "The Immigrants" and "The Hooked Ones" – both freighted with their own dose of bitter irony, considering the still-recent history of the region:

On the 28th day of February,
That important day
When we left El Paso
They took us out as contract labor . . .

We arrived at Laguna
Without any hope.
I asked the boss
If we were going to Oklahoma . . .

We arrived on the first day
And on the second began to work.
With picks in our hands
We set out tramping.

Some unloaded rails
And others unloaded ties,
And others of my companions
Threw out thousands of curses.

Said Jesús the Coyote,
As if he wanted to weep,
It would be better to be in Juárez
Even if we were without work.

These verses were composed
By a poor Mexican
To spread the word about
The American system.

And there were the Chinese, facing the insult since 1882 of being the first national group to have a prohibitive immigration law directed at them specifically. The Chinese Exclusion Act "set the precedent for barring people based on occupation and nation of origin." The Exclusion Act carried a double whammy: not only did it severely restrict further emigration from China (the Chinese having outlived their usefulness upon the completion of the transcontinental railroad), but it also secured the deportation of many thousands who had been building their lives in the USA for as long as three decades. Thousands of others were left stranded in the country: "Those who could not afford to go home permanently dared not leave at all. Those who had married before coming to the United States faced prolonged separations until they earned enough to finance a journey home. But those who had not married faced lifelong bachelorhood."

Since the 1870s, "more than 153 anti-Chinese riots [had] swept through the American West . . . and they included arson, property damage, murder, and lynch mobs." This anti-Chinese terror was backed by its own musical soundtrack. Amidst the San Francisco riots of 1877, Chinese people endured not only violence but also the ranting of the nativist "Working Men's Party," whose vigilantes rampaged through the streets chanting a song taken from that year's *Blue and Gray Songster* – yet more proof that the postbellum "romance of reunion" was carried on at the expense of nonwhite groups:

O workingmen dear, and did you hear
The news that's goin' round?
Another China steamer
Has been landed here in town.
Today I read the papers,
And it grieved my heart full sore
To see upon the title page,
O, just "Twelve Hundred More!"

O California's coming down,
As you can plainly see.
They are hiring all the Chinamen
And discharging you and me;
But strife will be in every town
Throughout the Pacific shore,
And the cry of old and young shall be,
"O, damn, 'Twelve Hundred More.'"

Another song from the early 1880s, "The Heathen Chinese," took its title from the popular narrative poem by Bret Harte, "Plain Language from Truthful James" (1870). Harte had hoped his poem would be seen as a critique of anti-Chinese bigotry; but as the song indicates, many nativists held no talent for perceiving Harte's irony. Nor was it the finest hour for the Knights of Labor:

As I walk round the streets of your city
In searching for employment and bread;
But alas! there's no work for a white man to do;
They're hiring the Chinese instead.
Come join hands with the bold Knights of Labor;
We will battle through fire and blood
To get rid of this leper, the curse of our country
The vampires that are sucking our blood.

Then a white man we'll put in the kitchen,
In the laundry poor widows there'll be;
On the railroads, the roundhouse, the ranches,
We'll fire the Heathen Chinese.
I will swear by my wife and children,
From the mountains all down to the sea;
I'll join hands with the bold Knights of Labor
To help fire out the Heathen Chinese.

The minstrel stage continued to treat the Chinese abominably with its endless recirculation of the yellowface "John Chinaman" figure. But in some cases, like W. S. Mullally and John E. Donnelly's "The Chinese, the Chinese, You Know" (1885), it is difficult to tell whether the true object of attack is the Chinese community or the anti-Chinese paranoia inscribed into the lyrics:

I'll sing of a subject, but your ears you must lend,
And listen to what I've to say.
We'll have to do something with this curse in our land,
For our business has gone to decay.

The merchants are idle, their goods on their hands,
And the cause of this terrible woe
I'll tell you my friends, and you'll say I am right,
It's the Chinese, the Chinese you know.

Added to the obscure intentions often lying behind such lyrics, one curious facet of white supremacism is reflected in many of the songs and character depictions of the Chinese during this period: exoticism – even outright desire for the nonwhite subject. For every degrading, dehumanizing stereotype of the pigtailed, bucktoothed John Chinaman careening about the stage and screeching "Me no shabee" ("I don't understand"), there is a fascinating, attractive figure – often but not always female and couched in a bewildering mélange in which Chinese, Japanese, and Arab figures are conflated into representations of general Oriental mystery, seduction, and sexual availability.

Cio-Cio-san in Puccini's *Madama Butterfly* would perhaps prove the apotheosis of this figure in the early twentieth century, but the outlines were already visible in the late nineteenth:

> The portrayal of Chinese women in American songs, skits, and musicals was in many ways similar to the depiction of non-Western women in the Orientalist opera tradition. Often works described these female characters as little more than pieces of porcelain or playthings for their lovers – and by extension, audiences. Some literally told stories about porcelain dolls that were either made in China or looked Chinese.

Mystery and desire underscored many songs along the lines of Max Hoffman's "On a Chinese Honeymoon" (1897), as well as operettas and musical comedies like *The Pearl of Pekin* (1888), *The Geisha* (1896), and *The Mandarin* (also 1896, and particularly confusing because, in spite of its title and a song called "Chin Chin Chinaman," it is "mostly Japanese-themed").

Like the members of the Chinese community itself, the neighborhoods in which they congregated soon contained the push-pull force of attraction and repulsion, reflected in musical productions like *A Trip to Chinatown* (1892) and *The Queen of Chinatown* (1899). As Krystyn Moon points out, by the 1890s, Chinatown – in whatever US city – had become "a musical subject and appeared as a site of both danger and pleasure," characterized by typical, familiar settings: "laundries, opium dens, and restaurants." But Chinatowns were important for one other crucial reason: they were the home of Chinese opera, by far the strongest form of cultural resistance to the twin degradations of minstrelsy and orientalism. Cantonese opera troupes first began touring the mining areas during the Gold Rush years, establishing themselves as regular fixtures on the stages of the Chinese theaters proliferating in San Francisco and other towns with large Chinese populations. Their productions, based on traditional Cantonese musical and lyrical sources widely known to their audiences, were nourishing beyond measure – to the extent that the opera historian Jack Chen would liken "the role of opera in the life of the immigrant bachelors to that of a religious institution for other immigrant groups." Unsurprisingly, Cantonese opera "achieved its greatest popularity as nativist bigotry intensified."

Indeed, Cantonese opera became so popular a phenomenon that it attracted the notice of white American commentators and audiences who saw it as another doorway to the exoticism and mystery of Chinatown. Like the Europeans first encountering Indigenous American and African music, they had no idea what to make of it. On the Chinese opera stage, "theatricality and artifice, rather than verisimilitude, were stressed. Movements, gestures, and text delivery were extremely stylized and conveyed symbolic meaning, obvious to seasoned Chinese opera-goers but baffling to most Westerners." As for the music itself, couched in ancient, traditional, non-Western tonalities and structures, and often improvised by the musicians, the critical response was often predictably ignorant: "Screams, goblings, brayings, barkings ... the mingled midnight music of forty cats."

The misunderstanding extended into the official realm with the belief that female Chinese opera singers were "a sexual danger to the American public," in reality "prostitutes who could spread venereal diseases to healthy European American men and produce children of mixed descent." Consequently, Congress passed the "Page Law" in 1875 – seven years before the more general Chinese Exclusion Act – "barring all prostitutes from immigrating, but because government officials were unable to distinguish a Chinese prostitute from other women, the law essentially barred all Chinese women." This restriction not only accounted for the high proportion of lonely bachelors among the Chinese immigrant population but also targeted female opera singers in particular, as "prostitutes were the only women permitted to sing and dance publicly in China during the nineteenth century." Hence the practice of men playing women's roles on the Chinese opera stages in the USA, another source of critical bafflement and derision.

If the misunderstanding of music marked the white critical response to Chinese opera, it proved positively lethal to Indigenous Americans, setting off a chain of deadly events that culminated in the massacre of the Lakota at Wounded Knee in 1890. To understand how such a tragedy could have unfolded, one needs to look back at the fearful – indeed paranoid – Euro-American encounters with Indigenous song and dance. From the white settlers on the overland trails shuddering between the extremes of "awesome silences" and the "threatening noises of whooping Indians and howling wolves," to the agents of the Bureau of Indian Affairs reporting that "medicine dances" and "singing doctors" were "deplorable obstacles in the way of Christianizing" the Indigenous people, by the late nineteenth century the decks were stacked against any culturally informed response to the music and dance of the First Americans.

White fear and hostility were exacerbated by the increasingly militant resistance of Plains tribes to the steady disappearance of the bison, the main source of food and warmth, at the hands (or, more precisely, guns) of white hunters and soldiers. The ensuing "Buffalo Wars" ended with the collapse of the entire ecology of the bison-hunting peoples. Amidst mass starvation, drought, winter freezes, and plagues of vermin, "millions of skeletons [and] carcasses rotted under an open sky." In the mid-1870s, the surrender of resistance leaders from the Southern Cheyenne, Kiowa, Comanche, and Arapaho tribes, and their consequent transportation to Fort Marion, Florida, marked "a turning point for the educational programming" of Indigenous peoples, one with great and tragic implications. The leading voice of this "programming," Lieutenant Richard Henry Pratt, declared with a half-appreciative nod to the brutal views of his Indian-hating superior, Phil Sheridan:

> A great General has said that the only good Indian is a dead one, and that high sanction of his destruction has been an enormous factor in promoting Indian massacres. In a sense I agree with the sentiment, but only in this; that all the Indian there is in a race should be dead. Kill the Indian and save the man.

Pratt became the supervisor of the Fort Marion prisoners. By the end of their incarceration in 1878, these former proud warriors and hunters had become, under his direction, "tourist attractions," in one instance "harmonizing an American-style ballad" in barbershop-quartet fashion:

> Lo we Red Men to your home,
> Came in silent sadness.
> From the far-off Plains where roam
> All our tribes in gladness.
> In this genial happy land
> Chiefs of many a nation,
> We find the welcome friendly hand,
> We find the true salvation.
> Here we've learned a nobler life,
> To do unto each other,
> The good we can,
> To conquer strife,
> And call the white man brother.

Privately, however, these prisoners of war refused to abandon their cultural traditions:

> As the imprisoned Apaches at Fort Marion fell ill due to the unhealthful coastal climate and cramped living conditions, they improvised a Gahe dance with whatever materials they could find ... When the prisoners departed from Florida, they left behind a picture of a Fire Dance Gahe etched into the walls of the old Spanish fort.

Leaving Fort Marion, Pratt went on to establish the Carlisle Indian Industrial School in Pennsylvania the following year, with an unforgiving assimilationist mission to indeed "kill the Indian and save the man." In addition to banning Indigenous languages, garments, and hair styles and enforcing "strict interpretations of Christianity," the curriculum obliged students "to study the piano, the cornet, the violin – the accoutrements of 'white music' ... at the expense of 'savage' musical practices, the 'Indian dances' of their parents." In 1883, a band of "civilized" Carlisle students played at the opening celebration of the Brooklyn Bridge before going on a tour of eastern churches.

Away from the off-reservation boarding schools – on the reservations themselves – enforcers from the BIA declared war on what they deemed "heathen" dances and their musical accompaniment, whether vocal or instrumental, beginning with the Lakota Sun Dance in 1882. The following year the BIA set up a "Court of Indian Offenses" on each reservation. Punishable crimes included "the sun dance, scalp dance, war dance, or any other similar feast." Offenders would face penalties including fines, reduced or withheld rations, forced labor, and imprisonment – "ten days for participation in a prohibited dance, and up to six months for employing 'the arts of a conjurer to prevent Indians from abandoning their barbarous rites and customs.'"

A similar cultural war was waged against the Indigenous people of Alaska, where children at both Federal- and church-sponsored schools sat in front of teachers who refused to learn their language and, worse, punished them for using it. At least in Alaska the Inuit children could exact revenge by making up "A-B-C songs" in which they took the "meaningless syllables" of their teachers' language, "under the pretext of learning them in order to become 'civilized,' and made a vehicle of satire from them." Nonetheless, the imposition of Western music was often distressing, as one missionary reported: "At St. Michael the men were invited into the Fur Company house where there was a small organ. . . . [A]n old man said that he did not understand what the noise says . . . 'It sounds confusedly in my ears and is strange to them. I like better to hear the drum and singing in the kashim, for I understand it.'" Even more distressing, surely, was the missionaries' determination to wipe out Indigenous festivals. One wrote in 1890, "We have condemned the masquerades and seek to suppress them," following up in 1894 with: "This has given us more heart and courage than anything else: there was no masquerade this year from Bethel to Ougavig, that is, in six prominent villages. A custom that has existed for generations and one about which these people have clung most tenaciously, has been put aside."

It soon got to the point – a nadir in both Indigenous and US cultural history – that the only way for some of the tribespeople to sing their songs and dance their dances would be to become, effectively, minstrel performers in the Wild West Shows fronted by Buffalo Bill Cody and other showmen. This included Sitting Bull, who gave up his resistance struggle in 1881 with the sad words: "I wish it to be remembered that I was the last man of my tribe to surrender his rifle." This was the occasion that marked Sitting Bull's own composition of a lament: "Once a famous warrior I was. It is all over and now a hard time I have." Four years later, he was in the cast of Buffalo Bill's Wild West Show. It was Sitting Bull who "drew in the crowds" for his reenactment as "the killer of Custer," to the accompaniment of Lakota war dances and victory songs – authentic and legitimate in themselves, but contained and diminished through their transformation into wholesome popular entertainment.

Figure 8.2 Sitting Bull and Buffalo Bill. Photograph by William Notman Studios, 1885. Library of Congress Prints and Photographs Division

Five years later, the Lakota and other Indigenous people – as well as Sitting Bull himself – faced the fatal penalty of singing their songs beyond the minstrel arena of Buffalo Bill's Wild West Show. It all began with the Ghost Dance, the messianic religious movement spearheaded by the semi-Christianized Paiute leader Jack Wilson, known as Wovoka ("the Cutter"), who had picked up and revived the Ghost Dance tradition that had had a brief flourishing in the 1870s. Wovoka had claimed: "I went up to heaven and saw God and all the people who had died a long time ago. God told me to come back and tell my people they must be good and love one another, and not fight, or steal, or lie. He gave me this dance to give to my people." He also claimed: "Jesus is now upon the earth. He came once long ago beyond the waters and the white people killed him. Now he is come to the Indians who never did him harm." By 1889, in the midst of Indigenous hunger and demoralization over the loss of the bison, the loss of their lands, the loss of their autonomy, and the loss of their cultural freedoms, the Ghost Dance movement had spread like fire throughout the western tribes, promising a return to the glorious days before the arrival of the white man: "The new world would be covered with green grass and herds of deer, elk, antelope, and buffalo, and the Indians would live in a paradise, untroubled by disease, wars, or famine."

Practitioners of the Ghost Dance wore Ghost Shirts, which they believed would protect them from gunfire, and often fell into trance-like states as the dance continued. An elderly Lakota man recalled:

> The leaders beat time and sang as the people danced ... They danced without rest, on and on ... Occasionally someone thoroughly exhausted and dizzy fell unconscious into the center and lay there "dead" ... They were now "dead" and seeing their dear ones. As each one came to, she, or he, slowly sat up and looked about, bewildered, and then began wailing inconsolably. ... Waking to the drab and wretched present after such a glowing vision, it was little wonder that they wailed as if their poor hearts would break in two with disillusionment.

A sympathetic folklore collector observed in 1900: "The ceremony is but an appeal to the unseen world to come near and to comfort those who have been overtaken in the land of their fathers."

Figure 8.3 Oglala Ghost Dance at Pine Ridge Agency, South Dakota. Illustration by Frederic Remington in *Harper's Weekly*, December 6, 1890.
Library of Congress Prints and Photographs Division

And yet, US authorities were terrified – terrified of a dance they couldn't understand and terrified of the many "shaman songs" that accompanied it, which they equally couldn't understand, even though some of them, if translated, would not look out of place in the Book of Exodus: "Clear the way / in a sacred manner / I come / the earth / is mine." As the Santee Dakota writer and physician Charles A. Eastman observed: "The 'Messiah craze' in itself was scarcely a source of danger, and one might almost as well call upon the army to suppress Billy Sunday and his hysterical followers." But on the Lakota's Standing Rock Reservation, "officials reported it as disturbing and unstoppable" – and they blamed Sitting Bull, whom they put under house arrest under armed guard. In December of 1890 he was killed by one of the guards, "not long after he physically tried to prevent the land selections at Standing Rock," which was in the process of being broken up into small allotments.

Still, the dancing and singing continued, not only at Standing Rock but also at Pine Ridge, nearly three hundred miles to the south, where, upon the news of Sitting Bull's death, the Lakota Chief Big Foot (Spotted Elk) led 350 of his starving people – men, women, and children – through the snow and sub-zero temperatures to throw themselves on the mercy of the US authorities. The aboriginals-turned-refugees were intercepted by army troops, who marched them to the camp beside a creek called Wounded Knee. Soon the troops were joined by a contingent of the Seventh Cavalry, which, fourteen years earlier, under the command of George Custer, had been mauled by the Lakota at the Battle of the Little Bighorn. Now they were back, and they remembered. They had Hotchkiss machine guns, and they had whiskey. Someone tried to grab someone's gun, someone else fired a shot, the machine guns opened fire, and within minutes three hundred unarmed Lakota – old and young; men, women, and children – lay dead in the snow, along with twenty-five soldiers killed by "friendly fire." The wounded were taken to a church nearby. As it was four days after Christmas, "the sanctuary was candlelit and decked with greenery. In the front, a banner read: PEACE ON EARTH AND GOOD WILL TO MEN."

The editor of a South Dakota newspaper wrote: "The Whites, by law of conquest, by justice of civilization, are masters of the American continent ... and the best safety of the frontier settlers will be secured by the total annihilation of the few remaining Indians." This was L. Frank Baum, who went on to write *The Wonderful Wizard of Oz.* One of the surviving Ghost Dancers, the Lakota shaman Short Bull, reflected: "Who would have thought that dancing would make such trouble, for the message that I brought was peace."

The settler-colonial conquest of the continent was complete. The massacre of the Ghost Dancers at Wounded Knee coincided, to the very year, with the US Census Bureau's declaration that the frontier was now gone – that, for all intents and purposes, there was no tract of the USA now free of non-Indigenous "settlement." But this was not the end of Manifest Destiny. There were still other frontiers to conquer; they just wouldn't be found on the continental land mass. The same year as the Wounded Knee massacre, Henry Adams and his close friend John La Farge found themselves in Hawai'i being "entertained by Judge Sanford Dole" (he of peach and pineapple fame) and "amused by King Kalākaua," whose songwriting sister, Lili'uokalani, would soon become the last monarch of Hawai'i, destined to be overthrown by the US annexationists led by Dole. La Farge (whose great-grandson, the singer-songwriter Peter La Farge, would become a champion of Indigenous rights) recalled Adams telling him: "The Pacific is our natural property. Our great coast borders it for a quarter of the world. We must either give up Hawaii, which will inevitably then go over to England, or take it willingly, if we need to keep the passage open to eastern Asia, the future battleground of commerce."

Within five years, Queen Lili'uokalani would be under house arrest, writing a hymn to God for strength and for forgiveness of those who had betrayed her:

> I live in sorrow
> Imprisoned,
> You are my light,
> Your glory my support.
>
> Behold not with malevolence
> The sins of man,
> But forgive
> And cleanse.

CHAPTER 9

Rule Anglo-Saxia

The last decade of the nineteenth century did have some bright moments. In 1890, Wyoming was admitted into the Union as the forty-fourth state. While it was still a territory – in 1869 – legislators had passed the Wyoming Suffrage Act, giving women the right to vote. Now, with statehood, it became the first in the USA to enshrine universal suffrage in law. Julia Mills Dunn's "Song of Wyoming" proclaimed the dawn of a new age to the tune of "John Brown's Body":

> From Wyoming's rocky valley to the wild New Hampshire hills,
> From our northern lakes of silver to the sunny southern rills,
> Lo! the clarion call of Freedom all the listening silence thrills!
> Our God shall lead us on . . .
>
> We have heard the voice of Freedom from that far-off western shore;
> We have heard the echoes calling, as our fathers heard of yore,
> Let us sing its stirring music, "Equal rights forevermore!"
> And God shall lead us on.

And, to the tune of "God Save the King," the Illinois suffragist Elizabeth Boynton Harbert sang of a "New America" while calling for the nation's male population to champion the movement for universal suffrage:

> Sons, will you longer see
> Mothers, on bended knee,
> For justice pray?
> Rise now in manhood's might,
> With earth's true souls unite
> To speed the dawning light
> Of freedom's day!

The Jewish "Sweatshop Poet" David Edelshtadt also saw great potential in a "new world" forged by an alliance of workers and suffragists – much as had occurred between abolitionists and suffragists before the Civil War. Edelshtadt boosted his argument in the form of ballads like "To the

Women Workers," published in New York's Yiddish-language anarchist newspaper, *Varheit* (Truth):

> Help us carry the red banner
> Forward, through storm and dark nights.
> Help us spread truth and light
> Among unknowing, lonely slaves.
>
> Help us lift the world from its filth;
> Be ready, as we are, to give up what you treasure.
> We'll struggle together, as might lions,
> For freedom, equality, and our ideal.

In Chicago, the Columbian Exposition of 1893 – the "World's Fair" commemorating the four hundredth anniversary of the European invasion of America (not that it was promoted as such) – brought a whole "new world" to Main Street. Well, it was "new" to those promenading along the Midway who had never before seen Arabs, South Asians, North Africans, Sub-Saharan Africans, Alaska Natives, and other groups, all gathered in what were, supposedly, their own authentic "living villages" but which were, in reality, exoticized exhibits situated in "a zone between ethnology and exploitation." There were the new architectural wonders of the dazzling White City (vying in hue with the whiteness of the supremacism that lay behind the "living villages" display). There was also a thrilling, newfangled adventure ride called the "Ferris Wheel." It was all so exciting that one Tin Pan Alley songsmith, Charles K. Allen, just *had* to deflate the hubbub and hype:

> After the Fair is over, just watch the rents come down,
> When all the rubes and hayseeds have skipped away from town;
> Many a man will be busted, people will tear their hair,
> Hyde Park will be dead and buried after the Fair.
>
> Oh, what a picnic this Fair will be
> What wondrous people at it we'll see;
> Indians from Indianapolis, Japs from Japan,
> Mr. Joe Bunko and the three card Monte man.
>
> Turks, French and Arabs and Esquimaux,
> Buffalo Bill and his great Wild West show;
> Things will be lively, money to spare,
> But oh, what a diff'rence after the Fair.

All cynicism aside, it is indeed true that the Chicago World's Fair was "a momentous occurrence in American social history." Musically, it was a particularly important event because it was there that "the American public discovered ragtime" – where they "first became familiar and intoxicated with the music." Ragtime had arrived in Chicago from the saloons and dives of the Mississippi River cities – Louisville, Memphis, St. Louis – where Black musicians improvised songs with intense syncopation, pushing it "to extremes not previously heard in Western music" and "imparting a restless, off-kilter energy to the music that no waltz or quadrille could match." In terms of melodic and harmonic sophistication, many of ragtime's signature pieces – particularly those composed by Scott Joplin – could give Schubert and Chopin a run for their money. European composers such as Claude Debussy, Erik Satie, and Igor Stravinsky would all attest to ragtime's influence upon their own work. Even before the ragtime "craze" of the early 1900s, a handful of notable white composers, like Joplin's protégé Joseph F. Lamb, became some of the genre's greatest champions and practitioners.

Ragtime is indeed "a paradoxical art form with a perplexing history," and its connection with racial struggle cannot be denied. Some music scholars have argued that ragtime's "earliest composers had no common racial identity, nor the desire to promote their music under an ethnic banner." But as the Black pianist and composer Eubie Blake recalled: "You have to know about the backrooms of bars, the incredible prejudice we had to deal with . . . You have to understand the background; you can't pretend it has nothing to do with ragtime." Joplin's own determination to elevate ragtime from its earliest associations with minstrelsy and the "coon song" is only one example of the struggle to establish Black American music as an art form in its own right, free from the degrading imagery of racist caricature.

As we have seen, sometimes Black composers and practitioners themselves were obliged, for financial or career reasons, to perpetuate some of that degrading imagery. How bitter an historical irony that George W. Johnson should have inaugurated Black American recording with "The Whistling Coon" of 1890, that the celebrated Black performers Bert Williams and George Walker should have to bill themselves as "The Two Real Coons," or that the poet Paul Laurence Dunbar and the classically-trained composer Will Marion Cook should feel the need to write: "Warm coons a-prancin', Swell coons a-dancin', / Tough coons who'll want to fight; / So bring 'long yo' blazahs, Fetch out yo' razahs, / Darktown is out to-night!"

The first association of ragtime with the "coon song" came with the sheet music of Ernest Hogan's "All Coons Look Alike to Me" (1896), which included "an optional syncopated accompaniment" called "A Negro Rag." Hogan was himself Black American, the first to both produce and star in a Broadway show (*The Oyster Man*, 1907) and who later expressed regret for having written the song that had kickstarted the "coon song" craze. Joplin himself was not immune to the temptation either, climbing onto the bandwagon with some awfully clichéd lyrics to his own "Ragtime Dance" of 1902:

> I attended a ball last Thursday night
> Given by the "Darktown" swells.
> Every coon came out in full dress, alright,
> And the girls were society belles.
>
> The hall was illuminated by electric lights;
> It certainly was a sight to see.
> So many colored folks there without a razor fight,
> 'Twas a great surprise to me.

Joplin's final labors to compose a full-scale "folk opera" – *Treemonisha*, about a Black woman's mission to lead her people "to freedom and equality through education" – are a further testament to his drive to unshackle ragtime from its early "coon song" associations. *Treemonisha* would remain unproduced until 1972, earning Joplin a posthumous Pulitzer Prize for Music in 1976.

Dunbar and Cook's "Darktown Is Out Tonight" was a featured song in their hit show, *Clorindy; or, The Origin of the Cakewalk*, which opened off-Broadway in April of 1898 and – problematic as it was in terms of "coon song" imagery – is "credited with giving birth to black musical comedy." (*Clorindy* also included such indicative songs as "Who Dat Say Chicken in Dis Crowd?" and "The Hottest Coon in Dixie.") It is telling that Cook, who had aspirations for a career as a serious composer, chose to write this show under the pen name "Will Marion" and that, in his next collaboration with Dunbar – *In Dahomey* (1902) – the show included the uplifting song "Swing Along," "a lilting melody with lyrics encouraging black children to be proud of who they are." It was an encouragement that the "Godfather of Soul," James Brown, would amplify and supercharge in the 1970s, in call-and-response mode with a Black children's chorus: "Say It Loud – I'm Black and I'm Proud." As Dunbar and Cook phrased it:

> Swing along, chillun, swing along de lane,
> Lif yo' head and yo' heels might high,
> Swing along chillun, 'tain't a-goin' to rain,
> Sun's as red as a rose in de sky.

> Come along Mandy, come along Sue,
> White folks watchin' and seein' what you do,
> White folks jealous when you'se walkin' two by two,
> So swing along, chillun, swing along!

While the dialect lyrics on the printed page may carry a tinge of minstrelsy for modern readers, the 1903 production of *In Dahomey* at the New York Theater in Times Square – the first full-length Black American musical to be produced on Broadway – was critically noted for its "mastery of sound, movement, timing, and the spoken word." It soon traveled to England, where it boasted over 250 performances in London, including a night at Buckingham Palace.

The battle against minstrelsy and the "coon song" was by now firmly entrenched. It had in fact come a long way since James Monroe Trotter had "established himself as America's first African American music historian" with his *Music and Some Highly Musical People* (1878). In this extended study of over forty Black composers, musicians, and touring groups, Trotter argued that "notwithstanding their lack of a scientific knowledge of music," Black Americans had "long furnished most of the best music that [had] been produced in nearly all of the Southern states." It was just a matter of time before Black music "of the most classical order" would be "rendered in a manner approved by the most exacting critic of the art."

In fact, such classical "rendering" was well under way. In the opera realm, the colatura soprano Marie Selika Williams and her husband, the baritone Sampson Williams, became the first Black Americans to sing at the White House – ironically, for Rutherford B. Hayes, the betrayer of Reconstruction, in 1878. They toured Europe four years later, to great acclaim – in France, Germany, Belgium, and England, where, like Elizabeth Taylor Greenfield before them, they sang at a royal command performance for Queen Victoria. In the 1890s, Sissieretta Jones, dubbed "the Black Patti" after the Italian soprano Adelina Patti, also sang at the White House as well as Carnegie Hall. Her great ambition had been to sing the role of the African queen Sélika in Giacomo Meyerbeer's grand opera *L'Africaine*, "but no white opera company of that day, in the United States, would have even considered such a possibility." Consequently, even while celebrated white mezzo-sopranos were blacking themselves up to play Sélika on the grand operatic stages, Jones was restricted to performing what she called "opera kaleidoscopes" with her concert troupe, the Black Patti Troubadours, offering arias from *Il Trovatore*, *Martha*, and *Lucia*, among other operas.

Figure 9.1 Sissieretta Jones. Concert poster, New York, 1899.
Library of Congress Prints and Photographs Division

It was indeed an uphill battle for Black composers and practitioners of what is still problematically called "serious" – meaning "classical" – music. The conservatory-trained baritone Carroll Clark "chafed at being allowed to sing only sentimental songs about the Old South." When he recorded a duet with the contralto Daisy Tapley in 1894, making Tapley possibly "the first African American woman to record commercially in the United States," their record label – Columbia – refrained from publishing their pictures or mentioning their race. Black musicians and singers would later face the same promotional censorship in the white-dominated country music arena. Both DeFord Bailey in the 1920s and Charley Pride in the 1960s surprised their first audiences on the Grand Ole Opry by being Black, their photographs having been withheld from public view.

By the turn of the century, "distinguished black composers, librettists, lyricists, and performers" – the likes of Cook, Dunbar, Harry T. Burleigh, James Weldon Johnson, J. Rosamond Johnson, and Bob Cole – were gathering for "serious discussions at Marshall's Hotel on West Fifty-third Street in Manhattan" to work out how to "elevate the image of the Negro as writer, composer, and performer" and "remove the minstrel mask from the musical stage." For a start, Cole and Rosamond Johnson removed the word "coon" from their duet performances, pointedly singing "All Boys Look Alike to Me." As Johnson recalled, the word "coon" had "always had a choking effect on their voices." Along with the tenor Sidney Woodward, Johnson also sang in John Isham's operatic review, *Oriental America* (1896), which included arias and choruses from *Rigoletto*, *Faust*, *Carmen*, and *Il Trovatore*, and was the first Black American operatic performance on Broadway. Meanwhile, over on Tin Pan Alley, Johnson's brother, the lyricist James Weldon Johnson, actively eschewed using "the rough, razor-wielding bully and other demeaning stereotypes" of the "coon song." It was he who would soon write the rousing, affirmative "Lift Every Voice and Sing," which in the twenty-first century would still be called "the Black National Anthem" by news outlets reporting the precedence of that song over "The Star-Spangled Banner" at some NFL football games, in solidarity with the Black Lives Matter movement.

But the "coon song" was nothing if not tenacious; and in 1899 a particularly strange raft of such songs began to appear – some of them written by Black songwriters like Irving Jones and *all* of them featuring Filipinos. They had titles like "My Own Manila Sue," "My Filipino Man (Coon Song and Chorus)," "My Filipino Baby," and "My Filipino Leana." The lyrics were truly appalling, as in Jones's "I Want a Filipino Man":

> There's a heap of trouble brewing up in Coontown,
> An' all the real swell coons are getting riled,
> Because a strange Jap just came from Manila,
> About him all the yaller girls are wild.
>
> He says that Aguinaldo is his cousin,
> In the Filipines [sic] he says he's the real gent.
> This black man doesn't talk the real coon rag-time,
> But this coon speaks with a rich Spanish accent.
>
> When that strange Jap struts through Coondom,
> All the wenches stare,
> You will hear them all declare,
> That coon's got white man's hair.

There was also Edgar Smith's equally cringeworthy "Belle ob de Philippines" ("Sung with great success" by Olive Redpath):

> All kin's ob coons yer see, in dis lan' ob de free,
> We'se all us had coons enough to spare.
> Yer can allus fin' a few on Seventh Avenue,
> Dere's more or less niggahs every where.

> But we'se just made a catch, ob a bran new yaller batch,
> Dat roun' about yere ain't been seen.
> She'll be yere might soon, dat pumpkin colored coon,
> Der high-toned belle ob de Philippines.

These and other songs marked one of the most bizarre musical developments to come out of the conflict that began with the sinking of the US battleship *Maine* in the harbor of Havana in February 1898. It ended with a changed America and a changed world. This was Manifest Destiny on overdrive – and it only took a few months, thanks to what President William McKinley's Secretary of State John Hay called "a splendid little war." Many people had seen it coming. José Martí, the Cuban poet and composer of the song "*Guantanamera*," predicted in his 1891 essay, "*Nuestra América*" (Our America): "The scorn of our formidable neighbour who does not know us is Our America's greatest danger. . . . Through ignorance it might even come to lay hands on us." (Martí died four years later, fighting for Cuba's independence from Spain.)

The Spanish colonial authorities maintained that the sinking of the *Maine* was a tragic accident – as many officials in the McKinley administration themselves believed. An apocryphal legend arose that the "Uncrowned King" of the yellow press, William Randolph Hearst, sent his illustrator Frederic Remington to Havana to report on the war build-up there. According to this account, Remington telegraphed to Hearst, "There is no trouble here. There will be no war. I wish to return," to which Hearst supposedly replied: "Please remain. You furnish the pictures, and I'll furnish the war." Whether or not this particular exchange ever took place, there is no doubt that the press did set out to whip up war hysteria, helped along, as it turned out, by a small army of songwriters. Indeed, one music historian reports: "While no precise figures exist for the number of titles published in response to the Maine tragedy, the activity of songwriters, promoters, and entertainers seems to have matched or surpassed that of the national press. More than 60 titles were published within weeks of the sinking of the ship." One songwriting duo known only as "The Brownings" "furnished" (pace Hearst) an indicative piece, oozing with melodrama and shot through with nationalist outrage. "Avenge the Good Ship Maine" was – as the sheet music declares – "Sung with Tremendous Applause by J. Aldrich Libbey and Others" on the vaudeville stage:

> In Havana's deep dark waters, the brave Yankee cruiser lay
> All on board were fast asleep, after the close of day
> While far away from home and friends, without their loved ones nigh
> They little thought how many souls would meet their God on high

Without a moment's warning, a fearful crash was heard
Like the roar of a thousand cannons: this nation's soul was stirred
By a terrible explosion underneath the good ship *Maine*
And we know our Yankee boys were killed by cowardly spies of Spain.

We shall now avenge the death of our brave sailors
Who gave their lives for glorious liberty
So hurrah for Uncle Sam and dear old Glory
For we'll whip Spain and set poor Cuba free.

Other songs were far too coarse to be unveiled on the genteel vaudeville stages: "Here's to the Spaniard, the son-of-a-bitch, / May his balls rot off with the Cuban itch. / May his prick shrivel up like a bamboo cane, / And his asshole whistle 'Remember the Maine.'"

Some historians have placed great emphasis on a telegram received by McKinley in March of 1898, a little more than a month after the *Maine*'s sinking, purportedly clinching his decision to declare war on Spain: "Big corporations here now believe we will have war. Believe all would welcome it as a relief to suspense." The USA did indeed have powerful sugar interests in Cuba, and they played their part; but there was something much more compelling that drove it into full-tilt imperialism in the Atlantic and the Pacific. This was expressed in September 1898 by Republican senatorial candidate Albert Beveridge in his address "The March of the Flag": "Distance and ocean are no arguments. The fact that all the territory our fathers bought and seized is contiguous is no argument ... Cuba not contiguous! Porto Rico not contiguous! Hawaii and the Philippines not contiguous! The oceans make them contiguous. And our navy will make them contiguous."

McKinley's troops quickly fanned out across land and sea, to the left and to the right of the US seaboards. On May Day of 1898, Admiral George Dewey's gunboats destroyed the Spanish fleet in Manila, where Spain had already been fighting off the determined Filipino resistance fighters under Emilio Aguinaldo. Jingoistic songwriters crowed, "Old Glory Holds the Bay":

We've heard of Dewey's vict'ry o'er the ocean,
Joyful tidings from old Glory in the bay,
We'll unite Anglo-Saxon for protection,
With six vessels Dewey's heroes won the day.
Are the noble race destined to save the people
We'll drive the cruel Spaniards from the sea.
Yet remember some are in the dungeon sleeping,
With a cannon ball chained to them, waiting thee.

In July, US Army troops and irregulars, Teddy Roosevelt's "Rough Riders" among them, charged up San Juan Hill in Cuba and defeated the Spanish forces. Two days later, the US Navy destroyed the Spanish fleet in Santiago Bay. Spain surrendered to the USA that month.

But did the Spanish surrender mean that the resistance fighters in Cuba and the Philippines now had a strong ally in the United States? Certainly not. As the disgusted Mark Twain put it: "There must be two Americas: one that sets the captive free, and one that takes a once-captive's new freedom away from him, and picks a quarrel with him with nothing to found it on; then kills him to get his land." With the "splendid little war" concluded by treaty in December 1898, the USA "acquired" Cuba, Puerto Rico, Guam, and the Philippines; it also annexed the Hawaiian Islands for good measure, although they had no connection with Spain. By 1900 the USA "had more than ten million native peoples as 'subjects' and had spread 'the race' ... 'from the rising to the setting sun,'" as the expansionist philosopher John Fiske phrased it. Tin Pan Alley duly composed the soundtrack, with jingoistic titles like "The King of the Sea," "Naval Heroes Waltz," and "For Victory of Our Country's Flag." Amidst all the hoopla, a lone, anonymous folk voice undercut the musical flatulence with satire:

McKinley called for volunteers,
Then I got my gun.
First Spaniard I saw coming,
I dropped my gun and run.
It was all about that Battleship of Maine.

Why are you running?
Are you afraid to die?
The reason that I'm running
Is because I cannot fly.
It was all about that Battleship of Maine.

This singer was conscious, too, of something else – something unlikely to be reflected in, say, James Ross and Karl Vincent's parlor number, "Rule Anglo-Saxia" (1898), whose sheet music trumpeted: "We Must Unite to Save the World for Freedom and Fair Trade." The singer of "The Battleship of Maine" had a few caustic words about "Fair Trade":

What kind of shoes
Do the Rough Riders wear?
Buttons on the side,
Cost five and a half a pair.
It was all about that Battleship of Maine.

What kind of shoes
Do the poor farmers wear?
Old brogans,
Cost a dollar a pair.
It was all about that Battleship of Maine.

Surveying the imperialist wars of 1898–1902 – not only the Spanish-American War but also the Philippine-American War that quickly followed it – Mark Twain predicted US tyranny and dictatorship, both abroad and at home, in a futuristic passage with chilling overtones for his time and ours: "But it was impossible to save the Great Republic. She was rotten to the heart. Lust of conquest had long ago done its work; trampling upon the helpless abroad had taught her, by a natural process, to endure with apathy the like at home."

The USA had had its eyes on Cuba a number of years before the sinking of the *Maine* provided a pretext for military invasion. In 1896, outgoing president Grover Cleveland worried that Cuba lay "so near to us as to be hardly separated from our own territory." Cleveland was even more worried over the possibility that, because of its heavily Black population, the insurgents' victory might lead to "the establishment of a white and black republic" or – even worse – an independent Black nation alongside a white-dominated one. Indeed, in hopes of achieving a US alliance against the Cuban freedom fighters, the Spanish ambassador wrote to Cleveland's Secretary of State Richard Olney: "In this revolution, the negro element has the most important part. Not only the principal leaders are colored men, but at least eight-tenths of their supporters . . . and the result of the war, if the Island can be declared independent, will be a secession of the black element and a black Republic." For this reason, McKinley refused to "recognize the rebels as belligerents or ask for Cuban independence" when he petitioned Congress for a war declaration, and, upon Spain's surrender, "no Cuban was allowed to confer on the surrender, or to sign it." The outcome of the US military adventure in Cuba – and the evident fear of Black power there – certainly problematizes the pride inscribed into a song that lauded the victory of the all-Black Tenth Cavalry Regiment against the Spanish at Las Guasimas, Cuba, at the start of the war:

We used to think the Negro
Didn't count for very much,
Light-fingered in the melon patch
And chicken yards and such.

But we've got to reconstruct our view
On color, more or less,
Now we know about the sentry
At Las Guasimas.

It would be too crude to say that the US soldiers in Cuba – Black and white – laid down their lives for nothing. After all:

> Americans began taking over railroad, mine, and sugar properties when the war ended. In a few years, $30 million of American capital was invested. United Fruit moved into the Cuban sugar industry. It bought 1,900,000 acres of land for about twenty cents an acre. The American Tobacco Company arrived. By the end of the occupation, in 1901 ... at least 80 percent of the export of Cuba's minerals were in American hands, mostly Bethlehem Steel.

As for the Puerto Rican people, who now saw themselves as colonial subjects without citizenship on an island that, above their heads, had been handed over from one imperial power to another through a treaty signed over four thousand miles away in Paris, there was little reason to cheer, however much they might have initially celebrated the Spanish defeat. As a popular song later composed by Rafael Hernández Marín – "*Pobre Borinquen*" (Poor Puerto Rico) – has it:

> With flowers we welcomed them
> With music and flags
> With guitars and violins
> We stared at the colors
> Of their starry banner
> And the enthusiastic island
> Never for once imagined
> It would find itself so hopeless
> When the Yankees took us over.

The historian Paul Ortiz lays out what unfolded, and what would further unfold, for the singers and subjects of "*Pobre Borinquen*":

> The United States exported its weaponized labor relations to Puerto Rico, where big sugar growers counted on police power to crush strikes ... Puerto Rico became, in the words of journalist Juan González, "the richest colony in American history," hugely profitable to US corporations, yet mired in poverty after generations of exploitation by the United States. An impoverished working class began a decades-long exodus to the United States in search of economic security.

On the other side of the globe, the "collective trauma" of the Philippines was being played out with the suppression of the independence struggle led by Aguinaldo – a war that by 1903 would leave more than a million dead, mostly Filipinos. US lawmakers and journalists dubbed Aguinaldo's anticolonial resistance fighters "insurrectionists, thereby delegitimizing their cause. In the US this conflict's name remained 'the Philippine Insurrection' until 1998." Characteristically, Theodore Roosevelt took to calling Aguinaldo a "'renegade Pawnee' and observed that Filipinos did not have the right to govern their country just because they happened to occupy it." The "Indian-hating" terminology was no coincidence: the US top command in the Philippines was led by veterans of the wars against the Lakota, Cheyenne, and Apache. Commodore Dewey referred to Aguinaldo's forces as "Indians" and "vowed to 'enter the city [Manila] and keep the Indians out.'" One US officer wrote to a journalist: "We exterminated the American Indians, and I guess most of us are proud of it, or, at least, believe the end justified the means; and we must have no scruples about exterminating this other race standing in the way of progress and enlightenment, if it is necessary." In a twist of the darkest irony, General Henry Ware Lawton was made commander of the US army of occupation – the same Lawton to whom the Apache chief Geronimo had surrendered in 1886. When Lawton was killed in 1899, it was at the hands of "Filipino insurgents under the leadership of a man named Geronimo."

The Philippines also saw the importation of a "Jim Crow architecture" based on the US belief that "the Negro and the Filipino got along too well together and thus endangered the well-being of the government." But like the Black "Buffalo Soldiers" who had taken up "the white man's burden" against the Indigenous warriors on the Plains, Black American soldiers in the Philippines found themselves in an anomalous position, at once victims and agents of racial defamation. On the one hand, many of their letters home indicate their outrage over the habitual use of the n-word to describe the Filipino resistance fighters. Yet, on the other hand, "they joined whites in calling them 'goo-goos' – as the invaders said, 'all goo-goos look alike to me.' They too took lovers they called 'squaws.'" But for some, like David Fagen, the most famous of the dozen-odd Black soldiers who deserted to join Aguinaldo's forces, the racism and brutality inflicted upon Filipinos by US forces was too much to endure. It was a racism and brutality encapsulated in a little-known song, "The Water Cure in the P.I. [Philippine Islands]," composed by white soldiers and sung, in spite of its "Battle Cry of Freedom" refrain, to the tune of the much more vindictive "Marching Through Georgia." The song celebrates the use of water torture as a means of obtaining information from captured Filipinos:

> Get the good old syringe boys and fill it to the brim
> We've caught another n——r and we'll operate on him
> Let someone take the handle who can work it with a vim
> Shouting the battle cry of freedom.
> (Chorus)

Hurrah Hurrah We bring the Jubilee
Hurrah Hurrah The flag that makes him free
Shove in the nozzle deep and let him taste of liberty
Shouting the battle cry of freedom.

For some at home, all that was left was war-weariness. This surely included the many *Nuevo mexicanos* – New Mexicans – whose fathers, brothers, sons, and husbands, "the sons of *conquistadores*," had ironically enlisted to fight the Spanish in both Cuba and the Philippines "to prove their loyalty to the United States." Their loved ones awaited their return and sang an *indita*, or "little Indian" song, praying for "San Gonzaga de Abaranda and the Virgin to stop the bloodshed":

St. Aloysius Gonzaga of Amarante
appeared on a bridge,
I composed this indita for you
when my son was absent.

St Aloysius Gonzaga of Amarante
appeared on the ocean,
grant me this miracle
I promised to dance for you.

They say the swallow
in one flight crossed the sea,
grant me this miracle
I promised to dance for you.

They say the swallow
in one flight crossed the sea,
in the Philippine Islands
they have finished fighting.

When the last of the blood had seeped into the ground of the Philippine Islands, one of McKinley's peace commissioners – Whitelaw Reid, editor of the *New-York Tribune* – purred with satisfaction at Aguinaldo's surrender and the collapse of the resistance: "The American people are in lawful possession of the Philippines with the assent of all Christendom, with a title as indisputable as its title to California." "Lawful possession": these words were uttered by the man whom Mark Twain had long been calling "Outlaw Reid."

The year of the Spanish-American War – 1898 – also saw the USA secure complete control of the Hawaiian Islands through annexation, although these islands had not been colonized by the Spanish and, on the face of it, had nothing to do with the war with Spain. But the USA was already in the neighborhood, as it were, having assumed military control of the islands in 1874 following the overthrow of Queen Lili'uokalani at the behest of the US planter interests. From that moment, Hawai'i and Hawaiian subjects became exotic fodder for vaudeville and Tin Pan Alley tunesmiths, who in a sense had found themselves in competition with the two final monarchs of the islands, both of whom were themselves established songwriters.

Lili'uokalani recalled in her memoirs, written under house arrest: "To compose was as natural to me as to breathe. . . . I have never yet numbered my compositions but am sure that they must run well up to the hundreds." One of these was the first Hawaiian national anthem, "*He Mele Lahui Hawai'i*," which Lili'uokalani composed in 1866. As she told it, the then-king Kamehameha

> brought to my notice the fact that the Hawaiian people had no national air. Each nation, he said, but ours had its statement of patriotism and love of country in its own music; but we were using for that purpose on state occasions the time-honored British anthem, "God Save the Queen." This he desired me to supplant by one of my own composition. In one week's time I notified the king that I had completed my task.

In 1874, Lili'uokalani's brother Kalākaua, the last king of Hawai'i, wrote what would become the anthem of both the short-lived Hawaiian Republic and, afterwards, the State of Hawai'i: "*Hawai'i Pono'ī*" (Hawai'i's Own), with music by his royal bandmaster, Henri Berger. The lyrics of the chorus are particularly bittersweet, given that the date of the song's composition coincides exactly with that of the US military takeover: "Royal father / Kamehameha / We shall defend / with spears." Music historian Marc Ferris writes: "With their control over the Hawaiian Islands slipping, the royal family fought back in song," but "'The Star-Spangled Banner' eventually drowned out both native Hawaiian anthems."

This fate lends special poignancy to the lyrics of a song that Lili'uokalani had composed in 1878, "*Aloha 'Oe*" (Farewell to Thee), by far her most popular song. "*Aloha 'Oe*" is known throughout the world even by those unaware of its composer. It has been used to signify "Hawaiian-ness" in cartoon series from *Looney Tunes* to *The Simpsons*, and was recorded by the likes of Bing Crosby, Les Paul, Andy Williams, Elvis Presley, Burl Ives, Tia Carrere, and – in his final recording session, on the verge of death – Johnny Cash. The Discogs recorded music database retrieves 5,430 pressings of "*Aloha 'Oe*" between 1910 and the present. The song is as much Lili'uokalani's love letter to her islands as an ode to romantic love: "*Aloha 'oe, aloha 'oe / E ke onaona noho i ka lipo* / A fond embrace, *a ho'i a'e au* / Until we meet again."

Figure 9.2 Lili'uokalani, the last queen of Hawai'i. Photo by Benine, c. 1917. Library of Congress Prints and Photographs Division

Of the many Hawaiian-themed songs and instrumentals coming out of Tin Pan Alley from the mid-1870s to the late 1890s, some of them appear to have honored (or at least sentimentally exploited) the noble tragedies of the last two monarchs, like Louis Bodecker's "Kalakaua March" (1874) or Defries and Libornio's "Queen Liliuokalani March and Songs" (1894). Indeed, some of these might be seen as one songwriter's homage to a fellow songwriter. Others were hardly so kind, such as John Wilson's "Lilikaloo," included in the songbook *National Campaigner (Marching Songs for Republican Clubs)* (1896), with an accompanying note chiding Lili'uokalani as "a foolish woman who simply threw her crown away" by resisting "the present Hawaiian government recognized by the United States." Wilson twisted the knife with a schoolyard taunt: "McKinley is Coming! O! ho! O! ho!" – which proved to be the case.

This was also the case, whether or not recorded in US history books: "In the nineteenth century, over a period of eighty years, the natives of Hawaii were observed to dwindle from diseases and demoralization introduced by Europeans and Euroamericans." And, like their mainland counterparts, the Indigenous Hawaiians faced cultural suppression on the part of white officials and missionaries who saw their ancient practices, like the *hula* dance with its accompanying chants and songs, as corrupting influences and impediments to "civilization." Hence a diatribe by the Hawaiian Evangelical Association damning "the native hulas" as

> a very great public evil, tending as we believe to demoralize the people very rapidly and very generally; to divert them from all industrial and intellectual pursuits; to lay waste their fields and gardens by neglect ... to foster idleness, dissipation and licentiousness; to produce poverty and distress among the people and thus create a strong temptation to supply their wants in unlawful ways.

Unsurprisingly, Hawaiian activists resisting the US takeover had their own musical weaponry in the form of the *Buke Mele Lahui* (Book of National Songs) compiled in 1895 "by F. J. Testa, editor of the proroyalist *Ka Makaainana*, from songs that had been printed and circulated in several Hawaiian-language newspapers." But such elitist musical manifestos were not truly equipped to reflect the human cost of US imperialism in the Hawaiian Islands. For this, we should look to the enormous body of immigration and work songs, most of them anonymously composed, wrung from the hearts of scattered and displaced peoples swept up in the whirlwind of US expansionism.

From roughly 1851 onwards, as the Hawaiian plantation economy expanded and the Indigenous population declined, large-scale sugar planters' associations had been drafting in waves of contract laborers from China, Japan, Micronesia, and – increasingly after the Spanish surrender – the Philippines and Puerto Rico. Groups of laborers also came from Spain itself, along with many from Portugal, Siberia, and even Norway. The Iberian group ("Latin peasants," as the planters liked to call them) arrived in substantial numbers in 1877, with imperialist newspapers editorializing along the racial lines that were typical for the mercantile and plantation classes: "They are a cleanly looking, well-behaved set, with the old fashioned polite manners of the Portuguese and Spanish races," the *Pacific Commercial Advertiser* announced shortly after their arrival in Honolulu. Comparing the Portuguese to the Chinese immigrants, the newspaper added: "The more we have of this sort of immigration the better. They are, as a race ... temperate, painstaking, thrifty and law abiding people." Yet, had a journalist or editor bothered to ask a Portuguese contract laborer how he felt sometime in 1880s, he or she might have heard a song of lamentation:

> Far from my land,
> And here without consolation,
> My heart conceals its apprehension
> Because of being in solitude.

Patience. It doesn't matter.
I shall wait on fate.
Today I shall have a good time
Seeing the death of a pig.

Filipino workers were brought to Hawai'i in increasing numbers, particularly because various exclusion orders from 1882 onwards had curtailed the importation of Chinese laborers. Filipinos were particularly hard-hit by racial stigmatization in Hawai'i, destined to be labeled criminals (or "poke-knives") by the Honolulu police department and constituting, by the middle of the next century, the largest group to face the death penalty – "nearly 80 percent of those executed" although only "one-sixth of Hawaii's population." The other large group "inherited" by the USA were Puerto Ricans, who made a considerable cultural impact on Hawai'i:

> Puerto Rico was considered a prime territory for cheap non-Asian labor, and the annexation of Puerto Rico, Hawai'i, Guam, and the Philippines by the United States in 1898 facilitated the transfer of Puerto Ricans from one US territory (Puerto Rico) to the other (Hawai'i). Between 1900 and 1901, 5,000 Puerto Ricans left the port of Guánica to immigrate to Hawai'i.

At the turn of the century, Hawai'i was under the complete domination of a US corporate oligarchy known as "the Big Five" – all sugarcane processing companies – who controlled the territory "as if it were their personal fiefdom" and, by exploiting ethnic divisions, aimed to "keep workers under control and in competition with one another. As Michael Haas notes, 'One of the ways that the plantation owners fostered inter-ethnic conflict was by intentionally recruiting Puerto Ricans as "scabs" to break up successful union strikes carried out by Japanese workers.'" The *Puertorriqueños* were virtual prisoners on the plantations. So restricted were their movements that they "could not move from one plantation to another without the planters' consent." The majority of early Puerto Rican workers were *jíbaros* – subsistence farmers – from highland areas devastated by hurricanes and depopulation. Their music is still heard in Hawai'i where it is known as *kachi kachi*; and their immigrant songs – some born of alienation and strife – still reside in the collective Puerto Rican consciousness in Hawai'i. One of these is Carlos Fraticelli's "*En Este País Hawaiiano*" (In This Hawaiian Land):

Thirty-three years we have been
In this distant land
As we came, we still are.
In vain do we despair,

The fatherland is far away;
We could be over there
cultivating a little vegetable garden;
For in this damned land,
There is no love, there is no friendship.

Of all the laboring groups brought to the Hawaiian Islands by the plantation elite, it was the Japanese who provided the most extensive body of song, in the form known as *hole hole bushi*. Beginning in the mid-1880s, large numbers of workers from Hiroshima, Wakayama, and Yamaguchi arrived, bringing with them "the Hiroshima rice-threshing melody '*to usu hiki uta*,'" which – like the ubiquitous twelve-bar, I–IV–V chord pattern at the base of innumerable blues songs – appears to have provided the musical setting of this largely female-owned genre. The term *hole hole* derives from the work generally reserved for women: "The Japanese male workers worked in the sugarcane fields cutting the long, rough stalks of cane while the women workers [did] the *hole hole* (the Hawaiian term for the work of stripping cane leaves off the cut stalks)." Song historian Franklin Odo notes: "*Hole hole* work was more than demanding; it required workers to be in the hot fields for ten hours a day, six and a half days every week . . . *Hole hole* work was often assigned to women because, although demanding and nasty, it was considered less arduous than other tasks."

Linguistically, *hole hole bushi* lyrics were couched in "the pidgin of the emerging creolized plantation culture, blending Japanese words with Hawaiian, Chinese, and Portuguese (the languages found among the multinational / multilingual work force) and English (the language of the plantation owners)." Thematically, they were "narratives of shifting landscapes of 'desire' and 'despair,' centered on broken dreams, arduous labor, homesickness, resistance, loneliness, vice, and social and economic inequality. Overall the *hole hole bushi* were found to be rooted in, and a result of, the larger struggles attributable to domination and autonomy common in the plantation structure." Politically, they could be fearless – as on one occasion in 1890 when 170 Japanese workers on the He'eia plantation rebelled against wage cuts and the brutality of the overseers (known by the Portuguese term *lunas*). Their representatives walked over ten miles to present a petition to a plantation official named Nakayama, who "threw their petition on the floor without even reading it and berated them for having the temerity to make complaints and told them that they should realize that they were nothing but mere contract laborers." They took their revenge in song, naming names, in the fields where all could hear them: "The laborers keep on coming / Overflowing these Islands / But it's only Inspector Nakayama / Who rakes in the profits." Other *hole hole bushi* went right to the top of the plantation food chain:

> Hawaii, Hawaii,
> But when I came
> What I saw
> Was hell.
> The boss was Satan,
> The *lunas*, his helpers.

Susan Asai likens the *hole hole bushi* to "the sorrow songs" of enslaved Black Americans before the Civil War: "The major exception is that the *hole hole bushi* conveyed a unique female expression of a Japanese American working-class identity shaped by the American plantation system in Hawaii and its exploitation of a unique form of gender oppression, the practice of recruiting Japanese women as picture brides." The songs indicate that some women tried to make the best of it:

> My husband cuts the cane
> While I do the *hole hole*
> With sweat and tears
> Together we get by
>
> My husband cuts the cane
> I carry the bundles
> Together, a couple,
> We get by.

Others, clearly, could not:

> In the morning darkness
> I endure the beating
> While my tears flow as I water
> The cane fields
> In the morning darkness
> Working without a break
> My tears flow as I water
> The cane fields.

At the very time these women were singing their *hole hole bushi* in the sugarcane fields, US music – and global music, for that matter – was on the brink of a momentous explosion sparked by the seizure of Hawai'i. After annexation, the US Provisional Government imposed a crackdown on the teaching of Indigenous Hawaiian language, song, and dance. As with Alaska Natives and Indigenous peoples on the mainland, the government of the day got what it set out to achieve: a long-lasting cultural eradication. Even today, "a large proportion of Hawaiians reportedly do not understand texts sung in Hawaiian." Consequently "singing or listening to songs sung in Hawaiian becomes an act of social protest."

With the governmental crackdown, Indigenous Hawaiian artists fled the islands to make their creative ways elsewhere – including the USA, for, unlike their colonized brothers and sisters from the Philippines and Puerto Rico, Indigenous Hawaiians "became US citizens after their region became a US Territory by force in 1900." (For *Puertorriqueños*, that mixed blessing would not be offered until 1917.) In 1904, a young Hawaiian named Joseph Kekuku stowed away on a freighter from Honolulu to San Francisco, carrying a new invention of his own making, the steel guitar, which, with its sliding, bending sounds, would soon transform the global soundscape:

Figure 9.3 Sheet music cover of "I Lost My Heart in Honolulu," composed by Will D. Cobb and Gus Edwards, 1916.
Library of Congress Music Division

> We can hear the instrument in Jimmie Rodgers and Son House recordings, or on the silver screen, accompanying Bing Crosby. For a while we see it in the hands of thousands of lei-bedecked haole boys and girls in places like Cleveland, Chicago, or Detroit. We hear it in Bollywood scores, even at the beginning of Warner Brothers cartoons.

There was also the ukulele, the small four-stringed guitar adapted from the Portuguese *cavaquinho* brought to the Hawaiian plantations in 1879 by contract laborers from Madeira. Before long, thanks to the likes of Ernest Kaai, "King" Bennie Nawahi, and George E. K. Awai and his Royal Hawaiian Quartet, the ukulele would infiltrate the consciousness of Tin Pan Alley, sounding "a promise of an island paradise" and sparking a Jazz Age craze for the instrument. As for the "island paradise" itself – a concept not shared by the Indigenous poor or the contract laborers whose songs never made it into the industry catalogs – Tin Pan Alley had its hands full in propagating that musical mythology: "Down in Honolulu in the land of paradise / There's a little hula maiden with dreamy goo goo eyes / She strums the ukulele and she dances in the breeze / And sings to me sweet songs of dear Hawaii."

And then there was "Hula Hula Dream Girl" and "My Bird of Paradise" and "Down Honolulu Way" and "Along the Way to Waikiki" and "Isles of Aloha (Isles of Love)" and "I Lost My Heart in Honolulu." There was "Yaaka Hula Hickey Dula" and "Oh! How She Could Yacki Hacki Wiki Wacki Woo" ("She had a Hula, Hula, Hicki, Boola, Boola in her walk, / She had a Ukalele Wicki, Waili in her talk"). There were scores of others to follow, drowning out the "sorrow songs" so comprehensively that one wouldn't think there could ever be trouble in Paradise.

CHAPTER 10

The Hand That Feeds You

It was all so heady, this new century. There were carriages without horses! A new song had recently appeared – "probably the first music to include the word 'automobile' in its title." This was Grace Walls Linn's "The Automobile Spin." Some of Tin Pan Alley's choicest offerings on the subject began to spin off the presses, as they would continue to do for the rest of the decade, the likes of "The Studebaker Grand March," "In My Merry Oldsmobile," "From Earth to Mars in a Jackson Car," "Mr. Ford's Little Jitney Bus," "Henry's Made a Lady Out of Lizzie," and "Give Me a Spin in Your Mitchell Bill." Specialists in the "coon song" also ran alongside and jumped onto the running board:

> I don't ride in no hitch like dat;
> Ole style buggy hitched to a rat,
> You come aroun' wid an automobile
> 'Lectric pow'r wid a blown up wheel,
> I'se outgrown a horse or a bike,
> Dey can't strike de gait I like.
> If wid me you want to speel
> Jes' come aroun' wid an automo-automobile.

The cities were expanding at a breathless pace, matched by an urban anxiety reflected symbiotically in the work of two brothers: Theodore Dreiser, whose novel *Sister Carrie* (1900) depicted the city as fatal siren for the restless rural soul, and Paul Dresser (né Dreiser), the Tin Pan Alley songwriter whose "She Went to the City" (1904) depicted, well, the same thing: "She grew kind o' restless and wanted to go, / Said she'd be back in a few weeks or so, / She went to the city with a tear in her eye, / But she never returned."

"Progress" was a thing – *the* thing. In 1904 the city of St. Louis stole the starry crown of Chicago, which eleven years earlier had hosted the Columbian Exposition. It was now time to mount the Louisiana Purchase Exposition commemorating Jefferson's doubling of US territory a century before. But how much "progress" had the country seen since

Chicago in 1893? On the one hand, the St. Louis Fair could boast its own "great white Palaces of Machinery and Electricity." These went well beyond the scope of Chicago's technological showpieces, which had been centered, for the most part, on rail transportation. On the other hand, some of the St. Louis exhibitions seemed to be running on re-treads, such as the poor excuses for ethnology in the form of "living exhibits" of "strange peoples" – "Inuits from the Arctic Circle in traditional dress" (in the middle of August) with "their panting sled dogs"; "African forest people"; and, from the newly subdued Philippines, a fresh bunch to marvel at: "Moro tree-dwellers," "Igorot dog-eaters," and "white-duck-attired Visayans who sang 'The Star-Spangled Banner' in American English." And then there was Geronimo, the broken Apache chief who now "had a booth in the Indian School [Exhibit], between Pueblo potters and Pueblo women grinding corn and making bread, where he made and sold bows and arrows, and sang and danced for customers."

"Progress" had certainly taken its toll on America's First Peoples. Since the Dawes Act of 1887, which broke up the Indigenous lands into separate allotments with the aim of inculcating individualism at the expense of a collective tribal identity, Indigenous culture had been under intense attack. The memories of the Ghost Dance were still fresh, and the zealots in the BIA were ever determined to eradicate religious dances and ceremonial music altogether. In addition to the "Indian Schools" with their curricula designed to "kill the Indian and save the man," there were devastating institutions like the Hiawatha Asylum for Insane Indians, which opened in 1903 in Canton, South Dakota. A historian writes: "Parents who opposed sending their children to boarding schools, individuals who restricted assimilation, those who argued with BIA agents, those too rowdy or bothersome, or those who steadfastly practiced indigenous religions, could be and often were committed to Hiawatha." Here it was forbidden to practice "Native dances and music, even to mourn the dead." As one Hiawatha alumna recalled, it was "spiritual murder."

Some lone white individuals fought against this spiritually and culturally murderous tide. One was the song collector Frances Densmore, who began her field work in 1907 among a vast array of peoples from the Chippewa to the Winnebago. She recalled: "I have met with much opposition in securing [songs], some of the old men insisting that it were better to let the songs die than to sing them for any fee less than a horse." At roughly the same time, Natalie Curtis was embarking on her mission to recover what music she could, a project culminating in *The Indians' Book* of 1907, which preserved the songs and folklore of eighteen tribes. As far as it could be achieved in the context of early, often paternalistic, ethnomusicology,

Curtis aimed to give Indigenous people ownership of the book, not only through their songs and narratives but also through their contributed artwork. She detested the BIA's cultural eradication policy, damning its effect as "racial suicide" and lamenting that the children at BIA boarding schools "must remain for five years without returning home. . . . It is not at all uncommon for the Indian child to have forgotten his own language during the school period, and so, on his return, to be unable to speak with his parents." Curtis made a point of including in *The Indians' Book* a translated lament sung to her by a young Lakota boarder recounting her departure for the school:

> For the last time, come greet me again,
> For the last time, come greet me again,
> Dear friend, I loved thee alone!
> Now to school I'm going away;
> For the last time, come greet me again,
> For the last time, come take my hand.

Like Densmore, Curtis faced reluctance from her Indigenous sources, so effective was the stigmatization and the fearful atmosphere imposed by the BIA. As one Hopi chief asked her: "Will not the superintendent be angry if you do this thing? Are you sure that you will not bring trouble upon us? White people try to stop our songs and dances, so I am fearful of your talk." Another chief, from the Pima people, was willing to lower his guard with the explanation:

> On our reservation no man dares to sing . . . White people do not like us to sing Indian songs. They think our songs are bad. . . . It is well that you have come to do this thing for us, but we have not money to offer you in return. The white people living up above us on the river have taken all the water, so that our fields are dry. We are poor.

One of Curtis's sources was Geronimo himself, interviewed just as he was completing his transformation from fugitive warrior to fairground exhibit. How defiant and soaring was his song for this white woman who had apparently gained his trust:

> Said Geronimo: "The song that I will sing is an old song, so old that no one knows who made it. It has been handed down through generations and was taught to me when I was but a little lad. It is now my own song. It belongs to me.
>
> "This is a holy song (medicine-song), and great is its power. The song tells how, as I sing, I go through the air to a holy place where Yusun [the Supreme Being] will give me power to do wonderful things. I am surrounded by little clouds, as I go through the air I change, becoming spirit only . . ."

O, ha le
O, ha le!
Through the air
I fly upon a cloud
Towards the sky, far, far, far,
O, ha le
O, ha le!
There to find the holy place,
Ah, now the change comes o'er me!

And what a contrast this spirit was to that of the "prisoner of war" performing at the St. Louis World's Fair under the watchful eyes of his "keeper" – the Christianized, hatted, be-suited old Geronimo who surely knew better than he let on when describing in his memoirs the music of his fellow sideshow performers, the Filipino Igorots. Of those "little brown people . . . that United States troops captured recently on some islands far away from here," Geronimo wrote:

> They did not wear much clothing, and I think that they should not have been allowed to come to the Fair. But they themselves did not seem to know any better. They had some little brass plates, and they tried to play music with these, but I did not think it was music – it was only a rattle. However, they danced to this noise and seemed to think they were giving a fine show.

Historian Richard Drinnon sums it up:

> So declaimed the great old man after taking that step to "civilization." At the time Geronimo was in his brief Christian phase, desperately wanted to return to his own country in Arizona to die, and treacherously said what whites had given him to understand they wanted him to say. Alas, it was not enough to get him home, but for this one revealing moment the ends of the empires came together, victims face to face.

Perhaps Geronimo *was* being "treacherous." Or, perhaps he would do and say anything to protect his people. After all, he had so debased himself as to ride in the inaugural procession for President Theodore Roosevelt in 1905, only to endure Roosevelt's public scolding:

> After the parade, Geronimo met with Roosevelt in what the *New York Tribune* reported was a "pathetic appeal" to allow him to return to Arizona. "Take the ropes from our hands," Geronimo begged, with tears "running down his bullet-scarred cheeks." Through an interpreter, Roosevelt told Geronimo that the Indian had a "bad heart." "You killed many of my people; you burned villages . . . and were not good Indians." The president would have to wait a while "and see how you and your people act" on their reservation.

Figure 10.1 Geronimo and Apaches on exhibit at the St. Louis World's Fair, 1904.
Library of Congress Prints and Photographs Division

What else could Geronimo do? He went so far as to commence his memoirs with a dedication: "Because he has given me permission to tell my story; because he has read that story and knows I try to speak the truth; because I believe that he is fair-minded and will cause my people to receive justice in the future; and because he is chief of a great people, I dedicate this story of my life to Theodore Roosevelt, President of the United States." Geronimo remained a prisoner until his death at Fort Sill, Oklahoma, in 1909. But at least his captors, in their magnanimity, had given him a 1905 Model C Locomobile to ride around in – the car bitterly memorialized in Michael Martin Murphey's 1972 anthem, "Geronimo's Cadillac." Now, that was progress.

Meanwhile, Tin Pan Alley was having a field day with a new, racist twist to the old "vanishing Indian" theme. The songwriting duo of Harry Williams and Egbert Van Alstyne came out in 1903 with "Navajo, Navajo," a "coon song" in which a Black suitor appeals to a Navajo maiden: "Nava, Nava, my Navajo / I have a love for you that will grow, / If you'll have a coon for a beau, / I'll have a Navajo." Among the "hundreds of Indian-themed songs" that followed were many that placed "Indianness in an unceasing array of thematic and often bizarre contexts." One of these was Jack Drislane and Theodore Morse's "Arrah Wanna: An Irish Indian Matrimonial Venture" (1906):

> 'Mid the wild and woolly prairies lived an Indian maid,
> Arrah Wanna queen of fairies of her tribe afraid
> Each night came an Irish laddie buck
> With a wedding ring,
> He would sit outside her tent and with his bag pipes loudly sing.
> "Arrah Wanna, on my honor, I'll take care of you,
> I'll be kind and true, we can love and bill and coo,
> In a wig-wam built of shamrocks green, we'll make those red men smile,
> When you're Misses Barney heap much Carney from Killarney's Isle."

Even the more serious, progressive musical efforts could be bogged down in retrograde racial imagery or exoticism at Indigenous people's expense. Opera historian John Dizikes points to Bob Cole and Rosamond Johnson's *The Red Moon* (1909), which "capitalized on the popularity of Native American themes and subjects" by presenting, for a plot,

> the improbable kidnapping and rescue of a young girl of mixed parentage, African American mother, Native American father. Clichés abounded in story and music. "Bleeding Moon" was a song about a Native American curse, "Big Red Shawl" a love song, while "Life Is a Game of Checkers" punned about reds and blacks mixing together. There was no pretense at using Native American music.

But after all, Black American composers, librettists, and performers were still facing problems with the whole idea of "progress" in their own music. Rosamond's brother, James Weldon Johnson, had written into the lyrics of "Lift Every Voice and Sing": "Sing us a song full of the faith that the dark past has taught us, / Sing a song full of the hope that the present has brought us." As Ian Peddie notes: "At the time when Johnson articulated his vision, there were many symphony orchestras and opera companies that prohibited black players." Some scholars have argued that, if anything, both Johnsons, as well as Cole, ultimately concluded that "progress" in Black American music would mean not only "clean[ing] up the caricature" (as Rosamond phrased it) but eradicating whatever it was that might flag up "a distinctive racial identity." Hence Lester Levy's conclusion: "In the lyrics of the most popular Cole and Johnson songs the team succeeded in cutting away the largely obnoxious racial stereotypes of the coon song, but they could only replace them with the equally stereotyped, through essentially non-racial, emotions of Tin Pan Alley."

But for Cole and the Johnson brothers, surely "a distinctive racial identity" was inscribed into the very origins and structures of the music that they absorbed and which they wished to advance. In 1903 they completed *The Evolution of Ragtime* – as they described it, "a musical suite of six songs illustrating Negro music," which modestly foretold the grander, historically themed compositions of Duke Ellington, Wynton Marsalis, and Irvin Mayfield. The "racial identity" of ragtime – whether played by Black or white musicians – would have been self-evident. It could hardly have been otherwise, given that the white musical establishment habitually associated ragtime with its Black origins, in whatever racially defamatory terms. The *Musical Courier* of New York, for instance, damned ragtime as "symbolic of the primitive morality and perceptible moral limitations of the negro type. With the latter, sexual restraint is almost unknown." It was partially in order to challenge such defamation that Cole and the Johnsons embarked upon their *Evolution of Ragtime* project.

The same year, Scott Joplin mounted his now-lost ragtime opera, *A Guest of Honor*, commemorating Booker T. Washington's 1901 invitation to dinner at the Roosevelt White House – an event that earned competing volumes of pride and scorn in the Black community. Washington's perceived accommodation with racial separatism would perhaps earn its greatest musical denunciation in the bluesman Gus Cannon's "Can You Blame the Colored Man?" (1927), which presents Washington as a minstrel clown making "goo-goo eyes" at the White House spread – a buffoon who "almost changed his color / When Roosevelt said to come in." But for Joplin, Cole, and the Johnsons, such a grand, public acknowledgment of a leading Black intellectual's stature was decidedly a signal of progress in itself.

What would *not* be accepted as a signal of progress was the steady "deracialization of ragtime," as white-penned songs proliferated with the snowballing of the ragtime craze in the first decades of the twentieth century. By the time of Lewis Muir's "Waiting for the Robert E. Lee" and Irving Berlin's "Alexander's Ragtime Band" and "Everybody's Doin' It" (all 1912, and all proclaiming themselves as authentic ragtime), James Weldon Johnson explicitly spelled out the claim to Black ownership:

> The first so-called Ragtime songs to be published were actually Negro secular folk songs that were set down by white men, who affixed their own names as composers. In fact, before the Negro succeeded fully in establishing his title as creator of his secular music the form was taken away from him and made national instead of racial.

In spite of this claim, Johnson was himself conflicted. He was proud of ragtime, but – as his novel *The Autobiography of an Ex-Colored Man* (1912) makes clear – ragtime would not come into its own until it was accepted as a legitimate "folk source" that could be assimilated "into the European classical tradition." The protagonist of Johnson's *Autobiography* is a ragtime pianist who harbors a wish "to voice all the joys and sorrows, the hopes and ambitions, of the American Negro in classic musical form." This same wish was expressed, that very year, by another leading figure in Black American musical history, the composer and bandleader James Reese Europe. In 1912, Europe staged a "Concert of Negro Music" at Carnegie Hall with the explicit intention of showing "to the public of New York what the Negro race has done and can do in music." Like many of his classically trained Black colleagues, Europe faced the dilemma of choosing between "a career as an unsuccessful serious musician or a career as a popular entertainer, playing music that the public expected Negro musicians to play." In fact, Europe aimed to help Black musicians achieve both. He established the Clef Club in New York in 1910, which focused on training in both popular music and the classics, and, the following year, cofounded the Music School Settlement for Colored People in Harlem.

A handful of Black artists were able to forge eminent careers by "transforming the spiritual into Western European-styled arias and hymns." The leading figure in this project was the composer and baritone Harry T. Burleigh. In 1893, Burleigh sang on "Colored American Day" at the Columbian Exposition in Chicago, followed by a series of performances with the Victor Herbert orchestra in New York's white resorts. He also sang with Sissieretta Jones – "the Black Patti" – in Washington, DC. In New York, Burleigh introduced the visiting Bohemian composer Antonin Dvořák to the African American spiritual. When Dvořák's Symphony No. 9, "From the New World," premiered in New York in 1893, it "incorporated elements of the spirituals that [Burleigh] had sung for the composer in his study."

Yet, for all Burleigh's deep immersion into the spirituals, the operas of Wagner and Puccini, the songs of Beethoven, Schubert, Schumann, and Grieg, and the compositions of his professed "models" Brahms and Debussy, even he had to take a dive occasionally into the dubious arena of popular orientalist desire. His *Saracen Songs* (1914), based on the "pseudo-Persian and East Indian lyrics" of Fred Bowles, fed into the public hunger for the "exotic" in the wake of the Columbian Exposition, the St. Louis World's Fair, and the continuing adventures of US imperialism in the Pacific. In this sense, Burleigh's "career-long efforts to counteract the negative presentation of black exoticism" did little to counteract the same with regard to Asian exoticism.

Not that Burleigh was alone in this lapse. As we have seen with respect to Hawai'i, Tin Pan Alley had no trouble in transforming the conquered landscape into "a backdrop for romance." Vague musical conceptions of the Middle East and South Asia followed, with North Africa sometimes thrown in, the songs freighted with "camels, temple bells, sand, and mystery." The "caravan" became a curiously strong figure, popping up in Irving Berlin's "Araby" (1915), Wallace and Weeks's "Hindustan" (1918), and Jones and Stern's "Turkestan" (1919). It is a testament to the tenacity of that particular signifier – "caravan" – that as late as 1936, Duke Ellington and Juan Tizol could apply it as a title to what became a jazz instrumental classic, with relatively few aware, even now, of the exoticized lyrics written by Irving Mills. As Ted Gioia notes, Ellington "understood the appeal of 'Caravan' almost from the start, especially since it fit perfectly with the musical exoticism that patrons were demanding at his regular gig at the Cotton Club in Harlem."

But why travel halfway around the world to look for the exotic, when you could find it in your own backyard? There was still Chinatown to rely on – of which Tin Pan Alley was well aware. "Chin Chin Chinaman," from the show *Chinatown Charlie* (1906); "Chinatown, My Chinatown," from *Up and Down Broadway* (1910); and "Dance Chinoise," "My Yellow Jacket Girl," "Down in Chinatown," "Chinese Waltz," "China Rose," and "Chu Chin Chow" (all between 1911 and 1917) were just a handful of the literally hundreds of Chinese-themed songs ushering in the new century. The old Gold Rush-era stereotypes of a Chinatown populated by the "'Heathen Chinee,' laundryman, or servant" had by now morphed into a realm of "'dreamy summer nights' (a subtle reference to the perception of widespread opium use) in the Chinese immigrant section of an unnamed American city."

Chinese American artists might try and counter the trend and take ownership of their own representations in a number of ways. They might step onto the vaudeville stage themselves and sing "Tin Pan Alley songs in Cantonese," or even in English with – as one critic wrote of the singer Chee Toy – "a purity of diction many American soubrettes might emulate." They might even put on blackface and sing "coon songs," as many did, sometimes confusing critics as to whether they were Chinese Americans made up as African Americans or "African Americans in yellowface." They could also turn the tables on the Irish minstrel performers who had for so long slandered them with the "John Chinaman" stereotype, and sing "My Irish Molly" or "Mother Machree" to critical acclaim: "The Chinaman's Irish dialect impersonation is said to be a screamingly funny act." Or they might ignore vaudeville altogether and turn to the nourishment of Cantonese opera, with theaters having sprung up "on every block" of San Francisco's Chinatown. Touring companies traveled to Chinatowns across the country with operatic epics of the classical Chinese "warrior-scholar" Kwan Kung or new operas based on the ordeal of immigration – in particular, imprisonment in the detention center on Angel Island in San Francisco Bay, the West Coast counterpart to New York's Ellis Island.

Angel Island also inspired the many songs of sorrow carved into the walls of the *Muk uk* or "Wooden Barracks" on *Tongsaan Matau* – "the China Dock," where newly arrived immigrants were "processed" in the wake of the Chinese Exclusion Act of 1882. Those who didn't fit into the restricted categories still permitted by the Exclusion Act (such as merchants, diplomats, clergy, and teachers) were "detained for several weeks, months, or even longer," and forbidden from "leaving the compound or meeting any visitors from the outside." As one verse reads in translation: "You don't uphold justice, you Americans, / You detain me in prison, guard me closely. / Your officials are wolves and tigers, / All ruthless, all wanting to bite me." Another:

> A weak nation can't speak up for herself.
> Chinese sojourners have come to a foreign country.
> Detained, put on trial, imprisoned in a hillside building;
> If deposition doesn't exactly match: the case is dead and in a bind.
> No chance for release.
> My fellow countrymen cry out injustice:
> The sole purpose is strict exclusion, to deport us all back to Hong
> Kong.
> Pity my fellow villagers and their flood of tears.

The anonymous verses spread themselves relentlessly across the walls of Angel Island, beginning in 1910 and continuing until 1940, when much of the detention center was destroyed by fire. Scholars have identified the Chinese "classical verse forms" in which all of the Angel Island writings were couched: the "*qi yan jeuju* or 'seven-character abbreviated verse,' *qi yan lüshi* or 'seven-character regulated verse,' *gu shi* or 'ancient verse,' and 'four syllable verse' patterned after works in the *Shi Jing* or *The Book of Poetry* (dating roughly from between the twelfth through the seventh centuries BCE)" – and all written by laborers and "commoners" deemed too lowly to be admitted into the USA. The loneliness of a detained immigrant, a woman likely to be deported, still resonates in history, long after the prison walls have crumbled:

In the quiet of night I heard the faint shrieking of wind
And out of this landscape of visions and shadows a poem grew.
The floating clouds, the fog, darken the sky.
The moon shines softly as the insects chirp.
Grief and bitterness are sent by heaven.
A lonely shadow sits, leaning by the window.

Another anonymous voice bursts out in anger:

American laws are fierce like tigers:
People are jailed inside wooden walls.
Detained, interrogated, and tortured,
Birds plunged into an open trap – O, sufferings!
Tragedy, to whom can I complain –
I yell to the sky: There is no way out!
If only I had known the difficulty of passing the Golden Gate!
Fed up with this treatment, I regret my journey here.

For those Chinese who had managed to pass through the Golden Gate on either side of the Chinese Exclusion Act, the songs of sorrow continued. Thousands of them were collected in San Francisco between 1911 and 1915 and compiled into a two-volume treasury, *Songs from Gold Mountain.* Many of the songs were based on folk forms such as the "*muk-yu go* (Cantonese wood-fishhead chants or songs), a thirty-six syllable verse poetic chant accompanied by the metrical beating of a fishhead-carved woodblock." Nearly all were composed by men, either the solitary bachelors who had grown old since their arrival in the Gold Rush days or the stranded family men whose memories of wives' and children's faces had grown dim. They sang of desolation:

A transient living beneath a stranger's
fence.
Cruelties increase day by day.
Though innocent, I am arrested and thrown
in jail;
Pathetic the lonely bachelors stranded in a
foreign land.
O, let's all go home.
Spare ourselves of this mighty tyrant.

They sang of familial heartbreak:

How was I to know I would be stranded here for so long?
Had I known, I wouldn't have come at all.
Separated by distant mountains and vast seas,
I've forsaken my wife and children for money.
O, my heart bleeds in pain –
A sojourner thousands of miles away from home.

Some even attempted to imagine and reconstruct the yearning – and even the bitterness – of those left behind:

> We were married for only a few nights;
> You left home for Gold Mountain.
> It has been a long twenty years and you haven't returned.
> For this, I embrace only resentment in my bedroom.
> Sigh after sigh –
> You've traveled far away; you are not coming home.
> Everything brings me sorrow, I no longer put on rouge.
> Endless longing for you only leads to streams of tears.

One of the most intriguing of the Angel Island verses speaks of an unhappy fellowship in suffering. It must have been carved into the walls sometime after 1929, when the "Undesirable Aliens Act," spearheaded by the white supremacist senator from South Carolina, Coleman Blease, began targeting Mexican immigrants specifically – for the first time since the top half of Mexico was lost to the USA. The imprisoned Chinese immigrant writes: "Detained in this wooden house for several tens of days / Because of the Mexican exclusion laws. / It's a pity heroes have no place to exercise their prowess. / I can only await the word so I can snap my whip and gallop."

That breathtaking image of snapping the whip and galloping – composed, as it was, from inside a prison fortress – might just as well have been used to describe one of the most legendary Mexican border figures of all time, "the Hispanic David to the American Goliath": the vaquero Gregorio Cortéz, who began to appear in border corridos from the moment of his capture by Texas Rangers in 1901. The various versions of "The Ballad of Gregorio Cortéz" focus on the hero's epic flight along the border after killing the "Anglo sheriff" who had killed his brother. All of them pit "the intelligence and courage of the vaquero" against the "stupidity and cowardice of the Anglo cowboy":

> In the ranch corral
> they managed to surround him.
> A little more than 300 men
> and there he gave them the slip.
> There around Encinal
> from all that they say
> They had a shoot-out
> and he killed another sheriff.
>
> Gregorio Cortéz said,
> with his pistol in his hand,
> "Don't run, you cowardly Rangers
> from one lone Mexican."

He turned toward Laredo
without a single fear,
"Follow me, you cowardly Rangers,
I am Gregorio Cortéz."

"The Ballad of Gregorio Cortéz" reflects, among other things, the bitter situation of all Mexicans in what became the US states of Texas, New Mexico, Arizona, and California in the decades following the Mexican–US War. Although the historical Cortéz was born in Mexico, he and his brother had settled in Texas, where new laws and authority figures had come to impose a racially and culturally discriminatory regime on the Mexicans who had lived there for centuries. The corrido accurately depicts what had in fact happened: an Anglo sheriff had come to question the Cortéz brothers about a stolen horse. Linguistic confusion led to a gunfight. The gunfight led to the birth of a solitary folk hero and a store of songs that have enabled "the collective voice of Mexican Americans to be heard."

The corrido developed in the borderlands "primarily as a mestizo cultural form, one associated with the rise of a national consciousness especially during the early decades of the twentieth century and in the context of border conflicts" between Mexico and the USA. Many corridos depict border crossings and the "Mexican strength of resistance to American culture and ideology." The hero figures need not all be gunfighters and fugitives like Joaquín Murieta, Gregorio Cortéz, and Pancho Villa; they may simply be poor workers who are better at their jobs than the gringos, as in the corrido "*Kiansas II*":

Five hundred steers there were,
All big and quick;
Thirty American cowboys
Could not keep them bunched together.

Then five Mexicans arrived,
All of them wearing good chaps;
And in less than a quarter-hour,
They had the steers penned up.

Those five Mexicans
Penned up the steers in a moment
And the thirty Americans
Were left staring in amazement.

Or they could simply be deportees – especially after the "Undesirable Aliens Act" of 1929 – thrown out of the land that their grandparents had called home:

Oh my beloved countrymen
I suffered a lot.
The light skinned men are very wicked.
They take advantage of the occasion.
And all the Mexicans
are treated without compassion.
There comes a large cloud of dust,
with no consideration.
Women, children and old ones
are being driven to the Border.
We are being kicked out of this country.
Good-bye beloved countrymen,
we are being deported.
But we are not bandits,
we came to work.

"We came to work": this was the mantra of millions. In 1850, the US census counted a little over two million foreign-born people living in the country; by the turn of the century it had risen to over ten million. By the start of World War I in Europe it would rise to over thirteen million. They all "came to work" – and many came to escape persecution and death. Some Tin Pan Alley voices suggested that they were not sufficiently grateful:

Last night as I lay a-sleeping,
A wonderful dream came to me,
I saw Uncle Sammy weeping
For his children from over the sea;
They had come to him friendless and starving,
When from tyrant's oppression they fled,
But now they abuse and revile him,
Till at last in just anger he said:

"If you don't like your Uncle Sammy,
Then go back to your home o'er the sea
To the land from where you came,
Whatever be its name;
But don't be ungrateful to me!
If you don't like the stars in Old Glory,
If you don't like the Red, White and Blue,
Then don't act like the cur in the story
Don't bite the hand that's feeding you."

In the borderlands between Tin Pan Alley and opera – the developing territory of musical theater – George M. Cohan, "the man who owned Broadway," began the century by planting the flag for both nativism and its hypocritical twin, imperialism. As his lyrics suggest, all-American values must be cherished and protected at home, but the USA should be ever at the ready to export those values to foreign shores, solicited or otherwise. Cohan's "Yankee Doodle Boy," from the musical *Little Johnny Jones* (1904), betrays a fondness for Roosevelt's Rough Riders in Cuba: "Father was so Yankee hearted / When the Spanish War was started / He slipped upon his uniform / And hopped up on a pony." The refrain suggests an American's right to go anywhere he pleases, anytime he pleases: "Yankee Doodle came to London / Just to ride the ponies / I am the Yankee Doodle boy." Cohan left no doubt where he stood two years later with the musical *George Washington, Jr.* (1906), which introduced one of his most famous anthems, "You're a Grand Old Flag." The lyrics burst with images of swelling military bands and armies ever at the ready to go "Over There" – wherever "There" might be.

Indeed, fifteen years before Cohan's "Over There" led the charge for US entry into World War I (1917), the Platt Amendment shoehorned into the constitution of newly independent Cuba the right and promise of US military intervention there (implicitly at times of the more powerful nation's choosing) as well as the right to secure Cuban lands for US military bases such as Guantánamo. At this very time, the Supreme Court was advising that civil control of the newly acquired territories might not go as smoothly as the champions of Manifest Destiny would hope: "If those possessions are inhabited by alien races, differing from us in religion, customs, laws, methods of taxation, and modes of thought, the administration of government and justice, according to Anglo-Saxon principles, may for a time be impossible." In which case, they shall "be governed by the military power under the control of the President as commander in chief." The protections of the Constitution may not follow the flag "Over There," but the armies can, and will.

But what of those millions who had cherished and acted upon their dreams of coming "Over Here"? As we have seen, Angel Island awaited them on the West Coast, where they carved their songs of sorrow into the walls. On the East Coast, the walls of Ellis Island, which "processed" arriving immigrants from 1892 to 1924, held their own secrets in the form of graffiti illustrations and writings in a kaleidoscopic array of languages: Arabic, Armenian, Chinese, Czech (Bohemian), French, German, Greek, Polish, Romanian, Russian, Slovenian, Spanish, and Yiddish. The walls of the Main Building, detention rooms, and dormitories were covered with voicings of hope and despair, revealed in the 1980s during Ellis Island's restoration and conversion into a museum. To be sure, not all the graffiti took the form of song lyrics, but some did – notably, some Greek verses based on established and widely recognized emigrant songs beginning with the curse "Damn you [anathema to you] America," for draining the villages of their young men. One faint, fragmented echo awaited discovery:

Anastasios Karatzias from village of
... Ntsiva
... located ... Greek in this prison
... the sins of the land ... America with the ... took all the young men ...
we are wandering, the poor souls, in order to make money ...
The foreign lands, the pains, the slavery ...
Travelling in the ocean ... To get to dry land ...
In Kasigkari of America in the unfair prison
Anastasios Karatzias
From Ntsiva

Pogroms raged, not only against Jews on the fringes of the Russian empire but also in Canada – in British Columbia, from whence, in 1907, the first substantial population of Sikhs arrived in the USA, fleeing "anti-Oriental riots." Upon settling in California, "they soon became isolated by restrictive immigration laws that prevented them from bringing brides or relatives from the Punjab to join them." Armenians fleeing Turkish massacres in 1894 and 1895 began the "mass exodus" that by 1914 saw "about 100,000 Armenians living in America." The New York-based Armenian Education Foundation published a collection of their "songs of despair and hope," such as Nahabed Kouchag's "*Bantookhd Ar Groong*" (The Migrant to the Crane):

I have left my vineyards and all my wealth.
I've gone so far away – my soul aches as I sigh.
O dear crane, stay a while – let your voice touch my soul.
O crane, do you have any word from our dear country?

In my letters I wrote that while I am here,
Not one single day of joy and happiness I know.
My dear ones, I yearn for you all.
O crane, do you have any word from our dear country?

Bulgarians in New York likewise appealed to nature for word of home and loved ones: "Tell me, white cloud, tell me please, I ask you, / Where you come from, say where have you been to? / Have you seen the house of my dear father, / Have you heard the voice of my dear mother?"

Workers from Poland – in the midst of that nation's "first wave" of US immigration, landed in the steel mills of Michigan, soon to lament:

> I came to that America,
> I found a job
> In the steel mill.
>
> I work, that's how I work, I watch my job
> And the English [i.e., the American] boss
> Still goddamns me.
>
> Let him goddamn me, I will not quit my job.
> When the Lord God will give me health,
> I will return to my country.

Hungarians had been arriving in small numbers since about 1800, a trickle that began to swell in the 1860s with emigrants fleeing the long and arduous military service in the Austro-Hungarian armies. Other reasons included escaping from local or regional blood feuds, or simply "the hard economic situation": "God damn the noble lords, / They thrash and beat the poor peasants. / You cannot subsist in this country, / You must emigrate to America!" A trio of Hungarian immigrant songs recorded in the Midwest just prior to the US entry into World War I reflects a store of emotion, from initial skepticism –

> America is the land of plenty and pure gold,
> Fried pigeons fly into one's mouth I'm told,
> Tell your tales, my good man, just go on,
> I'll get the best of you yet bye and bye . . .

– to disillusion and self-recrimination:

> Why did I come
> If not for cursed gold!
> No judge's sentence
> Compelled me to flee,
> Nor was it evil saying that pursued me;
> Just gold, shining gold
> Did I want to see . . .

– to a defiance born of ancient, poisonous bigotry, inevitably transported with its carrier across the Atlantic: "God save America forever. / I shall never leave her. / I prefer to dig in the mine / Rather than to be at home, the hired man of the Jew." Another song found among Hungarians in Connecticut begins with the same blessing – perhaps indicating a shared folk lyric – but with an opposite conclusion: "God save America forever, / But just let me get out of there!"

Many Slovakians traveled out from Ellis Island to the steel mills in the Midwest and Pennsylvania, where – in Pittsburgh – steelworker Andrew Kovaly was charged with the task of informing the newly arrived wife of a colleague that her husband had been killed on the job. Out of this tragedy came one of the most well-known immigrant songs, "He Lies in the American Land," with Kovaly's Slovak lyrics of 1900 translated and set to music by Pete Seeger and, later, forming the basis of Bruce Springsteen's song "American Land," on his album *Wrecking Ball* (2012). Kovaly's lyrics swiftly encapsulated, in four stanzas, the journey from hope to the grave:

> Ah, my God what is this land of America?
> So many people traveling there.
> I will go too, for I am still young,
> God the Lord will grant me good luck there.
>
> You my wife stay here till you hear from me.
> When you get my letter put everything in order.
> Mount a raven black steed, a horse like the wind,
> Fly across the ocean to join me here.
>
> Ah, but when she arrived in this strange land
> Here in McKeesport, this valley,
> This valley of fire,
> Only his grave, his blood did she find.
> Over it bitterly she cried.
>
> "Ah my husband, what have you done to this family of yours?
> What can you say to these children, to these children you orphaned?"
> "Tell them, my wife, not to wait, not to wait, not to wait for me.
> Tell them I lie here in the American land."

Some immigrant communities, notably the Lithuanian and the German, developed a strong tradition of socialist song within the broader arena of nationalist music activities. For the Lithuanians, a secular choral movement split off from its original church base, with the first Lithuanian secular choir founded in New York in 1894. With the arrival of the nationalist composers Mikas Petrauskas and Stasys Šimkus in 1907 and 1915 respectively, the choirs took on a particularly political bent. Hence the establishment of the *Susivienijimas Amerikos lietuvių sicuakustyų chorų*

(Union of American Lithuanian Socialist Choirs) in Chicago. Šimkus explained his musical mission in the Lithuanian American press: "I came to tell you about the misery of the Motherland and look for help for your shelterless and starving parents, brothers and sisters, wives and children."

German communities in the USA already had a well-established tradition of male choirs dating back to the 1830s and singing festivals, or *Sängerfest*, dating from 1849. These were mostly meant to bolster cultural pride and cohesion – a retention of "Germanness" and a connection to *die Heimat* (homeland) – based on a heavy component of Bach, Mozart, Beethoven, Wagner, and Brahms. By the turn of the century, a harder, more assertive edge had arrived with socialist workers' choirs sprung up in major centers of German immigration: Milwaukee, New York, Philadelphia, Chicago, and elsewhere. Conductors like Carl Sahm of the *New-York Sozialistischer Männerchoir* also composed some of the repertoire. Sahm's well known "*Bannerlied*" (Banner Song) "extolled the socialist color red as symbolizing the workers' flag – rage, hatred, and blood, with the red blood in the end being interpreted as a bond that united all workers." Sahm's "*Arbeiter Bundeslied*" (Workers' Federation Song) offers a fair taste of the genre's characteristic stridency:

> The times are grave, the days dull and hard;
> in the breath of wind, there is a sound like iron,
> it rumbles dully from a distance, as if the ocean would like to
> tear down many thousand-year-old dams!
> That means fight! We will win it,
> the long suffering must come to an end!
> The old does not want to give in to the new,
> so be it! We will overcome it!
> Close the ranks! The eye turned toward the enemy!

What a difference between this voice and that of the stereotyped German appearing on the vaudeville stages on either side of this new century. The comic "Dutchman" (from the common English mangling of *Deutsch*, or "German") was already a stock figure, long remembered in the routines, songs, and stage plays of Joseph K. Emmet, the yodeling, dialect-confused creator of Fritz Van Vonderblinkenstoffen. *The Adventures of Fritz (Our Cousin-German)*, *Fritz in Ireland*, *Fritz in Bohemia*, *Fritz among the Gypsies*, and, for good measure, *Fritz in a Madhouse* took no prisoners when it came to minstrel stereotypes. Complex human beings were reduced to crude patterns of "beer-drinking and sauerkraut-eating" to the waltz-time music of oom-pah bands. Interethnic collision became the stuff of comedy, as in Frank Wilson's yodel-driven comic song, "The German's Arrival" (1906), which began with a spoken introduction in an excruciatingly bad German accent: "'Handsome'? Who? Who's handsome? I'm not handsome – What's that? 'Hansom'?? Vy no, I don't vant a hansom cab. The last time I rode in a cab and come out, a lot of Irish, they throwed me a brick in the face!"

Straddling the turn of the century was a giant in German-language theater and song, Adolf Philipp: manager, actor, singer, composer, and "the most successful prolific writer of German American musical comedies." His musical pieces, plots, and characters all reflected "the steps to Americanization" taken by nominally successful immigrants, whether from Germany or elsewhere – "migration, ethnic maintenance, assimilation, and acculturation." In Philipp's case, it was all topped off with a heavy lathering of "nostalgia, sentiment, and emotion."

Philipp's productions were set in the *Klein Deutschland* (Little Germany) section of New York City, where homesickness and *die Heimat* resonated in the hearts of the local brewers, butchers, grocers, pawnbrokers, and landladies who were both his onstage characters and the greater part of his audience. In enormously popular shows such as *Der Corner Grocer aus der Avenue A* (The Corner Grocer on Avenue A), *Ein New Yorker Brauer* (A New York Brewer), *Der Butcher aus der Erste Avenue* (The Butcher on First Avenue), and *Die Landlady*, Philipp crafted his characters to tug at the heartstrings. Hence the character Hein Snut, the grocer from Hamburg (played by Philipp himself), singing "*Heimathlied*" (Song of Home) in *Der Corner Grocer*:

> We stop to think when we're alone
> What changes home has undergone.
> And to our parents' cottage we
> Oft sadly look afar across the sea.
>
> When the billows roar on the sandy shore,
> And the ship disappears on the distant sea,
> To the dear old land on our native strand,
> How we wish we were back where we used to be.

Philipp chose to call his productions "*Volksstücke*" – that is, "popular plays"; but inherent in the term "*Volk*" is a sense of nationhood. For him, the nation was Germany as a unified entity, retained even in the hearts of those who had come to the USA, settled in *Klein Deutschland*, and become the audience for the *Volksstücke* produced at his Germania Theater on Eighth Street. Philipp was a Jew – "an assimilated, secular German Jew" – but it was not anything he advertised, and many in his audience would not even have known. It was not necessarily a case of "closeting" his Jewishness, however; Philipp had no premonition of anything like a Third Reich gathering beyond the horizon. He simply wore his Germanness comfortably (as did so many subsequently surprised middle-class Jews in Hitler's Germany), to the extent that those in the know about his Jewishness queried his lack of identification. In one instance, a satirical writer for the *New York Figaro* magazine needled him with the suggestion that he should try mounting "a specifically Jewish *Volksstück* with acts centering on Jewish holidays."

Philipp would do no such thing. He kept his work firmly within the German-language arena of musical theater, leaving the Yiddish-language work to others who were at the forefront of the vibrant, expanding Yiddish theater of New York's Lower East Side – the likes of Abraham Goldfaden, Jacob Gordin, Boris and Bessie Thomashefsky, and Jacob Adler. Philipp did create a number of struggling, persevering Jewish characters – "Mandelbaum in *Der Corner Grocer aus der Avenue A*; Isaac Rosenstein, 'Clothing Store *Besitzer und* Wall Street Man' (Clothing Store Owner and Wall Street Man) in *Der Pawnbroker von der East Side* . . . and Moishe Rositsky in *From Across the Pond* of 1907." But, although the real-life counterparts of these characters would have spoken Yiddish, in Philipp's world they spoke German with Yiddish accents, thrown into the mix with "varying degrees of Germerican dialogue, low and high German, and English interpolations." Of course, there was a larger cultural issue. As Irving Howe explained, there was a perceptible schism between middle-class German Jews in the immigrant community and the more Orthodox Jews from the *shtetls* – villages – of Russia and Poland:

> With an ease the Russian and Polish Jews could not – indeed seldom cared to – emulate, the German Jews had thoroughly Americanized themselves, many of them finding a road to . . . bourgeois affluence. By the turn of the century, the tensions between the established German Jews and the insecure east European Jews had become severe, indeed, rather nasty.

It is partially a result of this bifurcation within the Jewish immigrant community that the Yiddish theater – and the songwork within it – remained in a world of its own; but it would nonetheless prove to be foundational in the development of American musical theater, cinema, and popular music. Many of its original alumni and those influenced by them – from Al Jolson and Eddie Cantor to Fanny Brice, Molly Picon, and Sophie Tucker to Irving Berlin, George Gershwin, and Leonard Bernstein – made their lasting mark on Tin Pan Alley, Broadway, and Hollywood. It began, as so much does, with terror. In 1883, "a complete government ban upon all Yiddish theater throughout tsarist Russia" had sparked the first wave of emigration among Jewish composers, writers, and performers. The earliest Yiddish song publication in the USA appeared in 1894, an instrumental march from Joseph Lateiner and Sigmund Mogulesco's operetta *Blihmeleh* (Little Blossom), which also included one of the most popular Yiddish wedding songs ever, "*Khosan kalleh mazel tov*" (Bridegroom and Bride, Good Luck).

Wishes of "good luck" were certainly needed. The Kishinev pogrom of 1903 alerted the world to the persecution of Tsarist Russia's Jews. That pogrom – the first of many – left forty-nine dead and "more than five hundred injured. Seven hundred houses and six hundred businesses were destroyed. In all, about two thousand families were left homeless." As the *New York Times* reported:

> The anti-Jewish riots in Kishinev, Bessarabia [modern Moldova], are worse than the censor will permit to publish. There was a well-laid-out plan for the general massacre of Jews on the day following the Russian Easter. The mob was led by priests, and the general cry, "Kill the Jews," was taken up all over the city.
>
> The Jews were taken wholly unaware and were slaughtered like sheep ... The scenes of horror attending this massacre are beyond description. Babes were literally torn to pieces by the frenzied and bloodthirsty mob. The local police made no attempt to check the reign of terror. At sunset the streets were piled with corpses and wounded. Those who could make their escape fled in terror, and the city is now practically deserted of Jews.

The Library of Congress database of Yiddish-American Popular Sheet Music, largely based on the collecting work of Irene Heskes, hosts a wealth of songs published in the USA on the pogroms and persecution, with translated titles the likes of "The Farewell of the Jews to Kishineff" (1903), "Have Mercy: Frug's Poem on the Kishineff Massacre" (1904), "Have Compassion: the Pogroms in Russia" (1906), "A Mother's Prayer" (1911), and "Wandering Jew" (1911). Solomon Smulewitz (Solomon Small), a leading songwriter and singer in New York's Yiddish theater, composed "one of the best-known songs about the czarist realm," "*A brivele fun rusland*" (A letter from Russia, 1912), which called on US Jews "to rescue the Russian brethren":

> Brothers of the free states, you're lucky, you're free.
> Our life is a shadow, our hope is past.
> Russia seeks false accusations against us, the charge of ritual murder
> [of Christians for their blood] is renewed.
> Hate, contempt, and abuse, horror from every boor.
> Be our liberators if Jewish life is dear to you.
> It keeps getting tighter, don't wait any longer, your help is needed now.

On the Lower East Side, three-year-old Stella Adler – the future legendary method-acting teacher of Marlon Brando and daughter of Jacob Adler – stood on the stage of her father's Yiddish theater with her "arms thrown wide" and appealed to her audience in song (here translated): "Jews, for the love of mercy, / Give of your charity! / For the dead, burial – / For the living, bread!" She then passed through the audience with her father's hat in hand: "People wept and emptied their pockets. Women with no money to give threw their wedding rings into his hat." Folksong collector Ruth Rubin uncovered further – unpublished, but certainly sung – lamentations: "There is a fire in Kishinev, / No smoke or flame can be seen, / Many Jews have been murdered, / In Kishinev there is a pogrom."

As New York's Yiddish theater developed in the first two decades of the new century, it absorbed topical material and transformed it through song into comedy, satire, and activism. Boris and Bessie Thomashefsky – grandparents of the symphony orchestra conductor Michael Tilson Thomas – were often at the forefront of this project. Boris Thomashefsky founded "the first theatrical union in the United States, the Hebrew Actors Union." In 1910 he produced the musical *Di sheyne amerikanerin* (The Beautiful American Girl), in which Bessie sang Herman Wohl and Arnold Perlmutter's "*Vayber, makht mir President*" (Women, Make Me President), drawing on the energies of the suffrage movement:

O women, women, women;
By God don't be "women"!
Let the men wash the diapers
If you hear an outcry.
Let them nibble from the pots
And let them have the children.
Let's have them catch bargains
At Wanamaker's store
And let the corset squeeze them
At least twice a year.

Bessie Thomashefsky returned as a tour de force in 1913 as the producer and lead in Rakow, Lillian, and Rumshinsky's *Chantshe in America*, a four-act homage to the persistence and progressive spirit in the Jewish immigrant community. In "*Weh dir kind von armuth*" (Woe to you, child of poverty), the young Chantshe sings (translated): "Slave of need, you must labor for bread from childhood to death. / All your life is a struggle to

Figure 10.2 Bessie Thomashefsky in *Chantshe in America*, 1913. Irene Heskes Collection, Library of Congress Music Division

survive, a battle against poverty." In the titular show-stopper, Chantshe is acclaimed: "What a lady is Chantshe. / They laughed at her, but now she is admired. / She's a suffragette and is for women's rights and independence." As Tilson Thomas recalled, *Chantshe in America* followed the "successful formula" of his grandmother's independent productions: "A woman disguised [as a man], spies out and exposes the perfidies of men," ultimately leading to their enlightenment and reform.

In 1915, Leo Frank, a Jewish factory superintendent from Atlanta, was lynched by a mob protesting the commutation of his death sentence for the murder of thirteen-year-old Mary Phagan in Marietta – a false conviction and miscarriage of justice now roundly accepted as being driven by anti-Semitism. Frank was posthumously pardoned by the State of Georgia in 1986. His lynching inspired Broadway director Hal Prince's

1998 musical *Parade*, written by Alfred Uhry and Jason Robert Brown, only one of the succeeding cultural interventions. Before that, indeed the very year of Frank's murder, country music pioneer and Klan member Fiddlin' John Carson wrote "Little Mary Phagan," which brazenly and deliberately fanned the flames of hatred and bigotry. As Peter La Chapelle notes:

> Carson's performances of his "Ballad of Mary Phagan" outside the courthouse were leading factors in fomenting public resentment in days leading up to the lynching. According to the *Atlanta Constitution*, Carson had "turned up with his fiddle at every Frank development within a 30 mile radius of Marietta since the day Mary Phagan's body was discovered," and further, upon Frank's death, had entertained crowds – disappointed that they could not get a glimpse of Frank's lifeless body – by standing in front of the courthouse and fiddling "a symphonic jubilee."

Here is a taste of Carson's serenade:

> She fell upon her knees, to Leo Frank she pled,
> Because she was virtuous, he hit her 'cross the head;
> The tears rolled down her rosy cheeks, the blood flowed down her back,
> She remembered telling her mother what time she would be back . . .
>
> Her mother sits a weeping, she weeps and mourns all day,
> She prays to meet her baby in a better world some day;
> Judge Roan passed the sentence, you bet he passed it well,
> Solicitor Hugh M. Dorsey sent Leo Frank to – .

In the intervening period between Frank's conviction and his lynching, Boris Thomashefsky produced his celebratory staging of Abraham Shomer's musical *The Green Millionaire*, which included Thomashefsky himself singing his own love letter to America, "*Leben Sol Columbus!*" (Long Live Columbus!), with the refrain (translated): "Long life to Columbus! Drink a toast, brothers. / Long life to Columbus and to this new land." The song included a verse with what may well be a critical reference to Carson. If so, it would mark one of the most unlikely conflicts in US musical history, that between Yiddish musical theater and early country music. There is no chance that Thomashefsky could have heard Carson's song, since it wasn't recorded until 1925. But every gruesome detail of the Frank case and its aftermath was reported in the Jewish newspapers (both in English and in Yiddish), and these details were discussed intensely in the community – so much so that Frank's conviction was cited as a main inspiration for the founding of the Anti-Defamation League in 1913 by the Jewish service organization B'nai

B'rith. Hence Thomashefsky's apparent dig at Carson's expense: "A slander's been cooked up against one of our Jews / A devil made music and Hamen played the fiddle." As it turned out, Thomashefsky's confidence in the outcome of the Frank case was woefully misplaced: "The lawyers, however, won't be silenced, they'll bring out the truth. / Believe me, Noah, it will turn out well: they won't hang a Jew!" Unsurprisingly, this verse disappeared from Thomashefsky's performances after Frank was lynched.

A stone's throw from New York's Lower East Side was the expanding Italian neighborhood still known as Little Italy, where, like their fellow immigrants from China, Ireland, and Germany, the newly arrived and settled Italians became the stuff of vaudeville stereotype – typically the garlic-eating, macaroni-scoffing, English-mangling, lazy good-for-nothing barber or organ grinder. Irving Berlin's "Pick, Pick, Pick, Pick on the Mandolin, Antonio" (1912) and his appalling "Hey Wop" (1914), whose lyrics deserve no repetition, are two of many possible examples. Charles Hamm points out that Berlin himself came to regret the crudeness of his early ethnic stereotyping and that, after "Hey Wop," he "was never again to publish a song in which an Italian protagonist was portrayed in what could be taken as a demeaning or ridiculous – even if supposedly comic – manner." Still, it remained – as ever – for members of the community to stand up and challenge the stereotypes imposed on them from the outside.

The leading Italian American performer in this struggle was Eduardo Migliaccio, who dominated the Italian vaudeville stages of Little Italy and the Lower East Side – as well as San Francisco – in the first two decades of the twentieth century. He was known as "the *Re dei macchiettisti*, the king of the *macchietta*" – "*macchietta*" being the comic, often satirical, character act in the Neapolitan tradition that Migliaccio brought to the USA and adapted as *macchiette coloniali*, peculiar to the Italian American experience. Under the stage name of "Farfariello" (the Little Butterfly), Migliaccio developed an elaborate song-and-spoken-word act that was "a blend of fourteenth-century Italian harlequin and the modern pantomime style of Charlie Chaplin," with exaggerated makeup and outlandish costume, "grimaces, gestures, and pantomime" mimicking "the *cafone*, a buffoon who adopted American clothes, mannerism, and slang, and yet was no more American than the most recent arrival from Italy." At times Migliaccio used his *macchiette coloniali* to critique US power structures, such as the judiciary, that were often heavy-handed in their dealings with the Italian immigrant community. One such *macchietta* was his "*Portame' a casa mia*" (Take me home), in which a drunken *cafone* – a greenhorn rustic – is hauled before a judge: "At night court / the judge said: 'Tell me / who sold you the drink? / I would like to go myself.'"

In other *macchiette coloniali*, Migliaccio sympathetically identified with the Italian immigrants struggling to adapt linguistically – often unsuccessfully – and who felt the impact in their own interpersonal relations, whether between family members, men and women in romantic situations, or immigrants and their US-born offspring. In so doing, he managed to assure his audience that they were not alone in "*la torre di Babele*" (the Tower of Babel) that was at once *Nuova Yorca* and *l'America* at large.

In the early twentieth century, Italian songs of struggle made their mark in one other important setting besides vaudeville: of course, this was opera. Giacomo Puccini's *Madama Butterfly* (1904), with a libretto by Luigi Illica and Giuseppe Giacosa, was based on a short story by John Luther Strong and a subsequent one-act play by David Belasco. Puccini's opera swept the stages with its depiction of US imperialism in the Pacific and its attendant swagger and carelessness. In *Madama Butterfly*, it is the naval Lieutenant Benjamin Franklin Pinkerton who brings disruption and ruin to Japan – personified by Cio-Cio-san – aboard the gunboat USS *Abraham Lincoln*. As the beguiled Cio-Cio-san sings early in Act I (here in translation): "I follow my destiny with full humility and bow to Mr. Pinkerton's God. . . . I will forsake my ancestral religion." Unaware that Pinkerton is faithless, Cio-Cio-san worships and weds him; she becomes his "butterfly," and he tells her, "I have caught you. I hold you as you tremble. You are mine." He then deserts her, leaving her to give birth to his child. When Pinkerton returns in Act II with a new American wife, determined to raise the child in the USA, Cio-Cio-san gives up her child, with a US flag planted in his hands, and takes her own life. She had been warned by Pinkerton himself in Act I (in "*Dovunque al mondo lo Yankee vagabondo*") that "the Yankee" will always seize anything he wants, wherever he finds it. For a recurring leitmotif to every despicable act and lie of Pinkerton's – and fully twenty-seven years before it was adopted as the national anthem – Puccini chose "The Star-Spangled Banner."

Six years later, in 1910, Puccini wrote a second opera based on US themes, again following a Belasco play: *La Fanciulla del West* (Girl of the Golden West), with a libretto by Guelfo Civinini. This opera, which hinges on interactions between Anglo, Mexican, and Indigenous characters in Gold Rush California, is important not only in its own right but also for the impact it had on an aspiring US opera composer, George Whitefield Chadwick. Upon seeing *La Fanciulla del West*, Chadwick set to work in 1913 on an opera that would not be produced in his lifetime, based on the exploitative practices of an Italian labor agent, or "*padrone*." In Chadwick's *The Padrone*, the lustful agent and tavern owner Catani manipulates the US immigration system to prevent the fiancé of his barmaid, Marietta, from entering the country, after she has given up her life's savings to pay his passage. (The fiancé, Marco, is barred entry as "a jailbird from Trapani" in Sicily.) In the final act, Marietta – Tosca-like – kills her antagonist and is thus herself doomed by the law and inevitable execution. In *The Padrone*, the "hopelessness of the Italians . . . is framed by the promise of America, the land of endless possibilities, where, as the tourists in the second act sing in its praise, 'milk and honey flow.'"

But in Chadwick's North Boston, there is, for Marietta, no tragic dimension worthy of the grand opera stage: "There is no Castello Sant'Angelo for her to leap from, as there was for Puccini's Tosca. Marietta is merely an Italian immigrant woman who has just stabbed someone to death." Chadwick's submission to the Metropolitan Opera was refused: "*The Padrone* with its realistic lower-class story neither contributed to the picturesque nor to the illusionary image of a spotlessly prospering America" in 1913. Indeed, for the majority of the working people of the country, not least those in the immigrant population disenthralled with the rhetoric of progress, this "illusionary image" had long been open to question. It was bound to remain so, even if the board members of the Metropolitan Opera thought otherwise.

CHAPTER 11

We Are Many

On March 25, 1911, tragedy struck the corner of Greene Street and Washington Place in New York City. The Triangle Shirtwaist Company went up in flames. Trapped on the upper floors, behind doors locked from the outside, were 800 garment workers, almost all of them girls and young women. Some managed to jump out a window, dying upon impact on the pavement below. Others perished through smoke inhalation and flame. All in all, 146 were killed – again, mostly girls and young women. Only two years previously, many of these women had led what became known as the "uprising of the 30,000," the US garment industry's first major strike. How they had been lionized in 1909:

> Hail the waist makers of 1909
> Making their stand on the picket line
>
> Breaking the power of those who reign
> Pointing the way and smashing the chain
>
> In the black winter of 1909
> When we froze and bled on the picket line
> We showed the world that women could fight
> And we rose and we won with women's might.

The following year, they fronted a second garment industry strike, this time leading over 115,000 workers into the streets. And now, in March of 1911, a newspaper reporter stood over the corpses laid out in a row before the blackened bricks of the Triangle Shirtwaist Factory: "I looked upon the dead bodies and I remembered these girls were the shirtwaist makers. I remembered their great strike of last year in which the same girls had demanded more sanitary conditions and more safety precautions in the shops. Their dead bodies were the answer." Most of these garment workers came from the immigrant communities of the Lower East Side. They were mourned in Yiddish elegies like Joseph Rumshinsky and Anshel Shor's "*Mamenyu!*" (Mother dear!):

> Woe unto you, orphan,
> You're a chopped-down tree . . .
> You're lonely everywhere . . .
> O mama, mama where are you? . . .
>
> "Oy vey, my child!" The mama tears her hair.
> For a piece of bread
> A terrible death
> Robbed me of my only child . . .
> My little girl lies dead
> Shrouds instead of a wedding gown
> Woe is me
> A child of sixteen
> Oy mama, mama, woe is me.

Figure 11.1 Victims of the Triangle Shirtwaist Factory fire being placed in their coffins, March 25, 1911.
Library of Congress Prints and Photographs Division

There was, of course, song and laughter still to be heard in the vaudeville theaters. Art song and opera still resounded in the concert halls. But other voices were filling the soundscape, like the Jewish workers' choirs of Chicago led by Jacob Shaefer, who had been "combining cantorial training with socialist ideas." There were individuals like the radical Italian balladeer Arturo Giovannitti, a leading light of New York's "La Lotta Club" (The Struggle Club), who proclaimed his manifesto in songs like "New York and I":

I shall sing of your slums where you bleed,
Your machines, iron claws of your greed,
And your jails, viscid coils of your mind,
The light of your eyes that dazzles the sun
And turns your midnights into moons,
The street where you buy and resell
Each day the whole world and mankind,
Your foundations that reach down to hell
And the glory of your nameless dead,
And the sword that shall hallow your hand,
And the dawn that shall garland your head!

In the coal mining country of West Virginia, 76-year-old Mary Harris Jones – the Irish-born schoolteacher and labor activist long known and revered as "Mother Jones" – was arrested, as she so often had been, for leading protests against the hideous conditions in the mines. Union miners across the country sang her praises:

The world of to-day is advancing,
   But Nero is yet on the throne;
And Croesus with iron rod ruling,
   The devil will soon take his own.
The light of millennium is dawning,
   The ages unborn will be blest;
Mother Jones will be ever remembered
   When her soul joins the heavenly rest.

They had sung for Mother Jones before, and they would sing for her again. In 1903, she'd led a children's march from Philadelphia to the New York doorstep of Theodore Roosevelt to condemn the flimsy child-labor laws in Pennsylvania's mills and mines. From these hellholes, Jones reported, children as young as five years old had been coming "into Union Headquarters, some with hands cut off, some with the thumb missing, some with their fingers off at the knuckle. They were stooped little things, round shouldered and skinny." Upon her death in 1930 at the age of ninety-three, she would be musically elegized by many, including "the Singing Cowboy," Gene Autry, whose pioneering recording of the anonymously penned "The Death of Mother Jones" was one of his earliest and most unlikely hits.

Triumph mingled with tragedy in the late adolescent and early teen years of the twentieth century. These were the years that brought to the fore the greatest song-driven labor organization in US history, the Industrial Workers of the World (IWW) – the "Wobblies," as they were nicknamed for a still-unknown reason. The IWW was established in Chicago in 1905, with a stirring manifesto:

> The working class and the employing class have nothing in common. There can be no peace so long as hunger and want are found among millions of the working people and the few, who make up the employing class, have all the good things of life.
>
> Between these two classes a struggle must go on until the workers of the world organise as a class, take possession of the means of production, abolish the wage system, and live in harmony with the Earth.

The IWW dove into some of the most acrid and bitter labor battles of the early twentieth century, beginning with the gold-mining strikes of Goldfield, Nevada, in 1906, and carrying on with the Pressed Steel Car Strike in Pittsburgh (1909); "free speech" battles throughout Washington State and California (1909); the great textile strike of Lawrence, Massachusetts (1912); the Paterson, New Jersey, silk strike of 1913; and the Minnesota Iron Range strike of 1916. The Wobblies pursued their goal of achieving "One Big Union" (OBU) for working people – as opposed to separate labor or craft unions which could easily be pitted against each other – through a range of approaches from organizing to direct action. The latter included wildcat strikes and sabotage, as represented by their trademark symbol, the snarling black cat – "Sabocat" – first drawn by the IWW activist, poet, and illustrator Ralph Chaplin. Chaplin also composed, to the tune of "Dixie," an ode to "That Sabo-Tabby Kitten" which reflects a typical Wobbly blend of humor, appeal, and implicit threat:

> This world should have but freemen in it,
> Let me show you how to win it,
> Hurry now! wonder how? MEOW – SABOTAGE!
> Perch will I on the System's coffin,
> On the hearse they take it off in.
> Hurry now! wonder how? MEOW – SABOTAGE!

Celebrated members of the IWW included William "Big Bill" Haywood, Mother Jones, Elizabeth Gurley Flynn, the Irish revolutionary James Connolly, Eugene Debs, and Helen Keller. Less known, but equally important, historically, was Roscoe T. Sims, "the union's first African American organizer." The IWW actively sought to redress the ongoing crime of the US labor movement most conspicuously evident in the exclusionary practices of the American Federation of Labor (AFL), whose "affiliated unions . . . were allowed to bar blacks from membership, even after the national charter forbid such discrimination." As Howard Zinn puts it, "racism was practical" for the AFL: "In general, the Negro was kept out of the trade union movement. W. E. B. Du Bois wrote in 1913: 'The net result of all this has been to convince the American Negro that his greatest enemy is not the employer who robs him, but his fellow white workingman.'" Consequently, the Wobblies had a "mission" to include "women, blacks, and unskilled workers excluded from the American Federation of Labor." In gratitude, one Black member, Paul Walker, penned "A Wobbly Good and True" to the tune of Ernest Ball and J. Keirn Brennan's parlor song, "Let the Rest of the World Go By" (1919):

I was riding one day
On a train far away,
Wishing there was a Wobbly near,
When it did just seem
Like someone in a dream,
Came a Wob with a hearty cheer.

With someone like you, a Wob good and true,
We'd like to rule this world and all that it produces.
Day and night, for the greedy parasites,
Just to give each slave his right.
And then we'd have peace,
The master class will cease
To divide us while we're on the job.
The boss will be surprised to find us organized
And every slave will be a Wob.

Now he said, Look here, Son,
I don't know where you're from,
But I know that you're true blue.
Let us hope that some day,
All wage slaves will say,
Hurrah for the O.B.U.

The most revered of the Wobblies' members were their songwriters, most of whom, like Walker, deliberately penned their verses to popular tunes that could easily be remembered and sung by the workers. Among the more celebrated "Wobbly bards" were the likes of Walker; Chaplin (who also composed the world-renowned "Solidarity Forever"); T-Bone Slim (Matti Valentine Huhta), who wrote "The Popular Wobbly" and "The Lumberjack's Prayer"; and Harry "Haywire Mac" McClintock, composer of "Hallelujah, I'm a Bum" and – so he claimed – "The Big Rock Candy Mountain." Towering above them all in the borderlands of history and legend was Joseph Hillström, formerly Joel Emmanuel Hägglund and subsequently – famously – Joe Hill. Hill, a Swedish-born immigrant and multi-instrumentalist, composed some of the best-known Wobbly songs, among them "Casey Jones – the Union Scab"; "There Is Power in a Union"; "The Rebel Girl"; "The Tramp"; and his supremely contemptuous parody of the Baptist hymn "In the Sweet By and By," "The Preacher and the Slave," which introduced the phrase "pie in the sky" into the English language ("You will eat by and by / in that glorious land up in the sky. / Work and pray, live on hay; / You'll get pie in the sky when you die"). Other Wobbly songwriters included a pantheon of women "hell-raisers": Laura Payne Emerson, Mary Marcy, Jane Street, Vera Moller, Matilda Robbins, Laura Tanne, and Agnes Thecla Fair among them. In 1909, the IWW published their first songbook, popularly known as the *Little Red Songbook*, dedicated to fanning "the flames of discontent." Over the years it has been expanded to include over 250 songs, and it has never been out of print. In 1914, Joe Hill perfectly articulated the musical strategy of the IWW: "A pamphlet, no matter how good, is never read more than once, but a song is learned by heart and repeated over and over ... Put a few cold, common sense facts into a song, and dress them up in a cloak of humor to take the dryness off of them."

Wobbly songs had – and still have – enormous influence in the multilingual, international labor movement. Italian radical songwriters such as Giovannitti and Efrem Bartoletti were IWW members. Giovannitti emerged into national renown, along with fellow Italian Wobbly Joseph Ettor, in the midst of the Lawrence strike of 1912, where the pair of them "risked capital punishment on the fabricated charges of inciting violence and being an accessory to murder." Bartoletti became a bard of the Minnesota Iron Range strike of 1916–1917, organizing members for the IWW and composing an anthem for the Italian miners, "*I ribelli del Minnesota*" (The Rebels of Minnesota), situating them among "all the oppressed of the world":

> An agonizing and desperate wail
> springs up from our chests; and from the dark
> mines, breathing the sweet pure air,
> each proud and indignant pariah rises . . .
>
> Sons of the Rhine, of the Danube and those
> of the Thames, of the Volga and the Seine,
> of the Tiber and of the Eridan we are brothers.

The IWW had particularly strong influence among the Finnish miners on the Minnesota Iron Range, who "engaged with the vibrant and melodic culture" of the Wobblies, gradually transforming songs brought from Finland into "derivations of IWW songs sung in Finnish with borrowed words from the American working class." Labor song historian Bucky Halker notes that "various editions of Finnish-language IWW songbooks printed by *Tyomies* (*The Worker*) in Superior, Wisconsin, made their way to Finland in the First World War era" and that the celebrated Finnish tenor Hannes Saari recorded Joe Hill's anthem "Workers of the World, Awaken!" for Columbia. For his part, Joe Hill was determined to spread the Wobbly songs and ethos as far abroad as he could: "In 1911, Hill was one of dozens of Wobblies who joined forces of the Partido Liberal Mexicano in Tijuana, Mexico, where his singing helped boost morale, and that same year he and a fellow Wobbly took passage to Hawai'i, a beehive of Wobbly activity among Chinese, Korean, Filipino, Hawaiian, and other workers."

During these teen years, three tragedies in particular had a profound impact not only on US labor history but also on US song history. In July of 1913 a strike was kicked off by the largely Finnish copper miners on the Keweenaw Peninsula of Upper Michigan. Since the late nineteenth century, Finnish immigrants had formed many vertebrae in the backbone of immigrant mining labor in the Upper Midwest – in the Vermilion and Mesabi iron ranges of Minnesota and in the Copper Country of Michigan. Finns were among the most politically militant of all immigrant groups:

> Around the turn of the century socialism began to gain ground among Finnish immigrants and many "Red Finns" took an active role in leftist politics and trade unions. This made the Finns the largest socialist group in the country and one of the most discriminated . . . While immigrants from English-speaking countries, Germans and Scandinavians were offered high-rank jobs, Finns, Slavs and Italians were given the most menial jobs.

It was a far cry from the "utopias" marketed by Midwestern land agencies that had been targeting would-be emigrants from Finland since the 1890s.

They brought with them their ancient folk songs and legends like the *Kalevala*, whose words, as sung by its central bardic figure, Väinämöinen, can only have taken on a bitter truth in the winter of 1913 in the mining country of Calumet, Michigan:

> Better dwell in one's own country
> There to drink its healthful waters
> From the simple cups of birchwood,
> Than in foreign lands to wander,
> There to drink the rarest liquors
> From the golden bowls of strangers.

On Christmas Eve of 1913, the largely Finnish members of the Western Miners Federation were into the fifth month of a doomed strike against the Calumet and Hecla Mining Company for fair wages and union recognition. They were having a Christmas party for their children on the second floor of Calumet's Italian Hall. At the end of what became known as the Italian Hall Disaster, sixty-three children and ten adults lay dead in a stairwell, crushed in a panic sparked by someone mendaciously yelling "Fire!" Finnish folklorist Anne Heimo links this tragedy to the "historical tales concerning so called Christmas panics in churches around Finland in the eighteenth and nineteenth century. These tales often include a false fire, people suffocating in stairways trying to flee and that many of the victims are children." But for the labor activist "Mother" Bloor – Ella Reeve Bloor – it was a "massacre of the innocents" by deputies of an American mining company, as she presented it in her autobiography, *We Are Many* (1940):

> What happened was this. In the panic a man with a child in his arms had fallen at the bottom of the stairs. There were two doors to the box entry, both opening outward. When the man fell, the child in his arms fell through one of the doors, out into the street. The deputies, who had been threatening to break up the entertainment, were standing outside of the door. They themselves had raised the cry of "Fire!" and knew what was happening . . . and both doors were held shut from the outside, so that no one could get out. . . . The staircase was made an air-tight coffin pen by those who wanted to create panic and disaster in order to discredit the union.

Whether or not the true culprit was in fact a member of the anti-union Citizens Alliance (as some survivors testified) or otherwise a management ally, Bloor's version of events was taken at face value by Woody Guthrie, whose song "1913 Massacre" (1941) – described as both "a post mortem" and "a description of a lost battle" – places the blame squarely on the "copper-boss thug men." Guthrie's "1913 Massacre" went on to influence more than one generation of singers and songwriters, including notably Ramblin' Jack Elliott and Bob Dylan. Indeed, Dylan not only performed "1913 Massacre" at his Carnegie Hall concert of 1961, but he also borrowed the tune for the setting of his own early eulogy, "Song to Woody."

Less than four months after the Italian Hall Disaster, a second tragedy – again with immigrants and their children as the victims – struck the coalfields of Ludlow, Colorado. John D. Rockefeller, Jr.'s, Colorado Fuel and Iron Company unleashed all the firepower of their hired guards and strikebreakers, backed up by the National Guard, against members of the UMW striking for union recognition, fair wages, a protected eight-hour work day, and freedom from the company store, company housing, and scrip payments. The strikers and their families, evicted from company housing, had set themselves up in a tent colony numbering about 1200 people under the stewardship of the Greek-born union leader Louis Tikas, surrounded by Rockefeller's hostile and trigger-happy forces. Again, Mother Bloor depicted a "massacre of the innocents":

> They were all very worried about their children. The tent colony was in an open field, surrounded on three sides by railroad bridges, where state soldiers were stationed watching every movement. Now and then they took a pot shot at a worker standing guard. One day a little boy went out to get a drink and was shot at by the soldiers. The women were terribly afraid some of their children would be killed.

Bloor then described the women's decision to "dig a cave inside the biggest tent and put all the children there at night" – which they did, sheltering "thirteen children and one pregnant woman."

> That night the soldiers waited until all the miners were asleep. They stole around the colony and soaked the bottoms of the tents with kerosene. Then they applied a match and there was a great burst of flame. The miners and their wives came running out of their tents, but there was a roaring wall of fire between them and the thirteen children and the pregnant woman in the cave. As they climbed out of the cave and before they could fight their way out of the blazing tent, the soldiers on the bridges started firing their Gatling guns. All the children who had been placed in the cave were killed – not by the fire, but by the bullets of the soldiers.

Bloor may have had her figures slightly wrong. Howard Zinn counts "the twisted bodies of eleven children and two women" discovered in the ashes of the cave among the "sixty-six men, women, and children [who] had been killed. Not one militiaman or mine guard had been indicted for a crime."

More certain, perhaps, than the accuracy of numbers is the impact of Bloor's account, once again, on Woody Guthrie, whose "Ludlow Massacre" (1941) appeared on the same album as his "1913 Massacre." This song, too, had long-lasting influence, not least on Zinn himself, who claims it as the catalyst for his leaving the shipbuilding trade and becoming a people's historian:

> I'd been a shipyard worker from the age of 18 to the age of 21, and I'd joined a union. And one day I heard a song by Woody Guthrie called "The Ludlow Massacre" – a dark, haunting, powerful song. And that led me to look in the library about this event, which nobody had ever mentioned in any of my history courses and which no textbook of mine had ever mentioned . . . The strike was lost, and the miners had to go back to work; but the event had a tremendous effect on lots of people around the country. Anybody who read about the Ludlow Massacre, anybody who heard about it, was bound to be affected by it.

Zinn concluded that the massacre was "the culminating act of perhaps the most violent struggle between corporate power and laboring men in American history."

Guthrie was not the only songwriter to memorialize the Ludlow Massacre. Indeed, shortly after the event itself, a number of songs appeared, emphasizing in the aggregate "the solidarity of the different ethnic groups who made up the strikers." A month after the tragedy, the *United Mine Workers Journal* published an elegiac ode to Louis Tikas, "Greek Louis," who had been murdered – beaten and shot in the back – on the day of the massacre:

> Who knows what deeds on ancient days
> Gave impulse, yearnings, tendencies?
> Who knows what blood flowed in his veins?
> Perhaps the blood of Pericles.
>
> He braved the assailants' iron might,
> Their brutal hate, unbridled, wild;
> His trust, the miners' naked home;
> His care, the mother and her child.
>
> And men in stress of coming days
> Shall win by strength his spirit gives;
> Who so for justice yield his life,
> He, dying, yet immortal lives.
>
> Oh, Louis Tikas, gallant soul,
> Defender of the helpless, weak;
> Knight of humanity, you were
> More than American or Greek.

Another songwriter – and witness to the massacre – was Colorado-born miner and musician Elias Baca, "the son of a half-Cherokee woman, Soledad Lopez, from Espanola, New Mexico, and Vicente Baca from Madrid, Spain." As historian Sarah Rudd notes, "Baca vividly recalled fighting scabs, the deaths of the women and children trapped in the Ludlow Black Hole, and marching through town in protest with only wood boards shaped to look like intimidating rifles since the militia had taken away their real weapons." Baca fused the Mexican corrido and union song forms to craft an homage to the Ludlow strikers and to Mother Jones, who, after being banned four times from entering Colorado, returned and was arrested in nearby Trinidad, where she was detained in a hospital. Baca recounts the Ludlow women and children marching on Trinidad to honor their imprisoned champion, resulting in an attack by the Colorado National Guard that subsequently became known as the "Mother Jones Riot." Baca titled his corrido "*¡Que viva la nación!*" (That the nation may live), erroneously locating the place of Mother Jones's imprisonment as Denver. More significantly, he adopted the time-honored corrido tradition of subjecting the adversarial Anglo forces to mockery:

From West Virginia came
very similar telegrams
that the 23rd of September
the mining would be stopped.

That the nation may live!
That the nation may live!
We're here fighting
in this powerful union.

The women over there in Denver
in loud voice cried out
that the companies sign
now that coal was lacking.

In the Denver hospital
the people were entering . . .

In the depot there . . .
there was a line
that we would fight
and in Ludlow, Colorado.

Those guards from Hastings,
those cool guards,
they stayed up by the hills
eaten by the birds.

Those guards from Delagua,
Such big, manly guards,
They stayed up by the hills
eaten by the coyotes.

One further important song emerged from the Ludlow Massacre, written some unidentified time after the event, by Alfred Hayes and Earl Robinson, excoriating the mine owner John D. Rockefeller, Jr. The song was certainly known to Woody Guthrie, who included it in the book he coedited with Alan Lomax and Pete Seeger, *Hard Hitting Songs for Hard-Hit People.* Hayes and Robinson's "Ludlow Massacre" pulled no punches in assigning culpability:

John D., he'd stacks of money,
John D., he'd silver and gold.
John D., he was warm in winter
While mining folks went cold.

He sent down his hired gunmen,
They'd orders to shoot on sight.
He sent down troops with helmets
To break the miners' fight.

John D., he was a Christian,
John D., the psalms he sung.
But he'd no mercy in his heart,
He shot down old and young.

Hayes and Robinson are perhaps better known for their musical commentary, written a little over two decades after the fact, on a third labor tragedy of the century's teen years. As their elegy begins, and as Paul Robeson famously sang: "I dreamed I saw Joe Hill last night / Alive as you and me. / Says I, 'But Joe, you're ten years dead.' / 'I never died,' says he. 'I never died,' says he." Upon his arrest in Salt Lake City in 1914 upon a dubious murder charge, Joe Hill knew that it was more than words and music that had turned him into a threat to the state and its capitalist interests; he was one of the IWW's most visible and inspiring activists. His biographer concludes: "Already enshrined by labor as an icon of courage and resistance, Hill had reached that extraordinary place that martyrs come to: the belief that he was worth infinitely more to the cause as a symbol than as an individual, and that by dying a dramatic death, the symbol would live in perpetuity." Following Hill's execution by firing squad in 1915, IWW founder "Big Bill" Haywood recounted the last words he'd received from his fellow Wobbly in prison: "Good bye Bill. I will die like a true blue rebel. Don't waste any time in mourning. Organize." Haywood had replied: "Good bye, Joe, you will live long in the hearts of the working class. Your songs will be sung wherever the workers toil, urging them to organize!"

Almost a century later, one of Joe Hill's posthumous disciples, the IWW balladeer Bruce "Utah" Phillips, explained the importance of Hill's activism and his songs:

> Kids don't have a little brother working in the coal mine, they don't have a little sister coughing her lungs out in the looms of the big mill towns of the Northeast. Why? Because we organized; we broke the back of the sweatshops in this country; we have child labor laws. Those were not benevolent gifts from enlightened management. They were fought for, they were bled for, they were died for by working people, by people like us. Kids ought to know that ... That's why I sing these songs. That's why I tell these stories, dammit. No root, no fruit!

The year after Hill's execution, and on a completely different performing stage than any likely to be occupied by an IWW balladeer, Dorothy Parker implied that something else quite subversive, if not revolutionary, was afoot. She voiced it in her "Musical Comedy Thought" (1916): "My heart is simply melting at the thought of Julian Eltinge; / His vice versa, Vesta Tilley, too. / Our language is so dexterous, let us call them ambisexterous – / Why hasn't this occurred before to you?" Julian Eltinge was the stage name of Massachusetts-born William Julian Dalton, a popular vaudeville performer. Vesta Tilley was his female British counterpart. Both were internationally renowned for cross-dressing onstage – Eltinge as a woman, Tilley as a man. In the USA, the destabilization of presumed sexual norms wasn't entirely new, at least in the arena of song performance. As far back as the 1870s, male impersonators such as Ella Wesner and Annie Hindle had made their careers by challenging "the models of middle-class masculinity" and "sexual virility" by coming onstage dressed as upper-class male "swells" and *bons vivants* in top hats and tails. They sang instructions to the men in the audience on what they should *really* know about lovemaking while intimating to women more than an acknowledgement of same-sex desire: "Lovely woman was made to be loved, / To be fondled and courted and kissed; / And the fellows who've never made love to a girl, / Well they don't know what fun they have missed."

But while male impersonation by female artists was an accepted, time-honored vaudeville tradition, men impersonating women apparently trod a more dangerous path. In 2020 the scholar Channing Gerard Joseph uncovered the ordeal of William Dorsey Swann – known by his friends and allies as "the Queen" – who was born into slavery circa 1858 and endured "the Civil War, racism, police surveillance, torture behind bars, and many other injustices." Swann was not only "the first American activist to lead a queer resistance group; he also became, in the same decade [the 1880s], the first known person to dub himself a 'queen of drag' – or, more familiarly, a drag queen." Swann was repeatedly – and violently – arrested in the 1880s for hosting "drag balls" in and around Washington, DC, "featuring folk songs and dances" enjoyed by "guests dressed in women's clothes, though some wore men's suits." In petitioning President Grover Cleveland for a formal pardon (unsuccessfully, as it turned out), Swann became "the earliest recorded American to take specific legal and political steps to defend the queer community's right to gather without the threat of criminalization, suppression, or police violence."

Whether or not it was known at the time, Swann helped to pave the way for "the popularity of female impersonation at the beginning of the twentieth century, with the carefully crafted femininity of Julian Eltinge and Bothwell Browne, turning them into major vaudeville stars." By the time Dorothy Parker wrote her comic ode to Eltinge and Tilly in 1916, a significant cultural barrier had been weakened, though not dismantled entirely. Eltinge had become so popular that he could run a New York theater named after him, star in numerous silent films, produce a beauty magazine for women, and sing songs written in collaboration with the likes of Jerome Kern and other leading theatrical composers, both gay and straight. But in spite of their popularity, Eltinge, Browne, and other female impersonators remained subject to severe cultural and legal policing. As Nan Alamilla Boyd points out, they "walked a fine line between respectable and deviant behaviors." Consequently, "booking agents nervously asked [female] impersonators to tone down their shows. Popular performers like Eltinge skirted accusations of sexual deviancy by asserting offstage masculinity." Queer male America still had a long struggle ahead.

So did female America, queer or otherwise. In 1916, the same year that Parker was punning on "ambi-sextrous" practices, birth-control advocates Margaret Sanger and Dr. Marie D. Equi were arrested, tried, and convicted in Portland, Oregon, for distributing Sanger's pamphlet, *Family Limitation*, which a male judge declared "indecent," "impure," and dangerous to "the marriage relation." Women folksingers had good reason to be singing a "radical version" of the traditional English ballad, "The Wagoner's Lad," which had been collected by Olive Dame Campbell: "Hard is the fortunes of all woman kind, / They're always controlled, they're always confined; / Controlled by their parents, until they are wives, / Then slaves to their husbands for the rest of their lives." Vaudeville and parlor singers were still gaining traction with Arthur J. Lamb and Harry Von Tilzer's lament to a loveless marriage, "A Bird in a Gilded Cage" (1900):

> She's only a bird in a gilded cage,
> A beautiful sight to see,
> You may think she's happy and free from care,
> She's not, though she seems to be,
> 'Tis sad when you think of her wasted life,
> For youth cannot mate with age,
> And her beauty was sold,
> For an old man's gold,
> She's a bird in a gilded cage.

In 1911, Charlotte Perkins Gilman turned from writing Gothic feminist tales such as *The Yellow Wallpaper* (1892) to songwriting for the suffragist cause. Gilman's "Another Star," from her collection *Suffrage Songs and Verses*, helped to push the campaign to success in California: "A ballot for the Lady! / For the home and for the Baby! / Come, vote ye for the Lady, / The Baby, the Home!" Her "Song for Equal Suffrage," in the same collection, cast a vision of a peaceful world no longer dominated by men in power: "Not for self but larger service has our cry for freedom grown, / There is crime, disease and warfare in a world of men alone, / In the name of love we're rising now to serve and save our own, / As Peace comes marching on!" Two years later, to the Irish marching tune "Garryowen" (which had accompanied George Custer's Seventh Cavalry on their less noble missions of Indigenous slaughter), Gilman vowed, "The Women Are Coming!" And they would be bearing the standard of Susan B. Anthony: "The great Aunt Susan, she went before, / And now we are following, more and more, / To help in the work and make it like home, / The women are coming, they come! they come!"

As her imagery and choice of tune setting made clear, Gilman was ironically promising peace in the midst of intense militancy – in particular, that of transatlantic activists such as Sylvia Pankhurst, whose Women's Social and Political Union had embarked on a program of direct action including a coordinated window-smashing campaign in London's West

Figure 11.2 Charlotte Perkins Gilman. Photograph by Francis B. Johnston, c. 1900. Library of Congress Prints and Photographs Division

End. Pankhurst's disappointingly small handful of US allies included Gilman and the celebrated operatic soprano Lillian Nordica, the latter of whom fronted a women's suffrage pageant at New York's Metropolitan Opera in May of 1912, wearing a crown of stars representing each of the states that had enshrined in law the right of women to vote. Nordica defended Pankhurst and all militant suffragettes:

> Smash windows? Yes! When men take the view that to gain an end warlike methods are excusable, they are heroes. A man has fought and gone to prison for his principles, and I think no great reform has been brought about without these. It is all very well for those in power to keep on their way, ignoring us. We have to draw attention to ourselves. If we are to be heard, why, we have to make ourselves obnoxious, perhaps, at times.

Still, Gilman sang of the "Peace to the World" that would come with the ascension of women into the corridors of power: "When motherlove the law shall mold, / The end of war has come; / Each child be safe in mother's hold, / And all the earth be home!" This was in 1913. Joe Hill was still alive, with his eye cast on some past wars and the great one to come – all of them laying waste the nurturing vision of Gilman's "motherlove." Hill looked back to "some time ago when Uncle Sam he had a war with Spain, / And many of the boys in blue were in the battle slain." He looked to the present, as Europe careened toward war and the USA built up what Dwight Eisenhower would eventually call its "military-industrial complex." For Hill, it was "the gold that pays the mighty fleet," laid upon "Mammon's altar":

> We're spending billions every year,
> For guns and ammunition.
> "Our Army" and "Our Navy" dear,
> To keep in good condition;
> While millions live in misery.

And, two years later, on the eve of his execution, with the global war commenced and the USA still on the sidelines, Hill looked at the shattering of Gilman's homely vision in one of his final songs. The setting was "a cabin across the sea" where a "little girl with her father stayed":

> Her mother dear in the cold grave lay; with her father
> she'd always be –
> But then one day the great war broke out and the father
> was told to go;
> The little girl pleaded – her father she needed.
> She begged, cried and pleaded so:
>
> *Chorus*
> Don't take my papa away from me, don't leave me there all alone.
> He has cared for me so tenderly, ever since mother was gone.
> Nobody ever like him can be, no one can so with me play.
> Don't take my papa away from me; please don't take papa away.

Prior to US entry into the war in April of 1917, such pacifist sentiments were freely sung and heard. Indeed, pacifism appears initially to have been a cash cow for Tin Pan Alley, with the likes of Alfred Bryan and Al Piantadosi's "I Didn't Raise My Boy to Be a Soldier" (1914) achieving "an enormous vogue" and its publisher, Leo Feist, boasting that "more than 700,000 copies were sold in the first eight weeks." Bryan's chorus chimed harmoniously with Gilman's evocation of "motherlove":

> I didn't raise my boy to be a soldier,
> I brought him up to be my pride and joy,
> Who dares to place a musket on his shoulder,
> To shoot some other mother's darling boy?
> Let nations arbitrate their future troubles,
> It's time to lay the sword and gun away,

There'd be no war today,
If mothers all would say,
"I didn't raise my boy to be a soldier."

Will Dillon and Albert Von Tilzer employed a similar trope in "Don't Take My Darling Boy Away" (1915), once again with a vision of the shattered hearth and home and the agony borne alone by a mother left behind:

Don't take my darling boy away from me,
Don't send him off to war.
You took his father and brothers three,
Now you've come back for more;
Who are the heroes that fight your wars,
Mothers who have no say,
But my duty's done, so for God's sake leave one,
And don't take my darling boy away.

However, as war fever heated up around 1916, some songwriters began to change the prevailing tune. The team of George Graff, Jr., and Jack Glogau sounded an alarm in "Wake Up, America!," which advocated precisely the same military-industrial build-up that Joe Hill had condemned:

Wake up, America
If we are called to war,
Are we prepared to give our lives for our sweethearts and our wives?
Are our mothers and our homes worth fighting for?
Let us pray, God, for peace, but peace with honor,
But let's get ready to answer duty's call,
So when Old Glory stands unfurled, let it mean to all the world,
America is ready, that's all.

Graff and Glogau's "Wake Up, America!" was introduced to the world by the country's most celebrated band leader, John Philip Sousa, who argued ambivalently in print: "Let America keep out of this fight. There is no reason for us to get into it, but we want to be prepared so that at no future time will any nation or nations feel that they can attack us with impunity. . . . I am for peace – and preparedness."

Parodies of the most popular pacifist songs began to appear under such titles as "I Did Not Raise My Boy to Be a Coward" (1915), "I Didn't Raise My Dog to Be a Sausage" (1915), and "I Didn't Raise My Boy to Be a Soldier, I'll Send My Girl to Be a Nurse" (1917). Such comedic derision could hardly mask the gathering sense of menace and paranoia infiltrating the official strata. Jon Meacham and Tim McGraw encapsulate this atmosphere of "turmoil, dissent, and passion" as the USA inched closer to war:

> In the name of national security, [President Woodrow] Wilson and the Congress restricted freedom of expression, passing legislation to protect the military draft from interference or protest; the Espionage Act of 1917 and the Sedition Act of 1918 criminalized dissent. As many as four hundred publications were censored, and Attorney General A. Mitchell Palmer was the architect, with J. Edgar Hoover, of controversial raids on suspected radicals. The Federal trespasses on basic constitutional norms during this "Red Scare" – so called because of fears that Soviet Bolshevism was a threat to the United States – led to the formation, in 1920, of the American Civil Liberties Union.

The holding cells on Ellis Island were swelling with immigrants detained on account of suspected Red or German sympathies and other threats to whatever "national security" entailed. In February of 1915, Harry T. Burleigh and James Reese Europe organized a series of concerts on the island for the detainees, with Europe's Clef Club Orchestra and Wanamaker's Colored Jubilee Club performing a program that included Burleigh's setting of James Weldon Johnson's "The Young Warrior." This song implicitly urged a hush upon any further expressions of resistant "motherlove": "Mother, shed no mournful tears, / But gird me on my sword, / And give no utt'rance to thy fears, / And bless me with thy word." Burleigh and Johnson's song was soon translated into Italian ("*Il giovane guerriero*") by Eduardo Petri; it became one of Italy's most celebrated wartime songs, both on the battlefield and off. In February of 1916 the Italian baritone Pasquale Amato performed "*Il giovane guerriero*" at New York's Biltmore Hotel "for an Italian war benefit concert . . . sponsored by the Italian ambassador . . . through the patronage of the Queen of Italy." As William Brooks observes: "The irony of an Italian marching song being written by two black Americans was duly noted but did not seem to harm its popularity." Burleigh went on to compose a suite of war songs based on European battlefield imagery, beginning with his setting of Margaret M. Harlan's "One Year: 1914–1915," musically recreating Harlan's "Battle birds in the sky; / Shriek of gun as they die; / Crash - and roar, bloody drench; / Black death in the trench." He followed with "Under a Blazing Star," referring to the devastation of an exploding star shell.

Woodrow Wilson had campaigned for his second presidential term in 1916 under the slogan, "He kept us out of war"; and so Tin Pan Alley sang of him, notably in Al Dubin, Joseph Burke, and George B. McConnell's "The Hero of the European War":

Is it Hindenburg or Joffre
Who will wear a hero's crown?
Who will be the one, just like Washington,
When the European war is done?
In my mind there's just one hero,
Woodrow Wilson's name will live forever more,
For there's no doubt of it, he kept us out of it,
And he's the hero of the European War.

One month after his inauguration, in April 1917, Wilson asked Congress to declare war on Imperial Germany, arguing: "The world must be made safe for democracy." One of the first casualties was the stable of German singers who summarily lost their contracts with the Metropolitan Opera. The Met frantically excised its entire German repertoire even though, in zeppelin-bombed London, Thomas Beecham "continued to conduct the operas of Mozart as well as Wagner in English translation." Elsewhere on the classical music front, the insurance agent and defiantly amateur composer Charles Ives began work on a series of art songs reflecting his and the country's dizzying journey from neutrality to full-scale militarism. "From Hanover Square North at the End of a Tragic Day, the Voice of the People Again Arose," "Tom Sails Away," "He Is There!" and "The Things Our Fathers Loved": all these works from 1917 drew on songs from the Civil War era (as well as offering quotations of "Yankee Doodle" and Cohan's "Over There") to establish Ives's "counterargument to neutrality and pacifism."

These militarist offerings stood in contrast to Ives's more somber setting, the same year, of John McCrae's poem "In Flanders Fields," which was also taken up by John Philip Sousa, who – having followed the same journey from neutrality to militarism – was lionized in the press for his jingoistic declaration: "I have had many triumphs in my life. I have done things of which I am proud, but the greatest ambition of my life is to lead a band down Wilhelmstrasse in Berlin playing 'The Star-Spangled Banner.' I will be satisfied with my life work when that is done." It never happened, although the vaudeville stage soon witnessed Sidney Phillips reciting Clyde Wilson's poem to the tune of Sousa's "The Stars and Stripes Forever": "I can see their metal flashing as they toot to beat the band, / And with blasts of mocking music raid the air of Kaiser land. / And they shoot like Yankee gunners, with a deadly Yankee grin, / Of the 'Stars and Stripes Forever,' played by Sousa in Berlin."

As Jill Lepore observes, Woodrow Wilson had narrowly won reelection through the votes of women whose campaign for equal suffrage he had spurned: "In the end it was women voters who, by rallying behind the peace movement, gained Wilson a narrow victory: he won ten out of the twelve states where women could vote." It was doubly ironic, then, that the Tin Pan Alley veterans Andrew B. Sterling and Arthur Lange could presume to speak on behalf of motherhood with their grotesque tub thumper, "America, Here's My Boy" (1917):

> America, I raised a boy for you,
> America, you'll find him staunch and true,
> Place a gun upon his shoulder,
> He is ready to die or do.
> America, he is my only one;
> My hope, my pride and joy,
> But if I had another, he would march beside his brother:
> America, here's my boy.

The song, of course, was a hit. Other Tin Pan Alley songsters followed suit, including Alfred Bryan, co-composer of "I Didn't Raise My Boy to Be a Soldier," who now jumped on the war wagon, along with Harry Tierney, with "It's Time for Every Boy to Be a Soldier." None could compete, however, with the stunning power of George M. Cohan's "Over There" as sung by the world's most popular operatic tenor, Enrico Caruso, whose bilingual Victrola recording in English and French made it "the most effective morale song of World War I." Patriotic songs tumbled from the presses, and for the next year the vaudeville industry's United Booking Office (UBO), bowing to government pressure, made sure that no songs that might possibly "be the result of German propaganda" would be performed by its artists – only "acts of the 'propaganda' type" would be sanctioned. Brian Holder notes:

> In March 1918 the government ordered the official collection of data on anyone who published or performed what the UBO dubbed a "peace song." Within the month, several new Leo Feist hit songs were restricted based on such information gathering. Music sheets for two songs, "It'll Be a Hot Time for the Old Boys When the Young Men Go to War" and "I Don't Want to Get Well, I'm in Love with a Beautiful Nurse," were seized from the counters of Woolworth, Kresge, and other stores nationwide.

Songs like W. Howard Johnson and George Meyer's "Just Like Washington Crossed the Delaware, General Pershing Will Cross the Rhine" and Mary Earl's musical triptych, "From Valley Forge to France," "My Sweetheart Is Somewhere in France," and "Lafayette We Hear You Calling" easily made it through the censor's gauntlet. A degree of familial concern was deemed understandable, so Al Jolson's recording of "Hello Central! Give Me No Man's Land" and The Shannon Four's

"There's a Vacant Chair in Every Home Tonight" escaped the official cull. Blind Lemon Jefferson, however, would have to wait until 1926 before he could release his critique of the African American draft, "Wartime Blues": "What you gonna do when they send your man to war? / Gonna drink muddy water and sleep in a holler log." Likewise Lead Belly, whose "Red Cross Store Blues" would not be published until 1936, the "Red Cross Sto'" being the army recruitment center, and the war itself just a "rich man's show." Other blues, apparently, slipped under the wire, such as Eldon B. Spofford's "Those Navy Blues," expressing the anxiety of an enlisted sailor: "Ev'ry time I try to sleep, I lie awake / Thinkin' 'bout the lovely corpse that I would make / If I ever sailed upon the deep blue sea, / Think what those torpedoes could be doin' for me." The Texas bluesmen Jimmie Marten and Mitch Le Blanc also got away with "War Bride Blues," drawing on the powerful, time-honored trope of the train – in this case, the 2:16 – that "done carried poor John away."

Indeed, the Selective Service Act of 1917 gave little choice to men between the ages of 21 and 30 (after September 1918, it would be expanded to men between 18 and 45). For Irving Berlin, the draft encouraged the development of his army camp show *Yip Yaphank* (1918), which not only introduced the subsequently discarded "God Bless America" but also nodded both to George M. Cohan and the growing jazz craze in the finale number of Act I: "Send a lot of jazz bands over there / To make the boys feel glad. / Send a troupe of Alexanders / With a ragtime band to Flanders."

But for the Black Americans who invented jazz and ragtime, it meant being drafted into a racially segregated army, where they would be relegated to performing the most menial tasks. During his service in France, the balladeer and folk song collector John Jacob Niles recorded a number of Black soldiers' songs, many of them reflecting the bitterness of their relegation to grave diggers' and ditch diggers' squads:

> I've got a grave-diggin' feelin' in my heart –
> I've got a grave-diggin' feelin' in my heart –
> Everybody died in de A.E.F. [American Expeditionary Force],
> Only one burial squad wuz left –
> I've got a grave-diggin' feelin' in my heart.
>
> Diggin', diggin', diggin' in Kentucky –
> Diggin' in Tennessee; diggin' in North Carolina –
> Diggin' in France.

It was a rare Black soldier who could escape such demeaning service. Some, like the legendary Eugene Bullard, chose to join the ranks of a more racially enlightened nation. Bullard became the first Black combat pilot – anywhere in the world – only by joining the French air force. Upon being made a *chevalier*, or knight, of the *Legion d'Honneur* (France's highest honor, on top of a slew of other French military honors awarded to him), Bullard reflected: "France taught me the true meaning of liberty, equality, and fraternity." James Reese Europe also managed to escape menial service through fronting a 60-piece military ensemble, the "Famous 369th US Infantry 'Hell Fighters' Band," which earned considerable notice on both sides of the Atlantic. While recovering from a gas attack in France, Europe joined Noble Sissle in crafting a highly modernist jazz – if not "proto-rap" – recreation of the battlefield, "On Patrol in No Man's Land," in which percussive instrumentation alternates with a commander's urgent

Figure 11.3 James Reese Europe conducts the 369th Infantry Regiment Band in the courtyard of a Paris hospital, 1918.
Library of Congress Prints and Photographs Division

orders: "Alert, gas! [sirens] Put on your mask, / Adjust it correctly and hurry up fast. / Drop! There's a rocket from the Boche barrage. / Down, hug the ground, close as you can, don't stand, / Creep and crawl, follow me, that's all."

Europe and Sissle offered a unique perspective on Black Americans' wartime experience. But for the majority of Black servicemen in the US forces, it meant watching from the sidelines – or from the kitchen, or from the bottom of a ditch: "All dese colored soldiers comin' over to France, / All dese soldiers and me, / Goin' to help de whites make de Kaiser dance, / All dese soldiers an' me." Many questioned why they were there at all, other than to escape privation at home: "Jined de army fur to git free clothes – / Lordy, turn your face on me – / What we're fightin' 'bout, nobody knows – / Lordy, turn your face on me."

Some Black American songs went beyond racial discrimination to reflect the class divisions enshrined in the military, as in previous war songs from the French and Indian War onwards:

I want to go home – I want to go home –
The war ain't so bad if you're wearin' a star –
But bein' a private don't get you so far.
So send me over the sea,
Where the tin hats they can't get at me –
Oh, my, I'm too young to die –
I want to go home.

In this regard, and perhaps only in this regard, Blacks and whites shared an equal fellowship, for, as a song retrieved by another collector indicates, the chain of command ensured the repression of the lowest class, regardless of any other distinctions:

If you want to know where the generals were . . .
Back in gay Paree.

If you want to know where the colonels were . . .
Way behind the lines.

If you want to know where the majors were . . .
Playing with the mademoiselles.

If you want to know where the captains were . . .
Down in the deep dugout.

If you want to know where the sergeants were . . .
Drinking up the privates' rum.

If you want to know where the privates were . . .
Up to their necks in mud!

For the "privates" and others in the lowest ranks singing new words to the revival hymn, "When the Roll Is Called Up Yonder," neither a general nor a colonel nor a major would be seen. They may as well have been as far away as the loved ones waiting back home:

> When your lungs are filled with gas,
> You'll be thinking of a lass,
> But you'll never see your sweetheart any more.
> Lying in the mud and rain,
> With a shrapnel in your brain,
> Oh, you'll never see your sweetheart any more.

Still, the war seemed to offer mixed blessings to some, at least in terms of song. Perhaps ironically, this included the Indigenous peoples of the USA. As Roxanne Dunbar-Ortiz has noted, Native Americans could, on the one hand, be found at the forefront of war resistance, as in their participation in the so-called Green Corn Rebellion of 1917, when a coalition of "white, Black, and Muskogee tenant farmers and sharecroppers in several eastern and southern Oklahoma counties took up arms to stop conscription" and marched toward Washington, DC, only to be scattered by "heavily armed posses supported by police and militias." Native Americans could also be the butts of the most heavy-handed, racist, and historically ignorant humor that Tin Pan Alley had to offer, as in Alfred Bryan, Edgar Leslie, and Maurice Abraham's "Big Chief Killa Hun" (1918):

> Big Chief put his war-paint on and kissed his squaw good bye;
> Threw away his pipe of peace, and went to do or die.
> He said, "Uncle Sammy feeds me, gives me all I get,
> Now that Uncle Sammy needs me, Big Chief no forget" . . .
>
> Big Chief's on his way to Berlin, just to do his share;
> Big Chief's goin' to make 'em squawk,
> When he hits 'em with his tomahawk.
> Big Chief's goin' to scalp the Kaiser, take away his fun;
> Oh! Oh! He have heap much fun;
> Good bye Herman, no more German, Big Chief Killa Hun.

If this song could have any redeeming feature, it lies in its (most likely inadvertent) acknowledgment of the part played by Indigenous people in an atmosphere of heightened emergency. William K. Powers notes:

> Fewer than 25 years after the infamous massacre of Wounded Knee, 1,200 Lakotas and other American Indians joined the United States military effort in World War I. While often viewed exclusively as an act of patriotism on

> the part of Native Americans (and surely this must have been the case for some), a more reasonable explanation is that they took up the gun to defend their own tribal land as well as the territory of the United States from potential foreign invasion.

The Lakotas' participation is particularly emphasized, given the brutal cultural suppression they faced after the Ghost Dance and the Wounded Knee massacre. With their warrior songs and tribal dances hitherto outlawed, World War I enabled them to "rejuvenate" their officially besieged traditions: "As Lakota soldiers went off to war, new songs were created to honor them, and their warrior deeds were memorialized in songs upon their return. The songs were often built on old warrior song texts and on Omaha Dance and Iwakicipi, or Victory Dance, melodies." The Lakotas' cultural need for this "rejuvenation" was such that "some tribes declared war on Germany independently of the United States." Even songs stemming from the Lakota victory against Custer at Little Big Horn were revised to fit the new context of a twentieth-century world war. Lakota warriors could now sing freely:

> *Eya ica wan maucanze ca*
> *Tamakoce na tawapaha ko*
> *Mak'uwakiye lo he ye he ye yo*
>
> The Germans made me mad
> So not only their land but flag
> Are what I made them give me *lo he ye he ye yo*
>
> *Tehatan natanpe lo* (4 times).
> *Iya ica kin ceya napape lo.*
> *Lakota ho ila tehantan natanpe lo.*
> *Iyašica kin ceya napape lo.*
>
> They are charging from afar (4 times).
> The Germans retreat crying.
> The Lakota boys they are charging from afar.
> The Germans retreat crying.

Regardless of the murky politics of World War I, it must be acknowledged that such warrior songs spoke "directly to the maintenance of Lakota identity," as historian Clyde Ellis argues: "These can be seen as resistance songs insofar as they insist on seeing these events through a Lakota cultural lens, and not through the assimilation lens that US officials hoped would be the case."

When the Armistice came into effect on the eleventh hour of the eleventh day of the eleventh month of 1918 (Parisian time), the boys began to come home. Some had their bodies and minds intact; many did not. There were parades, brass bands, ticker tape, confetti, windy speeches, and a soundtrack generating close to 14,000 song titles as collected by the Library of Congress. Some sang of laying down "swords and shields / Down by the riverside" and studying "war no more," as they had done through various versions since the Civil War. Tin Pan Alley also spared some thoughts for "The Boys Who Won't Come Home": "He gave his life to Uncle Sam / He's sleeping o'er the foam / So while you're cheering / Don't forget the boys who won't come home." There was a cascade of similarly sentimental parlor songs along the lines of Lora Starret and Leo Friedman's "Star of Gold" invoking the emblem of the boys who indeed wouldn't be coming home: "A mother old with tear dimmed eyes / A sorrowful story told. / As she pressed to her lips a service flag, / With its little star of gold." In the realm of art song, Harry T. Burleigh completed his war oeuvre with "The Victor" and "Down by the Sea," his setting of lines from George F. O'Connell's poetry collection *Memories* (1920), which he had apparently seen in manuscript. Burleigh dedicated his compositions "to all those who gave their lives for the Right: 'REQUIESCAT IN PACE.'"

For some, like the Ku Klux Klan, another war on the home front – the war for "100% Americanism" – was just beginning. Victorious Bolsheviks, International Jews, Popes in Rome, and dark-skinned peoples of all nations were the invading enemy, even if they had been born or already naturalized beneath the Stars and Stripes:

> Ten million men are marching,
> Ten million hearts a flame;
> Ten million Knights protect you,
> Your hearth, your home, your name
> The foreign hord[e]s advancing,
> We'll meet them man to man;
> The heart of all America
> Is centered in the Klan.

In this home-front war, there would be no Armistice – not now, not ever.

CHAPTER 12

100% American

It was always the foreigner's fault. In 2020 it was the "China virus" or the "Kung Flu," as Donald Trump perversely and persistently called it, sparking a rash of anti-Asian hate crimes during and after his xenophobic presidency. In 1918–1920 it was the "Spanish flu" or the "Spanish Lady" – not because it originated in Spain but because the Spanish press were simply the first to report it. In Spain itself, they pointed the finger at Italy, calling it "the Naples Soldier, after a song in a hit musical playing in Madrid." But in fact, the so-called Spanish flu – the virus H1N1 – may well have been 100% American, having first emerged on a US Army base, Fort Riley in Kansas, perhaps contracted on a nearby farm. It ended up killing anywhere between 20 million and 100 million people worldwide – the estimates vary widely. In the USA alone, 675,000 died from it. Then, as now, the disease was invoked for crude nationalist scapegoating – not against Spain but against Germany, the virus having emerged nine months before the Armistice. As one US Public Health Service officer told a Mississippi newspaper reporter: "The Hun resorts to unwanted murder of innocent noncombatants. ... He has been tempted to spread sickness and death through germs." Another paper reported: "The Germs are Coming. An epidemic of influenza is spreading or being spread (we wonder which)."

The vaudeville star Nora Bayes composed, along with Sam Downing and Abe Glatt, "The Man Who Put the Germ in Germany," laying the blame at the Kaiser's feet: "But the world is now aflame / At the 'Hell' in Wilhelm's name / The man who put the 'Germ' in Germany." The song concluded with a vow: "Now that our boys are in France, / If they just get half a chance / They'll disinfect that 'Germ' in Germany." If only. As the *New York Times* reported in August of 1918 upon a second viral wave: "A considerable number of American negroes, who have gone to France on horse transports, have contracted Spanish influenza on shore and died in French hospitals of pneumonia."

What is most surprising about this devastating global event is the cultural silence that followed it. Unlike the COVID-19 crisis of the 2020s, which produced a wealth of songs, published reflections from lockdown, short stories, and the promise of a raft of novels, the Spanish flu pandemic produced only the tiniest handful of cultural responses in the USA. Willa Cather's *One of Ours* (1922); Thomas Wolfe's *Look Homeward, Angel* (1929); William Keepers Maxwell, Jr.'s *They Came Like Swallows* (1937); and Katherine Anne Porter's *Pale Horse, Pale Rider* (1939) pretty well cover the literary output. The musical output was equally meager. Music historian Deniz Ertan observes that, for the most part, the task of musical commemoration fell to the blues: "As an intrinsically American music of grief and mourning, the blues suited well the subject of the influenza epidemic. Nevertheless, very few songwriters and composers tackled the topic, and when they did it was mainly through memory and observance, usually years or decades later." Ertan cites the likes of Blind Willie Johnson's "Jesus Is Coming Soon" and Essie Jenkins's "The 1919 Influenza Blues" – both of which cast the pandemic as divine retribution for human wickedness – as well as Frances Wallace's "Too Late, Too Late Blues (The Flu Blues)," which dwells on the loneliness of an abandoned woman suffering from the disease. Historians of the Spanish flu seem united in their assessment of the possible reasons behind the cultural silence. As one explains:

> After the twin horrors of world war and the Spanish flu, many Americans longed for a return to normalcy – a word used by President Warren G. Harding in his successful 1920 campaign for the presidency. It may be one of the reasons that very few people wrote or talked about the Spanish flu and that it largely disappeared from public memory – becoming a piece of hidden history.

One of the most curious aspects of this episode comes from the part that music and song appear to have played, not only in the actual onset of the pandemic but also in those precious few cultural responses to it. Unsurprisingly, the Spanish flu pandemic devastated the musical and performing community in the USA, just as COVID-19 did in the 2020s. Theaters and opera houses closed; eminent musicians and conductors succumbed to the disease, many of them fatally (such as Cleofonte Campanini, conductor of the Chicago Opera). Blues- and jazzman Lonnie Johnson lost ten brothers and sisters. Other victims included the operatic soprano Saba Doak, the composer Charles Tomlinson Griffes, and the composer and mentor of George Gershwin, Charles Hambitzer, all of whom died. John Philip Sousa almost did. Music critic Charles E. Watt wrote in January of 1919 of American musicians "groping in the dark," with the musical arena being a "chief sufferer" in the pandemic: "No one outside the profession will ever know the trials, the disappointments, the delays, the changes, the cancellations, the postponements and the general confusion and loss." Another critic, Joseph De Valdor, wrote at the same time that the pandemic had "affected the musical life of the country in a way which the war in itself [had] never done."

In fact, music appears to have been quite a malign accomplice in what would today be called "super-spreader events." Wartime newspapers reported on rallies and bond drives in which the bombast of patriotic songs often drowned out the sounds of warning and common sense. In San Francisco in September of 1918, the celebrated French tenor Lucien Muratore enthralled a crowd of fifty thousand from the steps of the Chronicle Building, where he sang

> an aria from *La Traviata*, the *Star Spangled Banner*, and *La Marseillaise* . . . In the middle of *La Marseillaise* the crowd had to divide to let an emergency ambulance down Market Street. "The singer, clutching the American and French flags resolutely, turned his eyes upward and did not observe the interruption to his song."

That same month, in Philadelphia, city officials – "confident that a vaccine for Spanish flu was imminent" – gave the go-ahead for a Liberty Loan parade in which two hundred thousand people pressed together along a twenty-three-block route: "Singing conductors and speakers were distributed among the marchers, and whenever the parade halted, they led the crowds in patriotic songs and harangued them to buy bonds." In voting against a mandatory masking ordinance in January of 1919, a San Francisco official argued that the measure "would mean 'the stilling of song in the throats of singers' and the arresting of musicians 'as they blow their horns going down the street.'" Given such musical culpability, it is no wonder that Katherine Anne Porter should have chosen a song of the Apocalypse by which to name her novella of death. As the protagonist Miranda lies sick with the flu, she asks her lover Adam – who will himself die from it – to join her in quietly singing "an old spiritual . . . 'Pale horse, pale rider, done taken my lover away . . . .'"

Even as the Spanish flu pandemic raged, reactionary figures were worried about another infection – the "virus" of Bolshevism in the wake of the communist overthrow of imperial Russia in 1917. The consequent backlash in the USA – the so-called Red Scare – is aptly summarized by Paul Ortiz as an official mission not only to stop Bolshevism in its tracks but also to "undermine immigrant working-class and Black militancy" under the guise of national security:

> This reactionary movement was led by future FBI director J. Edgar Hoover, Attorney General A. Mitchell Palmer, and others who used their authority to order the arrest, the detention, and ultimately, the expulsion of thousands of "alien" political activists ... State and Federal authorities used powers gained through the Espionage and Sedition Acts of 1917–18 to disrupt legitimate protest groups while ignoring real crimes that exacerbated racial tensions.

Lynchings, Klan raids, and the mass murder of Black Americans might go unpunished (Houston, East St. Louis, Waco, and Memphis in 1917; Valdosta, Georgia, in 1918; Elaine, Arkansas, and Washington, DC, in 1919; Ocoee, Florida, in 1920) and Black neighborhoods might be burned to the ground (Omaha and Chicago in 1919; Tulsa in 1921; Rosewood, Florida, in 1923). But the FBI was hardly interested in the racist depredations on either side of that peak period of white supremacist terror called the "Red Summer" – roughly April to September of 1919. The true, gold-standard, "newly minted public enemy" was not the home-grown white terrorist; it was the foreign Bolshevik and his home-grown agents. It wasn't the Red Summer that infected the popular music industry, but rather the Red Scare: "Several major song publishers began to produce songs that denounced Bolshevism in the name of Americanism. At the same time, both antiradical and antiunion sentiments began to run together." At the same time, too, the Ku Klux Klan was permitted to publish songbook after songbook dripping with anti-Black, anti-Jewish, and anti-Catholic hatred, under the cover of 100% Americanism.

One up-and-coming songwriter, Irving Berlin, attempted to walk a tightrope between affirmation and parody of the Red Scare with songs such as "Look Out for the Bolsheviki Man" ("You can tell him any place by the whiskers on his face") and – still riding on the coattails of Scott Joplin and other ragtime pioneers – "That Revolutionary Rag" ("It's not a melody / It's a crimson flag"). Meanwhile, and for over a decade, the Wobblies had been singing of that very flag: "Red's the color of our flag, it's stained with blood and tears." In 1918, in Chicago, 101 of them were put on trial for opposition to the war, accused of violating the Espionage Act and interfering with the Selective Service Act, not – at least on the face of it – for anything to do with labor or union organizing. IWW halls across the country were raided by Federal agents in what became known as "the Palmer Raids," and by the war's end the entire IWW leadership was either in prison or in exile. In Bisbee, Arizona, over a thousand striking miners led by the IWW were rounded up by vigilantes and, after a hasty trial in a kangaroo court, forcibly deported from the state and dumped on the Mexican border – a traumatic event memorialized in anonymous balladry:

> No farewells were then allowed us,
> Wives and babes were left behind;
> Tho' I saw their arms around us
> As I closed my eyes and wept.
>
> After what seemed weeks of torture,
> We were at our journey's end;
> Left to starve upon the border,
> Almost on Carranza's land.
>
> Then they rant of law and order,
> Love of God, and fellow man;
> Rave of freedom o'er the border,
> Being sent from promised lands.

IWW members, peace activists, and socialists such as Emma Goldman, Kate Richards O'Hare, and Eugene Debs languished in prison on dubious charges of sedition, while labor organizer Frank Little was dragged from his boarding house in Butte, Montana, and lynched from a railroad bridge. The remaining Wobblies sang of him:

> We'll remember you, Frank Little!
> They couldn't still your voice,
> So they strangled it;
> They couldn't chill your heart,
> So they stopped it;
> They couldn't dam your life blood
> So they spilled it . . .
>
> We'll remember you, Frank Little!
> The papers said: "So far as known,
> He made no outcry."
> No, not you. Half Indian, half white man,
> All IWW.

In Centralia, Washington, IWW members fought pitched gunfights against a band of American Legionnaires who had attacked their union hall. Four Legionnaires were killed. After a number of Wobblies were arrested, the prison guards handed one of them, 29-year-old war veteran Wesley Everest, over to an attacking lynch mob, who mutilated and tortured him, hanged him three times, shot him, and buried him in an unmarked grave – upon which the coroner "listed the cause of his death as suicide." No Legionnaires were ever charged; but Everest and the "Centralia Massacre" were memorialized in Loren Roberts's ballad, "The Tragedy of Sunset Land," set – with macabre irony – to the tune of a popular "memory lane piece" by C. H. Scoggins and Charles Avril, "Where the Silvery Colorado Wends Its Way":

> There's a little western city in the shadow of the hills,
> Where sleeps a brave young rebel 'neath the dew;
> Now he's free from life's long struggle, his name is with us still;
> We know that he was fearless, tried and true.
> In a homely pine-board coffin our warrior lies at rest.
> Those henchmen turned loose on him one day
> These parting words were spoken: "Boys, I did my best!"
> – Where the old Chehalis River flows its way.

Clearly, in the atmosphere of "100% Americanism" (as in the later atmosphere of "Make America Great Again") no one was truly safe – neither the foreigner nor the American-born; neither Black nor white; neither Indigenous nor Anglo; neither Wobblies on the defensive nor Legionnaires on the offensive. It was an atmosphere of hatred, division, paranoia, and scapegoating in which everybody lost something, whether lives, livelihood, freedom, or their own basic humanity and compassion. For the targeted, it often involved some particularly deft maneuvering. This was especially the case for German Americans, never fully supplanted by the Bolsheviks as enemies of the state. There was, perhaps, more safety in German American communities of the Upper Midwest, where "Dutchman polka bands" and other expressions of German folk culture flourished, with the accordion taking on renewed significance as a "bulwark" against alienation and "culture loss." There was also the cultural balm of the singers who "combined dialect comedy with familiar folk songs and tunes" – the likes of the Iowan Henry Moeller, honing his craft as "Herr Louie," champion of the outlandishly spiraling "*Schnitzelbank* Song" ("*Ist das nicht eine Schnitzelbank?*" "*Ja, das ist eine Schnitzelbank. . . .*" "*Ist das nicht ein Schnickelfritz?*" "*Ja, das ist ein Schnickelfritz*". . . . "*Ist das nicht ein Wagenrad?*" "*Ja, das ist . . .*"). Still, an aura of nativist menace was always hanging in the air, and what Kurt Vonnegut later claimed for German Americans after World War II surely applied to them after World War I as well: they should become "screamingly funny as soon as possible" – especially if they strayed from their own turf.

Neither were Irish Americans home free in the atmosphere of 100% Americanism – at least, not free from the musical hounds of the Ku Klux Klan. Tin Pan Alley songwriter Charles Lawlor, best known for "The

Sidewalks of New York," sought to remind everyone of the Irish contribution to the recent US war effort, in hopes of seeing the favor returned in support of an independent Ireland: "An Irish boy in Yankee land sailed across the sea, / To fight for Uncle Sam and France – for home and liberty, / He fought the fight and victory won – for freedom took his stand, / And freedom now is what he wants for his own native land." Yet, even with their war service, Irish Americans were clearly not American enough for the Klan. Their vile songbook *A Few 100% Selections to the Good Old Tunes We All Know* (1924) included "O No, My Brother," which threatened the Catholic community as well as any lingering disciples of the Molly Maguires:

O, yes, Old Molly,
Old Molly McGuire,
When you monkey with the Klan
You are playing with the fire,
Our guns are all loaded,
With the hottest kind of dope,
And we'll clean you to a frazzle,
From the Priest to the Pope.

Other groups shared the Irish Americans' musical victimization at the hands of the Klan. Italian Americans were caught up in the anti-Catholic vitriol, with the Klan warblers singing: "I'm going. I'm going, / to join the Ku Klux Klan, / And help them run the dagoes / Back to their home land." Not that some Italians needed the push, given the nativist bigotry to which they were often subjected in the period. One anonymous songwriter who had landed in West Virginia recounted his heartbreaking ordeal in "Nicolo Went to the USA":

My friend used to say, "Nico,
America is a nice country,
Tutti fanno planty money."

Like a stupid, I believed him,
I gave him my goat and then embarked.
You want to know the end of my story in America?

One night I was out on the street,
Someone gave me a punch with his fist,
Then I was afraid [there] was going to be more on the list.

I soon cried out aloud:
Police! Police! Help, help!
But when the police came, he arrested me.

No wonder the *cafone* sketches and songs of "Farfariello" – the "Little Butterfly," Eduardo Migliaccio – were still so popular in the Italian immigrant communities of New York and San Francisco, where brushes with bigoted policemen were comedically unpacked and refashioned on the vaudeville stage. No wonder a homesick immigrant might come home from, say, a variety performance of regional Italian dialect song by Gilda Mignonette (Gilda Andreatini), Teresa de Matienzo, or Rosina De Stafano, and sit down to write:

> I dreamed a strange dream, I dreamed of finding it in trees.
> Money, money, money!
> Stay right where you are
> If this is what America is like,
> I want to go back!

If Irish and Italian Americans could never be American enough, neither could Jewish Americans. They could sing their patriotic heads off in Yiddish – "*Columbus, ich hob zi dir gur nit*" (Columbus, I've no words against you): "America, land of freedom, I love you. Uncle Sam welcomes everyone, and Jews here are like other men. Columbus, you did a wonderful thing." They could remind whoever cared to listen of their wartime allegiance, as in "*Aza mazel aufin kaizer*" (Such [bad] luck upon the Kaiser): "Uncle Sam is at war, and our brave Yankee boys will win." They could sing of their late battlefield service, as in "*A grus fun die trenches*" (A greeting from the trenches): "I bring a letter from our boys in the trenches, a greeting from Uncle Sam's brave army." They could heap blessings on the head of the president at the war's end, as in "*Frieden*, Our Boys Are Coming Back" (Peace, our boys are coming back): "America, my Uncle Sam, your victory has been won. God bless President Wilson and our land." Irving Berlin could write a slew of patriotic songs in English, damn the Bolsheviks in any key (in either English or Yiddish), and work so assiduously to shed his ethnicity that, by 1942, few hoodless Klansmen singing "White Christmas" around the tree with their families would know that it was written by a Yiddish-speaking Russian Jew, born Israel Baelin. Early-career vaudeville performers like Fanny Brice and Sophie Tucker could work to demonstrate their cultural adaptability by putting a self-mocking Jewish twist to the minstrel show and the "coon song" (which surely the Klan songwriters should have appreciated, given their own tiresome and less witty appropriations from the same sources). But it was to no avail; the Jews could never be 100% enough. And so the Klan sang:

O Jew, O Jew, my huckleberry Jew,
Be careful what you do, do
The tide may turn most any time
And leave you in a stew, too,
So keep your tongue, and hold your peace
The very best you can,
For something's coming up the road,
That looks like the Ku Klux Klan.

The Klan had one particularly powerful ally when it came to using music to promote 100% Americanism and taking down the Jewish menace in the process: the industrialist Henry Ford, whose newspaper, the *Dearborn Independent*, published William J. Cameron's defamatory series *The International Jew* over ninety-one issues beginning in 1920. Amidst a host of conspiracy theories about global Jewish domination and corrupting influences was the argument that the ancient prayer "*Kol Nidre*" was actually a crafty ode to the skill of Jewish mendacity, a chanted promise of eternal betrayal; that the psalm "*Eli Eli*" was in fact a coded Jewish-Bolshevik war cry, and that "Yiddish song manufacturers" were responsible for the country's heinous musical degradation. "Jazz," Cameron said – with Ford's enthusiastic backing – was "a Jewish creation," degenerate as the race itself: "The mush, the slush, the sly suggestion, the abandoned sensuousness of sliding notes, are of Jewish origin." The chief culprit, Irving Berlin, had put "unashamed erotic suggestions" into the minds of American youth through "slimy" rhythms reeking of the "Congo." Ford's own highly publicized predilection for square dancing and old-time fiddling revivals must be seen in light of his campaign to protect America from the degrading influences of ragtime and jazz. As Peter La Chapelle argues, Ford built upon Fiddlin' John Carson's earlier use of "country music for anti-Semitic ends" while anticipating its later use in "racist or xenophobic movements" by Jim Crow politicians like Eugene Talmadge and George C. Wallace.

Of course, Cameron, Ford, and their allies in the Klan would never have considered the ridiculousness of the "International Jew" conspiracy theory even if they had thought of non-Jewish capitalists like the Rockefellers, Vanderbilts, Morgans, and Carnegies, or if they had heard any of the songs coming from the sweatshops of New York's Lower East Side, where poor Jewish immigrants, parted from their families in Europe, worked themselves to death as they sang:

Ludlow St . . . dreary tall dwellings,
Many dark stairways there . . .
Dear son, here lives your poor father!
Emaciated and weak is he.

Charity kitchen . . . putrid . . . stale bread . . .
Watery, bitter soup . . .
Dear son, here your poor father eats!
Complaining, he feeds on smoke . . .

He wants to buy a steamship ticket on payments,
Planning to return home for a long time now . . .
Dear son, "slack" is a dreadful period,
And it stands in your father's way.

In the end, Henry Ford professed shock and ignorance when a libel lawsuit forced him to apologize for his anti-Semitic ravings in print, and the *Dearborn Independent* was shut down. The Jewish theater impresario Billy Rose and his songwriting partners had a bitter field day with Ford's eleventh-hour apology:

I was sad and I was blue,
But now I'm just as good as you
Since Henry Ford apologized to me.
I've thrown away my little Chevrolet
And bought myself a Ford Coupe
Since Henry Ford apologized to me.

One can only imagine how the Klan songwriters would have dealt with the knowledge only recently uncovered by the musicologist and discographer Henry Sapoznik – that in their midst, in the 1920s, there was a flourishing fellowship of Black Jewish cantors, male and female, singing not only in Harlem's synagogues but also in concert halls and on the stage of the Yiddish theater. They included Thomas La Rue, known as "*der schvartzer khazn*" (the Black Cantor); "Mendel, *der Shvartzer Khazn*" (Mendel, the Black Cantor); Madame Sophie Kurtzer; "Dovid, *di Kalskrite Ha'Cohen der Falash*" (David Cohen, the Calligrapher from Abyssinia); "Goldye, *di Shvartze Khaznte*" (Goldye, the Black Female Cantor); and others numbering as many as a dozen. Moreover, the celebrated jazz pianist, Willie "the Lion" Smith, was raised in a Black Jewish household, spoke Yiddish, and billed himself on Yiddish business cards as "*der Yiddisher Khazn*" (the Yiddish Cantor) and on English cards as "the Hebrew Cantor."

On the one hand, knowledge of this Black-Jewish fellowship would have only confirmed the Ford–Klan–Cameron hysteria over "mongrelization," but, on the other hand, nothing could be more truly "100% American" than such a glorious admixture. Still, for many American Jews, again, it was to no avail – they could never be American enough – and the songs of exile proliferated in the interwar years:

I wander, old Reb Israel.
I've been wandering for thousands of years,
Driven into exile everywhere.
How long will I keep on wandering,
Seeking my home, my mother's lap.
Tell me, God, how much longer is the road that leads
Out of exile?

Perhaps less crudely stated than the Klan songs, but allied to their objectives, were the terms of the Immigration Act of 1917 (the "Barred Zone Act") and the Immigration Act of 1924 (the "Johnson–Reed Act" or "National Origins Quota Act"). These were "attempts by restrictionists to prohibit the immigration of certain racial and national groups that had been deemed racially inferior," designed "to make it difficult for almost all individuals – except those from northern and western Europe – to immigrate." In 1925, none other than Franklin D. Roosevelt penned a series of nine guest editorials for the Macon (Georgia) *Telegraph*, eventually collected as *Roosevelt Says*, urging the separation of white and Asian "races" – notably but not exclusively the Japanese. As FDR argued: "The mingling of white with oriental blood on an extensive scale is harmful to our future citizenship . . . As a corollary of this conviction, Americans object to the holding of large amounts of real property of land, by aliens or those descended from mixed marriages. Frankly, they do not want non-assimilable immigrants as citizens." Not only East Asians but those from the Indian subcontinent, too, were caught up in the restricted quota system enforced by a 1923 Supreme Court decision denying them citizenship on the grounds that "South Asians, who had previously been treated as Caucasians, were not 'free white persons' under the law. They were defined as Asian under immigration and naturalization procedures" – and so they fell into the jurisdiction of the "Asiatic Barred Zone." As for both North and sub-Saharan Africans: "Because they were seen as racially inferior and inassimilable to American civilization, government officials created a miniscule quota for all of Africa: only one thousand persons total" per year.

China was still sexy, inasmuch as it could be accessed through the filter of exotic stage and song performance. Yet, for actual Chinese performers, well, the Chinese Exclusion Act Case Files in the US National Archives are bursting with labor and entertainment lawyers' petitions for "entry permits, quotas, transfers, extensions, [and] travel," as well as petitions against "detention and deportation" – including "sizable files for six Cantonese opera theaters or troupes for the years 1921 to 1943 and numerous files of individual performers at all ports of entry." It was much easier to access the exotic fix through "yellowface" performances – not only in cabaret and vaudeville settings, where songs like "I Am Chu Chin Chow of China" and "China Dragon Blues" floated in an aural haze of "parallel fifths ... to simulate Asian music," but also on the grand opera stages with Chinese-themed heavyweights like Franco Leoni's *L'Oracolo* and Puccini's *Turandot.*

The besieged communities banded together. They needed cultural sustenance – and there was a market for it. This was the period that saw the emergence of ethnically based recording labels churning out 78-rpm discs of folk songs, dance music, and comic songs: "For example, Lebanese, Syrian, Palestinian, and Turkish Armenian musicians were engaged by major record labels such as Columbia, Victor, or His Master's Voice for their 'foreign language' series." Arab American labels included "Maloof, Macksoud, Ma'rouf, Star of the East, Abdel Ahad, Cleopatra, Nilephon, Metrophon, Arabphon, Golden Angel, and Orient," while "Turkish Armenian musicians established their own recording companies, including Kalaphon, Balkan, Parsekian, Metropolitan, and Stamboul."

This period also saw the emergence of the Black market for "race records," inaugurated by Mamie Smith's recording of Perry Bradford's "Crazy Blues" in 1920. (As Peter Muir points out, "This has had the remarkable consequence of 'Crazy Blues' being identified as the effective beginning of commercial blues ... thereby denying the existence of over four hundred blues that had been published and recorded before that date.") White-owned record companies appear to have exercised a fair degree of tyranny in trying to maintain the coherence of this market, forbidding Black bands from recording anything other than "hot jazz" or blues and promoting the primitivist fiction that Black musicians were only capable of wild improvisation. Pianist Eubie Blake recalled:

> Now, the white bands all had their music stands, see, but the people wanted to believe that Negroes couldn't learn to read music but had a natural talent for it. So we never played with no music. Now this is the truth. [James Reese] Europe's orchestra was filled with readin' sharks. That cornet player, Russell Smith! If a fly landed on the music, he'd play it, see, like that. But we weren't supposed to read music ... All the high-tone, big-time folks would say, "Isn't it wonderful how these untrained, primitive musicians can pick up all the latest songs instantly without being able to read music?"

Blake's own seminal opera, *Shuffle Along* (1921), written with Noble Sissle, should have put paid to such ignorant assumptions – just as his "finger-busting, virtuosic piano solos" should have done. This is not to mention the formal compositions of Europe, Burleigh, Cook, and Rosamond Johnson; the rags of Scott Joplin and his protégé, James Scott; the careers of the concert violinist Joseph Douglass (grandson of Frederick) and the autistic pianist and composer born into slavery, Thomas "Blind Tom" Wiggins; the choral complexities of the Fisk Jubilee Singers; the operatic and classical singing of Carroll Clark, Sidney Woodward, Sissieretta Jones, Marie Selika Williams, Sampson Williams, Thomas Bowers, Sarah Sedgwick Bowers, and Elizabeth Taylor Greenfield – indeed, the long train of Black American composition and performance dating back to Occramer Marycoo's *Promise Anthem* of 1764. It was partially the ignorance and inflexibility of white record producers that prompted the music publisher Harry Pace to establish the first Black-owned record label – Black Swan Records, named in honor of Greenfield, the "Black Swan" – in 1921, with the likes of James Weldon Johnson and William Grant Still on the Board of Directors and Fletcher Henderson as inhouse arranger and recording manager.

No wonder that amidst the racial defamation, cultural and political hostility, and naked violence that marked these years of "100% Americanism," liberation movements like Marcus Garvey's "Back to Africa" project should have been at their peak, with songwriters like I. E. Guinn proclaiming: "Arise, ye Garvey nation, home abroad, go forth; / Go forth across the seven seas, proclaim, / Proclaim a future year of freedom / When home across the sea shall meet at home sweet home." And no wonder that, for those who chose to remain in the country they had, after all, built with their own hands, the importation of West African "songs of derision" – dripping with satire and coded attacks – should have been taken up, via the West Indian diaspora, by the practitioners of the emerging musical genre calypso, whose "golden era" began in the 1920s.

Moreover, in the twisted logic of "100% Americanism," it appears that the least "American" of all were the Indigenous peoples below the forty-ninth parallel and the Alaska Natives above it. Why else would the Commissioner of Indian Affairs, Charles Burke, issue his infamous "special circular on Indian dances" in 1921, outlawing what he called the "dance evil" and its associated songs? (Apparently the Lakotas' wartime "victory songs" against the Kaiser had outlived their brief usefulness.) The aim of such official demonization, as ever, was to "prime" (or force) Indigenous Americans into shunning "their tribal identities and assimilate into American society." In Point Hope, Alaska, children resisting being schooled out of their tribal identity resorted, in song, to what the oppressed groups southward had long been resorting to: coded expressions of satire and derision at the expense of their oppressors. A song collector noted their mockery of an English song taught to them in the 1920s by a missionary from the lower USA: "The melody and the words are definitely not Inupiaq, but the sounds of the English words have been changed and distorted toward that of Eskimo words, while remaining meaningless. The melody sounds like that of 'Marching to Pretoria.' Its performance is always accompanied by great mirth." Less mirthful, however, was the missionaries' ultimate success in "wiping out all vestige of Eskimo musical forms" along Alaska's Kobuk River, as it was recalled in the 1970s: "Dancing is considered the work of the devil, and a few borrowed tapes, surreptitiously guarded, are all that remain of regularly held competitive dances, song partnerships, treasured family songs, and children's game songs."

And what of that other group of people who had lived on what became US territory *before* it became US territory? How did they fare in the atmosphere of "100% Americanism"? Not well, thanks to a particular catch in the 1917 Immigration Act, a literacy test and a head tax: "Although there was no language in either the Barred Zone Act or the National Origins Quota Act about controlling immigration from the Western Hemisphere, the literacy test and head tax often led to the deportation of Mexican immigrants." But Mexicans were always valued as cheap, temporary, contract labor north of the Río Grande, and so they endured countless indignities when they crossed the border. One of these measures led to the so-called Bath Riots on the border of El Paso and Juárez in 1917, when a seventeen-year-old girl named Carmelita Torres led a protest of Mexican workers being sprayed with toxic pesticides before being allowed into the country. (A similar affront was faced by Jews and other arrivals from Eastern and Southern Europe on Ellis Island.) The following year, in the twin cities of Ambos Nogales on the Arizona–Sonora border, Mexican and US border guards fought a gun battle against each other over the threatened detention of a lone Mexican worker crossing back into Sonora. At the end of it, three Americans and an estimated thirty Mexicans lay dead, with another fifty wounded on both sides. Out of this bitter tragedy came "*El corrido de Nogales*":

> Brave Nogalians
> Did their duty:
> They fought the gringos
> Until death or victory.

On the twenty-seventh of August,
At about four o'clock,
Rifle shots
Were heard on the border.

When a Mexican crossed
The border line,
A gringo fired a shot at him:
That was the beginning of the story.

After many stanzas, the corrido concludes:

Every vile Mexican
Who tramples on his flag
Is the slave of the gringos
And traitor to the nation ...

The man who composed this corrido
Sings it for fifty cents,
And he especially made it
For the heroes of Nogales.

Other corridos of the immediate postwar years tell of the misery of Texas-based Mexican Americans – nominally US citizens – facing the same hardships and bigotry endured by contract laborers from across the border:

In the year of 1923
Of the present era,
The beet-field workers went
To that Michigan, to their grief.

Here they come and they tell you
That we ought to go up there
Because there we will have everything
And we will not have a hard time.

But these are nothing but lies.
When we are over there
They begin to scold us
And we want to return ...

When we arrived at Houston,
Working night and day,
They didn't feed us anything,
Nothing more than watermelon.

Corridos of the period also fought fire with fire, challenging the sanctity of "100% Americanism" by extolling "that which was Mexican as opposed to that which was Yankee." Some undercut all patriotic bombast – Mexican or American – with ironic, self-mocking undertones similar to those of Migliaccio's Italian American *cafone*:

California is beautiful,
I had a great time there;
The thing I did not like,
Women are boss there.

I want to tell you about California
And about the state of Nevada,
Where Spanish is not spoken,
Only the American language . . .

The chicks from California
Do not know how to eat tortillas;
What they like on the table
Is bread and butter . . .

Mexico is horrible, they say,
Because of all the mixtures;
They speak in their own language,
And then they say "good-bye."

The gringos are so simple,
They do not know Sonora;
And when they want to say ten bits,
They say "dollar and a quarter."

The gringos are stupid,
They do not know Teocaltiche;
When they get mad at us,
They say "son of a bitch."

Other corridos make it clear that losing one's cultural identity to the tyranny of "100% Americanism" is a great loss indeed: "All of us want to speak / The American language, / Without understanding / Our own Spanish tongue."

But there was one final news flash: "100% American" didn't apply only to ethnicities and nationalities. It also applied to genders. There were specific ways for "real" American men and "real" American women to behave – at least, that's what the Klan songbooks taught. The musical indoctrination began very young, casting women as men's helpers and handmaidens, whiter than white and more Christian than Christian.

It would be found in *Ritual of the Tri-K-Klub* (1925), published by the "Tri-K-Klub, a Department of Women of the Ku Klux Klan for Teenage Girls," based in Little Rock, Arkansas. Or, it might be in the *Song Book for Women of the Ku Klux Klan*, published for "Mary I. Goodwin, Major Kleagle of Pennsylvania" in 1924. The *KKK Katechism and Song Book* (1924), published in Columbus, Ohio, would be an equally useful source. North or South, it didn't matter: "100% Americanism" was truly a national entity, as was the Klan itself. And all a good, 100% American Klanswoman needed to remember was this: "Carry me back to Old Virginia, / To the work of Women of the Ku Klux Klan; / Guard well our schools, our homes and our churches, / God keep them safe that they may forever stand."

But as long as the Deity was being invoked, thank God something else was afoot to undermine the monolithic monstrosity of "100% Americanism." It was signaled on the official stage in June of 1919 with the passage of the Nineteenth Amendment, which was sent to the states for ratification and became law in 1920. Women across the land could now vote. Of course their enfranchisement would be challenged and undermined, particularly in the Jim Crow South, where Black women would see their new, hard-won voting rights chipped away by the likes of poll taxes, literacy tests, and grandfather clauses. But on another stage – indeed, a completely different one – a quiet disturbance was rumbling along, marking currents of change beyond the reach and sterility of the Klanswoman's Katechism. Michael Bronski describes this stage as "an important social space where the concept of the new American woman – economically independent, sexually free, not necessarily heterosexual, and refusing to conform to social standards of beauty – was visible." It was the vaudeville stage, and onto it stepped one of the most gloriously nonconformist of all the century's musical figures. Her name was Eva Tanguay, and her signature song reflected the spirit that was needed to spit into the face of bigotry, sanctimony, and even terror – a spirit that, on the surface, belies the pain and commitment driving all liberating activism, as well as the necessity of holding one's nerve steady in the struggle against domination. The title of her song was "I Don't Care."

Jean Lenox and Harry O. Sutton published the song in 1905, but Tanguay had made it her own by 1922, when she recorded it. Hers wasn't a petulant "I Don't Care" – not the "I Don't Care" that Melania Trump had scrawled across the back of her jacket during a notorious visit to a migrant children's prison in Texas (a fashion choice that prompted considerable speculation). No, Tanguay's was a wholly different "I Don't

Care," one that her biographer Andrew Erdman sees as being embodied in her "self-determination and individual morality," as well as her challenge to "authorities" of all stripes. Tanguay shortened the original song, leaving out Lenox and Sutton's more ephemeral references to the political figures and events of their day (the 1904 presidential election, William Randoph Hearst, the Russian-Japanese War). She would periodically alter and substitute stanzas during her performing career, but she retained the song's core of individualism and personal autonomy in a new era already different from the composers' own:

> I don't care, I don't care
> What they may think of me;
> I'm happy-go-lucky, men say that I'm plucky,
> I'm happy and carefree.

Figure 12.1 Eva Tanguay on sheet music cover of Lenox and Sutton's "I Don't Care," c. 1922.
Public domain via Wikimedia Commons

I don't care, I don't care
If I should get a mean and stony stare.
And no one can faze me by calling me crazy,
'Cause I don't care.

Jody Rosen describes the dynamics of Tanguay's onstage performances: "She delivered her songs while executing dervishlike dances, complete with limb-flailing, leg kicks, breast-shaking, and violent tosses of the head; often, she seemed to be simulating orgasm." Rosen concludes: "In a country being remade by modernity – by new machines and new immigrants, by rising skylines and rising hemlines – Tanguay's madcap screech was audibly, if not scientifically, the soul of America." The purveyors of "100% Americanism" – not least those in the "Department of Women of the Ku Klux Klan for Teenage Girls" – would of course take issue with this construction of America's "soul"; but events tended to outrun them.

Events seem to have outrun a number of male songwriters as well. Some affected a degree of nervousness, although it wasn't always clear whether a parodical bluff was being played at resistant men's expense, as in Jack Stern and William Tracey's "You'd Better Be Nice to Them Now," a reflection on the late changes in the workforce brought about by the war and the Nineteenth Amendment:

Girls are filling men's positions nowadays
And making good at ev'rything they try.
They've found out they're useful in a lot of ways;
Go, get the money, is their battle cry.
Boys, you've got to hand it to the ladies,
Here's some good advice for you.
You'd –

Better be nice to them now.
Oh! you'd better be nice to them now.
Take your sweetie to a preacher right away;
She may come in handy for a rainy day.
It's all on account of the war.
Your job isn't safe anymore . . .

Ever since the nation granted women's right,
They've been preparing so they'd stand the test.
They've been sitting up and scheming ev'ry night,
And picking out the trade that they like best.
Pretty soon the girls will form a union;
Then you'll have no chance at all.
You'd –

Better be nice the them now . . .

"Flappers," "Modern Women," the "New Girl" – all of them, in their own way, saying "I Don't Care" – certainly got the goats of men in the more conservative, macho sectors of the culture. In the Mexican American community, *flapperismo* ("flapperdom") was a worry, and the *pelona* ("flapper") the subject of satire and ridicule from the pens of male songwriters and the singers of corridos: "Common fears were that wives and daughters were venturing out of the house, showing too much skin, working and dancing with Anglo-Americans, and losing both the Spanish language and Hispanic culture. In other words, *flapperismo* conflicted with the expected domesticity and modesty from women." Men exorcised their fears through songs like "*Las tres pelonas*" (The Three Flappers), "*Las pelonas*" (simply "The Flappers"), and "*Corrido de los pizcaores*" (The Cotton Pickers' Corrido, scorning the "Modern Women" and "New Girls" who refused to work in the fields).

Linking a discussion of *machismo* in corridos to that in calypso songs, Zena Moore points to the influence of conservative Catholic doctrine in both producing communities – the Latinx and the West Indian (including the diasporic) – instilling assumptions "about women as inferior, as fulfilling roles of submissive handmaids of the lords, and as responsible for the fall of men." These assumptions would remain in place for decades – at least to the extent that they could be simultaneously affirmed and undercut in parodical calypsos such as "Women Will Rule the World" by Atilla the Hun (Raymond Quevedo): "Long ago they chose to be schoolteachers, then they became stenographers, / We next hear of them as lecturers, authors, and engineers. / There is no limit to their ambition; they've gone in for aviation, / And if you men don't assert control, women will rule the world."

One important profession goes unmentioned by Atilla the Hun: classical music composition. While Eva Tanguay was at the height of her celebrity, earning $3500 a week ("out-earning the likes of Al Jolson, Harry Houdini, and Enrico Caruso"), two as yet unknown women – one white and one Black, neither of them wealthy – were quietly forging their compositional careers. In Chicago, Ruth Crawford, newly graduated from the American Conservatory of Music, began teaching piano to the daughters of Carl Sandburg and thought of setting some of his poems to music. At roughly the same time, in the same city, Florence Price – who'd had to "pass" as Mexican in order to get accepted into the New England Conservatory of Music – already had a string trio, some piano pieces, and a symphony under her belt. She also had an unhappy, stressful marriage to endure and two young daughters to care for. Price had yet to meet

Langston Hughes, whose lyrics she would put to music, along with those of Paul Laurence Dunbar. Through the music of these two women, the men's voices would sing. But both Crawford and Price would inevitably struggle to get past the blank faces of the men in the musical establishment – the builders of the canon – who would look at their work and say, in effect, "I Don't Care." Price and Crawford would have to make them care.

CHAPTER 13

We're Up Against It Now

Conjuring up an alternate universe in which Eugene Bullard might have flown for the USA instead of France, Blind Lemon Jefferson sang: "Got an airplane, baby, now I'm going to get a submarine. . . . / Going to get that Kaiser, and we'll be seldom seen." But what do you do with a fleet of slightly used Curtiss or De Havilland bi-planes and no foreign enemies to bomb? Answer: you sell them off as war surplus, which is precisely what the US Army Signal Corps did. A number of them ended up at the Curtis-Southwest airfield outside of Tulsa, Oklahoma.

In June of 1921, the "Tulsa Massacre," sparked by a baseless rumor of a young Black man assaulting a young white woman in an elevator, ended with the entire Greenwood district of the city – the prosperous "Black Wall Street" – burned to the ground. Close to three hundred people died, almost all of them Black Americans. A number of eyewitnesses – Black and white – reported seeing a squadron of privately owned Curtiss "Jennies" soaring over the city. One witness was the Tulsa lawyer Buck Colbert Franklin, father of the eminent Black historian John Hope Franklin. As he reported it:

> I could see planes circling in mid-air. They grew in number and hummed, darted and dipped low. I could hear something like hail falling upon the top of my office building. Down East Archer, I saw the old Mid-Way hotel on fire, burning from its top, and then another and another and another building began to burn from their top. . . . Lurid flames roared and belched and licked their forked tongues into the air. Smoke ascended the sky in thick, black volumes and amid it all, the planes – now a dozen or more in number – still hummed and darted here and there with the agility of natural birds of the air. . . . The side-walks were literally covered with burning turpentine balls. I knew all too well where they came from, and I knew all too well why every burning building first caught from the top. I paused and waited for an opportune time to escape. "Where oh where is our splendid fire department with its half dozen stations?" I asked myself. "Is the city in conspiracy with the mob?"

If such accounts are true, this would mark the first aerial bombing of a US city, twenty years before Pearl Harbor. At least one historian maintains that the Curtis Jenny would not have been equipped for effective aerial bombing, and that the planes were more likely used for psychological rather than tactical reasons – for purposes of domestic terrorization. Even so, that would have been bad enough, not least because it was an idea that was bound to catch on elsewhere.

And so it did, two months later, over Blair Mountain, West Virginia, where up to ten thousand armed coal miners fought against US Army troops and private detectives over the right to unionize. It was a battle that had been raging at fever pitch for over a month, sparked by the murder of a sympathetic police chief, Sid Hatfield, and other allies who had been siding with the striking miners in nearby Matewan. The World War I flying ace General William "Billy" Mitchell thought it would be a good idea to step in with a bit of aerial terror – in the first instance. As he reassured reporters upon his arrival in West Virginia: "You understand we wouldn't try to kill people at first. We'd drop tear gas all over the place. If they refused to disburse then we'd open up with artillery preparation and everything." In the end, the Army backed off from the idea; but the local sheriff hired three private airplanes to attack the miners with "tear gas and pipe bombs." The bombing was inept, and the missiles were either duds or fell wide of the mark. But this was beside the point: the willingness of lawmen to kill US citizens from the air was plain for all to see.

At less than two decades old, the airplane was still a source of wonder and romance in popular music, from Arthur Pryor's "Aeroplane Dip" (1904) to Alfred Bryan and Fred Fisher's "Come, Josephine, in My Flying Machine" (1910) to Fred Clifford and David Carver's "In Cupid's Biplane" (1916). The archives have not yet yielded up any songs commemorating these two particular examples of airborne domestic terror – Tulsa and Blair Mountain – but it would be apt to borrow a contemporary title from elsewhere to apply to these sorry episodes in US history: "We Are Up Against It Now."

The title of that Uncle Dave Macon song rang true for so many across the land, even as the stock market climbed toward its precipitous peak of October 1929. In social gatherings on Wall Street and in the leafy suburbs where the stockbrokers lived, young newbies to the profession – the runners and gofers – staged "impromptu cabaret" acts for their bosses and their wives, singing in harmony: "O hush thee, my babe, granny's bought some more shares, / Daddy's gone to play with the bulls and the bears, / Mother's buying on tips and she simply can't lose, / And baby shall have some expensive new shoes." At the same time, five hundred miles to the south and only a stone's throw from Matewan and Blair Mountain, a fiddler named Blind Alfred Reed was stringing together the words and notes that he would record right after the Wall Street Crash: "Officers kill without a cause, / Then complain about funny laws. / Tell me how can a poor man / Stand such times and live?"

The agricultural sector was particularly hard hit, and labor was well aware of it. Since the 1890s, farmers and union activists had been working together in various combinations using the hyphenated "Farmer-Labor" designation, but the impact of the Red Scare and the anti-union terror of the Ku Klux Klan in many agricultural areas strangled the movement by the late 1920s. Gone were such anthems as "The Farmers' Union Song" encouraging solidarity ("When we weaken and dishearten, as the ranks around us fall; Goodbye to selfish interest, farewell, strife to you, / For the Union is sure to triumph, if we all stay true"). Farmers now had to rely for their musical championship on the likes of Fiddlin' John Carson – hardly a voice for radical activism – who in 1924 revived Knowles Shaw's old populist philippic from the Grange days, "The Farmer Feeds Us All," recording it as "The Farmer Is the Man That Feeds Us All." It is highly ironic that in 1944, when the Special Committee on Un-American Activities began investigating the American Peace Mobilization, they cited Carson's words, as printed in *Songs of APM*, as incriminating evidence of "un-American propaganda activities":

> The farmer is the man, that farmer is the man, lives on credit till the fall,
> With the interest rate so high it's a wonder he don't die
> For the banker is the man who gets it all.
> When the banker says he's broke and the merchant's up in smoke,
> They forget that it's the farmer feeds them all;
> It would put them to a test if the farmer took a rest,
> Then they'd know that it's the farmer feeds them all.

Songs of defeat seemed to be everywhere. In 1929, the North Carolina string band, the Bently Boys, recast an earlier folk song, "Hard Times," as "Down on Penny's Farm." It would in turn become the inspiration for Bob Dylan's "Hard Times in New York Town" (1961). The Bentlys looked to the misery of the unprotected tenant farmer:

> George Penny's renters, they'll come into town,
> With their hands in their pockets, and their heads hanging down,
> Go in the store and the merchant will say:
> "Your mortgage is due and I'm looking for my pay" . . .

Down in his pocket with a trembling hand –
"Can't pay you all but I'll pay you what I can."
Then to the telephone the merchant makes a call,
"They'll put you on the chain gang if you don't pay it all."

It's hard times in the country,
Out on Penny's farm.

Even Tin Pan Alley was sympathetic to the farmers' plight. In 1928, soon after leaving Irving Berlin's music firm to start his own publishing company, the country and jazz arranger Bob Miller cowrote, with Emma Dermer, the hit song "Eleven Cent Cotton." Miller recorded the song as "Bob Ferguson," charting the descending spiral of the price of cotton from eleven cents a pound to five cents, while the price of meat remained at forty cents a pound. It was the mathematics of slow starvation: "Five cent cotton and forty cent meat, / How in the hell can a poor man eat? / Just look me over and you can see / That a good square meal is gonna kill poor me!"

The air of defeat drifted out beyond the agricultural sector. In the railroad depots, former militancy had turned to contrition in the wake of failed strike action. In 1923, between four and five thousand engineers and workers on the Virginia Railway had struck for better wages, better terms of service, and recognition of the Brotherhood of Locomotive Engineers. The strike was broken, and one former engineer, Roy Harvey, who sidelined as a guitarist for Charlie Poole's North Carolina Ramblers, wrote a song in hopes of getting his old job back: "I was one among the number that made the sad mistake, / And left my good old railroad job, my engine did forsake; / And now I'm sure downhearted, for I have no job at all, / But I'd like to run an engine on the Virginian again this fall." It was to no avail; there was no more working on the railroad for Roy Harvey.

To the south, an anonymous Mexican wrote and sang a corrido of *his* hopeless times working on the railroad (and elsewhere) as a nominally "illegal" immigrant in a land that within living memory had been Mexico:

One day, desperate from all the revolutions,
I crossed to the USA without paying the immigration . . .

Upon reaching the station, I came upon a "brother"
And he invited me to work for the "traque."

I thought "El Traque" was a fancy department store,
But it was fixing the rails where the trains run.

What a "brother"! What a "brother"!
How you took me to the railroad tracks!

When I got tired of "El Traque" he invited me again
To pick tomatoes and to hoe beets.

There I earned indulgences crawling on my knees,
Bowing down for three, four, and five miles . . .

I traveled on to California and saw all its orange groves
And all the huge tomato farms.

The beautiful state of Texas with its huge agricultural farms
Has many crops; all is very beautiful.

The gringuitos would ask me, "Do you like what you see?
It used to belong to the Mexicans, now it is all ours."

One immigrant from Finland, Arthur Kylander – former Wobbly, laborer, mandolinist, and songwriter – found himself in a New York recording studio a year before the Wall Street Crash, recalling his own hard times on the railroad in the song "*Siirtolaisen ensi vastuksia*" (The Immigrant's First Difficulties):

I left Finland behind me.
Like others I was headed to the golden land of the west.
I heard the echo of the strange language and I listened to it.
The first words I heard I still remember: No sir . . .

I heard that they needed men on the railroad.
I was hired, and thought that I could keep my job.
They yelled to me "hurry up," and other things.
I could not yet understand it so I replied: No sir . . .

Was any relief to be found anywhere? As ever, those who could afford it might spend a few cents to go to a stage show, where the collisions of race and nationality could be turned into uproarious comedy. And, as ever, great liberties were taken in the name of entertainment. Rodgers and Hart's *Chee-Chee* (1928), with a cast of Broadway stalwarts in yellowface, raised the roof at the expense of a young Chinese man fleeing from an impending career as a eunuch. George and Ira Gershwin's contribution to the Ziegfeld revue *East Meets West* (1929) was "In a Mandarin's Orchard Garden," one of the decade's many "superficially sinicized songs [that] proved exceptionally long-lived." Fortunately for the Chinese Americans in the vicinity of the Great China Theater in Seattle, as well as other stages of the Cantonese opera, there were still alternatives to these minstrel-show holdovers. There were "classical operas" celebrating the "warrior Xin Zhu," "contemporary melancholic operas with courtesan Xiao Dingxiang and the folk-style comic drama featuring local simpleton Shezi Ying" – all of which addressed "popular and common themes reflecting the everyday sentiments, aspirations, and difficulties of existence within the Chinese community of the United States."

The trials of immigration and assimilation were highly marketable on Broadway. Anne Nichols's *Abie's Irish Rose* – about a young Irish Catholic woman who marries a young Jewish man, Romeo-and-Juliet fashion (minus the tragedy) – was enjoying what was up until then the longest run in the history of the Great White Way. It spawned a musical response in the form of Leon De Costa's spin-off, *Kosher Kitty Kelly* (1925), in which the cross-romances between Irish and Jewish characters ultimately conclude with everyone remaining safer and happier within their own immigrant groups. The underlying message of the show seemed reactionary: stick to your own kind. The walls of prejudice separating people might be dismantled, but they might well be restored and even strengthened – a sobering prospect for the American-born children of immigrants hoping to build their own new world. If there was any doubt of the powerful hold of an older immigrant generation on the guilt-ridden consciences of the young, it was dispelled by Sophie Tucker's hit rendition of Jack Yellen and Lew Pollack's tearjerker, "My Yiddishe Momme" (1925), which "centers on the Americanized child's neglect of filial piety" – a neglect that the song's narrator recognizes only too late.

The same year of Tucker's recording, reactionism struck the heart of the country like a lightning bolt in the form of the Scopes Monkey Trial. A high school teacher in Dayton, Tennessee, John T. Scopes, instigated a test case of the state's law prohibiting the teaching of Charles Darwin's theories of evolution. The attorney for the defense was the celebrated civil rights lawyer Clarence Darrow. Prosecuting was the former Nebraska congressman and Secretary of State under Woodrow Wilson, the populist hero and religious conservative William Jennings Bryan. The trial attracted global attention through Darrow's novel decision to cross-examine Bryan as a biblical expert, the judge's guilty verdict, and Scopes's derisory fine of one hundred dollars, which seemed to send a deflating signal about the gravity of the offense. Songwriters drew their battle lines. On the side of the prosecution and the "old religion" was Vernon Dalhart, who recorded Carson J. Robison's "The John T. Scopes Trial" on the first day of the trial itself:

All the folks in Tennessee are as faithful as can be,
And they know the Bible teaches what is right;
They believe in God above and His great undying love,
And they know they are protected by His might . . .

Then, to Dayton came a man with his new ideas so grand,
And he said, "We came from monkeys long ago!"
But in teaching his belief, Mr. Scopes found only grief
For they would not let their old religion go.

A whirlwind of recording followed. The next year alone saw the likes of E. Arthur Lewis's "If I Came from a Monkey," Uncle Dave Macon's "The Bible's True," J. R. Baxter's "You Can't Make a Monkey Out of Me," and Charlie Poole's resurrection of Cal Stewart's twenty-year-old "Monkey on a String." Immigrant communities took note as well. Thus, for the defense and the forces of progressive, enlightened thought, the Finnish singer and songwriter Antti Syrjäniemi offered his "*Daytonin apinajuttu*" (Monkey Business in Dayton), which celebrated Darrow and mercilessly mocked Bryan:

When the arguments became heated,
Bryan's fan moved.
The air churned when Darrow shouted
And demanded an answer to his question:
"How could a whale swallow Jonah
When its throat was so damn narrow?
[How could] the earth revolve
While the sun is standing still?
 Give me a straight answer for once."
 "No, no, I trust the Lord!
 How could a monkey. . . ."

And on the ironic sidelines stood Fiddlin' John Carson with an adaptation of Wendell Hall's "Ain't Gonna Rain No More." Carson's "Ain't No Bugs on Me" mocked both fundamentalism (in the form of the popular evangelist Billy Sunday) and the teachings of Darwin:

Billy Sunday is a preacher,
His church is always full,
For the neighbors gather for miles around
To hear him shoot the bull.

The monkey swings by the end of his tail
And jumps from tree to tree.
There may be monkey in some of you guys,
There ain't no monkey in me.

In the same song, Carson also took a genial swipe at his pals in the Ku Klux Klan: "Well, the night was dark and drizzly, / And the air was full of sleet, / The old man joined the Ku Klux / And Ma, she lost her sheet." Some others did the same, such as Helen Marcell and Peggy Hedges, with "Daddy Swiped Our Last Clean Sheet (and Joined the Ku Klux Klan)" (1924). The problem with such musical jests, of course, was that the Klan enjoyed the notice and even saw them as endorsements, judging from their own recording and redistribution of them. Especially in the latter half of the 1920s, when they were at the height of their terror activities not only in the Jim Crow South but also in the Midwest, there was nothing funny about the Klan.

Famously, in 1927, Jerome Kern and Oscar Hammerstein II threw down a musical gauntlet in defense of the Klan's Black victims with their stage adaptation of Edna Ferber's novel *Show Boat*. They broke Broadway's color line with an interracial cast, a depicted interracial marriage, and a prominent mixed-race character. Moreover, their key song, "Ol' Man River," elevated an implicitly race-based anguish to tragic proportions. Two years later, in the same arena, the Black American team of Thomas "Fats" Waller and Andy Razaf collaborated with Harry Brooks on the musical *Hot Chocolates*, which saw the Broadway debut of Louis Armstrong in the pit orchestra and which hit out at Jim Crow racism with the song "(What Did I Do to Be So) Black and Blue?" This is the song that Ralph Ellison would later choose in his novel *Invisible Man* (1952) to signify the "invisibility" imposed upon Black Americans in a racist culture:

> I'd like to hear five recordings of Louis Armstrong playing and singing "What Did I Do to Be So Black and Blue" – all at the same time. Sometimes now I listen to Louis while I have my favorite dessert of vanilla ice cream and sloe gin. I pour the red liquid over the white mound, watching it glisten and the vapor rising as Louis bends that military instrument into a beam of lyrical sound. Perhaps I like Louis Armstrong because he's made poetry out of being invisible. I think it must be because he's unaware that he is invisible. And my own grasp of invisibility aids me to understand his music.

Blues singers of the period also sang of their invisibility. Against the wishful singing of Lonnie Johnson in "Life Saver Blues" (1927), which confidently asserted that "Uncle Sam's ship" was "coming painted in red, white and blue," others were decidedly more downbeat. Cow Cow Davenport's "Jim Crow Blues" (1927) imprisons the narrator in a potentially unbreakable circle of oppression. "Tired of being Jim Crowed," he vows "to leave this Jim Crow town"; but at the conclusion he is on the verge of going "back to my Jim Crow town." Big Bill Broonzy's "Starvation Blues" (1928) has the narrator facing "starvation in my kitchen"; and again, he is invisible: "Lord I walked to a store; I ain't got a dime. / When I asked for a darn neckbone: the clerk don't pay me no mind." In Tommy Johnson's "Canned Heat Blues" (1928), the singer slowly drinks himself to death with Sterno, "Cryin' mama mama mama / Cryin' canned heat is killin' me." But his cries go unheard and unanswered: "They took my soul, lord, / they gonna kill me dead." The singer of Roosevelt Sykes's "Fire Detective Blues" (1929) pleads: "My house burning down: the firemen are taking their time / Please Mr. fire detective: won't you save this old cabin of mine." His pleas, too, fall on deaf ears: "Let my house burn into ashes: didn't leave me one stick of wood."

The threat of invisibility extended into discussions about Black music itself. Just as James Weldon Johnson had felt obliged to reclaim ragtime from its white popularizers, it was now necessary to do the same with jazz. The first published book devoted to the genre, Henry O. Osgood's *So This Is Jazz* (1926), left no other choice. Osgood devoted his entire attention to the likes of Paul Whiteman, George Gershwin, Irving Berlin, and Ferde Grofé – white men all. He relegated Black input to a solitary footnote marred by precisely the same primitivist ignorance and slander that had so exasperated Eubie Blake:

> Nowhere have I gone into detail about negro jazz bands. There are so many good ones it would be hard to pick out a few for special mention. None of them, however, are as good as the best white bands, and very rarely are their best players as good as the best white virtuosos. Their playing makes up for what it may lack in smoothness and finish by abandon, dash, spirit and warmth. There are fewer trained musicians, consequently more of the improvisations and variations which characterized early jazz.

With all due respect to Osgood's white paragons and emerging white virtuosi like Bix Beiderbecke, Frankie Trumbauer, Joe Venuti, Eddie Lang, Benny Goodman, and Artie Shaw, such race-based condescension was already familiar and tiresome. It was always possible to fight back against it, and Black commentators and musical practitioners did just that. Importantly, they did so against the backdrop of Carter G. Woodson's campaign to promote the teaching of Black American history and culture in schools across the country – a campaign, he said, that was "much more important than the anti-lynching movement, because there would be no lynching if it did not start in the schoolroom."

In 1926, the same year that Osgood's negligent history of jazz appeared, Woodson inaugurated the celebration of Negro History Week, the forerunner of today's Black History Month. Music was central to Woodson's thesis. He argued for the formal teaching of music composition and performance precisely to counter the essentialist, primitivist, race-based assumptions of "natural" talent on the part of whites and Blacks alike: "The small number of Negro colleges and universities which undertake the training of the Negro in music is further evidence of the belief that the Negro is all but perfect in this field and should direct his attention to the traditional curricula." Woodson was particularly concerned with the international projection of African and Black American primitivism – for instance, in Paris, where Josephine Baker, the "Black Venus," enjoyed extraordinary celebrity for her erotic, often topless, "Danse Sauvage" and her habit of bringing her diamond-collared pet cheetah Chiquita onstage at the Folies Bergère and for promenades along the Champs-Élysées. Woodson wrote:

> Some Europeans rather regard the word Negro as romantic. Going now along the streets of Paris, one will see advertised such places as "l'Elan Noir," and the "Café au Nègre de Toulouse." In one of these cases the writer [that is, Woodson himself] was especially attracted by the "Choppe du Nègre" and took dinner there one day. The cuisine was excellent, the music rendered by the orchestra was charming, and a jolly crowd came to enjoy themselves. However, he was the only "Nègre" there.

With his concerns over primitivism thus voiced, Woodson also took pains to correct the "misguided" Black Americans "graduating from conservatories of music [who] dislike the singing of our folk songs." This was a position shared by Langston Hughes, whose seminal essay "The Negro Artist and the Racial Mountain" was published, again, the same year as Osgood's jazz history and Woodson's inauguration of Negro History Week. But for Hughes, the associations of Black vernacular music with the primitivism of the "tom-tom" were a good thing – "the tom-tom of revolt against weariness in a white world, a world of subway trains, and work, work, work; the tom-tom of joy and laughter, and pain swallowed in a smile." Primitivism was equally an assertive weapon for Zora Neale Hurston, who in 1928 published her essay "How It Feels to Be Colored Me," written five years earlier, with its oft-quoted, energetic passage on the experience of listening to jazz with a white friend in a Harlem club:

> I dance wildly inside myself; I yell within, I whoop; I shake my assegai above my head, I hurl it true to the mark *yeeeeooww*! I am in the jungle and living in the jungle way. My face is painted red and yellow and my body is painted blue. My pulse is throbbing like a war drum. I want to slaughter something – give pain, give death to what, I do not know. But the piece

> ends. The men of the orchestra wipe their lips and rest their fingers. I creep back slowly to the veneer we call civilization with the last tone and find the white friend sitting motionless in his seat, smoking calmly.
>
> "Good music they have here," he remarks, drumming the table with his fingertips.
>
> Music. The great blobs of purple and red emotion have not touched him. He has only heard what I felt. He is far away and I see him but dimly across the ocean and the continent that have fallen between us. He is so pale with his whiteness then and I am *so* colored.

And, as Hughes and Hurston wrote it, Duke Ellington played it, beginning a five-year residency at Harlem's Cotton Club in 1927. Surrounded by the deliberately primitivist imagery of the segregated club's decor – where slumming white patrons either got their exhilarating fix or, like Hurston's musically obtuse companion, missed it altogether – Ellington and his band filled the air with the likes of "Hottentot," "Jungle Jamboree," and "Jungle Night in Harlem." Ellington and his trumpeter, Bubber Miley, actually coined the term "jungle music" to describe the low, driving, "growling" sound driven by Miley's muted trumpet. It was a provocative, controversial gamble, appropriating a trope born in bigotry and white supremacism, and turning it on its head in an ironic gesture of cultural affirmation – much like the rap and hip-hop generation's later appropriations of the hated n-word.

In 1928, a musical genre emerged that was unfamiliar to the majority of Americans, although it had been steadily developing in the francophone areas of southwestern Louisiana since the establishment of the Acadian exile community in 1765. The commercial recording of Cajun music was inaugurated by vocalist Cléoma Breux and her soon-to-be husband, accordionist Joe Falcon, with the traditional "*Allons à Lafayette.*" It was a semi-comic song beloved of a community with historical memories of anti-Catholic victimization, exile, longing, and loss. The following year, Creole singer and accordionist Amédé Ardoin and fiddler Dennis McGee recorded six songs for Columbia Records, laying the groundwork for the commercialization of zydeco, the "musical voice" of the region's "diverse black groups" – the descendants of kidnapped Africans and *gens libres de coleur* (free persons of color) from revolutionary Haiti, as well as Indigenous Americans and the descendants of French and Spanish colonists. The cultural work of Cajun and zydeco music would prove crucial, not only in terms of interracial performance and appreciation but also against the continuing pressures of English dominance and the threat of linguistic eradication among the descendants of the original Acadians.

These descendants included the Falcons, who went on to teach their grandchildren the four-hundred-year-old ballads of Brittany, Normandy, and Poitou that had followed the refugee trail to Louisiana by way of Nova Scotia, "stories resonating with Cajun history of love, separation, and death."

Another marginalized – indeed, legally oppressed – group was also making its mark in song, the quiet start to a revolution that perhaps could only begin in a nod-nod, wink-wink fashion forty-three years before exploding into the Stonewall Riots of 1969. In 1926, George and Ira Gershwin wrote what was "probably the first song to use 'gay' to mean *gay*." Their song was called "Don't Ask," from the musical *Oh, Kay!* This was a year before Mae West was slapped with a jail term for her play *Sex*, which the New York authorities had shut down as soon as it opened – and the same year her play *The Drag* instigated "a law banning portrayals of homosexuals on the New York stage which lasted until 1967." Under such repressive circumstances, nodding and winking seemed the only option for the Gershwins: "If you're looking for a playmate / There's a chap whose praises I'd sing. / You will find that he's a gay mate, / If you care for that sort of thing." The Gershwin brothers appear to have been tiptoeing on the heels of Gus Kahn and Walter Donaldson, who had responded to "a big scandal about gay sex in the US Navy" that had been splashed across the headlines in 1921. Their song, "My Buddy" (1922) was "a sensual celebration of, supposedly, military buddies."

Tiptoeing around repression could take many forms. It might be the façade of comedic bewilderment, as in Edgar Leslie and James Monaco's "Masculine Women! Feminine Men!" (1925):

> Masculine women, feminine men
> Which is the rooster, which is the hen?
> It's hard to tell 'em apart today! And say!
> Sister is busy learning to shave,
> Brother just loves his permanent wave,
> It's hard to tell 'em apart today! Hey, hey!
> Girls were girls and boys were boys when I was a tot,
> Now we don't know who is who, or even what's what!
> Knickers and trousers, baggy and wide,
> Nobody knows who's walking inside,
> Those masculine women and feminine men!

Or one might share coded knowledge. In Oscar Wilde's time – the 1890s – it was the green carnation, "a dandy symbol and a covert badge of gayness." In the 1920s, it was "the red necktie." Hence Billy Jones and

Ernest Hare – on the radio as "The Happiness Boys" – with their "What! No Women?" (1926): "What was that girlish laughter just as I passed by? / Oh, that was just a fellow with a red necktie." By the time they recorded this, as Boze Hadleigh notes, "the red tie's meaning was commonly known. ... Gay men therefore stopped wearing them – score another one for the closet."

Following the green carnation and the red tie, the code was "lavender," which – in the next decade – culminated in an onscreen fistfight between the "singing cowboy," Gene Autry, and a heckler in the film *Tumbling Tumbleweeds* (1935), after said heckler taunted him, "Hey, we ain't got no use for lavender cowboys in this town." As Michael Duchemin encapsulates it: "Prominent references connecting 'lavender' with homosexual men stemmed from Carl Sandburg's use of the term to describe a young Abraham Lincoln in 1926. Cole Porter's reference in the song, 'I'm a Gigolo' (1929), included the lyrics: 'I'm a famous gigolo, and of lavender, my nature's got just a dash in it.'" The "Lavender Cowboy" became a well-known cultural figure, not only through the poem of that title by Harold Hersey (1923) but also through its being set to music and appearing in the 1930 western *Oklahoma Cyclone*. In spite of its comedic façade, "The Lavender Cowboy" betrays the anguish of the closeted gay man who represses his sexuality and must strive for acceptance according to the norms of a homophobic culture – in this case, with fatal results:

He was only a lavender cowboy,
The hairs on his chest were two.
He wanted to follow the heroes
To do as the he-men do.

But he was inwardly troubled
By dreams that gave no rest:
When he heard of heroes in action
He wanted more hairs on his chest.

Herpicide and many hair tonics
He rubbed in morning and night,
But when he looked into the mirror,
No new hairs grew in sight.

He battled for Red Nellie's honor
And cleaned out a hold-up nest.
He died with his six-gun a-smokin'
But only two hairs on his chest!

For at least two blues singers in the 1920s, there was no tiptoeing, no coded references, no nodding and winking: simply defiance. Ma Rainey's "Prove It On Me Blues" (1928) made it clear: "They say I do it, ain't nobody caught me / Sure got to prove it on me / Went out last night with a crowd of my friends / They must've been women, 'cause I don't like no men." Angela Davis cites this song as a "precursor to the lesbian cultural movement of the 1970s, which began to crystallize around the performance and recording of lesbian-affirming songs." Rainey's "Prove It On Me Blues" may well have lit an inspirational fire under Waymon "Sloppy" Henry, whose "Say I Do It," recorded the same year, appears to borrow some of Rainey's phrasing in making the case for gay male defiance (perhaps undercut with a hint of cautious closeting):

> Mose and Pete lived on Green Willow Street
> In northwest Baltimore.
> Pete run with Mose 'cause he powdered his nose
> And even wore ladies' hose.
> The two could be seen running hand in hand
> In all kinds of weather
> 'Til the neighbors, they began to signify
> 'Bout the birds that flock together.
> Mose, he began to sigh; Pete yelled out his reply:
>
> Say I do it, ain't nobody seed me,
> They sure got to prove it 'bout me.
> Can't identify a man with a cover over his head;
> When a crab is cooked, he's bound to turn red.
> It's true I use a powder puff and has a shiny face;
> I wears a red necktie 'cause I think it suits my taste.
> I know my voice is tenor, I reduce myself with lace,
> And when you see me with the gang you'll find me singing bass.
> They say I do it, ain't nobody see me,
> They sure got to prove it 'bout me.

Then, as now (and as ever), one's sexuality wasn't simply a "lifestyle choice" – and this was the most odious aspect of the repression that marked the legal and cultural landscape of the USA between the two world wars and long afterwards. But in the late 1920s, it wasn't only gay men and lesbians who had to tread lightly. Pacifists, anarchists, labor activists, and critics of US militarism had to contend with accusations of disloyalty, un-Americanism, anti-Americanism, and Bolshevism. Peace songs were fairly thin on the ground; it was a rare song like the Peerless

Quartet's "My Dream of the Big Parade" (1926), by Jimmy McHugh and Al Dubin, that could still pause to reflect on the boys who "didn't come home." The same year, Blind Lemon Jefferson had a sympathetic word for those who did come home, only to be insulted with the lip service of patriotism while their pockets remained empty – deprived, as they were, of a government bonus promised to them two years earlier: "Uncle Sam wasn't no woman, but didn't he grab your man. . . . / I wish Uncle Sam would hurry up, and pay these soldiers off." And for those pacifists who dared to raise their heads above the parapet, a strong word would be sung at them by the champions of the US Infantry – General Pershing's famous "Doughboys" – who scored a minor hit with their marching song, "The Infantry – Kings of the Highway" (1929), even though World War I was long over and a second one was not yet visible on the horizon: "Oh, the dashing, flashing, smashing, snarling Doughboys / Who for pacifism never give a damn / They hike as the Kings of the Highway / And fight like the sons of Uncle Sam."

In 1928, Blind Lemon Jefferson had something else on his mind, besides unpaid soldiers and patriotic hypocrisy: death – in particular, state murder, politely called "capital punishment." That year, the USA saw 144 executions by hanging and electrocution. The previous year – 1927 – saw 138. The designated crimes were murder, robbery-murder, rape, and attempted rape. In those two years, three white men were convicted of rape or attempted rape; the rest – 26 in all – were Black men, all in the Southern states. Without referring to any particular cases, it should be accepted that, in the Jim Crow South, charges of rape against Black men were useful tools in the maintenance of white supremacy and the masking of "white crimes" under the guise of protecting the sanctity of "white womanhood." As Kristina Du Rocher observes: "The assumption that white womanhood needed safeguarding was based on the belief that white women never desired to engage in sexual relationships with black men. The view of southern females as victims in need of protection also reinforced white men's exclusive sexual access to white women." Jefferson – a Texan – was well aware of this, as he dwelled in detail on the sensation of hanging in the context of a false accusation. His "Hangman's Blues" captures both the racist assumptions of the law and the courthouse mob, as well as the hopelessness of the accused:

> Hangman's rope, it's so tough and strong . . .
> They got to hang me, because I done something wrong.
>
> I want to tell you, the gallows, Lord, is a fearful sight . . .
> Hang me in the morning and cut me down at night.

Well, the mean old hangman, he went and tightened up that noose ...
Lord I'm so scared, I am trembling in my shoes.

Jury heard my case and it said my hand was red ...
And the judge is telling me, be hanging till I'm dead.

The crowd around the courthouse, and the time is growing fast ...
Soon a good-for-nothing killer is going to breathe his last.

Lord, I'm almost dying, gasping for my breath ...
And that trifling woman staying until I breaks my neck.

With equally insightful detail from the point of view of a loved one left behind in the aftermath of a state electrocution, Jefferson's "'Lectric Chair Blues" (1928) mentions no crime, but certainly presents more than one victim:

I walked to the jail with my partner, asked him how come he's here ...
"I had a ruckus with my family; they going to send me to the electric chair" ...

Going to get me a taxi to take me away from here ...
I didn't have but one friendly word, it's to be married to the electric chair.

I feel like jumping in the ocean, like jumping in the deep blue sea ...
Was nothing like that breaking of my heart, when they brought my electrocuted daddy to me.

Buried in the execution statistics for 1927 are two names that have left a legacy in the annals of US miscarriages of justice: Nicola Sacco and Bartolomeo Vanzetti, two Italian anarchists framed for the murder of a payroll guard in South Braintree, Massachusetts, seven years earlier. Convicted after a trial marred by obvious anti-Italian as well as antilabor bigotry – with the notorious judge Webster Thayer openly referring to them as "anarchistic bastards" – Sacco and Vanzetti's case sparked worldwide outcry and a global campaign for their acquittal. With the state impervious to appeals for clemency, the two were electrocuted in August of 1927. Fifty years later, the Governor of Massachusetts, Michael Dukakis, officially proclaimed that "any stigma and disgrace should be forever removed from the names of Nicola Sacco and Bartolomeo Vanzetti." Hanging over the notorious verdict was Judge Thayer's astounding courtroom instruction to the jury as he pointed at Vanzetti: "This man, although he may not actually have committed the crime attributed to him, is nevertheless morally culpable, because he is the enemy of our existing institutions." As Kurt Vonnegut was to marvel decades later: "Word of honor: This was said by a judge in an American court of law."

Figure 13.1 Demonstration in support of Sacco and Vanzetti, Boston, March 1, 1925. Unknown photographer.
Courtesy of the Boston Public Library / Massachusetts Digital Commonwealth

Tackling the case of Sacco and Vanzetti through song would prove to be an arduous task even for Woody Guthrie, commissioned by his producer Moe Asch to compose a concept album devoted to them in 1946. It was another eighteen years before the album was released. Guthrie had confessed to Asch the enormous difficulty in capturing the magnitude of the injustice in song: "I refuse to write these songs while I'm drunk and it looks like I'll be drunk for a long time." In the end, Guthrie's *Ballads of Sacco and Vanzetti* (1964) would prove to be the greatest musical monument to these innocent, martyred men. There was no shortage of literary commentary in the aftermath of the executions: Upton Sinclair's novel, *Boston* (1928); H. G. Wells's *Mr. Blettsworthy on Rampole Island* (1928); John Dos Passos's *The Big Money* (1936); and Howard Fast's *The Passion of Sacco and Vanzetti* (1953) are among the better-known works – Fast having taken his title from Ben Shahn's series of twenty-three paintings based on the case. But before Guthrie's album, musical responses were relatively rare, one noteworthy example being a setting of the Chinese immigrant H. T. Tsaing's poem, "Sacco, Vanzetti" (1928) by Ruth Crawford – by now, Ruth Crawford Seeger – in 1932. Through Crawford Seeger's jarring piano score, Tsaing's words echoed in a modernist discord that aptly reflected the dissonance between law and justice in the case itself:

> Look at your enemies.
> They are fishing,
> Smiling,
> Murdering,
> As ever.
> Shameful!
> It is an eternal disgrace to us all.

Other modernist composers would try their hand at capturing "the Passion of Sacco and Vanzetti," including Crawford Seeger's contemporary Marc Blitzstein, who died in 1964, with what he called his "magnum opus, the three-act opera *Sacco and Vanzetti*," uncompleted. The composer Leonard Lehrman finally completed it for him in 2000.

While most of the musical tributes to Sacco and Vanzetti were composed in the years and decades following their execution, one ephemeral song composed in Italian is particularly valuable because it captures the moment between the guilty verdict and the executions – when there was a still a glimmer of hope that justice might prevail. In 1927, with the executions pending, the celebrated Neapolitan tenor and immigrant, Alfredo Bascetta, recorded his dialect composition, "*Lacrime 'e cundannate*" (Bitter Tears and Two Condemned Men):

> The whole world is turned upside down
> For Sacco and Vanzetti both found guilty
> And those villains who scorned them
> Should never find a minute's rest!
>
> Everyone has been so cold-hearted
> Even the jury – what a cruel company!
> No they don't listen to reason or to innocence
> No this is not justice, this is only wicked vileness!

Another version has Bascetta capturing the intensity of the global appeals that came from Mexico, France, Argentina, Australia, Germany, Morocco, Venezuela, Italy, and further afield – as well as from such prominent individuals as Albert Einstein, Katherine Anne Porter, Thomas Mann, Marie Curie, H. G. Wells, George Bernard Shaw, and Diego Rivera, among many others:

From everywhere protests abound
Appealing for them to be given a pardon
After seven years of misery, incarcerated
Between life and death, for these wretched men
Now the sentence has been confirmed
There is no longer any way for them to be saved

Only the governor can give them justice
If God will stir up his conscience
The pardon he will give

They do not hear the reasons of the innocent ones
But this is not justice, it is cowardice
These wretches weep
They are resigned to their fate
And in their cell they await God's salvation.

"God's salvation" appears to have been in short supply in 1927, not only for Sacco and Vanzetti but also for thousands of people along the Mississippi River and its tributaries, which burst their banks and flooded over 26,000 square miles of land following heavy rains that had begun in the spring of 1926. Like Hurricane Katrina in 2005, the "Great Mississippi Flood of 1927" came to symbolize the height of official neglect and contempt for the poor, particularly the Black poor, who were the hardest hit. Of the roughly one million displaced refugees left in the flood's wake, many were the children of the slaves who had built the first levees. Many, too, were among the convicts and sharecroppers who built the later, largely rudimentary earthen ones. Only after the Great Flood would there be a major Federal initiative to modernize the levee system through the Flood Control Act of 1928. By then, the flood had secured its place as "the nation's greatest natural disaster" – "natural," yes, but one in which human malfeasance surely played a part.

A leading historian of the flood points to one particularly godforsaken place, Mounds Landing, outside of Greenville, Mississippi, where over two thousand Black men were dragooned into building up the bursting levee with sandbags "in a situation resembling slavery":

> Blacks were forced to unload supplies at gunpoint in Greenville and threatened with death if they tried to leave or refused work. If a local white person needed help clearing land or unloading supplies, any black person inside or outside a relief camp could be conscripted. . . . Stories circulated of black people being pulled out of their homes and off the street at gunpoint and physically taken to the levee.

When the levee burst at Mounds Landing, over one hundred Black men were killed.

Figure 13.2 Mississippi flood refugees on the Greenville levee. American Red Cross photograph, 1927.
Library of Congress Prints and Photographs Division

The blues became a great repository of flood memory. Blind Lemon Jefferson's "Rising High Water Blues" (1927), Sippie Wallace's "The Flood Blues" (1927), Porter Grainger's "Homeless Blues" (1927), Charlie Patton's "High Water Everywhere" (1929), and Joe McCoy's "When the Levee Breaks" (1929) are just a handful of indicative titles. Perhaps the best known of the contemporary blues normally associated with the Great Flood is Bessie Smith's "Back Water Blues":

When it rained five days and the skies turned dark as night . . .
Then trouble taken place in the lowlands at night.

I woke up this morning, can't even get out of my door . . .
There's enough trouble to make a poor girl wonder where she want to go.

Then they rowed a little boat about five miles across the pond . . .
I packed all my clothes, throwed them in and they rowed me along.

When it thunders and lightning and the wind begin to blow . . .
There's thousands of people ain't got no place to go.

Then I went and stood up on some high old lonesome hill . . .
Then looked down on my house where I used to live.

Backwater blues done caused me to pack up my things and go . . .
Because my house fell down and I can't live there no more.

Mmm, I can't move no more . . .
There ain't no place for a poor old girl to go.

While this blues powerfully reflects the hopelessness and misery of the 1927 flood victims, at least one scholar argues that it was actually written the previous year, based on the Cumberland River flood that hit Tennessee on Christmas Day of 1926. But rather than detracting from the tragedy of the 1927 Mississippi flood, Smith's "Back Water Blues" situates it in a broader history of natural disaster and human culpability. Indeed, only two years after the Great Mississippi Flood, the Río Grande burst its banks and flooded the railroad town of San Marcial, New Mexico. As it turned out, construction of the nearby Elephant Butte Dam and the creation of Elephant Butte Lake had so slowed the Río Grande's currents that a major flood would only have been a matter of time. In this case, it led to the abandonment of the once-thriving town, memorialized in a corrido by New Mexico's Ramón Luna:

On the 20th of August
I don't like to remember it,
the Río Grande flooded
the town of San Marcial.

It was a sad afternoon
On that date I remember,
that trains arrived from El Paso
to help the people.

The people were wandering frightened
and didn't know what to think,
whether to go to El Paso
or remain in San Marcial . . .

Oh, what a pitiful town,
how it was ruined!
In the middle of all the streets,
hills of sand remained . . .

I composed this corrido
for my countrymen from here,
I will tell them my name
so that they will remember me.

Well, my name is Ramón Luna
and I was born here,
and it's because I feel compassion
for the place where I was born.

When Bruce Springsteen updated Blind Alfred Reed's "How Can a Poor Man Stand Such Times and Live?" to comment on the tragedy of Hurricane Katrina, he included a chilling new couplet: "Them who's got, got out of town / And them who ain't got left to drown." Movement versus stasis; escape versus imprisonment: these contrasts were as fundamental to American life in the early twenty-first century as in the twentieth. In the 1920s, there was always the possibility of driving out of town, away from danger, toward a new promised land – if you could afford it, and if the infrastructure was there to support it. Songwriters, both well-known and anonymous, seemed to address this issue with particular fervor around 1927, the year that Henry Ford's Model T – the first "affordable" car for both the working and middle classes – was finally withdrawn from production. By then, the dehumanization of the automobile production line had become a topic of note, not least for the anonymous songwriter who set his lyrics to the tune of "John Brown's Body":

Mine eyes have seen the glories of the making of a Ford.
It's made under conditions that would offend even the Lord.
With a most ungodly hurry and amidst a wild uproar,
Production rushes on.

Hurry, hurry, hurry, hurry!
Hurry, hurry, hurry, hurry!
Hurry, hurry, hurry, hurry!
Production rushes on.

Be quick, my soul, to answer, and be quicker still, my feet;
Be fifty diff'rent places ev'ry time my heart doth beat.
The whip that drives me onward is my family must eat!
Production rushes on.

Hurry, hurry, hurry, hurry . . .

There was trouble, then, at the production end and trouble (as well as sardonic humor) at the purchasing end – that is, if you were a poor Spanish-speaking resident of the Southwest: "The first Model T Fords rolled into New Mexico with repair manuals written in English. With few translations, names for car parts were adapted directly into Spanish. Terms like '*cranque*' and '*esparque*' still provoke laughter." Hence "the most popular *relación* still performed in New Mexico . . . composed in the late 1920s by Severo Mondragón of Antón Chico":

I have a car so totally beat
Whoever has never driven it
Will never get it rolling . . .

The fenders are crooked
The tires are worn out
The roof is of cardboard.

The radiator is leaking.
The generator is shot,
The transmission is broken.

It doesn't even have a battery
I took it out the other day
Because it was in backwards . . .

"The auto's ruined the country," sang Uncle Dave Macon on the Grand Ole Opry; "Let's go back to the horse and buggy / And try to save some money." As a working wagoner and "dedicated mule-driver," Macon was in a position to comment trenchantly on the passing of an era. Among the litany of complaints in "We Are Up Against It Now" are the new road taxes and the monopolistic price-gouging of the auto dealerships:

We're up against it now,
There's no use to raise a row,
But of all the times I've ever seen
We're sure up against it now.

Since the highway's come,
They've taxed the farmer down
The road's so slick his team can't travel
And he has to walk to town.

Since the auto's come,
Mules and horses won't sell,
The farmer's land is mortgaged down
And the country's gone to, well . . .

A farmer bought him a tractor,
He raised quite an alarm,
He only broke one little piece
And he had to sell his farm.

Uncle Dave held out at least until the end of the decade, defiantly singing in 1928: "Been wagonin' for over twenty years and livin' on the farm, / I'll bet a hundred dollars to half a ginger-cake, I'm here when the trucks is gone." But by then, he had proved himself a martyr to progress in the form of the Ford "trucks" that had nailed shut the coffin of his old mule-and-wagon haulage business: "His answer was brief and to the point, a vintage Macon-style response: 'Boys, you can keep your trucks; just give me my banjo!' At midyear Dave closed the Macon Midway Mule & Mitchell Wagon Transportation Company rather than modernizing to truck transport." The last word was his: "I'm on my way to Heaven, and I tell you just how I feel: / I'd rather ride a wagon and go to Heaven, than to Hell in an automobile."

Modernity had arrived and it was here to stay. You could frail your banjo and complain or, like John Carson, saw your fiddle and complain – along with all those other fragile men still threatened by the advent of the "flappers" and the "new girls." "There's a Hard Time Coming," Carson warned, not least for the "old maids" who would now have to "bob off their hair" and "powder up their face" in order to get a man. The Mississippi singer and guitarist Dutch Coleman advised the same in "Granny Get Your Hair Cut" (1929), with the novel accusation that the "new girls" had ruined the farm economy:

> Some folks, they talk about the farm relief;
> Listen here folks, this is my belief.
> The boll weevil, he's an awful pest,
> But the flappers and the short skirts done the rest.
>
> So, Granny get your hair cut, paint your face and shine,
> Granny get your hair cut short like mine.
> If you want to kick high, have a big time,
> Granny get your hair cut short like mine.
>
> In eighteen hundred and ninety-two
> The women wore their dresses down to the top of their shoe;
> Nineteen hundred and twenty-three,
> They went to wearin' 'em up above their knee.
>
> If the women wear their dresses like they used to,
> Let me tell you farmers what it surely would do:
> Cause your cotton to go to twenty cents a pound –
> When the dresses went upward, why, the cotton went down.

Away from the farm, up in New York town, the Sicilian immigrant Leonardo Dia shook his head sadly as he sang of "*Li fimmini cu lu lipstick*" (The Women with Their Lipstick), with their short skirts and expensive lace fashions:

> Fashion these days is a curious thing,
> Girls, we don't know what they're up to.
> Father and mother are always splashing out money

And for the daughter, her wage just isn't enough
To buy lace and embroidery.

And in America you can't live
With this "fever" she has got
Even a handbag without laces
Just wouldn't be enough . . .

Grandmother would look in wonder,
Asking if you haven't got a longer skirt.
And do you know what else she would say?

There were women, too, for whom lipstick and lace were not the most urgent priorities in 1929. One of these was Ella May Wiggins, balladeer and union activist in the vanguard of the strike against the Loray textile mill in Gastonia, North Carolina, which began in April of that year. As she testified before a congressional investigating committee: "I'm the mother of nine. Four died with the whooping cough, all at once. I was working nights, I asked the super to put me on days, so's I could tend 'em when they had their bad spells. But he wouldn't. I don't know why. . . . So I had to quit, and then there wasn't no money for medicine, and they just died." The air was filled with songs about the atrocious working conditions in the mills and the meager pay, such as Dave McCarn's "Cotton Mill Colic" and "Poor Man, Rich Man (Cotton Mill Colic No. 2)" (both 1930). McCarn's strategic use of humor and exaggeration only served to highlight the awfulness on which his songs were based:

Twelve dollars a week is all we get,
How in the heck can we live on that?
I've got a wife and fourteen kids,
We all have to sleep on two bedsteads . . .

No use to colic; every day at noon
The kids get to crying in a different tune.
I'm a-gonna starve, and everybody will,
'Cause you can't make a living in a cotton mill.

From the vantage point of the 1940s, another textile mill worker, Dorsey Dixon, looked back on the conditions for child laborers in the 1920s. His "Babies in the Mill" (written 1945, recorded 1962) was based on his own recollections and those of his sister Nancy:

> "One night I was working," she remembered, "and I saw a little orphan boy, and he was a-sweeping. And he would get over his floor, and he'd crawl up in the waste box and go to sleep. And I'd wake him up a heap of

> times to keep them from getting after him. And one night they taken him down in the basement and whipped him, and when he come up the steps, he was just screaming as hard as he could. And then the next night, they didn't whip him, but they tied him to the waste box. And I told my father about it, and he told me to keep my mouth out of it."

Dixon captured the situation with pathos:

> I used to be a factory hand when things was moving slow,
> When children worked in cotton mills, each morning had to go.
> Every morning just at five the whistle blew on time,
> To call them babies out of bed at the age of eight or nine . . .
>
> To their jobs those little ones were strictly forced to go;
> Those babies had to be on time, through rain and sleet and snow.
> Many times when things went wrong, their bosses often frowned.
> Many times those little ones was kicked and shoved around.
>
> Come out of bed, little sleepy head, and get you a bite to eat.
> The factory whistle's calling you, there's no more time to sleep.

On the Gastonia front line, Ella May Wiggins was singing, in a sense, a mirror-image of "Babies in the Mill"; it was the despair of the working mother whose children were practically starving. Her most celebrated ballad was "Mill Mother's Lament" (1929):

> We leave our home in the morning, we kiss our children goodbye.
> While we slave for the bosses, our children scream and cry.
> And when we draw our money, our grocery bills to pay,
> Not a cent to spend for clothing, not a cent to lay away.
>
> And on that very evening, our little son will say,
> "I need some shoes, Mother, and so does sister May."
> How it grieves the heart of a mother, you, everyone, must know.
> But we can't buy for our children; our wages are too low.

But Wiggins didn't stop at pathos. She was an organizer for the National Textile Workers Union, which was at the forefront of the Gastonia strike, and her "Mill Mother's Lament" accurately reflected her commitment to both the strike and the union: "It is for our little children, that seem to us so dear; / But for us nor them, dear workers, the bosses do not care. / But understand, all workers, our union they do fear. / Let's stand together, workers, and have a union here." She was also a great voice for the International Labor Defense (ILD), founded in 1925 through the Communist International's "Red Aid" network. The ILD had defended Sacco and Vanzetti, were at the vanguard of the antilynching movement in the USA, and would go on to front the defense of the wrongfully imprisoned Scottsboro Boys – nine young Black Americans falsely convicted of raping two white woman in Alabama. The ILD also supported the struggles of the Gastonia textile workers, and Wiggins rewarded them in song: "Come and join the ILD," she wrote in "Toiling on Life's Pilgrim Pathway." Wiggins's singing was stopped by a bullet in the chest in September 1929, when she was confronted by armed goons as she drove to a union meeting in Gastonia. By then she had already survived "an earlier attempt to poison her water supply." As her coffin was lowered into the ground, mourners sang "Mill Mother's Lament." One of her co-workers concluded: "The bosses hated Ella May because she made up songs, and was always at the speakings. They aimed to git Ella May. They was after her." No one was ever convicted of her murder.

The historical magnitude of the Gastonia strike has threatened to obscure other struggles that were going on at the same time, the memories of which have also been preserved in song. One of these was the nearby strike by the United Textile Workers Union against the Marion Manufacturing Company in Marion, North Carolina. As one historian recounts it: "According to some reports, the working and living conditions in Marion were among the worst in the industry" – a situation that erupted into "the Marion Massacre" in October of 1929, after "mill owners reneged on their pledge that former strikers would not be blacklisted":

> On October 2, after two weeks of vain efforts to reinstate more than a hundred of their fellow workers, millhands working the night shift at the Baldwin mill walked off the job. As they congregated outside the mill in the hope of persuading workers arriving for the day shift to join their protest, the strikers were ordered by the sheriff to disperse. When they hesitated, the sheriff and his eleven deputies, most of whom were on the company's payroll, launched a murderous assault against the unarmed crowd. By the time the gunfire ended, four strikers were dead and more than two dozen, including two who later died, lay seriously wounded. In the aftermath of the carnage, R. W. Baldwin was overheard by several reporters to excitedly exclaim, "Some marksmanship that was. Any time I organize an army the sheriff and his men can join. It took five tons of lead to kill a man in the great war. It took only a few ounces to kill one here in Marion. Some shooting."

Both the strike and the union were broken, leaving in their wake a sad relic set to the tune of the spiritual, "We Are Climbing Jacob's Ladder" ("We won't budge until we conquer, / Workers in the mill!") and the eternal question posed in the struggles of labor against capitalist greed:

These men were only asking
Their rights and nothing more;
That their families would not suffer,
With a wolf at every door.

Why is it over money
These men from friends must part;
Leaving home and loved ones
With a bleeding, broken heart?

It was a question many others were asking in 1929. In New York's Spanish Harlem – *El Barrio* – a veteran of James Reese Europe's "Hell Fighters" Band, the songwriter and multi-instrumentalist Rafael Hernández Marín, was thinking of home. "Home" was a place called the Port of Riches – Puerto Rico – but the name was a cruel jest to the poor farmers, the *jíbaros* left behind as struggling colonial subjects of the USA. For this reason, in 1925, Hernández Marín had titled his damning critique of the US takeover "*Pobre Borinquen*" – Poor Borinquen (alternatively Borikén). He had chosen the name used by the island's original inhabitants, the Taínos, before the insult of "Puerto Rico" was imposed upon it by the Spanish colonizers. Hernández Marín's "*Lamento Borincano*" (Puerto Rican Lament), written in 1929, would become for Puerto Ricans what Yip Harburg and Jay Gorney's "Brother, Can You Spare a Dime?" would become for US Americans: "a virtual theme song for the Depression." "*Lamento Borincano*" tells "the tragic story of the *jíbaro*, the peasant, as he travels from the countryside to the city in Puerto Rico to sell his 'load' only to discover that there are no buyers":

He departs, overjoyed,
with his load for the city, ay, for the city . . .

He spends the entire morning
without anyone being able to
buy his goods, ay, buy his goods . . .

You can hear this lament everywhere
in my wretched Borikén, yes.

Then, of course, on or about October 29, the world changed. As Uncle Dave Macon put it: "The engineer pulled the throttle, the conductor rang the bell, / The brakeman hollered 'all aboard' and the banks all went to hell." A former industrialist with a company on the New York Stock Exchange recalled that "Black Tuesday":

October 29, 1929, yeah. A frenzy. I must have gotten calls from a dozen and a half friends who were desperate. In each case, there was no sense in loaning them the money that they would give the broker. Tomorrow they'd be worse off than yesterday. Suicides, left and right, made a terrific impression on me, of course. People I knew. It was heartbreaking. One day you saw the prices at a hundred, the next day at $20, at $15.

On Wall Street, the people walked around like zombies. It was like *Death Takes a Holiday*. It was very dark. You saw people who yesterday rode around in Cadillacs lucky now to have carfare.

One of my friends said to me, "If things keep on as they are, we'll all have to go begging." I asked, "Who from?"

Figure 13.3 "Toward Los Angeles, Calif." Farm Security Administration photo by Dorothea Lange, 1937.
Library of Congress Prints and Photographs Division

In Memphis, the self-proclaimed "Father of the Blues," W. C. Handy, looked northward, along with his sometime lyricist, Margaret Gregory. She spelled out what had happened with admirable brevity:

> Margin-callin' brokers, miles of tickertape,
> Got many a poor, old sap-head a-wearin' crepe.
> Wailin' Wall Street, I just can't enthuse.
> Boo-hoo-hoo-in', I've got the Wall Street Blues.

CHAPTER 14

The Panic Is On

In another eight years, Edgar Yipsel Harburg – they called him "Yip" – would captivate the world with his lyrics to "Over the Rainbow" and all the other songs in *The Wizard of Oz* (1939). But for now, he was thinking of something else: "The fellow in the breadline, just back from the wars . . . a bewildered hero with a medal on his chest ignominiously dumped into a breadline. I wanted a song that would express his indignation over having worked hard in the system only to be discarded when the system had no use for him." With Ira Gershwin's encouragement and Jay Gorney's music, Harburg wrote the song that became the anthem of the Depression. As one account has it:

> Harburg had some lyrics in mind, but the team couldn't think up a title. They decided to take a break and take a walk in New York's Central Park. A young man approached Gorney, his collar turned up and his hat pulled low. "Buddy, can you spare a dime?" he asked. The two songwriters glanced at each other and knew they'd found the words they'd been searching for.

"Buddy" became "Brother" in the title; but it was retained in the song's final, intense line, somehow making it more "military – and militant." As "Brother, Can You Spare a Dime?" (1931) makes clear, the tin medal on the chest, the hearty pat on the back, the "Yankee Dood-lee Dum" – it all rang hollow now.

In December of 1931, a coordinated National Hunger March of over 1600 delegates from all over the USA – many of them the financially desperate World War I veterans defended by Blind Lemon Jefferson – converged on Washington, DC. Their goal was to petition Congress for unemployment insurance, winter relief, housing protection, and "full and immediate payment" of the veterans' bonus. They had their own music "provided by the Unemployed Workers Club Martini Horn Band. This ensemble consisted of a drum major, a snare drum, a bass drum, a cornet, five martini horns, and an instrument made up of sixteen pan pipes.

At times the band burst forth with what the *Evening Graphic* called 'revolutionary tunes'" – meaning, in particular, "The Internationale": "Arise, ye prisoners of starvation . . ." Upon reaching the Capitol Building, they were rebuffed, and they melted away, dejected.

Immediately upon their heels, on January 6, 1932, 12,000 marchers under the leadership of Father James Renshaw Cox – "Cox's Army" – arrived in the capital, singing less militant songs such as "America" and "Keep the Home Fires Burning." They were rebuffed, too, only more gently. Still, the vets continued to sing, as did their champions, such as the Arkansas fiddler Bert Layne – an occasional member of Gid Tanner's Skillet Lickers – who memorialized the "Forgotten Soldier Boy" in 1930. Layne's song was later recorded by the bluegrass pioneers Bill and Charlie Monroe, "one of the rare topical songs the brothers recorded." As they sang:

I saw my buddies dying, and some shell-shocked and torn,
Although we never faltered at the Battle of the Marne.
And we were told when we left home, we'd be heroes of the land,
So we came back and found no one would lend a helping hand.

They promised gold and silver and bid us all adieu.
They said they'd welcome us back home when the terrible war was through.
We fought until the war was o'er, they said we'd won the fight;
But we have no job nor money, no place to sleep at night.

They called us wandering boys, bums, asking for shelter and bread;
Although we fought in No Man's Land and many a poor boy is dead.
So listen to my story and lend a helping hand
To the poor forgotten soldier boy who fought to save our land.

In the early summer of 1932, yet a third army of veterans marched on Washington, the "Bonus Army" some 17,000 strong, plus their families, which swelled the numbers to over 40,000. They camped for almost two months in a hastily built shantytown of shacks and tents on a swampland just across the river from the seat of government. On July 28, President Herbert Hoover ordered the army to disperse the marchers and clear the camp. Under the command of General Douglas MacArthur (who had immediately declared the march a communist conspiracy) and with direction from subordinate officers George Patton and Dwight Eisenhower, US Army troops attacked their fellow citizens with tanks, tear gas, bayonets, and rifles. By the time the camp was cleared, two veterans – William Hushka and Eric Carlson – lay fatally wounded. Their final, ironic honor was to be buried in Arlington National Cemetery with no shortage of Yankee Doodlee Dum. By then, "pictures and movies of the burning shacks filled newsreels across the country." The marchers drifted away, many to join the ranks of the other "forgotten men" on the breadlines and in the hobo jungles sprawling on the edges of towns and cities across the country. Some of these men were likely to be singing: "I've been working in the army, I've been working on a farm, / And all I've got to show is the muscle in my arm. / And it looks like I'm never going to cease my wandering."

In Detroit, labor attorney and amateur songwriter Maurice Sugar composed a sardonic anthem to the tune of "My Bonnie Lies Over the Ocean":

I'm spending my nights at the flophouse,
I'm spending my days on the street,
I'm looking for work and I find none,
I wish I had something to eat.

Soo-oup, soo-oup,
They give me a bowl of soo-oup.
Soo-oup, soo-oup,
They give me a bowl of soup.

For some, like the Tennessee blueswoman Pearl Dickson, the onset of the Depression merely overlaid one added misery on top of another. Her "Tallahatchie River Blues," composed in 1930, depicted an entire population just struggling to their feet after the disastrous floods of 1927:

Tallahatchie River rising: Lord it's mighty bad
Some peoples on the Tallahatchie: done lost everything they had
Some people in the Delta: wondering what to do
They don't build some levees: I don't know what become of you
High water rising: get me troubled in mind
I got to go: and leave my daddy behind.

As farm prices crashed, the Arkansas boogie-woogie pianist, Roosevelt Sykes – recording as "Easy Papa Johnson," one of his multiple pseudonyms – sang of the desperation he had perceived among the cotton farmers on his way northward to record in New York. His "Cotton Seed Blues" (1930) unpacked the economic misery in a slow, steady drag:

Lord, I ain't gonna make no more cotton, Mama,
Lord, I'll tell you the reason that I say so . . .
I don't get nothin' out of my seed
And the cotton price is so doggone low.

The boss man told me to go to the commissary,
I could get anything that I need . . .
He said I didn't have to have no money right away,
Lord, he said he would take it out of my seed.

Lord make a cotton crop, Mama,
Lord, it's just the same as shootin' dice . . .
Lord, you work the whole year 'round,
And then cotton won't be no price.

Lord, I plowed all this summer long,
And the sun would burn my skin . . .
And then the cotton sold for twelve and a half cents;
You know, no way that I could win.

The desperation in the cotton fields was a major source of musical commentary from Black and white alike. Tampa Red and Georgia Tom recorded a guitar and piano version of Sykes's "Cotton Seed Blues" three months after he did, suggesting the song's powerful currency in the blues community. Austin and Lee Allen – the Chattanooga Boys – sang their "Price of Cotton Blues" with a comedic jug-band inflection (thanks to their kazoo) that didn't quite dispel the underlying Depression anxiety (which they would soon experience personally, abandoning their musical careers in 1934 through lack of work). Although they weren't themselves cotton farmers, the Allens seemed to know what they were singing about: "We can't borrow money from the banks no more, / 'Cause the price of cotton done gone too low. / Cotton's gone to seven cents a pound; / Get me a club and run a jackrabbit down."

Everything was connected. As it went for the cotton farmers, so it inevitably went for the cotton-mill workers. Dave McCarn's "Serves Them Fine (Cotton Mill Colic no. 3)" looked back wistfully to the flush times of ten years before: "Now people, in the year nineteen and twenty, / The mills ran good, everybody had plenty." Cut to the Wall Street Crash and the collapse of the rural economy:

Now in the year 19-and-30,
They don't pay nothing and they do us dirty;
If we ever do manage to get ahead,
It seems like all of the mills go dead;
We're down in a hole, getting deeper every day,
If we ever get even, it'll be Judgement Day;
There's no use to colic and there's no use to shirk,
For there's more people loafing than there are at work.

In 1930, the Georgia fiddler Lowe Stokes surely caught the mood of the depressed cotton farmer – most likely a tenant – who'd "worked the whole year round" and gone to town to sell his cotton, only to come back home wishing "I'd-a bought me half a pint and stayed in the wagon yard." But

Stokes also knew that even procuring that measly "half a pint," while easy enough in practice, would reveal something rotten in the land. Prohibition seemed to help only the dishonest, the power-mad, and the black marketeers: "Prohibition is a failure, most anyone can see; / For whiskey's sold in every town in the good old USA. / Oh, the policeman will arrest you, he'll lock you up in jail, / He'll drink up all your liquor, and turn you out on bail." But Stokes also had his finger in the air as the political winds showed signs of turning: "Oh, at the next election, I'm sure you all will see, / We'll have light wines and good old beer in 1933." The Allen Brothers sang a similar warning: "Mr. Hoover came to office feeling kind of raw, / With a strong determination to enforce the law. / 'You can't have liquor, I'll tell you right now. / If you drink anything, you'll get it from a cow.'" But November of 1932 would surely change Mr. Hoover's tune: "Now the day am coming, and it won't be long / 'Til you find, Mr. Hoover, you done gone wrong. / The folks gonna say, next election day, / 'Step out, Mr. Hoover, you've had your way.'"

Was Herbert Hoover really all that bad – Hoover, the architect of the massive European relief program after World War I? Why would someone with such a record of generosity now have the squalid migrant camps, wherever they sprang up across the land – outside the city dumps, under the railroad bridges, along the river bottoms – named after him? Why should they be called "Hoovervilles"? And why should the patches on the torn and mended clothes of the Southern poor be called, of all things, "Hoover badges"? H. L. Mencken, for one, thought that Hoover was simply in the wrong place at the wrong time. As he argued, Hoover's predecessor, Calvin Coolidge, had had "a volcano boiling under him, but he did not know it, and was not singed. When it burst forth at last, it was Hoover who got its blast, and was fried, boiled, roasted and fricasseed."

But a number of factors had turned the people against Hoover. There was Prohibition, yes; but that alone couldn't have been enough. There was the attack he had ordered against the Bonus Army – both a moral and political debacle. And there was his hostility toward any thought of Federal relief for the victims of the Depression, in spite of his earlier record in international aid. "I am opposed to any government dole," he told Congress in 1932. It was, he said, "an abhorrent notion" – and even "local relief should be kept as distasteful as possible to avoid encouraging shiftlessness." To be fair, there is one historical error that should be cleared up: "Hoover never declared that prosperity was 'just around the corner' (that fatuous statement came from the vice president, Charles Curtis), but he did refuse to face reality." In fact, Hoover would be forever associated with "that fatuous statement," for which songwriters like Carson J. Robison had only contempt:

Prosperity is just around the corner!
(What we'd like to know is, which corner? We've turned so many corners now we're dizzy.)
But still I'm positive we'll soon be busy!
Why I read in Monday's paper that 10,000 men were hired!
(Yes, but Tuesday they forgot to say 12,000 more were fired.)
Well, I insist that this land of ours is stable!
(Stable? Sounds like horses to me.)

In a chilling high tenor plummeting to the baritone, the Delta blues singer Skip James sang of America as a "killin' floor," with "the people ... drifting from door to door." His was a ghostly, Gothic landscape, redolent of the stockyard slaughterhouse. But, for the former minstrel-show guitarist and singer Hezekiah Jenkins, the landscape was more of a perverse Boschean carnival, with reality seemingly cut loose from its moorings:

Saw a man this morning walking down the street
In his BVDs, no shoes on his feet.
You ought to seen the women curlin' in their flats;
I could hear 'em saying, "What kind of man is that?"
Doggone, I mean the panic is on ...

Some play numbers, some read your mind;
They all got a racket of some kind.
Some trimmin' corns off of people's feet –
They got to do something to make ends meet.
Doggone, I mean the panic is on ...

I pawned my clothes and everything,
Pawned my jewelry, watch and my ring;
Pawned my razor and my gun,
So if luck don't change, there'll be some stealin' done.
Doggone, I mean the panic is on.

On Tin Pan Alley, the lyricist Sam Lewis (Samuel M. Levine) had been enjoying great success with songs like "Dinah" (1925) and "Has Anybody Seen My Gal" (1925) as well as the old wartime hits "Hello Central! Give Me No Man's Land" (1918) and "Rock-a-Bye Your Baby with a Dixie Melody" (1918). In 1931 he teamed up with Abel Baer, composer of "Lucky Lindy!" (1927), to write a chastening ode to all the cocksure high flyers who had gambled everything on the stock market and lost, taking the country down with them: "If I ever get a job again, / I will never be a snob again; / I'll live within my means, / Carry a dollar in my jeans, / If I ever get a job again."

Hard times for some meant worse times for others. This was surely the case for Mexicans on both sides of the border. In Texas, an anonymous corridista sang of "*Efectos de la crisis*" (Effects of the Crisis), particularly on the fabric of the struggling household, where "Lots of prickly pear is eaten / For lack of other food":

Probably everybody knows
About these many evils;
That there are homes without food,
In which our children cry . . .

The pianolas no longer play,
The dances are fewer and fewer;
The sad little flappers pray
To have the gaiety return . . .

Divorces have increased
In these last years;
Depression has decreed it
With its sad disillusion.

And so I take my leave,
May you all be happy.
Here ends the song,
But the Depression goes on forever.

Song collector María Herrera-Sobek writes that, in these times of scarce resources, "families that had lived (for some generations) on US soil . . . were now being 'encouraged' to leave." The dismal "*Corrido de Immigración*" recounts the effect of such "encouragement" upon a Mexican community in California:

Ever since the year 1923
Up until the present date
We were having a prosperous time
But now we have to leave . . .

Some are going with their families
As the occasion arises
Others are being deported
From California to El Paso.

In the San Joaquin Valley
It pains one's heart
To see the poor families
Now being deported . . .

In the town of San Fernando
This is no laughing matter
They blocked off the whole town
On Ash Wednesday.

They made a big hullabaloo
Keep this in mind
In the Barrio of Rebote
There they gathered all the people.

They demanded passports,
Women and children crying;
They took my daddy,
God only knows when I'll see him again.

As ever, the hypocrisy of such nativist bigotry was breathtaking, especially when US interests were, at that very moment, flexing their muscles far beyond the national borders – for instance, in Honduras, where, in January of 1932, martial law was declared on behalf of the United Fruit Company, fighting off a rebellion by workers on the banana plantations. As a historian of United Fruit explains:

> One sphere in which United Fruit excelled was in the handling of labor. It had its own labor laws and any that its host countries might have had were suspended in United Fruit's areas. It hired, fired, and controlled through its own security forces, a network of charge-hands, superintendents, police and spies. The latter were known as *oidos en el suelo*, "ears in the ground," whose function was not only to be listening out for political troublemakers, but also those who complained too much about working conditions.

The Chilean poet Pablo Neruda based one of his celebrated cantos, "*La* United Fruit Co." (1950) on this deadly neocolonial power:

Among the bloodthirsty flies
the Fruit Company lands its ships,
taking off the coffee and the fruit;
the treasure of our submerged
territories flows as though
on plates into the ships.
Meanwhile Indians are falling

Into the sugared chasms
of the harbors, wrapped
for burial in the mist of the dawn:
a body rolls, a thing
that has no name, a fallen cipher,
a cluster of dead fruit
thrown down on the dump.

But at precisely the same time, if you were, say, a suspected Mexican presuming to tread on the sacred soil of Miami, Arizona, you might be singing a grim corrido of your own as your hour of deportation approached – particularly if you had been caught doing what half the country had long been doing: making their own beer.

You hear only the complaints
Of all without distinction;
Men, children, and old people,
All have to go to prison . . .

If you want to be happy
When you have crossed the Bravo,
Show this country clearly
That you have not broken its laws.

If you used to make beer
And operate a still,
Just scratch your head
And don't admit anything.

Meanwhile, in Puerto Rico, the American Sugar Refining Company (today's Domino Sugar), owned by the colony's former US governor, Charles Herbert Allen, now controlled over 40 percent of the island's agricultural land, as well as the coastal railroads and major ports. American Sugar pulled the political strings in Puerto Rico, whether it had to do with labor laws, tariffs, water rights, land grants, property seizures and foreclosures, or tax subsidies. In New York, Rafael Hernández Marín might well sing of a "bucolic" Puerto Rican past in "*Los Carreteros*" (1931), where rural cart drivers "sang along with the tempo of the wheels of their oxcarts":

Day breaks, day breaks,
From the linnets is heard the happy wakeup call.
Day breaks, day breaks,
And the dew is drying upon the grass.

And the flowers are waking
And in the mountains the cartdrivers are heard singing.

But, amidst the realities of neocolonialism, such a "pastoral paradise" was bound to be "a more distant memory than many migrants' songs might lead the listener to believe" – including such a song as "*Los Carreteros.*" After all, the "cartdrivers," the impoverished *jíbaros*, saw the island's wealth being stripped out from under them, filling the coffers of the American

Sugar Refining Company and the local sugar barons who supplied them. Not for nothing would Neruda include the poem "*Puerto Rico, puerto pobre*" (Rich Port, Poor Port) in his *Cancíon de Gesta* (Song of Protest, 1960); and not for nothing had Hernández Marín already composed his own "*Lamento Borincano.*"

A similar stripping-out of wealth was going on in the coal fields of Harlan County, Kentucky, even as the Coal Operators' Association determined to cut miners' wages by 10 percent in February of 1931. This marked the commencement of the Harlan County War – "Bloody Harlan" – between the operators and the UMW. One of that union's greatest musical champions, Florence Reece, composed the anthem that would be revived time and again in labor struggles around the world, well into the present century:

> Come all of you good workers
> Good news to you I'll tell
> Of how that good old union
> Has come in here to dwell
>
> Which side are you on?
> Which side are you on?

Years later, Reece described the origins of the song, born amidst a long, bitter strike and vicious terrorization on the part of gun thugs hired by the company, who ranged across the coal fields, hunting down UMW organizers – ambushing them or dragging them from their homes; beating them, jailing them, and killing them. As Reece recalled:

> Sheriff J. H. Blair and his men came to our house in search of Sam – that's my husband – he was one of the union leaders. I was home alone with our seven children. They ransacked the whole house and then kept watch outside, waiting to shoot Sam down when he came back. But he didn't come home that night. Afterward I tore a sheet from a calendar on the wall and wrote the words to the labor song, "Which Side Are You On?" to an old Baptist hymn, "Lay the Lily Low." My songs always go to the underdog – to the worker. I'm one of them and I feel like I've got to be with them. There's no such thing as neutral. You have to be on one side or the other. Some people say, I don't take sides – I'm neutral. There's no such thing. In your mind you're on one side or the other. In Harlan County there wasn't no neutral. If you wasn't a gun thug, you was a union man. You had to be.

When the novelist Theodore Dreiser came to Harlan in 1931 along with Sherwood Anderson, John Dos Passos, and others in the National

Committee for the Defense of Political Prisoners (as many union members had been jailed), they listened to another songwriter-activist, Aunt Molly Jackson, sing her "Ragged, Hungry Blues": "I'm sad and weary, I've got the hungry ragged blues, / Not a penny in the pocket to buy one thing I need to use. / I woke up this morning, with the worst blues I ever had in my life. / Not a bit to cook for breakfast, a poor coal miner's wife." Jackson, a midwife – hence her designation "Aunt" – later recalled the origins of another song, "Dreadful Memories":

> Thirty-seven babies died in my arms in the last three months of 1931. Their little stomachs busted open; they was mortified inside. Oh, what an awful way for a baby to die. Not a thing to give our babies to eat but the strong soup from soup beans, and that took the lining from their little stomachs, so that they bled inside and mortified and died. And died so hard that before we got help from other states my nerves was so stirred up for four years afterward, the memory of them babies suffering and dying in my arms, and me sitting by their little dead bodies three or four hours before daylight in the dark to keep some hungry dog or cat from eating up their little dead bodies. Then four years later I still had such sad memories of these babies that I wrote this song.

And she sang: "I can't forget them, coal miners' children, / That starved to death without one drop of milk, / While the coal operators and their wives and children / Were all dressed in jewels and silk."

The autobiographical authority of Jackson's singing, as well as her testimony, made a huge impact on the Dreiser Committee. It was an authority that carried through in such songs as "Poor Miner's Farewell," which remains one of the best-known songs to emerge from Bloody Harlan: "When I'm in Kentucky so often I meet / Poor coal miners' children out on the street. / 'How are you doing?' to them I have said; / 'We are hungry, Aunt Molly, we're begging for bread.'" As Jackson told song collector John Greenway:

> The day I composed this song I never will forget; it was about three weeks after my own dear brother was killed. I found my brother's three oldest children out on the street. They told me they had been over to a store to try to get some food. They said, "We are out of money, and we have been all over town trying to get some groceries on time, but everyone has turned us down." Then my brother's little blue-eyed boy looked up at me so sweet and said to me, "Aunt Molly, will you get us some food to eat?"

The Dreiser Committee's findings were published in 1932 as *Harlan Miners Speak: Report on Terrorism in the Kentucky Coal Fields.* One committee member reported on the partiality and outright hostility of the press reports surrounding the strike:

> The Associated Press man occasionally asked questions of witnesses to bring out testimony favourable to the operators. And once, when Aunt Molly Jackson, who works among her fellow-sufferers of Straight Creek, ministering to the sick and delivering babies, was testifying that seventeen babies had died of flux during the summer, the Associated Press man skeptically inquired: "Can we see the graves?" It was plain why Associated Press writers enjoyed immunity in the Kentucky coalfields.

Jackson herself had a few words for the convenient accusation that all the striking miners were, by definition, "communists" and "subversives." It is true that after the failure of the UMW in the first stage of the strike, which was broken by the Kentucky National Guard in May of 1931, the Communist-led National Miners Union (NMU) briefly took up the baton of leadership. But nonetheless these were Americans defending Americans. Jackson's "I Am a Union Woman" ridiculed the paranoiac connections with the Kremlin while revealing the seriousness of the resultant blacklist for all those connected with the NMU:

> I was raised in Kentucky,
> In Kentucky born and bred;
> And when I joined the union
> They called me a Rooshian red.
>
> When my husband asked the boss for a job
> This is the words he said:
> "Bill Jackson, I can't work you sir,
> Your wife's a Rooshian red."
>
> This is the worst time on earth
> That I have ever saw;
> To get shot down by gun thugs
> And framed up by the law.

Jackson's other songs memorializing Bloody Harlan included her "Lonesome Jailhouse Blues" (1931), which, she told Greenway, "originated from a bunch of 'em a-gettin' mad at me because I took part in a strike, and they framed me and had me put in jail." She used the song as a message to her fellow activists to petition the ILD for aid, which duly arrived:

> I am locked up in prison,
> Just as lonesome as I can be;
> I want you to write me a letter,
> To the dear old ILD.
>
> Tell them that I am in prison,
> Then they will know what to do.
> The bosses had me put in jail
> For joining the NMU.

If Bloody Harlan had only produced Florence Reece and Aunt Molly Jackson, that would have been impressive enough. But Jackson herself was one of a family who would carry the musical legacy of Harlan to New York later in the decade, inspiring many of the central figures of the folk revival there – Alan Lomax, Woody Guthrie, Pete Seeger, Lead Belly, Burl Ives, and others. Jackson's younger half-sister, Sarah Ogan Gunning, was as musically militant as she was, composing such renowned union anthems as "I'm Goin' to Organize, Baby Mine" (1932) and "Down on the Picket Line" (1932):

> Come on, friends, an' let's go down,
> Let's go down, let's go down,
> Come on friends, an' let's go down,
> Down on the picket line.
> As we went down on the picket line
> To keep the scabs out of the mine,
> Who's goin' to win the strike,
> Come on an' we'll show you the way.
> We went out one mornin' before daylight
> An' I was sure we'd have a fight,
> But the scabs was cowardly, ran away,
> We went back the very next day.

Gunning's older brother, Jim Garland, completed the family trio. He was "a coal miner who had been blacklisted for union activity" in Harlan, known particularly for two songs emerging from the struggle: "The Death of Harry Simms" (1932), cowritten with Jackson, and "I Don't Want Your Millions, Mister" (1932). Garland was a close friend of Simms (Harry Simms Hersh), a young Jewish union organizer who hailed from Massachusetts, where he had worked in textile mills from the age of fourteen. He came to Brush Creek, Kentucky, to join the NMU miners' fight and, at the age of nineteen, was murdered by a deputy-sheriff moonlighting as a mining company guard. Reportedly, Simms and Garland each had a $1000 bounty placed on their heads by the Bush Creek coal operators, and Garland believed – quite reasonably, in light of the murder of Ella May Wiggins in Gastonia – that "the bullet that killed Harry Simms was meant for him." As Garland and Jackson elegized him:

> Harry Simms was a pal of mine,
> We labored side by side,
> Expecting to be shot on sight
> Or taken for a ride
> By some life-stealing gun thug
> That roams from town to town
> To shoot and kill our union men
> Where e'er they may be found . . .

Harry Simms was killed on Brush Creek
In nineteen thirty-two;
He organized the miners
Into the NMU;
He gave his life in struggle,
'Twas all that he could do;
He died for the union,
He died for me and you.

Garland went on to be a senior figure in the folk revival of the 1960s, appearing with Pete Seeger at the Newport Folk Festival, by which time his song "I Don't Want Your Millions, Mister" had become known as one of the major anthems of the Depression:

I don't want your millions, mister;
I don't want your diamond ring.
All I want is the right to live, mister;
Give me back my job again.

I don't want your Rolls-Royce, mister,
I don't want your pleasure yacht;
All I want is food for my babies;
Give to me my old job back.

Woody Guthrie would later write: "Well, I hated that song and argued about it all across the country and back. I said the workers do want your millions, Mister, do want your pleasure yacht, do want your pleasure car, do want your watch and chain, and they do want lots more than, 'just the right to live, Mister' or 'my old job back again.'"

The Bloody Harlan conflict, which lasted from 1931 to 1939, has been seen as the major labor struggle of the 1930s, and it was highly inspirational to workers in other industries, such as the striking United Textile Workers Union in Tennessee, in 1933. One of these operatives, Eleanor Kellogg, wrote "My Children Are Seven in Number," which deftly drew in the miners' struggle as one of her own, given the general onslaught against organized labor in the midst of the Depression:

They shot Barney Graham, our leader,
His spirit abides with us still;
The spirit of strength for justice,
No bullets have the power to kill . . .

Oh, miners, go on with the union,
Oh, miners, go on with the fight;
For we're in the struggle for justice
And we're in the struggle for right.

This was in fact the spirit of old Mother Jones, who had given up her ghost at the age of ninety-three in November of 1930. In 1912, the year he won the highest popular vote that any Socialist Party candidate for the presidency had achieved or ever would again, Eugene Debs had set the tone for the manner in which Mother Jones would be remembered:

> She has spent weeks and months in the bleak hills of West Virginia, Pennsylvania and other states, where the official machine that maligned her dare not go, standing on the firing line, face to face with guns and bayonets, fighting the battles of the workers; she has been in jail all over this country again and again enjoined by the courts; she has gone to prison where strikers were locked up, "ignorant foreigners," afflicted with the smallpox and nursed them as tenderly as if they had been children; she has been routed out of her bed at midnight by armed ruffians, corporation murderers, and made to leave a coal camp alone at that hour.

Whether it was for textile operatives, coal miners, foundry workers, or child laborers across all industries, Mother Jones had carried on the unitary mission of the IWW – which she had cofounded – to the end. But it was the coal miners, in particular, who embraced her as their patron saint. Gene Autry and others began to sing of her as early as 1931, in a song whose composer remains unknown: "The world today's in mourning for the death of Mother Jones. / Gloom and sorrow hover around the miners' homes. / This grand old champion of labor was known in every land. / She fought for right and justice; she took a noble stand." But of the many songs sung for her, one in particular stands out as a reflection of the struggle carried on by labor activists – during the Depression and before – against the legalized thuggery of capital. A West Virginia miner named Orville J. Jenks left this elegy:

> Mother Jones is not forgotten
> By the miners of this field,
> She's gone to rest above, God bless her soul.
> Tried to lead the boys to vict'ry,
> But was punished here in jail,
> For the price of just a little lump of coal.

In March of 1931, there were some Americans who didn't need to join a union, front a strike, or consort with suspected communists in order to be slung into jail. All they needed was to be Black, male, and hoboing on the wrong train between Chattanooga and Memphis. Successful in defending themselves against a gang of white attackers on that train, nine young Black Americans were accused of rape by two young white women – unemployed millworkers – who, perhaps, thought it might have prevented them from being jailed for vagrancy, since they, too, were hoboing on that train (better to be an outraged Southern white woman than a common vagrant). As Woody Guthrie later surmised: "Lots of girls rode the trains. With the railroad bulls so tough and the police so mean, you are suspicioned all of the time, and investigated to boot for everything that goes wrong. Something happened. The cops and the girls had some words." Tragically and mendaciously, one of those words was "rape."

The train had briefly dipped across the state line into Paint Rock, Alabama, where the altercation occurred. The nine Black men – well, boys, since the oldest was nineteen and the youngest was thirteen – were tied up and carted off to the jail in nearby Scottsboro. Although one of the women soon retracted her accusation and campaigned actively for the boys' acquittal, not until twelve years and three trials later would the first seven of them be released. Another was freed in 1946, and the last one escaped to the North in 1948. By then, the case of the "Scottsboro Boys" had seared the conscience of the world (and even some parts of Alabama). One of the wrongfully accused young men was seventeen-year-old Olen Montgomery, nearly blind, with a cataract in one eye and a talent for song writing and guitar playing. He had boarded the ill-fated freight train in order to find work so that he could earn the two dollars he needed to buy a pair of eyeglasses. As he later wrote to his attorney: "I was on my way to Memphis on a oil tank By My Self a lone and I was Not Worried With any one untell I Got to Paint Rock Alabama and they Just made a Frame up on us Boys Just Cause they Cud."

Unfortunately for the Scottsboro Boys, they found themselves pawns in a much larger game. Their cause had been taken up by the Communist Party of the USA (CPUSA) and the ILD, which – along with the NAACP – hired one of the country's top criminal lawyers, Samuel Liebowitz, a Romanian-born Jewish lawyer from New York (and, in spite of the source of his paycheck, an ardent anti-communist). No matter his effectiveness, he could never be an Atticus Finch. The county prosecutor shamelessly appealed to the all-white jury early in the trial: "Show them . . . show them that Alabama justice cannot be bought and sold with Jew money from New York."

It seemed that the Southern battle against the tyranny of Reconstruction and Northern carpetbaggery was being fought out all over again, with the added ingredients of Jews and Communists descending upon Alabama. Only a year before the arrest of the Scottsboro Boys, a group of white Southern poets, essayists, and novelists, collectively known as the Nashville

Agrarians (or "Twelve Southerners," as they called themselves) had published their manifesto, *I'll Take My Stand* (1930). Dominated by Allen Tate, John Crowe Ransom, Robert Penn Warren, and Donald Davidson, the group lashed out at presumed Northern cultural and intellectual arrogance, which had been par for the course since the end of the Civil War, if not before. But what was novel – indeed, bizarre – was the assumption inscribed into their original title. Before settling on *I'll Take My Stand,* they'd titled their manifesto *Tracts Against Communism,* for reasons known only to them. (It had something to do with their stated belief that Northern industrialism would inevitably lead to "much the same economic system as that imposed by violence upon Russia in 1917.")

To Olen Montgomery, this was all irrelevant: "She hollered 'Rape.' Nine of us went to jail over it. She changed her mind and said we was innocent, but they wouldn't let us out." And from the depths of the Kilby Prison in Mt. Meigs, Alabama, Montgomery composed the most harrowing musical document to emerge from the whole affair, "Lonesome Jailhouse Blues":

All last night I walked my cell and cried
Because this old jailhouse got lonesome and I just can't be satisfied.

I tried to eat my breakfast this morning, but I couldn't for shedding tears, mama,
It almost breaks my heart to think of those five long years.

Oh Lord, Oh Lord, what am I going to do?
I have walked around in this old jail so long I can't even wear my shoes.

I wouldn't even treat a dog like these people treats poor me,
They treats me just like I'm some kind of an animal they ain't never seen.

I don't know anything about Alabama, 'cause it's not my home.
But ever since I been here I have regretted the day I was born.

I'm singing this song because I wants everybody to know
How a poor boy feels when he is down so low.

North of the Mason-Dixon Line, protesters in the streets marched to jarring, militant anthems like "The Scottsboro Boys Shall Not Die!" (1933), by Charles Abron and L. E. Swift (the pseudonym of modernist composer Elie Siegmeister):

Workers, farmers, Negro and white,
The lynching bosses we must fight.
Close your fists and raise them high,
Labor Defense is our battle cry.

> The Scottsboro boys shall not die,
> The Scottsboro boys shall not die,
> Workers led by ILD will set them free.
> Set them free!

As the lyrics indicate, the Scottsboro Boys were a valuable cause célèbre for the CPUSA, which was understandably enjoying its brief heyday during the Depression. While charges of propagandic opportunism are certainly credible, it was still the case that both the Party and its legal arm, the ILD, were at the forefront of the decade's most concerted activism in the defense of labor and civil rights – not only in Gastonia, Harlan, and Scottsboro, but also in the fields and orchards of California, where Mexican, Chinese, Japanese, and Filipino workers, soon to be joined by refugees from the Dust Bowl, fought for better wages and conditions under the auspices of communist-led unions like the Cannery and Agricultural Workers Industrial Union. Inevitably they got as good as they gave, as historian Michael Denning notes:

> They were the largest strikes in the history of American agriculture and the great majority succeeded in winning wage increases. Because of the remarkable successes of the strikes, the factory-farm owners together with the railroads and the canning companies organized the Associated Farmers, which used vigilante violence, deportation and anti-picketing laws to imprison the union's leaders and crush the union.

This was the situation that would greet Woody Guthrie upon his arrival in California in 1937.

Musically, the CPUSA and the broader communist movement were facing an ideological crisis within the ranks. After all, song was meant to be revolutionary, if it was to mean anything at all. Aaron Copland laid out the Party line in 1934:

> Every participant in revolutionary activity knows from his own experience that a good mass song is a powerful weapon in the class struggle. It creates solidarity and inspires action. No other form of collective art activity exerts so far-reaching and all-pervading an influence. The song the mass itself sings is a cultural symbol which helps to give continuity to the day-to-day struggle of the proletariat.

All right, so what should "revolutionary" music sound like? For Copland at that time, as well as the other doctrinaire members of the Party's "Composers' Collective," the more modern sounding – or modernist – the better. One telling example came from Charles Seeger (now the husband of Ruth Crawford), who, in order to protect his university teaching position, wrote criticism and composed under the pseudonym "Carl Sands." Seeger pointed to a musical diatribe of his own, "in five-four time with five-measure phrases. . . . We really did sing away, but it didn't catch on very much." Copland fared little better with his setting of Alfred Hayes's "Into the Streets May First!" The lyrics were typically strident, perhaps a touch New York-centric (which probably didn't go down too well in the mill and foundry towns to the south and west), but not difficult to remember:

Into the streets May First!
Into the roaring Square!
Shake the midtown towers!
Shatter the downtown air!
Come with a storm of banners,
Come with an earthquake tread,
Bells, hurl out of your belfries,
Red flag, leap out your red!

The real problem was the music. As a worried Seeger asked Copland, "Do you think it will ever be sung on the picket line?" And, although Seeger himself had awarded Copland the Collective's first prize for the composition, he would later cite "Into the Streets May First!" as a sterling example of flawed "revolutionary music – freak modulations, big skips of sevenths, dissonances, numerous key changes." No wonder the *New Masses* editor Mike Gold heard in the Collective's music only "geometric bitterness and the angles and glass splinters of pure technic . . . written for an assortment of mechanical canaries." And he asked, famously: "Why don't American workers sing? The Wobblies knew how, but we have still to develop a Communist Joe Hill." Seeger eventually found the answer, and he could almost pinpoint the date of his epiphany:

> I was trying to write music for protest marches and union gatherings. An old woman named Aunt Molly Jackson had come to one of the meetings of the Composers' Collective, and I learned her songs and discovered that they were folk songs simply dolled up, with new words and perhaps a few touches of her own, and that the people could sing their songs and they couldn't sing our songs. So I went up to her and I said, Molly, you're on the right track and we're on the wrong track, and I gave up the Collective. We were all on the wrong track – it was professionals trying to write music for the people and not in the people's idiom.

This was the farthest cry from the "Carl Sands" who had written in 1934 that folk songs were, for the most part, "complacent, melancholy, defeatist, intended to make slaves endure their lot – pretty but not the stuff for a militant proletariat to feed upon." Seeger's conversion marked the CPUSA's pivot away from "revolutionary" modernist music and into its wholesale embrace of folk music as "the people's idiom." No more Hanns Eisler and Arnold Schoenberg as guiding spirits. Now it was cowboy singers, musical loggers and roustabouts, Alan Lomax, Aunt Molly Jackson, Sarah Ogan Gunning, Lead Belly, Josh White, and – very soon – Woody Guthrie and Pete Seeger. It was all the songs in Carl Sandburg's *American Songbag* (1927), Ray and Lida Auville's *Songs of the American Worker* (1934), Lawrence Gellert's *Negro Songs of Protest* (1936) and *Me and My Captain* (1939), and J. Rosamond Johnson's *Rolling Along in Song* (1937). It was the "vernacular" forms and cadences now willingly – even voraciously – absorbed by Copland, emerging in signature works like *El Salón México* (1936), *Billy the Kid* (1938), *Rodeo* (1942), and *Appalachian Spring* (1944). It was Ruth Crawford Seeger's more gradual farewell to the modernist discords of her "Three Chants for Female Chorus" (1930) and her decidedly nonvernacular "Three Songs to Carl Sandburg Poems" (1930–1932). She would soon set these aside for the Appalachian sounds discovered on field trips with her husband ("a conversion experience" for her), working the likes of Bascom Lamar Lunsford's *30 and 1 Folk Songs from the Southern Mountains* (1929) into her future compositions.

Of course, Black composers never needed the imprimatur of the Communist Party in the first place when it came to knowing full well the value of their own folk and vernacular sources. After all, these were the fountainhead of not only their music but of almost all non-Indigenous American music. Florence Price was following no party line in threading the spiritual, the blues, and the juba dance into, variously, "The New Moon" and "Moon Bridge" (1930), her *Symphony in E Minor* (1932), her *Piano Concerto in One Movement* (1934), her settings for Paul Laurence Dunbar's "Dreamin' Town" and "The Wind and the Sea," and Langston Hughes's "My Dream" (1935), or any number of other piano and choral arrangements by mid-decade.

Meanwhile, the "mixed blessing" of the Gershwin–Dubose Hayward "folk opera" *Porgy and Bess* (1935) brought Black vernacular sources to the wide attention of both the classical and musical theater worlds as though for the first time, to the point that its historical dominance has threatened to obscure other landmarks by Black composers of the same period. As the Harlem-based choral conductor Eva Jessye observed shortly after the premiere of *Porgy and Bess*, George Gershwin was "definitely gifted. . . . He studied a great deal, but I've been black longer than he has. . . . I was black all day and he wasn't. . . . His stuff sounds quite white." *Porgy and*

Bess certainly deserves credit for having opened up opportunities for Black singers and actors. One historian goes so far as to cite it as "the high point in Negro artistic participation for the decade." This participation extended to the performer playing the small role of the bogus lawyer, Frazier, in the premiere: one J. Rosamond Johnson, "who a generation earlier had himself tried with little success to advance the cause of both black performers in general and the musical stage as a whole."

But *Porgy and Bess* pushed to the margins the likes of William Dawson's *Negro Folk Symphony* (1934), which premiered under the baton of Leopold Stokowski conducting the Philadelphia Orchestra, and William Grant Still's *Afro-American Symphony* of 1930 (which didn't see its premiere until 1935 with the New York Philharmonic). Both these symphonies were constructed around movements representing the progression of Black American life and history as the composers saw it, "from 'The Bond of Africa' to 'O Lem-me Shine!' in Dawson's work, from 'Longing' to 'Aspiration' in Still's."

In 1933, the Metropolitan Opera premiered Louis Gruenberg's *The Emperor Jones*, based on Eugene O'Neill's stage play of 1920. The titular role was sung by the white baritone Lawrence Tibbett in blackface; "however, the production was notable for breaking the color line: Helmsley Winfield, an African American, danced the role of the Witch Doctor." For some Black commentators, such a staging would raise two cheers at best, not only because of Tibbett's blackface minstrel overtones and the professional affront to Winfield, but also because it played directly into the white primitivist discourse that had driven much of the cultural response to the US occupation of Haiti that had begun in 1915. As Clare Corbould notes:

> In most of these mainstream accounts Haiti was a backward place where travelers could experience the primitive culture of Africa, only closer to home. These were lurid treatments of Haitian culture, sold as "reportage." Tales and images of voodoo ceremonies, cannibalism, child sacrifice, and zombies, not to mention drumming and half-naked bodies, became bestselling books and much-seen films.

O'Neill's play had emerged in the midst of this cultural fascination, fed on its energy, and helped to perpetuate it – so much so that the poet Haines J. Washington was moved to publish his critique, "Death of the Emperor Jones," in the *Negro World* in May 1930:

> I'm tired;
> Weary from drums
> Pounding in my ears,
> Banging in my head,
> Drumming in my heart,
> Drums – white drums

Bursting fear
Into my brain,
Sweating agony
Over my body,
Drums, drums driving,
Driving to madness.

But just as Langston Hughes, Zora Neale Hurston, and Duke Ellington had seized on the "tom-tom" and "jungle music" as affirmative entities, the Black American team of Clarence Cameron White and John Frederick Matheus did the same with their opera of revolutionary Haiti, *Ouanga*, completed in 1932 but not staged until 1949 (the same year that saw the premiere of Still's Haitian opera, *Troubled Island*). Set during the last years of the Haitian war of independence, *Ouanga* pits the "modernizing will" of Jean-Jacques Dessalines – the Emperor Jacques I – against voodoo as "a serious belief system, integral to Haitian life" and "a celebration of autonomous black culture."

However, if Haiti indeed offered access to a version of Africa that was "closer to home," it did not and never would eclipse the cultural draw of Africa itself, even after the peak of Marcus Garvey's influence in the 1920s. "Garveyism" had run like an incandescent lava stream through the intellectual and political landscapes of the Harlem Renaissance and beyond, encapsulated in Garvey's declaration of 1920:

> Wheresoever I go, whether it is England, France, or Germany, I am told, "This is a white man's country." Wheresoever I travel throughout the United States of America, I am made to understand that I am a "n——r." If the Englishman claims England as his native habitat, and the Frenchman claims France, the time has come for 400 million Negroes to claim Africa as their native land. . . . If you believe that the Negro should have a place in the sun; if you believe that Africa should be one vast empire, controlled by the Negro, then arise.

As late as 1934, the Trinidad-born calypso star, Wilmoth Houdini, would still be singing the praises of Garvey's "Back to Africa" movement in his "African Love Call":

Some people say give me Booker T.,
But I say give me Marcus Garvey.
They said Marcus Garvey was looking for war,
So I asked them what Booker T. did before.
They said he gave the Negro nation high-class education,
And that was Booker T.'s chief ambition.
But His Honor Marcus Garvey start the fight for liberty
Universally.

But for composers like Still, whose "long-lost masterpiece," the orchestral suite *Africa,* coincided with his *Afro-American Symphony* but would not be recorded until 2005, it was enough to invoke Mother Africa as a source of celebration rather than an actual destination. (His biographer notes that, while he could not have avoided the debates surrounding Garveyism in the midst of the Harlem Renaissance, "it was highly unlikely" that he would have been "a member of Garvey's movement.") Africa would best serve as a creative source to Still. Hence the fourth movement of his *Afro-American Symphony,* which initially had as its epigraph the final stanza of Paul Laurence Dunbar's "Ode to Ethiopia":

Go on and up! Our souls and eyes
Shall follow thy continuous rise;
Our ears shall list thy story
From bards who from thy root shall spring,
And proudly turn their lyres to sing
Of Ethiopia's Glory.

For another pioneering Black composer, Hall Johnson, the inspiration of Africa fed into his otherwise overwhelmingly American musical, *Run, Little Chillun* (1933), which, as "a new form, the Negro folk drama," staked a strong foundational claim two years before the premiere of *Porgy and Bess.* Johnson had provided both the spiritual arrangements and the choir for the white playwright Marc Connelly's Pulitzer Prize-winning Broadway production of *The Green Pastures* (1930), based on another white author's depictions of Black spirituality, Roark Bradford's *Ol' Man Adam an' His Chillun* (1928). As Johnson later wrote: "*The Green Pastures,* a third-hand derivation from a second-hand book, was never more than a white-washed burlesque of the religious thought of the Negro." In his own musical, Johnson sought to maintain Africa as a distant but maternal power, with an African mother figure who "looks like a powerful conjure woman" and a "Dance of the Full Moon," which, as the stage directions explain, represents "something approaching voodoo – not too directly African, but with a strong African flavor." Following its successful Broadway run of 1933, *Run, Little Chillun* was staged as a Federal Theater Project (FTP) production on the West Coast, becoming "the longest running and most enthusiastically received production of any of the New Deal cultural programs."

Off the Broadway stage, the spiritual – Hall Johnson's forte – had begun to transform the US labor movement, along with other vernacular music sources. Mike Gold's *cri de coeur* – "Why don't American workers sing?" – betrayed, perhaps, a New York-based ignorance as to what was already

Figure 14.1 Poster for Federal Theater Project presentation of Hall Johnson's *Run, Little Chillun* at the Savoy Theater, San Diego, c. 1936.
Works Progress Administration Poster Collection, Library of Congress

being sung, even as the members of the Composers' Collective were arguing over the revolutionary potential of the five-four time signature. Indeed, while the Party wasn't yet declaring itself ready for folk music, much of the singing beyond the environs of New York had at least given the nod to the Party. The balladeers of Gastonia and Harlan – Ella May Wiggins, Sarah Ogan Gunning, and Aunt Molly Jackson – all celebrated the ILD in their various verses. The CPUSA maintained informal (if sometimes testy) affiliations with the Brookwood Labor College in Katonah, New York; Commonwealth College in Arkansas; and the Highlander Folk School in Tennessee – all of which put folk song at the heart of their organizing curricula.

There were many Southern Black workers drawn to the CPUSA and its affiliated organizations in the 1930s, and they brought with them a treasure trove of song. In 1931, striking members of the West Virginia Miners Union had taken the venerable "I Shall Not Be Moved" and collectivized it into "We Shall Not Be Moved." One activist, Brookwood alumna Helen Norton Starr, later said:

> I could remember the first time I heard "We Shall Not Be Moved." The only place that could be secured for the meeting in that particular valley was the front of a dilapidated Negro schoolhouse that stood in a depression among the hills. . . . On the steps of the schoolhouse stood a mixed group of white and Negro miners and their wives, singing out their story and their hopes. The summer sun blazed down on them and on the miners' families seated on the slope in front. On the road above a group of state "po-lice" and mine guards watched, their guns conspicuously displayed.

Black communists in Alabama transformed "Give Me That Old Time Religion" into "Give Me That Old Communist Spirit" as well as "The Scottsboro Song." "A Stone Came Rolling Out of Babylon" became "the 'official' ILD song in the South," retitled "We Got a Stone," and numerous blues songs were adopted as "efficacious example[s] of resistance."

The Southern Tenant Farmers Union, founded in 1934 and headquartered in Memphis but active throughout the South, had a hugely influential songwriter among its ranks, the Black tenant farmer and organizer John Handcox, known as "the Sharecropper's Troubadour." Handcox wrote some of the most celebrated labor songs of the twentieth century, among them "There's Mean Things Happening in This Land," "Raggedy, Raggedy Are We," and – often co-credited with Lee Hays and the Reverend Claude Williams – "Roll the Union On":

> If the planter's in the way,
> We're gonna roll it over him,
> Gonna roll it over him,
> Gonna roll it over him.
> If the planter's in the way,
> We're gonna roll it over him,
> Gonna roll the union on.

As Handcox recalled:

> The songs I wrote was to try and tell the laboring people, the ones where I was trying to organize, to try to reveal to them the things that they was doing, you know, and it was forced on them. It wasn't because they had asked for it but it was being forced on them by the landlords. And to show that they deserve a better life than what they were getting. They were producing everything and getting nothing.

Handcox's compositional strategy was to change or "zipper in" new words to traditional spirituals, a practice derived from Black church singing. Thus, the spiritual "How Beautiful Heaven Must Be" became, in his hands, "Raggedy, Raggedy Are We," flexible enough for new words to be "zippered in" to account for any number of scenarios:

> Raggedy, raggedy are we,
> Just as raggedy as raggedy can be,
> We don't get nothing for our labor,
> So raggedy, raggedy are we.
>
> So hungry, hungry are we,
> Just as hungry, as hungry can be . . .
>
> So homeless, homeless, are we . . .
>
> So landless, landless are we . . .
>
> So cowless, cowless, are we . . .
>
> So cornless, cornless are we . . .
>
> So pitiful, pitiful are we . . .

It was a compositional strategy that would later characterize the most celebrated anthems of the Civil Rights Movement, notably "We Shall Overcome," initially the spiritual "I'll Overcome Someday" as sung by members of the Negro Food and Tobacco Union in Charleston, South Carolina, who changed it pointedly to "We Will Overcome." Zilphia Horton, a director of the Highlander Folk School, picked it up from the union singers and taught it to Pete Seeger. "No one is certain who changed 'will' to 'shall,'" Seeger later recalled. "It could have been me, but it might have been Septima Clarke, the director of education at Highlander. She always preferred 'shall,' since it opens up the voice and sings better." Seeger, in turn, taught "We Shall Overcome" to the world, and it became the defining musical signature of civil rights activists at home and abroad. But he never forgot its origins in the Black churches and on the union picket lines of the South.

There was much to overcome, too, in the industrial cities of the North at mid-decade. In 1934, general strikes rocked the auto parts industry of

Toledo, the haulage industry of Minneapolis, and the longshore and maritime industries of San Francisco. These cities were completely shut down. By far the bloodiest battle was in San Francisco, when strikebreakers hired by the Industrial Association, backed up by police, tried to force open the city's port, leading to a day-long gun battle between police and strike supporters that left two dead and scores wounded. The San Francisco strike sparked sympathy walkouts across the major port cities of the West Coast, leading eventually to the establishment of the International Longshore and Warehouse Union. It also produced a powerful ballad in the tradition of the Wobblies, Gastonia, and Bloody Harlan, the anonymously composed "Ballad of Bloody Thursday," clearly based on the cowboy ballad, "The Streets of Laredo":

It was there on the line that I marched with my brothers,
It was there on the line as we proudly walked by;
The cops and the soldiers they brought up their rifles,
I'm shot in the breast and I know I must die.

Four hundred strikers were brutally wounded;
Four hundred strikers and I left to die;
Remember the day, sir, to all of your children,
This bloody Thursday, the fifth of July.

Don't beat the drums slowly, don't play the pipes lowly,
Don't play the dead march as they carry me along;
There's wrongs that need righting, so keep right on fighting,
And lift your proud voices in proud union songs.

It was a period, Michael Denning writes, of "insurgency, upheaval, and hope," with currents and events such as these leading to the rise of the Congress of Industrial Organizations (CIO) and the "laboring of American culture," the "first time in the history of the United States that the left – the tradition of radical democratic movements for social transformation – had a central, indeed shaping impact on American culture." Historians like Denning have tended to look, quite rightly, at the centrality of proletarian struggle in this "social transformation." Indeed, the most familiar Depression-era imagery reflects it, from the novels of John Steinbeck, John Dos Passos, and Richard Wright to the photographs of Dorothea Lange, Walker Evans, and Margaret Bourke-White to the songs of Yip Harburg and Woody Guthrie. But another, generally unremarked "social transformation" was also going on, not so much proletarian as sexual, and it was marked by two phenomena. One was the so-called pansy craze – more affirmative, defiant, and revolutionary than the phrase might suggest – and the other, the culture of the "bulldagger" or "mannish lesbian." As with almost everything else in American life, both were tied up with issues of race.

As Michael Bronski notes, Black Americans and homosexuals in the 1930s "shared a sense of social stigmatization, marginalization, and criminalization." Hence the relatively liberating atmospheres of both Greenwich Village and Harlem in New York City:

> Greenwich Village was in many ways accepting of people of color. Harlem, a primarily African American community was accepting of homosexuals of color as well as some white homosexuals. . . . Harlem's world of jazz clubs, speakeasies, cellar clubs, and low-end and upscale nightclubs (the latter frequented by wealthy white patrons) encouraged sexualized performances. In the early 1930s, performers such as African American Gladys Bentley, who performed dressed as a man, and "Gloria Swanson," a renowned Chicago drag queen who moved to Harlem to open his own club, were extraordinarily popular. The sites of arts and entertainment that blossomed around African American and same-sex communities continued in the sexual tradition of nineteenth-century same-sex-loving artists to turn homosociality into sexual fluidity.

New York had the Pansy Club, the Rubaiyat, the Club Abbey, and the Argonaut, among others, where drag artists and female impersonators enjoyed enormous success when they weren't dodging the police who periodically shut down the clubs in the crusade against vice and drink. Chicago had its Ballyhoo Café, and Hollywood had the Bali, where the celebrated gay nightclub singer Bruz Fletcher made it clear in "The Simple Things in Life" (1936) that all were welcome to sit at his tables, whether gay stalwarts or straight slummers:

> I want a cozy little nest, somewhere in the West
> Where the best of all the worst will always be.
> I want an extensive, expensive excursion
> To the realms of "in," "per," and "di"-version.
> It's the simple things in life for me.

The pansy craze, as Darryl Bullock summarizes it, marked

> a short period when gay men and lesbians were feted by royalty, courted by Hollywood (before the Hays Code, which effectively banned Hollywood from portraying homosexual characters or movies having positive LGBT storylines) and celebrated nationally for their work. The Pansy Craze was a by-product of the open defiance of America's recently enacted prohibition laws, and the moral crusaders of the Woman's Christian Temperance Union and their allies would have been furious had they realised that their

> success in banning alcohol sales across the United States would create a thriving black market for bootleg booze, a bustling underground club scene and a vicious criminal underworld.

The performer who, more than any other, ruled the pansy craze of the 1930s was Brooklyn-born Jean/Gene Malin (Victor Malinovsky), "the highest-paid nightclub entertainer of 1930 . . . an openly gay man (although he, like many others, would later marry), who bleached his hair platinum blond but dressed in expensive suits and dinner jackets when he performed." Malin wooed New York with his versions of Eugene Conrad's "I'd Rather Be Spanish (Than Mannish)" (1932) and his own "That's What's the Matter With Me" (1931), which mischievously played with the rigid expectations of binary sexuality:

> I don't know whether I'm mister, miss, or missus;
> I'm on the spot, as you can plainly see.
> Before my birth, my mother had just flowers on her mind;
> The doctor who attended her was just so good and kind;
> And when he arrived, he brought the biggest pansy he could find,
> So that's what's the matter with me. That's all!

As theater reviewer Mark Hellinger noted, Malin had given New York audiences their "first glimpse of pansy nightlife. . . . Before the mainstream knew what was happening, there was a hand on a hip for every light on Broadway."

The pansy became a stock figure in many knowing popular songs of the day, particularly those composed by gay songwriters, such as Lorenz Hart's "Ten Cents a Dance" (1930) and Cole Porter's "I'm Unlucky at Gambling," in which "the sophisticated lady finds out her favorite croupier is gay and shrugs it off to happenstance." A surprising number of Black male blues singers also gave the pansy a more or less playful nod. Kokomo Arnold's "Sissy Man Blues" (1935) was recorded three times within the year following his own premiere recording – by Josh White (as Pinewood Tom), George Noble, and Connie McLean's Rhythm Boys – all of them including the groundbreaking line: "Lord, if you can't send me no woman, please send me some sissy man." Kokomo Arnold and Speckled Red both recorded classic versions of "The Dirty Dozens" (alternatively "The Twelves"): "I like your mama, I like your sister too / I *did* like your daddy, but your daddy wouldn't do / Met your daddy on the corner the other day / You know about that, that he was funny that way." Tom Delaney's "Down on Pennsylvania Avenue" (1929) depicts "that cabaret / Where they turn night into day" and where "You can't tell the he's from the she's."

Al Miller's "Somebody's Been Using That Thing" (1929) also made the rounds in versions by the Hokum Boys, Tampa Red, and Milton Brown and His Brownies (among others), cheering on the man who "puts paint and powder on his face" and the "women who walked and talked like men." Tampa Red and Frankie "Half Pint" Jaxon took on James Bernie Barbour's "My Daddy Rocks Me (With One Steady Roll)," originally recorded by Trixie Smith in 1923 as "My Man Rocks Me": "There's no slippin' when once he takes hold. / I looked at the clock and the clock struck one. / I said, 'Now Daddy, ain't we got fun.' / He kept rockin' with one steady roll." These lines obviously took on an entirely new meaning when sung by men. And, as the openly gay George Hannah wrote and sang in "Freakish Man Blues" (1930): "There was a time when I was alone, my freakish ways to see / But they're so common now, you get one every day in the week."

In contrast to the "pansies," lesbians did not enjoy the same popular-culture celebrity. Bronski surmises that this was possibly because "the mannish lesbian, recognizable by her masculine clothing and short-cropped hair ... was associated with progressive causes such as suffrage, and was specifically, not generally, subversive." Lesbians were *serious*, pansies playful: "For this reason – as well as because the pansy was more flagrantly sexual and instantly recognizable, fluttering his hands and fussing over women's clothing – the pansy image enjoyed much wider appeal." Enter Lucille Bogan (as the pseudonymous Bessie Jackson), whose "B. D. Woman's Blues" (1935) championed the self-reliance and strength of the "bulldagger":

> Comin' a time, B.D. women, they ain't going to need no men ...
> 'Cause the way they treat us is a lowdown and dirty sin.
>
> B.D. women, you sure can't understand ...
> They got a head like a sweet angel and they walk just like a natural man.
>
> B.D. women, they all done learned their plan ...
> They can lay their jive just like a natural man.
>
> B.D. women, B.D. women, you know they sure is rough ...
> They all drink up plenty whiskey and they sure will strut their stuff.
>
> B.D. women, you know they work and make their dough ...
> And when they get ready to spend it, they know they have to go.

Bogan's song came seven years on the heels of "Worried Blues" (1928) by Gladys Bentley, the top-hat-and-tails-wearing "250-pound black lesbian" and "avowed 'bulldagger'" for whom women are "to be both respected and feared." Bentley's challenge was uncompromising, with her verses backed up by her own mouth-trumpet rasp:

> What makes you menfolk treat us women like you do? . . .
> I don't want no man that I got to give my money to . . .
>
> Give my man everything from a diamond ring on down . . .
> Next thing I'm gonna give him: six feet in the cold, cold ground.
>
> You can never tell what an old, old man can do . . .
> Keep your eyes open, girls, 'cause he'll put that thing on you.

In 1930, George Hannah sang an ode to lesbian sex in "The Boy in the Boat," with piano accompaniment by Meade "Lux" Lewis. Bullock notes that "the phrase 'boy in the boat' is a euphemism for the clitoris and the clitoral hood." But the song's most important lines are not about "that boy in the boat." Rather, they are the opening couplet, a primary lesson for homophobes and bigots of all stripes: "When you see two women walking hand in hand / Just look 'em over and try to understand." Perhaps it was nothing more – and nothing less – than a precursor to President Barack Obama's declaration eighty-five years later, on the legalization of same-sex marriage, that "all people should be treated equally, regardless of who they are or who they love" – that, in the end, "love is love."

CHAPTER 15

To Thee We Sing

Franklin D. Roosevelt was up for reelection in 1936. Four years earlier he'd been swept into office with the promise of a "New Deal" for the American people and a request for executive power "to wage war against the emergency" – a power as great as that for a president facing "invasion by a foreign foe." But as Woody Guthrie observed, the threat was already there, on FDR's doorstep: "On the skeeter bit end of th' garbage dump, / 30 million people slump / Down where the big rats run an' jump / In Hooversville." Of course, not all the country's unemployed were living in the "Hooverville" camps, and Guthrie's numbers were overstated. During the first year of Roosevelt's presidency, just under 13 million were unemployed, or one-quarter of the civilian workforce. By 1936, that number had dropped to just under 8 million.

Driven by the ideas of Roosevelt's controversial "Brain Trust" and backed up by a US Government check for billions of imaginary dollars, the face of American legislation began a cautious but unprecedented transformation during the first three years of Roosevelt's presidency, what some historians refer to as the "First New Deal" period. From the Agricultural Adjustment Administration (AAA) to the National Recovery Administration (NRA), and from the Civilian Conservation Corps (CCC) to the Federal Housing Administration (FHA) – and many other departments and initiatives, all with their corresponding acronyms and abbreviations – a whole alphabet of government programs had been set in motion to combat the worst effects of the Depression. And yet, by now the inescapable limitations of the New Deal had been revealed: the invisibility of reforms at the worst levels of poverty outside its catchment areas, the failure of the program to enforce an atmosphere for effective union organization, and the lasting shame of the vagrant and migrant homeless ever on the move and thus out of reach of many of the program's reforms.

All these factors gave rise to a mixed bag of cultural responses. For Langston Hughes, by 1934 it was already time to "stop waitin' on Roosevelt."

The shift from the Hoover era to the Roosevelt era had appeared so monumental that a traditional ballad on the assassination of William McKinley, "McKinley's Gone," quickly began to recirculate in the Appalachian Mountains as the "White House Blues." Its composer has never been identified, but he or she caught the initial euphoria of the first Roosevelt election:

> Look here, Mr. Hoover, it's see what you done;
> You went off a-fishin', let the country go to ruin.
> Now he's gone, I'm glad he's gone.
>
> Roosevelt's in the White House, doin' his best,
> While old Hoover is layin' round and takin' his rest.
> Now he's gone, I'm glad he's gone . . .
>
> People all angry, they all got the blues,
> Wearing patched britches and old tennis shoes.
> Now he's gone, I'm glad he's gone.

Inevitably Roosevelt's initiatives prompted charges of executive overreach and unconstitutionality from conservative and laissez-faire activists. Among them were the so-called Four Horsemen of the Supreme Court, four right-wing justices who worked tirelessly in the name of unfettered capitalism to void the earliest New Deal acts and who, consequently, incurred the wrath of some poor communities to the point of being hanged in effigy. Ed Sturgill – a West Virginia coal miner, UMW activist, and banjo player – memorialized the battle between Roosevelt and the Court in his "'31 Depression Blues," which also celebrated the establishment of the Federal Deposit Insurance Corporation in 1933:

> The Depression is gone and I'm glad it's gone.
> Oh the year that it happened, nineteen hundred thirty one.
> When the NRA, it was done late one night
> And the big supreme judge then he said it wasn't right.
>
> Then Roosevelt stepped in, he was doing his best.
> Then he closed all the banks and he give them a rest.
> Then he opened them up when he put them on their feet,
> He said, "Boys, you can deposit now, your money can't be beat."

Southern country music and blues players responded in great numbers to the New Deal initiatives. Peter La Chapelle notes:

> Several hillbilly bands and performers including Fiddlin' John Carson, the Skillet Lickers, the Allen Brothers, the Light Crust Doughboys, and Milton Brown and his Musical Brownies took it upon themselves to support Roosevelt with specialized recordings or endorsements of other kinds – a stance that staked out not just the traditional Democratic tendencies of the South but also the affinity with which many Southerners, poor or not, had for FDR and his social programs for farmers and the distressed.

Hence Bill Cox's "NRA Blues" of 1933, with its wry anti-capitalist slant on the NRA:

> When you goin' to join the NRA,
> Sweet thing, sweet thing,
> When you goin' to join the NRA,
> I never heard the big boss say,
> Sweet thing, yes, baby mine.

The Tennessee Valley Authority, established in 1933 and whose dam-building and electrification projects were crucial to large areas of the South (in spite of their devastating environmental and cultural impact), reflected a particularly strong Federal challenge to the greed and capriciousness of privately owned energy companies. For this reason Alan Lomax, Woody Guthrie, and Pete Seeger took special care to include the "Ballad of the TVA" by the Kentucky fiddler Jilson Setters (James William Day) in their song collection, *Hard Hitting Songs for Hard-Hit People.* Guthrie's notes presented it as a "love song":

> 'Course you know as well as I do that once in a while some boy and girl will haul off and fall in love in spite of everything the bankers can do about it. I been around this country and seen 'em fall in. So you see you're dealing with an old goes. This here song is a good one. Love song. This ballad spread all through the Mountains of Kentucky and Tennessee and often would change the names of places and people around to fit their own locality. It even spread up to New York City.

Setters indeed couched his eulogy to the TVA in the form of a traditional love ballad:

> I meant to marry Sally
> But work I could not find;
> The TVA was started
> And surely eased my mind.

I'm writing her a letter
These words I'll surely say:
"The Government has surely saved us,
Just name our wedding day."

We'll build a little cabin
On Cove Creek near her home;
We'll settle down forever
And never care to roam.

For things are surely movin'
Down here in Tennessee;
Good times for all the valley
For Sally and for me.

Black blues singers also composed their New Deal accolades, such as Alabama-born Joe Pullum's "CWA Blues" of 1934, boosting the new Civil Works Administration: "CWA, you're the best pal we ever knew, / You're killing Old Man Depression, and the breadlines too." The Chicago pianist and singer Jimmie Gordon composed "Don't Take Away My PWA" (recorded 1936) to celebrate the Public Works Administration that had taken as many as three million men and women out of unemployment to provide the labor and administration for new schools, hospitals, tunnels, bridges, dams, roads, and waterworks across the country – "a splendidly improved national estate." Gordon's plea was passionate: "Oh, Mister President, listen to what I'm going to say. / You can take away all of the alphabets, / But please leave that PWA."

In a 1932 radio address, then-Governor Roosevelt had spoken of "the forgotten man at the bottom of the economic pyramid," a phrase borrowed from the nineteenth-century Yale philosopher William Graham Sumner. In the 1930s the phrase came to epitomize "the poor man, the old man, labor, or any other recipient of government help." Tin Pan Alley was quick to take note, with Bob Miller (writing as Bill Palmer) giving notice of who would determine the outcome of that year's election: "Who's gonna vote on election day? / Who's finally gonna have his say? / Who's gonna cause a change, hey hey! / It's the poor forgotten man!" While Miller's prediction did come true, it was only a year later that Al Dubin and Harry Warren were already pleading – as sung by the pointedly biracial duo of Etta Moten and Joan Blondell in the film *Gold Diggers of 1933* – "Remember My Forgotten Man":

Remember my forgotten man.
You put a rifle in his hand;
You sent him far away,
You shouted: "Hip-hooray!"
But look at him today.

Remember my forgotten man.
You had him cultivate the land;
He walked behind the plow,
The sweat fell from his brow.
But look at him right now.

The same year, the pianist and singer Ramona (Estrild Raymona Meyers) recorded – along with Roy Bargy and the Paul Whiteman Orchestra – Ted Koehler and Harold Arlen's "Raisin' the Rent," which suggested that "better times" were "taking too long" – even though Roosevelt had only just begun his first term:

I'm buried in worry, surrounded by woe;
No end to my trouble I can see.
Depression has got me, won't let me go;
It's trying to double up on me.

Good luck has crossed me, bad luck has forced me,
Down to my one last cent.
I'm right in the middle of solving the riddle,
Known as raising the rent.

Taken together, these songs reflect both the desperation and the high hopes faced by the first Roosevelt administration immediately upon taking office in March of 1933. The task of recovery was monumental; and in the midst of the economic depression, it seemed that natural forces were also conspiring to thwart any mortal's best efforts. Just as the Mississippi Flood of 1927 had broken through the prosperous bull-market veneer of the "Roaring Twenties," from about 1931 until the end of the decade it was the great dust storms of what became known as the "Dirty Thirties."

There had always been periods of drought on the Southern and Midwestern plains of North America. Over many centuries the Indigenous inhabitants came naturally to expect extreme periods of drought every twenty years or so, but through patience and conservation they learned how to ride out the dry times. Along with the drought there was always the dust – but again, for centuries the worst of it had been held in check by the native prairie grasses locking down the soil with their deep roots. With the arrival of the Euro-American plainsmen – the "sod busters," as they proudly and arrogantly called themselves – the protective grasses gave way to the harshest of cash crops, in particular wheat and cotton. By the second decade of the twentieth century, with the aid of Henry Ford's tractors and combine harvesters, cash crops had outstripped the grass on an industrial scale. Land speculators, oil prospectors, railroad magnates, and coal operators had seized most of the fertile lands in Oklahoma and adjacent areas, leasing their holdings to be worked by a poor, hardscrabble class of renters and tenant farmers. Already trapped in the ever-spiraling credit-and-debt cycle of the crop lien system, the hard-hit farmers on the plains faced one of their century's greatest catastrophes, brought about – in historian Donald Worster's words – by "one of the three worst ecological blunders in history." The first had been the deforestation of the Chinese highlands in 3000 BCE, leading to floods of biblical proportion. The second was the destruction of Mediterranean flora through livestock farming, turning the once-fertile lands to semi-desert. And now came the Dust Bowl of the 1930s, when the rains failed to come, the temperatures soared, the drought returned, and the ravaged land exacted its revenge.

In November 1933, the dust of five thousand square miles of outraged farmland buried Chicago. The following spring it buried Chicago again – as well as Albany and Buffalo, New York. Sailors three hundred miles out in the Atlantic reported the settling of a fine patina of dry, red prairie dust on their decks and railings. The dust continued to blow throughout the decade, but no storm was as terrifying as that of Palm Sunday – "Black Sunday" – April 14, 1935. On that day, the Midwestern skies grew black and red with thousands of tons of roiling dust. Across the plains, animals and people choked to death. Toddlers wandered out into dust drifts and suffocated. The fervently religious – Baptists and Pentacostals – proclaimed it the Day of Judgment. But in reality it was, in Worster's words, "the inevitable outcome of a culture that deliberately, self-consciously, set itself the task of dominating and exploiting the land for all it was worth."

Twenty-three-year-old Woody Guthrie and his young family watched the storm approach the Texas Panhandle town of Pampa, where he had moved from Oklahoma in 1929. He recalled the vision for Alan Lomax:

> And so we watched the dust storm come up like the Red Sea closin' in on the Israel children . . . So we got to talking, you know. And a lot of people in the crowd that was religious minded, and they was up pretty well on the Scriptures, and they said, "Well, boys, girls, friends and relatives, this is the end. . . . This is the end of the world."

Guthrie later wrote: "For every farmer who was dusted out or tractored out, another ten were chased out by bankers." Guthrie himself was not a farmer; he was the middle-class son of a real estate speculator fallen on hard times. But a future singing partner of his, Agnes "Sis" Cunningham, recalled the end of her farming days in the Dust Bowl:

> Along with other hundreds of thousands of dirt farmers, we fought to survive. We battled crop failures, hunger, illness without doctors, hail and windstorms, gully washes, the death of livestock, fires. We could have endured these normal disasters, but there was no way in God's world to escape the shark's teeth of the bankers.

Thus began what Guthrie's biographer Joe Klein called "a human convulsion of epic proportions." With the snowballing evictions of Dust Bowl farmers and laborers, "the whole countryside seemed to heave and groan as the farms emptied and the highways filled." "Sis" Cunningham retrospectively and succinctly captured the migrants' dilemma in her song, "How Can You Keep on Movin'?" (1945):

> How can you keep on movin' unless you migrate too?
> They tell you to keep on movin', but migrate you must not do.
> I'll tell you why I'm movin': the reason why I roam
> Is to get to a new location and find myself a home . . .
>
> And if you pitch your little tent along the broad highway,
> The Board of Sanitation says, "Sorry, you cannot stay."
> "Go on, get along and get movin'" is their everlasting cry.
> Can't stay, can't go back, and can't migrate, so where in the heck am I?

Woody Guthrie would soon make his name with his *Dust Bowl Ballads* (1940), but he was not the only "Dust Bowl Balladeer." For example, Jack Bryant, a farmer from Okomogee, Oklahoma, left a field recording with the Library of Congress on his experience as a migrant headed for California, where he ended up in Firebaugh, one of the handful of camps set up by the Farm Security Administration (FSA). His first-person narrative in "Arizona" fairly complements the second-person narrative in Guthrie's more famous "(If You Ain't Got the) Do Re Mi," while the influence of Jimmie Rodgers on Bryant's singing and playing is immediately apparent:

> We were out in Arizona on the Painted Desert ground;
> We had no place to call our own home, and work could not be found.
> We started to California, but our money, it didn't last long.
> I want to be back in Oklahoma, be back in my old home.
>
> Away out on the desert, where water is hard to find,
> It's a hundred miles to Tempe and the wind blows all the time.
> You will burn up in the daytime, yet you're cold when the sun goes down.
> I want to be back in Oklahoma, be back in my home town.
>
> You people in Oklahoma, if you ever come west,
> Have your pockets full of money, and you better be well dressed.
> If you wind up in the desert, you're gonna wish that you were dead.
> You'll be longing for Oklahoma and your good old feather bed.

Lester Hunter was another "Dust Bowl refugee" at the Shafter camp, also run by the FSA. He, too, left a field recording for the Library of Congress, "We'd Rather Not Be on Relief" (1938). It was, in a sense, a musical reinforcement of Guthrie's scathing reply to the hostile *Los Angeles Times* reporter, Kenneth Crist, who had condemned the Dust Bowl migrants as filthy grifters in search of easy handouts. As Guthrie wrote in his "Woody Sez" column for the *People's World*:

> The Author was trying to make you believe that these weatherbeaten, browbeaten, homeless people are really robbers at heart ... people who were living like wild hogs in a boggy river bottom for a whole year in order to get some of that easy Relief Gold. ... No, Kenneth ... it ain't the "Easy Relief Money Us Folks Is After" – it's jest a chanct to work an' earn our livin' ... sorta like you earn yore livin'....
>
> But before I'd make my livin' by writin' articles that make fun of the Hungery folks, and the Workin' folks,
>
> I'd go on Relief.

For Lester Hunter in the Shafter camp, there was a lesson for all the Kenneth Crists and the vigilante thugs and deputies in the hire of the Associated Farmers, who – as Guthrie would recount in his famous Dust Bowl ballad "Vigilante Man" – set out with violence to break the union organization of migrant workers: "I'd rather not be on the rolls of relief or work on the WPA; / We'd rather work for the farmer, if the farmer could raise the pay ... / The times are going to get better, and I guess you'd like to know; / I'll tell you all about it: I've joined the CIO."

Periods of deep economic depression are always dangerous. In the 1930s, the near collapse of capitalism inevitably raised opportunities for demagogues – an epithet often slung by conservatives at Roosevelt himself. However, as Amity Shlaes notes, there was an alternative "story line" to the Roosevelt years: "Without the New Deal, the country would have followed a demagogue, Huey Long, or worse, Father Coughlin." The first of these, Huey Long, was the populist Louisiana governor – afterwards senator – assassinated in 1935 on the steps of the state capitol building. Long has been cited by historians and commentators as "the first true dictator out of the soil of America," an "incipient fascist," and, most recently, a "Trumpian figure." Alternatively, he was simply "a good mass leader," the poor man's champion, and "the 'original' Bernie Sanders." The second figure – Father Charles Coughlin – has earned a less divided reputation: he was a demagogic radio broadcaster, fierce anti-Semite, and admirer of Hitler and Mussolini. Coughlin was also, perhaps, the greatest American celebrity of the 1930s, enjoying "national popularity of bewildering proportions" before "a strain of megalomania wore away his self-restraint until finally his excesses destroyed him." Both Long and Coughlin were staunch supporters of Roosevelt before violently turning on him as the Depression deepened.

Huey P. Long was himself a songwriter. As La Chapelle notes: "In 1935, Long gained national attention for co-writing and singing 'Every Man a King,' his own self-promoting jazz-pop slogan song, which took its title and message from his 1933 autobiography of the same name." Long would habitually "switch" the song "from marches to jazz to hillbilly as it pleased him or suited his public relations." Ultimately it would be "slowed down and turned into a dirge" for his funeral, the same year that he cowrote the song with Castro Carazo. The lyrics might help to explain Long's popular appeal among Louisiana's poor in the midst of the Depression:

> Why weep or slumber, America?
> Land of brave and true,
> With castles, clothing, and food for all
> All belongs to you.
> Ev'ry man a king, ev'ry man a king,
> For you can be a millionaire;
> If there's something belonging to others,
> There's enough for all people to share.
> When it's sunny June and December, too,
> Or in the wintertime or spring,
> There'll be peace without end.
> Ev'ry neighbor a friend,
> And ev'ry man a king.

Alan Brinkley accounts for "the unwavering support, even adulation" that Long enjoyed among Louisiana's poor:

> It was for them, he claimed, that he built hundreds of miles of paved highways, provided free textbooks, constructed bridges, hospitals, schools, and a major university. It was for them that he revised the state tax codes, for them that he railed against the oil companies and utilities that had dominated Louisiana for decades.

More than one admirer answered Long's song with their own, such as an imprisoned jailbird named Theodore Buckner:

> Just walking in the moon light
> For the night so long
> If yo wants to meat A Real man
> Meat H. P. Long

Some People are glad Some People are so
But he will bring the baken back where Ever He go
And if yo wants to be Reborn
Just keep on voten for H. P. Long
Don't Pull up your Cotton Crop
Give the kids an Edecasion and bring them to the top.

Now this Song is coming to an end
So stick to H. P. Long He is yo only Friend.

Among the many musical elegies that appeared after Long's assassination, it is *possible* that one was written by Bob Miller, indicating the appeal for the controversial populist among some sectors of the Left. "The Death of Huey P. Long" was released by the early country singer Hank Warner on September 13, 1935, three days after Long's death: "Oh, they shot Huey Long in Louisiana, / As he walked down the capitol steps. / Yes, they killed Huey Long in Louisiana / As he took on the capitalist." Long was also the inspiration for some conflicting literary representations, most notably the populist demagogue Buzz Windrip, who leads the US into fascism in Sinclair Lewis's *It Can't Happen Here* (1935), and the equally demagogic Willie Stark in Robert Penn Warren's *All the King's Men* (1946). But perhaps the most unsettling, because most ambivalent, depiction comes from the Black Louisianian Ernest J. Gaines, whose 103-year-old narrator in *The Autobiography of Miss Jane Pittman* (1971) lays bare both the man's social commitment and his muscular racism: "I agree he did call the colored people n——r. But when he said n——r he said, 'Here a book, n——r. Go read your name.' When other ones said n——r they said, 'Here a sack, n——r. Go pick that cotton.'"

As for Father Coughlin, most literary and musical representations have been appropriately scornful. Sinclair Lewis, again in *It Can't Happen Here*, and Woody Guthrie, in the song "Lindbergh" (1944), both give him a resounding thumbs down for his Hitler-loving demagoguery. Philip Roth's fictional autobiography, *The Plot Against America* (2004), presents "the 'Radio Priest' Father Coughlin and his Jew-hating Christian Front" as chief enablers of the fascist, anti-Semitic president Charles A. Lindbergh. For any laudatory song, one must turn to the ephemera of printed sheet music to discover the likes of Clarence Gaskill's "Shepherd of the Air" (1933), Muriel Magerl Kyle's "The Golden Call" (1935), and Kenyon Scott's "Father Coughlin Came Along" (1935), all now fortunately sunk into oblivion.

Whether or not the New Deal was indeed responsible for short-circuiting the triumph of demagoguery in the USA, the 1936 election approached with Roosevelt groping his way toward the more radical "Second New Deal" that included social security, slum clearance, and the "new program of emergency public employment" that became the Works Progress Administration (WPA). What was most new and striking about the WPA was its expansion of the concept of public labor beyond the bounds of physical infrastructure – road building, dam building etc. – to include writers, artists, musicians, actors, and others working in creative arenas. Under the umbrella of "Federal Project Number One," Roosevelt's team inaugurated the Federal Writers Project (FWP), the Federal Music Project (FMP), the Federal Theater Project (FTP), the Federal Art Project (FAP), and the Historical Records Survey (HRS). The reach – and enduring legacy – of the WPA was prodigious. As historian Nick Taylor asserts: "There was not a county in the United States that the agency had not touched in some way, and scarcely a possibility for work that had not been exploited."

If certain contemporary song lyrics are an indication, Roosevelt had been backed into a corner, with the likes of the Piedmont bluesman Carl Martin's "Let's Have a New Deal" warning in 1935 – already two years *into* the New Deal – "Because I've got to make a living: if I have to rob and steal." It was a threat repeated that same year by Kokomo Arnold: "I ain't got no airplane, / Ain't got no automobile, / I ain't got no money, / I guess I have to rob and steal." Sleepy John Estes, from Tennessee, celebrated the "government money" that would "furnish you a milkcow: a rooster and some portion of hen." But as Roosevelt had declared to Congress in announcing the Second New Deal: "The Federal Government must and shall quit this business of relief." What then for Aunt Molly Jackson, who sang of "Christmas Eve in the East Side": "My heart it is breaking, it's Christmas eve night, / I'm in the slums on the East Side without any light. / I've no gas or electric to make myself a cup of tea. / Oh tell me, fellow workers, how can this be?" On the other hand, other, more ephemeral lyricists were adamant that "this business of relief" must indeed end. "O Listen While We Sing About the Billions Spent," complained one anonymously in 1936. "The Nation of Our Fathers Is Assailed by Foes Within," warned another – also anonymously – that same year. "O Give Me a Home Where No Brain Trusters Roam," sang yet a third, all three lending their efforts to the anti-Roosevelt *Campaign Songs for the Liberty Quartette*.

Roosevelt's answer to the charges of "easy relief" was, in effect, the WPA itself. Guido van Rijn notes that "the first blues artist to comment on the new agency was William 'Casey Bill' Weldon" from Arkansas, whose

"WPA Blues" presents "a poor man who has rented a house that is part of a WPA slum clearance project." It was hardly a resounding vote of confidence for the WPA in its earliest days:

> Everybody's workin' in this town, and it's worried me night and day,
> It's that mean workin' crew that works for the WPA.
> Well, well, the landlord come this morning, and he knocked on my door,
> Asked me if I was goin' to pay my rent no more.
>
> He said, "You have to move, if you can't pay,"
> And then he turned and he walked slowly away,
> So I have to try, find me some other place to stay,
> That house wreckin' crew is coming, from that WPA.

In mid-1936, a California songwriter named Charles Hammond gloated in his song title that it was "The End of the New Deal Dream (WPA, AAA, IECX, or What Have We?)." His sheet music sported an illustration of a toddler playing with a pile of alphabet blocks and babbling, "Big AAA house fa' down." If the cover is to be believed, it was "Today's Most Popular Song," with lyrics proclaiming: "There's a dreamer in the White House / Building castles in the air, / Like a child with lettered blocks, / That he piles with greatest care."

But apparently the rest of the country believed that it was only the *beginning* of the New Deal dream, for in November that year they renewed Roosevelt's mandate by a landslide. It was the greatest electoral and popular vote enjoyed by any presidential candidate since 1820. Bill Cox, the "Dixie Songbird," rushed straight to the recording studio the following week, along with his singing partner Cliff Hobbs, and cut two euphoric sides. One was "The Democratic Donkey," eulogizing the mascot of the Democratic Party:

> I've been a good old donkey, but they'd turned me out to die.
> They had me on the common, where the grass don't grow so high.
> But now I'm in the clover, in a field of golden grain:
> I'm back in old Columbee, in the same old stall again . . .
>
> Hee-haw-hallelujah! Hee-haw-hallelujah!
> I'm back in old Columbee, in the same old stall again.

On the other side was "Franklin D. Roosevelt's Back Again," which celebrated the repeal of Prohibition as much as the "money in our jeans": "I'll take a drink of brandy and let myself be handy. / Good old times are coming back again (hallelujah!) / You can laugh and tell a joke, / You can dance and drink and smoke; / We've got Franklin D. Roosevelt back again."

Soon the harmonica-playing bluesman Sonny Boy Williamson was boosting the WPA's road-building program, which promised to open new vistas and mobility, at least in the creative imagination.

Williamson's "Project Highway" (1937) offered the prospect of a vibrant life beyond the doldrums of the Depression: "Well, I've got to get some money; I wants to buy a V-8 Ford. . . . / I wants to ride this new highway that the project just completed a week ago. / Well, I gots to ride this new highway, Lord, and I'm gonna cross the Gulf of Mexico; /And I ain't gonna stop ridin', well, until I park in front of my baby's door."

But all the euphoria and boosting of Roosevelt and the Second New Deal did not eclipse the voices of struggle. The commercially successful blues singer and guitarist Josh White – not yet having emerged from behind his "Pinewood Tom" alter ego – recorded his first "contemporary protest pieces" in 1936, both written by Bob Miller: "No More Ball and Chain," about twenty prisoners killed in "a jailhouse fire," and "Silicosis Is Killin' Me" ("Silicosis Blues"), sung, it is usually assumed, from the point of view of a coal miner suffering from "black lung." White's biographer, Elijah Wald, stresses the impossibility of saying conclusively "why he chose to make a protest record at this time, or what importance he may have attached to it. The songs were certainly not of the sort he would have been playing at Harlem rent parties. . . . Nonetheless, no other major race artist [had] recorded anything comparable" by 1936.

"Silicosis Is Killin' Me" points to a strain of labor and industrial unease utterly impervious to New Deal reforms. Indeed, what if the narrator wasn't a coal miner with "black lung," but rather a tunnel blaster working on a road-building project and suffering from "white lung"? He would then be a victim of the acknowledged "silicosis crisis" of the Depression era, when "government officials and business leaders believed that 'silica dust is probably the most serious occupational disease hazard in existence today,'" typifying "'the whole occupational disease' problem." The lyrics then would add an extra twist to the critical knife:

> Now, silicosis, you're a dirty robber and a thief . . .
> Robbed me of my right to live,
> And all you brought poor me is grief.
>
> I was there diggin' that tunnel for just six bits a day . . .
> Didn't know I was diggin' my own grave,
> Silicosis was eatin' my lungs away.

Guthrie's own notes to the song in *Hard Hitting Songs for Hard-Hit People* reinforce the conflict between labor and capital that seemed to go on and on, right through the years of the New Deal:

> You get the silicosis a working in hard rock tunnels. . . . It killed an average of a man a week on rock drilling jobs in New York City. Sixteen Union

> men died in 4 months from it. No masks to keep it out of your lungs. They'd set off the dynamite and then make you go right in; the law says you got to wait thirty minutes for the dust to settle. To hell with the law, the big shots figured, and they hired spies to stand in the mouth of the tunnel and holler when a inspector was a coming, so's they could hide their illegal tools, the ones that makes so much dust.
>
> Wanted: More and bigger and better Cuss Words to tell what I think of a man that would do a thing like this just to squeeze a extry dollar out of a working man's dead body.

The CIO was only one year old when White recorded "Silicosis Is Killin' Me." It had frantically been organizing workers in major industries across the country – rubber, steel, agriculture, food processing, and textiles among them. In spite of the reputation Roosevelt enjoyed as "labor's friend," and with the CIO brandishing on their recruitment posters a quote attributed to him – "If I went to work in a factory, the first thing I'd do is join a union" – anti-union backlash flourished during the New Deal years. And the conflict wasn't only in the factories. The same year as White's recording, the Southern Tenant Farmers Union, only two years old, called a strike that brought on an assault from the Arkansas National Guard. Vigilantes set out to find the strike organizers, dragging them and their families from their homes and throwing their belongings into the road. It was this sight that prompted John Handcox to write "There's Mean Things Happening in This Land" before he himself was targeted. As he recalled:

> A friend of mine, a white fellow, he'd been up at the store and overheard them say, "that n——r John Handcox, we gonna hang him. We got the rope and we got the limb, all we want is him". . . . I went over on the highway. At that time they just had a gravel road. Two lanes, one going, one coming. I caught a Greyhound. I caught that puppy to Memphis.

And, in "The Strike in Arkansas," he sang: "If you go through Arkansas, you better drive fast. / How the labor is being treated, you better not ask."

Anti-union hostility continued through the Kentucky and West Virginia mine patches, where Jilson Setters revived the memories of the Coal Creek Wars of the 1890s to comment on the ongoing "Harlan County War" between, on one side, the CIO and the UMW, and, on the other, the coal operators:

> My song is founded on the truth: in poverty we stand.
> How hard the millionaire will crush upon the laboring man.
> The miner's toiling underground to earn his daily bread,
> To clothe his wife and children and see that they are fed.

Some are from Kentucky, the place known as my birth,
As true and honest-hearted men as ever trod the earth.
The governor sent the convicts here and works them in the bank;
The captain and his soldiers are leading by in rank.

Sarah Ogan Gunning recorded a store of ballads for Alan Lomax in 1937, many of which were focused on the Harlan coal dispute and its causes. "Thinking Tonight of an Old Southern Town" was hardly an ode to the moonlight and magnolias of the Old South. On the contrary it was about the coal operators' terror tactics in wresting the subsistence farmers' coal-rich land out from under them for a pittance, much as the railroad speculators had done to the farmers and homesteaders further west in the previous century:

Thinking tonight of one old southern town
And my loved ones that I left behind.
I know that they're naked and hungry, too,
And it sure does worry my mind.

Oh, poor little children, so hungry and cold,
The rich mighty captains so big and so bold;
They stole all our land and they stole all our coal:
We get starvation while they get the gold.

Gunning's "Come All You Coal Miners" reinforced both the continuing struggle to organize and the broader economic structures behind it: "Coal mining is the most dangerous work in our land today, / With plenty of dirty, slaving work, and very little pay. / Coal miner, won't you wake up and open your eyes and see / What the dirty capitalist system is doing to you and me." Other Gunning songs recorded by Lomax that year, some of which would become classics in the US folk music revival of the 1940s–1960s, included "Down on the Picket Line," "I'm Goin' to Organize, Baby Mine," and "I Hate the Capitalist System."

The ongoing coal struggles also produced a store of anti-union ballads particularly aimed at the CIO and its founding leader, John L. Lewis, as well as the UMW:

Children lying in the bed,
Crying, "Daddy, please bring home some bread."
Picket line says, "You can't go through;
We'll beat you up if you try to."

John L.'s pay is big and fat;
I wish I had a tenth of that.
I don't like to sit at home
And hear my wife and young 'uns moan.

Thought I'd work 'cause I'm almost broke,
Dig for Donegal Coal and Coke;
Three hundred pickets came around,
Beat me bloody to the ground.

In nearby Kentucky, the ballad collector Jean Thomas found this:

The Ashland Tannery was where I worked,
The men, like me, I know
Were satisfied with their own jobs,
Then came the CIO.

They spread ill feeling around the men,
The bosses and laborers alike.
Then came the day the men were forced
To organize and strike.

The pickets were placed in front and back
And men kept out by force.
Instead of settling in a peaceful way,
They took the roughest course.

As far as the CIO was concerned, there was no "settling in a peaceful way." Violent events all across the country had been proving it – events like the 1937 "Memorial Day Massacre" in Chicago, when police killed ten unarmed CIO strikers who were protesting over the refusal of smaller companies like Republic Steel ("Little Steel") to agree to a contract already signed by "Big Steel," the United States Steel Corporation. Shortly afterwards, Earl Robinson composed "Ballad of the Chicago Steel Massacre," which took direct aim at the chairman of Republic Steel, Tom M. Girdler:

On dark Republic's bloody ground, the thirtieth of May:
Oh, brothers, lift your voices high for them that died that day.
The men who make our country's steel, the toilers in the mill,
They said, "In Union is our strength and Justice is our will."

We will not be Tom Girdler's slaves, but free men we will be.
List to the voices from their graves: "We died to set you free."
In ordered ranks they all marched on to picket Girdler's mill.
They did not know that Girdler's cops had orders: Shoot to kill!

"Sit-down" strikes swept the country in the years 1936 and 1937, beginning with rubber workers against the Goodyear Tire and Rubber Company in Akron, Ohio. This was followed by a strike against Woolworth's department store in Detroit, where low wages, institutional sexism, racism, and union nonrecognition were the main issues of dispute.

By far the biggest sit-down strike of the period was in Flint, Michigan, where workers took over the General Motors (GM) plant "in one of the first successful attempts at unionization in the auto industry." This strike produced some noteworthy songs, such as an anonymously composed parody of Johnny Mercer and Matty Malneck's popular hit, "Goody, Goody" (1936):

> When we walked out on you,
> we set you back on your heels,
> Goody, goody!
> So you lost some money and now
> you know how it feels.
> Goody, goody!

Maurice Sugar, composer of "The Soup Song" and now the attorney for the United Auto Workers union (UAW), wrote the most famous song to come out of the Flint strike, "Sit Down":

> When they tie the can to a union man,
> Sit down! Sit down!
> When they give him the sack, they'll take him back.
> Sit down! Sit down!
>
> Sit down, just take a seat,
> Sit down, and rest your feet,
> Sit down, you've got 'em beat.
> Sit down! Sit down!

Other songs emerging from the Flint strike included a parody of the minstrel show favorite, "A Hot Time in the Old Town," composed spontaneously in the aftermath of the "Battle of the Running Bulls," when – on the 11th of January, 1937 – police assaulted the strikers with tear gas and guns, only to be held off by a barrage of bottles, bolts, hinges, and other missiles hurled at them from inside the plant:

> Tear Gas Bombs
> Were flying thick and fast
> The lousy police
> They knew they couldn't last
> Because in all their lives they never
> ran so fast
> As in that hot time in this old
> town last nite.

During the strike, fifty women met to form the "Women's Emergency Brigade" and the "Women's Auxiliary" to assist the auto workers inside and outside the GM plant. They had their own theme song, set to the tune of "Marching Through Georgia":

> The women got together and they formed a
> mighty throng,
> Every worker's wife and mom and sister will
> belong,
> They will fight beside the men to help the cause
> along,
> Shouting the Union forever!

In the end, the Flint strike was successful in that it achieved its objective of winning GM recognition for the UAW, but in 1939 the Supreme Court ruled that such strikes were "a high-handed show without shadow of legal right" – arguably a sign of their effectiveness, if ever there was one.

The Flint strikers also drew great sustenance from singing the rousing song that had emerged among the West Virginia Miners Union five years earlier: "We Shall Not Be Moved." This song continued to travel, landing in the care of the striking Mexican American pecan shellers of San Antonio, Texas, in the new year of 1938. Sitting in the jail they called "the black hole of Texas," they sang it as "*No nos moverán,*" the first time the historical record shows it being sung in Spanish. One participant, George Lambert of the CIO, recalled its origin:

> I remember spending one night in a cell, which was made for about six people, and there was about twenty some-odd people in there. Twenty or more of us were in there, so we couldn't lay down. [Santos] Vásquez was in there with me, and I gave him the words to a number of labor songs – the English words – and he translated them into Spanish. The only one that I can remember now was "We Shall Not Be Moved." . . . The words go "just like a tree planted by the water" and he puzzled with that for quite some time and decided that the closest translation he could get was in the Spanish words for "just like a rock that stands against the windstorm" – "*como peñón que resiste el viento.*" . . . We got the people in that jail singing that night! They were all packed in there. . . . The jailers were trying to quiet it down. There was some talk about using the [fire] hoses on us. . . . These labor songs were just pouring out of there in Spanish all that night.

Meanwhile, in a neglected corner of the US empire – the environs of Ponce, Puerto Rico – the people were still reeling from the massacre of Palm Sunday, 1937, when a peaceful march organized by the Puerto Rican Nationalist Party ended with the slaughter of twenty-one unarmed marchers and the wounding of another 150 at the hands of the Insular Police Force, which was under the direct command of the US governor of the island, General Blanton Winship. Rafael Hernández Marín, eight years after having composed his "*Lamento Borincano*," responded to the Ponce Massacre with the bolero "*Preciosa*" (recorded 1937):

> Precious you are called by the bards
> who sing your history.
> It's not important that the tyrant treats you
> with black evil.
> Precious you'd be without a flag,
> without laurels, or glory.
> Precious, precious, you are called
> by the children of liberty.

As Ruth Glasser notes: "No one who heard the song . . . doubted to whom *el tirano* (tyrant) referred."

The year 1937 also saw the genesis of what was arguably the century's most damning musical commentary on US tyranny – not necessarily *state* tyranny, but not wholly unconnected to it, either. It began as a poem prompted by a widely-circulated photograph of two Black men lynched in Marion, Indiana, Thomas Shipp and Abram Smith. A high school teacher in the Bronx, Abel Meeropol, published his poem "Bitter Fruit" in the union newspaper *New York Teacher*. Whether or not Meeropol's empathy had been heightened by particular cases like the lynching of Leo Frank in 1915, he later wrote:

> I am a Jew,
> How can I tell?
> The Negro lynched
> Reminds me as well.
> I am a Jew.

If, by the 1930s, lynching of Black Americans by whites had indeed begun to decline from its peak in 1892, it was no thanks to the Federal government. As David Meyer observes, "in the 1930s, President Roosevelt saw more to lose than to gain by embracing the cause of civil rights . . . in the form of an antilynching law." When two Democratic senators, Edward Costigan and Robert F. Wagner, cosponsored a Federal antilynching bill in 1934, they presented it to Roosevelt, who dismissed it out of hand. As Roosevelt explained to the NAACP secretary Walter White the following year, it was all about the Southern vote: "The Southerners . . . occupy strategic places on most of the Senate and House committees. If I come out for the antilynching bill now, they will block every bill I ask Congress to pass to keep America from collapsing. I just can't take that risk."

The death of innocents seemed to haunt Meeropol, to the extent that he published his poem under the pen name of Lewis Allan – the combined names of his two stillborn children. (Meeropol and his wife Anne would later adopt the two orphaned sons of Julius and Ethel Rosenberg after their execution on confused charges of espionage in 1953.) Meeropol's sardonic irony – the "Pastoral scene of the gallant South" reflected in the "bulging eyes and the twisted mouth" of the lynched victims – drove the song, retitled "Strange Fruit," that would become the blues singer Billie Holiday's career hit in 1939. It was also circulated that year to US senators debating, yet again, the passage of an antilynching bill. Eighty-two years later, in January of 2021, the Emmett Till Antilynching Act was introduced to Congress. The legislation – given by Skopos policy analysts that month a "1% chance of being enacted" – faced determined obstruction by largely Southern conservative senators, even though the Senate had "formally apologized in 2005 for failing to outlaw the practice." The stack of unpassed Federal antilynching bills remained – as late as 2021, when "all lives" supposedly mattered – "a strange and bitter crop" indeed.

By 1937, the same year as Meeropol's "Bitter Fruit," the blues singer Huddie Ledbetter was already widely known across the country as Lead Belly, having emerged from Angola Prison in Louisiana three years earlier into the controlling management of the folksong collector John Lomax. Theirs was an "exploitative relationship" that the novelist Richard Wright called "one of the most amazing cultural swindles in American history." Not only had Lomax been taking "50 percent of Lead Belly's profits (along with full control over his bookings)," but he had also "demanded" that Lead Belly

> perform and take promotional photographs dressed in prison stripes and/or bandanaed and barefoot in sharecropper's overalls. Even Angola's prisoners no longer wore stripes; in 1930, then-governor of Louisiana R. G. Pleasant censured the practice because it "degraded and humiliated them unnecessarily." Ledbetter – a fastidious dresser, particularly while performing – found Lomax's representational demands demeaning and offensive.

Moreover, such imagery threatened to imprison Lead Belly in the default position of presumed Black criminality that had, since the end of Reconstruction, perpetuated slavery by other means within the legal system and, outside of that system, allowed lynching to flourish.

After breaking with Lomax, Lead Belly remained on good terms with his son, Alan, and in 1937 traveled to Washington, DC, to record his songs for the younger Lomax at the Library of Congress. He was meant to stay at

Alan Lomax's rented apartment, but was "kicked out by the landlord because of his race." As Jeff Place recounts it: "They found they couldn't even find him a place to eat or stay in the black areas because he was with white people. In exasperation, someone in the group commented that Washington was a 'bourgeois' town." Out of this bitter experience came one of Lead Belly's greatest protest songs, "Bourgeois Blues" (1938):

> Some white folk in Washington, they know just how
> To call a colored man a n——r just to see him bow . . .
>
> Home of the brave, land of the free;
> I don't want to be mistreated by no bourgeoisie,
> Lord, in a bourgeois town.
> Hmmm, the bourgeois town.
> I got the bourgeois blues;
> Gonna spread the news all around.

Clearly, then, race and ethnicity remained at the center of much struggle and song in the midst of the Second New Deal. Moreover, the battle over what constituted "100% Americanism" had hardly been decided. If anything, it had intensified. In 1936, the CPUSA president, Earl Browder, had declared Communism to be simply "Twentieth-century Americanism" – a slogan, Robbie Lieberman notes, that was "taken to heart by cultural and political workers." In this scenario, Marx, Engels, and Lenin joined the ranks of Jefferson, Paine, and – above all others – Lincoln.

Although he himself was no Communist, Carl Sandburg had done much to prime Abraham Lincoln for his adoption by the CPUSA and the Popular Front. In 1936, the first two volumes of Sandburg's six-volume biography had appeared as *Abraham Lincoln: The Prairie Years.* This was the same year that Sandburg's poetry collection, *The People, Yes,* was published, reinforcing his established reputation – with his guitar and his *American Songbag* – as the songster of the common man and woman. As for Sandburg's Lincoln, he was no capitalist stooge – not the shrewd corporate lawyer who, in history, plotted the tax avoidance of the Illinois Central Railroad and had a town named after him as a gesture of gratitude by the Chicago & Alton Railroad. Rather, he was a proletarian rail-splitter sprung from the American grain itself, akin to "a tall horse chestnut tree or a rangy horse or a big wagon or a log barn full of new-mown hay." Indeed, in *The American Songbag,* an entire section of traditional ballads is devoted to "the Lincolns and the Hankses" simply on the grounds that Lincoln and his family *might* have known or sung them. Only two of the songs are actually about Lincoln: "Old Abe Lincoln Came Out of the Wilderness" and – the most useful for proletarian purposes – "Lincoln and Liberty," the campaign song that completely elides Lincoln's history as a wealthy railroad lawyer: "They'll find what by felling and mauling, / Our rail-maker statesman can do; For the people are everywhere calling / For Lincoln and Liberty too."

It was no great leap from Sandburg to a number of other musical practitioners who found Lincoln a suitable symbol of American virtue and progressivism – even radicalism – in the New Deal years. The composer Daniel Gregory Mason, grandson of Lowell Mason, spent two years working on his *Lincoln Symphony* (Symphony no. 3, 1935–1936), building upon the ground already laid out in his *String Quartet on Negro Themes* (1918–1919) by inextricably linking settings of spirituals and a "lament of the slaves" to a recurring "three-note motive of wide skips" representing Lincoln's moods ("pity," "inner struggle," "rough gaiety," and "poignant sorrow"). And, in 2009, there were discovered among the papers of Florence Price two complete settings of Vachel Lindsay's poem, "Abraham Lincoln Walks at Midnight" (1914): "one setting for orchestra, organ, chorus, and soloists" and one "for chorus and soloists and piano accompaniment." Michael Driscoll, music director for the Andover (Massachusetts) Choral Society, which premiered a recording of the latter setting in 2019, notes that Price's diary indicates that the work could have been composed anytime between 1914 and 1949.

There is no evidence that either Mason or Price would have allied themselves ideologically with the Popular Front or the CPUSA, but the figure of Lincoln was certainly brought into the communist orbit as an embodiment of both proletarian struggle and anti-fascism, not least through one other musical setting of Lindsay's poem, that of the Composers' Collective renegade, Elie Siegmeister, in 1937. As a devotee of both Sandburg and Aunt Molly Jackson, Siegmeister knew about the relationship between music, political activism, and propaganda, citing in his Marxist pamphlet, *Music and Society* (1938), two contemporary examples:

> 1. The shameless perversion in present-day Germany of Beethoven's *Eroica* Symphony, dedicated originally to a great liberator and democrat (the young Napoleon), performed today in honor of Adolf Hitler; and 2. The distortion of the traditional popular Christmas hymn, *Heilige Nacht* [Silent Night], which teaches peace and brotherhood, into a Nazi-Pagan hymn of hate.

Siegmeister was only two years away from publishing his own Sandburg-inspired collection, *A Treasury of American Song* (1940), and a year away from establishing his own six-person choral group, the American Ballad Singers (1939). Through Siegmeister's choral setting, Lindsay's Lincoln was reborn as a Popular Front revolutionary: "He cannot rest until a spirit-dawn / Shall come; – the shining hope of Europe free; / A league of sober folk, the workers' earth, / Bringing long peace to Cornland, Alp and Sea."

For Siegmeister's musical colleague Earl Robinson, Lincoln was best filtered through the pen of Alfred Hayes, who had written "Abe Lincoln" in 1936, the same year that the pair had collaborated on "I Dreamed I Saw Joe Hill Last Night" while teaching together at the left-wing Camp Unity in New York State. With lines from Lincoln's First Inaugural Address interspersed with original lyrics by Hayes, the song came from a particular historical place, as Robinson recalled in the liner notes to his own recording of the song in 1963:

> Consider the Depression and the roaring 30's. Consider seventeen million unemployed in a nation of only 120 million. Reflect on the needs and problems and consequent moods of "one third of a nation, ill clad, ill nourished and ill housed" [FDR]. People were in motion, forced to organize against starvation, for a living wage, for a union of their own choice, for a decent life. By the millions, they were joining the big industrial unions, building the CIO . . . And there was a need not only to look to the future but to seek back in the past, through our own history, for help to face and understand the stormy present. The word "revolutionary" was not a fearsome word to the majority.

In Robinson and Hayes's construction, the "revolutionary" was Lincoln himself, based on the lines from his First Inaugural Address, repeated as the song's refrain:

> This country with its institutions belongs to the people who inhabit it;
> This country with its constitution belong to us who live in it;
> Whenever they shall grow weary of the existing government
> They can exercise their constitutional right of amending it,
> Or their revolutionary right to dismember or overthrow it.

These lines dovetailed with Hayes's own:

> Now old Abe Lincoln, a great big giant of a man was he,
> Yes sir!
> He was born in an old log cabin and he worked for a living,
> Splittin' rails.

Robinson later reflected on the ultimate destination of "Abe Lincoln," in a curious indication of how far popular culture was prepared to go, in those years, to absorb the Popular Front's conception of a "radical"

American: "The most amazing thing of all was its being bought by the Schuberts for inclusion in the Broadway production of *Hellzapoppin.* In that zany Olsen-Johnson highjinx, our strong radical Abe Lincoln song sung with nice dignity by a Negro quartet, was a quiet spot." John "Ole" Olsen and Harold "Chic" Johnson's slapstick revue, *Hellzapoppin* (1938) was briefly Broadway's longest running musical, and, given Gerald Bordman's summary of it as "zany, happy, and irrelevant," one must indeed wonder what "Abe Lincoln" was doing in the midst of it:

> A filmed sequence that opened the evening offered praise for the revue from Hitler (speaking with a Yiddish accent), Mussolini (ranting in a Negro dialect), and Roosevelt (talking gibberish). "Workmen" lumbered through the rows of seats with large ladders, forcing patrons to get up and out of their way; in the middle of the performance a woman screamed she had left her baby at the Automat and rushed out of the theatre. A man walked up and down the aisles attempting to give a lady a plant she had ordered; the plant grew bigger with each appearance, and by the end of the evening departing crowds could see the man sitting in the lobby with a small tree and still forlornly calling out the lady's name. Sirens, firecrackers, and guns were going off incessantly. In a show such as this there was little use for good music.

The mind still boggles at what the producers' – the Shuberts' – intentions were in buying "Abe Lincoln" for the show. Perhaps it was part of the anarchic *zeitgeist* of the most extreme Depression-era comedy, a type that so unnerved Charlie Chaplin that he would confess in 1936: "Modern humor frightens me a little. The Marx Brothers are frightening. Thurber, Stewart, Joe Cook, Benchley – yes, all of them. ... Acquiescence in everything disintegrating. Knocking everything down. Annihilating everything." If Hayes and Robinson's Lincoln – harmonically elegized by a Black quartet no less – fit somewhere in the carnivalesque scheme of *Hellzapoppin*, then surely the more earnest purveyors of Popular Front ideology had something to worry about.

After all, there were some more serious – deadly serious – things afoot, and "Abe Lincoln" was wrapped up in them, too. As Robinson recalled: "It was sung in Spain by members of the Abraham Lincoln Brigade, in the struggle of the Spanish Loyalists against Franco." In some respects, the currents of the Spanish Civil War of 1936–1939 were as confusing as the plot of *Hellzapoppin*, though hardly comedic. On the one hand, there was the Marxist poet George Witter Sherman making a startling comparison in "Moon Over Spain" (1938) via a moon "sorrowing at Lincoln's tomb in Springfield and / At Lenin's tomb in Red Square." On the other hand, there was Maxwell Anderson in his play *Key Largo* (1939) denying any exclusive claim of the Communist International or the CPUSA on the fighters of the Lincoln Battalion: "They're Anarchists, Communists, Leftists, Rightists, Leftist-rightists, Rightist-leftists, Socialists, Leftist-Socialists, Rightist-Socialists, Anti-clericals, Clerical-Communists, Loyalist soldiers, police, crazy people, and once in a while just a plain farmer, all fighting Franco!" And there was Ernest Hemingway in *For Whom the Bell Tolls* (1941), with his protagonist Robert Jordan – based on the commander of the Lincoln Battalion, Robert Hale Merriman – confessing to himself: "You're not a Marxist and you know it. You believe in Liberty, Equality and Fraternity. You believe in Life, Liberty and the Pursuit of Happiness. Don't ever kid yourself with too much dialectics. They are for some, but not for you."

But each US fighter was there for a reason, and many of them sang and wrote songs – even as the still unknown Woody Guthrie was singing for them at fund-raising benefits up and down the West Coast in the years 1937 and 1938, establishing a kinship in his mind between the refugees from Franco and the refugees from the Dust Bowl. Indeed, Guthrie has often been miscredited with the composition of the most famous English-language song to emerge from the Spanish Civil War: "Jarama Valley," which he recorded in the late 1940s but which was composed by the Scottish fighter Alex McDade, who died in the Battle of Brunete in July 1937. "Jarama Valley" was one of many songs known to have been sung by the US fighters in the Lincoln Battalion. Others included "Cookhouse," or "The Young Man from Alcalá," "Quartermaster Song," "*Viva la Quince Brigada*" (Long Live the 15th Brigade), "*El Quinto Regimiento*" (The 5th Regiment), and "*Si Me Quieres Escribir*" (If You Want to Write to Me), as well as the legendary "*Los Cuatro Generales*" composed by Federico García Lorca.

With the fascist dictator Francisco Franco's victory secured in 1939, "Sis" Cunningham recalled: "Several personal friends and acquaintances of mine were volunteers in Spain – all but one came back. In a manner of speaking, all of us, even if we never left the United States, had to come back from Spain." What did they find when they came back? Among other things, they would have found a Depression "which had seemed to be lifting" until, in 1937–1938, it "took a turn for the worse." In the midst of the economic downturn, however, there had been some bright spots on the musical front. The composer Marc Blitzstein, his producer John Houseman, and his director Orson Welles had managed to stage their radical opera *The Cradle Will Rock* (1937) – "about industrial violence in the steel industry" – in an impromptu, scaled-down version in defiance of the FTP, which had withdrawn its sponsorship and funding due to anti-CIO hostility and the Roosevelt administration's consequent cold feet. In the end, the opera ran for two weeks, "with little publicity but to mostly sold-out houses." On the immediate heels of *The Cradle Will Rock* came the Harold Rome musical revue *Pins and Needles* (1937), produced with members of the International Ladies Garment Workers' Union and boasting indicative song titles like "One Big Union for Two," "Doing the Reactionary," and its defining paean to political and social activism in the form of a love song, "Sing Me a Song with Social Significance":

> Sing me of wars and sing me of breadlines;
> Tell me of front-page news.
> Sing me of strikes and last minute headlines,
> Dress your observation in syncopation.
>
> Sing me a song with social significance;
> There's nothing else that will do.
> It must get hot with what is what,
> Or I won't love you.

Pins and Needles turned out to be "a completely unanticipated hit," running until 1940 and setting "a record for musicals of the 1930s with 1,108 performances" on Broadway.

In spite of its hostility to *The Cradle Will Rock*, the New Deal government was responsible for supporting a number of African American productions that benefitted from its sponsorship. William Grant Still's *Lenox Avenue*, an orchestra and choral work featuring a narrative and scenario by Verna Arvey, was an evocative presentation of Harlem life first broadcast on CBS radio in May 1937. It was staged the following year as a ballet with the FMP at the Dance Theater of Los Angeles, where the *Los Angeles Times* praised it for the choreography, and the Harlem Renaissance intellectual Alain Locke perceived in the classical, jazz, and spiritual mix an "inner mastery of mood and spirit."

The same year, Helen Tamiris, chief choreographer for the Federal Dance Theater in New York City, staged *How Long, Brethren?*, based on Lawrence Gellert's *Negro Songs of Protest*, which had been published the year before. It "ran for an unprecedented ten weeks, playing to 24,235 people." *How Long, Brethren?* was "a suite of seven dances" based on the songs "Pickin' off de Cotton," "Upon de Mountain," "Railroad," "Scottsboro," "Sistern an' Brethren," "Let's Go to de Buryin'," and – the finale – "How Long, Brethren." Elizabeth Cooper notes that, in its entirety, the production conveyed through dance, orchestra, and full African American chorus "a history of poverty, starvation, injustice, and death, and ending with a plea to end the oppression and suffering." But indeed, the finale was more than a "plea." As the song collected by Gellert makes clear, it was a Black finger pointed in outrage as well as a wakeup call to action:

> So long my people been asleep
> White folks plowin' n——r's soul down deep.
> How long, how long, brethren, how long? . . .
>
> White folks ain't Jesus, he just a man,
> Grabbin' biscuit out of poor n——r's hand.
> Too long, too long, brethren, too long.

Gellert's friend and sometime collaborator, Langston Hughes, had written a foreword – unused, in the end – to *Negro Songs of Protest*, in which he wrote:

> These songs collected by Lawrence Gellert from plantations, chain gangs, lumber camps, and jails are of inestimable value, if they do nothing more than show that not all Negroes are shouting spirituals, cheering endowed football teams, dancing to the blues, or mouthing inter-racial oratory. Some of them are tired of being poor, and picturesque, and hungry. Terribly and bitterly tired.

In April 1938, Hughes himself built upon this history of "tiredness" in his own production, *Don't You Want to Be Free?*, which starred Robert Earl Jones – father of James Earl Jones – in what Hughes called "a continuous panorama of the emotional history of the Negro from Africa to the present." It was, in Arnold Rampersad's words, a hardhitting, multifaceted production in which "music, especially the blues and spirituals, was integral," one that used "techniques borrowed from musical comedy, religious pageants, and the 'living newspaper,' but [was] most heavily dependent on Hughes's poems." *Don't You Want to Be Free?* was a stark homespun production, staged for "an overflow crowd of almost 200" in a Harlem loft with a "curtainless stage; in plain sight were three chairs, a table, a screen, a slave block, and a tree stump. An American flag was hanging left of center; a heavy rope tied in a noose dangled at the center; also on stage was a carpet sweeper." From that bare, dusty stage the likes of Nat Turner, Denmark Vesey, Harriet Tubman, and Sojourner Truth reminded the Depression generation what it meant to fight, rather than to plead.

But how downscale it was, compared to another gala event that December at Carnegie Hall. The first of John Hammond's *From*

Spirituals to Swing concerts offered a different "panorama," a sweeping musical history reflected in the program's title and introducing an all-Black roster that included the Golden Gate Quartet, the Count Basie Orchestra, Jimmy Rushing, James P. Johnson, Sonny Terry, Big Bill Broonzy, Sister Rosetta Tharpe, Big Joe Turner, Meade "Lux" Lewis, and Albert Ammons, among others. The concert was both a musical and political milestone funded by the CPUSA magazine *New Masses* and the leftist Theater Arts Committee, since an integrated audience sitting before a stage full of Black performers meant that Hammond could secure no other funding. The first concert was so successful that it was repeated the following December, this time with a racially integrated performance roster that included the Benny Goodman Sextet. As Ted Gioia observes: "In the context of American society, these were earthshaking moves. Popular music was the first important sphere in American society to desegregate, and the superstar jazz musicians led the way."

By the time of the second *From Spirituals to Swing* concerts, another issue had driven itself toward the top of Roosevelt's agenda. For two years, a cross-section of the country had been wondering precisely what Earl Robinson and Harold Schachter had expressed in their "Spring Song" of 1937: "Oh, I wonder will there be a war this spring? / Will we be fighting while the robins sing? / Will the bayonets be bristling and bullets do the whistling / When the world is all in bloom in the spring?" Even before the Nazi–Soviet invasion of Poland in September 1939, the issue was already complicated (to put it mildly) for the US Left, thanks to the nonaggression pact – the Hitler–Stalin pact – signed the previous month. Fascism and Nazism were bad, bad, bad, of course . . . but after all, the Soviet Union was the "Mother of the Revolution." As Al Richmond, editor of the West Coast Communist newspaper, the *People's World*, put it: "One argument for the treaty was that it created a zone of peace. From this I deduced that surely Hitler would not strike eastward." And yet, he did, followed by Stalin from the east, two weeks later. World War II was underway in Europe. "The Yanks Aren't Coming" was the new song that Harold Rome hastily added to the 1939 production of *Pins and Needles*. "(If They'd Only Fight Their Battles with) Little Toy Men," wrote Tin Pan Alley's Malvin Franklin and Bill Gaston.

For Roosevelt, timing was everything. Even before the British found themselves formally at war with the Axis Powers, they needed – as Winston Churchill had been arguing – to build up their war machine, just as Hitler had been doing in contravention of the Versailles Treaty that had concluded World War I. Kristine McCusker describes the part that an all-women Appalachian string band, "a troupe of 'Negro' singers from the WPA," a "black opera singer," a "white Metropolitan Opera baritone," and a "white popular singer" played in the unfolding of events. The bigger picture was this:

> Roosevelt knew he had to name the British his allies so he could support their military buildup, but he could not be assured that all Americans would be pro-British. The American Nazi Party had a substantial presence in the United States during the 1930s, attracting American luminaries such as Charles Lindbergh. American companies – General Motors, Ford, IBM, and Du Pont – sold material to Hitler as he illegally rearmed Germany. Finally, there was a substantial German-American population and an Irish-American population in the United States that was vehemently anti-British.

Against this backdrop, enter Lily May Ledford and the Coon Creek Girls, the WPA singers, Marian Anderson, Lawrence Tibbett, and Kate Smith, invited by the Roosevelts to perform for King George VI and Queen Mary of England at the White House on June 8, 1939. With a musical program designed to reinforce "the bonds of friendship that link our two peoples" (as Roosevelt declared in his opening toast), the performances were meant to signal "the transition from an isolationist American culture to one that was ready to fight the Nazis."

Four months before this royal performance, Marian Anderson had been barred by the Daughters of the American Revolution (DAR) from performing in their Constitution Hall because she was Black – an affront that led Eleanor Roosevelt to resign her membership from the organization. At the White House, there was a delicious moment when Anderson was introduced formally to Queen Mary while shamefaced members of the DAR were forced to look on, unintroduced. Fresh in everyone's memory, no doubt, was Anderson's legendary Easter Day performance on the steps of the Lincoln Memorial, secured by Eleanor Roosevelt, before a crowd of seventy-five thousand, for whom she sang – among other songs – the spirituals "Gospel Train," "Trampin'," and "My Soul Is Anchored in the Lord," as well as a pointedly adjusted verse of "America":

> My country 'tis of thee,
> Sweet land of liberty,
> *To* thee *we* sing.

As the Black civil rights leader and educator Mary McLeod Bethune declared: "Through the Marian Anderson protest concert we made our triumphant entry into the democratic spirit of American life."

Figure 15.1 Marian Anderson. Portrait by Carl Van Vechten, 1940. Library of Congress Prints and Photographs Division

It is possible that no one can precisely define "the democratic spirit of American life" – perhaps because the phrase has been up for grabs ever since Hector St. Jean de Crevecoeur asked in 1782, "What Is an American?" But in 1939, John La Touche and Earl Robinson took a stab at it with their cantata originally titled "The Ballad for Uncle Sam," written for an FTP revue called *Sing for Your Supper.* The revue ran for only two months before the House Committee on Un-American Activities saw that both the show and the FTP were defunded and terminated as hotbeds of rampant communism. Radio producer Norman Corwin then took the cantata, retitled it "Ballad for Americans," and hired Paul Robeson to sing it on a coast-to-coast broadcast of the CBS radio show *The Pursuit of Happiness* on Sunday, November 5. It quickly became so popular that Bing Crosby recorded it in 1940, the same year that it was performed in its entirety at both the Republican National Convention and the annual convention of the CPUSA – an irony that is also quite problematic in terms of what it signals about the relationship between popularity, radicalism, and conservatism.

Indeed, although it was a signal production of the Popular Front in its waning years, "Ballad for Americans" was both radical – to an extent – and conservative. In its class consciousness and gender consciousness it aimed to be inclusive:

> What's your racket? What do you do for a living?
> Well, I'm an engineer, musician, street cleaner, carpenter, teacher –
> How about a farmer?
> Also.
> Office clerk?
> Yes, ma'am.
> Mechanic?
> That's right.
> Housewife?
> Certainly!
> Factory worker?
> You said it.
> Stenographer?
> Uh huh.
> Beauty Specialist?
> Absotively!
> Bartender?
> Posolutely!
> Truck driver?
> Definitely!
> Miner, seamstress, ditchdigger?
> All of them. I am the "etceteras" and the "and so forths" that do the work.

In terms of race and ethnicity, it aimed likewise (although neither Latinx nor Indigenous people got a look-in):

> Am I an American?
> I'm just an Irish, Negro, Jewish, Italian,
> French and English, Spanish, Russian,
> Chinese, Polish, Scotch, Hungarian,
> Litvak, Swedish, Finnish, Canadian,
> Greek and Turk and Czech
> And double-check American.

And perhaps most disturbing, but also in keeping with the Popular Front's calculated absorption of the American mythos, "Ballad for Americans" is highly selective in its catalog of national crimes. It condemns slavery, "the murders and lynching," and "the patriotic spouting," but it appears unable to critique the ugliness of US imperialism with its Trails of Tears, its Sand Creek massacres, its Wounded Knees, and its seizures of half of Mexico and Cuba, Puerto Rico, the Philippines, and the Hawaiian Islands – all based on what Richard Drinnon memorably called (with a

Figure 15.2 Paul Robeson, 1942. Photograph by Gordon Parks for the Office of War Information, 1942.
Public Domain via Wikimedia Commons

nod to Melville) "the metaphysics of Indian-hating and empire-building," without which the USA, in any and all of its formations, could never have existed. The fact that "Ballad for Americans" *didn't* engage with these "metaphysics" is precisely what enabled the Republican National Committee to adopt it for their 1940 convention. When it came to westward expansion, the song's cast of characters – and the narrative itself (if unrhymed) – could have come from any of John Ford's most sentimental, patriotic westerns:

> Building a nation is awful tough.
> The people found the going rough.
> And thirteen states weren't large enough.
> So they started to expand –
> Into the western lands . . .
>
> But Lewis and Clark and the pioneers,
> Driven by hunger, haunted by fears,
> The Klondike miners and the Forty-Niners,
> Some wanted freedom and some wanted riches,
> Some liked to loaf while others dug ditches.

Perhaps without knowing it, the composers of "Ballad for Americans" had raised the nation's primal question – its Ur-question. In the 447 years since the Columbian invasion of 1492, that question – Whose land is this, anyway? – had been fought over and never conclusively answered. How many millions had died *trying* to answer it? Could or would it ever be answered? "Ballad for Americans" had tried and failed. It was left for others to try again.

Conclusion
Whose Land?

"If an observer from another world had trained his eye on a two-mile-square area bounded by Greenwich Village to the south and Times Square to the north, with the participants drawing together from Louisiana, New York, and Oklahoma's Dust Bowl, he would have witnessed an art form – the modern protest song – in the making." So writes Pete Seeger's biographer. The Louisianian was Lead Belly, the New Yorker was Seeger, and the Oklahoman was Woodrow Wilson Guthrie. The date they all first met was October 3, 1940. Alan Lomax later said: "You can date the renaissance of American folk song from that night."

The Oklahoman's Klan-loving father had named him after a racist Southern Democrat. As Guthrie later remembered:

> At the age of about four or five years old, a long time before I went to school, I remember my dad used to teach me little political speeches and rhymes. And I'd climb up in a hay wagon around all the political meetings and rallies they had on the streets, and I'd make my little speeches. And it might be that I've turned out now where I don't believe the speeches anymore, and I make speeches just the opposite.

He had traveled far – far from his father and from the town of Okemah, where he was born and raised; far from Pampa, Texas, where he matured, married, and became a father himself; far from the heart of the Dust Bowl and far from California, where he'd been politically awakened and transformed in the midst of deprivation, repression, anti-"Okie" bigotry, and Popular Front activism.

Shortly before meeting Seeger and Lead Belly, Guthrie had completed an epic transcontinental journey "from California to the New York island," a phrase he committed to paper on the 23rd of February in a cheap rooming house on the corner of Forty-third Street and Sixth Avenue. En route to New York – outside Harrisburg – he'd nearly succumbed in a snowdrift during one of the worst blizzards of the century.

Figure C.1a Pete Seeger and Woody Guthrie, c. 1940. Photographer unknown. American Folklife Center, Library of Congress

Figure C.1b Lead Belly (Huddie Ledbetter), c. 1940. Photographer unknown. American Folklife Center, Library of Congress

Seeger later recalled: "Woody was hitchhiking through Pennsylvania in the month of February. It was freezing cold – can you imagine him on the side of the highway with his thumb stuck out and the cars going *zzzoom, zzooom* past him? But if he had a nickel he'd go into a roadside diner and get a cup of coffee, and the juke box was playing Kate Smith singing 'God Bless America.'"

"America." Whose "America" was this, anyway? This was the question driven into Guthrie's mind, not only by Irving Berlin's latest hit as sung by Kate Smith but also by his own store of experiences – already more than enough for any man's lifetime, but a store that, nevertheless, he had yet to build upon. As an autodidact who had never finished high school, his knowledge was inevitably patchy. As an obsessive listener and record collector, he knew about all kinds of American music.

Even while still a young boy in Oklahoma, he knew that his father – an ambitious and often unlucky real estate swindler – had been adept at buying and selling Indigenous people's oil-rich lands out from under them. Guthrie later recalled: "They used dope, they used opium, they used every kind of a trick to get these Indians to sign over their lands." When his cousin "Oklahoma Jack" Guthrie took his song "Oklahoma Hills," recorded it and claimed credit for writing it, Woody's greatest objection was that he'd left out "the best parts of the whole song": the names of the "Chickasaw, Choctaw, Cherokee, Creek, and Seminole" whose land he knew it was.

In 1931, when he was nineteen years old, Guthrie had traveled with his father and his Uncle Jeff to the Texas–Mexico borderlands in search of a fabled, illusory gold mine his grandfather had supposedly staked out. It was there, as he recalled in his autobiographical novel *Seeds of Man* (posthumously published in 1976), that he was first exposed to the misery of the Mexican contract workers whom he would later memorialize in his song "Deportee" (1948). He'd heard their "Crying. Wailing . . . Like it was something between life and death. Like something was gone bad wrong." As he later wrote to his producer Moe Asch: "The Mexicans catch the roughest end of it all. They are allowed to come in, make their trip north, and then are herded back out as aliens and undesireables every year as the birds fly; only the birds are lots more welcome and fed better." In 1938 he'd spent a few brief months broadcasting from a Mexican border station, where he might have been exposed to the music of the era's most popular *canción ranchera* singers – the likes of Los Hermanos Chavarría; Gaitán y Cantú; Rocha y Martínez; and, especially, Lydia Mendoza, known as "*la alondra de la frontera*" (the Lark of the Border) and "*la cancionera de los pobres*" (the Poor People's Singer). There is no telling precisely what music Guthrie absorbed along that borderland, but he knew whose land it had been and whose it now was: those north of the Río Grande with Spanish names and US passports, whose citizenship had yet to be translated into equal rights, equal access, and equal justice.

Did this land belong to the Japanese American citizens whom Guthrie had seen amidst the union struggles in the Californian fruit fields, and whom Franklin Roosevelt would begin to intern in concentration camps two years from now? As he would soon write in *Bound for Glory* (1943), just a year into the Japanese internment program: "These little Japanese farmers that you see up and down the country here, and these Japanese people that run the little old cafés and gin joints, they can't help it because they happen to be Japanese." Did they have an equal claim to – an equal stake in – this land?

Did this land belong to Lead Belly, who two years earlier couldn't find a place to stay in the "bourgeois town" of Washington, DC, because of the color of his skin? Did it belong to the young Black man in California who had heard Guthrie play the appalling minstrel song "Run, N——r, Run" on his radio show one night in October of 1937? His letter, brimming with dignified outrage, had so awakened Guthrie that he felt compelled to read it over the air the next day:

> You were getting along quite well in your program this evening until you announced your "N——r Blues." I am a Negro, a young Negro in college and I certainly resented your remark. No person, or person of any intelligence, uses that word over the radio today . . . I don't know just how many Negroes listened to your program tonight, but I, for one, am letting you know that it was deeply resented.

Which land had belonged to Laura and Lawrence Nelson, a mother and her fourteen-year-old son lynched from the Okemah railroad bridge a year before Guthrie's birth – possibly, though by no means certainly, with his own father's participation? Guthrie would memorialize them later in songs like "Slipknot" and "Don't Kill My Baby and My Son," which he would dedicate to "the many Negro mothers, fathers, and sons alike, that was lynched and hanged under the bridge of the Canadian River, seven miles south of Okemah, Okla., and to the day when such will be no more."

In "God Bless America," Irving Berlin – the former Israel Baelin from Tolochin, Belarus, survivor of the pogroms – called this land his "home sweet home." Guthrie surely understood why, sensitive as he was to the plight of refugees, whether from Europe or from the Dust Bowl. He could recall a cousin in California who had "built him a shack in one of those flood basins out there . . . a big packing box that he got down at the water front and all over it was painted the name of a family of people that managed to get out of Germany just as the Nazis were taking over. My cousin called it his Hitler box." In another two years he would marry into a Jewish family and witness the trauma of anti-Semitism faced by his wife when, in Alton, Illinois, she would be confronted with a sign outside a swimming pool: "No dogs or Jews allowed." It was just like the signs they'd posted in California: "Okies and dogs not allowed inside." In the midst of the war, Guthrie would tell his wife: "I think of what fascism is trying to do to you and to your relatives, to me and mine, and seeing what they've done and are doing in the nations they've already overrun, it makes me even fuller of hate for them."

What bone, then, could Guthrie possibly have had to pick with Irving Berlin? The song he had just completed – the "angry song," Bruce Springsteen later called it – was titled "God Blessed America for Me" in a direct clapback at Berlin's hit. Why? Perhaps the answer lay in the injunction Guthrie scrawled at the bottom of the manuscript lyrics to his song, which he would soon retitle "This Land Is Your Land": "All you can write is what you see." Whatever else Berlin may have seen, he chose to mention only the mountains, prairies, and white-foamed oceans. Guthrie had seen some beautiful things, too, on his travels – waving wheat fields and golden valleys; endless blue skies and redwood forests. He'd seen some awesome things, like enormous, rolling dust clouds and ribbons of highway disappearing to the vanishing point. But he'd also seen some ugly things: high walls and fences with signs proclaiming "Private Property" and "No Trespassing"; lines of his hungry and destitute people, seeking relief; vigilantes and deputies forcing them to go where they didn't want to go. All these went into the song that, he concluded, was about a land that had been "made for you and me" – for whomever "you and me" happened to be. Perhaps in being so vague and so general, he was being evasive. Perhaps he was being as all-inclusive as it was humanly possible to be. As soon as he finished writing it, Guthrie set his new song aside and promptly forgot about it. There were other things to sing about.

By the time "This Land Is Your Land" became somewhat of an unofficial national anthem – sometime in the early 1960s – Guthrie had begun his final descent into the darkening twilight of Huntington's disease, which took his life in October of 1967. He never got to see Seeger and Springsteen performing it on the steps of the Lincoln Memorial in January 2009, televised for a global audience tuned in to Barack Obama's first inaugural concert. He never got to see Jennifer Lopez sing it for Joe Biden's inauguration in January 2021. And he had no idea of the controversy that his song would generate, even before the worst of his disease took hold. As early as 1958, *The Bosses' Songbook* edited by Dave Van Ronk and Dick Ellington included a savage parody, "This Land Is Not Our Land," later recorded by the IWW balladeer Utah Phillips:

> This land is their land, it is not our land.
> From your plush apartment to your Cadillac car-land;
> From your Wall Street office to your Hollywood star-land,
> This land is not for you and me.
>
> So take your slogan and kindly stow it;
> If this is our land, you'd never know it.
> Let's get together and overthrow it:
> This land was made for you and me.

Years later, Seeger recalled a tense moment during the Poor People's March on Washington in 1968, when he and two Black singers, Jimmy Collier and Rev. Fred Kirkpatrick, kicked off a rousing singalong of "This Land":

> Henry Crow Dog of the Sioux Indian delegation came up and punched his finger in Jimmy's chest. "Hey, you're both wrong. It belongs to me." Jimmy stopped and added seriously, "Should we not sing this song?" Then a big grin came over Henry Crow Dog's face. "No, it's okay. Go ahead and sing it. As long as we are all down here together to get something done."

But Seeger was shaken to the core. Only two years earlier, the Cree songwriter Buffy Sainte-Marie had refused to sing "This Land" with him. "I just cried through it," she said. "I thought, 'This used to be my land and you guys aren't even smart enough to be sensitive to this?'" And now, he'd put his foot in it again. His friend Bernice Johnson Reagon – one of the Freedom Singers and, later, the founder of Sweet Honey in the Rock – reflected:

> That song was the basis of Pete's principles, him and good old Woody. And it's the basis of the American dream – coming in and building a country, freedom, blah blah. . . . And I remember Pete talking constantly about that exchange with Kirkpatrick and Collier around Chief Crow Dog, and how he then had a hard time doing "This Land Is Your Land." It felt like he didn't know what to sing . . . he was not sure what his function was.

Later, Seeger sometimes attempted to ease his troubled conscience in performance by adding a verse penned by the singer and activist Carolyn "Cappy" Israel to acknowledge the theft of Indigenous land:

This land is your land, but it once was my land
Before we sold you Manhattan Island.
You pushed my nation to the reservation:
This land was stole by you from me.

But these parodical and revisionist efforts of the 1950s and 1960s have not put the issue to rest. Henry Crow Dog's "big grin" has not been shared by all those in the Indigenous communities of the USA, many of whom continue to see "This Land" as an anthem of settler colonialism, a repository of "the unconscious manifest destiny we live with." In the period between the Obama and Biden inaugural performances, the Abenaki musician and singer Mali Obomsawin wrote of being shaken up "like a soda can" every time she heard a performance of "This Land Is Your Land":

> Woody Guthrie's protest anthem exemplifies the particular blind spot that Americans have in regard to Natives: American patriotism erases us, even if it comes in the form of a leftist protest song. Why? Because this land "was" our land. Through genocide, broken treaties and a legal system created by and for the colonial interest, this land "became" American land.

Inevitably, Obomsawin's patient and reasoned argument gave the right-wing pundits a field day. They were delighted to witness the internecine strife among the "fascist woketards" of the US left.

But Obomsawin had a point, one that would not go away. It resurfaced in the immediate aftermath of J-Lo's performance at the Biden inauguration, when a host of Indigenous commentators stood up to shine a light on the "blind spot" in Guthrie's song. "You know, maybe he had good intentions," said one, "and he wrote a dumb verse that now has taken on a new meaning, but why is that the point? Why is the point not: In this moment of symbolic significance for the United States, why are we going through this ceremony erasing Indigenous people?"

* * *

Erasing Indigenous people. We appear to have come full circle, at least in terms of description, from the depredations of Cortés and Guzmán through the massacre at Wounded Knee to the deliberate silences of the late and unlamented 1776 Commission that began our discussion hundreds of pages ago. Regardless of any attempted silencing or erasure – and there will surely be more of that, as school curricula and teachers are attacked (sometimes physically) by angry crusaders against "wokeness" and something they've been told is "Critical Race Theory" – it is a discussion that will continue outside the pages of this book, both in song and beyond song. And the more we run from it, the more we will run into it.

Notes and Sources

Preface

xiii One type of song: Tom Lehrer, "Folk Song Army," on Lehrer, *That Was the Year That Was* (Reprise Records, 1965), Track A4.

xiii I'm not part of no Movement: Bob Dylan in Nat Hentoff, "The Crackin', Shakin', Breakin' Sounds," *New Yorker,* October 24, 1964, in Jonathan Cott, ed., *Bob Dylan: The Essential Interviews* (New York: Simon & Schuster, 2017), 28.

xiii finger-pointing songs: Dylan in Nat Hentoff, "Bob Dylan, the Wanderer," *New Yorker,* October 16, 1964, in Cott, 17.

xiv Fender Stratocaster: Elijah Wald, *Dylan Goes Electric! Newport, Seeger, Dylan, and the Night That Split the Sixties* (New York: Dey St., 2015), 257.

xiv "Judas": Howard Sounes, *Down the Highway: The Life of Bob Dylan* (New York: Doubleday, 2001), 213.

xiv FBI files: Aaron J. Leonard, *The Folk Singers and the Bureau: The FBI, the Folk Artists, and the Suppression of the Communist Party, USA – 1939–1956* (London: Repeater Books, 2020), *passim.*

xiv a tool of Communist psychological: *When Is Folk Music NOT Folk Music?* (Los Angeles: Fire and Police Research Association, 1963), n. p. See also William Steuart McBirnie, *Songs of Subversion* (Glendale, CA: Voice of Americanism, 1965); Jere Real, "Folk Music and Red Tubthumpers," *American Opinion* 7 (December 1964), 19–24; Herbert Philbrick, "Subverting Youth with Folksinging," in Kenneth W. Ingwalson, ed., *Your Church – Their Target: What's Going on in the Protestant Churches* (Arlington, VA: Better Books, 1966), 167–177; David Noebel, *Rhythm, Riots, and Revolution: An Analysis of the Communist Use of Music, the Communist Master Music Plan* (Tulsa: Christian Crusade Publications, 1966); David Noebel, *The Marxist Minstrels: A Handbook on Communist Subversion of Music* (Tulsa: Christian Crusade Publications, 1974).

xiv At one time I called myself: Tex Ritter quoted in Richard A. Reuss with JoAnne C. Reuss, *American Folk Music and Left-Wing Politics, 1927–1957* (Lanham, MD: Scarecrow Press, 2000), 253.

xiv By 1940: See Dorian Lynskey, *33 Revolutions per Minute: A History of Protest Songs* (London: Faber, 2010); Ronald D. Cohen, *Rainbow Quest: The Folk Music Revival and American Society, 1940–1970* (Amherst: University of Massachusetts Press, 2002); Dick Weissman, *Which Side Are You On? An Inside History of the Folk Music Revival in America* (New York: Continuum Books, 2006); Jerome L. Rodnitzsky, *Minstrels of the Dawn: The Folk-Protest Singer as a Cultural Hero* (Chicago: Nelson-Hall, 1976).

xiv criticism, persuasion, complaint: Alan Lomax, Compiler's Postscript, in Lomax, Woody Guthrie, and Pete Seeger, eds., *Hard Hitting Songs for Hard-Hit People* (New York: Oak Publications, 1967), 365. See also John Greenway, *American Folk Songs of Protest* (New York: A. S. Barnes & Co., 1953), and R. Serge Denisoff, *Great Day Coming: Folk Music and the American Left* (Baltimore: Penguin, 1973).

xiv rhetorical, magnetic, deliberative, epideictic: Elizabeth Kizer, "Protest Song Lyrics as Rhetoric," *Popular Music and Society* 9, no. 1 (January 1983): 3–11.

xiv If you want to: Martin Carthy on *Bob Dylan's Big Freeze*, prod. Katrina Fallon and Patrick Humphries, BBC Radio 2, broadcast November 25, 2008.

xiv Woody's insistence: Moses Asch, liner notes to Woody Guthrie, *Struggle* (Folkways Records, 1976).

xv–xvi Our children are instructed: "Remarks by President Trump at the White House Conference on American History," September 17, 2020: www.whitehouse.gov/briefings-statements/remarks-president-trump-white-house-conference-american-history (subsequently removed from White House website).

xvi 1619 Project: *New York Times*, 1619 Project: www.nytimes.com/interactive/2019/08/14/magazine/1619-america-slavery.html.

xvi The more we run: Wynton Marsalis on Ken Burns, dir., *Jazz* (Florentine Films/PBS, 2001).

Introduction: The Work of Recovery

1 When we entered: Charlevoix quoted in Charles Hamm, *Music in the New World* (New York: Norton, 1983), 11.

1 songwork: Gary Tomlinson, *The Singing of the New World: Indigenous Voices in the Era of European Contact* (Cambridge: Cambridge University Press, 2007), 5.

1 When it came: Glenda Goodman, "'But They Differ from Us in Sound': Indian Psalmody and the Soundscape of Colonialism, 1651–75," *William and Mary Quarterly* 69, no. 4 (October 2012): 793–822 (p. 797, n. 9).

2 Indian words: Paula Mitchell Marks, *In a Barren Land: The American Indian Quest for Cultural Survival, 1607 to the Present* (New York: Perennial Books, 2002), 3.

2 the singers: Robert Stein quoted in Michael Hauser, *Traditional Inuit Songs from the Thule Area* (Njalsgade, Denmark: Museum Tusculanum Press, 2010), 32.

2 The words: Margaret Uyauperk Aniksak, quoted in John Bennett and Susan Rowley, eds., *Uqalurait: An Oral History of Nunavut* (Montreal: McGill-Queen's University Press, 2005), 108.

2 acts of world: Tomlinson, 6–7.

2 power objects: Dale A. Olsen, *The Music of El Dorado: The Ethnomusicology of Ancient South American Cultures* (Jacksonville: University Press of Florida, 2005), 14.

2 sticks and stones: Ted Gioia, *Music: A Subversive History* (New York: Basic Books, 2019), 21–22.

3 Smithsonian Folkways: *The Promised Land: American Indian Songs of Lament and Protest*, originated and performed by Periwinkle (Smithsonian Folkways FHS37254, 1981).

3 Once a famous warrior: Sitting Bull quoted in Reginald Laubin and Gladys Laubin, *Indian Dances of North America* (Norman: University of Oklahoma Press, 1989), 94.

3 *Hlin Biyin*: Natalie Curtis, *The Indians' Book* (New York: Harper & Bros., 1907), 361–362.

3 solemn quest for horses; sacred missions: Elizabeth A. H. John, *Storms Brewed in Other Men's Worlds: The Confrontation of Indians, Spanish, and French in the Southwest, 1540–1795* (Norman: University of Oklahoma Press, 1996), 62–63; LaVerne Harrell Clark, *They Sang for Horses: The Impact of the Horse on Navajo and Apache Folklore* (Boulder: University Press of Colorado, 2001), xiii.

3–4 *Cantaras mexicanos*: Tomlinson, 28–82 *passim*.

1 Broken Spears and Songs of Sorrow

5 no war music: Kirkpatrick Sale, *Christopher Columbus and the Conquest of Paradise* (New York: I. B. Tauris, 2006), 99.

5 Columbus's *Journal*: Christopher Columbus, *Journal of the First Voyage*, in Julius E. Olson and Edward Gaylord Bourne, eds., *The Northmen, Columbus and Cabot, 985–1503* (New York: Charles Scribner's Sons, 1906), 111–202 *passim.*

6 first recorded instance: John Ogasapian, *Music of the Colonial and Revolutionary Era* (Westport: Greenwood Press, 2004), 12.

6 Las Casas; *Historia de las Indias*; With great rejoicing: Olson and Bourne, 331–335.

6 Iere: K. M. Laurence, "Notes of Iere, the Amerindian Name for Trinidad," *Caribbean Quarterly* 13, no. 3 (September 1967): 45–51.

6 This escalating exchange: Craig Harris, *Heartbeat, Warble, and the Electric Powwow: American Indian Music* (Norman: University of Oklahoma Press, 2016), ix.

7 Of the five hundred slaves: Michael Bronski, *A Queer History of the United States* (Boston: Beacon Press, 2011), 5.

7 rarely took the trouble: Ogasapian, 12.

7 their major accomplishment: Miguel Leon-Portilla, ed., *The Broken Spears: The Aztec Account of the Conquest of Mexico*, trans. Lysander Kemp (Boston: Beacon Press, 1962), xlvi–xlvii.

7 When a Spanish armada: Howard Zinn, *A People's History of the United States* (New York: HarperCollins, 2005), 11.

7–8 Then they arrayed: Leon-Portilla, 23–26.

8–9 The celebrants: "The Story of the Conquest as Told by the Anonymous Authors of Tlatelolco," in Susan Castillo and Ivy Schweitzer, eds., *The Literatures of Colonial America* (Oxford: Blackwell, 2001), 66.

9 The Indians thought: Sagahún quoted in David E. Stannard, *American Holocaust: The Conquest of the New World* (New York: Oxford University Press, 1992), 76.

9 When the dance was loveliest: Leon-Portilla, 74.

9 They advanced cautiously: Leon-Portilla, 105–106.

9 genocidal enterprises: Stannard, 81.

10 It is said: Las Casas quoted in Francis A. MacNutt, *Bartholomew de Las Casas: His Life, Apostolate, and Writings* (Cleveland: Arthur H. Clark Co., 1909), 344–345.

11 In many provinces: Bartolomé de Las Casas, *An Account, Much Abbreviated, of the Destruction of the Indies with Related Texts*, ed. Franklin W. Night and trans. Andrew Hurley (Indianapolis: Hackett Publishing Co., 2003), 65–66.

11 Nothing but flowers: "Flowers and Songs of Sorrow," in Castillo and Schweitzer, 71.

11 From this day: Las Casas, *An Account*, 34.

11–12 Broken spears: *Icnocuicatl* (threnody), in Leon-Portilla, 137–138.

12 Indigenous peoples were less than human: Stannard, 77.

12 When a religion was bad: Francis Jennings, *The Invasion of America: Indians, Colonialism, and the Cant of Conquest* (New York: W. W. Norton, 1976), 43.

12 the creation of the world: MacNutt, 192, 204.

12 Indigenous musical instruments: Harris, 23.

12 one Spanish missionary: Ogasapian, 26.

13 The folk-tinged Catholicism: Ogasapian, 12.

13 If, after their conversion: Sahagún quoted in Tomlinson, 57.

13 trail of the Camino Real: Jack Loeffler, *La Música de los Viejitos: Hispano Folk Music of the Río Grande del Norte* (Albuquerque: University of New Mexico Press, 1999), ix.

13 first organ: Federal Writers Project, *The WPA Guide to New Mexico: The Colorful State* (San Antonio, TX: Trinity University Press, 2014 [1940]), 143–144.

13 and the Spanish settlers enjoyed: Ogasapian, 25.

13–14 The imperial scramble for the Americas: Jennings, 5; Felipe Fernández-Armesto, *The Americas: A Hemispheric History* (New York: Modern Library, 2003), *passim*.

14 [It brought] greate terrour: Jennings, 168.

14 A commemorative plaque: Newfoundland and Labrador Heritage Website, Memorial University of Newfoundland: www.heritage.nf.ca/first-world-war/gallery/commemorations/index.php.

15 bells, looking-glasses: George Best quoted in Renee Fossett, *In Order to Live Untroubled: Inuit of the Central Arctic, 1550–1940* (Winnipeg: University of Manitoba Press, 2001), 34.

15 That point: Fossett, 36–38.

15 tooke great delight: Fossett, 40.

15 When they came unto us: John Janes, *The first voyage of Master John Davis, undertaken in June 1585, for the Discoverie of the Northwest Passage*, in Albert Hastings Markham, ed., *The Voyages and Works of John Davis the Navigator* (Burlington, VT: Ashgate, 2010 [1880]), 6–7.

15 transcribed three Micmac melodies: Victoria Lindsay Levine, ed. *Writing American Indian Music: Historic Transcriptions, Notations, and Arrangements* (Middleton, WI: American Musicological Society / A-R Editions, Inc., 2002), xxi.

16 primitive, heathen, and inferior: Levine, xxi–xxii.

16 Champlain, "Algoumenquin," "Tabagie": Conrad E. Heidenreich and K. Janet R. Ritch, eds., *Samuel de Champlain before 1604:* Des Sauvages *and Other Documents Relating to the Period* (Toronto: The Champlain Society, 2010), 263, 269.

2 Good Newes from Virginia

17 Roanoke, CRO, CROATOAN: Scott Dawson, *The Lost Colony and Hatteras Island* (Charleston, SC: The History Press, 2020), 18 and *passim.*

17 sounded with a trumpet: Giles Milton, *Big Chief Elizabeth: The Adventures and Fate of the First English Colonists in America* (New York: Picador, 2001), 232–233.

18 thicke cane: John Smith quoted in Charles Hamm, *Music in the New World* (New York: Norton, 1983), 8, 11.

18 most dolefullest noyse: Smith quoted in Jennifer I. M. Reid, *Worse than Beasts: An Anatomy of Melancholy and the Literature of Travel in 17th and 18th Century England* (Aurora, CO: Davis Group Publishers, 2005), 42.

18 What will it availe you: Powhatan quoted in Colin G. Calloway, ed., *The World Turned Upside Down: Indian Voices from Early America* (New York: Bedford Books of St. Martin's Press, 1994), 39.

18 Some soldiers: Howard Zinn, *A People's History of the United States* (New York: HarperCollins, 2005), 12.

18 We, who hitherto: Edward Waterhouse quoted in Francis Jennings, *The Invasion of America: Indians, Colonialism, and the Cant of Conquest* (New York: Norton, 1976), 80.

19 No English heart: "Good Newes from Virginia, 1623," *William and Mary Quarterly* 5, no. 3 (July 1948): 351–358; some spelling and typography updated.

19 guile and merciless treatment: Alden T. Vaughan, "'Expulsion of the Salvages': English Policy and the Virginia Massacre of 1622," *William and Mary Quarterly* 35, no. 1 (January 1978): 20, 57–84 (p. 67).

19 that unmanned wild Countrey: Samuel Purchase quoted in Jennings, 80.

19 land without people: Israel Zangwill quoted in Lorenzo Veracini, *Settler Colonialism: A Theoretical Overview* (London: Palgrave Macmillan, 2010), 83.

20 aural landscape: Sarah Keyes, "'Like a Roaring Lion': The Overland Trail as Sonic Conquest," *Journal of American History* 96, no. 1 (June 2009): 19–43 (pp. 20–21).

21 San Miguel de Guadalpe: Paul E. Hoffman, *A New Andalucia and a Way to the Orient: The American Southeast during the Sixteenth Century* (Baton Rouge: Louisiana State University Press, 2004), 73–79.

21 anomalous situation: Dena J. Epstein, *Sinful Tunes and Spirituals: Black Folk Music to the Civil War* (Urbana: University of Illinois Press, 2003), 21.

21 so discernible; passing comments; John Josselyn: Ronald M. Radano, *Lying up a Nation: Race and Black Music* (Chicago: University of Chicago Press, 2003), 67–68.

21–22 Falconbridge; Claxton; Towne: House of Commons witnesses quoted in Epstein, 8–9.

22 One slaver testified: Katrina Dyonne Thompson, *Ring Shout, Wheel About: The Racial Politics of Music and Dance in North American Slavery* (Urbana: University of Illinois Press, 2014), 53–54.

22 politely called plantations: Isabel Wilkerson, *Caste: The Lies That Divide Us* (New York: Allen Lane, 2020), 46.

22 They have little varieties: Richard Jobson quoted in Eileen Southern, ed., *Readings in Black American Music* (New York: Norton, 1983), 2.

23 relatively simple; calls: Shane White and Graham White, *The Sounds of Slavery* (Boston: Beacon Press, 2005), 20.

23 cries: Ashenafi Kebede quoted in Robert Darden, *People Get Ready! A New History of Black Gospel Music* (London: Bloomsbury, 2013), 43–44.

23 A silent slave: John Dizikes, *Opera in America: A Cultural History* (New Haven, CT: Yale University Press, 1993), 382.

23 The masters encouraged: Eugene D. Genovese, *Roll, Jordon, Roll: The World the Slaves Made* (New York: Vintage, 1976), 324.

24 the basic difference: LeRoi Jones (Amiri Baraka), *Blues People* (Edinburgh: Canongate, 1995), 20.

24 first black music: Kent A. Bowman, *Voices of Combat: A Century of Liberty and War Songs, 1765–1865* (Westport, CT: Greenwood Press, 1987), x.

24 coded meanings; Gates; new African Americans: Ted Gioia, *Music: A Subversive History* (New York: Basic Books, 2019), 159; Darden, 46.

24 religious truth: Darden, 2.

24 Protest songs: Gioia, 326.

24 not until 1861: Epstein, 245.

24 spirited, nabbed, kidnapped: Peter Linebaugh and Marcus Rediker, *The Many-Headed Hydra: The Hidden History of the Revolutionary Atlantic* (London: Verso, 2000), 110.

25 These people: Howard Zinn and Anthony Arnove, eds., *Voices of a People's History of the United States* (London: Seven Stories Press, 2009), 63.

25 active agents in the dispossession: Roxanne Dunbar-Ortiz, *An Indigenous People's History of the United States* (Boston: Beacon Press, 2014), 35.

25 rogues and vagabonds: Zinn, *A People's History*, 42–43.

25–26 Seven long years: "The Virginia Maid's Lament," in Norm Cohen, ed., *American Folk Songs: A Regional Encyclopedia* (Westport, CT: Greenwood Press, 2008), I: 186.

26 decidedly non-Puritan colony; bestial sodomy: Michael Bronski, *A Queer History of the United States* (Boston: Beacon Press, 2011), 13–14.

27 ode to Hymen; reeling with drink: Richard Slotkin, *Regeneration through Violence: The Mythology of the American Frontier, 1600–1860* (Norman: University of Oklahoma Press, 1973), 63–64.

27 Drink and be merry: Thomas Morton, *New English Canaan*, ed. Jack Dempsey (Scituate, MA: Digital Scanning, Inc, 2000 [1637]), 137.

27 archetypal male lovers: Bronski, 14.

27 lasses in beaver coats: Morton, 138.

27–28 They then fell: William Bradford, *Of Plymouth Plantation, 1620–1647*, ed. Samuel Eliot Morison (New York: Alfred A. Knopf, 2002), 205–206.

28 political tracts: Bronski, 14.

28–29 Jollity and gloom: Nathaniel Hawthorne, "The May-Pole of Merrymount," in Hawthorne, *Tales and Sketches*, Library of America edition (New York: Literary Classics of the United States, 1982), 360–370 *passim*.

29 no rude shows: Nathaniel Hawthorne, *The Scarlet Letter*, in Hawthorne, *Collected Novels*, Library of America edition (New York: Literary Classics of the United States, 1983), 317.

29 Sewall and Bradstreet: Ronald L. Davis, *A History of Music in American Life: Volume 1 – The Formative Years, 1620–1865* (Malabar, FL: Robert Kreiger Publishing Co., 1982), 3–4.

29 wonderful preparation: Veracini, 83.

30 "filthiness" was sin: Jennings, 49–50.

30 alternative genders: Will Roscoe quoted in Gunlög Fur, "Weibe-Town and the Delawares-as-Women: Gender Crossing and Same-Sex Relations in Eighteenth-Century Northeastern Indian Culture," in Thomas A. Foster, ed., *Long before Stonewall: Histories of Same-Sex Sexuality in Early America* (New York: New York University Press, 2007), 32–50 (p. 34).

30 a falsehood: M. K. Bennett, "The Food Economy of the New England Indians, 1605–75," *Journal of Political Economy* 63, no. 5 (October 1955): 369–397.

30 Responding to scrupulous objections: Jennings, 82.

30 first Anglo-Indian war: Alfred A. Cave, *The Pequot War* (Amherst: University of Massachusetts Press, 1996), 1.

30 a white trader: Zinn, *A People's History*, 14.

30 In 1638; executive termination: Veracini, 49.

30 Thames; New London: Richard Drinnon, *Facing West: The Metaphysics of Indian-Hating and Empire-Building* (New York: Schocken Books, 1990), 55.

31 Men in a Dream: John Mason quoted in Drinnon, 56.

31 native bardic myth-historians: Slotkin, 42.

31–32 praying Indians; first book published: Craig Harris, *Heartbeat, Warble, and the Electric Powwow: American Indian Music* (Norman: University of Oklahoma Press, 2016), 60.

32 Puritan auditors: Glenda Goodman, "'But They Differ from Us in Sound': Indian Psalmody and the Soundscape of Colonialism, 1651–75," *William and Mary Quarterly* 69, no. 4 (October 2012): 793–822 (pp. 802–803).

32 no Biblical sanction; King David; St. Peter: Davis, *A History of Music*, 6.

32 If therefore the verses: *The Bay Psalm Book, Being a Facsimile Reprint of the First Edition, Printed by Stephen Daye at Cambridge, in New England in 1640* (New York: Dodd, Meade & Co., 1903), 38–39, antique spelling updated.

33 The Protestant ethic: Davis, *A History of Music*, vii.

33 outright witchcraft: Peter G. Davis, *The American Opera Singer* (New York: Anchor Books, 1997), 28.

33 Would it not greatly tend: Thomas Symmes quoted in Hamm, *Music in the New World*, 39.

33 If we once begin: unhappy correspondent quoted in Davis, *A History of Music*, 13.

33 Intended for the assistance: Cotton Mather quoted in Michael L. Mark, *A Concise History of American Music Education* (Lanham, MD: Rowman & Littlefield Education, 2008), 29.

34 reworking of Psalm 100: Esther R. Crookshank, "'We're Marching to Zion': Isaac Watts in America," in Tara Browner & Thomas L. Riis, eds., *Rethinking American Music* (Urbana: University of Illinois Press, 2019), 103–137 (pp. 104–105).

34 My Method: Samson Occom quoted in Calloway, 59.

34 divert young people: Symmes quoted in Davis, *A History of Music*, 13.

34 single sheets of paper: National Library of Scotland, "Broadsides and other single-sheet items": www.nls.uk/collections/rare-books/collections/broadsides.

34 austere religious interpretation: Ola Elizabeth Winslow, ed. *American Broadside Verse: From Imprints of the 17th and 18th Centuries* (New Haven, CT: Yale University Press, 1930), xviii.

35 Death like a murth'ring Jesuite: Percival Lowell, "A Funeral Elegie (Written Many years Since) on the Death of the memorable and Truly Honourable John Winthrope Esq.," in Winslow, 3.

35 Pueblo Revolt: Calloway, 115.

35 psychological weapons: Goodman, 816.

35 the name he [had] asked for: Jennings, 290.

35 war of conquest: Zinn, *A People's History*, 16.

35 They continued *shooting*: Thomas Wheeler quoted in Goodman, 817–818.

36 O New-England: Wait Winthrop, "Some Meditations . . .," in Carlton Sprague Smith, "Broadsides and Their Music in Colonial America," Proceedings of the Colonial Society of Massachusetts, Vol. 53: *Music in Colonial Massachusetts, 1630–1820: Music in Public Places*, 157–367 (p. 184): www.colonialsociety.org/node/2012.

36 roaring, and singing: Mary Rowlandson, *The Sovereignty and Goodness of God* (1682), in Gordon M. Sayre, ed., *American Captivity Narratives* (Boston: Wadsworth Cengage Learning, 2000), 140, 168.

37 cold war mentality: Eric B. Schultz and Michael J. Touglas, *King Philip's War: The History and Legacy of America's Forgotten Conflict* (New York: Norton / Countryman Press, 2017), 25.

37 farmers in England: "An Invitation to North America," in Irwin Silber, ed., *Songs of Independence* (Harrisburg, PA: Stackpole Books, 1973), 19.

37 uprisings and strikes: Zinn, *passim.*

37 Bacon's Rebellion: Linebaugh and Rediker, 136–137.

37–38 Our hopes of safety: "Bacon's Epitaph, Made by His Man," in Louis Untermeyer, ed., *Early American Poets* (Lincoln, NE: iUniverse, 2000 [1952]), 21.

38 Anglo settler-farmers: Dunbar-Ortiz, 61–62.

38 richest one percent; local residents: Zinn and Arnove, 68.

38 Billy broke locks: "The Escape of Old John Webber," in Silber, *Songs of Independence*, 25–26.

38–39 Zenger: Silber, *Songs of Independence*, 30.

39 Stono rebellion: Epstein, 39–40.

39 repressive legislation: Epstein, 59–60.

39 Where the use of the African drum: Baraka (Jones), 60.

40 They took away my brogues: "Felix the Soldier," in Silber, *Songs of Independence*, 32.

3 A Capital Chop

41 the majority mention: Kent A. Bowman, *Voices of Combat: A Century of Liberty and War Songs, 1765–1865* (Westport, CT: Greenwood Press, 1987), 3.

41 itinerant ballad-singers: Carolyn Rabson, *Songbook of the American Revolution* (Park Island, ME: NEO Press, 1974), 1.

41 To the English colonists: Vera Brodsky Lawrence, *Music for Patriots, Politicians and Presidents: Harmonies and Discords of the First Hundred Years* (New York: Macmillan, 1975), 22.

41 printed from woodcuts: Ronald L. Davis, *A History of Music in American Life, Volume I: The Formative Years, 1620–1865* (Malabar, FL: Robert Kreiger Publishing Co., 1982), 78.

42 For a hundred years: Howard Zinn and Anthony Arnove, eds., *Voices of a People's History of the United States* (London: Seven Stories Press, 2009), 93.

42 By the year 1760: Zinn and Arnove, 79.

42 On the North American continent: Peter Linebaugh and Marcus Rediker, *The Many-Headed Hydra: The Hidden History of the Revolutionary Atlantic* (London: Verso, 2000), 224, 226.

42 Nicholas Cresswell: Eileen Southern, *The Music of Black Americans* (New York: W. W. Norton, 1983), 49; Lawrence W. Levine, *Black Culture and Black Consciousness* (Oxford: Oxford University Press, 1977), 12.

43 For lo! the days come: Occramer Marycoo (Newport Gardner), "Promise Anthem," in Southern, 70.

43 few songs radical in sentiments: Bowman, 13.

44 a rallying cry: Charles Adams, *For Good and Evil: The Impact of Taxes on the Course of Civilization* (Lanham, MD: Madison Books, 1992), 263.

44 But while I stood: "Liberty, Property and No Excise," in Lawrence, 17.

44 *Boston Evening-Post*: Lawrence, 19.

44 mob energy against England; rhetorical device: Zinn, 57, 65.

44 opening anthem: Irwin Silber, ed., *Songs of Independence* (Harrisburg, PA: Stackpole Books, 1973), 36.

44–45 To what you have commanded: Samuel or Peter St. John, "American Taxation," Library of Congress, Rare Books and Special Collections, American Song Sheets: www.loc.gov/item/amss.as100260. Some of this ballad's later verses referencing George Washington indicate that it was revised sometime after the commencement of military hostilities in 1775.

45 On our brow: "Hearts of Oak Are We Still," in Silber, *Songs of Independence*, 42.

45 Townshend Acts: Peter D. G. Thomas, *The Townshend Duties Crisis: The Second Phase of the American Revolution, 1767–1775* (Oxford: Clarendon Press, 1987), 128, 200–234 *passim.*

46 HERE then: John Dickinson, *Letters from a Farmer in Pennsylvania, to the Inhabitants of the British Colonies*, ed. R. T. H. Halsey (New York: The Outlook Company, 1903), 24.

46 I inclose you a song: Dickinson quoted in Frank Moore, ed., *Songs and Ballads of the American Revolution* (New York: Hurst & Co., 1905), 38.

47 created as forcible an impact: Lawrence, 27.

47 HOW sweet: John Dickinson, "A New Song," in *The Writings of John Dickinson*, Vol. I, ed. Paul Leicester Ford (Beford, MA: Applewood Books, 2018 [1895]), 431.

47 Given Dickenson's moderate: Silber, *Songs of Independence*, 43.
47 Then join: Dickinson, "A New Song," 432.
48 And as one: "Young Ladies in Town," in John Anthony Scott, *The Ballad of America: The History of the United States in Song and Story* (New York: Bantam Pathfinder, 1966), 58.
48 motley rabble; image of revolution: Linebaugh and Rediker, 233.
48 By cruel Soldiers: "On the Death of Five Young Men," in Winslow, 45.
48 When the *Foes*: "A Song for the 5th of March," in Lawrence, 48.
49 December 16, 1773: Benjamin Woods Labaree, *The Boston Tea Party* (Boston: Northeastern University Press, 1979), 141–144.
49 Cursed weed: "The Destruction of the Tea," in Moore, 52–53.
49 KING and PRINCE: "Tea Destroyed by Indians," Library of Congress, Printed Ephemera Collection: www.loc.gov/resource/rbpe.0370240a.
49 A number of females: Abigail Adams quoted in Zinn, 109–110.
50 implicitly the Daughters of Liberty: Susan Branson, *From Daughters of Liberty to Women in the Republic: American Women in the Era of the American Revolution* (New Brunswick, NJ: Rutgers University Press, 2007), 51.
50 island queen: "The Rich Lady over the Sea," in Scott, 59–61.
51 Her Orders: Benjamin Franklin (possibly), "The Mother Country: A Song," in Lawrence, 43.
51 beauties of common speech: Franklin quoted in Gilbert Chase, *America's Music: From the Pilgrims to the Present* (New York: McGraw-Hill, 1955), 95.
51 encourage frugality; suspension of civic amusements: Davis, *A History of Music*, 39, 78.
51 Hearts of oak were our sires: "The Glorious Seventy-Four," in J. Heneage Jesse, *Memoirs of the Life and Reign of King George the Third* (London: Tinsley Brothers, 1867), I, 567–568.
52 Instead of *bread*: "Epigram. On the Poor of Boston being Employed in Paving the Streets, 1774," in Winthrop Sargent, ed., *The Loyalist Poetry of the Revolution* (Philadelphia: Winthrop Sargent, by Subscription, 1857), 55.
52 Bostonia first: "Gage's Proclamation," in Moore, 58.
52 At *Lexington*: "Bloody Butchery by the British Troops," Massachusetts Historical Society Collections Online: www.masshist.org/database/viewer.php?item_id=467.

52 How brave: "Paddy," in Kenneth Silverman, *A Cultural History of the American Revolution* (New York: Thomas Y. Crowell Co., 1976), 274–275.

53 When the Second Brigade: Unnamed newspaper quoted in Silverman, 275–276.

53 probably originated: Ted Gioia, *Music: A Subversive History* (New York: Basic Books, 2019), 319.

53 from England, Ireland, or Scotland: Davis, *A History of Music*, 78.

53 Hungarian, Hessian: Lawrence, 32.

53 Barton, "Yankee Doodle": in John Shaw, *This Land That I Love: Irving Berlin, Woody Guthrie, and the Story of Two American Anthems* (New York: Public Affairs, 2013), 45–46.

54 no cure but a capital chop: "Fish and Tea," in Silber, *Songs of Independence*, 68.

54 When Congress sent: "Adam's Fall / The Trip to Cambridge," in Moore, 83.

54 And there was captain Washington: "The Farmer and His Son's return . . ." ("Yankee Doodle"), in Lawrence, 61.

54 class resentment: Zinn, 79.

55 petty privileges: Silber, *Songs of Independence*, 110.

55 New lords: Unnamed army chaplain quoted in Zinn, 79.

55 by paying for substitutes: Zinn, 75.

55 And to you my lovely officers: "A New Song, Written by a Soldier," in Silber, *Songs of Independence*, 111.

55 I do not know: Joel Barlow quoted in Moore, 80.

55–56 To see a town: Barlow, "Breed's Hill," in Moore, 80–82.

56 a series of incendiary ballads: Davis, *A History of Music*, 60.

56 the Credit of being: Francis Hopkinson quoted in Charles Hamm, *Yesterdays: Popular Song in America* (New York: W. W. Norton, 1983), 89.

56 By the Rivers of Watertown: William Billings, "Lamentation Over Boston," in Lawrence, 46.

56 played on fifes; one of the most popular: Rabson, 70.

56 Billings withheld from publication: H. Wiley Hitchcock, *Music in the United States: A Historical Introduction* (Englewood Cliffs: Prentice-Hall, 1988), 11.

56 Let tyrants shake: Billings, in Davis, *A History of Music, 66.*

56 The essential contradiction: Silber, *Songs of Independence*, 116.

57 I am a jolly soldier: "The Soldier's Lamentation," in Silber, *Songs of Independence*, 116.

57 the CRUELTY exercised: "A New Privateering Song," in Lawrence, 69.
57 In vaults: "Verses Written in Captivity," in Sargent, 108.
57 Adams, "dull as beetles"; Stansbury, "A New Song": Lawrence, 74.
58 the Patriots' decision: Paul Ortiz, *An African American and LatinX History of the United States* (Boston: Beacon Press, 2018), 14–15.
58 No one bothered: Southern, 66.
58 Town Destroyer; war of extermination; I have now looked: Calloway, 146–156 *passim*.
59 most tribes eventually supported the British: Calloway, 146.
59 Choctaws, Chickasaws: Untitled English ballad of 1779, in Moore, 197.
59 America, the song hints: Scott, 62.
59 What though your cannon raze: "The Folks on t'Other Side the Wave," in Scott, 62–63.
60 Unhappy times of late: "Unhappy Times," in Oscar Brand, ed., *Songs of '76: A Folksinger's History of the Revolution* (New York: M. Evans & Co., 1972), 160–161.
60 debunked by military historians: William Weir, *Secrets of Warfare: Exposing the Myths and Hidden History of Weapons and Battles* (Pompton Plains, NJ: Career Press, 2011), 107–110.

4 If I Had but a Small Loaf of Bread

61 independent in *literature*: Noah Webster quoted in Joshua Kendall, *The Forgotten Founding Father: Noah Webster's Obsession and the Creation of an American Culture* (New York: G. P. Putnam's Sons, 2010), 6.
61 any Rules for Composition; not confined to rules: William Billings, *The New-England Psalm-Singer; or, American Chorister* (1770) and *Continental Harmony* (1794), quoted in H. Wiley Hitchcock, *Music in the United States: A Historical Introduction* (Englewood Cliffs, NJ: Prentice-Hall, 1988), 10, 11.
61 influenced by the British models: Ronald L. Davis, *A History of Music in American Life: Volume I – The Formative Years, 1620–1865* (Malabar, FL: Robert Kreiger Publishing Co., 1982), 66.
61 ban lifted in 1793: John Dizikes, *Opera in America: A Cultural History* (New Haven, CT: Yale University Press, 1993), 150.

61 vernacular British opera; English music to the core: Charles Hamm, *Yesterdays: Popular Song in America* (New York: W. W. Norton, 1983), 23.

61 the most popular song in America: Hamm, 23.

62 *Oh! think on my fate*: J. C. Cross and William Reeve, *The Purse, or, The Benevolent Tar: A Musical Entertainment in One Act* (London: J. Dicks, no publication date), 28–29. Retrieved from the Library of Congress: www.loc.gov/item/2010667343.

62 On Afric's wide plains: William Reeve, "The Desponding Negro," in Vera Brodsky Lawrence, *Music for Patriots, Politicians and Presidents: Harmonies and Discords of the First Hundred Years* (New York: Macmillan, 1975), 127.

62–63 May the head be corrected: "Favorite Song," in Lawrence, 127.

63 At night they would sing: Unnamed overseer quoted in Shane White and Graham White, *The Sounds of Slavery* (Boston: Beacon Press, 2005), x–xi.

63 the great water spirit: Geordie Buxton, *Haunted Plantations: Ghosts of Slavery and Legends of the Cotton Kingdoms* (Charleston, SC: Arcadia Publishing, 2007), 59.

63 singing of Jacobin songs: Dena J. Epstein, *Sinful Tunes and Spirituals: Black Folk Music to the Civil War* (Urbana: University of Illinois Press, 2003), 72.

63–64 Jean St. Malo (Juan San Malo): Gilbert C. Din, "*Cimarrones* and the San Malo Band in Spanish Louisiana," *Journal of the Louisiana Historical Association* 21, no. 3 (Summer 1980): 237–262 *passim.*

64 They hauled him: "The Dirge of St. Malo," in Philip S. Foner, ed., *American Labor Songs of the Nineteenth Century* (Urbana: University of Illinois Press, 1975), 93.

64 conducted two trials: Carla Gerona, "With a Song in Their Hands: Incendiary *Décimas* from the Texas and Louisiana Borderlands during a Revolutionary Age," *Early American Studies* 12, no. 1 (Winter 2014): 93–142 (p. 93).

64 poems of ten octosyllabic verses: Patricia Manning Lestrade, "The Last of the Louisiana *Décimas,*" *Hispania* 87, no. 3 (September 2004): 447–452 (p. 447).

64 Vicente is a rich man: translation of Nacogdoches *décima* in Gerona, 95.

64 With quarrels every day: translation in Gerona, 126.

65 Then under full sail: Alexander Reinagle, "America, Commerce, and Freedom," in Richard Crawford, *The American Musical Landscape* (Berkeley: University of California Press, 1993), 63.

65 Oh let the sacred fire: "Rights of Woman," in Danny O. Crew, *Suffragist Sheet Music* (Jefferson, NC: McFarland & Co., 2002), 9.

65 Cordwainers: John McIlvaine, "Address to the Journeymen Cordwainers," in Foner, 11.

65 guilty of a combination: Foner, 13.

66 I have been greatly abused: Plough Jogger quoted in Howard Zinn, Preface to William Loren Katz and Laurie R. Lehman, eds., *The Cruel Years: American Voices at the Dawn of the Twentieth Century* (Boston: Beacon Press, 2003), xi.

66 a central government: Howard Zinn and Anthony Arnove, eds., *Voices of a People's History of the United States* (London: Seven Stories Press, 2009), 104.

66 Here Plenty: "The Grand Constitution; or, the Palladium of Columbia," in William McCarty, ed. *Songs, Odes, and Other Poems, on National Subjects; Compiled from Various Sources* (Philadelphia: Wm. McCarty, 1842), 251.

66 The Master of Life: Indigenous deputation quoted in Patricia Cleary, *The World, the Flesh, and the Devil: A History of Colonial St. Louis* (Columbia: University of Missouri Press, 2011), 250.

67 a vast empire: Gary Clayton Anderson, *Ethnic Cleansing and the Indian: The Crime That Should Haunt America* (Norman: University of Oklahoma Press, 2014), 88.

67 Beginning with such songs: John W. Finson, *The Voices That Are Gone: Themes in 19th-Century American Popular Song* (New York: Oxford University Press, 1997), 241.

67 Operatic melodrama: Hitchcock, 42.

67 not created equal: Michel-Rolph Trouillot, *Silencing the Past: Power and the Production of History* (Boston: Beacon Books, 2015), 47.

67 One collector: Danny O. Crew, *Presidential Sheet Music: An Illustrated Catalogue* (Jefferson, NC: McFarland & Co., Inc., 2001), 295, 329, 465.

67 Adams; Alien and Sedition Acts: Zinn, 100.

68 Let our patriots: "Adams and Liberty," in Carolyn Rabson, *Songbook of the American Revolution* (Peaks Island, ME: NEO Press, 1974), 83.

68 Men in power: untitled Jeffersonian ballad in Irwin Silber, ed., *Songs of Independence* (Harrisburg, PA: Stackpole Books, 1973), 185–186.

68 three-fifths' that of a white person: Constitution of the United States, Article 1, Section 2, Clause 3, Library of Congress, Books and Printed Materials Division: www.loc.gov/item/11008400.

68 Our ships: "The Embargo," in Lawrence, 185.

68 Here's milk; Tumble Up; Sweep: Franklin Folsom, *America before Welfare* (New York: New York University Press, 1991), 6.

68–69 Good Peter had said: George C. Shattuck, *The Oneida Land Claims: A Legal History* (Syracuse, NY: Syracuse University Press, 1991), 60.

69 Without arms: Michael Fortune, "The Acquisition of Louisiana," in Lester S. Levy, *Give Me Yesterday: American History in Song, 1890–1920* (Norman: University of Oklahoma Press, 1975), 259.

69 War of the Quadrilles: Ann Ostendorf, *Sounds American: National Identity and the Music Cultures of the Lower Mississippi River Valley, 1800–1860* (Athens: University of Georgia Press, 2011), 73, 83, 86.

69 "negotiating" the cession: Lawrence, 192.

70 Where today are the Pequot: Tecumseh quoted in Bruce Elliott Johansen, *The Native Peoples of North America: A History* (Westport, CT: Praeger, 2005), I, 191.

70 Hark hark: in Lawrence, 192.

70 land speculator, merchant: Zinn, 127.

71 English drinking song: Lawrence, 192.

71 Plumbers, founders, dyers: "The Patriotic Diggers," in Foner, 13–14.

71 Is there one: "An Ode for the Brave," in McCarty, 135–136.

71 Lo! he fought: Charles Miner, "James Bird," in Silber, 201.

71 Jackson and friends: Zinn, 128.

72 When a maiden's: C. E. Horn, "But Mind to Slip OBEY," in Crew, *Suffragist Sheet Music*, 10.

72 unending cycles: Folsom, 16.

72 If I had but a small loaf: "A Loaf of Bread," in Foner, 14.

72 organized labor's song tradition: Robert Weir, "Music and Labor," in Weir and James P. Hanlan, eds., *Historical Encyclopedia of American Labor* (Westport, CT: Greenwood Press, 2004), 327.

72 Adieu, my weekly wash: "The Washerwoman versus the Steam Washing Company," in George Stuyvesant Jackson, ed., *Early Songs of Uncle Sam* (Boston: Bruce Humphries Publishers, 1933), 44.

73 the railroads: "The Hackney Coachman," in Jackson, 44.

73 five out of every six: John Greenway, *American Folksongs of Protest* (New York: A. S. Barnes, 1960), 24.

73 machine in the garden: Leo Marx, *The Machine in the Garden: Technology and the Pastoral Ideal in America* (New York: Oxford University Press, 1964).

73 first environmental protest song: George Pope Morris and Henry Russell, "Woodman, Spare That Tree": www.amaranthpublishing.com/woodman.htm.

73 Thus *Merrymak*: Samuel Sewell, "Upon the Drying Up that Ancient River, the River Merrymak," in Ola Elizabeth Winslow, ed., *American Broadside Verse: From Imprints of the 17th and 18th Centuries* (New Haven, CT: Yale University Press, 1930), 161. Some typography updated.

73 docile and easily managed: Zinn and Arnove, 121.

73 Oh! Isn't it a pity: "I Will Not Be a Slave," in Ted Gioia, *Work Songs* (Durham, NC: Duke University Press, 2006), 93.

73–74 Paterson, New Jersey: Zinn, 230–231.

74 Oh! who would wish: Untitled ballad in Foner, 41.

74 Hark! Don't you hear: Thomas Mann, untitled ballad quoted in Mark M. Smith, *Listening to Nineteenth-Century America* (Chapel Hill: University of North Carolina Press, 2001), 138.

74 By the end of 1836: Zinn, 230; Foner, 45.

74 rioting for flour: Zinn, 225.

74 "the mill has shut down!": in Foner, 45.

74 Oh – curse upon the banks: "Hard Times," in Jackson, 33.

74 three-fourths of Alabama; land grabs; sign another treaty: Zinn, 128–129.

74–75 Seminole Indians: Andrew Jackson quoted in Richard Drinnon, *Facing West: The Metaphysics of Indian Hating and Empire Building* (New York: Schocken Books, 1990), 107.

75 John Quincy Adams: Paul Ortiz, *An African American and LatinX History of the United States* (Boston: Beacon Press, 2018), 37.

75 Jackson justified the carnage: Drinnon, 107.

75 turning Indigenous peoples into refugees: Lorenzo Veracini, *Settler Colonialism: A Theoretical Overview* (London: Palgrave Macmillan, 2010), 35.

75 inescapably colonized: Gary Tomlinson, *The Singing of the New World: Indigenous Voice in the Era of European Contact* (Cambridge: Cambridge University Press, 2007), 82.

75 I have no more land: Creek removal song, in Paula Mitchell Marks, *In a Barren Land: The American Indian Quest for Cultural Survival, 1607 to the Present* (New York: Perennial, 2002), 89.

75 They are taking us: "They Are Taking Us beyond Miami," in Norm Cohen, *American Folk Songs: A Regional Encyclopedia* (Westport, CT: Greenwood Press, 2008), I, 319.

75–76 elicit our pity: Finson, 240–241.

76 O give me back: "The American Indian Girl," in Finson, 242.

76 Does the flush: Eliza Cook and William R. Dempster, "O Why Does the White Man Follow My Path?" (Boston: Oliver Ditson, 1846), Library of Congress, Music Division: www.loc.gov/item/sm1846.420070.

76 I once had a sister: John Hutchinson, "The Indian's Lament," in Michael V. Pisani, *Imagining Native America in Music* (New Haven, CT: Yale University Press, 2005), 114.

76 Oh, bring me the arrow'd raven: S. S. Steele and Benjamin Franklin Baker, "The Death of Osceola" (Boston: Henry Tolman, 1847), Library of Congress, Music Division: www.loc.gov/resource/sm1847.420540.0.

76 exalted musical style: Finson, 241.

76 theatrical practice: Eric Lott, *Love and Theft: Blackface Minstrelsy and the American Working Class* (New York: Oxford University Press, 1993), 3.

76 probably the first: Charles Hamm, *Music in the New World* (New York: Norton, 1983), 183.

76 Ole Zip Coon: George Washington Dixon, "Old Zip Coon," quoted in Finson, 170.

76 Weel about: Thomas Dartmouth Rice, "Jump Jim Crow," quoted in Will Kaufman, *The Civil War in American Culture* (Edinburgh: Edinburgh University Press, 2006), 9.

76 a broad streak of carmine: minstrel show manual quoted in Kaufman, 10.

76–77 fiddle, banjo, bones: Crawford, 75.

77 We'll put for de souf: Stephen Foster, "We'll Put for De Souf," in Kaufman, 11.

77 queer words: Edwin P. Christy quoted in Crawford, 76.

77–78 Congo Square; one of the few places: Terry Waldo, *This Is Ragtime* (New York: Da Capo Press, 1991), 15.

78 filthy scum: Frederick Douglass quoted in Lott, 15.

78 caricature; debased melodies: W. E. B. Du Bois, *The Souls of Black Folk*, in Du Bois, *Writings* (New York: Literary Classics of the United States, Inc., 1986), 538.

78 They say slaves are happy: John Little quoted in Zinn, 172.

78 walking advertisements: Katrina Dyonne Thompson, *Ring Shout, Wheel About: The Racial Politics of Music and Dance in North American Slavery* (Urbana: University of Illinois Press, 2014), 143.

78 The fiddle sing: "Old Virginia Never Tire," in Thompson, 130.

79 Blow the clarion's warlike blast: in Foner, 93.

79 You mought be rich: "Nat Turner," in Foner, 94.

80 After that, the low whites: Charity Bowery quoted in Epstein, 229–230.

80 Steal away; summoning code: Thompson, 127.

80 variations of African American slavery: Barbara Krauthammer, *Black Slaves, Indian Masters: Slavery, Emancipation, and Citizenship in the Native American South* (Chapel Hill: University of North Carolina Press, 2013), *passim.*

81 one visit to Baltimore: Caroline Moseley, "The Hutchinson Family: The Function of Their Song in Ante-Bellum America," in Timothy Scheurer, ed., *The Nineteenth Century and Tin Pan Alley: Readings from the Popular Press* (Bowling Green, OH: Bowling Green State University Popular Press, 1989): 63–74 (p. 66).

81 Hear the mighty car wheels: Hutchinson Family Singers, "Get Off the Track," in Lawrence, 305.

81 With fingers weary: "The Song of the Shirt," in Hamm, *Yesterdays*, 154.

81 patroonship system: Zinn, 211.

81 Keep out of the way: S. H. Foster, "The End of Big Bill Snyder," in Greenway, 30.

82 radical insurgency: Zinn, 214.

83 These are the men: "Landholders' Victory," in Greenway, 35.

83 Although our chosen guide: "Suffrage Pledge," in Foner, 40.

83 while tens of thousands more: William H. A. Williams, *'Twas Only an Irishman's Dream: The Image of Ireland and the Irish in American Popular Song Lyrics, 1800–1920* (Urbana: University of Illinois Press, 1996), 15.

83 the most popular, widely sung: Hamm, *Yesterdays*, 44.

83 glorious past; dismal present; The harp that once: Hamm, *Yesterdays*, 51–52.

83 Give me three grains: A. M. Edmond, "Give Me Three Grains of Corn," in Nicholas E. Tawa, *Sweet Songs for Gentle Americans: The Parlor Song in America, 1790–1869* (Bowling Green, OH: Bowling Green University Popular Press, 1980), 145.
84 the cold in winter: Williams, 91.
84 Arise! Degraded sons: Mike Walsh, "The Tarriers' Song," in Ronald D. Cohen, *Work and Sing: A History of Occupational and Labor Union Songs in the United States* (Crockett, CA: Carquinez Press, 2010), 2.
84 Ten thousand Micks: in Williams, 91.
84 Oh, de Natives: "De Philadelphia Riots," in Cohen, *American Folk Songs*, I, 144.
85 palpable violation: Mexican Congressional statement in Ortiz 41.
85 Africans, the descendants of Africans, and Indians: Constitution of the Republic of Texas (1836): Tarlton Law Library, Jamail Center for Legal Research: https://tarltonapps.law.utexas.edu/constitutions/texas1836/general_provisions.
85 *Crockett in Texas*: James Fisher, *Historical Dictionary of American Theater: Beginnings* (Lanham, MD: Rowman & Littlefield, 2015), 123.
85 R. T. Conrad's, "The Alamo": Danny O. Crew, *American Political Music: A State-by-State Catalog* (Jefferson, NC: McFarland & Co., 2006), II, 666.
86 "Go Ahead . . . A March": Crew, *American Political Music*, II, 666.
86 a certain provocation: Lawrence, 306.
86 He is to expel: Ethan Allen Hitchcock quoted in Zinn, 149.
86 We are the nation: John L. O'Sullivan, "The Great Nation of Futurity" (1839), in Gary Noy, ed., *Distant Horizon: Documents from the Nineteenth-Century American West* (Lincoln: University of Nebraska Press, 1999), 6–8 (p. 7).

5 Where Today Are the Pequot?

87 one of the most unjust; to provoke a fight: Ulysses S. Grant, *Memoirs and Selected Letters* (New York: Literary Classics of the United States, Inc., 1990), 41, 50.
87 In the wake of the $15 million pittance: Howard Zinn, *A People's History of the United States* (New York: HarperCollins, 2005), 169.
87 racialization: Paul Ortiz, *An African American and LatinX History of the United States* (Boston: Beacon Press, 2018), 56.

87 *Nosotros no cruzamos la frontera*: Martha I. Chew Sánchez, *Corridos in Migrant Memory* (Albuquerque: University of New Mexico Press, 2006), 4.

88 sentimental, patriotic, and moral: David Warren Steel, "Secular Music in Shape Notes," in Tara Browner and Thomas L. Riis, eds., *Rethinking American Music* (Urbana: University of Illinois Press, 2019), 50–67 (pp. 56–57).

88 racist and jingoistic: Ronald L. Davis, *A History of Music in American Life: Volume I – The Formative Years, 1620–1865* (Malabar, FL: Robert Kreiger Publishing Co., 1982), 83.

88 The Mexicans are doomed to fall: "We're the Boys for Mexico," in George Stuyvesant Jackson, *Early Songs of Uncle Sam* (Boston: Bruce Humphries Publishers, 1933), 34.

88 Heed not the Spanish battle yell: "Remember the Alamo!" in Irwin Silber, ed., *Songs of the Great American West* (New York: Macmillan, 1967), 48.

88 O Boys, we're goin' far: "Way Down in Mexico," in John A. Lomax, ed., *Cowboy Songs and Other Frontier Ballads* (New York: Macmillan, 1922), 314.

88 Texas Rangers, Quick Steps, Volunteers for Glory, All for Texas: Danny O. Crew, *American Political Music: A State-by-State Catalog* (Jefferson, NC: McFarland & Co., 2006), II, 666 and 711.

88 quite a number of British seamen: Stan Hugill, *Shanties from the Seven Seas* (Mystic, CT: Mystic Seaport Museum, 1994), 75.

88 Oh, Santy Anna: "Santy Anna," in Silber, *Songs of the Great American West*, 52.

88 American anti-war songs: Kent A. Bowman, *Voices of Combat: A Century of Liberty and War Songs, 1765–1865* (Westport, CT: Greenwood Press, 1987), 69, 85.

89 War and slavery perplex: "The Old Granite State," in Charles Hamm, *Yesterdays: Popular Song in America* (New York: Norton, 1983), 152.

89 the present Mexican war: Henry David Thoreau, "Civil Disobedience," in Thoreau, *Collected Essays and Poems* (New York: Literary Classics of the United States, Inc., 2001), 203.

89 St. Patrick's Battalion / *San Patricios*: Paul Foos, *A Short, Offhand, Killing Affair: Soldiers and Social Conflict during the Mexican-American War* (Chapel Hill: University of North Carolina Press, 2002), 107–108.

89 Derry Down; Sergeant, buck him: "Buck and Gag Him," in Edward Arthur Dolph, *"Sound Off!" Soldier Songs from the Revolution to World War II* (New York: Farrar & Rinehart, Inc., 1942), 394.

89 graphic testimony: Manuel Peña, *Música Tejana: The Cultural Economy of Artistic Transformation* (College Station: Texas A&M University Press, 2002), 43.

89 That General Cortina: translation of "*El General Cortina*," in Peña, 43.

89 mustangers, buffalo hunters: Américo Parades, *A Texas-Mexican Cancionero: Folksongs of the Lower Border* (Austin: University of Texas Press, 2001), 4.

90 looms large: María Herrera-Sobek, *Northward Bound: The Mexican Immigrant Experience in Ballad and Song* (Bloomington: Indiana University Press, 1993), 18.

90 five or perhaps more: Norm Cohen, *American Folk Songs: A Regional Encyclopedia* (Westport, CT: Greenwood Press, 2008), II, 647.

90 Murieta does not like: translation of "*Corrido de Joaquín Murrieta*," in Cohen, *American Folk Songs*, II, 645.

92 all verbatim song titles: "The Lousy Miner" in Silber, *Songs of the Great American West*, 118–119; "The Fools of Forty-Nine" in John Anthony Scott, *The Ballad of America: The History of the United States in Song and Story* (New York: Bantam Pathfinder, 1966), 184–185; "Steam Navigation Thieves" in Silber, 125; "Humbug Steamship Companies" in Silber, 126–129.

92 Listen, brother: "The Dying Californian," in Scott, 188–189.

92–93 You journeyed away: translation of "*Ved en Persons Hjemkomst, Der Har Seet Fristaterne og Kalifornien*," in Theodore C. Blegen and Martin B. Ruud, eds., *Norwegian Emigrant Songs and Ballads* (Minneapolis: University of Minnesota Press, 1936), 230–234.

93 Ducks and chickens; This is where bird Phoenix lives: Translated Swedish and Danish emigrant ballads, in E. Gustav Johnson, "A Swedish Emigrant Ballad," *Scandinavian Studies* 20, no. 4 (November 1948): 193–201 (p. 194).

93 Good men of Norway: translation of "*Bedre End Guld*" in Blegen and Ruud, 184.

93 the most famous of all: Blegen and Ruud, 191–192.

93–94 Then, ho! Boys ho: "Ho! For California," in Silber, *Songs of the Great American West*, 10–11.

94 Though California: Ortiz, 57.

94 Oh, husband: "The Wisconsin Emigrant," in Scott, 163.

94–95 Plains Indians seemed; While camped near Fort Laramie: Michael L. Tate, *Indians and Emigrants: Encounters on the Overland Trails* (Norman: University of Oklahoma Press, 2014), 95–96.

95 from *aboriginal ... to refugees*: Lorenzo Veracini, *Settler Colonialism: A Theoretical Overview* (London: Palgrave Macmillan, 2010), 35.

95 March, march, Choctaw: "Choctaw and Cherokee," in Jackson, 38.

95 vacant lands: Thomas Jefferson quoted in Dana Brand, *The Spectator and the City in Nineteenth-Century American Literature* (New York: Cambridge University Press, 1991), 64.

96 Immigration during the first five years: James M. McPherson, *Battle Cry of Freedom: The Civil War Era* (New York: Oxford University Press, 1988), 131.

96 Since freedom has been lost: translation of Swabian emigrant song, c. 1848, in Max Paul Friedman, "Beyond 'Voting with Their Feet': Toward a Conceptual History of 'America' in European Migrant Sending Communities, 1860s to 1914," *Journal of Social History* 40, no. 3 (Spring 2007): 557–575 (p. 564).

96 I am a little Communist: "The Little Communist," translated in Foner, 84.

96 Then the famine came stalking: L. V. H. Crosby, "The Emigrant's Farewell," in John W. Finson, *The Voices That Are Gone: Themes in 19th-Century American Popular Song* (New York: Oxford University Press, 1997), 287.

97 GIRL WANTED: Mark Bulik, "1854: No Irish Need Apply," *New York Times*, September 8, 2015: www.nytimes.com/2015/09/08/insider/1854-no-irish-need-apply.html.

97 I thought you'd cut your queue off: "John Chinaman," in Foner, 109.

97 John Chinaman; similar function: Krystyn R. Moon, *Yellowface: Creating the Chinese in American Popular Music and Performance, 1850s–1920s* (New Brunswick, NJ: Rutgers Press, 2004), 32.

98 Oh, now my friends: Mart Taylor, "John Chinaman's Appeal" (1856), in Moon, 35.

98 With a pillow: translation of Taishan emigrant song in Marlon Kau Hom, "Some Cantonese Folksongs on the American Experience," *Western Folklore* 42, no. 2 (April 1983): 126–139 (pp. 127–128).

98 hefty foreign miners' tax: Marlon Kau Hom, *Songs of Gold Mountain: Cantonese Rhymes from San Francisco Chinatown* (Berkeley: University of California Press, 1987), 92.

98 O, sojourner: translation in Hom, "Some Cantonese Folksongs," 128.

98 My husband: translation in Hom, "Some Cantonese Folksongs," 129.

99 the futile violence: Zinn, 227.

99 The Astor Place Opera House: John Dizikes, *Opera in America: A Cultural History* (New Haven, CT: Yale University Press, 1993), 160–161. Dizikes mistakenly places the riot in 1848.

99 the boom in railroads and manufacturing: Zinn, 227–228.

99 The times are so tight: George Morris, "Money Is a Hard Thing to Borrow" (1854), Library of Congress, Music Division: www.loc.gov/resource/sm1854.561880.0.

100 cited the lack of married woman's property rights: Judith Wellman, *The Road to Seneca Falls: Elizabeth Cady Stanton and the First Women's Rights Convention* (Urbana: University of Illinois Press, 2004), 154.

100 thirty songs published: Danny O. Crew, *Suffragist Sheet Music* (Jefferson, NC: McFarland & Co., 2002), 17–44.

100 'Tis woman's Right: Kate Horn, "Woman's Rights," in Crew, *Suffragist Sheet Music*, 37.

100 Come prepared: "The Great Convention, or Woman's Rights," in Crew, *Suffragist Sheet Music*, 33.

100 hurled her first spear; her advanced editorial policy: Vera Brodsky Lawrence, *Music for Patriots, Politicians and Presidents: Harmonies and Discords of the First Hundred Years* (New York: Macmillan, 1975), 327.

101 piano pieces: Crew, *Suffragist Sheet Music*, 19–35 *passim*.

101 Dear me: "The Bloomer's Complaint," in Lawrence, 327.

101–02 And ain't I a woman: Sojourner Truth quoted in Frances D. Gage, "Reminiscences of Sojourner Truth," in Elizabeth Cady Stanton et al., eds., *History of Woman Suffrage* (Rochester, NY: Fowler & Wells, 1881–1922), I, 115–117 (p. 116).

102 scholarly debate: Nell Irvin Painter, *Sojourner Truth: A Life, a Symbol* (New York: W. W. Norton, 1997), 125–126.

102–03 I am pleading: Sojourner Truth, "I Am Pleading for My People," in Molefi Kete Asante and Abu S. Abarry, eds., *African Intellectual Heritage: A Book of Sources* (Philadelphia: Temple University Press, 1996), 770.

104 The South have their school: Judson Hutchinson, "Slavery Is a Hard Foe to Battle" (1855), Library of Congress, Music Division: www.loc.gov/item/sm1855.751680.

104 Tom Shows: Will Kaufman, *The Civil War in American Culture* (Edinburgh: Edinburgh University Press, 2006), 18–20.

104 parody shows; lyrics: Gerald Bordman, *American Musical Theater: A Chronicle* (New York: Oxford University Press, 2010), 13.

105 sheet music market with the likes of: Crew, 71–72; Davis, I, 184.

105 Hurrah, hurrah: "My Massa's Old Plantation," in Marcello Truzzi, "The 100% American Songbag: Conservative Folksongs in America," *Western Folklore* 28, no. 1 (January 1969): 27–40 (pp. 34–35).

105 Oh, this is the tale: "Alabama" / "John Cherokee," in Hugill, 330.

105–06 Here you see a man: "Escape from Slavery of Henry Box Brown," in Foner, 91.

106 I'm on my way to Canada: George N. Allen, "Underground Rail Car! or, Song of the Fugitive" (1854), Lester S. Levy Sheet Music Collection, Johns Hopkins University: https://levysheetmusic.mse.jhu.edu/collection/059/117.

106 unless something was done: Shane White and Graham White, *The Sounds of Slavery* (Boston: Beacon Press, 2005), 177.

106–07 spirituals; peg-legged sailor; Foller the drinkin' gou'd: Robert Darden, *People Get Ready! A New History of Black Gospel Music* (London: Bloomsbury, 2013), 4–5, 83.

107 Shadrach Minkins; Jerry: Zinn, 181.

107 probably represented the views: A. Leon Higginbotham, Jr., *Shades of Freedom: Racial Politics and Presumptions of the American Legal Process* (New York: Oxford University Press, 1996), 7.

108 These were the last written words: W. E. B. Du Bois, *John Brown* (New York: Modern Library, 2001), 219.

108 Weird John Brown: Herman Melville, "The Portent," in *Battle Pieces: The Civil War Poems of Herman Melville* (Edison, NJ: Castle Books, 2000), 11.

108 William Steffe; converted more people: Hamm, *Yesterdays*, 156, 236.

108 The New Testament: John Brown quoted in Du Bois, 216.

108 cease to exaggerate: Frederick Douglass quoted in R. J. M. Blackett, "Cracks in the Antislavery Wall," in Alan J. Rice and Martin Crawford, eds., *Liberating Sojourn: Frederick Douglass and Transatlantic Reform* (Athens: University of Georgia Press, 1999), 187–206 (p. 200).

108 still remembered and revered: Kaufman, 15–16.

109 The bills of the Concert; blind listening: Jennifer Lynn Stoever, *The Sonic Color Line: Race and the Cultural Politics of Listening* (New York: New York University Press, 2016), 132.

109 Under these circumstances: quoted in Peter G. Davis, *The American Opera Singer* (New York: Anchor Books, 1997), 324–325.

109 What induced me: Thomas Bowers quoted in Lawrence Schenbeck, *Racial Uplift and American Music, 1878–1943* (Jackson: University Press of Mississippi, 2012), 12.

109 I had the intention: Stephen Foster quoted in Timothy E. Scheurer, ed., *The Nineteenth Century and Tin Pan Alley: Readings from the Popular Press* (Bowling Green, OH: Bowling Green State University Popular Press, 1989), 43.

109–10 Way down upon de Swanee ribber: Stephen Foster, "Old Folks at Home" (words and music credited to E. P. Christy, 1851), Library of Congress, Music Division: www.loc.gov/resource/ihas.200187242.0.

110 fluency in black culture: Ted Gioia, *Music: A Subversive History* (New York: Basic Books, 2019), 314–315.

110 One hundred years hence: "A Hundred Years Hence," in Lawrence, 470.

6 There Is a Fountain Filled with Blood

111 the first woman; On the appointed day: Jack Loeffler, *La Música de los Viejitos: Hispano Folk Music of the Río Grande del Norte* (Albuquerque: University of New Mexico Press, 1999), 35–36.

111 In the countryside: "The Late Pablita" (*La finada Pablita*), translation in Loeffler, 37.

111–12 Oregon passed a "race tax": Paul Ortiz, *An African American and LatinX History of the United States* (Boston: Beacon Press, 2018), 59.

112 first railroad labor union: Christian Wolmar, *The Great Railroad Revolution: The History of Trains in America* (New York: Public Affairs, 2013), 231–232.

112 the following year: Patricia A. Cooper, *Once a Cigar Maker: Men, Women, and Work Culture in American Cigar Factories, 1900–1919* (Urbana: University of Illinois Press, 1987), 76.

112 in his own hand: Thom Hatch, *The Blue, the Gray, and the Red: Indian Campaigns of the Civil War* (Mechanicsburg, PA: Stackpole Books, 2003), 101–102.

112 Lincoln campaign songs: Danny O. Crew, *Presidential Sheet Music: An Illustrated Catalog* (Jefferson, NC: McFarland & Co., 2001), 53–95 *passim.*

112 Sprung from the race: Untitled Lincoln campaign song in Ray B. Browne, ed., *Lincoln-Lore: Lincoln in the Popular Mind* (Bowling Green, OH: Bowling Green State University Popular Press, 1996), 205.

112 Karl Marx; quintessential bourgeois; corporate lawyer: Allan Kulikoff, *Abraham Lincoln and Karl Marx in Dialogue* (New York: Oxford University Press, 2018), 14.

113 skilfully blend: Howard Zinn, *A People's History of the United States* (New York: HarperCollins, 2005), 187.

113 preëminently the white man's President: Frederick Douglass, "Oration in Memory of Abraham Lincoln" (1876), in Douglass, *Selected Speeches and Writings*, ed. Philip S. Foner (Chicago: Lawrence Hill Books, 1999), 618.

113 Black Republican: Elizabeth Young, *Disarming the Nation: Women's Writing and the American Civil War* (Chicago: University of Chicago Press, 1999), 49–50.

113 picked up a good deal of money: Anon., *Abraham Africanus I, His Secret Life as Revealed Under the Mesmeric Influence* (New York: J. F. Feeks, 1861), 32.

113 apocryphal story: Benjamin B. Thomas, *Abraham Lincoln: A Biography* (Carbondale: Southern Illinois University Press, 2008), 24.

113 After being hunted: John Wilkes Booth, diary entry for April 21, 1865, in *"Right or Wrong, God Judge Me": The Writings of John Wilkes Booth*, ed. John Rhodehamel and Louise Taper (Urbana: University of Illinois Press, 2001), 154.

113 Our Brutus: Thomas J. Kernan, "Vilification or Problematization?: John Wilkes Booth in Popular Songs and Musicals," in Joseph E. Morgan and Gregory N. Reish, eds., *Tyranny and Music* (Lanham, MD: Lexington Books, 2018), 93–110 (pp. 96–97); Crew, *Presidential Sheet Music*, 8.

114 an ironic glimpse: John Dizikes, *Opera in America: A Cultural History* (New Haven, CT: Yale University Press, 1993), 174.

114 Isabella Hinckley; "singing lesson" scene: Peter G. Davis, *The American Opera Singer* (New York: Anchor Books, 1997), 49.

114 first American war fought to music: Christian McWhirter, *Battle Hymns: The Power and Popularity of Music in the Civil War* (Chapel Hill: University of North Carolina Press, 2012), 1.

114 a people's war: Charles Hamm, *Yesterdays: Popular Song in America* (New York: Norton, 1983), 252.

114 common soldiers and citizens: McWhirter, 4.

114 African American stevedores: McWhirter, 177.

114–15 We live in hard and stirring times: Stephen Foster, "That's What's the Matter," in Irwin Silber, ed., *Songs of the Civil War* (New York: Dover, 1995), 12.

115 Old songs! New songs: Stephen Foster, "The Song of All Songs," in McWhirter, 7–8.

115 cheap pocket songsters; swap shared songs: Hamm, *Yesterdays*, 231.

116 Mammy, is Ol' Massa; My old Mistis: WPA slave narrations from Alabama and Arkansas, in Lawrence W. Levine, *Black Culture and Black Consciousness* (New York: Oxford University Press, 1977), 13, 15.

116 My army cross ober: "My Army Cross Over," in William Francis Allen et al., *Slave Songs of the United States* (Bedford, MA: Applewood Books, 1996 [1867]), 38.

116 "My God! What Is All This For": in Danny O. Crew, *American Political Music: A State-by-State Catalog of Printed and Recorded Music* (Jefferson, NC: McFarland & Co., 2006), I, 66.

116 My paramount object: Lincoln quoted in James M. McPherson, *Battle Cry of Freedom: The Civil War Era* (New York: Oxford University Press, 1988), 510.

116 Lincoln had in fact: McPherson, 545.

116 political pow-wowing: Ronald L. Davis, *A History of Music in American Life: Volume I – The Formative Years, 1620–1865* (Malabar, FL: Robert Kreiger Publishing Co., 1982), 257.

116 so destructive of morale: Hamm, *Yesterdays*, 240.

117 death on the battlefield: John W. Finson, *The Voices That Are Gone: Themes in 19th-Century American Popular Song* (New York: Oxford University Press, 1997), 97.

117 to tug at the heartstrings: Steven H. Cornelius, *Music of the Civil War Era* (Westport, CT: Greenwood Press, 2004), 62.

117 a watershed in the history; naïve; innocent: Gillian M. Rodger, *Champagne Charlie and Pretty Jemima: Variety Theater in the Nineteenth Century* (Urbana: University of Illinois Press, 2010), 60, 64.

117 first publication: Dena J. Epstein, *Sinful Tunes and Spirituals: Black Folk Music to the Civil War* (Urbana: University of Illinois Press, 2003), 244–245.

117 Washington a rebel was: "Rebel," in Silber, *Songs of the Civil War*, 49.

117 My homespun dress: A. E. Blackmar, "The Southern Girl" (1865), Library of Congress, Civil War Sheet Music Collection: www.loc.gov/resource/ihas.200002584.0.

118 They called them: "The Maryland Martyrs" (c. 1861), Library of Congress, American Song Sheets, Rare Books and Special Collections: www.loc.gov/resource/amss.cw201180.0.

118 William Wells Brown; Go down, Abraham: Eileen Southern, *The Music of Black Americans* (New York: W. W. Norton, 1983), 214.

118 McClellan went to Richmond: Tom Craig, "Colored Volunteer," in Vera Brodsky Lawrence, *Music for Patriots, Politicians and Presidents: Harmonies and Discords of the First Hundred Years* (New York: Macmillan, 1975), 385.

119 the only wartime effort: Crystal M. Fleming, *How to Be Less Stupid About Race* (Boston: Beacon Press, 2018), 62.

119 Oh, we're the bully soldiers: Capt. Lindley Miller, "Marching Song of the First Arkansas (Negro) Regiment," in Silber, *Songs of the Civil War*, 26.

119 worthless: Andrew F. Smith, *Starving the South: How the North Won the Civil War* (New York: St. Martin's Press, 2011), 57.

119 Now Northern goods: Carrie Bell Sinclair, "The Homespun Dress," in Silber, *Songs of the Civil War*, 68.

119 We're coming, Father Abra'am: Dan Emmett, "How Are You, Greenbacks," in Davis, *A History of Music*, 262.

120 somewhere between the documented figure; thousands of blacks: Barnet Schecter, *The Devil's Own Work: The Civil War Draft Riots*

and the Fight to Reconstruct America (New York: Walker & Co., 2005), 251–252.

120 Smaller anti-draft riots: Zinn, 236.

120–21 My true love is a soldier: Septimus Winner, "He's Gone to the Arms of Abraham," in Cornelius, 63.

121 Oh, Jimmy farewell: Henry Clay Work, "Grafted into the Army," in Lawrence, 371.

121 I am a broker: John L. Zieber, "The Substitute Broker" (1864), Library of Congress, Civil War Sheet Music Collection: www.loc.gov/item/ihas.200002328.

121 The Conscription Act: "Johnny, Fill Up the Bowl," in Lawrence, 397.

121 The Irish, who, at home: Frederick Douglass quoted in Noel Ignatiev, *How the Irish Became White* (London: Routledge, 1995), v.

121 Irish effort; black struggle: Ignatiev, 6, 120.

122–23 "No!" he says; Ould Ireland: John F. Poole, "No Irish Need Apply" (c. 1865), Library of Congress, American Song Sheets: www.loc.gov/resource/amss.as109730.0.

123 But now a bright sunshine: "The Irish Volunteer," in Rodger, 119–120.

123 Kathleen O'Neil; un-American: Finson, 290–291.

123 But now on every side: "The Irish Are Preferred," in William H. A. Williams, *'Twas Only an Irishman's Dream: The Image of Ireland and the Irish in American Popular Song Lyrics, 1800–1920* (Urbana: University of Illinois Press, 1996), 114.

123 30,000 Irish troops: Philip Thomas Tucker, *Irish Confederates: The Civil War's Forgotten Soldiers* (Abilene, TX: McWhiney Foundation Press, 2006), 12, 17.

123 Och! de Rebels: John Ross Dix, "Paddy's Lament" (1864), Library of Congress, Rare Books and Special Collections: www.loc.gov/resource/amss.hc00011a.

124 The Confederacy, outraged: Benjamin G. Cloyd, *Haunted by Atrocity: Civil War Prisons in American Memory* (Baton Rouge: Louisiana State University Press, 2010), 8.

124 black flag policy: Cloyd, 11

124 music setting for hymns; labor songs; Irish freedom songs: Kent A. Bowman, *Voices of Combat: A Century of Liberty and War Songs, 1765–1865* (Westport, CT: Greenwood Press, 1987), 131.

124 Tramp, tramp, tramp: George Frederick Root, "Tramp! Tramp! Tramp!" in Richard Crawford, ed., *The Civil War Songbook* (New York: Dover Publications, 1977), 46–47.

124 replacing "the starry flag": Confederate version of "Tramp! Tramp! Tramp!" in Silber, *Songs of the Civil War*, 37.

124 remember Andersonville: Cloyd, 35.

125 Had they fallen in battle: George Frederick Root, "Starved in Prison" (1865), Library of Congress, Civil War Sheet Music Collection: www.loc.gov/resource/ihas.200001908.0.

125 War is cruelty; make old and young: William T. Sherman quoted in McPherson, 809.

125 when they heard the joyful sound; thoroughfare for Freedom: Henry Clay Work, "Marching Through Georgia," in Crawford, *Civil War Songbook*, 34–37.

125 to listen to a song; I wish I had a dollar: Noah Andre Trudeau, *Southern Storm: Sherman's March to the Sea* (New York: Harper Perennial, 2008), 537.

126 Oh where shall we go; I can't remember the tune: James Calhart James quoted in Eileen Southern, ed., *Readings in Black American Music* (New York: W. W. Norton, 1983), 120.

126 Sherman; Special Field Order 15; Andrew Johnson; restored this land: Zinn, 197.

126 Sun, you be here: Susie Melton quoted in Zinn, 195–196.

126 Lincoln, himself: Kevin Lane Dearinger, *The Bard in the Bluegrass: Two Centuries of Shakespearean Performance in Lexington, Kentucky* (Jefferson, NC: McFarland & Co., 2007), 68.

127 Of all the actors: "Booth Killed Lincoln," in Silber, *Songs of the Civil War*, 112.

127 Lincoln odes, marches, elegies: in Crew, *Presidential Sheet Music*, 51–100 *passim*.

127 Shall we let our soldiers perish: Thomas MacKellar and J. Henry Wolsieffer, "Shall We Let Our Soldiers Perish?" (1865), Lester S. Levy Sheet Music Collection, Johns Hopkins University: https://levysheetmusic.mse.jhu.edu/collection/089/163.

127 all women thought a wound: Louisa May Alcott quoted in Kim E. Nielsen, *A Disability History of the United States* (Boston: Beacon Press, 2012), 78.

127 To accept my hand: lyrics by Thomas A. Perrine, in Nielsen, 78–79.

127 Care was lost: E. Ludewig Kurtz, "The Union Restored" (1865), Library of Congress, Civil War Sheet Music Collection: www.loc.gov/resource/ihas.200001524.0.

128 To the Memory of Abraham Lincoln: William Willing, "The Union Restored" (1865), Library of Congress, Sheet Music from the Alfred Whital Stern Collection of Lincolniana: www.loc.gov/resource/lprbscsm.scsm0204.

128 Arouse ye! arouse ye: "M. M.," "Workmen, Arouse Ye!" in Foner, 99.

128 Appalachian oil-producing basin: Harold F. Williamson et al., *The American Petroleum Industry* (Evanston, IL: Northwestern University Press, 1963), 16.

128 Tis strange: C. Archer, "Pa Has Struck Ile" (1865), Lester S. Levy Sheet Music Collection, Johns Hopkins University: https://levysheetmusic.mse.jhu.edu/collection/053/035.

128 The lawyers, doctors: Joseph Eastburn Winner, "Oil on the Brain" (1865), Lester S. Levy Sheet Music Collection, Johns Hopkins University: https://levysheetmusic.mse.jhu.edu/collection/053/020.

128 'Tis very strange, but I declare: O. I. L. Wells, "Petroleum, Petroleum; or, Oil Upon the Brain" (1865), University of Michigan digitization from Hathi Trust: https://babel.hathitrust.org/cgi/pt?id=mdp.39015096606515&view=1up&seq=1.

129 To Messrs. Swindle'em: "Famous Oil Firms" (1865), Lester S. Levy Sheet Music Collection, Johns Hopkins University: https://levysheetmusic.mse.jhu.edu/collection/051/034.

129 a system of control: Michelle Alexander, *The New Jim Crow: Mass Incarceration in the Age of Colorblindness* (New York: The New Press, 2012), 30.

7 A Tragedy That Beggared the Greek

130 Who shall rule: Henry Clay Work, "Who Shall Rule This American Nation?" in Timothy E. Scheurer, *Born in the USA: The Myth of America in Popular Music from Colonial Times to the Present* (Jackson: University Press of Mississippi, 1991), 65.

130 *Pas Nègres*: Untitled Louisiana field song in Alyn Shipton, *A New History of Jazz* (London: Bloomsbury, 2010), 15.

130 I will be your Moses: J. H. McNaughton, "Where Is Our Moses?" in Danny O. Crew, *Presidential Sheet Music: An Illustrated Catalog* (Jefferson, NC: McFarland & Co., 2001), 49.

130–31 O. O. Howard; "Nobody Knows the Trouble I've Seen": Robert Darden, *People Get Ready: A New History of Black Gospel Music* (London: Bloomsbury, 2010), 112.

131 romance of reunion; conciliatory culture: Nina Silber, *The Romance of Reunion: Northerners and the South, 1865–1900* (Chapel Hill: University of North Carolina Press, 1993), 2.

131 more equitable: Eric Foner, "Why Reconstruction Matters," *New York Times*, March 28, 2015: www.nytimes.com/2015/03/29/opinion/sunday/why-reconstruction-matters.html; Foner, *Reconstruction: America's Unfinished Revolution, 1863–1877* (New York: Perennial Classics, 1988), *passim.*

131 O I'm a good old rebel: Innes Randolph, "O I'm a Good Old Rebel" (c. 1867), in Vera Brodsky Lawrence, *Music for Patriots, Politicians and Presidents: Harmonies and Discords of the First Hundred Years* (New York: Macmillan, 1975), 437.

131 satire on the unreconstructable rebel: Alan Lomax, *The Folk Songs of North America* (Garden City: Doubleday & Co., 1960), 252.

131–32 Freedmen's Buro; lyin', thievin' Yankees etc.: Randolph, "Good Old Rebel," in Lawrence, 437.

132 was received with shouts: Lomax, 252.

132 the only role for blacks: David W. Blight, *Race and Reunion: The Civil War in American Memory* (Cambridge, MA: Harvard University Press, 2002), 386.

132 I fought beneath: W. Dexter Smith, Jr., and Fred Clemence, "I'll Never Be a Slave Again" (1866), Library of Congress, Civil War Sheet Music Collection: www.loc.gov/resource/ihas.200000412.0.

132 Throughout 1867: Blair Murphy Kelley, *Right to Ride: Streetcar Boycotts and African American Citizenship in the Era of* Plessy *v.* Ferguson (Chapel Hill: University of North Carolina Press, 2010), 92, 147 and *passim.*

133 the finest effort; tragedy that beggared the Greek: W. E. B. Du Bois quoted in Paul Ortiz, *An African American and LatinX History of the United States* (Boston: Beacon Press, 2018), 94.

133 Now, peace on earth: John W. Hutchinson, "The Fatherhood of God and the Brotherhood of Man" (1868), in Lawrence, 446.

133 I'm a gay old Carpet-Bagger: T. E. Garrett and Alfred von Rochow, "The Carpet-Bagger" (1868), Library of Congress, Civil War Sheet Music Collection: www.loc.gov/item/ihas.200002527.

134 just in case African Americans: Ortiz, 59.

134 considered it the destiny: Roxanne Dunbar-Ortiz, *An Indigenous People's History of the United States* (Boston: Beacon Press, 2014), 163.

134 BIA; Christianize and "civilize"; what a white man wants: Thomas F. Johnston, "The Eskimo Songs of Northwestern Alaska," *Arctic* 29, no. 1 (March 1976): 7–19 (p. 8); Diane Hirshberg, "'It Was Bad or It Was Good': Alaska Natives in Past Boarding Schools," *Journal of American Indian Education* 47, no. 3 (2008): 5–30 (p. 5); James H. Ducker, "Curriculum for a New Culture: A Case Study of Schools and Alaska Natives, 1884–1947," *Pacific Northwest Quarterly* 92, no. 2 (Spring 2000): 71–83 (p. 74).

134 The "medicine dances": Tisa Wenger, "Indian Dances and the Politics of Religious Freedom, 1870–1930," *Journal of the American Academy of Religion* 79, no. 4 (December 2011): 850–878 (p. 856).

134 intercultural conflict: Manuel Peña, Foreword, in Américo Parades, *A Texas-Mexican Cancionero: Folksongs of the Lower Border* (Austin: University of Texas Press, 2001), xxix.

134 We got to the Salado River: translation of "*El corrido de Kansas*" (Kansas I), in María Herrera-Sobek, *Northward Bound: The Mexican Immigrant Experience in Ballad and Song* (Bloomington: Indiana University Press, 1993), 8.

135 We reach out: George F. Root, "The Pacific Railroad," in Irwin Silber, ed., *Songs of the Great American West* (New York: Macmillan, 1967), 40–41.

135 Shall Arizona woo me: "Westward Ho," in John A. Lomax, ed., *Cowboy Songs and Other Frontier Ballads* (New York: Macmillan, 1922), 37.

135–36 Now Coolie labor is the cry: Tony Pastor, "John Chinaman," in Philip S. Foner, ed., *American Labor Songs of the Nineteenth Century* (Urbana: University of Illinois Press, 1975), 110–111.

136–37 For I kin wash: "Since the Chinese Ruint the Thrade," in Foner, *American Labor Songs*, 110.

137 "The White Man's Banner": in Crew, *Presidential Sheet Music*, 320.

137 KKK dance numbers: in Danny O. Crew, *Ku Klux Klan Sheet Music: An Illustrated Catalog of Published Music, 1867–2002* (Jefferson, NC: McFarland & Co., 2003), 6–11 *passim.*

137 Upon the breeze: "K. K. K." in Crew, *Ku Klux Klan Sheet Music*, 8.

137 Thomas Mundy Peterson; Hiram Rhodes Revels: Molefi Kete Asante, *The African American People: A Global History* (New York: Routledge, 2012), 118, 354.

138 You say you have emancipated us: Frederick Douglass quoted in Roy Morris, Jr., *Fraud of the Century: Rutherford B. Hayes, Samuel Tilden, and the Stolen Election of 1876* (New York: Simon & Schuster, 2003), 72–73.

139 Three states not yet counted: Howard Zinn, *A People's History of the United States* (New York: HarperCollins, 2005), 205.

139 The South will: William H. Long and J. G. Kuhn, "Tilden and Reform" (1876), Lester S. Levy Sheet Music Collection, Johns Hopkins University: https://levysheetmusic.mse.jhu.edu/collection/007/121.

139 For Tennessee is a hard slavery state: "The Land That Gives Birth to Freedom," in Philip S. Foner, ed., *American Labor Songs of the Nineteenth Century* (Urbana: University of Illinois Press, 1975), 134.

139 fled . . . as if under a spell: Isabel Wilkerson, *The Warmth of Other Suns: The Epic Story of America's Great Migration* (New York: Random House, 2010), 8.

139 plantation nostalgia songs: John W. Finson, *The Voices That Are Gone: Themes in 19th-Century American Popular Song* (New York: Oxford University Press, 1997), 206.

139 one of the most hackneyed clichés: Blight, 284.

140 like our first orbital lunar flight: Harold Courlander quoted in Darden, 100.

140 platforms for expression: Ted Gioia, *Music: A Subversive History* (New York: Basic Books, 2019), 324.

140 an unlikely band: Darden, 115.

140 the slave songs . . . so deeply: W. E. B. Du Bois, *The Souls of Black Folk* (London: Penguin, 1996 [1903]), 205.

141 see their black faces: Du Bois quoted in Jennifer Lynn Stoever, *The Sonic Color Line: Race and the Cultural Politics of Listening* (New York: New York University Press, 2016), 132.

141 trick style . . . I say again: Zora Neale Hurston quoted in Darden, 121.

141 "Go Down, Moses"; "O Brother"; reflect white musical practice: Charles Hamm, *Yesterdays: Popular Song in America* (New York: W. W. Norton, 1983), 377; Shipton, 8.

141 did provide stage training: James Weldon Johnson quoted in Finson, 238.

141 Oh, the old home: Charles A. White, "The Old Home Ain't What It Used to Be" (1874), in Hamm, *Yesterdays*, 270–271.

142 an odious aristocracy: Susan B. Anthony, address to US Circuit Court for the Northern District of New York, in Ann. D. Gordon, ed., *The Selected Papers of Elizabeth Cady Stanton and Susan B. Anthony, Vol. II: Against an Aristocracy of Sex, 1866 to 1873* (New Brunswick, NJ: Rutgers University Press, 2000), 577–578.

142 A vassal state: William Lloyd Garrison, "Human Equality" (1871), Library of Congress, Rare Book and Special Collections Division: www.loc.gov/item/amss.as105600.

142 But when from her position: R. A. Cohen, "Female Suffrage" (1867), in Danny O. Crew, *Suffragist Sheet Music* (Jefferson, NC: McFarland & Co., 2002), 46–47.

143 O, men whom the people: Elizabeth B. Dewing and Joseph Philbrick Webster, "All Rights for All!" (1868), University of Michigan, Thomas A. Edison Collection of American Sheet Music: https://hdl.handle.net/2027/mdp.39015096602639.

143 Shiv'ring and cold: Charles A. Van Anden, "Poverty's Child" (1870), Library of Congress, Music for the Nation: American Sheet Music, ca. 1870 to 1885: www.loc.gov/item/sm1870.04369.

143–44 The Colonel's tongue: Mark Twain and Charles Dudley Warner, *The Gilded Age*, in Twain, *The Gilded Age and Later Novels*, Library of America edition (New York: Literary Classics of the United States, Inc., 2002), 63–64.

144 I can hire one half: Jay Gould quoted in Paul Le Blanc, *Work and Struggle: Voices from US Labor Radicalism* (New York: Routledge, 2011), vii.

144 a further irritant: Jenny Bourne, *In Essentials, Unity: An Economic History of the Grange Movement* (Athens: Ohio University Press, 2017), 5–6.

144 experiment with greenbacks: Bourne, 7.

144 There are speculators: Knowles Shaw, "The Farmer Feeds Us All" (1874), in James L. Orr, ed., *Grange Melodies* (Philadelphia: George S. Ferguson, 1911), 193–194.

144 Police clubs: Unidentified New York newspaper quoted in Zinn, 243.

144–45 J. C. J.: "The Increase of Crime" (1873), Lester S. Levy Sheet Music Collection, Johns Hopkins University: https://levysheetmusic.mse.jhu.edu/collection/032/051a.

145 Agitation: John Greenway, *American Folksongs of Protest* (New York: A. S. Barnes, 1960), 36–37.

145 James Brown's body toils: E. R. Place, "James Brown," in Foner, *American Labor Songs of the Nineteenth Century*, 220–221.

146 a mass action: Ronald L. Filippelli, *Labor Conflict in the United States: An Encyclopedia* (New York: Garland Publishing, 1990), 24–25.

146 racial egalitarianism: Matthew Hild, "Organizing across the Color Line: The Knights of Labor and Black Recruitment Efforts in Small-Town Georgia," *Georgia Historical Quarterly* 81, no. 2 (Summer 1997): 287–310 (p. 290).

146 Base oppressors: "If We Will, We Can Be Free," in Greenway, 47.

146 the first major uprising: Filippelli, 13.

147 What's that you say: "What Makes Us Strike?" in George Korson, *Minstrels of the Mine Patch: Songs and Stories of the Anthracite Industry* (Hatboro, PA: Folklore Associates, Inc., 1964 [1938]), 219–220.

147 Having more potent weapons: Korson, 210.

147 Go back to yer work: "W. B. A.," in Korson, 221.

147 other ethnicities: Filippelli, 13; Zinn, 244.

148 drunken underclass; label of terrorism: Harold W. Aurand, "Molly Maguires," in Filippelli, 333.

148 The intensity of class conflict: Clark D. Halker, *For Democracy, Workers, and God: Labor Song-Poems and Labor Protest, 1865–95* (Urbana: University of Illinois Press, 1991), 81–82.

148 He was self-taught: Korson, 295.

148 transmigration of souls: Mark Twain, *A Connecticut Yankee in King Arthur's Court*, ed. M. Thomas Inge (Oxford: Oxford University Press, 1998), 7.

148–49 Thomas Duffy and James Carroll: Martin Mulhall, "Thomas Duffy," in Korson, 266.

149 We Are the 99 Percent: David Graeber, *The Democracy Project: A History, a Crisis, a Movement* (New York: Penguin Books, 2013), 41.

149 They toil in the fields: Elizabeth Rose Smith, "Labor's Ninety and Nine," in Halker, 124.

8 Muscle, Blood, and Steel

150 first nationwide work stoppage: Roxanne Dunbar-Ortiz, *An Indigenous People's History of the United States* (Boston: Beacon Press, 2014), 166.

150 Shall banks and railroad kings: B. M. Lawrence, "When Workingmen Combine," in Clark D. Halker, *For Democracy, Workers, and God: Labor Song-Poems and Labor Protest, 1865–95* (Urbana: University of Illinois Press, 1991), 123.

150–51 There's Field, Jay Gould: "The Freight Handlers' Strike," in John Greenway, *American Folksongs of Protest* (New York: A. S. Barnes, 1960 [1953]), 52–53.

151 one hundred thousand homeless children: William Loren Katz and Laurie R. Lehmen, *The Cruel Years: American Voices at the Dawn of the Twentieth Century* (Boston: Beacon Press, 2003), 11.

151 As it moves: "Anti-Monopoly War Song" (1882), Library of Congress, "Music for the Nation: American Sheet Music, ca. 1870–1885": www.loc.gov/item/sm1882.20639.

151 Britain, Australia and beyond: Ronald D. Cohen, *Work and Sing: A History of Occupational and Labor Union Songs in the United States* (Crockett, CA: Carquinez Press, 2010), 4.

152 Strong intrenched: "Our Battle Song," in Philip S. Foner, *American Labor Songs of the Nineteenth Century* (Urbana: University of Illinois Press, 1975), 269.

152–53 wave of strikes: Ronald L. Filippelli, ed., *Labor Conflict in the United States: An Encyclopedia* (New York: Garland Publishing, 1990), xxi.

153 famine, floods, and earthquakes: Ella Lodge, "Come Join the Knights of Labor; or, The Great Railway Strike" (1886), Lester S. Levy Sheet Music Collection, Johns Hopkins University: https://jscholarship.library.jhu.edu/handle/1774.2/7637.

153 the first time May Day; If Satan took the blacklegs: "The Eight Hour Day," in Edith Fowker and Joe Glazer, *Songs of Work and Protest* (New York: Dover, 1973), 26–27.

153 Bay View Massacre: Leon Fink, *Workingmen's Democracy: The Knights of Labor and American Politics* (Urbana: University of Illinois Press, 1983), 194–195.

153 Ev'ry day that passes by: Will J. Hardman, "The Unions" (1886), in Lester S. Levy, *Give Me Yesterday: American History in Song, 1890–1920* (Norman: University of Oklahoma Press, 1975), 359.

153 Haymarket bombing: Norm Cohen, *American Folk Songs: A Regional Encyclopedia* (Westport, CT: Greenwood Press, 2008), II, 447.

154 Thibodaux, Louisiana: John DeSantis, *The Thibodaux Massacre: Racial Violence and the 1887 Sugar Cane Labor Strike* (Charleston, SC: The History Press, 2016), *passim.*

154 Let us save our noble brothers: Arthur Cheesewright, "A Shout of Protest," in Foner, *American Labor Songs*, 228.

154 no songs honoring: See Mary Gauthier and Catie Curtis, "Sugar Cane" (2013): www.youtube.com/watch?v=EErWvLlYY7Q; John DeSantis, "The Ballad of Jack Conrad" (2016): www.youtube.com/watch?v=bCBWxgkNN1A.

154 strikes continued into 1889: Filippelli, xxii.

154 struggle between players and owners: Filippelli, 35.

154 Pay me my money down: "Pay Me the Money Down," in Laura Alexandrine Smith, *The Music of the Waters: A Collection of the Sailors' Chanties, or Working Songs of the Sea, of All Maritime Nations* (London: Kegan Paul, Trench & Co., 1888), 23–24; Peter J. Ling, "Developing Freedom Songs: Guy Carawan and the African American Traditions of the South Carolina Sea Islands," *History Workshop Journal* 44 (Autumn 1997): 198–231 (p. 207).

154 defrauded in land grabs; Santa Fe Ring; *Las Gorras Blancas*: F. Arturo Rosales, *Chicano! The History of the Mexican American Civil Rights Movement* (Houston: Arte Público Press, 1997), 8–9.

154–55 flimsy evidence; John Brown's Body: David Correia, "'Retribution Will Be Their Reward': New Mexico's *Las Gorras Blancas* and the Fight for the Las Vegas Land Grant Commons," *Radical History Review* 108 (Fall 2010), 49–72 (pp. 60–61).

155 banks; railroads; local law officials: Norm Cohen, *American Folk Songs: A Regional Encyclopedia* (Westport, CT: Greenwood Press, 2008), II, 489.

155 I once was a tool of oppression: "The Hayseed," in Peter Gough, *Sounds of the New Deal: The Federal Music Project in the West* (Urbana: University of Illinois Press, 2015), 29.

155 Let us work and vote together: in Omar H. Ali, *In the Lion's Mouth: Black Populism in the New South, 1886–1900* (Jackson: University Press of Mississippi, 2010), 89.

155 New Orleans; railroad switchmen; copper miners: Howard Zinn, *A People's History of the United States* (New York: HarperCollins, 2005), 276.

155–56 Coal Creek songs: "Buddy, Won't You Roll Down the Line," in Foner, *American Labor Songs*, 205; also Cohen, *American Folk Songs*, I, 271–272; Neil V. Rosenberg, "Revival, Aesthetics, and the 'Coal Creek March,'" in Archie Green, ed., *Songs about Work: Essays in Occupational Culture* (Bloomington: Folklore Institute of Indiana University Bloomington, 1993): 163–183 (pp. 164–165).

156 Homestead; Carnegie; Frick: Zinn, 276.

156 When a bunch of bum detectives: Michael McGovern, "The Homestead Strike," in Pete Seeger and Bob Reiser, *Carry It On! A History and Song and Picture of the Working Men and Women of America* (Poole, UK: Blandford Press, 1986), 61–63.

156 Ye prating politicians: William W. Delaney, "Father Was Killed by the Pinkerton Men," in Michael K. Rosenow, *Death and Dying in the Working Class, 1865–1920* (Urbana: University of Illinois Press, 2015), 107.

156–57 A third of the railroads: Katz and Lehman, 2.

157 in no mood to cooperate: Zinn, 279.

157 drifted to other railroads: Carl Sandburg, *The American Songbag* (San Diego: Harcourt Brace Jovanovich, 1990 [1927]), 190.

157 Been on the hummer: "A. R. U.," in Sandburg, 191.

157 petition with boots: David S. Meyer, *The Politics of Protest: Social Movements in America* (New York: Oxford University Press, 2007), 164.

157–58 "A Petition of the Unemployed": Franklin Folsom, *America before Welfare* (New York: New York University Press, 1991), 450.

158 trivial offense: Foner, *American Labor Songs*, 253.

158 Yes, we have Union men: Willie Wildwave (William W. Delaney), "Coxey Army!" in Foner, *American Labor Songs*, 253.

158 O say, can you see: "The National Grass Plot," in Greenway, 63.

158 spontaneous uprising; first agreement: Robert V. Wells, *Life Flows On in Endless Song: Folk Songs and American History* (Urbana: University of Illinois Press, 2009), 88.

158 We sign then a contract: Isaac Hanna, "The Company Store," in David C. Duke, *Writers and Miners: Activism and Imagery in America* (Lexington: University Press of Kentucky, 2002), 177.

159 America! America: Katherine Lee Bates, "America the Beautiful" (1895), in John Shaw, *This Land That I Love: Irving Berlin, Woody Guthrie, and the Story of Two American Anthems* (New York: Public Affairs, 2013), 29.

159 Into this boiling cauldron: Katz and Lehman, 3.

159 German socialist and anarchist societies and songs: Tom Goyens, *Beer and Revolution: The German Anarchist Movement in New York City, 1880–1914* (Urbana: University of Illinois Press, 2007), 168, 171; Cohen, *Work and Sing*, 25.

159 Polish singing societies: Stanislaus A. Blejwas, "'To Sing Out the Future of Our Beloved Fatherland': Choral Nationalism and the Polish Singers Alliance of America, 1889–1939," *Journal of American Ethnic History* 19, no. 1 (Fall 1999): 3–25 (pp. 3–4); Helen Stankiewicz Zand, "Polish Institutional Folkways in the United States," *Polish American Studies* 14, nos. 1–2 (January–June 1957): 24–32 (pp. 25–26).

159 Immigrants from southern and eastern Europe; Polish population: John Radzilowski, "In American Eyes: Views of Polish Peasants in Europe and the United States, 1890s–1930s," *Polish Review* 47, no. 4 (2002), 393–406 (p. 394).

159 Organ Grinder; Dagoe Banana Peddler: John W. Finson, *The Voices That Are Gone: Themes in 19th-Century American Popular Song* (New York: Oxford University Press, 1997), 305–306.

160 Nothing work: "Song of an Italian Workman" (c. 1890), in Foner, *American Labor Songs*, 286.

160 2.5 million: Mark Slobin, *Tenement Songs: The Popular Music of the Jewish Immigrants* (Urbana: University of Illinois Press, 1996), 12.

160 Ponder on these bitter times: Untitled emigrant song in Ruth Rubin, *Voices of a People: The Story of Yiddish Folksong* (New York: Mc-Graw-Hill, 1973), 344–345.

160–61 Your daddy's in America: translation of Sholem Aleichem, "*Schlof mayn kind*" (Sleep, My Child), in Rubin, 40.

161 first victories; Weary days: translation of "*Ot Ozoy Neyt a Shnayder*" (Weary Days Are a Tailor's) and commentary in John Anthony Scott, *The Ballad of America: The History of the United States in Song and Story* (New York: Bantam Pathfinder, 1966), 286–287.

161–62 Everywhere, on both sides: translation of Morris Winchevsky, "*Hert ir kinder*" (Children, Do You Hear?) and commentary in Rubin, 349–350.

162 The merchants are jealous: Frank Dumont, "Jacob and Solomon Rosenstein," in Finson, 304.

162 They say some of our people: Ned Harrigan and David Braham, "They Never Tell All What They Know," in Finson, 305.

163 On the 28th day of February: translation of "The Immigrants" ("The Hooked Ones"), in María Herrera-Sobek, *Northward Bound: The Mexican Immigrant Experience in Ballad and Song* (Bloomington: Indiana University Press, 1993), 43–44.

163 set the precedent: Krystyn R. Moon, "On a Temporary Basis: Immigration, Labor Unions, and the American Entertainment Industry, 1880s–1930s," *Journal of American History* 99, no. 3 (December 2012): 771–792 (p. 771).

163–64 Those who could not afford: Marlon Kau Hom, *Songs of Gold Mountain: Cantonese Rhymes from San Francisco Chinatown* (Berkeley: University of California Press, 1987), 270.

164 more than 153 anti-Chinese riots: Nancy Yunhwa Rao, *Chinatown Opera Theater in North America* (Urbana: University of Illinois Press, 2017), 44–45.

164 O workingmen dear: "Twelve Hundred More," in Foner, *American Labor Songs*, 135.

164–65 As I walk round the streets: "The Heathen Chinese," in Marcello Truzzi, "The 100% American Songbag: Conservative Folksongs in America," *Western Folklore* 28, no. 1 (January 1969): 27–40 (pp. 22–23).

165 I'll sing of a subject: W. S. Mullally and John E. Donnelly, "The Chinese, the Chinese, You Know," in Philip Furia and Michael Lasser, *America's Songs: The Stories behind the Songs of Broadway, Hollywood, and Tin Pan Alley* (New York: Routledge, 2006), 14.

165 Exoticism and desire: Michael Saffle, "Eastern Fantasies on Western Stages: Chinese-Themed Operettas and Musical Comedies in Turn-of-the-Last Century London and New York," in Yang Hon-Lun and Michael Saffle, eds., *China and the West: Music, Representation, and Reception* (Ann Arbor: University of Michigan Press, 2017), 87–118 (p. 95); Krystyn R. Moon, *Yellowface: Creating the Chinese in American Popular Music and Performance, 1850s–1920s* (New Brunswick, NJ: Rutgers University Press, 2004), 144.

165 The portrayal of Chinese women: Moon, *Yellowface,* 123–124.

166 mostly Japanese-themed: Saffle, 91, 97.

166 a musical subject; laundries, opium dens: Moon, *Yellowface,* 119, 121.

166 Cantonese opera troupes: Rao, 22.

166 the role of opera: Jack Chen paraphrased in Mina Yang, "Orientalism and the Music of Asian Immigrant Communities in California, 1924–1945," *American Music* 19, no. 4 (Winter 2001): 385–416 (p. 392).

166 achieved its greatest popularity: John Dizikes, *Opera in America: A Cultural History* (New Haven, CT: Yale University Press, 1993), 272.

166 theatricality and artifice: Yang, 392.

166 screams, goblings: review quoted in Dizikes, 110.

166–67 sexual danger; Page Law: Moon, "On a Temporary Basis," 778.

167 awesome silences; threatening noises: Sarah Keyes, "'Like a Roaring Lion': The Overland Trail as a Sonic Conquest," *Journal of American History* 96, no. 1 (June 2009): 19–43 (p. 23).

167 deplorable obstacles: BIA agent William Forbes, quoted in Tisa Wenger, "Indian Dances and the Politics of Religious Freedom, 1870–1930," *Journal of the American Academy of Religion* 79, no. 4 (December 2011): 850–878 (p. 856).

167 disappearance of the bison: Jeffrey Ostler, "'They Regard Their Passing as Wakan': Interpreting the Western Sioux Explanations for the Bison's Decline," *Western Historical Quarterly* 30, no. 4 (1999): 475–497 (pp. 483–484).

167–68 millions of skeletons; educational programming; A great General: Brad D. Lookingbill, *War Dance at Fort Marion: Plains Indian War Prisoners* (Norman: University of Oklahoma Press, 2014), 5–7, 33.

168 tourist attractions; harmonizing; Lo we Red Men: Lookingbill, 161–162.

168 As the imprisoned Apaches: T. Christopher Alpin, "'This Is Our Dance': The Fire Dance of the Fort Sill Chiricahua Warm Springs Apache," in Tara Browner, ed., *Music of the First Nations: Tradition and Innovation in Native North America* (Urbana: University of Illinois Press, 2009), 92–112 (p. 102).

168 strict interpretations; study the piano: John W. Troutman, *Indian Blues: American Indians and the Politics of Music, 1879–1934* (Norman: University of Oklahoma Press, 2012), 7–8.

168 Carlisle students at Brooklyn Bridge: Dunbar-Ortiz, 157.
168 BIA war on "heathen" dances: Troutman, 31.
169 Court of Indian Offenses; ten days for participation: Wenger, 855.
169 A-B-C songs; vehicle of satire: Thomas F. Johnston, "The Social Background of Eskimo Music in Northwest Alaska," *Journal of American Folklore* 89, no. 354 (October–December 1976): 438–448 (p. 442).
169 At St. Michael: Thomas F. Johnston, "Alaskan Eskimo Music Is Revitalized," *Journal of American Indian Education* 17, no. 3 (May 1978): 1–7 (p. 2).
169 We have condemned; This has given us: Missionary quoted in Johnston, "Alaskan Eskimo Music," 2.
169 I wish it to be remembered: Sitting Bull quoted in Gary Clayton Anderson, *Ethnic Cleansing and the Indian: The Crime That Should Haunt America* (Norman: University of Oklahoma Press, 2014), 306.
169 Once a famous warrior I was: Sitting Bull quoted in Reginald Laubin and Gladys Laubin, *Indian Dances of North America* (Norman: University of Oklahoma Press, 1989), 94.
169 drew in the crowds; the killer of Custer: Linda Scarangella McNenly, *Native Performers in Wild West Shows: From Buffalo Bill to Euro Disney* (Norman: University of Oklahoma Press, 2015), 25, 81–82.
170 Wovoka; I went up to heaven; Jesus is now upon the earth: Craig Harris, *Heartbeat, Warble, and the Electric Powwow: American Indian Music* (Norman: University of Oklahoma Press, 2016), 9–10.
171 The new world: James Mooney quoted in Harris, 10.
171 The leaders beat time: quoted in Dunbar-Ortiz, 153–154.
171 The ceremony is but an appeal: Alice C. Fletcher, *Indian Story and Song from North America* (Lincoln: University of Nebraska Press, 1995 [1900]), 96–97.
172 Clear the way: translation of Ghost Dance song in Paula Mitchell Marks, *In a Barren Land: The American Indian Quest for Cultural Survival, 1607 to the Present* (New York: Perennial, 2002), xv.
172 The Messiah craze: Charles A. Eastman quoted in Lawana Trout, ed., *Native American Literature: An Anthology* (Lincolnwood, IL: NTC Publishing Group, 1999), 269.

172 officials reported; not long after he physically tried: Dunbar-Ortiz, 154; Anderson, 335–336.

172 Wounded Knee; the sanctuary was candlelit: Dunbar-Ortiz, 154–155.

172 The Whites: L. Frank Baum quoted in Howard Zinn and Anthony Arnove, *Voices of a People's History of the United States* (London: Seven Stories Press, 2009), 148.

172 Who would have thought: Short Bull quoted in Harris, 11.

173 US Census Bureau: Gerald D. Nash, "The Census of 1890 and the Closing of the Frontier," *Pacific Northwest Quarterly* 71, no. 3 (July 1980): 98–100 (p. 98).

173 entertained; amused; The Pacific is our natural property: Richard Drinnon, *Facing West: The Metaphysics of Indian Hating and Empire Building* (New York: Schocken Books, 1990), 245, 249.

173 I live in sorrow: translation of Lili'uokalani, "*Ke Aloha O Ka Haku*" (The Queen's Prayer), in Cheryl A. Harstad and James R. Harstad, eds., *Island Fire: An Anthology of Literature from Hawai'i* (Honolulu: University of Hawai'i Press, 2002), 7.

9 Rule Anglo-Saxia

174 From Wyoming's rocky valley: Julia Mills Dunn, "Song of Wyoming," in Danny O. Crew, *Suffragist Sheet Music* (Jefferson, NC: McFarland & Co., 2002), 109.

174 Sons, will you longer see: Elizabeth Boynton Harbert, "New America," in Crew, 119.

175 Help us carry: translation of David Edelshtadt, "To the Women Workers," in Philip S. Foner, ed., *American Labor Songs of the Nineteenth Century* (Urbana: University of Illinois Press, 1975), 318.

175 zone between ethnology and exploitation: Larry Hamberlin, "Visions of Salome: The Femme Fatale in American Popular Songs before 1920," *Journal of the American Musicological Society* 59, no. 3 (Fall 2006): 631–696 (p. 646).

175 After the Fair is over: Charles K. Harris, "After the Fair," in John W. Finson, *The Voices That Are Gone: Themes in 19th-Century American Popular Song* (New York: Oxford University Press, 1997), 154.

175–76 momentous occurrence; discovered ragtime: Edward A. Berlin, *Reflections and Research on Ragtime* (Brooklyn, NY: Institute for Studies in American Music, Brooklyn College of the City University of New York, 1987), 1–2.

176 extremes not previously heard; imparting a restless: Ted Gioia, *Music: A Subversive History* (New York: Basic Books, 2019), 328; Finson, 228–229.

176 paradoxical art form; earliest composers: David A. Jasen and Trebor Jay Tichenor, *Rags and Ragtime: A Musical History* (New York: Dover Publications, 1978), 1–2.

176 You have to know: Eubie Blake quoted in Terry Waldo, *This Is Ragtime* (New York: Da Capo Press, 1991), viii.

176 inaugurated African American recording: Tim Brooks, *Lost Sounds: Blacks and the Birth of the Recording Industry, 1890–1919* (Urbana: University of Illinois Press, 2005), 28.

176 The Two Real Coons: Edward A. Berlin, *King of Ragtime: Scott Joplin and His Era* (New York: Oxford University Press, 1995), 79.

176 Warm coons: Paul Laurence Dunbar and Will Marion Cook, "Darktown Is Out Tonight," in Berlin, 79.

177 optional syncopated accompaniment: H. Wiley Hitchcock, *Music in the United States: A Historical Introduction* (Englewood Cliffs: Prentice-Hall, 1988), 134.

177 later expressed regret: Karen L. Cox, *Dreaming of Dixie: How the South Was Created in American Popular Culture* (Chapel Hill: University of North Carolina Press, 2011), 15.

177 I attended a ball: Scott Joplin, "Ragtime Dance," in Waldo, 32.

177 to freedom and equality: Rudi Blesh, "Scott Joplin: Black-American Classicist," in Vera Brodsky Lawrence, ed., *Scott Joplin: Collected Piano Works* (New York: New York Public Library, 1972), xiii–xl (pp. xxxvii–xxxviii).

177 Pulitzer Prize: Berlin, 251–252.

177 credited with giving birth: Brooks, 293.

177 a lilting melody: Brooks, 295.

177–78 Swing along, chillun: Paul Laurence Dunbar and Will Marion Cook, "Swing Along," in Brooks, 295.

178 mastery of sound; Buckingham Palace: Marva Giffin Carter, "Removing the 'Minstrel Mask' in the Musicals of Will Marion Cook," *Musical Quarterly* 84, no. 2 (Summer 2000): 206–220 (p. 209).

178 established himself: Guthrie P. Ramsey, Jr., "Cosmopolitan or Provincial? Ideology in Early Black Music Historiography, 1867–1940," *Black Music Research Journal* 16, no. 1 (Spring 1996): 11–42 (p. 15).

178 notwithstanding their lack: James Monroe Trotter quoted in Stephen Blum, "Musical Enactment of Attitudes toward Conflict in the United States," in John Morgan O'Connell and Salwa el-Shawan Castelo-Branco, eds., *Music and Conflict* (Urbana: University of Illinois Press, 2010): 232–242 (p. 237).

178 Marie Selika Williams and Sampson Williams: Peter G. Davis, *The American Opera Singer* (New York: Anchor Books, 1997), 326–327.

178 but no white opera company; opera kaleidoscopes: John Dizikes, *Opera in America: A Cultural History* (New Haven, CT: Yale University Press, 1993), 385.

179 chafed at being allowed; the first African American woman: Brooks, 3, 254–255.

179 DeFord Bailey: Patrick Huber, "Black Hillbillies," in Diane Pecknold, ed., *Hidden in the Mix: The African American Presence in Country Music* (Durham, NC: Duke University Press, 2013), 19–81 (p. 39).

179 Charley Pride: Charles L. Hughes, *Country Soul: Making Music and Making Race in the American South* (Chapel Hill: University of North Carolina Press, 2015), 133–134.

179 distinguished black composers: Carter, 206–207.

180 always had a choking effect: Eugene Levy, "Ragtime and Race Pride: The Career of James Weldon Johnson," in Timothy E. Scheurer, ed., *The Nineteenth Century and Tin Pan Alley: Readings from the Popular Press* (Bowling Green, OH: Bowling Green State University Popular Press, 1989), 92–103 (p. 97).

180 *Oriental America*: Dizikes, 386–387.

180 rough, razor-wielding bully: Berlin, 36.

180 the Black National Anthem: Jabari Jackson and Jill Martin, "The NFL Plans to Play the Black National Anthem before Week 1 Games," CNN *Edition* online, July 3, 2020: https://edition.cnn.com/2020/07/02/sport/nfl-black-national-anthem-week-1-spt-intl/index.html.

180 There's a heap of trouble: Irving Jones, "I Want a Filipino Man," in Thomas P. Walsh, *Tin Pan Alley and the Philippines:*

American Songs of War and Love, 1898–1946 (Lanham, MD: Scarecrow Press, 2013), 74.

180–81 All kin's ob coons: Edgar Smith, "Belle ob de Philippines," in Walsh, 78.

181 splendid little war: John Hay quoted in Richard Drinnon, *Facing West: The Metaphysics of Indian Hating and Empire Building* (New York: Schocken Books, 1990), 270.

181 The scorn: José Martí quoted in Vicki L. Ruiz, "*Nuestra América*: Latino History as United States History," *Journal of American History* 93, no. 3 (December 2006): 655–672 (p. 662).

181 There is no trouble here; Please remain: Remington and Hearst apocryphally quoted in Kenneth Whyte, *The Uncrowned King: The Sensational Rise of William Randolph Hearst* (Berkeley, CA: Counterpoint Press, 2009), 301.

181 While no precise figures: Jill DeTemple, "Singing the Maine: The Popular Image of Cuba in Sheet Music of the Spanish-American War," *The Historian* 63, no. 4 (Summer 2001): 715–729 (p. 722).

181–82 In Havana's deep dark waters: The Brownings, "Avenge the Good Ship Maine," in DeTemple, 722–723.

182 Here's to the Spaniard: Untitled verse in James P. Leary, *Folksongs of Another America: Field Recordings from the Upper Midwest, 1937–1946* (Madison, and Atlanta, GA: University of Wisconsin Press and Dust-to-Digital, 2015), 127–128.

182 Big corporations: Quoted in Zinn, 305.

182 powerful sugar interests in Cuba: Richard F. Hamilton, *President McKinley, War, and Empire* (New York: Routledge, 2017), I, 130–131.

182 Distance and ocean: Albert Beveridge quoted in Drinnon, 312.

182 We've heard of Dewey's vict'ry: Jas. C. Dunn, "Old Glory Holds the Bay," in Walsh, 40.

183 There must be two Americas: Mark Twain, "To the Person Sitting in Darkness," in Twain, *Tales, Speeches, Essays, and Sketches*, ed. Tom Quirk (New York: Penguin, 1994), 272.

183 had more than ten million native peoples: Drinnon, 241.

183 jingoistic titles: Danny O. Crew, *American Political Music: A State-by-State Catalog* (Jefferson, NC: McFarland & Co., 2006), I, 2.

183 McKinley called for volunteers: "The Battleship of Maine," in John Cohen and Mike Seeger, eds., *Old-Time String Band Songbook* (New York: Oak Publications, 1976), 100.

183 "Rule Anglo-Saxia": James D. Ross and Karl Vincent, "Rule Anglo-Saxia," in Danny O. Crew, *Presidential Sheet Music* (Jefferson, NC: McFarland & Co., 2001), 249.

183–84 What kind of shoes: "The Battleship of Maine," in Cohen and Seeger, 101.

184 But it was impossible: Mark Twain, "Passage from 'Outlines of History' (suppressed)," quoted in Hunt Hawkins, "Mark Twain's Anti-Imperialism," *American Literary Realism, 1870–1910*, 25, no. 2 (Winter 1993): 31–45 (p. 38).

184 so near to us: Grover Cleveland quoted in Drinnon, 269.

184 In this revolution: Enrique Dupuy de Lome quoted in Zinn, along with commentary, 303.

184 recognize the rebels; no Cuban was allowed: Zinn, 305, 309.

184 We used to think the Negro: Anon., "The Negro Soldier," in Glenn Watkins, *Proof through the Night: Music and the Great War* (Berkeley: University of California Press, 2003), 312.

185 Americans began taking: Zinn, 310.

185 With flowers we welcomed them: translation of Rafael Hernández Marín, "*Pobre Borinquen*," in Dick Weissman, *Talkin' 'Bout a Revolution: Music and Social Change in America* (New York: Backbeat Books, 2010), 248.

185 The United States exported: Paul Ortiz, *An African American and LatinX History of the United States* (Boston: Beacon Press, 2018), 101–102.

185 collective trauma: E. San Juan, Jr., "The Filipino Diaspora," *Philippine Studies* 49, no. 2 (2001): 255–264 (pp. 259–260).

185 insurrectionists: Faye C. Caronan, "Memories of US Imperialism Narratives of the Homeland in Filipino and Puerto Rican Homes in the United States," *Philippine Studies: Historical and Ethnic Viewpoints* 60, no. 3 (September 2012): 336–366 (p. 350).

186 renegade Pawnee: Roxanne Dunbar-Ortiz, *An Indigenous People's History of the United States* (Boston: Beacon Press, 2014), 165–166.

186 We exterminated the American Indians: Unnamed US officer quoted in Drinnon, 314.

186 Filipino insurgents: Dunbar-Ortiz, 164–165.

186 Jim Crow architecture: T. Thomas Fortune quoted in Ortiz, 101.

186 they joined whites: Drinnon, 313.

186–87 Get the good old syringe: "The Water Cure in the P. I.," in Phillip W. Hoffman, *David Fagen: Turncoat Hero* (Staunton, VA: American History Press, 2017), 160.

187 the sons of *conquistadores*; to prove their loyalty; St. Aloysius Gonzaga: translation of "*Indita de San Luis Gonzaga*" and accompanying commentary in Jack Loeffler, *La Música de los Viejitos: Hispano Folk Music of the Río Grande del Norte* (Albuquerque: University of New Mexico Press, 1999), 25–27.

187 The American people: Whitelaw Reid quoted in Drinnon, 312.

187 Outlaw Reid: Henry Nash Smith and William Gibson, eds., *Mark Twain–Howells Letters* (Cambridge, MA: Belknap Press of Harvard University Press, 1960), I, 390.

188 To compose; brought to my notice: Lili'uokalani, *Hawaii's Story by Hawaii's Queen* (Boston: Lee & Shepard, 1898), 30.

188 Royal father: translation of Kalākaua, "*Hawai'i Pono'ī*," in Ku'ualoha Ho'omanawanui, "*He Lei Ho'oheno no nā Kau a Kau*: Language, Performance, and Form in Hawaiian Poetry," *The Contemporary Pacific* 17, no. 1 (2005): 29–81 (p. 48).

188 With their control: Marc Ferris, *Star-Spangled Banner: The Unlikely Story of America's National Anthem* (Baltimore: Johns Hopkins University Press, 2014), 96.

188 5430 pressings: "*Aloha 'Oe*," Discogs search: www.discogs.com.

188 *Aloha 'oe, aloha 'oe*: Lili'uokalani, "*Aloha 'Oe*," in Amy K. Stillman, "Published Hawaiian Songbooks," *Notes* 44, no. 2 (December 1987): 221–239 (p. 226).

189 Songs on Lili'uokalani: All in Crew, *American Political Music*, I, 109.

189 In the nineteenth century: Francis Jennings, *The Invasion of America: Indians, Colonialism, and the Cant of Conquest* (New York: W. W. Norton, 1976), 21.

190 the native hulas; very great public evil: Hawaiian Evangelical Association appeal quoted in James Revell Carr, *Hawaiian Music in Motion: Mariners, Missionaries, and Minstrels* (Urbana: University of Illinois Press, 2014), 111.

190 by F. J. Testa: Darlaine Mahealani Dudoit, "Against Extinction: A Legacy of Native Hawaiian Resistance Literature," in Ibrahim G. Aoudé, ed., *The Ethnic Studies Story: Politics and Social Movements in Hawai'i*, Vol. 39 (Honolulu: University of Hawai'i Press, 1999), 226–248 (p. 234).

190 contract laborers: Beverly Lozano, "The Andalucía–Hawaii–California Migration: A Study in Macrostructure and Microhistory," in Phylis Cancilla Martinelli and Ana Varela-Lago, eds., *Hidden Out in the Open: Spanish Migration to the United States, 1875–1930* (Boulder: University Press of Colorado, 2018), 66–90 (pp. 68, 75–76).

190 The Iberian group; Latin peasants; cleanly looking etc.: Ronald Takaki, *Pau Hana: Plantation Life and Labor in Hawaii, 1835–1920* (Honolulu: University of Hawaii Press, 1984), 35.

190–91 Far from my land: translation of an anonymously composed Portuguese-Hawaiian immigrant song, in Takaki, 36.

191 poke-knives; nearly 80 percent; one-sixth: Jonathan Y. Okamura, *Ethnicity and Inequality in Hawai'i* (Philadelphia: Temple University Press, 2008), 156, 160; San Juan, Jr., 259.

191 Puerto Rico was considered: Iris López, "Borinkis and Chop Suey: Puerto Rican Identity in Hawai'i, 1900 to 2000," in Carmen Teresa Whalen and Victor Vázquez-Hernández, eds., *Puerto Rican Diaspora: Historical Perspectives* (Philadelphia: Temple University Press, 2005), 43–67 (p. 44).

191 their personal fiefdom; keep workers under control: López, 45–46.

191 could not move: López, 47.

191–92 Thirty-three years: translation of Carlos Fraticelli, "*En Este País Hawaiiano,*" in Ted Solís, "Disconnections: Puerto Rican Diasporic Musical Identity in Hawai'i," in Birgit Abels, ed., *Austronesian Soundscapes: Performing Arts in Oceania and Southeast Asia* (Amsterdam: Amsterdam University Press, 2011), 241–259 (pp. 244–245). Also López, 53.

192 Hiroshima rice-threshing melody: Susan Asai, "*Hole Hole Bushi*: Cultural/Musical Resistance by Japanese Women Plantation Workers in Early Twentieth-Century Hawaii," in Diane C. Fujino, ed., *Wicked Theory, Naked Practice: A Fred Ho Reader* (Minneapolis: University of Minnesota Press, 2009), 274–280 (p. 278).

192 The Japanese male workers: Fred Ho, "Bamboo that Snaps Back! Resistance and Revolution in Asian Pacific American Working-Class and Left-Wing Expressive Culture," in Fujino, *Wicked Theory, Naked Practice*, 247–269 (p. 255).

192 *Hole hole* work: Franklin Odo, *Voices from the Canefields: Folksongs from Japanese Immigrant Workers in Hawai'i* (New York: Oxford University Press, 2013), xxiii.

192 the pidgin of the emerging: Asai, 277.

192 narratives of shifting landscapes: Aaron Kingsbury, "Music in the Fields: Constructing Narratives of the Late 19th-Century Hawaiian Plantation Cultural Landscape," *Yearbook of the Association of Pacific Coast Geographers* 70 (2008): 45–58 (p. 55).

192 threw their petition: Gary Y. Okihiro, *Cane Fires: The Anti-Japanese Movement in Hawaii, 1865–1945* (Philadelphia: Temple University Press, 1991), 26.

193 The laborers keep on coming: translation in Okihiro, 26–27.

193 Hawaii, Hawaii: translation of untitled *hole hole bushi*, in Norm Cohen, *American Folk Songs: A Regional Encyclopedia* (Westport, CT: Greenwood Press, 2008), II, 692.

193 The major exception: Asai, 280.

193 My husband cuts the cane: translation in Odo, 160.

193 In the morning darkness: translation in Odo, 162.

194 a large proportion; singing or listening: Ron Emoff, "A Cajun Poetics of Loss and Longing," *Ethnomusicology* 42, no. 2 (Spring–Summer 1998): 283–310 (p. 288).

194 became US citizens: JoAnna Poblete, *Islanders in the Empire: Filipino and Puerto Rican Laborers in Hawai'i* (Urbana: University of Illinois Press, 2014), 6.

195 We can hear: John W. Troutman, *Kila Kila: How the Hawaiian Steel Guitar Changed the Sound of Modern Music* (Chapel Hill: University of North Carolina Press, 2016), 6–7.

195 a promise of an island paradise: Jim Tranquada and John King, *The 'Ukulele: A History* (Honolulu: University of Hawai'i Press, 2012), 2.

195 Down in Honolulu: Jerald N. Johnson and Henry Kalimai, "My Honolulu Ukulele Baby" (New York: Jerome H. Remick & Co., 1916), 1.

195 And then there was: Timothy E. Scheurer, "'Thou Witty': The Evolution and Triumph of Style in Lyric Writing, 1890–1950," in Scheurer, *The Nineteenth Century and Tin Pan Alley*, 104–119 (p. 110).

10 The Hand That Feeds You

196 probably the first music; choicest offerings: Lester S. Levy, *Give Me Yesterday: American History in Song, 1890–1920* (Norman: University of Oklahoma Press, 1975), 67–73 *passim.*

196 I don't ride: R. Melville Baker and Josephine Sherwood, "Just Come Aroun' Wid an Automobile" (1902), in Levy, 66.

196 She grew kind o' restless: Paul Dresser, "She Went to the City" (1904), in Charles Hamm, *Yesterdays: Popular Song in America* (New York: Norton, 1983), 306.

197 great white Palaces; Inuits; panting sled dogs, etc.; had a booth: Richard Drinnon, *Facing West: The Metaphysics of Indian Hating and Empire Building* (New York: Schocken Books, 1990), 340–341, 344.

197 BIA: Tara Browner, "Ferruccio Busoni and *The Indians' Book*," in Browner, ed., *Music of the First Nations: Tradition and Innovation in Native North America* (Urbana: University of Illinois Press, 2009): 131–140 (p. 292, n. 7).

197 Parents who opposed; spiritual murder: Kim E. Nielsen, *A Disability History of the United States* (Boston: Beacon Press, 2012), 120, 121.

197 I have met with much opposition: Frances Densmore quoted in Craig Harris, *Heartbeat, Warble, and the Electric Powwow: American Indian Music* (Norman: University of Oklahoma Press, 2016), 64.

198 Curtis aimed: Browner, 285.

198 racial suicide; must remain; For the last time: Natalie Curtis, *The Indians' Book* (New York: Harper & Bros., 1907), xxxiii, 57–58.

198 Will not the superintendent: Hopi chief Lolollomai quoted in Curtis, 475–476.

198 On our reservation: Unnamed Pima chief quoted in Curtis, 314.

198–99 Said Geronimo: in Curtis, 234.

199 little brown people; they did not wear: Geronimo, *My Life*, as told to S. M. Barrett (Mineola, NY: Dover Publications, 2005 [1906]), 119.

199 So declaimed: Drinnon, 340–341.

199 After the parade: Gilbert King, "Geronimo's Appeal to Theodore Roosevelt," *Smithsonian Magazine*, November 9, 2012: www.smithsonianmag.com/history/geronimos-appeal-to-theodore-roosevelt-117859516.

200 Because he has given: Geronimo, iv.

200 Geronimo's Cadillac: William M. Clements, *Imagining Geronimo: An Apache Icon in Popular Culture* (Albuquerque: University of New Mexico Press, 2013), 197–198.

200 Nava, Nava: Harry Williams and Egbert Van Alstyne, "Navajo, Navajo" (1903), in Dick Weissman, *Talkin' 'Bout a Revolution: Music and Social Change in America* (New York: Backbeat Books, 2010), 30–31.

201 Hundreds of Indian-themed songs; Indianness: John W. Troutman, *Indian Blues: American Indians and the Politics of Music, 1879–1934* (Norman: University of Oklahoma Press, 2012), 206.

201 'Mid the wild: Jack Drislane and Theodore Morse, "Arrah Wanna" (1906), in Troutman, 206.

201 capitalized on the popularity; the improbable kidnapping: John Dizikes, *Opera in America: A Cultural History* (New Haven, CT: Yale University Press, 1993), 390–391.

201 Sing us a song: James Weldon Johnson and Rosamond Johnson, "Lift Every Voice and Sing" (1900), in Ian Peddie, "Music, Religion and Protest," in Christopher Partridge and Marcus Moberg, eds., *The Bloomsbury Handbook of Religion and Popular Music* (London: Bloomsbury, 2018), 32–42 (p. 33).

201 At the time: Peddie, "Music, Religion and Protest," 33.

201 In the lyrics: Levy, *Give Me Yesterday,* 100; Rosamond Johnson quoted in Michael Lasser, *America's Songs II: Songs from the 1890s to the Post-War Years* (New York: Routledge, 2014), 21.

202 a musical suite; Ellington, Marsalis, and Mayfield: Stephen Blum, "Musical Enactment of Attitudes toward Conflict in the United States," in John Morgan O'Connell and Salwa el-Shawan Castelo-Branco, eds., *Music and Conflict* (Urbana: University of Illinois Press, 2010), 232–242 (p. 235).

202 symbolic of the primitive morality: Quoted in Ted Gioia, *Music: A Subversive History* (New York: Basic Books, 2019), 330.

202 *A Guest of Honor*: Edward A. Berlin, *King of Ragtime: Scott Joplin and His Era* (New York: Oxford University Press, 1995), 130.

202 goo-goo eyes; almost changed his color: Gus Cannon, "Can You Blame the Colored Man?" in Dom Flemons, "Can You Blame Gus Cannon?" *Oxford American* 83 (Winter 2013): www.oxfordamerican.org/magazine/item/160-can-you-blame-gus-cannon.

202 The first so-called Ragtime songs: James Weldon Johnson quoted in Edward A. Berlin, *Ragtime: A Musical and Cultural History* (Berkeley: University of California Press 1984), 5–6.

203 folk source; into the European classical tradition: Edward A. Berlin, *Reflections and Research on Ragtime* (Brooklyn: Institute for Studies in American Music, Brooklyn College of the City University of New York, 1987), 61; also Levy, 100.

203 to voice all the joys; to the public of New York: Johnson and Europe quoted in Blum, 238.

203 a career: Samuel Charters and Leonard Kunstadt quoted in Alyn Shipton, *A New History of Jazz* (London: Bloomsbury, 2010), 7.

203 Clef Club and Music School Settlement: Tim Brooks, *Lost Sounds: Blacks and the Birth of the Recording Industry, 1890–1919* (Urbana: University of Illinois Press, 2005), 270.

203 transforming the spiritual; incorporated elements: Brooks, 474–475.

203 models; pseudo-Persian and East Indian lyrics; career-long efforts: Jean E. Snyder, *Harry T. Burleigh: From the Spiritual to the Harlem Renaissance* (Urbana: University of Illinois Press, 2016), 271–272.

204 a backdrop for romance; camels, temple bells; caravan: Timothy E. Scheurer, "'Thou Witty': The Evolution and Triumph of Style in Lyric Writing, 1890–1950," in Scheurer, ed., *The Nineteenth Century and Tin Pan Alley: Readings from the Popular Press* (Bowling Green, OH: Bowling Green State University Popular Press, 1989), 104–119 (p. 109).

204 understood the appeal: Ted Gioia, *The Jazz Standards: A Guide to the Repertoire* (New York: Oxford University Press, 2012), 58.

204 Chinese-themed songs: Michael Saffle, "Eastern Fantasies on Western Stages: Chinese-Themed Operettas and Musical Comedies in Turn-of-the-Last-Century London and New York," in Yan Hon-Lun and Michael Saffle, eds., *China and the West: Music, Representation, and Reception* (Ann Arbor: University of Michigan Press, 2017), 87–118 (pp. 91, 97).

204 Heathen Chinee; dreamy summer nights: Krystyn R. Moon, *Yellowface: Creating the Chinese in American Popular Music and*

Performance, 1850s–1920s (New Brunswick, NJ: Rutgers University Press, 2004), 119, 161–162.

204 Tin Pan Alley songs in Cantonese; purity of diction: Moon, 157–158.

204–05 African Americans in yellowface; Irish minstrel performers: Moon, 158, 259.

205 on every block; warrior scholar: Fred Ho, "Bamboo That Snaps Back! Resistance and Revolution in Asian Pacific American Working-Class and Left-Wing Expressive Culture," in Diane C. Fujino, ed., *Wicked Theory, Naked Practice: A Fred Ho Reader* (Minneapolis: University of Minnesota Press, 2009), 247–269 (pp. 251–253).

205 detained for several weeks: Cyrus R. K. Patell, *Emergent US Literatures: From Multiculturalism to Cosmopolitanism in the Late-Twentieth Century* (New York: New York University Press, 2014), 82.

205 You don't uphold justice: translation in Patell, 83.

205 A weak nation: translation in Patell, 83.

205 classical verse forms; commoners: Steven G. Yao, "Transplantation and Modernity: The Chinese/American Poems of Angel Island," in Eric Hayot, Haun Saussy, and Steven G. Yao, eds., *Sinographies: Writing China* (Minneapolis: University of Minnesota Press, 2007), 300–329 (pp. 300, 310).

206 In the quiet of night: translation in Judy Yung, "'A Bowlful of Tears': Chinese Women Immigrants on Angel Island," *Frontiers: A Journal of Women Studies* 2, no. 2 (Summer 1977): 52–55 (p. 52).

206 American laws are fierce: translation in Marlon Kau Hom, "Some Cantonese Folksongs on the American Experience," *Western Folklore* 42, no. 2 (April 1983): 126–139 (p. 132).

206 *muk-yu go*: Ho, 254.

206 A transient: translation in Marlon Kau Hom, *Songs of Gold Mountain: Cantonese Rhymes from San Francisco Chinatown* (Berkeley: University of California Press, 1987), 90.

206 How was I to know: translation in Hom, "Some Cantonese Folksongs," 134.

207 We were married: translation in Hom, "Some Cantonese Folksongs," 135.

207 Detained: translation in Yung, 52.

207 the Hispanic David: Norm Cohen, *American Folk Songs: A Regional Encyclopedia* (Westport, CT: Greenwood Press, 2008), II, 528.

207–08 intelligence and courage; stupidity and cowardice; In the ranch corral: translation and commentary in Patell, 56–57.

208 the collective voice: Sarah M. Rudd, "Harmonizing Corrido and Union Song at the Ludlow Massacre," *Western Folklore* 61, no. 1 (Spring 2002): 21–42 (p. 29).

208 primarily as a mestizo cultural form: John H. McDowell, *Poetry and Violence: The Ballad Tradition of Mexico's Costa Chica* (Urbana: University of Illinois Press, 2008), 26.

208 Mexican strength of resistance: Zena Moore, "Post-Colonial Influences in Spanish Diaspora: Christian Doctrine and the Depiction of Women in Tejano Border Songs and Calypso," *Counterpoints* 96 (1999): 215–233 (p. 222).

208 Five hundred steers: translation of "*Kiansis II*," in María Herrera-Sobek, *Northward Bound: The Mexican Immigrant Experience in Ballad and Song* (Bloomington: Indiana University Press, 1993), 9.

209 Oh my beloved countrymen: translation of "*El Deportado*," in Patell, 59.

209 two million; ten million; thirteen million: Campbell Gibson and Emily Lennon, *Historical Census Statistics on the Foreign-Born Population of the United States, 1850 to 1900* (Washington, DC: US Bureau of the Census, 1999): www.census.gov/history/pdf/1910foreignbornpop.pdf.

209 Last night as I lay a-sleeping: Thomas Hoier and Jimmie Morgan, "Don't Bite the Hand That's Feeding You" (1915), Library of Congress, Historic Sheet Music Collection, 1800–1922: https://loc.gov/item/ihas.100007833.

210 Father was so Yankee hearted: George M. Cohan, "Yankee Doodle Boy," and commentary in Dizikes, 373–374.

210 Platt Amendment: Ruiz, 663.

210 If those possessions: *US Reports*, *Downes* v. *Bidwell*, 182 US 244 (1901), 287, 345, Library of Congress: https://tile.loc.gov/storage-services/service/ll/usrep/usrep182/usrep182244/usrep182244.

211 Damn you [anathema to you]: Katherine Reed, "'The Prison, By God, Where I Have Found Myself': Graffiti at Ellis Island Immigration Station, New York, c. 1900–1923," *Journal of American Ethnic History* 38, no. 3 (Spring 2019): 5–35 (p. 19).

211 Anastasios Karatzias: translation in Reed, 21.

211 anti-Oriental riots; from the Punjab: Raymond Brad Williams, "Asian Indian and Pakistani Religions in the United States," *Annals of the American Academy of Political and Social Science* 558 (July 1998): 178–195 (p. 184).

211 mass exodus; 100,000 Armenians; songs of despair and hope; I have left my vineyards: translation of Nahabed Kouchag, "*Bantookhd Ar Groong*" (The Migrant to the Crane) and commentary, in Jerry Silverman, *Immigrant Songbook* (Pacific, MO: Mel Bay Publications, 2008), 17.

211 Tell me, white cloud: translation of "*Ya Kazhi Mi, Oblache Le Byalo*" (Tell Me, White Cloud), in Silverman, 20.

212 I came to that America: translation of "*W zelaznej fabryce*" (In the Steel Mill), in James P. Leary, *Folksongs of Another America: Field Recordings from the Upper Midwest, 1937–1946* (Madison, and Atlanta, GA: University Wisconsin Press and Dust-to-Digital, 2015), 153.

212 the hard economic situation; God damn the noble lords: translation of Hungarian emigrant song from Cigánd village, Bodrogköz region, with commentary in Béla Gunda, "America in the Hungarian Folk Tradition," *Journal of American Folklore* 83, no. 330 (October-December 1970): 406–416 (pp. 406, 408).

212 America is the land: translation in Helen Ware, "American-Hungarian Folk-Song," *Musical Quarterly* 2, no. 3 (July 1916): 434–444 (p. 440).

212 Why did I come: translation in Ware, 438.

212–13 God save America: translation in Gunda, 406.

213 God save America forever: translation in Max Paul Friedman, "Beyond 'Voting with Their Feet': Toward a Conceptual History of 'America' in European Migrant Sending Communities, 1860s to 1914," *Journal of Social History* 40, no. 3 (Spring 2007): 557–575 (p. 566).

213 Ah, my God: translation of Andrew Kovaly, "In the American Land" (1900), on Pete Seeger, *American Industrial Ballads* (Smithsonian Folkways, 1992), Track 10.

213–14 Lithuanian choirs; I came to tell you: Danuté Petrauskaité, "Lithuanian Music in America, 1870–1920," *Journal of Baltic Studies* 31, no. 1 (Spring 2000): 60–79 (pp. 65–67, 75).

214 *Sängerfest*; Germanness; *die Heimat*: Christopher G. Ogburn, "Brews, Brotherhood, and Beethoven: The 1865 New York City *Sängerfest* and the Fostering of German American Identity," *American Music* 33, no. 4 (Winter 2015): 405–444 (pp. 405–406).

214 German socialist workers' choirs; extolled the socialist color red: Heike Bungert, "The Singing Festivals of German Americans, 1849–1914," *American Music* 34, no. 2 (Summer 2016): 141–179 (p. 159).

214 The times are grave: translation of Carl Sahm, "*Arbeiter Bundeslied*," in Bungert, 159–160.

214 Fritz Van Vonderblinkenstoffen; beer-drinking and sauerkraut-eating: Timothy Wise, "Lullabies, Laments, and Ragtime Cowboys: Yodeling at the Turn of the Twentieth Century," *American Music* 26, no. 1 (Spring 2008): 13–36 (pp. 14, 17).

215 "Handsome"? Who: Frank Wilson, "The German's Arrival" (1906): Victor recording, Library of Congress, National Jukebox: www.loc.gov/jukebox.

215 most successful; steps to Americanization; migration; nostalgia: John Koegel, "Adolf Philipp and Ethnic Musical Comedy in New York's Little Germany," *American Music* 24, no. 3 (Autumn 2006): 267–319 (pp. 270, 284).

215 We stop to think: translation of Adolf Philipp, "Heimathlied," in Koegel, 280.

215 *Volksstücke*: Sabine Haenni, *The Immigrant Scene: Ethnic Amusements in New York, 1880–1920* (Minneapolis: University of Minnesota Press, 2008), 69–70.

215 assimilated, secular German Jew: Koegel, 293.

216 a specifically Jewish *Volksstück*: Haenni, 72.

216 struggling, persevering Jewish characters; varying degrees of Germerican: Koegel, 293.

216 With an ease: Irving Howe, *World of Our Fathers: The Journey of the East European Jews to America and the Life They Found and Made* (New York: Simon & Schuster, 1976), 229.

216 original alumni and those influenced by them: Jack Gottlieb, *Funny, It Doesn't Sound Jewish: How Yiddish Songs and Synagogue Melodies Influenced Tin Pan Alley, Broadway, and Hollywood* (Albany: State University of New York Press, 2004), *passim*.

216–17 a complete government ban: Irene Heskes, *Passport to Jewish Music: Its History, Traditions, and Culture* (Westport, CT: Greenwood Press, 1994), 139.

217 earliest Yiddish song publication: Heskes, 136, 144 n. 4.

217 more than five hundred injured: Lawrence J. Epstein, *At the Edge of a Dream: The Story of Jewish Immigrants on New York's Lower East Side, 1880–1920* (San Francisco: John Wiley & Sons, 2007), 11.

217 The anti-Jewish riots in Kishinev: *New York Times*, April 28, 1903, quoted in Epstein, 11.

217 Library of Congress database: Library of Congress, Yiddish American Popular Sheet Music: www.loc.gov/collections/yiddish-american-popular-sheet-music.

217 Brothers of the free states: translation of Solomon Smulewitz, "*A brivele fun rusland*," with commentary, in Mark Slobin, *Tenement Songs: The Popular Music of the Jewish Immigrants* (Urbana: University of Illinois Press, 1996), 152–153, formatting adjusted.

218 arms thrown wide; Jews, for the love of mercy; People wept: Stella Adler and Lulla Rosenfeld quoted in Slobin, 6.

218 There is a fire in Kishinev: translation of untitled lament in Ruth Rubin, *Voices of a People: The Story of Yiddish Folksong* (New York: McGraw-Hill, 1973), 220.

218 the first theatrical union: Michael Tilson Thomas, *The Thomashefskys: Music and Memories of a Life in the Yiddish Theater*, dir. Gary Halvorson (New York: WNET/Thomashefsky Film Project, 2012).

218 O women, women, women: translation of Herman Wohl and Arnold Perlmutter, "*Vayber, makht mir president*," in Slobin, 131, formatting adjusted.

218–19 Slave of need: translation of Nahum Rakow, Isidore Lillian, and Joseph Rumshinsky, "*Weh dir kind von armuth*," Library of Congress, Yiddish American Popular Sheet Music: www.loc.gov/item/ihas.200182190/.

219 What a lady is Chantshe: translation of Rakow, Lillian, and Rumshinsky, "Chantshe in America," Library of Congress, Yiddish American Popular Sheet Music: www.loc.gov/item/ihas.200182187.

219 successful formula; a woman disguised: Tilson Thomas, *The Thomashefskys*.

219 Leo Frank; miscarriage of justice; posthumous pardon: Robert Seitz Frey and Nancy C. Thompson, with Foreword by John Seigenthaler, *The Silent and the Damned: The Murder of Mary Phagan and the Lynching of Leo Frank* (New York: Cooper Square Press, 2002), xv–xvii and *passim.*

220 Carson's performances: Peter La Chapelle, *I'd Fight the World: A Political History of Old-Time, Hillbilly, and Country Music* (Chicago: University of Chicago Press, 2019), 27.

220 She fell upon her knees: Fiddlin' John Carson, "Little Mary Phagan," in Cohen, *American Folk Songs*, I, 314.

220 Long life to Columbus: translation of Boris Thomashefsky, "*Leben Sol Columbus!*" in Jane Peppler, *Yiddish Penny Songs: Tenement Song Broadsides of Theater and Variety Show Songs, 1895–1925*: www.yiddishpennysongs.com/2015/09/lebn-zol-kolumbus-aka-leben-sol.html.

220 wasn't recorded until 1925: Tony Russell, *Rural Rhythm: The Story of Old-Time Country Music in 78 Records* (New York: Oxford University Press, 2021), 17.

220 Anti-Defamation League: Deborah Dash Moore, *B'nai B'rith and the Challenge of Ethnic Leadership* (Albany: State University of New York Press, 1981), 108.

221 never again to publish: Charles Hamm, *Irving Berlin: Songs from the Melting Pot: The Formative Years, 1907–1914* (New York: Oxford University Press, 1997), 39.

221 *macchietta*; *macchiette coloniali*: Isabella Livorni, "'*Parla Comme T'Ha Fatta Memmeta*'? Identity Formation through Sonic Code-Switching in 1920s Italian American Song," *Italian American Review* 9, no. 1 (Winter 2019): 26–48 (p. 34).

221 a blend of fourteenth-century Italian harlequin: Deanna Paoli Gumina, "*Connazionali*, Stenterello, and Farfariello: Italian Variety Theater in San Francisco," *California Historical Quarterly* 54, no. 1 (Spring 1975): 27–36 (p. 33).

222 At night court: translation of Eduardo Migliaccio, "*Portame' a casa mia*," in Michael La Sorte, *La Merica: Images of Italian Greenhorn Experience* (Philadelphia: Temple University Press, 1985), 174.

222 *la torre di Babele*; *Nuova Yorca*; *l'America*: Nancy N. Carnevale, *A New Language, a New World: Italian Immigrants in the United States, 1890–1945* (Urbana: University of Illinois Press, 2009), 120.

222 I follow my destiny: in Burton D. Fisher, ed., *Puccini's Madama Butterfly* (Miami, FL: Opera Journeys Publishing, 2005), 53.

222 I have caught you: in Fisher, 59.

222 the Yankee: Fisher, 17.

222 "The Star-Spangled Banner" as leitmotif: Glenn Watkins, *Proof through the Night: Music and the Great War* (Berkeley: University of California Press, 2003), 289.

222–23 George Whitefield Chadwick: Linda B. Fairtile, "'Real Americans Mean Much More': Race, Ethnicity, and Authenticity in Belasco's *Girl of the Golden West* and Puccini's *La Fanciulla Del West*," *Studi Pucciniani: Rassegna sull musica e sul teatro musicale nell'epoca di Giacomo Puccini*, ed. Leo S. Olsche (Firenze: Centro Studi Giacomo Puccini, 2010): 89–101 *passim.*

223 a jailbird from Trapani: George Whitfield Chadwick, *The Padrone*, ed. Marianne Betz (Middleton, WI: A-R Editions, Inc., 2017), 333.

223 hopelessness of the Italians: Marianne Betz, in Chadwick, xxx.

223 There is no Castello Sant'Angelo: Betz, in Chadwick, xlii.

223 *The Padrone* with its realistic lower class story: Marianne Betz, "American Women as Opera Figures: *Puccini's Fanciulla del West* versus Chadwick's Marietta in *The Padrone*," *Journal of the American Music Research Center* 12 (2002): 1–9 (p. 6).

11 We Are Many

224 Hail the waist makers: Untitled ode in Elizabeth Ewen, *Immigrant Women* (New York: New York University Press/ Monthly Review Press, 1985), 256.

224 I looked upon: Quoted in Ewen, 260.

225 Woe unto you: translation of Joseph Rumshinsky and Anshel Shor, "*Mamenyu!*" (1911), in Mark Slobin, *Tenement Songs: The Popular Music of the Jewish Immigrants* (Urbana: University of Illinois Press, 1996), 134, formatting adjusted.

226 combining cantorial training: Slobin, 25.

226 I shall sing: translation of Arturo Giovannitti, "New York and I," in Marcella Bencivenni, *Italian Immigrant Radical Culture: The Idealism of the Sovversivi in the United States, 1899–1940* (New York: New York University Press, 2011), 162.

226 The world of to-day: Jenkin D. Resse, "Welcome, Mother Jones," in George Korson, *Coal Dust on the Fiddle: Songs and Stories of the Bituminous Industry* (Hatboro, PA: Folklore Associates, Inc., 1965 [1943]), 348.

226–27 into Union Headquarters: Mother Jones quoted in William Loren Katz and Laurie R. Lehmen, eds., *The Cruel Years: American Voices at the Dawn of the Twentieth Century* (Boston: Beacon Press, 2003), 10–11.

227 earliest and most unlikely hits: Archie Green, *The Death of Mother Jones: How a Labor Union Song Became a Folksong* (Urbana: University of Illinois Press, 1960), 1–15 *passim.*

227 The working class: Preamble to I. W. W. Constitution, in Joyce Kornbluh, ed., *Rebel Voices: An IWW Anthology* (Oakland, CA: PM Press, 2011), 12.

227 This world should have: Ralph Chaplin, "That Sabo-Tabby Kitten," in Archie Green, David Roediger, Franklin Rosemont, and Salvatore Salerno, eds., *The Big Red Songbook* (Chicago: Charles H. Kerr, 2007), 155–156.

228 the union's first African American organizer; affiliated unions: Paul Garon and Gene Tomko, *What's the Use of Walking if There's a Freight Train Going Your Way?: Black Hoboes and Their Songs* (Chicago: Charles H. Kerr Publishing Co., 2006), 200.

228 racism was practical; in general: Howard Zinn, *A People's History of the United States* (New York: HarperCollins, 2005), 328–329.

228 mission; women, blacks: David King Dunaway and Molly Beer, *Singing Out: An Oral History of America's Folk Music Revivals* (New York: Oxford University Press, 2010), 37.

228 I was riding one day: Paul Walker, "A Wobbly Good and True," in Garon and Tomko, 201, formatting adjusted.

229 hell-raisers: Franklin Rosemont, "Lost and Found: Other IWW Songs and Poems," in Green et al., *Big Red Songbook*: 13–22 (p. 15).

229 In 1909: Archie Green, Preface, *Big Red Songbook*, 4.

229 A pamphlet: Joe Hill quoted in Gibbs Smith, *Joe Hill* (Layton, UT: Peregrine Smith, 1969), 19.

229 risked capital punishment: Bencivenni, 155–156.

229–30 all the oppressed; An agonizing and desperate wail: translation of Efrem Bartoletti, "*I Ribelli del Minnesota*," and commentary in Thierry Rinaldetti, "Efrem Bartoletti in the Mesabi Range: A Wobbly's Efforts to Mobilize Immigrant Italian Miners," *Italian American Review* 5, no. 1: 1–26 (p. 11).

230 engaged with the vibrant; derivations: Gary Kaunonen, *Flames of Discontent: The 1916 Minnesota Iron Ore Strike* (Minneapolis: University of Minnesota Press, 2017), 99–100.

230 various editions: Bucky Halker, "Tramp, Tramp, Tramp: The Songs of Joe Hill around the World," in Peter Cole, David Struthers, and Kenyon Zimmer, eds., *Wobblies of the World: A Global History of the IWW* (London: Pluto Press, 2017), 288–298 (p. 292).

230 In 1911: Halker, "Tramp, Tramp, Tramp," 290.

230 Since the late nineteenth century: John Ilmari Kolehmainen, "The Finnish Pioneers of Minnesota," *Minnesota History* 25, no. 4 (December 1944): 317–328 (p. 319).

230 Around the turn of the century: Anne Heimo, "The Italian Hall Tragedy, 1913: A Hundred Years of Remediated Memories," in Tea Sindbæk Andersen and Barbara Törnquist-Plewa, eds., *The Twentieth Century in European Memory: Transcultural Mediation and Reception* (Leiden: Brill Publishing, 2017), 240–267 (p. 246).

230 utopias: Carl Ross, "The Utopian Vision of Finnish Immigrants, 1900–30," *Scandinavian Studies* 60, no. 4 (Autumn 1988): 481–496 (p. 482).

231 "*Kalevala*"; Better dwell: Marjorie Edgar, "Finnish Folk Songs in Minnesota," *Minnesota History* 16, no. 3 (September 1935): 319–321 (p. 320); "*Kalevala*" quoted in Kolehmainen, 322.

231 historical tales: Heimo, 240.

231 massacre; What happened: Ella Reeve Bloor, *We Are Many: An Autobiography* (New York: International Publishers, 1940), 123–124.

231 Citizens Alliance; management ally: Steve Lehto, *Death's Door: The Truth behind Michigan's Largest Mass Murder* (Troy, MI: Momentum Books, 2013), *passim.*

231–32 post-mortem; description; copper-boss thug men: Woody Guthrie, "1913 Massacre," on Guthrie, *Struggle* (Smithsonian Folkways, 1990 [1941]), Track 12; Daniel Wolff, *Grown-Up Anger: The Connected Mysteries of Bob Dylan, Woody Guthrie, and the Calumet Massacre of 1913* (New York: Harper Collins, 2017), 16.

232 Song to Woody: Bob Dylan, "Song to Woody," on *Bob Dylan* (Sony Legacy CD, 2006 [1962]), Track 12.

232 They were all very worried: Bloor, 132.

232 the twisted bodies; sixty-six: Zinn, *People's History of the United States*, 355–356.

233 Ludlow Massacre: Woody Guthrie, "Ludlow Massacre," on *Struggle*, Track 11.

233 I'd been a shipyard worker: Howard Zinn on Deb Ellis and Denis Mueller, *Howard Zinn: You Can't Be Neutral on a Moving Train* (First Run Features documentary, 2010).

233 the culminating act: Howard Zinn, *The Politics of History* (Urbana: University of Illinois Press, 1990), 79.

233 the solidarity: Archaeologist Mark Walker quoted in Sarah M. Rudd, "Harmonizing Corrido and Union Song at the Ludlow Massacre," *Western Folklore* 61, no. 1 (Spring 2002): 21–42 (p. 37).

233 Who knows what deeds: "Louis Tikas, Ludlow Martyr," in Korson, *Coal Dust on the Fiddle*, 390–391.

234 the son; Baca vividly recalled: Rudd, 23–24.

234 The Mother Jones Riot: Rudd, 22.

234–35 From West Virginia came: translation of Elias Baca, "*¡Que viva la nación!*" in Rudd, 31–32.

235 John D: Alfred Hayes and Earl Robinson, "Ludlow Massacre," in Alan Lomax, Woody Guthrie, and Pete Seeger, eds., *Hard Hitting Songs for Hard-Hit People* (New York: Oak Publications, 1967), 333.

235 I dreamed: Alfred Hayes and Earl Robinson, "Joe Hill," in Pete Seeger and Rob Reiser, *Carry It On! A History in Song and Picture of the Working Men and Women of America* (Poole, UK: Blandford Press, 1986), 111.

235–36 Already enshrined: William M. Adler, *The Man Who Never Died: The Life, Times, and Legacy of Joe Hill, American Labor Icon* (New York: Bloomsbury USA, 2011), 314.

236 Good bye Bill; Good bye, Joe: Joe Hill and "Big Bill" Haywood quoted in Adler, 13.

236 Kids don't have: Bruce "Utah" Phillips, on Robert Shetterly, *Americans Who Tell the Truth*: www.americanswhotellthetruth .org/portraits/bruce-utah-phillips.

236 My heart: Dorothy Parker, "A Musical Comedy Thought," quoted in Michael Bronski, *A Queer History of the United States* (Boston: Beacon Press, 2011), 114.

236 the models; sexual virility; swells: Gilliam M. Rodger, *Just One of the Boys: Female-to-Male Cross-Dressing on the American Variety Stage* (Urbana: University of Illinois Press, 2018), 37; Gillian Rodger, "'He Isn't a Marrying Man': Gender and Sexuality in the Repertoire of Male Impersonators, 1870–1930," in Sophie Fuller and Lloyd Whitesell, eds., *Queer Episodes in Music and Modern*

Identity (Urbana: University of Illinois Press, 2002), 105–133 (pp. 112, 114).

236 Lovely woman: J. F. Mitchell, "Hi Waiter! A Dozen More Bottles," quoted in Rodger, *Just One of the Boys*, 43.

237 William Dorsey Swann: Channing Gerard Joseph, "The First Drag Queen Was a Former Slave." *The Nation*, January 31, 2020: www.thenation.com/article/society/drag-queen-slave-ball.

237 the popularity of female impersonation: Barry Reay, *Trans America: A Counter History* (New York: Polity Press, 2020), n. p. (e-book).

237 Eltinge had become so popular: Mark Berger, *The Julian Eltinge Project* (2005): www.julianeltingeproject.com.

237 walked a fine line; booking agents: Nan Alamilla Boyd, *Wide Open Town: A History of Queer San Francisco to 1965* (Berkeley: University of California Press, 2003), 33–34.

237–38 indecent; impure; marriage relation: Michael Helquist, "'Lewd, Obscene and Indecent': The 1916 Portland Edition of *Family Limitation*," *Oregon Historical Quarterly* 117, no. 2 (2016): 274–287 (p. 277).

238 radical version; Hard is the fortunes: "The Wagoner's Lad" and commentary in Dick Weissman, *A New History of American and Canadian Folk Music* (New York: Bloomsbury Academic, 2020), 40.

238 She's only a bird: Arthur J. Lamb and Harry Von Tilzer, "A Bird in a Gilded Cage," in John W. Finson, *The Voices That Are Gone: Themes in 19th-Century American Popular Song* (New York: Oxford University Press, 1997), 74.

238 A ballot for the Lady: Charlotte Perkins Gilman, "Another Star," in Gilman, *Suffrage Songs and Verses* (New York: The Charlton Company, 1911), 23–24.

238 Not for self: Gilman, "Song for Equal Suffrage," *Suffrage Songs and Verses*, 22–23.

238 The great Aunt Susan: Gilman, "The Women Are Coming!" in *The Complete Poetry of Charlotte Perkins Gilman, 1884–1935*, ed. Jacquelyn K. Markham (Lewiston, NY: Edwin Mellen Press, 2014), 443.

239 Smash windows: Lillian Nordica quoted in John Dizikes, *Opera in America: A Cultural History* (New Haven, CT: Yale University Press, 1993), 306.

239 When motherlove: Gilman, "Peace to the World" (1913), *Complete Poetry*, 439.

240 Some time ago: Joe Hill, "Stung Right" (1913), *Big Red Songbook*, 120.

240 the gold; Mammon's altar; We're spending: Joe Hill, "Should I Ever Be a Soldier" (1913), *Big Red Songbook*, 111.

240 cabin; little girl; Her mother: Joe Hill, "Don't Take My Papa Away from Me" (1915), *Big Red Songbook*, 172–173.

240 an enormous vogue; more than 700,000: Glenn Watkins, *Proof through the Night: Music and the Great War* (Berkeley: University of California Press, 2003), 249.

240–41 I didn't raise my boy: Alfred Bryan and Al Piantadosi, "I Didn't Raise My Boy to Be a Soldier," in Jon Meacham and Tim McGraw, *Songs of America: Patriotism, Protest, and the Music that Made a Nation* (New York: Random House, 2019), 112.

241 Don't take: Will Dillon and Albert Von Tilzer, "Don't Take My Darling Boy Away" (1915), Library of Congress, World War I Sheet Music Collection: www.loc.gov/item/2013569497.

241 Wake up: George Graff, Jr., and Jack Glogau, "Wake Up, America!" (1916), in Lester S. Levy, *Give Me Yesterday: American History in Song 1890–1920* (Norman: University of Oklahoma Press, 1975), 136–137.

241 Let America: John Philip Sousa quoted in Patrick Warfield, "Profitable Patriotism: John Philip Sousa and the Great War," in William Brooks, Christina Bashford, and Gayle Magee, eds., *Over Here, Over There: Transatlantic Conversations on the Music of World War I* (Urbana: University of Illinois Press, 2019): 73–96 (p. 78).

241 Parodies: Nicholas Slonimsky, *Slonimsky's Book of Musical Anecdotes* (New York: Routledge, 2013 [1948]), 75.

242 turmoil; In the name: Meacham and McGraw, 112.

242 Mother, shed: James Weldon Johnson, "The Young Warrior," quoted in William Brooks, "Of Stars, Soldiers, Mothers, and Mourning," *Over Here, Over There*, 199–223 (p. 478).

242 for an Italian war benefit: Jean E. Snyder, *Harry T. Burleigh: From the Spiritual to the Harlem Renaissance* (Urbana: University of Illinois Press, 2016), 283.

242 The irony: Brooks, "Of Stars," 478.

242 Battle birds: Harry T. Burleigh, "One Year: 1914–1915," libretto by Margaret M. Harlan (London: G. Ricordi & Co., 1916).

242 Under a Blazing Star: Snyder, 286.

243 Is it Hindenburg: Al Dubin, Joseph Burke, and George B. McConnell, "The Hero of the European War," in Levy, *Give Me Yesterday*, 135.

243 continued to conduct: Watkins, 309.

243 counterargument to neutrality: Gayle Magee, "'Every Man in New York': Charles Ives and the First World War," in Brooks et al., *Over Here, Over There*, 37–57 (pp. 38, 50).

243 I have had many triumphs: John Philip Sousa quoted in Warfield, 89.

243 I can see: Clyde B. Wilson, "'The Stars and Stripes Forever' Played by Sousa in Berlin" (1919), in Warfield, 89–90.

243–44 In the end: Jill Lepore, *These Truths: A History of the United States* (New York: W. W. Norton & Co., 2019), 393–394.

244 America, I raised: Andrew B. Sterling and Arthur Lange, "America, Here's My Boy," in Levy, 138.

244 It's Time for Every Boy: Ronald D. Cohen and Will Kaufman, *Singing for Peace: Antiwar Songs in American History* (New York: Routledge, 2015), 24.

244 the most effective morale song: Dizikes, 374.

244 German propaganda; In March 1918: Brian Holder, "Americanization as a Cure for Bolshevism: Anti-Revolutionary Popular Song in 1919," *American Music* 25, no. 3 (Fall 2007): 334–352 (pp. 338–339).

244–45 Songs like: Danny O. Crew, *Presidential Sheet Music: An Illustrated Catalog* (Jefferson, NC: McFarland & Co., 2001), 251, 256.

245 What you gonna do: Blind Lemon Jefferson, "Wartime Blues" (1926), on Jefferson, *Dry Southern Blues: 1925–1929 Recordings* (Soul Jam Records, 2018), Disc 1, Track 14.

245 Red Cross Sto'; rich man's show: Lead Belly, "Red Cross Store Blues," in Timothy E. Scheurer, *Born in the USA: The Myth of America in Popular Music from Colonial Times to the Present* (Jackson: University Press of Mississippi, 1991), 141; Jeff Place, *Lead Belly: The Smithsonian Folkways Collection*, accompanying text (Washington, DC: Smithsonian Folkways Recordings, 2015), n. p.

245 Ev'ry time I try: Eldon B. Spofford, "Those Navy Blues" (1917), in Peter C. Muir, *Long Lost Blues: Popular Blues in America, 1850–1920* (Urbana: University of Illinois Press, 2010), 46.

245 done carried poor John: Jimmie Marten and Mitch Le Blanc, "War Bride Blues" (1917), in Muir, 46.

245 Send a lot of jazz bands: Irving Berlin, "Send a Lot of Jazz Bands Over There" (1918), in Jeffrey Magee, "From the Great War to *White Christmas*: The Long Reach of Irving Berlin's *Yip Yip Yaphank*," in Brooks et al., eds. *Over Here, Over There*: 97–114 (p. 105).

245 I've got a grave-diggin' feelin': "Grave Diggers," in John Jacob Niles, *Singing Soldiers* (New York: Charles Scribner's Sons, 1927), 132.

245 Diggin', diggin', diggin': "Diggin'," in Niles, 30.

246 France taught me: Eugene Bullard quoted in Craig Lloyd, *Eugene Bullard: Black Expatriate in Jazz-Age Paris* (Athens: University of Georgia Press, 2006), 140.

247 Alert, gas: James Reese Europe and Noble Sissle, "On Patrol in No Man's Land" (1918), in Watkins, 320.

247 All dese colored soldiers: "Deep Sea Blues," in Niles, 99.

247 Jined de army: "Lordy, Turn Your Face," in Niles, 50.

247 I want to go home: "Going Home Song," in Niles, 3.

247 If you want to know: "I'll Tell You Where They Were," in Edward Arthur Dolph, *"Sound Off!" Soldier Songs from the Revolution to World War II* (New York: Farrar & Rinehart, Inc., 1942), 87–88.

248 When your lungs: "When the Guns Are Rolling Yonder," in Watkins, 267.

248 white, Black, and Muskogee: Roxanne Dunbar-Ortiz, *An Indigenous People's History of the United States* (Boston: Beacon Press, 2014), 166–167.

248 Big Chief put his war-paint on: Alfred Bryan, Edgar Leslie, and Maurice Abrahams, "Big Chief Killa Hun," in Michael A. Amundson, *Talking Machine West: A History and Catalogue of Tin Pan Alley's Western Recordings, 1902–1918* (Norman: University of Oklahoma Press, 2017), 184–185.

248–49 Fewer than 25 years: William K. Powers, *The Lakota Warrior Tradition: Three Essays on Lakotas at War* (Kendall Park, NJ: Lakota Books, 2001), 32.

249 As Lakota soldiers; some tribes declared: John W. Troutman, *Indian Blues: American Indians and the Politics of Music, 1879–1934* (Norman: University of Oklahoma Press, 2012), 54.

249 revised to fit the new context: Linda Scarangella McNenly, *Native Performers in Wild West Shows: From Buffalo Bill to Euro Disney* (Norman: University of Oklahoma Press, 2015), 80.

249 *Eya ica wan maucanze ca*: Lakota war song, in Troutman, 54.

249 *Tehatan natanpe lo*: Lakota war song, in Troutman, 54–55.

249 directly to the maintenance; These can be seen: Clyde Ellis, email to author, May 14, 2018.

250 close to 14,000 song titles: Library of Congress, World War I Sheet Music Collection: www.loc.gov/collections/world-war-i-sheet-music/about-this-collection.

250 swords and shields: "Down by the Riverside" / "Study War No More," in Cohen and Kaufman, 22.

250 He gave his life: Harry Hamilton and Ed Thomas, "The Boys Who Won't Come Home" (1919), in Cohen and Kaufman, 25–26.

250 A mother old: Lora Starret and Leo Friedman, "Star of Gold" (1919), in Brooks, "Of Stars," 215.

250 to all those: Snyder 286–287.

250 Ten million men: "The Creed of the Ku Klux Klan" (Written by A. Klansman for The Klan) (c. 1923), in Danny O. Crew, *Ku Klux Klan Sheet Music: An Illustrated Catalog of Published Music, 1867–2002* (Jefferson, NC: McFarland & Co., 2003), 38.

12 100% American

251 anti-Asian attacks: Kimmy Yam, "Biden Signs Memorandum to Combat Bias Incidents toward Asian Americans," NBC News, January 26, 2021: www.nbcnews.com/news/asian-america/biden-signs-executive-order-combat-bias-incidents-toward-asian-americans-n1255713.

251 the Naples Soldier: Kenneth C. Davis, *More Deadly than War: The Hidden History of Spanish Flu and the First World War* (New York: Henry Holt & Co., 2018), 51.

251 The Hun; The Germs: Quoted in Deniz Ertan, "The Beginning of the End of Something," in William Brooks, Christina Bashford, and Gayle Magee, eds., *Over Here, Over There: Transatlantic Conversations on the Music of World War I* (Urbana: University of Illinois Press, 2019), 224–244 (p. 225).

251 But the world: Nora Bayes, Sam Downing, and Abe Glatt, "The Man Who Put the Germ in Germany" (1918), in Ertan, 232.

251 A considerable number: *New York Times*, quoted in Davis, 50–51.

252 literary output: Alice Vincent, "Will We Ever Be Ready for the Covid-19 Novel?," Penguin Books *Features*, July 7, 2020: www.penguin.co.uk/articles/2020/july/covid-fiction-pandemic-corona-literature.html.

252 As an intrinsically American: Ertan, 233.

252 After the twin: Davis, 204.

252–53 eminent musicians and conductors; Watt; De Valdor: Ertan, 229.

253 an aria from *La Traviata*: Alfred W. Crosby, *America's Forgotten Pandemic: The Influenza of 1918* (New York: Cambridge University Press, 2003), 93.

253 confident that a vaccine; Singing conductors: Catherine Arnold, *Pandemic 1918: Eyewitness Accounts from the Greatest Medical Holocaust in Modern History* (New York: St. Martin's Griffin, 2018), 116–117.

253 the stilling of song: Crosby, 111–112.

253 an old spiritual: Katherine Anne Porter, *Pale Horse, Pale Rider* (New York: The Modern Library, 1939), 240.

254 undermine immigrant; This reactionary movement: Paul Ortiz, *An African American and LatinX History of the United States* (Boston: Beacon Press, 2018), 128.

254 Red Summer: Cameron McWhirter, *Red Summer: The Summer of 1919 and the Awakening of Black America* (New York: Henry Holt & Co., 2011); Robert Whitaker, *On the Laps of Gods: The Red Summer of 1919 and the Struggle for Justice that Remade a Nation* (New York: Crown Publishers, 2008).

254 newly minted public enemy; Several song publishers: Brian Holder, "Americanization as a Cure for Bolshevism: Anti-Revolutionary Popular Song in 1919," *American Music* 25, no. 3 (Fall 2007): 334–352 (p. 340).

254 You can tell him; It's not a melody: Irving Berlin, "Look Out for the Bolsheviki Man" and "That Revolutionary Rag," in Holder, 344, 346.

254 Red's the color: Ralph Chaplin and Elmer Rumbaugh, "Paint 'Er Red," in Archie Green et al., eds. *The Big Red Songbook* (Chicago: Charles H. Kerr, 2007), 157.

255 No farewells: "Bisbee!" in Norm Cohen, *American Folk Songs: A Regional Encyclopedia* (Westport, CT: Greenwood Press, 2008), II, 538–539.

255 We'll remember you: Phillips Russell, "Frank Little," in Green et al., *Big Red Songbook*, 180–181.

255–56 listed the cause: Cohen, *American Folk Songs,* II, 627.

256 memory lane piece; There's a little western city: Loren Roberts, "The Tragedy of Sunset Land," with commentary in Green et al., *Big Red Songbook*, 230.

256 Dutchman polka bands; bulwark; culture loss: Marion Jacobson, *Squeeze This! A Cultural History of the Accordion in America* (Urbana: University of Illinois Press, 2012), 118.

256 combined dialect comedy; Schnitzelbank Song: James P. Leary, "Herr Louie, the Weasel, and the Hungry Five: German American Performers on Midwestern Radio," *Lied und populäre Kultur / Song and Popular Culture* 55 (2010): 101–133 (pp. 103–104, 124).

256 screamingly funny: Kurt Vonnegut, *Palm Sunday* (London: Jonathan Cape, 1991), 182.

257 An Irish boy: Charles Lawlor, "Irish Liberty" (1920), in William H. A. Williams, *'Twas Only an Irishman's Dream: The Image of Ireland and the Irish in American Popular Song Lyrics, 1800–1920* (Urbana: University of Illinois Press, 1996), 188.

257 O, yes, Old Molly: "O No, My Brother," in Danny O. Crew, *Ku Klux Klan Sheet Music: An Illustrated Catalog of Published Music, 1867–2002* (Jefferson, NC: McFarland & Co., 2003), 70.

257 I'm going: "Gone Are the Days," in Crew, *Ku Klux Klan Sheet Music,* 131.

257 My friend used to say: translation of "Nicolo Went to the USA," in Victor Greene, *A Singing Ambivalence: American Immigrants between Old World and New, 1830–1930* (Kent, OH: Kent State University Press, 2004), 87–88.

258 I dreamed a strange dream: translation of "The Disillusioned Immigrant," in Greene, 86. For Mignonette, De Matienzo and De Stefano, see Simona Frasca, "Investigating Gilda Mignonette as a 'Newpolitan' Approach to Popular Culture," in Pellegrino D'Acierno and Stanislao G. Pugliese, eds., *Delirious Naples: A Cultural History of the City of the Sun* (New York: Fordham University Press, 2019): 120–132.

258 America, land of freedom: translation of Isidore Solotarefsky, "*Columbus, ich hob zi dir gur nit*" (1920), Library of Congress, Yiddish American Popular Sheet Music Collection: www.loc.gov/item/ihas.200182380/.

258 Uncle Sam is at war: translation of Morris Goldberg, "*Aza mazel aufin kaizer*" (1918), Library of Congress, Yiddish American Popular Sheet Music Collection: www.loc.gov/item/ihas.200182331/.

258 I bring a letter: translation of Isidore Lillian, "*A grus fun die trenches*" (1918), Library of Congress, Yiddish American Popular Sheet Music Collection: www.loc.gov/item/ihas.200182325/.

258 America, my Uncle Sam: translation of David Meyerowitz, "*Frieden*, our boys are coming back" (1918), Library of Congress, Yiddish American Popular Sheet Music Collection: www.loc.gov/item/ihas.200155189/.

258 Fanny Brice and Sophie Tucker; coon song: Stephanie Vander Wel, *Hillbilly Maidens, Okies, and Cowgirls: Women's Country Music, 1930–1960* (Urbana: University of Illinois Press, 2020), 55.

259 O Jew: "O Jew," in Crew, *Ku Klux Klan Sheet Music*, 70.

259 Ford and Cameron: Quotes from *The International Jew* and contextual discussion in Peter La Chapelle, *I'd Fight the World: A Political History of Old-Time, Hillbilly, and Country Music* (Chicago: University of Chicago Press, 2019), 45.

259 Ford's own highly publicized predilection: Bill C. Malone and Tracey E. W. Laird, *Country Music USA: 50th Anniversary Edition* (Austin: University of Texas Press, 2018), 49.

259 country music for anti-Semitic ends; racist or xenophobic movements: La Chapelle, 60.

259–60 Ludlow St: translation of Michl Kaplan, "Ludlow Street," in Ruth Rubin, *Voices of a People: The Story of Yiddish Folksong* (New York: McGraw-Hill, 1973), 361–362.

260 I was sad: Ballard MacDonald, Billy Rose, and Dave Stamper, "Since Henry Ford Apologized to Me," on *From Avenue A to the Great White Way: Yiddish and American Popular Songs from 1914–1940* (Columbia/Legacy Recordings, 2002), Disc 2, Track 10.

260 Black Cantors: Renee Ghert-Zand, "Yiddisher Black Cantors from 100 Years Ago Rediscovered Thanks to Rare Recording," *The Times*

of Israel, November 1, 2020: www.timesofisrael.com/yiddisher-black-cantors-from-100-years-ago-rediscovered-thanks-to-rare-recording. See also the Henry Sapoznik Research Blog: www.henrysapoznik.com/research-blog.

261 I wander: translation of "*Der eybiker vanderer*" (The Eternal Wanderer), in Mark Slobin, *Tenement Songs: The Popular Music of the Jewish Immigrants* (Urbana: University of Illinois Press, 1996), 151.

261 attempts by restrictionists: Krystyn R. Moon, "On a Temporary Basis: Immigration, Labor Unions, and the American Entertainment Industry, 1880s–1930s," *Journal of American History* 99, no. 3 (December 2012): 771–792 (p. 779).

261 The mingling: Franklin D. Roosevelt quoted in Crystal M. Fleming, *How to Be Less Stupid about Race* (Boston: Beacon Press, 2018), 112–113.

261 South Asians: Raymond Brady Williams, "Asian Indian and Pakistani Regions in the United States," *Annals of the American Academy of Political and Social Science* 558 (July 1998): 178–195 (p. 180).

261 Because they were seen: Moon, "On a Temporary Basis," 781.

261–62 entry permits; detention and deportation; sizable files: Nancy Yunhwa Rao, *Chinatown Opera Theater in North America* (Urbana: University of Illinois Press, 2017), 10–11.

262 parallel fifths: Philip Furia and Michael Lasser, *America's Songs: The Stories behind the Songs of Broadway, Hollywood, and Tin Pan Alley* (New York: Routledge, 2006), 15.

262 *L'Oracolo* and *Turandot*: Rao, 15–16.

262 for example, Lebanese; Maloof, Macksoud; Turkish Armenian: Anne K. Rasmussen, "Made in America: Historical and Contemporary Recordings of Middle Eastern Music in the United States," *Middle East Studies Association Bulletin* 31, no. 2 (December 1997): 158–162 (pp. 158–159).

262 This has had: Peter C. Muir, *Long Lost Blues: Popular Blues in America, 1850–1920* (Urbana: University of Illinois Press, 2010), 3–4.

262 Now, the white bands: Eubie Blake quoted in Ofer Gazit, "Passing Tones: Shifting National, Social, and Musical Borders in Jazz-Age Harlem," *Jazz and Culture* 3, no. 1 (Spring–Summer 2020): 1–21 (p. 8).

263 finger-busting, virtuosic piano solos: Richard Carlin and Ken Bloom, *Eubie Blake: Rags, Rhythm, and Race* (New York: Oxford University Press, 2020), xi.

263 Black Swan Records: Tim Brooks, *Lost Sounds: Blacks and the Birth of the Recording Industry, 1890–1919* (Urbana: University of Illinois Press, 2005), 168.

263 Arise, ye Garvey nation: I. E. Guinn, "Arise, Ye Garvey Nation," in John Greenway, *American Folksongs of Protest* (New York: A. S. Barnes, 1960 [1953]), 108.

263 songs of derision: Theodore van Dam, "The Influence of West African Songs of Derision in the New World," *African Music* 1, no. 1 (1954): 53–56 (p. 53); Zena Moore, "Post-Colonial Influences in Spanish Diaspora: Christian Doctrine and the Depiction of Women in Tejano Border Songs and Calypso," *Counterpoints* 96 (1999): 215–233 (p. 219).

263 special circular; dance evil: Tara Browner, "Ferruccio Busoni and *The Indians' Book*," in Tara Browner and Thomas L. Riis, eds., *Rethinking American Music* (Urbana: University of Illinois Press, 2019), 283–294 (p. 292, n. 7).

263 prime; their tribal identities: John W. Troutman, *Indian Blues: American Indians and the Politics of Music, 1879–1934* (Norman: University of Oklahoma Press, 2012), 67.

264 The melody and the words; wiping out all vestige; Dancing is considered: Thomas F. Johnston, "The Social Background of Eskimo Music in Northwest Alaska," *Journal of American Folklore* 89, no. 354 (October–December 1976): 438–448 (p. 443).

264 Although there was no language: Moon, "On a Temporary Basis," 780–781.

264 Bath Riots; similar affront: David Dorado Romo, *Ringside Seat to a Revolution: An Underground Cultural History of El Paso and Juárez, 1893–1923* (El Paso: Cinco Puntos Press, 2005), 243.

264–65 Brave Nogalians: translation of "*El corrido de Nogales*," with commentary in Cohen, *American Folk Songs*, II, 541–543.

265 In the year of 1923: translation of "*Versos de los betabeleros*" (Verses of the Beet-Field Workers), in María Herrera-Sobek, *Northward Bound: The Mexican Immigrant Experience in Ballad and Song* (Bloomington: Indiana University Press, 1993), 90–91.

266 that which was Mexican; California is beautiful: translation of "*Las pollas de California*" (The Chicks from California), with commentary in Herrera-Sobek, 106–107.

266 All of us want to speak: translation of "*Los Mexicanos que hablan inglés*" (Mexicans Who Speak English), in Herrera-Sobek, 110.

267 Tri-K-Klub: Crew, *Ku Klux Klan Sheet Music*, 216.

267 *Song Book for Women*: Crew, 139.

267 *KKK Katechism*: Crew, 85.

267 Carry me back: "Carry Me Back to Klancraft," in Crew, 117.

267 an important social space: Michael Bronski, *A Queer History of the United States* (Boston: Beacon Press, 2011), 121.

267 a fashion choice: "Melania Trump Jacket: Five Things 'I Don't Care' Could Mean," BBC News Online, June 22, 2018: www.bbc.co.uk/news/world-us-canada-44574499.

268 embodied; self-determination: Andrew L. Erdman, *Queen of Vaudeville: The Story of Eva Tanguay* (Ithaca, NY: Cornell University Press, 2012), 171.

268 Tanguay shortened the original song: Jean Lenox and Harry O. Sutton, "I Don't Care" (1905), Temple University Digital Collections: https://cdm16002.contentdm.oclc.org/digital/collection/p15037coll1/id/2761.

268–69 I don't care: Eva Tanguay, "I Don't Care" (1922), on various artists, *They Stopped the Show* (Audio Fidelity, 2020), Track 6.

269 She delivered her songs; In a country: Jody Rosen, "Vanishing Act: In Search of Eva Tanguay, the First Rock Star," *Slate*, December 1, 2009: www.slate.com/articles/arts/music_box/2009/12/vanishing_act.html.

269 Girls are filling: Jack Stern and William Tracey, "You'd Better Be Nice to Them Now," Library of Congress, Women's Suffrage in Sheet Music: www.loc.gov/item/2017562359.

270 Common fears: Maria Montserrat Feu López, "The US Hispanic Flapper: *Pelonas* and *Flapperismo* in US Spanish-Language Newspapers, 1920–1929," *Studies in American Humor* 1, no. 2 (2015): 192–217 (pp. 193, 210–211).

270 about women as inferior: Moore, 217.

270 Long ago they chose: Atilla the Hun (Raymond Quevedo), "Women Will Rule the World" (1935), on various artists, *Fall of Man: Calypsos on the Human Condition* (Rounder CD, 1999), Track 3.

270 out-earning: Rosen, "Vanishing Act."

270 Ruth Crawford: Judith Tick, *Ruth Crawford Seeger: A Composer's Search for American Music* (New York: Oxford University Press, 1997), 57.

270–71 Florence Price: Rae Linda Brown, *The Heart of a Woman: The Life and Music of Florence B. Price* (Urbana: University of Illinois Press, 2020), 54.

13 We're Up Against It Now

272 Got an airplane: Blind Lemon Jefferson, "Rabbit Foot Blues" (1926), on Blind Lemon Jefferson, *Dry Southern Blues: 1925–1929 Recordings* (Soul Jam Records, 2018), Disc 1, Track 17.

272 I could see planes: Buck Colbert Franklin quoted in Allison Keyes, "A Long-Lost Manuscript Contains a Searing Eyewitness Account of the Tulsa Race Massacre of 1921," *Smithsonian Magazine*, May 27, 2016: www.smithsonianmag.com/smithsonian-institution/long-lost-manuscript-contains-searing-eyewitness-account-tulsa-race-massacre-1921-180959251.

273 psychological rather than tactical: Randy Krehbiel, *Tulsa, 1921: Reporting a Massacre* (Norman: University of Oklahoma Press, 2019), 76.

273 You understand: Billy Mitchell quoted in Robert Shogan, *The Battle of Blair Mountain: The Story of America's Largest Labor Uprising* (Boulder, CO: Basic Books, 2006), 180.

273 tear gas and pipe bombs: Shogan, 198.

273 wonder and romance: Titles chosen from Bella C. Landaeur Collection of Aeronautical Sheet Music, Smithsonian Libraries: www.sil.si.edu/ondisplay/music/collection.htm.

273 impromptu cabaret; O hush thee: Gordon Thomas and Max Morgan-Witts, *The Day the Bubble Burst: A Social History of the Wall Street Crash of 1929* (New York: Doubleday, 1982), 6.

274 Officers kill: Blind Alfred Reed, "How Can a Poor Man Stand Such Times and Live?" (1929), on Blind Alfred Reed, *Complete Recorded Works, 1927–1929* (Document Records, 2012), Track 17.

274 Farm-Labor: James R. Green, *Grass Roots Socialism: Radical Movements in the Southwest, 1895–1943* (Baton Rouge: Louisiana State University Press, 1978), 405.

274 When we weaken: "Farmers' Union Song," in Norm Cohen, *American Folk Songs: A Regional Encyclopedia* (Westport, CT: Greenwood Press, 2008), II, 567.

274 The farmer is the man: "The Farmer Is the Man That Feeds Them All," in United States Congress, Special Committee on

Un-American Activities (1938–1944), *Investigation of Un-American Propaganda Activities in the United States* (Washington, DC: US Government Printing Office, 1944), 439.

274–75 George Penny's renters: The Bently Boys, "Down on Penny's Farm" (1929), on *Anthology of American Folk Music,* ed. Harry Smith (Smithsonian Folkways, 1997), Disc 2, Track 25.

275 Bob Miller: Richard Carlin, *The Big Book of Country Music: A Biographical Encyclopedia* (New York: Penguin, 1995), 299.

275 Five cent cotton: Bob Miller and Emma Dermer, "Eleven Cent Cotton," in Ronald D. Cohen and David Samuelson, eds., *Songs for Political Action: Folk Music, Topical Songs, and the American Left, 1926–1953* (Holste-Oldendorf, Germany: Bear Family Records, 1996), companion text, 63.

275 I was one: Roy Harvey, "The Virginia Strike of '23," in Cohen, *American Folk Songs*, I, 225.

275–76 One day, desperate: translation of "*De 'El Traque'*" (The Railroad Worker), in María Herrera-Sobek, *Northward Bound: The Mexican Immigrant Experience in Ballad and Song* (Bloomington: Indiana University Press, 1993), 46–47.

276 I left Finland: translation of Arthur Kylander, "*Siirtolaisen ensi vastuksia,*" on *Stranded in the USA: Early Songs of Emigration*, comp. Christoph Wagner (Trikont Records, 2004), Track 17.

276 superficially sinicized: Michael Saffle, "Eastern Fantasies on Western Stages: Chinese-Themed Operettas and Musical Comedies in Turn-of-the-Last Century London and New York," in Yang Ho-Lun and Michael Saffle, eds., *China and the West: Music, Representation, and Reception* (Ann Arbor: University of Michigan Press, 2017), 87–118 (p. 98).

277 classical operas; contemporary melancholic; popular and common themes: Nancy Yunhwa Rao, *Chinatown Opera Theater in North America* (Urbana: University of Illinois Press, 2017), 195.

277 *Abie's Irish Rose*; *Kosher Kitty Kelly*; within their own immigrant groups: Gerald Bordman, *American Musical Theater: A Chronicle* (New York: Oxford University Press, 2010), 455.

277 centers on the Americanized child's: Mark Slobin, *Tenement Songs: The Popular Music of the Jewish Immigrants* (Urbana: University of Illinois Press, 1996), 125.

278 All the folks in Tennessee: Carson J. Robison (as Carlos B. McAfee), "The John T. Scopes Trial" (1925), in Cohen, *American Folk Songs*, I, 278–279.

278 The next year alone saw: Tony Russell, *Rural Rhythm: The Story of Old-Time Country Music in 78 Records* (New York: Oxford University Press, 2021), 60.

278 When the arguments: translation of Antti Syrjäniemi, "*Daytonin apinajuttu*" (1929), Richard K. Spottswood, comp., *Folk Music in America,* Vol. 10: *Songs of War and History* (Library of Congress, Archive of Folk Song, 1976), Track A6 (and liner notes pp. 5–6).

278 Billy Sunday is a preacher: Fiddlin' John Carson, "Ain't No Bugs on Me" (1928), in John Cohen and Mike Seeger, eds., *Old-Time String Band Songbook* (New York: Oak Publications, 1976), 226.

279 Well, the night: in Cohen and Seeger, 226.

279 Daddy Swiped: Danny O. Crew, *Ku Klux Klan Sheet Music: An Illustrated Catalogue of Published Music, 1867–2002* (Jefferson, NC: McFarland & Co., 2002), 60, 229.

279 *Show Boat*: Todd Decker, "The 'Most Distinctive and Biggest Benefit that Broadway Has Ever Known'," in Tara Browner and Thomas L. Riis, eds., *Rethinking American Music* (Urbana: University of Illinois Press, 2019), 221–246 (p. 223); John Dizikes, *Opera in America: A Cultural History* (New Haven, CT: Yale University Press, 1993), 450–451.

279 I'd like to hear: Ralph Ellison, *Invisible Man* (New York: Vintage International, 2010 [1952]), 7–8.

279 Uncle Sam's ship: Lonnie Johnson, "Life Saver Blues," in Timothy E. Scheurer, *Born in the USA: The Myth of America in Popular Music from Colonial Times to the Present* (Jackson: University Press of Mississippi, 1991), 142.

279–80 Tired of being Jim Crowed: Cow Cow Davenport, "Jim Crow Blues," on Richard K. Spottswood, comp., *Folk Music in America,* Vol. 6: *Songs of Migration and Immigration* (Library of Congress, Archive of Folk Song, 1976), Track A5, liner notes 4–5.

280 starvation in my kitchen: Big Bill Broonzy, "Starvation Blues," in Michael Taft, ed., *Talkin' to Myself: Blues Lyrics, 1921–1942* (London: Routledge, 2005), 78.

280 Cryin' mama: Tommy Johnson, "Canned Heat Blues," in Eric Sackheim, ed., *The Blues Line: Blues Lyrics from Leadbelly to Muddy Waters* (New York: Thunder's Mouth Press, 1969), 157.

280 My house burning down: Roosevelt Sykes, "Fire Detective Blues," in Taft, *Talkin' to Myself,* 581.

280 Nowhere have I gone: Henry O. Osgood, *So This Is Jazz* (Boston: Da Capo Press, 1978 [1926]), 103.

280 much more important: Carter G. Woodson, *The Mis-Education of the Negro* (Mineola, NY: Dover Publications, 2005 [1933]), 2.

281 The small number: Woodson, 52.

281 Josephine Baker: Jean-Claude Baker and Chris Chase, *Josephine: The Hungry Heart* (New York: Cooper Square Press, 1993), 170.

281 Some Europeans: Woodson, 129.

281 misguided; graduating: Woodson, 91.

281 tom-tom of revolt: Langston Hughes, "The Negro Artist and the Racial Mountain" (1926), The Poetry Foundation: www.poetryfoundation.org/articles/69395/the-negro-artist-and-the-racial-mountain.

281–82 I dance wildly: Zora Neale Hurston, "How It Feels to Be Colored Me," in Alice Walker, ed., *I Love Myself when I Am Laughing: A Zora Neale Hurston Reader* (New York: The Feminist Press of the City University of New York, 1979), 154.

282 Ellington; Cotton Club: Charles Hamm, *Music in the New World* (New York: W. W. Norton, 1983), 522–523.

282 jungle music; growling: Michael Lasser, *America's Songs II: Songs from the 1890s to the Post-War Years* (New York: Routledge, 2014), 23.

282 Cajun music; "*Allons à Lafayette*": Ron Emoff, "A Cajun Poetics of Loss and Longing," *Ethnomusicology* 42, no. 2 (Spring–Summer 1998): 283–301 (p. 286); Mark Mattern, *Acting in Concert: Music, Community, and Political Action* (New Brunswick, NJ: Rutgers University Press, 1998), 80–81, 97.

282 zydeco; musical voice; diverse black groups: Michael Tisserand, *The Kingdom of Zydeco* (New York: Arcade Publishing, 1998), 2, 57–58.

283 stories resonating: Mattern, 81–82.

283 probably the first song: Boze Hadleigh, *Sing Out! Gays and Lesbians in the Music World* (New York: Barricade Books, 1997), 29.

283 Mae West; *Sex*: Michael Bronski, *A Queer History of the United States* (Boston: Beacon Press, 2011), 117.

283 a law banning: Margaret Cruikshank, *The Gay and Lesbian Liberation Movement* (New York: Routledge, 1992), 127.

283 If you're looking: George and Ira Gershwin, "Don't Ask" (1926), in Robert Kimball, ed., *The Complete Lyrics of Ira Gershwin* (New York: Da Capo Press, 1998), 79.

283 a big scandal; a sensual celebration: Hadleigh, 29.

283 Masculine women: Edgar Leslie and James Monaco, "Masculine Women! Feminine Men!" (1925), in David Zirin, *A People's History of Sports in the United States: 250 Years of Politics, Protest, People, and Play* (New York: The New Press, 2008), 51.

283 a dandy symbol; the red necktie: Hadleigh, 30.

284 What was that girlish laughter: Billy Jones and Ernest Hare, "What! No Women?" (1926), *Collected Works of Billy Jones and Ernest Hare*, Track 56, Internet Archive: https://archive.org/details/BillyJonesErnestHare.

284 the red tie's meaning: Hadleigh, 30.

284 Hey, we ain't got; Prominent references: Michael Duchemin, *New Deal Cowboy: Gene Autry and Public Diplomacy* (Norman: University of Oklahoma Press, 2016), 61–62.

284 He was only a lavender cowboy: Harold Hersey, "The Lavender Cowboy," in Jim Elledge, ed., *Masquerade: Queer Poetry in America to the End of World War II* (Bloomington: Indiana University Press, 2004), 15–16.

285 They say I do it: Gertrude "Ma" Rainey, "Prove It On Me Blues" (1928), on Ma Rainey, *The Complete 1928 Sessions* (Document Records, 1993), Track 5.

285 precursor: Angela Y. Davis, *Blues Legacies and Black Feminism: Gertrude "Ma" Rainey, Bessie Smith, and Billie Holiday* (New York: Vintage Books, 1999), 40.

285 Mose and Pete: Waymon "Sloppy" Henry, "Say I Do It" (1928), on *Atlanta Blues: Big City Blues from the Heartland* (London: JSP Records, 2005), Disc 4, Track 15.

286 didn't come home: Jimmy McHugh and Al Dubin, "My Dream of the Big Parade," in Ronald D. Cohen and Will Kaufman, *Singing for Peace: Antiwar Songs in American History* (New York: Routledge, 2015), 26.

286 Uncle Sam wasn't no woman: Blind Lemon Jefferson, "Dry Southern Blues" (1926), on Jefferson, *Dry Southern Blues*, Disc 1, Track 3.

286 Oh, the dashing: R. J. Burt, Sr., "The Infantry – Kings of the Highway," in Edward Artur Dolph, *"Sound Off!": Soldier Songs*

from the Revolution to World War II (New York: Farrar & Rinehart, Inc., 1942), xix.

286 executions: Statistics from DeathPenaltyUSA, "Database of Executions in the United States of America": https://deathpenaltyusa.org.

286 The assumption: Kristina DuRocher, *Raising Racists: The Socialization of White Children in the Jim Crow South* (Lexington: University Press of Kentucky, 2011), 132.

286–87 Hangman's rope: Blind Lemon Jefferson, "Hangman's Blues" (1928), on *Dry Southern Blues*, Disc 2, Track 10.

287 I walked to the jail: Blind Lemon Jefferson, "'Lectric Chair Blues," on *Dry Southern Blues*, Disc 2, Track 2.

287 Sacco and Vanzetti; Thayer; any stigma and disgrace: Bruce Watson, *Sacco and Vanzetti: The Men, the Murders, and the Judgment of Mankind* (New York: Viking, 2007), 160, 365.

287 This man: Webster Thayer quoted in Nicholas N. Kittrie and Eldon D. Wedlock, Jr., eds., *The Tree of Liberty: A Documentary History of Rebellion and Political Crime in America* (Baltimore: Johns Hopkins University Press, 1998), 543.

287 Word of honor: Kurt Vonnegut, *Jailbird* (New York: Delta, 1999 [1979]), 235.

288 I refuse: Woody Guthrie quoted in Joseph P. Cosco, "'I Just Want to Sing Your Name': Woody Guthrie's Struggles with *Ballads of Sacco and Vanzetti*," *Italian American Review* 1, no. 1 (Winter 2011): 35–51 (p. 35).

288 Fast; Ben Shahn: Ben Shahn, *The Passion of Sacco and Vanzetti* (1931–1932), Whitney Museum of American Art: https://whitney.org/collection/works/1022.

289 Look at your enemies: H. T. Tsaing and Ruth Crawford Seeger, "Sacco, Vanzetti" (1932), on Oliver Knussen et al., *Ruth Crawford Seeger: Portrait* (Deutsche Grammophon, 1997), Track 14.

289 magnum opus: Leonard Lehrman, "Unifying the Cultural Left: Edith Segal, Emma Goldman, and the Completion of Marc Blitzstein's *Sacco and Vanzetti*," in Jerome H. Delamater and Mary Anne Trasciatti, eds., *Representing Sacco and Vanzetti* (New York: Palgrave Macmillan, 2005), 91–100 (pp. 93–94).

289 The whole world: translation of Alfredo Bascetta, "*Lacrime 'e cundannate*," in Richard Polenberg, *Hear My Sad Story: The True Tales that Inspired Stagolee, John Henry, and Other*

Traditional American Folk Songs (Ithaca, NY: Cornell University Press, 2015), 258.

289 global appeals: Lisa McGirr, "The Passion of Sacco and Vanzetti: A Global History," *Journal of American History* 93, no. 4 (March 2007): 1085–1115 *passim.*

290 From everywhere: translation of Bascetta, "*Lacrime 'e cundannate,*" on Wagner, *Stranded in the USA*, Track 22.

290 the nation's greatest natural disaster: Christopher Morris, *The Big Muddy: An Environmental History of the Mississippi and Its Peoples from Hernando de Soto to Hurricane Katrina* (New York: Oxford University Press, 2012), 165.

290 in a situation resembling slavery; Blacks were forced: Richard M. Mizelle, Jr., *Backwater Blues: The Mississippi Flood of 1927 in the African American Imagination* (Minneapolis: University of Minnesota Press, 2014), 37.

290 over 100: Morris, 164.

291–92 When it rained: Bessie Smith, "Back Water Blues" (1926/1927), on *Bessie Smith Sings the Blues* (Sony Music Special Editions, 1995), Track 4.

292 Cumberland River flood: David Evans, "Bessie Smith's 'Back Water Blues': The Story Behind the Song," *Popular Music* 26, no. 1 (2007): 97–116 *passim.*

292–93 On the 20th of August: translation of Ramón Luna, "*El corrido de San Marcial*" (1930), with commentary in Jack Loeffler, *La Música de los Viejitos: Hispano Folk Music of the Río Grande del Norte* (Albuquerque: University of New Mexico Press, 1999), 53.

293 Them who's got: Bruce Springsteen, "How Can a Poor Man Stand Such Times and Live?" on Springsteen, *We Shall Overcome: The Seeger Sessions* (Sony Music Entertainment, 2006), Track 16.

293 Model T; affordable: Hazel Arnott, *I Hear America Singing! Great Folk Songs from the Revolution to Rock* (New York: Praeger, 1975), 151.

293 Mine eyes have seen: "Hurry, Hurry, Hurry, Hurry!" (c. 1925), in Pete Seeger and Bob Reiser, *Carry It On! A History in Song and Picture of the Working Men and Women of America* (Poole, UK: Blandford Press, 1986), 123.

293 The first Model T Fords: Loeffler, 21.

294 I have a car: translation of Severo Mondragón, "*Mi carrito pasaedo*" (My Jalopy), in Loeffler, 21.

294 The auto's ruined: Uncle Dave Macon, "Jordan Is a Hard Road to Travel" (1927), on Uncle Dave Macon, *Classic Sides, 1924–1938* (JSP Records, 2004), Disc B, Track 25.

294 dedicated mule-driver: Carlin, 280.

294 We're up against it now: Uncle Dave Macon, "We Are Up Against It Now" (1926), on *Classic Sides,* Disc A, Track 21.

294 Been wagonin': Uncle Dave Macon, "From Earth to Heaven" (1920), on *Classic Sides*, Disc C, Track 10.

295 His answer was brief: Michael D. Doubler, *Dixie Dewdrop: The Uncle Dave Macon Story* (Urbana: University of Illinois Press, 2018), 61–62.

295 I'm on my way: Uncle Dave Macon, "From Earth to Heaven."

295 old maids; bob off their hair; powder up their face: Fiddlin' John Carson, "There's a Hard Time Coming" (1925), in Patrick Huber, *Linthead Stomp: The Creation of Country Music in the Piedmont South* (Chapel Hill: University of North Carolina Press, 2008), 87.

295 Some folks: Dutch Coleman, "Granny Get Your Hair Cut" (1929), on Richard K. Spottswood, comp., *Folk Music in America,* Vol. 7*: Songs of Complaint and Protest* (Library of Congress, Archive of Folk Song, 1976), Track A3.

295–96 Fashion these days: translation of Leonardo Dia, "*Li fimmini cu lu lipstick*" (1929), on Wagner, comp., *Stranded in the USA*, Track 13.

296 I'm a mother of nine: Ella May Wiggins quoted in Mat Callahan and Yvonne Moore, *Working Class Heroes: A History of Struggle in Song* (Oakland, CA: PM Press, 2019), 19.

296 Twelve dollars a week: Dave McCarn, "Cotton Mill Colic," on *Gastonia Gallop: Cotton Mill Songs and Hillbilly Blues* (Old Hat Records, 2009), Track 4.

296–97 One night I was working: Huber, 267, 269.

297 I used to be a factory hand: Dorsey Dixon, "Babies in the Mill," on Dixon et al., *Babies in the Mill: Carolina Traditional, Industrial, Sacred Songs* (HighTone Records, 1997), Track 1.

297 We leave our home; It is for our little children: Ella May Wiggins, "Mill Mother's Lament" (1929), as sung by Pete Seeger on *American Industrial Ballads* (Smithsonian Folkways, 1992), Track 15.

298 Come and join: Ella May Wiggins, "Toiling of Life's Pilgrim Pathway," in Callahan and Moore, 10–11.

298 an earlier attempt; The bosses hated: Quotations and commentary in Timothy Lynch, *Strike Songs of the Depression* (Jackson: University Press of Mississippi, 2001), 12.

298 According to some reports; mill owners reneged; On October 2: Clete Daniel, *Culture of Misfortune: An Interpretive History of Textile Unionism in the United States* (Ithaca, NY: Cornell University Press, 2001), 32, 34.

298 We won't budge: "We Are Building a Strong Union" (1929), in Edith Fowke and Joe Glazer, *Songs of Work and Protest* (New York: Dover, 1973), 73.

299 These men were only asking: "The Marion Massacre" (1929), in Cohen, *American Folk Songs*, I, 239–240.

299 a virtual theme song for the Depression: Ruth Glasser, *My Music Is My Flag: Puerto Rican Musicians and Their New York Communities, 1917–1940* (Berkeley: University of California Press, 1997), 2.

299 the tragic story; He departs: translation of Rafael Hernández Marín, "*Lamento Borincano*," and commentary in Mario C. Cancel-Bigay, "'*Lamento Borincano' – Canario y Su Grupo (1930)*," Washington, DC: National Recording Preservation Board, Library of Congress, 2017: www.loc.gov/static/programs/national-recording-preservation-board/documents/LamentoBorincano.pdf, 1–2.

299 The engineer pulled: Uncle Dave Macon, "Wreck of the Tennessee Gravy Train," on *Classic Sides*, Disc D, Track 8.

300 October 29, 1929, yeah: Arthur A. Robertson quoted in Studs Terkel, *My American Century* (London: Phoenix Giant, 1998), 101.

301 Margin-callin' brokers: Margaret Gregory and W. C. Handy, "Wall Street Blues" (1929), as sung by Lee Hunter on *The Face on the Dime: A Musical History of the FDR Years* (Smithsonian Folkways/Collector Records, 1989), Track 1.

14 The Panic Is On

302 The fellow: E. Y. Harburg quoted in Philip Furia, *The Poets of Tin Pan Alley: A History of America's Great Lyricists* (New York: Oxford University Press, 1992), 204.

302 Harburg had some lyrics: Sean McCullum, "'Brother Can You Spare a Dime?': The Story Behind the Song," John F. Kennedy

Center for the Performing Arts, ARTSEDGE project (2019): www.kennedy-center.org/education/resources-for-educators/classroom-resources/media-and-interactives/media/music/story-behind-the-song/the-story-behind-the-song/brother-can-you-spare-a-dime/.

302 military – and militant: Furia, 205.

302–03 National Hunger March; full and immediate payment, etc.: Franklin Folsom, *America before Welfare* (New York: New York University Press, 1991), 286, 293.

303 Cox's Army: Folsom, 299.

303 one of the rare topical songs: Neil V. Rosenberg and Charles K. Wolfe, *The Music of Bill Monroe* (Urbana: University of Illinois Press, 2007), 11–12.

303 I saw my buddies: Bert Layne, "The Forgotten Soldier Boy," as sung by the Monroe Brothers on *Bill Monroe: Blue Moon of Kentucky, 1936–1949* (Bear Family Records, 2002), Disc 1, Track 25.

303–04 Bonus Army; pictures and movies: David S. Meyer, *The Politics of Protest: Social Movements in America* (New York: Oxford University Press, 2007), 163.

304 I've been working: "Wandering," in John Anthony Scott, *The Ballad of America: The History of the United States in Song and Story* (New York: Bantam Pathfinder, 1966), 336.

304 I'm spending my nights: Maurice Sugar, "The Soup Song" (1931), in Ronald D. Cohen, *Depression Folk: Grassroots Music and Left-Wing Politics in 1930s America* (Chapel Hill: University of North Carolina Press, 2016), 35.

304 Tallahatchie River rising: Pearl Dickson, "Tallahatchie River Blues," in Michael Taft, ed., *Talkin' to Myself: Blues Lyrics, 1921–1942* (London: Routledge, 2005), 163.

304–05 Lord, I ain't gonna: Easy Papa Johnson (Roosevelt Sykes), "Cotton Seed Blues," on Roosevelt Sykes, *Complete Recorded Works*, Vol. 2 (Document Records, 1992), Track 8.

305 Tampa Red and Georgia Tom recorded: Tampa Red and Georgia Tom, "Cotton Seed Blues," on *Tampa Red and Georgia Tom: 1929–1931* (Document Records, 1990), Track B7.

305 abandoning their musical careers: Kurt Wolff and Orla Duane, *Country Music: The Rough Guide* (London: Rough Guides, 2000), 8.

305 We can't borrow: The Allen Brothers, "Price of Cotton Blues" (1930), on *The Allen Brothers with Other Country Brother Acts* (JSP Records, 2015), Disc 1, Track 13.

305 Now people; Now in the year: Dave McCarn, "Serves Them Fine" (1931), in John Cohen and Mike Seeger, eds., *Old-Time String Band Songbook* (New York: Oak Publications, 1976), 235.

305 worked the whole year; I'd-a bought me: Lowe Stokes, "I Wish I'd Stayed in the Wagon Yard," in Bill C. Malone, *Don't Get above Your Raisin': Country Music and the Southern Working Class* (Urbana: University of Illinois Press, 2002), 178–179.

306 Prohibition is a failure; Oh, at the next election: Lowe Stokes, "Prohibition Is a Failure" (1930), on Lowe Stokes, *Complete Recorded Works,* Vol. 1 (Document Records, 1999), Track 18.

306 Mr. Hoover came; Now the day am coming: The Allen Brothers, "The Enforcement Blues" (1930), on *The Allen Brothers with Other Country Brother Acts,* (JSP Records, 2015), Disc 1, Track 8.

306 Hoover badges: Cohen and Seeger, *Old-Time String Band Songbook,* 228.

306 a volcano: H. L. Mencken, *A Mencken Chrestomathy: His Own Selection of His Choicest Writings* (New York: Vintage, 1982), 253.

306 I am opposed; an abhorrent notion; local relief: Herbert Hoover quoted in Pete Seeger and Bob Reiser, *Carry It On! A History in Song and Picture of the Working Men and Women of America* (Poole, UK: Blandford Press, 1985), 129.

306 Hoover never declared: William E. Leuchtenburg, *Herbert Hoover* (New York: Times Books, 2009), 107.

307 Prosperity is just around the corner: Carson J. Robison, "Prosperity Is Just Around the Corner" (1932), on *Top 100 Classics: The Very Best of Carson Robison* (GRR Music, 2015), Track 75.

307 killin' floor; the people: Skip James, "Hard Time Killin' Floor Blues" (1931), on Skip James, *Hard Time Killin' Floor* (Yazoo, 2005), Track 3.

307 Saw a man: Hezekiah Jenkins, "The Panic Is On" (1931), on *Blues and Jazz Obscurities* (Document Records, 1996), Track 11.

307–08 If I ever get a job: Sam Lewis and Abel Baer, "If I Ever Get a Job Again" (1932), in Diane Holloway and Bob Cheney, *American History in Song: Lyrics from 1900 to 1945* (San Jose: Authors Choice Press, 2001), 312.

308 Lots of prickly pear; Probably everybody knows: translation of "*Efectos de la crisis,*" in María Herrera-Sobek, *Northward Bound: The Mexican Immigrant Experience in Ballad and Song* (Bloomington: Indiana University Press, 1993), 130–131.

308 families that had lived: Herrera-Sobek, 126.

308–09 Ever since the year: translation of "*Corrido de Immigración,*" in Herrera-Sobek, 139–141.

309 One sphere: Peter Chapman, *Bananas: How the United Fruit Company Shaped the World* (New York: Canongate, 2007), 75.

309 Among the bloodthirsty: Pablo Neruda, "*La* United Fruit Co.," in Robert Bly, ed. and trans., *Neruda and Vallejo: Selected Poems* (Boston: Beacon Press, 1993), 87.

310 You hear only: translation of "*Corrido de la emigración*" (Corrido of the Immigration Officers), in Herrera-Sobek, 135–137.

310 American Sugar: Federico Ribes Tovar, *Albizu Campos: Puerto Rican Revolutionary* (San Juan: Plus Ultra Educational Publishers, 1971), 122–144, 197–204.

310 bucolic; sang along; day breaks: translation of Rafael Hernandez Marín, "*Los Carreteros,*" with commentary in Ruth Glasser, *My Music Is My Flag: Puerto Rican Musicians and Their New York Communities* (Berkeley: University of California Press, 1997), 15–16.

310 pastoral paradise; more distant memory: Glasser, 16.

311 "*Puerto Rico, puerto pobre*": Julio Marzán, "Pablo Neruda's Dilemma," *Massachusetts Review* 40, no. 4 (Winter 1999/2000): 675–681 (p. 679).

311 Come all of you: Florence Reece, "Which Side Are You On?" (1931), in Edith Fowke and Joe Glazer, *Songs of Work and Protest* (New York: Dover Publications, 1973), 55.

311 Sheriff J. H. Blair: Florence Reece quoted in David Greene, *Unfit to Be a Slave: A Guide to Adult Education for Liberation* (Boston: Sense Publishers, 2014), 5.

312 I'm sad and weary: Aunt Molly Jackson, "Ragged, Hungry Blues" (1931), on Ronald D. Cohen and David Samuelson, comp., *Songs for Political Action: Folk Music, Topical Songs, and the American Left: 1926–1953* (Bear Family Records, 1996), Disc 1, Track 7.

312 Thirty-seven babies: Aunt Molly Jackson quoted in Timothy Lynch, *Strike Songs of the Depression* (Jackson: University Press of Mississippi, 2001), 49.

312 I can't forget them: Aunt Molly Jackson, "Dreadful Memories" (1935), in John Greenway, *American Folksongs of Protest* (New York: A. S. Barnes, 1960 [1953]), 275.

312 When I'm in Kentucky: Aunt Molly Jackson, "Poor Miner's Farewell," in Greenway, 263.

312 The day I composed: Aunt Molly Jackson quoted in Greenway, 263.

313 The Associated Press: Members of the National Committee for the Defense of Political Prisoners, *Harlan Miners Speak: Report on Terrorism in the Kentucky Coal Fields* (Lexington: University Press of Kentucky, 2008 [1932]), 79.

313 took up the baton of leadership: John W. Hevener, *Which Side Are You On? The Harlan County Coal Miners, 1931–39* (Urbana: University of Illinois Press, 2002), 42–47, 56–88.

313 I was raised in Kentucky: Aunt Molly Jackson, "I Am a Union Woman" (1931), in Charlotte Nekola and Paula Rabinowitz, eds., *Writing Red: An Anthology of American Women Writers, 1930–1940* (New York: Feminist Press, 1987), 184.

313 originated; I am locked up in prison: Aunt Molly Jackson, "Lonesome Jailhouse Blues," in Greenway, 265–266.

314 Come on, friends: Sarah Ogan Gunning, "Down on the Picket Line" (1932), in Holloway and Cheney, 306.

314 a coal miner who had been blacklisted: Fowke and Glazer, 161.

314 Harry Simms Hersh: Alessandro Portelli, *They Say in Harlan County: An Oral History* (New York: Oxford University Press, 2000), 200.

314 the bullet that killed Harry Simms: Mat Callahan and Yvonne Moore, *Working Class Heroes: A History of Struggle in Song* (Oakland: PM Press, 2019), 21.

314–15 Harry Simms was a pal: Jim Garland and Aunt Molly Jackson, "The Death of Harry Simms" (1932), in Greenway, 272–273.

315 I don't want your millions: Jim Garland, "I Don't Want Your Millions, Mister" (1932), in Fowke and Glazer, 161.

315 Well, I hated that song: Woody Guthrie quoted in Will Kaufman, *Woody Guthrie, American Radical* (Urbana: University of Illinois Press, 2011), 123.

315 They shot Barney Graham: Eleanor Kellogg, "My Children Are Seven in Number" (1933), in Norm Cohen, *American Folk Songs: A Regional Encyclopedia* (Westport, CT: Greenwood Press, 2008), I, 282.

316 She has spent weeks: Eugene Debs quoted in Elliott J. Gorn, *Mother Jones: The Most Dangerous Woman in America* (New York: Hill & Wang, 2001), 164–165.

316 The world today's: "The Death of Mother Jones," as recorded by Gene Autry (1931), on *Gene Autry: Early Sides* (JSP Records, 2008), Disc 3, Track 21.

316 Mother Jones is not forgotten: Orville J. Jenks, "Sprinkle Coal Dust on My Grave" (rec. 1940), in George Korson, *Coal Dust on the Fiddle: Songs and Stories of the Bituminous Industry* (Hatboro, PA: Folklore Associates, Inc., 1965 [1943]), 65–66.

317 Lots of girls: Woody Guthrie, in Alan Lomax, Woody Guthrie, and Pete Seeger, eds. *Hard Hitting Songs for Hard-Hit People* (New York: Oak Publications, 1967), 80.

317 I was on my way: Olen Montgomery, in Kwando M. Kinshasa, ed., *The Scottsboro Boys in Their Own Words: Selected Letters, 1931–1950* (Jefferson, NC: McFarland & Co., 2014), 4.

317 Show them: Wade Wright quoted in Dan T. Carter, *Scottsboro: A Tragedy of the American South* (Baton Rouge: Louisiana State University Press, 2007), 235.

318 to much the same economic system: "Twelve Southerners," *I'll Take My Stand: The South and the Agrarian Tradition* (Baton Rouge: Louisiana State University Press, 1977 [1930]), xlii.

318 She hollered: Olen Montgomery quoted in Lomax, Guthrie, and Seeger, *Hard Hitting Songs*, 80.

318 All last night: Olen Montgomery, "Lonesome Jailhouse Blues," in Lomax, Guthrie, and Seeger, *Hard Hitting Songs*, 81.

318–19 Workers, farmers: Charles Abron and L. E. Swift, "The Scottsboro Boys Shall Not Die," *The Workers Songbook* (New York: Workers Music League, 1934), 7.

319 They were the largest strikes: Michael Denning, *The Cultural Front: The Laboring of American Culture in the Twentieth Century* (London: Verso, 1998), 260.

319 Every participant: Aaron Copland, "Workers Sing!" in *Aaron Copland: A Reader: Selected Writings, 1923–72*, ed. Richard Kostelanetz (New York: Routledge, 2004), 88.

320 in four-five time: Charles Seeger quoted in David King Dunaway, "Charles Seeger and Carl Sands: The Composers' Collective Years," *Ethnomusicology* 24, no. 2 (May 1980), 159–168 (p. 163).

320 Into the streets: Alfred Hayes and Aaron Copland, "Into the Streets May First" (1934), in Archie Green, *Wobblies, Pile Butts, and Other Heroes: Laborlore Explorations* (Urbana: University of Illinois Press, 1993), 88.

320 Do you think: Charles Seeger quoted in Green, 87.

320 revolutionary music: Green, 87.

320 geometric bitterness; Why don't American workers: Mike Gold quoted in John Shaw, *This Land That I Love: Irving Berlin, Woody Guthrie, and the Story of Two American Anthems* (New York: Public Affairs, 2013), 94.

320 I was trying: Charles Seeger quoted in Gayle Murchison, *The American Stravinsky: The Style and Aesthetics of Copland's New American Music, The Early Works, 1921–1938* (Ann Arbor: University of Michigan Press, 2012), 183.

320–21 complacent, melancholy: Charles Seeger (Carl Sands) quoted in Robbie Lieberman, *"My Song Is My Weapon": People's Songs, American Communism, and the Politics of Culture, 1930–50* (Urbana: University of Illinois Press, 1995), 30.

321 the people's idiom: Richard Reuss and Joanne C. Reuss, *American Folk Music and Left-Wing Politics, 1927–1957* (Lanham, MD: Scarecrow Press, 2000), 73–74; Murchison, 187.

321 vernacular: Howard Pollack, *Aaron Copland* (New York: Henry Holt & Co., 1999), 186.

321 a conversion experience: Judith Tick, *Ruth Crawford Seeger: A Composer's Search for American Music* (New York: Oxford University Press, 1997), 239.

321 Florence Price was following: Rae Linda Brown, *The Heart of a Woman: The Life and Music of Florence B. Price* (Urbana: University of Illinois Press, 2020), 8–9 and *passim.*

321 mixed blessing; folk opera; definitely gifted: Commentary and Eva Jessye quotation in John Dizikes, *Opera in America: A Cultural History* (New Haven, CT: Yale University Press, 1993), 461.

322 the high point: Orrin Clayton Suthern II, "Minstrelsy and Popular Culture," in Timothy E. Scheurer, ed., *The Nineteenth Century and Tin Pan Alley: Readings from the Popular Press* (Bowling Green, OH: Bowling Green State University Popular Press, 1989), 75–85 (p. 84).

322 who a generation earlier: Gerald Bordman, *American Musical Theater: A Chronicle* (New York: Oxford University Press, 2010), 552.

322 Dawson, *Negro Folk Symphony*, and Still, *Afro-American Symphony*: Ellen Noonan, *The Strange Career of Porgy and*

Bess: Race, Culture, and America's Most Famous Opera (Chapel Hill: University of North Carolina Press, 2012), 149.

322 from "the Bond of Africa": Stephen Blum, "Musical Enactment of Attitudes toward Conflict in the United States," in John Morgan O'Connell and Salwa El-Shawan Castelo-Branco, eds., *Music and Conflict* (Urbana: University of Illinois Press, 2010): 232–242 (p. 236).

322 however, the production: Dizikes, 454.

322 In most of these mainstream: Clare Corbould, "At the Feet of Dessalines: Performing Haiti's Revolution during the New Negro Renaissance," in W. Fitzhugh Brundage, ed., *Beyond Blackface: African Americans and the Creation of American Popular Culture, 1890–1930* (Chapel Hill: University of North Carolina Press, 2011), 259–288 (p. 262).

322–23 I'm tired: Haines J. Washington, "Death of the Emperor Jones," in Corbould, 255–256.

323 modernizing will; a serious belief system; a celebration: Corbould, 271.

323 Wheresoever I go: Marcus Garvey quoted in Colin Grant, *Negro with a Hat: The Rise and Fall of Marcus Garvey* (New York: Oxford University Press, 2010), 246–247.

323 Some people say: Wilmoth Houdini, "African Love Call," on Wilmoth Houdini, *Poor but Ambitious* (Arhoolie Records, 1993), Track 22.

324 long-lost masterpiece; highly unlikely; member of Garvey's: Catherine Parsons Smith, *William Grant Still* (Urbana: University of Illinois Press, 2008), 51–52.

324 Go on and up: Paul Laurence Dunbar, "Ode to Ethiopia," in Peter Gough, *Sounds of the New Deal: The Federal Music Project in the West* (Urbana: University of Illinois Press, 2015), 122.

324 a new form: Eugene Thamon Simpson, *Hall Johnson: His Life, His Sprit, and His Music* (Lanham, MD: Scarecrow Press, 2008), 14.

324 *The Green Pastures*: Hall Johnson quoted in Judith Weisenfeld, "'The Secret at the Root': Performing African American Religious Modernity in Hall Johnson's *Run, Little Chillun*," *Religion and American Culture: A Journal of Interpretation* 21, no. 1 (Winter 2011): 39–80 (p. 44).

324 looks like a powerful; Dance of the Full Moon; something approaching voodoo: Weisenfeld, 49–50.

324 the longest running: Gough, 115.

326 CPUSA; Southern Black workers: Robin D. G. Kelley, "'Comrades, Praise Gawd for Lenin and Them!': Ideology and Culture among Black Communists in Alabama, 1930–1935," *Science and Society* 52, no. 1 (Spring 1988): 59–82 (pp. 59–60).

326 I could remember: Helen Norton Starr quoted in Fowke and Glazer, 39.

326 the "official" ILD song; efficacious example[s]: Kelley, 74–76.

326 If the planter's: John Handcox, Lee Hays, and Claude Williams, "Roll the Union On," in Cohen, *Depression Folk*, 81; Fowke and Glazer, 45.

327 The songs I wrote: John Handcox quoted in Rebecca B. Schroeder and Donald M. Lance, "John Handcox: 'There Is Still Mean Things Happening,'" in Archie Green, ed., *Songs about Work: Essays in Occupational Culture* (Bloomington: Folklore Institute of Indiana University Bloomington, 1993), 184–207 (p. 185).

327 zipper in: Michael K. Honey, *Sharecropper's Troubadour: John L. Handcox, the Southern Tenant Farmers' Union, and the African American Song Tradition* (New York: Palgrave Macmillan, 2013), 96.

327 Raggedy, raggedy: John Handcox, "Raggedy, Raggedy Are We," in Lomax, Guthrie, and Seeger, *Hard Hitting Songs*, 265.

327 "We Shall Overcome"; Horton; Seeger: Guy and Candie Carawan, *Sing for Freedom: The Story of the Civil Rights Movement through Its Songs* (Montgomery, AL: NewSouth Books, 2007), 8.

327 No one is certain: Pete Seeger, *Where Have All the Flowers Gone: A Singalong Memoir* (New York: Sing Out! / W. W. Norton, 2009), 32.

328 Toledo; Minneapolis; San Francisco: Callahan and Moore, 7.

328 It was there on the line: "The Ballad of Bloody Thursday," with commentary in Cohen, *American Folk Songs*, II, 668–669.

328 insurgency; laboring; first time: Denning, 3.

329 shared a sense; Greenwich Village: Michael Bronski, *A Queer History of the United States* (Boston: Beacon Press, 2011), 112–113.

329 I want a cozy little nest: Bruz Fletcher, "The Simple Things in Life," in Bronski, 122.

329–30 a short period: Darryl W. Bullock, *David Bowie Made Me Gay: 100 Years of LGBT Music* (London: Duckworth Overlook, 2018), 58.

330 highest paid nightclub entertainer: Bullock, 60.

330 I don't know whether: Jean/Gene Malin, "That's What's the Matter With Me," (Columbia Records, 1931): www.youtube.com/watch?v=KNkdI8-88eE.

330 first glimpse: Mark Hellinger quoted in Bullock, 60.

330 the sophisticated lady: Boze Hadleigh, *Sing Out! Gays and Lesbians in the Music World* (New York: Barricade Books, 1997), 30.

330 Lord, if you can't: Kokomo Arnold, "Sissy Man Blues," on *Kokomo Arnold: Old Original Kokomo Blues* (Catfish Records, 1997), Track 13.

330 I like your mama: "The Dirty Dozens," in Eric Sackheim, *The Blues Line: Blues Lyrics from Leadbelly to Muddy Waters* (New York: Thunder's Mouth Press, 1969), 397; "The Twelves," in Taft, *Talkin' to Myself*, 11–12.

330 that cabaret: Tom Delaney, "Down on Pennsylvania Avenue," as sung by Bertha Idaho on *Female Blues Singers*, Vol. 10 (Document Records, 1996), Track 8.

331 puts paint and powder: Al Miller, "Somebody's Been Using That Thing" (1929), on *Al Miller, 1927–1936* (Document Records, 1994), Track 20.

331 There's no slippin': J. Bernie Barbour, "My Daddy Rocks Me (With One Steady Roll)," as sung by Tampa Red's Hokum Jug Band on *Tampa Red in Chronological Order* (Document Records, 1991), Track 10.

331 There was a time: George Hannah, "Freakish Man Blues," in Taft, *Talkin' to Myself*, 220.

331 mannish lesbian; For this reason: Bronski, 115.

331 Comin' a time: Lucille Bogan (Bessie Jackson), "B. D. Woman's Blues," on *Shave 'Em Dry: The Best of Lucille Bogan* (Columbia / Legacy, 2004), Track 3.

331 250-pound black lesbian; avowed; to be both respected: James F. Wilson, *Bulldaggers, Pansies, and Chocolate Babies: Performance, Race, and Sexuality in the Harlem Renaissance* (Ann Arbor: University of Michigan Press, 2011), 155, 166.

332 What makes you menfolk: Gladys Bentley, "Worried Blues," on *Maggie Jones and Gladys Bentley: Complete Recorded Works* (Document Records, 1995), Track 18.

332 the phrase: Bullock, 47.

332 When you see two women: George Hannah and Meade "Lux" Lewis, "The Boy in the Boat," on *Sissy Man Blues: 25 Authentic*

Straight and Gay Blues and Jazz Vocals (Jass Records, 1996), Track 5.

332 all people; love is love: "Transcript: Obama's Remarks on Supreme Court Ruling on Same-Sex Marriage," *Washington Post*, June 26, 2015: www.washingtonpost.com/news/post-nation/wp/2015/06/26/transcript-obamas-remarks-on-supreme-court-ruling-on-same-sex-marriage.

15 To Thee We Sing

333 New Deal; wage war; invasion: Franklin D. Roosevelt, First Inaugural Address, in Davis W. Houck, *FDR and Fear Itself: The First Inaugural Address* (College Station: Texas A&M University Press, 2002), 7.

333 On the skeeter bit: Woody Guthrie, "Hooversville," quoted in Will Kaufman, *Woody Guthrie, American Radical* (Urbana: University of Illinois Press, 2011), 7.

333 13 million; 8 million: Irving Bernstein, "Americans in Depression and War," US Department of Labor: www.dol.gov/general/aboutdol/history/chapter5.

333 Brain Trust; First New Deal Period: Arthur M. Schlesinger, Jr., *The Coming of the New* Deal, *1933–1935* (New York: Houghton Mifflin, 2003), 179–181.

334 stop waitin': Langston Hughes, "Waitin' on Roosevelt" ("Ballad of Roosevelt"), in Alan Lomax, Woody Guthrie, and Pete Seeger, eds., *Hard Hitting Songs for Hard-Hit People* (New York: Oak Publications, 1967), 210.

334 Look here, Mr. Hoover: "White House Blues," in John Cohen and Mike Seeger, eds., *Old-Time String Band Songbook* (New York: Oak Publications, 1976), 228.

334 Four Horsemen: Edward Lazarus, *Closed Chambers: The Rise, Fall, and Future of the Modern Supreme Court* (New York: Penguin, 1999), 284.

334 The Depression is gone: Ed Sturgill, "'31 Depression Blues," as sung by the New Lost City Ramblers on *Modern Times* (Folkways Records, 1968), Track A2.

335 Several hillbilly bands: Peter La Chapelle, *I'd Fight the World: A Political History of Old-Time, Hillbilly, and Country Music* (Chicago: University of Chicago Press, 2019), 80.

335 When you goin': Bill Cox, "NRA Blues," in Lomax, Guthrie, and Seeger, *Hard Hitting Songs*, 192.

335 'Course you know: Woody Guthrie in *Hard Hitting Songs*, 196.

335–36 I meant to marry Sally: Jilson Setters, "Ballad of the TVA," in *Hard Hitting Songs*, 196.

336 CWA, you're the best: Joe Pullum, "CWA Blues," in Allan Moore, *The Cambridge Companion to Blues and Gospel Music* (Cambridge: Cambridge University Press, 2002), 155.

336 a splendidly improved: Schlesinger, 288.

336 Oh, Mister President: Jimmie Gordon, "Don't Take Away My PWA," in Lomax, Guthrie, and Seeger, *Hard Hitting Songs*, 191.

336 the forgotten man; the poor man: Amity Shlaes, *The Forgotten Man: A New History of the Great Depression* (New York: HarperCollins, 2007), 12.

336 Who's gonna vote: Bob Miller, "The Poor Forgotten Man" (1932), on Ronald D. Cohen and Dave Samuelson, comp., *Songs for Political Action: Folk Music, Topical Songs, and the American Left: 1926–1953* (Bear Family Records, 1996), Disc 1, Track 22.

336–37 Remember: Al Dubin and Harry Warren, "Remember My Forgotten Man," on *Lullaby of Broadway: The Best of Busby Berkeley at Warner Bros.* (Sony Music, 1995), Disc 1, Track 7.

337 I'm buried: Ted Koehler and Harold Arlen, "Raisin' the Rent" (1933), as performed by Ramona, Roy Bargy, and the Paul Whiteman Orchestra, on *Poor Man's Heaven* (Bluebird, 2003), Track 6.

338 one of the three worst: Donald Worster, *Dust Bowl: The Southern Plains in the 1930s* (New York: Oxford University Press, 2004), 4.

338 the inevitable outcome: Worster, 4.

338 And so we watched: Woody Guthrie on *Library of Congress Recordings* (Rounder Records, 1988), Disc 1, Track 8.

338 For every farmer: Woody Guthrie quoted in Ed Cray, *Ramblin' Man: The Life and Times of Woody Guthrie* (New York: W. W. Norton, 2004), 134.

339 Along with other: Agnes "Sis" Cunningham quoted in Fred Metting, *The Unbroken Circle: Tradition and Innovation in the Music of Ry Cooder and Taj Mahal* (Lanham, MD: Scarecrow Press, 2001), 121.

339 epic proportions; the whole countryside: Joe Klein, *Woody Guthrie: A Life* (New York: Delta, 1980), 77.

339 How can you keep on: Agnes "Sis" Cunningham, "How Can You Keep on Movin'?" on *Sundown: Agnes "Sis" Cunningham Sings Her Own Songs and a Few Old Favorites* (Folkways Records, 2007), Track A2.

339 We were out in Arizona: Jack Bryant, "Arizona" (c. 1940), Library of Congress, "Voices from the Dust Bowl: The Charles L. Todd and Robert Sonkin Migrant Worker Collection, 1940 to 1941": www.loc.gov/item/toddbib000194.

340 The Author was trying: Woody Guthrie quoted in Mark Allan Jackson, *Prophet Singer: The Voice and Vision of Woody Guthrie* (Jackson: University Press of Mississippi, 2007), 87–89.

340 I'd rather not: Lester Hunter, "We'd Rather Not Be on Relief" (1939), Library of Congress, sound recording, American Folklife Center: www.loc.gov/item/afc9999005.10491/.

340 Without the New Deal: Shlaes, 4.

340 the first true dictator: Hodding Carter quoted in Dylan Hayley Leavitt, "Huey Long's Life and Legacy," PBS Online, February 24, 2014: www.pbs.org/wgbh/roadshow/stories/articles/2014/2/24/huey-longs-life-and-legacy.

340 incipient fascist: Victor Ferkiss quoted in Alan Brinkley, "Huey Long, the Share Our Wealth Movement, and the Limits of Depression Dissidence," *Louisiana History* 22, no. 2 (1981): 117–134 (p. 119).

340 Trumpian figure: Annika Neklason, "When Demagogic Populism Swings Left," *The Atlantic*, March 3, 2019: https://web.archive.org/web/20191120033234/https://www.theatlantic.com/politics/archive/2019/03/huey-long-was-donald-trumps-left-wing-counterpart/583933.

340 a good mass leader: T. Harry Williams quoted in Alan Brinkley, *Voices of Protest: Huey Long, Father Coughlin, and the Great Depression* (New York: Vintage, 1983), xi.

340 "original" Bernie Sanders: Fernando Ramiriz, "Huey Long, the 'Original' Bernie Sanders, Died 81 Years Ago," *Houston Chronicle*, September 9, 2016: www.chron.com/politics/article/Huey-Long-the-original-Bernie-Sanders-died-81-9212821.php.

340–41 national popularity; a strain of megalomania: Brinkley, *Voices of Protest*, 83.

341 In 1935; marches to jazz; slowed down: La Chapelle, 77.

341 Why weep or slumber: Huey Long and Castro Carazo, "Every Man a King," in Scott Myers-Lipton, *Social Solutions to Poverty: America's Struggle to Build a Just Society* (New York: Routledge, 2016), 187.

341 unwavering support; It was for them: Brinkley, *Voices of Protest*, 9.

341–42 Just walking: Theodore Buckner, untitled ode to Huey Long, in Brinkley, *Voices of Protest*, 9–10.

342 Oh, they shot: "The Death of Huey P. Long," as sung by Hank Warner (Conqueror Records, 1935); Tony Russell, *Country Music Records: A Discography, 1921–1942* (New York: Oxford University Press, 2004), 940.

342 I agree: Ernest J. Gaines, *The Autobiography of Miss Jane Pittman* (New York: Dial Press, 1971), 158–159.

342 the "Radio Priest": Philip Roth, *The Plot against America* (New York: Vintage, 2004), 264.

342 printed sheet music: Danny O. Crew, *American Political Music: A State-by-State Catalog* (Jefferson, NC: McFarland & Co., 2006), I, 295–296.

343 Second New Deal; new program: Franklin D. Roosevelt, Annual Message to Congress (January 4, 1935), in Deborah Kalb, Gerhard Peters, and John T. Woolley, eds., *State of the Union: Presidential Rhetoric from Woodrow Wilson to George W. Bush* (Washington, DC: CQ Press, 2007), 261.

343 There was not a county: Nick Taylor, *American-Made: The Enduring Legacy of the WPA* (New York: Bantam, 2008), 330.

343 Because I've got to: Carl Martin, "Let's Have a New Deal," in Timothy E. Scheurer, *Born in the USA: The Myth of America in Popular Music from Colonial Times to the Present* (Jackson: University Press of Mississippi, 1991), 143.

343 I ain't got no airplane: Kokomo Arnold, "Down and Out" (1935), in Lomax, Guthrie, and Seeger, *Hard Hitting Songs*, 50.

343 government money; furnish you: Sleepy John Estes, "Government Money" (1935), in Michael Taft, ed., *Talkin' to Myself: Blues Lyrics, 1921–1942* (London: Routledge, 2005), 181.

343 The Federal Government must: Roosevelt, Annual Message to Congress, in Kalb et al., *State of the Union*, 260.

343 My heart is breaking: Aunt Molly Jackson, "Christmas Eve in the East Side" (1936), on *Aunt Molly Jackson: Library of Congress Recordings* (Rounder Records, 1972), Track A5.

343 O Listen; The Nation; O Give Me: Crew, *American Political Music*, I, 78, 349.

343–44 the first blues artist; a poor man: Guido van Rijn, *Roosevelt's Blues: African American Blues and Gospel Songs on FDR* (Jackson: University of Mississippi Press, 1997), 81.

344 Everybody's workin': Casey Bill Weldon, "WPA Blues" (c. 1936), in van Rijn, 81–82.

344 There's a dreamer: Charles Hammond, "The End of the New Deal Dream" (1936), in Danny O. Crew, *Presidential Sheet Music: An Illustrated Catalogue* (Jefferson, NC: McFarland & Co., 2001), 189.

344 greatest electoral and popular vote: Marian C. McKenna, *Franklin Roosevelt and the Great Constitutional War* (New York: Fordham University Press, 2002), 242–243.

344 I've been a good old donkey: Bill Cox and Cliff Hobbs, "The Democratic Donkey" (ARC Records, 1936): www.youtube.com/watch?v=w78NwmT2xEY.

344 money in our jeans; drink of brandy: Bill Cox and Cliff Hobbs, "Franklin D. Roosevelt's Back Again" (ARC Records, 1936): www.youtube.com/watch?v=mKVTzKhD9tM.

345 Well, I've got to get some money: Sonny Boy Williamson, "Project Highway" (1937), on *The Original Sonny Boy Williamson,* Vol. 1 (JSP Records, 2007), Disc 1, Track 21.

345 contemporary protest pieces; why he chose: Elijah Wald, *Josh White: Society Blues* (New York: Routledge, 2013), 45.

345 white lung; silicosis crisis: Gerald Markowitz and David Rosner, "The Illusion of Medical Certainty: Silicosis and the Politics of Industrial Disability, 1930–1960," *The Millbank Quarterly* 67, part 1 (1989): 228–253 (p. 230).

345 Now, silicosis: Bob Miller, "Silicosis Is Killin' Me" (Silicosis Blues) (1936), as performed by Josh White (Pinewood Tom) on *Josh White: Blues Singer, 1932–1936* (Columbia, 1996), Track 18.

345–46 You get the silicosis: Guthrie, *Hard Hitting Songs,* 134.

346 If I went to work: CIO poster cited in Michael Kazin, *The Populist Persuasion: An American History* (Ithaca, NY: Cornell University Press, 1998), 135.

346 A friend of mine: John Handcox quoted in Rebecca Schroeder and Donald M. Lance, "John L. Handcox: 'There Is Still Mean Things Happening,'" in Archie Green, ed., *Songs about Work:*

Essays in Occupational Culture (Bloomington: Folklore Institute of Indiana University Bloomington, 1993), 184–207 (pp. 186–187).

346 If you go: John Handcox, "The Strike in Arkansas" (1936), in Schroeder and Lance, 200.

346–47 My song is founded: Jilson Setters (James William Day), "Coal Creek Troubles" (1937), on *The Lomax Kentucky Recordings*, online project: https://lomaxky.omeka.net/items/show/97.

347 Thinking tonight: Sarah Ogan Gunning, "Thinking Tonight of an Old Southern Town" (1937), *Lomax Kentucky Recordings*: https://lomaxky.omeka.net/items/show/187.

347 Coal mining is the most dangerous: Sarah Ogan Gunning, "Come All You Coal Miners" (1937), *Lomax Kentucky Recordings*: https://lomaxky.omeka.net/items/show/188.

347–48 Children lying: Anon., "Flag of Blue, White, and Red" (1937), in Marcello Truzzi, "The 100% American Songbag: Conservative Folksongs in America," *Western Folklore* 28, no. 1 (January 1969): 27–40 (pp. 30–31).

348 The Ashland Tannery: Untitled Kentucky ballad in Truzzi, 29–30.

348 On dark Republic's: Earl Robinson, "The Memorial Day Massacre" ("Ballad of the Chicago Steel Massacre") (1939), as sung by Joe Glazer on *Songs of Steel and Struggle: The Story of the Steelworkers* (Collector Records, 1975), Track A7.

349 in one of the first: Norm Cohen, *American Folk Songs: A Regional Encyclopedia* (Westport, CT: Greenwood Press, 2008), II, 416.

349 When we walked out: Parody of "Goody, Goody" (c. 1937), in Jerome L. Rodnitzky, *Minstrels of the Dawn: The Folk-Protest Singer as a Cultural Hero* (Chicago: Nelson-Hall, 1976), 6.

349 When they tie the can: Maurice Sugar, "Sit Down" (1937), as performed by The Manhattan Chorus on Cohen and Samuelson, *Songs for Political Action*, Disc 1, Track 32.

349 Tear Gas Bombs: Parody of "A Hot Time in the Old Town," in Sidney Fine, *Sit-Down: The General Motors Strike of 1936–1937* (Ann Arbor: University of Michigan Press, 2020), 8.

350 The women got together: Flint women's strike song quoted in Fine, 200.

350 a high-handed show: *NLRB* v. *Fansteel Metallurgical Corporation*, 306 US 240 (1939), quoted in Fine, 176.

350 I remember spending: George Lambert quoted in David Spener, *We Shall Not Be Moved / No nos moverán: Biography of a Song of Struggle* (Philadelphia: Temple University Press, 2016), 80.

350–51 Ponce massacre: Faye C. Caronan, "Memories of US Imperialism Narrative of the Homeland in Filipino and Puerto Rican Homes in the United States," *Philippine Studies: Historical and Ethnic Viewpoints* 60, no. 3 (September 2012): 336–366 (p. 350).

351 Precious you; no one who heard: translation of Rafael Hernández Marín, "*Preciosa*" and commentary in Ruth Glasser, *My Music Is My Flag: Puerto Rican Musicians and Their New York Communities, 1917–1940* (Berkeley: University of California Press, 1997), 202.

351 Bitter Fruit: Dorian Lynskey, *33 Revolutions per Minute: A History of Protest Songs* (London: Faber & Faber, 2010), 9.

351 I am a Jew: Abel Meeropol quoted in James Sullivan, *Which Side Are You On? 20th-Century American History in 100 Protest Songs* (New York: Oxford University Press, 2019), 48.

351 peak in 1892: Leigh Raiford, *Imprisoned in a Luminous Glare: Photography and the African American Freedom Struggle* (Chapel Hill: University of North Carolina Press, 2011), 36.

351 in the 1930s: David S. Meyer, *The Politics of Protest: Social Movements in America* (New York: Oxford University Press, 2007), 30.

351 The Southerners: Franklin D. Roosevelt quoted in Daniel Kato, *Liberalizing Lynching: Building a New Racialized State* (New York: Oxford University Press, 2016), 50.

352 the combined names: Sullivan, 47.

352 adopt the two orphaned sons: David Margolick, *Strange Fruit: The Biography of a Song* (New York: The Ecco Press, 2001), 11.

352 circulated that year to US senators: Sullivan, 48.

352 1% chance: Skopos Labs analysis quoted on GovTrack.US: www.govtrack.us/congress/bills/117/hr55.

352 Senate formally apologized: Nicholas Fandos, "Frustration and Fury as Rand Paul Holds up Anti-Lynching Bill in Senate," *New York Times*, June 5, 2020: www.nytimes.com/2020/06/05/us/politics/rand-paul-anti-lynching-bill-senate.html; Sheryl Gay Stolberg, "Senate Issues Apology over Failure on Lynching Law," *New York Times*, June 14, 2005: www.nytimes.com/2005/06/14/politics/senate-issues-apology-over-failure-on-lynching-law.html.

352 strange and bitter crop: Lewis Allen (Abel Meeropol), "Strange Fruit," as sung by Billie Holiday on *Billie Holiday: The Platinum Collection* (Not Now Music, 2017), Disc 2, Track 1.

352 exploitative relationship; cultural swindles: Richard Wright quoted in Jennifer Lynn Stoever, *The Sonic Color Line: Race and the Cultural Politics of Listening* (New York: New York University Press, 2016), 193.

352 50 percent; perform and take: Stoever, 180, 193.

352 slavery by other means: Michelle Alexander, *The New Jim Crow: Mass Incarceration in the Age of Colorblindness* (New York: The New Press, 2012), *passim.*

353 kicked out; They found: Jeff Place, *Lead Belly: The Smithsonian Folkways Collection* (Smithsonian Folkways Recordings, 2015), accompanying text, 30.

353 Some white folk: Lead Belly, "Bourgeois Blues," on *Lead Belly: The Smithsonian Folkways Collection*, Disc 1, Track 2.

353 taken to heart: Robbie Lieberman, *"My Song Is My Weapon": People's Songs, American Communism, and the Politics of Culture, 1930–50* (Urbana: University of Illinois Press, 1995), 39–40.

353 shrewd railroad lawyer: Jan Morris, *Lincoln: A Foreigner's Quest* (New York: Viking, 1999), 69–70.

353 tall horse chestnut tree: Carl Sandburg, *Abraham Lincoln: The Prairie Years and the War Years* (New York: Harvest/Harcourt, 1982 [1926, 1939]), 147.

354 They'll find: "Lincoln and Liberty," in Carl Sandburg, *The American Songbag* (San Diego: Harcourt Brace Jovanovich, 1990 [1927]), 167.

354 lament; three-note motive: Burnet C. Tuthill, "Daniel Gregory Mason," *The Musical Quarterly* 34, no. 1 (January 1948): 46–60 (pp. 53–55).

354 one setting; between 1914 and 1949: Michael Driscoll, program notes to Andover Choral Society's May 2019 performance of Florence Price's *Abraham Lincoln Walks at Midnight*: www.andoverchoralsociety.org/2018-2019-season/abraham-lincoln-walks/abraham-lincoln-walks-at-midnight-program-notes.

354 The shameless perversion: Elie Siegmeister, *Music and Society* (New York: Critics Group Press, 1938), 6.

354 Sandburg-inspired; American Ballad Singers: Carol J. Oja, "Composer with a Conscience: Elie Siegmeister in Profile," *American Music* 6, no. 2 (Summer 1988): 158–180 (p. 170).

355 He cannot rest: Vachel Lindsay, "Abraham Lincoln Walks at Midnight," in Richard Marius, ed., *The Columbia Book of Civil War Poetry* (New York: Columbia University Press, 1994), 355–356.

355 Consider the Depression: Earl Robinson, liner notes to "Abe Lincoln," on *Earl Robinson Sings* (Folkways Records, 1963).

355 Now old Abe Lincoln: Alfred Hayes and Earl Robinson, "Abe Lincoln," as performed by Earl Robinson on *Earl Robinson Sings*, Track A4.

356 The most amazing thing: Robinson, liner notes to "Abe Lincoln," *Earl Robinson Sings.*

356 zany; A filmed sequence: Gerald Bordman, *American Musical Theatre: A Chronicle* (New York: Oxford University Press, 2010), 569.

356 Modern humor: Charlie Chaplin quoted in Max Eastman, *Enjoyment of Laughter* (New York: Simon & Schuster, 1936), 108.

356 It was sung in Spain: Robinson, liner notes, *Earl Robinson Sings.*

356 sorrowing at Lincoln's tomb: George Witter Sherman, "Moon Over Spain," in Alan Guttman, *The Wound in the Heart: America and the Spanish Civil War* (New York: Free Press of Glencoe, 1962), 154.

357 They're Anarchists: Maxwell Anderson, *Key Largo* (Washington, DC: Anderson House, 1939), 9.

357 You're not a Marxist: Ernest Hemingway, *For Whom the Bell Tolls* (London: Jonathan Cape, 1978 [1941]), 288.

357 Guthrie; "Jarama Valley": Will Kaufman, "Woody Guthrie's Songs Against Franco," *Atlantis* 39, no. 1 (June 2017): 91–111 (pp. 93, 96).

357 sung by the US fighters: Pete Seeger et al., Songs of the Lincoln Brigade on *Songs of the Spanish Civil War* (Smithsonian Folkways Recordings, 2014).

357 Several personal friends: Agnes "Sis" Cunningham in Cunningham and Gordon Friesen, *Red Dust and Broadsides: A Joint Autobiography*, ed. Ronald D. Cohen (Amherst: University of Massachusetts Press, 1999), 177.

357 which had seemed; took a turn: Bordman, 561.

357-58 about industrial violence; with little publicity: John Dizikes, *Opera in America: A Cultural History* (New Haven, CT: Yale University Press, 1993), 464, 466.

358 Sing me of wars: Harold Rome, "Sing Me a Song with Social Significance," as performed by Rose Marie Jun on *Pins and Needles: Twenty-Fifth Anniversary Edition* (Columbia Records, 1993), Track 1.

358 completely unanticipated; a record: William H. Young and Nancy K. Young, *Music of the Great Depression* (Westport, CT: Greenwood Press, 2005), 87–88.

358 *Lenox Avenue*; inner mastery: Jon Michael Spencer, "William Grant Still, *Lenox Avenue*, 1937," *Lenox Avenue: A Journal of Interarts Inquiry* 2 (1996): ii–vi (p. iii); Peter Gough, *Sounds of the New Deal: The Federal Music Project in the West* (Urbana: University of Illinois Press, 2015), 110.

358–59 ran for an unprecedented; suite; history of poverty: Elizabeth Cooper, "Tamaris and the Federal Dance Theater, 1936–1939: Socially Relevant Dance Amidst the Policies and Politics of the New Deal Era," *Dance Research Journal* 29, no. 2 (Autumn 1997): 23–48 (pp. 31–33).

359 So long my people: "How Long, Brethren?" in Steven P. Garabedian, *A Sound History: Lawrence Gellert, Black Musical Protest, and White Denial* (Amherst: University of Massachusetts Press, 2020), 2–3.

359 These songs: Langston Hughes quoted in Garabedian, 1.

359 a continuous panorama; music; techniques: Langston Hughes quoted, with commentary, in Arnold Rampersad, *The Life of Langston Hughes, Volume 1: 1902–1941: I, Too, Sing America* (New York: Oxford University Press, 2002), 358.

359 an overflow crowd; curtainless stage: Rampersad, 358.

359–60 *From Spirituals to Swing*: Young and Young, 126–127.

360 In the context: Ted Gioia, *Music: A Subversive History* (New York: Basic Books, 2019), 351.

360 Oh, I wonder: Earl Robinson and Harold Schacter, "Spring Song," in Ronald D. Cohen, *Depression Folk: Grassroots Music and Left-Wing Politics in 1930s America* (Chapel Hill: University of North Carolina Press, 2016), 106.

360 One argument: Al Richmond, *A Long View from the Left: Memoirs of an American Revolutionary* (New York: Delta, 1972), 283.

360 "The Yanks Aren't Coming"; "Little Toy Men": Ronald D. Cohen and Will Kaufman, *Singing for Peace: Antiwar Songs in American History* (New York: Routledge, 2015), 27.

361 a troupe; black opera singer; white Metropolitan Opera baritone; white popular singer; Roosevelt knew: Kristine N. McCusker, *Lonesome Cowgirls and Honky-Tonk Angels: The Women of Barn Dance Radio* (Urbana: University of Illinois Press, 2008), 99–101.

361 the bonds of friendship; the transition: McCusker, 83.

361 introduced formally: McCusker, 101.

361 *To* thee *we* sing: John Shaw, *This Land That I Love: Irving Berlin, Woody Guthrie, and the Story of Two American Anthems* (New York: Public Affairs, 2013), 148.

361 Through the Marian Anderson protest concert: Mary McLeod Bethune quoted in Shaw, 149.

362 What Is an American: J. Hector St. John de Crevecoeur, *Letters from an American Farmer and Other Essays*, ed. Dennis D. Moore (Cambridge: Belknap Press, 2013), 28.

362 FTP: Barry B. Witham, *The Federal Theatre Project: A Case Study* (Cambridge: Cambridge University Press, 2003), 130.

362 "Ballad for Americans": Morris Dickstein, *Dancing in the Dark: A Cultural History of the Great Depression* (New York: W. W. Norton, 2009), 426.

363 What's your racket; Am I an American; murders; patriotic spouting: John La Touche and Earl Robinson, "Ballad for Americans," as performed by Paul Robeson and ensemble on Paul Robeson, *Ballad for Americans (And Great Songs of Faith, Love, and Patriotism)* (Vanguard, 1989), Track 22.

364 metaphysics of Indian hating: Richard Drinnon, *Facing West: The Metaphysics of Indian-Hating and Empire-Building* (New York: Schocken Books, 1990), *passim.* Melville coined the phrase "the metaphysics of Indian-hating" in Chapter 26 of *The Confidence-Man* (1857).

364 Building a nation: La Touche and Robinson, "Ballad for Americans."

Conclusion: Whose Land?

366 If an observer: David King Dunaway, *How Can I Keep from Singing? The Ballad of Pete Seeger* (New York: Villard Books, 2008), 65.

366 You can date: Alan Lomax quoted in Dunaway, 69.

366 At the age of about four: Woody Guthrie, "How Much, How Long," on *The Live Wire Woody Guthrie* (Woody Guthrie Archives, 2007), Track 1.

368 Woody was hitchhiking: Pete Seeger on *Pete Seeger at 90*, prod. Vincent Dowd, BBC Radio 4, first broadcast May 1, 2009.

368 They used dope: Woody Guthrie, "How Much, How Long," on *The Live Wire Woody Guthrie* (Woody Guthrie Archives, 2007), Track 1.

368 the best parts: Guthrie quoted in Will Kaufman, *Woody Guthrie, American Radical* (Urbana: University of Illinois Press, 2011), 154.

368 Crying. Wailing: Woody Guthrie, *Seeds of Man* (New York: Pocket Books, 1977), 159.

368 The Mexicans catch: Guthrie quoted in Kaufman, 231, n. 34.

368–69 most popular *canción ranchera* singers: Manuel Peña, *Música Tejana: The Cultural Economy of Artistic Transformation* (College Station: Texas A&M University Press, 2002), 51–53; Lydia Mendoza, "The Lark of the Border," in *Ethnic Recordings in America: A Neglected Heritage* (Washington, DC: American Folklife Center, Library of Congress, 1982), 119–131 (p. 130).

369 These little Japanese farmers: Woody Guthrie, *Bound for Glory* (New York: E. P. Dutton, 1943), 354.

369 You were getting along: Anonymous KFVD listener quoted in Kaufman, 150; I don't know just how many: same listener quoted in Ed Cray, *Ramblin' Man: The Life and Times of Woody Guthrie* (New York: W. W. Norton, 2004), 109.

369 Laura and Lawrence Nelson: Mark Allan Jackson, *Prophet Singer: The Voice and Vision of Woody Guthrie* (Jackson: University Press of Mississippi, 2007), 136.

369 the many Negro mothers: Guthrie quoted in Kaufman, 147.

369–70 built him a shack: Guthrie quoted in Will Kaufman, *Woody Guthrie's Modern World Blues* (Norman: University of Oklahoma Press, 2017), 210.

370 No dogs or Jews: Joe Klein, *Woody Guthrie: A Life* (New York: Delta, 1980), 308.

370 Okies and dogs: Philippe Bourgois, "The Symbolic Violence of Primitive Accumulation in the United States," Foreword in Seth M. Holmes, *Fresh Fruit, Broken Bodies: Migrant Farmworkers in the United States* (Berkeley: University of California Press, 2013), xii.

370 I think of what fascism: Guthrie quoted in Kaufman, *Woody Guthrie's Modern World Blues*, 212.

370 angry song: Bruce Springsteen, introduction to "This Land Is Your Land," on *Bruce Springsteen and the E Street Band, Live / 1975–85* (CBS Records, 1986), Disc 2, Track 9.

370 All you can write: Guthrie quoted in Klein, 145.

371 "This Land Is Not Our Land": on Utah Phillips, *Making Speech Free* (Free Dirt Records, 2011), Track 20.

371 Henry Crow Dog: Pete Seeger, *Where Have All the Flowers Gone: A Singalong Memoir* (New York: Sing Out! / W. W. Norton, 2009), 144.

371 I just cried: Buffy Sainte-Marie quoted in Sam Yellowhorse Kesler, "The Blind Spot in the Great American Protest Song," *NPR Music*, February 3, 2021: www.npr.org/2021/02/03/963185860/the-blind-spot-in-the-great-american-protest-song.

371 That song: Bernice Reagon Johnson quoted in Dunaway, 343–345.

371–72 Carolyn "Cappy" Israel, This Land: in Seeger, 144.

372 unconscious manifest destiny: Roxanne Dunbar-Ortiz, *An Indigenous People's History of the United States* (Boston: Beacon Press, 2014), 3.

372 Woody Guthrie's protest anthem: Mali Obomsawin, "This Land Is Whose Land? Indian Country and the Shortcomings of Settler Protest," *Smithsonian Folklife Magazine*, June 14, 2019: https://folklife.si.edu/magazine/this-land-is-whose-land-indian-country-settler-protest.

372 fascist woketards: John Nolte, "Commie Folksinger Woody Guthrie Not Woke Enough for Mob," *Breitbart*, June 18, 2019: www.breitbart.com/entertainment/2019/06/18/commie-folk-singer-woody-guthrie-not-woke-enough-for-mob.

372 You know: Rebecca Nagle (Cherokee), in Yellowhorse Kesler.

Song Index

Untitled songs are referenced through their first quoted lines

General Index